Perspectives on Property Law

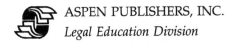

Perspectives on Property Law

Third Edition

Robert C. Ellickson

Walter E. Meyer Professor of Property and Urban Law,
Yale University

Carol M. Rose

Gordon Bradford Tweedy Professor of Law
  and Organization,
Yale University

Bruce A. Ackerman

Sterling Professor of Law and Political Science,
Yale University

ASPEN LAW & BUSINESS
A Division of Aspen Publishers, Inc.
New York   Gaithersburg

Permissions
Aspen Law & Business
1185 Avenue of the Americas
New York, NY   10036

Printed in the United States of America

1 2 3 4 5 6 7 8 9 0

ISBN 0-7355-2874-8

Library of Congress Cataloging-in-Publication Data

Perspectives on property law / [edited by] Robert C. Ellickson, Carol M. Rose, Bruce A. Ackerman — 3rd ed.
    p. cm.
    Includes bibliographical references.
    ISBN 0-7355-2874-8 (alk. paper)
    1. Right of property — United States.   2. Property — United States.   I. Ellickson, Robert C.   II. Rose, Carol M.   III. Ackerman, Bruce A.

    KF562.E25 2002
    346.7304 — dc21

                                                        2001056052

About Aspen Law & Business Legal Education Division

With a dedication to preserving and strengthening the long-standing tradition of publishing excellence in legal education, Aspen Law & Business continues to provide the highest quality teaching and learning resources for today's law school community. Careful development, meticulous editing, and an unmatched responsiveness to the evolving needs of today's discerning educators combine in the creation of our outstanding casebooks, coursebooks, textbooks, and study aids.

ASPEN LAW & BUSINESS
A Division of Aspen Publishers, Inc.
A Wolters Kluwer Company
www.aspenpublishers.com

To Jenny and Owen
R.C.E.

To Hugh and Marie
C.M.R.

Summary of Contents

Contents

Preface

Property is a term that triggers strong emotions. For some, including the Founders, it carries the promise of prosperity and freedom from tyranny. For others, it signifies blind defense of a status quo characterized by unequal wealth. Issues of property have inspired philosophical comment at least since Plato; unlike many philosophic issues, however, they have also provoked intense popular concern. Wars and revolutions are commonly fought over property rules and property distributions. Property teachers can deservedly note that issues in torts and contracts (the other foundational private-law subjects) are rarely so explosive.

Despite its highly charged subject matter, property law often strikes law students as a confusing jumble of doctrines that apply to relatively unconnected sets of disputes. To counter that impression, we have designed this reader primarily for use in an introductory course on property law, most predictably as a supplement to a casebook or other compendium of primary legal materials. Because the structure of property institutions has increasingly attracted interdisciplinary study, we expect that students and researchers in other fields may also benefit from both the selections and our notes and questions.

Although we have consciously included a highly diverse set of readings in this volume, we aim not to add to the confusion but to help the student to identify fundamental questions linking conventionally separated pockets of property law. An understanding of these interconnections should provide a foundation for advanced study in highly diverse property-related fields: to name just the most obvious, environmental policy, poverty law, intellectual property, real estate, family wealth transactions, taxation, urban government, natural resources, and legal history.

This reader builds on and indeed is a successor to Bruce Ack-

xviii   Perspectives on Property Law

erman's Economic Foundations of Property Law, published in 1975. In his preface to that edition, Ackerman observed that "[t]he institution of private property . . . serves as the linchpin of our economic organization, and it would be remarkable if its proper study could not enlighten the fundamental premises of a wide range of legal phenomena." Whether supported by law or customary practice, *private property* denotes a regime that entitles an individual owner to exercise dominion over a scarce resource. At maximum, this control includes the rights to use the resource, to exclude others from it, and to transfer it to others. In many contexts, however, societies — including our own — dilute this pure form of private property; for example, the legal system may support a political protester's right to leaflet in a shopping center whose legal title belongs to someone else. Moreover, societies routinely make room for other forms of property. University students who jointly use a dormitory's common room have a casual form of *communal property*. Streets, beaches, and even languages and jokes may be *open-access property*, available for all to use. The selections in this volume should help the reader to untangle these different property regimes and to reflect upon the reasons why every society ends up with such an eclectic variety of them.

In the first edition of this collection, Ackerman included *Economic* in the title. His decision to do so was faithful to the spirit of the time — as is our collective decision to delete the word from the title of subsequent editions. The 1970s were an ascendant period for law and economics. Ackerman's preface to the first edition unassailably asserted that scholars applying tools of economics had produced "the most dynamic body of research in the field" of property. A generation later, however, most observers no longer regard law and economics as a dynamic upstart, but rather as "normal science" (to borrow a phrase from Thomas Kuhn), at least in a predominantly private-law field such as property.

This edition does contain many seminal works in law and economics. But we have widened our net to take in authors adopting "upstart" perspectives that aim either to complement or to displace the normal science of law and economics. Even in the first edition, Ackerman noted that "the insights of the economist must be placed in a larger structure in which sociological, psychological and historical theory have their rightful place. Consequently, it would be quite appropriate for the instructor to supplement the readings in this volume with others. . . ." Because recent interdisciplinary work on property has been so rich, the editors now can assist instructors who share this aspiration. We include here selections taken not only from sociology, psychology, and history (the disciplines Ackerman mentioned), but also philosophy, gender studies, game theory, critical legal studies, and law and literature. Which, if any, of these perspectives will make lasting contributions to legal thought presently remains murky; the readers of this volume are members of one of the juries that will decide.

Robert Ellickson and Carol Rose, who assumed entire editorial responsibility thereafter, wish to acknowledge Bruce Ackerman's pioneering accomplishments in the first edition. Bruce's 1975 preface asserted that property courses at the time often consisted of a thin base of historical accounts of struggles between English landowners and the Crown, a Langdellian superstructure of American common-law precedent, all incongruously finished off with oddments of constitutional law and recent statutory reforms. The success of his first edition demonstrated the strong latent demand for a volume that added spice and structure to property instruction. Moreover, simply by its appearance, the first edition helped establish a canon that has significantly influenced the course of scholarship on property law. In the 1960s, property was generally regarded as a sleepy field. Since then it has become one of the most vibrant, varied, and contested fields of legal scholarship.

The selections appearing here have been rigorously edited. Most footnotes have been deleted; those that remain retain their original numbers, and readers will notice large gaps in the sequences. Any reader who finds an excerpt stimulating is urged to consult the fuller original. After all, these excerpts were chosen not only to clarify, but to provoke.

Robert C. Ellickson
Carol M. Rose

January 2002
New Haven

Acknowledgments

Acheson, James M., excerpts 48-49, 73-76, 142-144 from The Lobster Gangs of Maine, Copyright © 1988 by University Press of New England. Reprinted by permission.

Ackerman, Bruce A., Regulating Slum Housing Markets on Behalf of the Poor: Of Housing Codes, Housing Subsidies and Income Redistribution Policy, 80 Yale Law Journal, 1102-1106. Copyright © 1971. Reprinted by permission of The Yale Law Journal Company and Fred B. Rothman & Company.

Allen, Douglas W. & Lueck, Dean, The "Back Forty" on a Handshake: Specific Assets, Reputation, and the Structure of Farmland Contracts, Journal of Law, Economics; and Organization 8(2), 366-371, 375. Copyright © 1992. Reprinted by permission of Oxford University Press.

Arnott, Richard, Rent Control: The International Experience, 1 Journal of Real Estate, Finance, and Economics, 203-206, 209-210. Copyright © 1988. Reprinted by permission of Kluwer Academic Publishers.

Axelrod, Robert, The Evolution of Cooperation, 3-12,19-21, 30-35. Copyright © 1984 by Robert Axelrod. Reprinted by permission of BasicBooks, a division of Perseus Books, L.L.C.

Ayres, Ian & Gertner, Robert, Filling Gaps in Incomplete Contracts: An Economic Theory of Default Rules, 99 Yale Law Journal, 87-89, 91-94, 97-100, 125-127. Copyright © 1989. Reprinted by permission of The Yale Law Journal Company and Fred B. Rothman & Company.

Banner, Stuart, Two Properties, One Land: Law and Space in Nineteenth Century New Zealand, Law and Social Inquiry 24:4, 807-813, 823-828, 830-836, 844-847, Copyright ©1999. Reprinted by permission of The University of Chicago Press.

Blackstone, William, 2 Commentaries on the Laws of England,

Perspectives on Property Law

Chapter 1

The Debate over Private Property

A. Culture and Human Nature

Asylums: Essays on the Social Situation of Mental Patients and Other Inmates*

Erving Goffman

The admission procedure can be characterized as a leaving off and a taking on, with the midpoint marked by physical nakedness. Leaving off of course entails a dispossession of property, important because persons invest self feelings in their possessions. Perhaps the most significant of these possessions is not physical at all, one's full name; whatever one is thereafter called, loss of one's name can be a great curtailment of the self. . . .

Once the inmate is stripped of his possessions, at least some replacements must be made by the establishment, but these take the form of standard issue uniform in character and uniformly distributed. These substitute possessions are clearly marked as really belonging to the institution and in some cases are recalled at regular intervals to be, as it were, disinfected of identifications. With objects that can be used up — for example, pencils — the inmate may be required to return the remnants before obtaining a reissue. Failure to provide inmates with individual lockers and periodic searches and confiscations of accumulated personal property re-

*Source: pp. 18-21, 244-254 (1961).

inforce property dispossession. Religious orders have appreciated the implications for self of such separation from belongings. Inmates may be required to change their cells once a year so as not to become attached to them. The Benedictine Rule is explicit:

> For their bedding let a mattress, a blanket, a coverlet, and a pillow suffice. These beds must be frequently inspected by the Abbot, because of private property which may be found therein. If anyone be discovered to have what he has not received from the Abbot, let him be most severely punished. And in order that this vice of private ownership may be completely rooted out, let all things that are necessary be supplied by the Abbot: that is, cowl, tunic, stockings, shoes, girdle, knife, pen, needle, handkerchief, and tablets; so that all plea of necessity may be taken away. And let the Abbot always consider that passage in the Acts of the Apostles: "Distribution was made to each according as anyone had need."[21]

One set of the individual's possessions has a special relation to self. The individual ordinarily expects to exert some control over the guise in which he appears before others. For this he needs cosmetic and clothing supplies, tools for applying, arranging, and repairing them, and an accessible, secure place to store these supplies and tools — in short, the individual will need an "identity kit" for the management of his personal front. He will also need access to decoration specialists such as barbers and clothiers.

On admission to a total institution, however, the individual is likely to be stripped of his usual appearance and of the equipment and services by which he maintains it, thus suffering a personal defacement. Clothing, combs, needle and thread, cosmetics, towels, soap, shaving sets, bathing facilities — all these may be taken away or denied him, although some may be kept in inaccessible storage, to be returned if and when he leaves. In the words of St. Benedict's Holy Rule:

> Then forthwith he shall, there in the oratory, be divested of his own garments with which he is clothed and be clad in those of the monastery. Those garments of which he is divested shall be placed in the wardrobe, there to be kept, so that if, perchance, he should ever be persuaded by the devil to leave the monastery (which God forbid), he may be stripped of the monastic habit and cast forth.[22]

As suggested, the institutional issue provided as a substitute for what has been taken away is typically of a "coarse" variety, ill-suited, often old, and the same for large categories of inmates. The

---

21. The Holy Rule of St. Benedict, Ch. 55.
22. The Holy Rule of St. Benedict, Ch. 58.

impact of this substitution is described in a report on imprisoned prostitutes:

> First, there is the shower officer who forces them to undress, takes their own clothes away, sees to it that they take showers and get their prison clothes — one pair of black oxfords with cuban heels, two pairs of much-mended ankle socks, three cotton dresses, two cotton slips, two pairs of panties, and a couple of bras. Practically all the bras are flat and useless. No corsets or girdles are issued.
>
> There is not a sadder sight than some of the obese prisoners who, if nothing else, have been managing to keep themselves looking decent on the outside, confronted by the first sight of themselves in prison issue.[23] . . .

In mental hospitals and similar institutions the basic kind of personal territory is, perhaps, the private sleeping room, officially available to around five or ten per cent of the ward population. In Central Hospital such a room was sometimes given in exchange for doing ward work. Once obtained, a private room could be stocked with objects that could lend comfort, pleasure, and control to the patient's life. Pin-up pictures, a radio, a box of paper-back detective stories, a bag of fruit, coffee-making equipment, matches, shaving equipment — these were some of the objects, many of them illicit, that were introduced by patients.

Patients who had been on a given ward for several months tended to develop personal territories in the day room, at least to the degree that some inmates developed favorite sitting or standing places and would make some effort to dislodge anybody who usurped them. Thus, on one continued treatment ward, one elderly patient in contact was by mutual consent accorded a free-standing radiator; by spreading paper on top, he managed to be able to sit on it, and sit on it he usually did. Behind the radiator he kept some of his personal effects, which further marked off the area as his place. A few feet from him, in a corner of the room, a working patient had what amounted to his "office," this being the place where staff knew they could find him when he was wanted. He had sat so long in this corner that there was a soiled dent in the plaster wall where his head usually came to rest. On the same ward, another patient laid claim to a chair that was directly in front of the TV set; although a few patients would contest this place, he generally could sustain his claim upon it.

Territory formation on wards has a special relation to mental

---

23. John M. Murtagh & Sara Harris, Cast the First Stone (New York: Pocket Books, 1958), pp. 239-240. . . .

disorder. In many civilian situations an equalitarian rule such as "first come, first served" prevails, and some disguise conceals another organizing principle, "strongest takes what he wants." This last rule operated to some extent on bad wards, just as the first rule did on good wards. Another dimension must be introduced, however. The alignment to ward life that many back-ward patients took, for whatever voluntary reason or from whatever involuntary cause, led them to remain silent and unprotesting and to move away from any commotion involving themselves. Such a person could be dislodged from a seat or place regardless of his size or strength. Hence, on the bad wards, a special pecking order of a sort occurred, with vocal patients in good contact taking favorite chairs and benches from those not in contact. This was carried to a point where one patient might force a mute one off a footrest, leaving the vocal patient with a chair *and* a footrest, and the mute patient with nothing at all — a difference that is not negligible considering the fact that except for breaks at mealtime some patients spent the whole of the day on these wards doing nothing but sitting or standing in one place.

Perhaps the minimum space that was built into a personal territory was that provided by a patient's blanket. In some wards, a few patients would carry their blankets around with them during the day and, in an act thought to be highly regressive, each would curl up on the floor with his blanket completely covering him; within this covered space each had some margin of control.

As may be expected, a personal territory can develop within a free place or group territory. For example, in the recreation room of a chronic male service one of the two large wooden armchairs favorably situated close to the light and the radiator was regularly taken by an elderly respected patient, both patients and staff recognizing his right to it.

One of the most elaborate illustrations of territory formation in a free place in Central Hospital occurred in the disused basement of one of the continued-treatment buildings. Here a few of the more intact rooms had been taken over by lower-echelon staff to use as supply rooms; thus there was a paint room and a room where grounds-care equipment was stored. In each of these rooms a patient helper held semi-official dominion. Pin-ups, a radio, a relatively soft chair, and supplies of hospital tobacco were to be found. A few of the remaining less usable rooms had been appropriated by aging long-term parole patients, each of whom had managed to stock his nest with something, if only a broken chair and stacks of old Life magazines. In the rare event of any of these patients being needed during the day by a member of staff, a message would be sent directly to his basement office, not his ward.

In some cases, an assignment provided a personal territory. For example, the working patients who looked after their ward's clothing and supply room were allowed to stay in this room when no chores were to be done; and there they could sit or lie on the floor away from the alterations of commotion and pall in the day room. . . . In everyday life, legitimate possessions employed in primary adjustments are typically stored, when not in use, in special places of safekeeping which can be gotten to at will, such as footlockers, cabinets, bureau drawers, and safe deposit boxes. These storage places protect the object from damage, misuse, and misappropriation, and allow the user to conceal what he possesses from others. More important, these places can represent an extension of the self and its autonomy, becoming more important as the individual foregoes other repositories of selfhood. If nothing can be kept only for oneself, and everything one uses is used by others, too, then little protection from social contamination by others is possible. Further, some of the things one must give up are those with which one has become especially identified and which one employs for self-identification to others. It is thus that a man in a monastery may be concerned about his one privacy, his letterbox, and a man on a frigate about his canvas clothes bag.

Where such private storage places are not allowed, it is understandable that they will be illicitly developed. Further, if one is to possess an object illicitly, then the place in which it is stored may itself have to be concealed. A personal storage space that is concealed and/or locked not merely to thwart illegitimate interlopers but also legitimate authority is sometimes called a *stash* in the criminal and near-criminal world, and will be called this here. . . .

When patients entered Central Hospital, especially if they were excited or depressed on admission, they were denied a private, accessible place to store things. Their personal clothing, for example, might be stored in a room that was beyond their discretionary use. Their money was kept in the administration building, unobtainable without medical and/or their legal agents' permission. Valuables or breakables, such as false teeth, eyeglasses, wrist watches, often an integral part of body image, might be locked up safely out of their owners' reach. Official papers of self-identification might also be retained by the institution. Cosmetics, needed to present oneself properly to others, were collectivized, being made accessible to patients only at certain times. On convalescent wards, bed boxes were available, but since they were unlocked they were subject to theft from other patients and from staff, and in any case were often located in rooms locked to patients during the day.

If people were selfless, or were required to be selfless, there would of course be a logic to having no private storage place. . . . But all have some self. Given the curtailment implied by loss of places of safekeeping, it is understandable that patients in Central Hospital developed places of their own.

It seemed characteristic of hospital life that the most common form of stash was one that could be carried around on one's person wherever one went. One such device for female patients was a large handbag; a parallel technique for a man was a jacket with commodious pockets, worn even in the hottest weather. While these containers are quite usual ones in the wider community, there was a special burden placed upon them in the hospital: books, writing materials, washcloths, fruit, small valuables, scarves, playing cards, soap, shaving equipment (on the part of men), containers of salt, pepper, and sugar, bottles of milk — these were some of the objects sometimes carried in this manner. So common was this practice that one of the most reliable symbols of patient status in the hospital was bulging pockets. Another portable storage device was a shopping bag lined with another shopping bag. (When partly full, this frequently employed stash also served as a cushion and back rest.) Among men, a small stash was sometimes created out of a long sock: by knotting the open end and twisting this end around his belt, the patient could let a kind of moneybag inconspicuously hang down inside his trouser leg. . . .

I would like to repeat that there were some good reasons for these bulky carryings-on. Many of the amenities of life, such as soap, toilet paper, or cards, which are ordinarily available in many depots of comfort in civil society, are not thus available to patients, so that the day's needs had to be partly provided for at the beginning of the day.

Fixed stashes, as well as portable ones, were employed, too; they were most often found in free places and territories. Some patients attempted to keep their valuables under their mattresses but, as previously suggested, the general hospital rule making dormitories off-limits during the day reduced the usefulness of this device. The half-concealed lips of window sills were sometimes used. Patients with private rooms and friendly relations with the attendant used their rooms as stashes. Female patients sometimes hid matches and cigarettes in the compacts they left in their rooms. And a favorite exemplary tale in the hospital was of an old man who was claimed to have hid his money, $1200, in a cigar box in a tree on the hospital grounds.

NOTES AND QUESTIONS ON PROPERTY AND THE SENSE OF SELF

1. Why does the author make so much of an inmate's use of property (or possessions) to present a personal appearance? Are such uses of property a good thing, or do they imply that property merely serves vanity and deception? Why did the Benedictines restrict the monks' property? What other institutions do so, and why? For related critiques of property, see, for example, E.M. Forster, My Wood, *in* Abinger Harvest 22 (1964), suggesting that property makes the holder pompous and self-important; Thorstein Veblen, The Theory of the Leisure Class (1899), arguing that the wealthy use property for "conspicuous consumption."

2. Why is "first come, first served" a principle identified with the asylum's "good wards," whereas "strongest takes what he wants" is a principle identified with the "bad wards"? What is the matter with the rule of the stronger? See Thomas Hobbes, Leviathan (1651). First possession is a widespread rule for property formation; see Chapter 3, infra, on The Significance of Possession. But does this make first possession more morally justifiable than the rule of the stronger? Which would latecomers prefer? Is first possession justifiable on efficiency grounds? Compare Duncan Kennedy and Frank Michelman, Are Property and Contract Efficient?, infra p. 63.

3. How do you account for the pervasive "territory formation" among inmates? Do you see similar patterns in other persons, such as the homeless, who ostensibly own very little property? Do these patterns suggest that some sort of territoriality is "hardwired" in the human psyche, as is argued by sociobiologists? See Richard Pipes, Human Nature and the Fall of Communism, infra p. 20. For variations on this theme, see Elizabeth Cashdan, Spatial Organization and Habitat Use, *in* Eric Alden Smith & Bruce Winterhalder, Evolutionary Ecology and Human Behavior (1992). Or is the inmates' territory formation grounded on functional needs, culture, or both?

Property and Personhood*

Margaret Jane Radin

This article explores the relationship between property and personhood, a relationship that has commonly been both ignored and taken for granted in legal thought. The premise underlying the personhood perspective is that to achieve proper self-development — to be a *person* — an individual needs some control over resources in the external environment. The necessary assurances of control take the form of property rights. Although explicit elaboration of this perspective is wanting in modern writing on property, the personhood perspective is often implicit in the connections that courts and commentators find between property and privacy or between property and liberty. In addition to its power to explain certain aspects of existing schemes of property entitlement, the personhood perspective can also serve as an explicit source of values for making moral distinctions in property disputes, and hence for either justifying or criticizing current law. . . . It is not surprising that personhood has played a part in property theories all along the political spectrum. Conservatives rely on an absolute conception of property as sacred to personal autonomy. Communitarians believe that changing conceptions of property reflect and shape the changing nature of persons and communities. Welfare rights liberals find entitlement to a minimal level of resources necessary to the dignity of persons even when the entitlement must curtail the property rights of others. This article does not emphasize how the notion of personhood might figure in the most prevalent traditional lines of liberal property theory: the Lockean labor-desert theory, which focuses on individual autonomy, or the utilitarian theory, which focuses on welfare maximization. It rather attempts to clarify a third strand of liberal property theory that focuses on personal embodiment or self-constitution in terms of "things." . . .

In what follows I shall discuss the personhood perspective as Hegel developed it in Philosophy of Right, trace some of its later permutations and entanglements with other perspectives on property, and try to develop a contemporary view useful in the context of the American legal system. . . .

*Source: 34 Stanford Law Review 957-973, 977-979, 984-991, 1002-1006 (1982).

I. Property for Personhood: An Intuitive View

Most people possess certain objects they feel are almost part of themselves. These objects are closely bound up with personhood because they are part of the way we constitute ourselves as continuing personal entities in the world. They may be as different as people are different, but some common examples might be a wedding ring, a portrait, an heirloom, or a house.

One may gauge the strength or significance of someone's relationship with an object by the kind of pain that would be occasioned by its loss. On this view, an object is closely related to one's personhood if its loss causes pain that cannot be relieved by the object's replacement. If so, that particular object is bound up with the holder. For instance, if a wedding ring is stolen from a jeweler, insurance proceeds can reimburse the jeweler, but if a wedding ring is stolen from a loving wearer, the price of a replacement will not restore the status quo — perhaps no amount of money can do so.

The opposite of holding an object that has become a part of oneself is holding an object that is perfectly replaceable with other goods of equal market value. One holds such an object for purely instrumental reasons. The archetype of such a good is, of course, money, which is almost always held only to buy other things. A dollar is worth no more than what one chooses to buy with it, and one dollar bill is as good as another. Other examples are the wedding ring in the hands of the jeweler, the automobile in the hands of the dealer, the land in the hands of the developer, or the apartment in the hands of the commercial landlord. I shall call these theoretical opposites — property that is bound up with a person and property that is held purely instrumentally — personal property and fungible property respectively. . . .

Once we admit that a person can be bound up with an external "thing" in some constitutive sense, we can argue that by virtue of this connection the person should be accorded broad liberty with respect to control over that "thing." But here liberty follows from property for personhood; personhood is the basic concept, not liberty. Of course, if liberty is viewed not as freedom from interference, or "negative freedom," but rather as some positive will that by acting on the external world is constitutive of the person, then liberty comes closer to capturing the idea of the self being intimately bound up with things in the external world.

It intuitively appears that there is such a thing as property for personhood because people become bound up with "things." But this intuitive view does not compel the conclusion that property for personhood deserves moral recognition or legal protection, because arguably there is bad as well as good in being bound up with external objects. If there is a traditional understanding that a well-developed person must invest herself to some extent in external objects, there is no less a traditional understanding that one should not invest oneself *in the wrong way* or *to too great an extent* in external objects. Property is damnation as well as salvation, object-fetishism as well as moral groundwork. In this view, the relationship between the shoe fetishist and his shoe will not be respected like that between the spouse and her wedding ring. At the extreme, anyone who lives only for material objects is considered not to be a well-developed person, but rather to be lacking some important attribute of humanity.

II. The Role of the Concept of Person . . .

A. Theories of the Person

The polymorphous nature of the word "person" inevitably creates problems for a moral thesis about property built upon notions of personhood. "Person" stems from the Latin *persona*, meaning, among other things, a theatrical role. In Roman law, *persona* came to mean simply an entity possessing legal rights and duties. Today it commonly signifies any human being. . . .

B. Property Theories and Theories of the Person

[L]et us begin with the person conceived as bodily continuity. Locke says that "every Man has a *Property* in his own *Person*," from which it immediately follows that "[t]he *Labour* of his Body, and the *Work* of his hands . . . are properly his."[28] Though . . . Locke elsewhere considers the person as reflective consciousness and memory, he may well mean here that one literally owns one's limbs and hence must own their product. If not, perhaps property in one's person should be understood to mean simply that an individual has an entitlement to be a person or to be treated as a person. This would probably include the right to self-preservation on which Locke bases the right to appropriate.

If it makes sense to say that one owns one's body, then, on the embodiment theory of personhood, the body is quintessentially personal property because it is literally constitutive of one's per-

---

28. J. Locke [Second Treatise of Government], ch. V, §27.

sonhood. If the body is property, then objectively it is property for personhood. This line of thinking leads to a property theory for the tort of assault and battery: Interference with my body is interference with my personal property. Certain external things, for example, the shirt off my back, may also be considered personal property if they are closely enough connected with the body.

The idea of property in one's body presents some interesting paradoxes. In some cases, bodily parts can become fungible commodities, just as other personal property can become fungible with a change in its relationship with the owner: Blood can be withdrawn and used in a transfusion; hair can be cut off and used by a wig-maker; organs can be transplanted. On the other hand, bodily parts may be too "personal" to be property at all. . . .

Finally, let us consider the view that what is important in personhood is a continuing character structure encompassing future projects or plans, as well as past events and feelings. The general idea of expressing one's character through property is quite familiar. It is frequently remarked that dogs resemble their masters; the attributes of many material goods, such as cars and clothes, can proclaim character traits of their owners. Of course, many would say that becoming too enthralled with property takes away time and energy needed to develop other faculties constitutive of personhood. But, for example, if you express your generosity by giving away fruits that grow in your orchard, then if the orchard ceases to be your property, you are no longer able to express your character. This at least suggests that property may have an important relationship to certain character traits that partly constitute a person.

This view of personhood also gives us insight into why protecting people's "expectations" of continuing control over objects seems so important. If an object you now control is bound up in your future plans or in your anticipation of your future self, and it is partly these plans for your own continuity that make you a person, then your personhood depends on the realization of these expectations. . . .

C. The Problem of Fetishism

We must construct sufficiently objective criteria to identify close object relations that should be excluded from recognition as personal property because the particular nature of the relationship works to hinder rather than to support healthy self-constitution. A key to distinguishing these cases is "healthy." We can tell the difference between personal property and fetishism the same way we can tell the difference between a healthy person and a sick person, or between a sane person and an insane person. In fact, the concepts of sanity and personhood are intertwined: At some point we question whether the insane person is a person at all. Using the word "we" here, however, implies that a consensus exists and can be discerned. Because I seek a source of objective judgments about property for personhood, but do not wish to rely on natural law or simple moral realism, consensus must be a sufficient source of objective moral criteria — and I believe it can be, sometimes, without destroying the meaning of objectivity. In the context of property for personhood, then, a "thing" that someone claims to be bound up with nevertheless should not be treated as personal vis-à-vis other people's claimed rights and interests when there is an objective moral consensus that to be bound up with that category of "thing" is inconsistent with personhood or healthy self-constitution.

Judgments of insanity or fetishism are both made on the basis of the minimum indicia it takes to recognize an individual as one of us. There does not seem to be the same reason to restrain a private fetishist as there would be to restrain an insane person prone to violence against others. But the restraint of denying the fetishist's property special recognition as personal is less severe than that imposed on someone deemed violently insane. To refuse on moral grounds to call fetishist property personal is not to refuse to call it property at all. The immediate consequence of denying personal status to something is merely to treat that thing as fungible property, and hence to deny only those claims that might rely on a preferred status of personal property.

A broader aspect of the problem of fetishism is suggested by Marx's "fetishism of commodities."[47] Marx attributed power in a market society to the commodities that form the market. He believed that people become subordinate in their relations to these commodities. In other words, under capitalism property itself is antipersonhood.

Even if one does not accept that all capitalist market relations with objects destroy personhood, it is probably true that most people view the caricature capitalist with distaste. Most people might consider her lacking in some essential attribute of personhood, such as the capacity to respect other people or the environment. If there is some moral cut-off point, beyond which one is attached too much or in the wrong way to property, the extent to which someone may emulate the caricature capitalist and still claim property for personhood is not clear, but is not unlimited. Although the

47. K. Marx, Capital, ch. 1.

caricature capitalist cannot express her nature without control over a vast quantity of things and other people, her need for this control to constitute herself the complete capitalist could not objectively be recognized as personal property because at some point there is an objective moral consensus that such control is destroying personhood rather than fostering it.

III. Hegel, Property, and Personhood

A. Hegel's Philosophy of Right

The property theory of Hegel's Philosophy of Right,[49] although based on a conception of persons, does not immediately invoke the intuitive personhood perspective. . . .

Because the person in Hegel's conception is merely an abstract unit of free will or autonomy, it has no concrete existence until that will acts on the external world. "[T]he person must give its freedom an external sphere in order to exist as Idea."[52] At this level of particularization, the external sphere "capable of embodying [the person's] freedom" consists of the rest of the world, everything that is distinct from the person.

From the need to embody the person's will to take free will from the abstract realm to the actual, Hegel concludes that the person becomes a real self only by engaging in a property relationship with something external. Such a relationship is the *goal* of the person. . . . Hegel at least clearly makes the claim that a human being can only become properly developed — actualize her freedom — in the context of a community of others. Thus, though he speaks of the person in the sphere of abstract right only in the Kantian sense of abstract rationality, he implicitly claims that personhood in the richer sense of self-development and differentiation presupposes the context of human community. If accepted, this claim has important ramifications for a theory of personal property which does rely on that richer sense of personhood. . . .

IV. Two Kinds of Property: The Dichotomy as Critique

One element of the intuitive personhood perspective is that property for personhood gives rise to a stronger moral claim than other

---

49. . . . (T. Knox trans. 1942) [hereinafter cited as PR]. . . .
52. PR §41.

property. This division of property resembles a recurrent kind of critique of real-world property arrangements. The underlying insight of the many dualist property theories seems to be that some property is accorded more stringent legal protection than other property, or is otherwise deemed more important than other property by social consensus. . . .

B. A Utilitarian Dichotomy

In apparent contrast to these assertions that certain property claims are stronger than others, some utilitarians might claim that since there is only one social goal, maximization of welfare, so there is only one kind of property — that which results in maximization of welfare. In this utilitarian scheme, there will also be no reason for distinctions between property entitlements and other kinds of individual entitlements except for deference to linguistic tradition. Posner's position represents this view: Efficiency will be maximized only when anything that is scarce in the relevant human society during the relevant time period (thus, a "good" and not merely an undifferentiated attribute of the environment) is the subject of an entitlement.[92]

Yet those who espouse utilitarianism in the form of instrumental economics have elaborated a hierarchy of *remedies*. The Calabresi-Melamed distinction between protecting entitlements with "property rules" or "liability rules" is now a widely recognized tool of economic analysis.[93] An entitlement is protected by a property rule if B can obtain it from A only by paying whatever price A sets as a willing seller, or if A can obtain an injunction to prevent B's interference. An entitlement is protected by a liability rule if B can obtain it from A by paying some extrinsically determined price (such as the "market" price), even if A is not a willing seller, or if A can obtain only damages on account of B's interference. To some extent, this system does not correspond to the ordinary meaning of property. Most rights traditionally called property are protected against the government only by a liability rule. On the other hand, some rights not traditionally called property, like freedom from bodily intrusion, are protected by property rules. . . .

---

92. R. Posner [Economic Analysis of Law (2d ed. 1977)].
93. . . . Property Rules, Liability Rules, and Inalienability: One View of the Cathedral, 85 Harv. L. Rev. 1089 (1972). . . .

C. *The Personhood Dichotomy*

The personhood dichotomy comes about in the following way: A general justification of property entitlements in terms of their relationship to personhood could hold that the rights that come within the general justification form a continuum from fungible to personal. It then might hold that those rights near one end of the continuum — fungible property rights — can be overridden in some cases in which those near the other — personal property rights — cannot be. This is to argue not that fungible property rights are unrelated to personhood, but simply that distinctions are sometimes warranted depending upon the character or strength of the connection. Thus, the personhood perspective generates a hierarchy of entitlements: The more closely connected with personhood, the stronger the entitlement.

Does it make sense to speak of two levels of property, personal and fungible? I think the answer is yes in many situations, no in many others. Since the personhood perspective depends partly on the subjective nature of the relationships between person and thing, it makes more sense to think of a continuum that ranges from a thing indispensable to someone's being to a thing wholly interchangeable with money. Many relationships between persons and things will fall somewhere in the middle of this continuum. Perhaps the entrepreneur factory owner has ownership of a particular factory and its machines bound up with her being to some degree. If a dichotomy telescoping this continuum to two end points is to be useful, it must be because within a given social context certain types of person-thing relationships are understood to fall close to one end or the other of the continuum, so that decision makers within that social context can use the dichotomy as a guide to determine which property is worthier of protection. For example, in our social context a house that is owned by someone who resides there is generally understood to be toward the personal end of the continuum. There is both a positive sense that people are bound up with their homes and a normative sense that this is not fetishistic. . . .

D. *Welfare Rights and a Dichotomy in Property . . .*

A welfare rights or minimal entitlement theory of just distribution might hold that a government that respects personhood must guarantee citizens all entitlements necessary for personhood. If the personhood dichotomy in property is taken as the source of a distributive mandate as part of such a general theory, it would suggest that government should make it possible for all citizens to have whatever property is necessary for personhood. But a welfare rights theory incorporating property for personhood would suggest not only that government distribute largess in order to make it possible for people to buy property in which to constitute themselves but would further suggest that government should rearrange property rights so that fungible property of some people does not overwhelm the opportunities of the rest to constitute themselves in property. That is, a welfare rights theory incorporating the right to personal property would tell the government to cease allowing one person to impinge on the personhood of another by means of her control over tangible resources, rather than simply tell the government to dole out resources.

Curtailing fungible property rights that impinge on others' opportunities for self-constitution may seem a more radical sort of reform than wealth redistribution through taxation. But purely fungible property is just like any other form of wealth. If a welfare rights theory of distribution makes personhood interests take precedence over some claims to wealth, permitting taxation to provide largess for the poor, it may equally permit curtailing fungible property rights that impinge on the poor, unless doing so only for the holders of certain assets would under the circumstances violate accepted norms of equality.

V. Two Kinds of Property: A Selective Survey

This Part surveys a number of disparate legal issues from the viewpoint of property for personhood. These issues represent types of cases in which the rough dichotomy between personal and fungible property approximates the world well enough to be useful. . . .

[Professor Radin first discusses several legal rules providing special consideration to the "sanctity of the home," notably privacy protections, allowing persons to own and read the literature of their choice in the privacy of their homes. She also discusses laws protecting tenants and constitutional safeguards against unreasonable searches.]

B. Aspects of the Taking Problem

The whole question of government regulation and "taking" of private property is the most difficult, yet most promising area for applying the personhood dichotomy. The personhood perspective cannot generate a comprehensive theory of property rights vis-à-vis the government; it can only add another moral inquiry that helps clarify some cases. But this is a field in which a unified theory has not been forthcoming. . . .

[T]he theory of personal property suggests that not all object-loss is equally important. Some objects may approach the fungible end of the continuum so that the justification for protecting them as specially related to persons disappears. . . .

On the other hand, a few objects may be so close to the personal end of the continuum that no compensation could be "just." That is, hypothetically, if some object were so bound up with me that I would cease to be "myself" if it were taken, then a government that must respect persons ought not to take it. If my kidney may be called my property, it is not property subject to condemnation for the general public welfare. Hence, in the context of a legal system, one might expect to find the characteristic use of standards of review and burdens of proof designed to shift risk of error away from protected interests in personal property. For instance, if there were reason to suspect that some object were close to the personal end of the continuum, there might be a prima facie case against taking it. That prima facie case might be rebutted if the government could show that the object is not personal, or perhaps that the object is not "too" personal compared with the importance to the government of acquiring that particular object for social purposes.

This suggests that if the personhood perspective is expressed in law, one might expect to find an implied limitation on the eminent domain power. That is, one might expect to find that a special class of property like a family home is protected against the government by a "property rule" and not just a "liability rule." Or one might expect to find that a special class of property is protected against taking unless the government shows a "compelling state interest" and that taking it is the "least intrusive alternative."

This general limitation has not developed. Perhaps the personhood perspective is not strong enough to outweigh other concerns, especially the government's need to appear even-handed and the lower administrative costs associated with simpler rules. For example, perhaps we are unwilling to presume that all single-family homes are personal because many houses are held only for investment, and a subjective inquiry into each case slows down government too much. On the other hand, perhaps the personhood perspective is so deeply embedded that, without focusing on the problem, we expect that the condemning authority will take fungible property where possible. We may simply take for granted that the government will not take homesteads when parking lots will do. Still, the fact that the personhood perspective has not surfaced to give some explicit protection to family homes from government taking, such as stricter scrutiny, seems to be anomalous. . . .

NOTES AND QUESTIONS ON THE "PERSONHOOD" THEORY OF PROPERTY

1. Reconsider the selection from Goffman: Does Radin's account of "personhood" property explain the inmates' distress at losing what seem to be relatively trivial items, or their anxiety to establish ways to keep such items? By her account, which entitlements should be most important to them? Why?

2. How plausible are Radin's intuitions about the sort of property that people become "bound up with"? For evidence on the matter, see Mihaly Csikszentmihalyi & Eugene Rochberg-Halton, The Meaning of Things: Domestic Symbols and the Self (1981).

3. Does the distinction between personhood property and fungible property stand up, in the sense that some identifiable properties are more important than others in people's ability to carry out their personal projects? Might a business be personhood property? What about the bank account that an elderly couple has saved for retirement?

Consider the remark that a quadriplegic law student made to one of the editors of this volume: He regards money (rather than heirlooms, clothes, or any other specific item) as his most important asset because money enables him to hire the assistants he needs for dressing, eating, transportation, writing, and the like; thus money enables him to carry out a meaningful and useful life. Is his money personhood property? Or is it fungible property? How do you know the difference?

4. Note that Radin characterizes a wedding ring "in the hands of the jeweler" as instrumental or fungible property. If the personhood/fungible attributes of a given item depend on the characteristics of the individual in possession of that item, can the personhood/fungible distinction function as a rule of law? Why does the distinction carry some implicit legal weight in protecting the privacy of the home, but do little to protect the home from eminent domain? For more on eminent domain and takings of property, see Chapter 9, section D, infra. For another author's contemporaneous and somewhat similar thesis about the graded importance of different kinds of property, and some suggestions

about the legal consequences for eminent domain, see William Rogers, Bringing People Back: Toward a Comprehensive Theory of Taking in Natural Resources Law, 10 Ecol. L.Q. 205 (1982).

5. What is wrong with fetishism? How does anyone know a healthy attachment from a sick or fetishistic one? Does the concept of fetishistic property, as opposed to personhood property, entail a theory of the healthy personality? For Radin's more recent consideration of the relationships between property and the healthy personality, see her Contested Commodities 54-78 (1996), where she makes particular use of the philosopher Martha Nussbaum's work on human "capabilities."

6. Radin discusses a "personhood" interest in a minimal level of economic support. Who should provide this support, and how? Are the personhood claims of recipients compatible with the personhood claims of what may be involuntary donors?

A seminal article on the property-like characteristics of welfare payments and other governmentally created benefits is Charles Reich, The New Property, 73 Yale L.J. 957 (1964). Reich argued that recipients of such benefits should have a cognizable property interest in what had previously been thought to be mere governmental "largesse." Among other things, Reich suggested that welfare recipients need secure property in order to play genuine roles as citizens. How does that argument compare to Radin's personhood thesis? Is political participation an aspect of personhood, and how does it depend on property ownership? Reich's article spawned an enormous literature on the "new property," as well as some well-known case law, notably Goldberg v. Kelly, 397 U.S. 254 (1970).

For other arguments on minimal levels of support, see John Rawls, A Theory of Justice, infra p. 94, and the notes following that selection.

7. "Personhood" theories of property have received considerable play as a basis for intellectual property rights, particularly in the "moral rights" theory prevalent in Europe, which accords authors and artists continuing artistic control over their works even after sale. For a discussion of a number of related issues, see Justin Hughes, "Recoding" Intellectual Property and Overlooked Audience Interests, 77 Tex. L. Rev. 923 (1999).

8. For further consideration of the idea of body parts as property, see the selection from Radin's Market-Inalienability, infra p. 336.

Human Nature and the Fall of Communism*

Richard Pipes

. . . All empires have sooner or later suffered collapse, but they have done so either as a result of slow internal decay or war. The Soviet Union vanished in a matter of days and in a time of peace. What accounts for the abrupt disappearance of a power that only a few years earlier had boasted it would inherit the earth?

Various explanations come to mind: the intolerable burden of defense expenditures, . . . the precipitous decline in the 1980s of world commodity prices, notably that of petroleum, which had brought Moscow the lion's share of its hard-currency earnings; the humiliation of the Red Army in Afghanistan; the resistance of dissidents. To these internal causes must be added the steadfast resolve of the Western alliance. . . . Historians will long argue how much importance to attach to each of these factors. . . .

My purpose . . . is to probe deeper, beneath the political, economic, and military levels of causation. I wish to ask whether a regime based on Communist principles was viable even under the best of circumstances, whether it could maintain itself in power by means other than terror, and whether terror makes for long-term stability — in other words, whether, even if mistakes had not been committed and misfortunes had not struck, the Soviet Union could have survived. Rather than ask, "Why has the Soviet Union collapsed so quickly?" we may inquire, "How did such a regime manage to hold on for so long?" For, as I propose to show, not just the practice but the very principles of Communism violated everything we have learned from sociobiology, anthropology, and the psychology of human nature, the building blocks of every social order. . . . I shall focus on only one [feature] — namely, the abolition of private property, which Marx and Engels, in *The Communist Manifesto*, proclaimed the quintessence of their movement. I shall argue that a government that monopolizes a nation's wealth and prohibits its citizens from accumulating any property beyond mere personal effects ensures its own destruction — if not from social or political explosion, then from chronic apathy, the sociopolitical equivalent of pernicious anemia. . . .

[The Bolshevik revolutionaries] were determined to abolish private property in all its forms, from great fortunes to small plots of land cultivated by peasant families, because they saw in property

*Source: Am. Acad. Arts & Sci. Bull., Jan. 1996, at 38-52.

the basis of class divisions — the cause of exploitation, oppression, and war. They adopted the view Engels had derived from the writings of the American anthropologist Lewis Morgan: that in its original state, mankind knew only communal property, and that private ownership was a transient, historically conditioned institution bound to disappear in due course. Faithful to this thesis, immediately on coming to power they nationalized all agricultural land, urban real estate, and industry. They outlawed inheritance. Next they proceeded, by unrestrained printing of banknotes, to devalue money to the point that by the early 1920s it was hardly worth the paper on which it was printed. Stalin completed Lenin's work by nationalizing the peasants' crops and livestock. When Stalin died in 1953, some 99 percent of the country's productive wealth belonged to the state, or, more precisely, the Communist Party.

The Communists felt certain that by concentrating all human and material resources in their hands, they would be able to allocate resources more rationally than the capitalists, whose investment decisions, driven by the quest for private profit, led to wasteful competition. Indeed, they proved time and again that by mobilizing capital and labor they could carry out gigantic crash programs. What eluded them to the end was a balanced economy capable of promoting a work ethic and generating innovation. Only the minuscule private sector confined to the small garden plots left to the disposal of peasant families showed any dynamism: the 1.5 percent of the Soviet Union's cultivated land allocated to private initiative and subject to market forces provided the country with nearly one-third of its produce. The state sector languished. . . .

Is private property really a transient, historically conditioned phenomenon, as the Communists assumed? Are there grounds for arguing that in their "natural" condition, living creatures, human beings included, neither need nor crave to own?

Let us begin with animals. Ethology, the systematic study of animal behavior in the wild, is a relatively new science, its origins dating mainly to the 1920s and 1930s. Among the earliest findings of the pioneering studies by Nicholas Tinbergen and Konrad Lorenz was that defense of territory is one of the consistent traits of animal life. Nearly all creatures, from insects to primates, display possessiveness in regard to the territory where they live, draw nourishment, and breed. They mark its boundaries and, if challenged, defend it by chasing away intruders. There is nothing surprising in this, because animals in their natural condition, being wholly dependent on the bounty of nature, perish if deprived of their habitat.

Ornithologists were among the first to observe this fact. In 1920 H. Eliot Howard published *Territory in Bird Life*, an extraordinary account of the relationship between birds and their environment. Howard described in poetic detail how finches, which live peacefully side by side during the winter, with the advent of spring undergo a marked change of personality, turning aggressively possessive. As the time to breed approaches, male finches separate themselves from the group and take possession of a defined area, be it a tree or a hedge, title to which they proclaim by singing. (The bird songs that so charm us are typically title claims to real estate proclaimed by males, mainly during the courtship and breeding seasons.) The tenacity with which birds fight off intruders has to do with the fact that the newly hatched brood is extremely sensitive to cold and liable to perish if the parents have to fly far away to obtain food for them. For the hatchlings to survive, they need a nearby area for exclusive use.

Most other animals display similar possessiveness in regard to territory; it has been said that even protozoa, the most primitive of living creatures, form territorial communities. . . . According to Edward Wilson, a few simple animals have no territory: the vast majority, including nearly all vertebrates and most of the advanced invertebrates, "conduct their lives according to precise rules of land tenure, spacing and dominance."

I am aware of the controversies raging over the claims of sociobiology to find in animal behavior clues to the social behavior of human beings. . . . But whoever believes in evolution — and this belief is surely universal among scientists — is hardly in a position to disassociate animal from human behavior. Is it conceivable that humans, who share with animals so many physical traits, can differ from them entirely in psyche and conduct?

In other words, if, as seems amply demonstrated, possessiveness is virtually universal in the animal world, then it is hard to see how one can deny that it is also an attribute of human beings. Whereas for animals it applies largely to territory, for mankind, in addition to territory, it touches on everything that human ingenuity is capable of creating, from tools and weapons to ideas and works of art. And even as mankind frees itself from dependence on the bounty of nature, competition over territory continues to play a significant role in the relations of peoples as well as governments. In *The Federalist*, Alexander Hamilton asserted that "territorial disputes have at all times been found one of the most fertile sources of hostility among nations. Perhaps the greatest proportion of wars that have desolated the earth have sprung from this origin." And, in fact, today, two hundred years since those words were written, what inspires the bloodiest conflicts — between Serbians and Bosnians, Israelis and Arabs, Russians and Chechens, Peruvians and Ecuadorians, the Gikuyus and Masais of Kenya — if not competition over space? And what lies behind the mounting resistance to illegal and semilegal immigrants — in France, Germany, California — if not the desire to protect one's territory from outsiders? It may well be that in the twenty-first century the most unsettling catalyst will be the demographic pressures and encroachments of the poorer regions of the world on those more affluent and more committed to social welfare.

Next, let us turn our inquiry concerning property to primitive societies. Lewis Morgan's influential treatise *Ancient Society* (1877), which popularized the notion that early mankind was ignorant of private property, originated under the inspiration of Darwin. . . . Subsequent studies of primitive societies showed [Morgan's assumptions] to be untenable, with the result that evolutionary sociology is today quite discredited. Field studies revealed that there are no universal phases of social evolution, each phase defined by institutions and practices unique to it. Primitive and advanced forms frequently flourish side by side, and nearly everything true of highly developed societies can also be found, even if less prominently, among the most primitive ones. The alleged absence of religion and marriage in prehistoric communities proved a mirage. And so did the alleged ignorance of private property.

Contemporary anthropologists are virtually at one that there is no society so crude as to be a stranger to private property. Hunters and gatherers, the most primitive of all human groups, typically hold in common the land from which they draw their sustenance and, like animals, expel or kill trespassers. But they also acknowledge as private property that which their members acquire through personal effort, be it food, weapons, utensils, clothes, adornments, dwellings, and even songs and legends. . . . The universal condemnation and punishment of theft in all known societies attests to the universality of private property.

The importance of private property rises as societies evolve from nomadic to sedentary life, from hunting and gathering to full-time agriculture and then, still further, to commercial and industrial occupations.

Although there are exceptions — the Russian *mir*, or peasant commune, being the best known — cultivated land is, as a rule, held privately. Where it is not in family possession, ownership is usually restricted to the broader kinship group. Possessiveness in regard to cultivated land is explainable not only by economic considerations — namely, the desire to reap the benefits of the labor invested in the soil — but also by the fact that the land is the site of the family residence. Religious faith comes into play as well — namely, the widespread belief that the spirits of one's ancestors continue to dwell on the land that they had in their time cleared and farmed.

Property in the form of liquid capital is by its nature private. It was the growth of capital in the West since the sixteenth century and the great social inequalities to which it had given rise that inspired socialism and the notion that private ownership was not only immoral but "unnatural."

If private property is a universal phenomenon, observable among all societies at all times, on what grounds can it be denied that it is an attribute of the human personality? What but preconceived notions of human beings — not as they are but as they ought to be — can inspire visions of a propertyless world?

The universal prevalence of private property, especially in regard to territory, is explainable, among humans as among animals, first and foremost by economic considerations. But ownership is known also to have significant psychological ramifications. . . .

. . . In her researches among small children, Lita Furby has found that they develop very early a sense of ownership that obviously has nothing to do with economics but a great deal to do with their sense of identity. According to Furby, possession is one of the first concepts to which toddlers give expression when they begin to utter two-word phrases (for instance, "Daddy chair"). It turns out that the child's awareness of self — who he or she is — is closely related to the knowledge of what objects the child controls (that is, owns): "I" is that which can dispose of certain objects or a certain territory; "mine" helps define "me." To paraphrase Descartes's "I think, therefore I am," psychologically it holds true to say of small children, "I own, therefore I am."

Property disputes are a major preoccupation of preschool children. Another child psychologist, Helen C. Dawe, found that 73.5 percent of quarrels among toddlers 18 to 29 months old are over possession. Lest it be objected that the children she studied had been raised in and conditioned by a property-centered environment, Furby extended her investigations to Israeli kibbutzim organized on the Communist principle. The results were the same. On the basis of these findings, she reached two conclusions: one, that there is a "sense of personal control or competence associated with possession," and two, that there exists an "association between possessions and one's sense of self." . . .

With these general considerations in mind, let us revert to the Soviet Union and its demise. . . .

As stated previously, during their first ten years in power, the Bolsheviks liquidated every form of productive property and converted all citizens into wage-earning employees of the state. In theory, the entire wealth of the country became public possession. But since the amorphous abstraction called "the people" cannot manage a nation's assets, Russia's wealth became, in fact, the property of the Communist Party, or, more precisely, of that party's leadership, which by 1930 meant one man: Joseph Stalin. What were the consequences?

First and foremost, corruption: stupendous, ubiquitous corruption that extended from the ranking figures of the party to the lowest-paid laborer and farm hand. In his rise to power, Stalin made certain that the central party apparatus, which served as his political base, received unique privileges in the form of special food rations, housing, and health care, along with everything else that was in short supply in that impoverished land. These privileges subsequently became institutionalized. Proceeding from the top, the cancer of corruption metastasized throughout the body politic. . . .

Another consequence was the destruction of the public spirit. The Communists wanted their citizens to give up, along with private property, personal ambitions, and to dedicate themselves wholly to the collective good. This aspiration has proven very difficult to realize, even in small utopian communities composed of idealistic volunteers. It was utterly unattainable in a vast empire held together by force. Rather than devote themselves 100 percent to the good of all, the vast majority of Soviet citizens dedicated themselves 100 percent to their private welfare. To members of the elite, the regime was an inexhaustible cornucopia that they skimmed mercilessly. Ordinary citizens interpreted the nationalization of all assets to mean that they had no stake in the country, since it belonged to someone else: since "they" owned it, let "them" take care of it. As a Soviet joke had it, "They pretend to pay us; we pretend to work." Such attitudes resulted in a progressive alienation of the citizenry from the body politic.

Another consequence of the expropriation of property was that the state assumed responsibility for the management of human and material resources that vastly exceeded its capacity to handle. The Soviet government was the world's largest conglomerate: it insisted on controlling everything, from mammoth automobile factories and steel mills to two-chair barber shops. Capitalist enterprises long ago discovered the limits to the effective centralization of management. The Communists failed to heed this lesson: they persisted in trying to manage from a single bureaucratic center nearly 300 million people dispersed across 13 time zones, and they did so because their power and privileges depended on it. . . .

Finally, among the consequences of the abolition of private property were the imponderable but very real, psychological side effects. The Communists persecuted as criminal activity any manifestation of private initiative, any action that suggested a striving for economic self-betterment. . . . A kind of regressive evolution was set in motion, under which those least fit to survive under normal conditions — that is, the most docile and unenterprising — outlived their betters. And these survivors ultimately settled into a kind of dumb stupor in which alcohol offered the favored means of escape from a hopeless existence.

Gradually, the inhabitants of Communist countries lost the very will to live and procreate. Russia, which under the tsarist regime had evinced the most rapid population growth in Europe — an annual excess of 15 to 18 births over deaths per 1,000 inhabitants — ended up, in the final years of Communism, with negative growth. . . .

When I first visited the Soviet Union nearly forty years ago, what struck me most was not the prevailing poverty and backwardness but the dispirited condition of the people. I had been to even poorer, more backward countries, yet had found many of them brimming with life and good cheer. Here I witnessed for the first time something resembling a collective depression. Is it farfetched to attribute this mood, at least in part, to the ruin of self caused by the inability to claim the fruits of one's labor? . . .

The Communist authorities finally recognized in the 1980s that with a population sunk in such inertia, so estranged from their government and each other, the Soviet Union could not maintain its place as a great world power. Thus, they initiated, at first cautiously and then more boldly, reforms intended to give their citizens a sense of belonging and having a purpose in life. Unfortunately for them, their regime turned out to be of a piece: once the windows were opened to let in the fresh winds of free speech and private initiative, the whole structure collapsed in a heap. The speed and finality of the crash only emphasized how unnatural that structure had been.

The collapse of Communism has released instincts that had been restrained for three quarters of a century. An explosion of frenetic acquisitiveness, bridled by neither law nor conscience, has been tearing the country apart. . . . Crime has been privatized, and gangster bands of all sorts are extorting protection money. Anything goes in today's Russia. Excesses occur; people suffer. It is, indeed, a sorry sight — but what else can one expect of a people whose natural desire to own and to better themselves has been so long thwarted and whom harsh experience had conditioned to look out only for themselves?

It ill behooves us to condemn such behavior. And there certainly is no reason to regret the demise of the Communist system, which was the root cause of such uncivil behavior. It seems to me that what we are witnessing in Russia today is the unavoidable and painful transition, a rapacious interlude in which healthy instincts, long suppressed, are reasserting themselves in rather savage ways. . . .

NOTES AND QUESTIONS ON PROPERTY AND HUMAN NATURE

1. For an extensive elaboration of the themes of this essay, see Richard Pipes, Property and Freedom (1999).

2. Is it true that human beings languish without private property? How would one then explain the durability of the Benedictines (described in Goffman, supra p. 1) and of the Russian peasant communes (*miri*) that Pipes mentions? (On *miri*, see Robert C. Ellickson, Property in Land, 102 Yale L.J. 1315, 1393-1394 (1993).) How would one explain the prevalent sharing and partial property arrangements that many people enter voluntarily, such as condominiums, co-ops, and other planned communities? See Epstein, infra p. 423; see also Hanoch Dagan & Michael Heller, The Liberal Commons, 110 Yale L.J. 549 (2000), arguing that human sociability leads people into shared property arrangements. Compare also Marshall P. Sahlins's observation that tribal peoples make an effort *not* to own property. See Sahlins, The Original Affluent Society, *in* Stone Age Economics 1-39 (1972).

3. Pipes roundly rejects Morgan's theory of evolutionary stages of mankind. Does a kind of evolutionary theory reappear in Pipes' own discussion of greater importance of property in agrarian and industrial societies? Notice the parallels to the evolutionary stories in Blackstone, infra p. 45, and Demsetz, infra p. 135.

4. Does Pipes' sociobiological discussion elide an important difference between *possession* and *property*? Compare other selections in this reader, e.g., Blackstone, infra p. 45, describing possession or "occupancy" as a stage prior to and different from property; Rose, Possession, infra p. 180, describing possession as different

from property because the latter entails social recognition as opposed to mere force; Goffman, supra p. 1, describing the "bad" regimes in which stronger inmates refused to recognize others' earlier possession as conferring a kind of durable entitlement. Does animal territoriality say anything at all about *property* as an entitlement generally recognized by others? Or is territoriality merely an instance of an instinct toward "possession"? Consider disputes over national borders: Does the contentiousness over the physical occupancy of various territories suggest that possession is different from property?

5. References to the presence or absence of property in the now-defunct Soviet Union will appear in several places in this book, notably in the selection by Friedman, infra p. 75, and Heller & Eisenberg, infra pp. 160-161. Notice the very different view of Heller & Eisenberg of Soviet property relations, namely that the property-like entitlements in that system were *over-* rather than *under*developed.

6. Pipes describes the corruption of the Soviet Union, as well as the continued corruption in post-Soviet Russia. For more on the latter issue, see Stephen Handelman, Comrade Criminal: Russia's New Mafiya (1995).

Property as Storytelling: Perspectives from Game Theory, Narrative Theory, Feminist Theory*

Carol M. Rose

Introduction

Many of our modern views about property, and indeed about political and economic matters generally, come from the works of seventeenth and eighteenth century theorists who hoped to find a firmly scientific basis for the study of "political economy."[1] Their systematic approach suggests that these theorists' accounts of property might be purely analytic — "synchronic" as the linguists call it. An account of this sort would treat the subject as if all its

---

*Source: 2 Yale J.L. & Human. 37-57 (1990).
1. T. Hobbes, Leviathan, ch. 20, at 261 (C.B. McPherson ed. 1968) (1651): "The skill of making, and maintaining Common-wealths, consisteth in certain rules, as doth Arithmetique and Geometry; not (as Tennis-play) on Practice onely"; see also J. Locke, Two Treatises of Government, editor's introduction at 104 (P. Laslett rev. ed. 1963) (3d ed. 1698) [hereinafter Locke]. . . .

parts occur at once, in an interlocking whole whose various aspects can be inferred logically and verified empirically, without reference to origins or to transformative changes over time. On such an account, one might indeed perceive that things change as time passes, but if one has a proper grip on the overall analytic framework, any changes would occur according to set patterns, so that future states are predictable from past states. This would be, more or less, a scientific approach: all changes in a given system are predictable from a proper synchronic analysis of the system itself.

But however much these early modern theorists hoped to ground political economy as a science, one notices that their discussions of property at some point take a striking turn toward a narrative or "diachronic" explanatory mode, treating property regimes as if they had origins and as if they developed over time. Locke is undoubtedly the most influential of the classic property theorists, and Locke used this narrative approach in his famous discussion of property in the Second Treatise of Government. Although the parts are somewhat scattered, the Treatise clearly unfolds a story line, beginning in a plenteous state of nature, carrying through the growing individual appropriation of goods, then proceeding to the development of a trading money economy, and culminating in the creation of government to safeguard property. Indeed Locke's choice of a narrative mode is all the more striking because he appears to have been indifferent to the factual accuracy of the story as a genuine history.

Almost a century later, William Blackstone launched into a quite similar pseudo-history in explaining property as an institution with an origin and evolution: he too described human beings as beginning in a state of plenty, gradually accumulating personal and landed property, and finally creating government and laws to protect property.[9] And in more recent days, the modern economist Harold Demsetz has chosen to illustrate his theory of property rights by reference to a narrative history of an evolving property regime among fur-hunting Indians on the American continent.[10]

Why have these theorists turned to storytelling to discuss property? Why have they chosen a narrative explanatory mode, which often diverges from scientific/predictive modes, and instead envisions events as unfolding in ways that, at least arguably, are only understandable after the fact? That is the subject of this paper,

9. 2 W. Blackstone, Commentaries on the Laws of England 3-9 (1766 & reprint 1979) [hereinafter Blackstone].

10. Demsetz, Toward a Theory of Property Rights, 1967 Am. Econ. Rev. 347 (Papers & Proceedings).

or at least one of its subjects. The larger subject is the relation of property to storytelling generally: the reasons why in our general discussions of who has what, and how property gets distributed, we turn to narratives instead of looking exclusively to scientific or predictive analytic approaches. In treating that subject, the paper will borrow especially from game theory, narrative theory and feminist theory. . . .

I. The Preference Orderings in the Classical Analysis of Property

We often think of property as some version of entitlement to things: I have a right to this thing or that. In a more sophisticated version of property, of course, we see property as a way of defining our relationships with other people. On such versions, my right to this thing or that isn't about controlling the "thing," so much as it is about my relationship with *you*, and with everybody else in the world: if I have a property right to this thing or that, I can keep you from exercising any control over it or having any access to it at all. That was Blackstone's benchmark for property: property was not just a "sole and despotic dominion," but it was a dominion that empowered the holder to the "total exclusion of the right of any other individual in the universe."[14]

In fact, that is the standard economic version of property: property as an institution revolves around the desire for resources themselves, but it also revolves around the desire to control others' access to those resources, at least when the resources are scarce. On this classical view, the institution of property mediates peoples' conflicting desires about resources, and it does so by allocating exclusive rights. If there were no property rights in the berry patch, all of us would just have to fight all the time for the berries. But instead, a property regime allocates this part of the patch to X, and that part to Y; and this (or any other) allocation gives each owner a sense of security, so that she invests in cultivation and tending the plants — which she won't do if she thinks she is going to wind up having to share the berries later with a lot of interloping loafers. Besides that, exclusive property rights identify who has what, and allow all of us owners to trade instead of fighting. As a result, everything gets more valuable. It all gets more valuable because the property regime encourages us to work, and then to trade the

14. 2 Blackstone 2.

results of our work, instead of wasting time and effort in bickering and fighting.

So when we break down this very standard version of property, we find several critical points. The first point is that desire — that is, a desire for resources — is at the center of the whole institution of property. The second point is that we need the capacity to shut out others from the resources that are the objects of our desire, at least when those objects become scarce. And the third point is that by allocating exclusive control of resources to individuals, a property regime winds up by satisfying even more desires, because it mediates conflicts between individuals and encourages everyone to work and trade instead of fighting, thus making possible an even greater satisfaction of desires.

There is another element hidden in this analysis, though: it is the idea that we already know, at least roughly, how people are going to order their desires, or more technically, their *preferences* about themselves and others, and about their respective access to desired resources.

What is that understood ordering? Like many of our interesting ideas in this area, it comes to us from the seventeenth century, and most particularly from Hobbes first and later Locke. Hobbes' major point about human preferences is that individuals want to *live*. Our desire to stay alive is just *there*, omnipresent and undeniable; it needs no further explanation. When push comes to shove, Hobbes thought, we will prefer our own lives over other peoples',[20] and by and large, we will also prefer our lives over highfalutin' causes, however noble. That is why in battle, for example, as Hobbes put it, "there is on one side, or both, a running away."[21]

Locke's major addendum to this picture was to show the relevance of property to the desire to live. He pointed out that life depends on property, in a very primitive sense; if one cannot literally *appropriate* those berries and fruits, one will simply die.[22]

And so acquisitiveness, the desire to have property, is "just there" too, also universal and omnipresent; thus one can always predict a human desire to have things for one's self, or as they say more lately, the human propensity to be a self-interested rational utility maximizer. The propensity is just a kind of fact of life, and the eighteenth century political economists took it for granted, rejecting as unrealistic the earlier condemnations of acquisitiveness. They attempted instead to carry forward the new science of polit-

20. Hobbes, ch. 13, at 184.
21. Hobbes, ch. 21.
22. Locke, 2d Treatise §28.

ical economy on the firm ground of irreducible self-interest, and indeed they toned down the language of "avarice" into that of the more benign "interest."

Indeed, if we do take these preferences for life and acquisition as givens, then economics can make a bid to be a kind of logical science in politics and law. With these preferences understood, we can sensibly talk about how the law gives people incentives to do this thing and that, and we can manipulate future welfare by institutionalizing the proper *ex-ante* approaches. Shifts of entitlements become predictable because we know how people order their preferences; with that knowledge, we can predict their responses and moves under different states of affairs.

That is what modern neoclassical economists do, more or less taking these utility-maximizing preference orderings for granted, and using them to perform some very powerful and sophisticated predictions of property-related behavior under varying circumstances. They make predictions about the production or consumption shifts that follow from shifts of costs, and may predict, for example, a lowered provision of rental housing in the wake of added landlord repair costs. Underlying such predictions is an idea that people prefer more for themselves rather than less, and that this preference ordering is an irreducible fact that needs no further explanation — it is just there.

Note, however, that if we do *not* have that starting point of a predictable set of preferences for "more" rather than "less," then the ways that people trade and otherwise shift their entitlements will be a little weird and unpredictable; and in talking about property, and about the ways people deal with it, at least sometimes we may have to turn to post-hoc explanatory approaches to supplement our logical predictions. That is, we may only be able to understand property arrangements through narrative discourses like literature and history, discourses that construct a story of how things got to be that way — a story in which there were genuine choices along the way, and in which things were not really predictable in advance, and did not have to wind up the way they did.

II. The Humdrum and the Weird; or, Predictable and Unpredictable Preferences

This part of the paper questions the idea that any given preference orderings are "just there," as they seem to be in the standard classical and neoclassical economic view. It suggests instead that even if one is quite sympathetic to the classical view of self-interest, there are a lot of leftover preference orderings that would not have been predicted, and that have to be explained in some way through an after-the-fact story. This part makes that point through a series of thought experiments on the ways that people order their preferences about their own and other people's access to resources.

These thought experiments present scenarios about preference orderings, in a situation where there are two people (you and I) and some Resource X that both of us desire. The scenarios presume five possible outcomes, to wit:

> I get a lot of X, and so do you;
> I get pretty much X (where "pretty much" is something over one-half of "a lot"), and so do you;
> I get a little X, and so do you;
> I get a lot of X, and you get nothing; and
> I get nothing, and you get a lot of X.

Obviously these outcomes would not be exhaustive in the real world, but they are enough to work with for now. In each of the following scenarios, "I" order my preferences among these possible outcomes, beginning with the outcome that I desire most, and moving downward to the outcome that I desire least. Again, there is some mathematically large number of ways that people might line up these outcomes, but I have chosen six that are probably familiar to most readers, and have given them names so that they can be identified more easily:

> Number 1: John Doe (JD). This perfectly ordinary person has the following order of preferences:
> Choice #1:   I get a lot, you get a lot.
>   2:   I get a lot, you get zip.
>   3:   I get pretty much, you get pretty much.
>   4:   I get a little, you get a little.
>   5:   I get zip, you get a lot.
> JD seems to be quite compatible with classical property thinking. His order of preferences is based on a kind of self-interest that is "just there." He is not mean, and is happy to have you get a lot of X where there is plenty to be had, but not if your share cuts into his. In general, he just prefers getting more over getting less, no matter what you get.
> Number 2: King of the Mountain (KOM). A somewhat more competitive type orders his preferences as follows:
> Choice #1:   I get a lot, you get zip.

2: I get a lot, you get a lot.
3: I get pretty much, you get pretty much.
4: I get a little, you get a little.
5: I get zip, you get a lot.

KOM is getting a bit slippery, from the point of view of the standard predicted preferences. He reverses John Doe's first and second preferences: he doesn't prefer the situation of maximum combined utility (both get a lot), but rather prefers the situation where he is the only winner. Still, economic prediction might be able to accommodate KOM; after all, KOM is just like JD insofar as he maximizes his own take, and his choices always put getting *more* over getting *less*. He just competes a bit more with the other guy. A little later, I will argue that with respect to property, JD and KOM are pretty much identical.

Number 3: Malice Aforethought (MA). This is a nastier character:

Choice #1: I get a lot, you get zip.
2: I get a little, you get a little.
3: I get pretty much, you get pretty much.
4: I get a lot, you get a lot.
5: I get zip, you get a lot.

MA is *very* slippery. MA would rather lose a great deal than have the other guy win; his preference ordering is based on keeping the other guy down. He is not looking very self-interested any more, at least in the usual sense. The reason is that he is "distracted" by interpersonal matters.

Number 4: Mom (or Good Citizen). Mom is a more comfortable figure, and orders her preferences this way:

Choice #1: I get a lot, you get a lot.
2: I get pretty much, you get pretty much.
3: I get zip, you get a lot.
4: I get a lot, you get zip (?).
5: I get a little, you get a little (?).

Interestingly enough, Mom too is out of line for a prediction based on self-interest: her first choice is like JD's (both get a lot), but after that she prefers that both get a reasonably good deal, and thereafter she puts the other person first. Why would a self-interested utility maximizer do that? S/he wouldn't. Again, Mom seems to be distracted by interpersonal matters. But note, Mom's orderings choose highest *joint* utility first, the next highest next and so forth. As for the question marks by 4 and 5: if Mom gets a lot, maybe she can give you some; if she can't do that, she might prefer 5 to 4.

Number 5: Portnoy's Mom (PM). She will be the first to tell you that her order of preference is:

Choice #1: I get zip, you get a lot.
  2: I get a lot, you get a lot.
  3: I get pretty much, you get pretty much.
  4: I get a little, you get a little.
  5: I get a lot, you get zip.

PM is even more out of line with a predicted preference ordering of self-interested maximization. She would rather have the other person come in first — but she's not completely crazy, either, since her second choice is to do well herself, as long as the other guy does too.

Number 6: Hit Me. This is a kind of natural victim:

Choice #1: I get zip, you get a lot.
  2: I get a little, you get a little.
  3: I get pretty much, you get pretty much.
  4: I get a lot, you get a lot.
  5: I get a lot, you get zip.

This character is out of the economic predictor's ballpark. She is a mirror image of Malice Aforethought: She wants to lose, she wants to be beaten, preferably by somebody else. . . .

Now I want to return to the main argument. Which of our preference orderings can be predicted on the classical assumptions of self-interested maximization? John Doe certainly can be, and King of the Mountain too, if we assume that self interest simply means indifference about others. Both are maximizing their own "take," both consistently choosing more over less; and preference orderings like that are assumed to be "just there," without any need for further explanation.

But how about the others? However odd they are, and however small their numbers, characters with the offbeat and unpredicted preference orderings of Numbers 3 to 6 do indeed seem to be around too, at least in most people's repertoire of experience. How do we know that? Well, for one thing, we see these characters in actual narratives, both historical and fictional. Shakespeare and Gibbon, to take two illustrious examples, are all full of tales about Malice Aforethought and his vengeance and spite. Mom and the Good Citizen might be less dramatic, but they too are all over the place in heroic novels and tales; and according to feminist literature, the cooperative, helpful character is really quite common. Roth of course told the story of Portnoy's Mom,[34] in a way that is apparently readily recognizable by a substantial segment of the population; and feminist literature has a good deal to say about Hit Me and about victimization generally.

Those other characters certainly make themselves felt in the law as well. Here as in literature and history, some of the most interesting examples revolve about the Malice Aforethought character. In property law, there is a whole category of cases about people who build the so-called "spite fence"; their story revolves about a character who goes to considerable expense to wall in a neighbor's windows, or put up some repulsive object to ruin the neighbor's view of the sunset. An example from a few years ago involved a disappointed Vermont landowner, whose neighbors blocked his efforts to rezone his lot for motel use; he decided to use the property for a piggery instead. One needs to know the story, the narrative, to figure out how such people got that way.

Much sadder are the cases of Hit Me, the victims. The criminal law is now seeing persons who give away all they have, even their lives, and appear to defer consistently to some others in what seems to be a kind of pathology of other-regarding behavior. Perhaps such persons are not very common, and perhaps their motives are exceedingly complex, but their plight does seem to attract an extraordinary level of popular fascination, and perhaps self-comparison.

The Good Citizen or Mom is another category that shows up constantly in law, and generally speaking, the law tries to encourage her cooperative behavior. The law allows people to set up all kinds of cooperative arrangements; people can form contracts and partnerships, hold joint bank accounts, and own property in various forms of common tenure. The law also polices cooperative arrangements and disfavors those in which one person seems to take advantage of another, even though the advantage-taking may fall within the formal terms of a given agreement. Moreover, while the law does not generally require that anyone assist another who is in trouble, it does recognize that some people will volunteer anyway, and protects those "Good Samaritans." Thus if John Doe's carelessness causes an accident, and Mom stops to assist the victim, tort law may make John Doe responsible for Mom as well as for

---

34. P. Roth, Portnoy's Complaint (1969).

the original victim, on the theory that he should have realized that she would try to help.

The point of all this is that legal doctrines reflect the knowledge that these other preference orderings exist; certainly there is no monolithic legal expectation that everyone will behave as an individual self-interested utility maximizer. The further point is that all these offbeat preference orderings suggest an element of indeterminacy in the ways that people use property, trade it, transfer it. There is no single ordering of preferences in the real world, and everyone knows it. . . .

What does that mean? It means that even if we think the classical property view is generally true, we are going to have to make some allowances for oddities in the way people actually do order their preferences, at least some of the time. And that in turn means that the way we fix and trade entitlements is not going to be perfectly predictable, from a set of maximizing preferences that are just there. At least some of the time, in order to figure out how entitlements have shifted and settled as they have, we are going to have to explain things after the fact, post hoc — that is, we are going to have to tell a story.

III. Narrativity and the Property Regime

I want to go now to the point where the weakness of a single ordering of preferences is most telling. That point has to do with the very regime of property itself. But to get to that point, I have to begin with an explanation of a particular kind of property, that is, common property.

Common property is a kind of property system that often emerges when it is impractical or expensive to have individualized property in a given resource. For example, it might be awfully expensive to establish and police individual rights to fish in a large lake. At the same time, though, the fish are a finite resource, and it might be important to restrain the total "take," so that the fishery doesn't get overused or ruined, and so that the fish can regenerate. What our fishermen have to do, then, is to agree on some way that they can limit the times they fish, or the numbers they take, or the way they re-stock the lake — or do something else to protect the fish against decimation.

Note that our fishermen now cannot follow the preference choice "I get a lot, you get a lot," and just let all the fishermen take all the fish they want. That is the choice of plenty, and these fish are not infinitely plenteous, but are rather a limited resource. But the fishery resource is not easily divided up among the fishermen, either; it would be conserved and used most productively if all the parties were simply to exercise some forbearance. And so, they could be faced with what is conventionally called the "Prisoner's Dilemma": all parties have to give up something for the sake of a higher long-term collective total, but it is not at all clear that they will do so, especially since each has some individual motive to cheat on any cooperative arrangement.

Now, this common-property problem creates a modification of the way we can picture the preference choices that were available to our earlier cast of characters. If we rule out the choice of Plenty (i.e., "I get a lot, you get a lot,"), the remaining options fall into the familiar Prisoner's Dilemma square:

	You cooperate	*You cheat*
I cooperate	(A) I get pretty much, you get pretty much.	(B) I get zip, you get lots.
I cheat	(C) I get lots, you get zip.	(D) I get little, you get little.

Of course, the best choice from the point of view of joint utility maximization is Box (A), where each fisherman cooperates and curtails some of his fishing for the sake of preserving the resource indefinitely for the whole group; that choice would mean that everyone would get pretty much over the long run, and the total fish taken would be maximized because the underlying resource would be able to renew itself. But for each fisherman, the *individual's* maximizing choice would be Box (C), in which he cheats while the others cooperate; thus he would prefer that all the others follow the rules and cooperate to curtail overfishing, while he "defects," or cheats, and takes all he can. But if each fisherman chooses this strategy of cheating, the whole system is driven toward Box (D), where all parties cheat, and the joint product winds up at a relatively puny level, because the fish are too depleted to regenerate. Thus the "cheating" choice can turn a renewable resource — a "positive-sum game" resource where there are gains from cooperation — into a wasting asset, a "zero-sum" resource in which all individual gains are at the expense of others, and in which the resource eventually depletes, to the ultimate detriment of all the players.

Now let us review the choices of our cast of characters: How would each character choose, if we rule out the option of Plenty (I get a lot, you get a lot)? And most important, would any of these characters be able to sustain a cooperative arrangement, and choose the optimal Box (A), where everyone acts to get "pretty much," but not the individual maximum?

First and most important, John Doe and King of the Mountain would not choose this cooperative Box (A). Where the option of Plenty is gone, they would have identical preference orderings. In a situation of finite or scarce resources, when we have to strike out the preference for everyone getting a lot, we see for both JD and KOM the following ordering:

1:   C)   I get lots, you get zip.
2:   A)   I get pretty much, you get pretty much.
3:   D)   I get little, you get little.
4:   B)   I get zip, you get lots.

When resources are limited, the cooperative management of common property is a second choice for both John Doe and King of the Mountain. Instead, in this situation of scarcity, they both have the same first choice: to take the mostest fustest. Hence the standard political economists' prediction, which is based on these characters, is what is called the Tragedy of the Commons: unless restrained by some outside compulsion, each tries to get the most for himself, and in the ensuing race, a resource that could be renewable is driven toward ruination instead.[45]

Malice Aforethought wouldn't put Box (A) first either. Striking the option of Plenty makes no difference to his first choice, which is (C) (I get lots, you get zip). In this he is like John Doe and King of the Mountain, even though his next choices would diverge from theirs. Mrs. Portnoy wouldn't choose box (A) either: her first choice remains (B) (I get zip, you get lots), which of course just encourages Malice Aforethought. And Hit-Me is like Portnoy's Mom in putting choice (B) first.

The heroine of the piece, then, is Mom (or the Good Citizen) who does not put her own well-being above yours, but is not a fool about needless self-sacrifice either: After the ruled-out choice of Plenty (I get a lot, you get a lot), her next — and now first — choice is the cooperative choice (A), (I get pretty much, you get pretty much). This is the most productive choice in a world where

45. Hardin, The Tragedy of the Commons, 162 Science 1243 (1968).

scarce resources have to be managed cooperatively; it is the choice that forbears from taking the largest individual portion and instead maximizes the joint product.

Now, here is the kicker. The larger implication of all this is that a property *regime* generally, taken as an entire system, has the same structure as a common property. This is most notable at the formative stage. At the outset of private property, people have to cooperate to set up the system — they have to get themselves organized, go to the meetings, discuss the options, figure out who gets what and how the entitlements will be protected. Even if the property regime is just a matter of customary practices that develop over time, the participants have to cooperate to the extent of recognizing and abiding by the indicia of ownership that their customs set out. And indeed, even after a property regime is in place, people have to respect each others' individual entitlements out of cooperative impulses, because it is impossible to have a continuous system of policing and/or retaliation for cheating. Thus a property system depends on people not stealing, cheating and so forth, even when they have the chance — that is, all the participants, or at least a substantial number of them, have to cooperate to make a property regime work.

A property regime, in short, presupposes a kind of character who is *not* predicted in the standard story about property. And that, I suggest, is why the classic theories of property turned to narrative at crucial moments, particularly in explaining the origin of property regimes, where the need for cooperation is most obvious: Their narrative stories allowed them to slide smoothly over the cooperative gap in their systematic analyses of self-interest.

One can see the point in the various parts of Locke's story about property. He starts off with a tale of people in a state of nature, acquiring natural products like acorns and apples through the very labor of gathering them; and then realizing that wealth could be stored through the collection of durables (like nuts and little pieces of gold); and finally, growing nervous at the "very unsafe, very unsecure" enjoyment of property in the state of nature, and joining with others to establish the civil society that will protect everyone's hard-earned property.[52]

Hold it right there: joining with others? Just how did they form that civil society and its government, anyway? Who put in the time and effort of schmoozing, and getting the special committees together, and hammering out the terms? Why didn't they

---

52. [Locke] §123.

all just loaf around, as John Doe would, choosing Box (C) in the hopes that other people would do all the organizing work? And if they did let George do it, who is this George character anyway? If there is a George, he looks an awful lot like Mom, or the Good Citizen — somebody who would be willing to do some work for the sake of the common good.

Blackstone's story is a more connected narrative, but it slides over the point even more easily. After a long tale of the way in which people started to hold onto increasing numbers of objects for themselves, as they became more talented and numerous, he points out that the "earth would not produce her fruits in sufficient quantities, without the assistance of tillage: but who would be at the pains of tilling it, if another might watch an opportunity to seize upon and enjoy the product of his industry, art and labour?" Here is the happy conclusion: "Necessity begat property, and in order to insure that property, recourse was had to civil society."[56] And that's it.

Now wait a minute: If nobody would be at pains of tilling unless they could capture the rewards, why should they be at pains of setting up a civil society? Why don't Blackstone's characters sit around waiting for George too?

In short, there is a gap between the kind of self-interested individual who needs exclusive property to induce him to labor, and the kind of individual who has to be there to create, maintain, and protect a property regime. The existence of a property regime is not predictable from a starting point of rational self-interest; and consequently, from that perspective, property needs a tale, a story, a post-hoc explanation.

That, I think, is one reason Locke and Blackstone, and their modern-day successors, are so fond of telling stories when they talk about the origin of property. It is the story that fills the gap in the classical theory, and, as Hayden White might put it, that makes property "plausible." Narrative gives us a smooth tale of property as an institution that could come about through time, effort, and above all through cooperative choices.

Cooperation, then, is a preference ordering that the classical property theorists weren't counting on in theory, but that they can't do without. And so they have to tell a story to explain it, and rely on our imaginative reconstruction from narrative to paint a plausible picture about how we got these property regimes in the first place.

56. [2 Blackstone, at 2-8.]

IV.   Reprise: The "Natural-ness" of Self-Interest and the "Moral-ness" of the Property Story

Quite aside from the thought experiments we have run through, and quite aside from the striking case of the cooperative preferences that we need for the institution of property itself, it should be pretty obvious that John Doe's self-interested preference ordering is only one among a number of options. In the real world, his orderings have to be explained too; they have a history too, and need a story just like anybody else's. The Critical Legal Studies movement has been around long enough to get across the idea that John Doe is just another story; it is instead the endless repetition of JD's "naturalness" that has made us think that his preferences are "just there," needing no further explanation or narration.

Feminist theorists have made the point in another way: at least since Carol Gilligan,[60] and really for some time before, we have realized that Mom or the Good Citizen — the caring, cooperative person generally — is just as much "there" as the indifferent non-cooperator, John Doe. Indeed, the feminist theorists have pointed out the importance of narrative in arriving at preference choices: Mom talks things over, and arrives at her preference orderings through discussion and negotiation — perhaps at least sometimes because she has little to begin with, and hence little capacity to retaliate against non-cooperators. Presumably, from Mom's (or Good Citizen George's) perspective, cooperation would be the predictable set of preferences, while John Doe's self-interest would be the oddity, and John Doe would have to be explained by some kind of story about how he got that way.

So why is cooperation the preference ordering that seems to need the story? There is, of course, the point that is made so tellingly by critical theory, and even more so by feminist theory: the dominant storyteller can make his position seem to be the natural one. . . .

But there is more to be said about these characters than their identity as a dominating group of storytellers. Consider Mom's big problem: suppose that she encounters John Doe, the blandest of these three noncooperating characters. However much she may prefer cooperative solutions, when she meets this non-cooperator, she has to choose between two roles she does not want. One of her choices is to be a Hit-Me victim, since her choice to cooperate would only meet John Doe's choice to cheat, which would put her

60. C. Gilligan [In a Different Voice (1982)].

in the worst of all possible positions. Her other choice is to mimic John Doe himself, by choosing mutual non-cooperation — but that is a role that she realizes would lead to a collective loss, which she also does not want. Thus unless she is dealing with another Mom, another cooperator, she is stuck with a choice between Boxes (B) or (D): the choice between cooperating and the great risk of domination, or of cheating and the certainty of the relative mutual impoverishment of "I get a little, you get a little."

And that, I would suggest, is a big reason why John Doe seems like nature, like something that is "just there," while Mom seems to need a narrative. John Doe chooses the safe route, the route that might lead to the jackpot if the opposite number is a cooperator/sucker, and that at least lets him get a little bit if the other guy is another noncooperative John Doe.

But Mom the cooperator takes risks for a common good. When it works, everyone is better off, but when it doesn't, she may lose horribly. And she makes you wonder, how did she get that way? Why didn't she take the safe route and cheat, like John Doe? . . . *What's her story, anyway?*

Thus we are back to storytelling — and not just the story about Mom, but also to the story that she can tell: her storytelling can both create a sense of commonality, and reorder her audience's ways of dealing with the world. According to the narrative theorists, the teller of the tales has a vision of some kind of community, even if it is only a community of two.[64] The storyteller places herself with the audience experiencing the tale; she takes a clutch of occurrences and through narrative reveals them for her audience as *actions*, with beginnings, middles, and ends — actions in which the audience can imagine themselves as common participants or common observers. . . . In this sense, narratives change our minds, and give us an opportunity to reconsider and reorder our approach to events; we can recollect them as actions taken and not taken, and act differently in the future, instead of endlessly repeating some formulaic, repetitive, and predictable response, as rocks respond to gravity. Perhaps this is what Mom is aiming at: Narrative theory coincides with feminist theory in suggesting that preference orderings don't just come out of nowhere; they may be constructs of narrative and negotiation, and may change over time, as we digest the stories of the places that our preferences have led us, or may lead us in the future, unless we act to lead them instead. . . .

Perhaps now we can take another guess at why Locke and

64. D. Carr, Time, Narrative and History 61-62, 153-156 (1986).

Blackstone and their successors have been telling those siren tales about property, too. Their theoretical self-interest had a fatal weakness too when it came to establishing a property regime. But if their tales could just get us John Does over the hump of our conservative, unimaginative, play-it-safe self-interest, they might get us to establish property regimes; they might get us to recognize that if we all respect each others' claims, we can encourage everyone to expend labor on the resources of the world, and we all will be better off in the end.

And maybe that is the real story about why they told those stories, and why their successors continue to tell them. They may have been right or wrong in their argument that property improves the lot of humankind; and their smooth tales of property's cooperative origins may well have slighted the emotional context in which cooperation takes place. But those tales are moral ones all the same, just as much as Aesop's Fables, speaking to and constituting a kind of moral community, and urging that community to change its ways.

NOTES AND QUESTIONS ON NARRATIVE APPROACHES

1. Several of the authors discussed here are represented in selections in this volume, including William Blackstone, Harold Demsetz, and Garrett Hardin.

2. What is the picture of human nature and human desires that Rose attributes to the classical property thinkers? How does this differ from the picture presented by Goffman? By Radin? What consequences might follow for the structuring of property regimes? For other depictions of human preferences about property, see the selections by Pipes, supra p. 20, and Sugden, infra p. 170.

3. Rose's analysis of the supposed flaws of the classical property theory revolves around the problem conventionally identified as the "prisoner's dilemma" (PD). Rose says that a character like "Mom" — someone with some level of altruistic or other-directed preferences — is needed to overcome PD problems. Is this true? Robert Axelrod, The Evolution of Cooperation (1984), reproduced in part at p. 261, infra argues that cooperation can emerge from purely self-interested motivations. But compare Robert Frank, Passions Within Reason: The Strategic Role of the Emotions (1988), who argues that cooperation rests fundamentally on emotions that cannot be derived from rational self-interest.

4. Rose's "post-modern" presentation suggests that there is no single dominating set of human preferences. Is that true? Why, then, is the classical property story so persuasive? Does its persuasive power suggest some kind of underlying dominating preferences? Or does it only suggest that stories help people to believe inconsistent things?

5. In discussing the theory of narrative as a persuasive strategy, Rose relies chiefly on David Carr, Time, Narrative and History (1986), which relates narrative to the theory of action. The classical study of rhetoric, which revolved around the question of persuasion, is no longer studied in a systematic fashion at most universities. Interest in rhetoric is increasing, however, stimulated by the view that even persons in the predictive sciences are influenced by arguments that are merely *persuasive* without being *demonstrative* — sometimes on the premise that there is no conclusively demonstrable truth at all. For a version of this position with respect to the physical sciences, see Thomas Kuhn, The Structure of Scientific Revolutions (1962); for the argument that economics is also basically rhetorical, see Donald McCloskey, The Rhetoric of Economics (1985).

Do people really use "stories" to change their own and other peoples' minds and behaviors? How important, for example, are stories for lawyers? The burgeoning literature on legal storytelling received a stinging critique in Daniel Farber & Suzanna Sherry, Telling Stories Out of School: An Essay on Legal Narratives, 45 Stan. L. Rev. 807 (1993).

6. Isn't this selection a piece of rhetoric too? Why, for example, do the characters have the names they do? Why do the possible preference orderings ("I get a lot, you get a little," for instance) wind up falling so neatly into a prisoner's dilemma box?

B. Property and Prosperity

*Commentaries on the Laws of England**

William Blackstone

There is nothing which so generally strikes the imagination, and engages the affections of mankind, as the right of property; or

*Source: Vol. 2, *2-*11 (1766).

that sole and despotic dominion which one man claims and exercises over the external things of the world, in total exclusion of the right of any other individual in the universe. And yet there are very few that will give themselves the trouble to consider the original and foundation of this right. Pleased as we are with the possession, we seem afraid to look back to the means by which it was acquired, as if fearful of some defect in our title; or at best we rest satisfied with the decision of the laws in our favor, without examining the reason or authority upon which those laws have been built. We think it enough that our title is derived by the grant of the former proprietor, by descent from our ancestors, or by the last will and testament of the dying owner; not caring to reflect that (accurately and strictly speaking) there is no foundation in nature or in natural law, why a set of words upon parchment should convey the dominion of land: why the son should have a right to exclude his fellow-creatures from a determinate spot of ground, because his father had done so before him: or why the occupier of a particular field or of a jewel, when lying on his death-bed, and no longer able to maintain possession, should be entitled to tell the rest of the world which of them should enjoy it after him. These inquiries, it must be owned, would be useless and even troublesome in common life. It is well if the mass of mankind will obey the laws when made, without scrutinizing too nicely into the reason for making them. But, when law is to be considered not only as a matter of practice, but also as a rational science, it cannot be improper or useless to examine more deeply the rudiments and grounds of these positive constitutions of society.

In the beginning of the world, we are informed by holy writ, the all-bountiful Creator gave to man "dominion over all the earth, and over the fish of the sea, and over the fowl of the air, and over every living thing that moveth upon the earth."[a] This is the only true and solid foundation of man's dominion over external things, whatever airy metaphysical notions may have been started by fanciful writers upon this subject. The earth, therefore, and all things therein, are the general property of all mankind, exclusive of other beings, from the immediate gift of the Creator. And, while the earth continued bare of inhabitants, it is reasonable to suppose that all was in common among them, and that every one took from the public stock to his own use such things as his immediate necessities required.

These general notions of property were then sufficient to an-

(a) Gen. i. 28.

swer all the purposes of human life; and might perhaps still have answered them had it been possible for mankind to have remained in a state of primeval simplicity: as may be collected from the manners of many American nations when first discovered by the Europeans; and from the ancient method of living among the first Europeans themselves, if we may credit either the memorials of them preserved in the golden age of the poets, or the uniform accounts given by historians of those times. . . . Not that this communion of goods seems ever to have been applicable, even in the earliest stages, to aught but the *substance* of the thing; nor could it be extended to the *use* of it. For, by the law of nature and reason, he, who first began to use it, acquired therein a kind of transient property, that lasted so long as he was using it, and no longer: or, to speak with greater precision, the *right* of possession continued for the same time only that the *act* of possession lasted. Thus the ground was in common, and no part of it was the permanent property of any man in particular; yet whoever was in the occupation of any determined spot of it, for rest, for shade, or the like, acquired for the time a sort of ownership, from which it would have been unjust, and contrary to the law of nature, to have driven him by force: but the instant that he quitted the use or occupation of it, another might seize it, without injustice. Thus also a vine or other tree might be said to be in common, as all men were equally entitled to its produce; and yet any private individual might gain the sole property of the fruit, which he had gathered for his own repast. A doctrine well illustrated by Cicero, who compares the world to a great theatre, which is common to the public, and yet the place which any man has taken is for the time his own.

But when mankind increased in number, craft, and ambition, it became necessary to entertain conceptions of more permanent dominions; and to appropriate to individuals not the immediate *use* only, but the very *substance* of the thing to be used. Otherwise innumerable tumults must have arisen, and the good order of the world be continually broken and disturbed, while a variety of persons were striving who should get the first occupation of the same thing, or disputing which of them had actually gained it. As human life also grew more and more refined, abundance of conveniences were devised to render it more easy, commodious, and agreeable; as, habitations for shelter and safety, and raiment for warmth and decency. But no man would be at the trouble to provide either, so long as he had only an usufructuary property in them, which was to cease the instant that he quitted possession; if, as soon as he walked out of his tent, or pulled off his garments, the next stranger who came by would have a right to inhabit the one, and to wear the other. In the case of habitations in particular, it was natural to observe, that even the brute creation, to whom every thing else was in common, maintained a kind of permanent property in their dwellings, especially for the protection of their young; that the birds of the air had nests, and the beasts of the field had caverns, the invasion of which they esteemed a very flagrant injustice, and would sacrifice their lives to preserve them. Hence a property was soon established in every man's house and home-stall: which seem to have been originally mere temporary huts or movable cabins, suited to the design of Providence for more speedily peopling the earth, and suited to the wandering life of their owners, before any extensive property in the soil or ground was established. And there can be no doubt, but that movables of every kind became sooner appropriated than the permanent substantial soil: partly because they were more susceptible of a long occupancy, which might be continued for months together without any sensible interruption, and at length by usage ripen into an established right; but principally because few of them could be fit for use, till improved and ameliorated by the bodily labor of the occupant, which bodily labor, bestowed upon any subject which before lay in common to all men, is universally allowed to give the fairest and most reasonable title to an exclusive property therein.

The article of food was a more immediate call, and therefore a more early consideration. Such as were not contented with the spontaneous product of the earth, sought for a more solid refreshment in the flesh of beasts, which they obtained by hunting. But the frequent disappointments incident to that method of provision, induced them to gather together such animals as were of a more tame and sequacious nature, and to establish a permanent property in their flocks and herds, in order to sustain themselves in a less precarious manner, partly by the milk of the dams, and partly by the flesh of the young. The support of these their cattle made the article of *water* also a very important point. And therefore the book of Genesis (the most venerable monument of antiquity, considered merely with a view to history) will furnish us with frequent instances of violent contentions concerning wells; the exclusive property of which appears to have been established in the first digger or occupant, even in such places where the ground and herbage remained yet in common. Thus we find Abraham, who was but a sojourner, asserting his right to a well in the country of Abimelech, and exacting an oath for his security, "because he had digged that well."[e] And Isaac, about ninety years afterwards, reclaimed that as his father's property, and after much contention with the Philistines was suffered to enjoy it in peace.[f]

All this while the soil and pasture of the earth remained still in common as before, and open to every occupant: except perhaps in the neighborhood of towns, where the necessity of a sole and exclusive property in lands (for the sake of agriculture) was earlier felt, and therefore more readily complied with. Otherwise, when the multitude of men and cattle had consumed every convenience on one spot of ground, it was deemed a natural right to seize upon and occupy such other lands as would more easily supply their necessities. This practice is still retained among the wild and uncultivated nations that have never been formed into civil states, like the Tartars and others in the east; where the climate itself, and the boundless extent of their territory, conspire to retain them still in the same savage state of vagrant liberty, which was universal in the earliest ages, and which, Tacitus informs us, continued among the Germans till the decline of the Roman empire. We have also a striking example of the same kind in the history of Abraham and his nephew Lot.[h] When their joint substance became so great that pasture and other conveniences grew scarce, the natural consequence was, that a strife arose between their servants; so that it was no longer practicable to dwell together. This contention Abraham thus endeavored to compose: — "Let there be no strife, I pray thee, between thee and me. Is not the whole land before thee? Separate thyself, I pray thee, from me. If thou wilt take the left hand, then I will go to the right; or if thou depart to the right hand, then I will go to the left." This plainly implies an acknowledged right, in either, to occupy whatever ground he pleased, that was not preoccupied by other tribes. "And Lot lifted up his eyes, and beheld all the plain of Jordan, that it was well watered everywhere, even as the garden of the Lord. Then Lot choose him all the plain of Jordan, and journeyed east; and Abraham dwelt in the land of Canaan."

Upon the same principle was founded the right of migration, or sending colonies to find out new habitations when the mother-country was overcharged with inhabitants; which was practiced as well by the Phoenicians and Greeks, as the Germans, Scythians, and other northern people. And, so long as it was confined to the

(e) Gen. xxi. 30.
(f) Gen. xxvi. 15, 18, etc.
(h) Gen. c. xiii.

stocking and cultivation of desert uninhabited countries, it kept strictly within the limits of the law of nature. But how far the seizing on countries already peopled, and driving out or massa-cring the innocent and defenceless natives, merely because they differed from their invaders in language, in religion, in customs, in government, or in color; how far such a conduct was consonant to nature, to reason, or to Christianity, deserved well to be consid-ered by those who have rendered their names immortal by thus civilizing mankind.

As the world by degrees grew more populous, it daily became more difficult to find out new spots to inhabit, without encroaching upon former occupants: and, by constantly occupying the same individual spot, the fruits of the earth were consumed, and its spontaneous produce destroyed, without any provision for future supply or succession. It therefore became necessary to pursue some regular method of providing a constant subsistence; and this ne-cessity produced, or at least promoted and encouraged, the art of agriculture. And the art of agriculture, by a regular connection and consequence, introduced and established the idea of a more per-manent property in the soil than had hitherto been received and adopted. It was clear that the earth would not produce her fruits in sufficient quantities without the assistance of tillage; but who would be at the pains of tilling it, if another might watch an op-portunity to seize upon and enjoy the product of his industry, art, and labor? Had not therefore a separate property in lands as well as movables been vested in some individuals, the world must have continued a forest, and men have been mere animals of prey, which, according to some philosophers, is the genuine state of na-ture. Whereas now (so graciously has Providence interwoven our duty and our happiness together) the result of this very necessity has been the ennobling of the human species, by giving it oppor-tunities of improving its *rational* faculties, as well as of exerting its *natural*. Necessity begat property; and, in order to insure that prop-erty, recourse was had to civil society, which brought along with it a long train of inseparable concomitants, — states, government, laws, punishments, and the public exercise of religious duties. Thus connected together, it was found that a part only of society was sufficient to provide, by their manual labor, for the necessary subsistence of all; and leisure was given to others to cultivate the human mind, to invent useful arts, and to lay the foundations of science.

The only question remaining is, how this property became ac-tually invested, or what it is that gave a man an exclusive right to retain in a permanent manner that specific *land*, which before belonged generally to everybody, but particularly to nobody. And, as we before observed that occupancy gave the right to the temporary *use* of the soil, so it is agreed upon all hands, that occupancy gave also the original right to the permanent property in the *substance* of the earth itself; which excludes every one else but the owner from the use of it. There is indeed some difference among the writers on natural law concerning the reason why occupancy should convey this right, and invest one with this absolute property: Grotius and Puffendorf insisting that this right of occupancy is founded on a tacit and implied assent of all mankind that the first occupant should become the owner; and Barbeyrac, Titius, Mr. Locke, and others, holding that there is no such implied assent, neither is it necessary that there should be; for that the very act of occupancy alone, being a degree of bodily labor, is, from a principle of natural justice, without any consent or compact, sufficient of itself to gain a title; — a dispute that savors too much of nice and scholastic refinement. However, both sides agree in this, that occupancy is the thing by which the title was in fact originally gained; every man seizing to his own continued use such spots of ground as he found most agreeable to his own convenience, provided he found them unoccupied by any one else.

Property, both in lands and movables, being thus originally acquired by the first taker, which taking amounts to a declaration that he intends to appropriate the thing to his own use, it remains in him, by the principles of universal law, till such time as he does some other act which shows an intention to abandon it; for then it becomes, naturally speaking, *publici juris* once more, and is liable to be again appropriated by the next occupant. . . .

But this method of one man's abandoning his property, and another seizing the vacant possession, however well founded in theory, could not long subsist in fact. It was calculated merely for the rudiments of civil society, and necessarily ceased among the complicated interests and artificial refinements of polite and established governments. In these it was found, that what became inconvenient or useless to one man, was highly convenient and useful to another, who was ready to give in exchange for it some equivalent that was equally desirable to the former proprietor. Thus mutual convenience introduced commercial traffic, and the reciprocal transfer of property by sale, grant, or conveyance; which may be considered either as a continuance of the original possession which the first occupant had, or as an abandoning of the thing by the present owner, and an immediate successive occupancy of the same by the new proprietor. . . .

The most universal and effectual way of abandoning property, is by the death of the occupant: when, both the actual possession and intention of keeping possession ceasing, the property which is founded upon such possession and intention ought also to cease of course. For, naturally speaking, the instant a man ceases to be, he ceases to have any dominion: else, if he had a right to dispose of his acquisitions one moment beyond his life, he would also have a right to direct their disposal for a million of ages after him: which would be highly absurd and inconvenient. All property must therefore cease upon death, considering men as absolute individuals, and unconnected with civil society: for, then, by the principles before established, the next immediate occupant would acquire a right in all that the deceased possessed. But as, under civilized governments, which are calculated for the peace of mankind, such a constitution would be productive of endless disturbances, the universal law of almost every nation (which is a kind of secondary law of nature) has either given the dying person a power of continuing his property, by disposing of his possessions by will; or, in case he neglects to dispose of it, or is not permitted to make any disposition at all, the municipal law of the country then steps in, and declares who shall be the successor, representative, or heir of the deceased; that is, who alone shall have a right to enter upon this vacant possession, in order to avoid that confusion which its becoming again common would occasion. . . .

NOTES AND QUESTIONS ON THE BLACKSTONIAN VISION

1. Blackstone begins by remarking on people's uneasiness about the basis of property. Does this suggest, as some have said, that property is ultimately based on theft, and that, moreover, people realize this and hence are nervous about their own titles? The view that property is theft was most famously stated by P. J. Proudhon, What Is Property? (1840). Marx's view was somewhat similar; see The So-Called Primitive Accumulation, *in* Capital, pt. 8 (3d ed. 1883).

On Blackstone's account, what does property *do* for people? Why have property regimes if property makes people nervous?

2. Blackstone names several "principles" upon which property may be based, including (a) God's bequest to all mankind, (b) an analogy to animal nesting behavior, (c) reward to labor, (d) "necessity" for agriculture, and (e) occupancy. How do these principles fit together, if they do? Which, if any, overcome the charge that

property is theft? Do you think that Blackstone really cared? (Note, for example, his comment on the "scholastic" dispute between Grotius and Locke.)

3. Blackstone suggests that certain types of objects were turned into property before others, and that property rights themselves evolved from temporary usage to more permanent entitlement. What accounts for these evolutionary patterns? Are there modern sequels, in the American West, for instance? See Terry L. Anderson & P. J. Hill, The Evolution of Property Rights: A Study of the American West, 18 J.L. & Econ. 163 (1975), describing evolving property regimes in such resources as water and livestock range. Are there contemporary examples of emerging property rights in previously unowned resources, in such places as the South American rainforest or the ocean seabed?

4. Blackstone's comment that property entails "sole and despotic dominion" in "total exclusion" of the rights of others is one of the most quoted lines in the literature of property. But how important is "exclusivity" to property? Compare Thomas W. Merrill, Property and the Right to Exclude, 77 Neb. L. Rev. 730 (1998) (exclusion essential to property) with Carol M. Rose, Canons of Property Talk, or, Blackstone's Anxiety, 198 Yale L.J. 601 (1998) (exclusion more metaphoric than real in property).

5. Rose, Storytelling, supra p. 28, suggests that Blackstone's account was just a "story," and indeed basically the same optimistic story that is told by Demsetz, infra p. 135. How persuasive is the story? Is it any more persuasive than the story that "property is theft"? Does your answer depend on your views about how likely human beings are to cooperate? See Robert Axelrod, The Evolution of Cooperation, infra p. 261.

6. In the final two paragraphs of this selection, Blackstone offers reasons why owners of private property should be entitled to transfer their belongings by sale and by disposition at death (either by will or rules of intestate succession). How persuasive are these passages? These issues — alienability and the appropriate time span of private ownership — are revisited infra in Chapter 7C and in Note 5, pp. 380-381.

*Economic Analysis of Law**

Richard A. Posner

§3.1   The Economic Theory of Property Rights: Static and Dynamic Aspects

To understand the economics of property rights, it is first necessary to grasp the economist's distinction between *static* and *dynamic* analysis. Static analysis suppresses the time dimension of economic activity: All adjustments to change are assumed to occur instantaneously. The assumption is unrealistic but often fruitful. . . .

Dynamic analysis, in which the assumption of instantaneous adjustment to change is relaxed, is usually more complex than static analysis. So it is surprising that the economic basis of property rights was first perceived in dynamic terms. Imagine a society in which all property rights have been abolished. A farmer plants corn, fertilizes it, and erects scarecrows, but when the corn is ripe his neighbor reaps it and takes it away for his own use. The farmer has no legal remedy against his neighbor's conduct since he owns neither the land that he sowed nor the crop. Unless defensive measures are feasible (and let us assume for the moment that they are not), after a few such incidents the cultivation of land will be abandoned and society will shift to methods of subsistence (such as hunting) that involve less preparatory investment.

As this example suggests, legal protection of property rights creates incentives to use resources efficiently. Although the value of the crop in our example, as measured by consumers' willingness to pay, may have greatly exceeded its cost in labor, materials, and forgone alternative uses of the land, without property rights there is no incentive to incur these costs because there is no reasonably assured reward for incurring them. The proper incentives are created by parceling out mutually exclusive rights to the use of particular resources among the members of society. If every piece of land is owned by someone — if there is always someone who can exclude all others from access to any given area — then individuals will endeavor by cultivation or other improvements to maximize the value of land. Of course, land is just an example. The principle applies to all valuable resources.

*Source: pp. 36-45 (5th ed. 1998).

All this has been well known for hundreds of years.[1] In contrast, the static analysis of property rights is little more than 70 years old. Imagine that a number of farmers own a pasture in common; that is, none has the right to exclude any of the others and hence none can charge the others for the use of the pasture. We can abstract from the dynamic aspects of the problem by assuming that the pasture is a natural (uncultivated) one, so there is no question of improving it by investment. Even so, pasturing additional cows will impose a cost on all the farmers. The cows will have to graze more in order to eat the same amount of grass, and this will reduce their weight. But because none of the farmers pays for the use of the pasture, none will take this cost into account in deciding how many additional cows to pasture, with the result that more cows will be pastured than would be efficient. (Can you see an analogy to highway congestion?)

The problem would disappear if one person owned the pasture and charged each farmer for its use (for purposes of this analysis, disregard the cost of levying such a charge). The charge to each farmer would include the cost he imposes on the other farmers by pasturing additional cows, because that cost reduces the value of the pasture to the other farmers and hence the price they are willing to pay the owner for the right to graze.

The creation of individual (as distinct from collective) ownership rights is a necessary rather than a sufficient condition for the efficient use of resources. The rights also must be transferable. Suppose the farmer in our first example owns the land that he sows but is a bad farmer; his land would be more productive in someone else's hands. Efficiency requires a mechanism by which

---

1. See, e.g., 2 William Blackstone, Commentaries on the Laws of England 4, 7 (1766). And property-rights systems are prehistoric in their origins. Vernon L. Smith, The Primitive Hunter Culture, Pleistocene Extinction, and the Rise of Agriculture, 83 J. Pol. Econ. 727 (1975).

The proposition that enforcing property rights will lead to a greater output is questioned by Frank I. Michelman in Ethics, Economics, and the Law of Property, 24 Nomos 3, 25 (1982). He suggests that the farmer who knows that half his crop will be stolen may just plant twice as much. This suggestion overlooks

  (1) the added incentive to theft that will be created by planting a larger crop and the resulting likelihood that more than one-half of the larger crop will be stolen;

  (2) the unlikelihood that farming would be so much more profitable than substitute activities not entailing preparatory investment as to keep people in farming; and

  (3) the likelihood that the farmer, if he remained in farming, would divert some of his resources from growing crops to protecting them with walls, guards, etc.

the farmer can be induced to transfer the property to someone who can work it more productively. A transferable property right is such a mechanism. Suppose Farmer A owns a piece of land that he anticipates will yield him $100 a year above his labor and other costs, indefinitely. Just as the price of a share of common stock is equal to the present value of the anticipated earnings to which the shareholder will be entitled, so the present value of a parcel of land that is expected to yield an annual net income of $100 can be calculated and is the minimum price that A will accept in exchange for his property right. Suppose Farmer B believes that he can use A's land more productively than A. The present value of B's expected earnings stream will therefore exceed the present value calculated by A. Suppose the present value calculated by A is $1,000 and by B $1,500. Then at any price between $1,000 and $1,500 both A and B will be made better off by a sale. Thus, there are strong incentives for a voluntary exchange of A's land for B's money.

The discussion to this point may seem to imply that if every valuable (meaning scarce as well as desired) resource were owned by someone (the criterion of universality), ownership connoted the unqualified power to exclude everybody else from using the resource (exclusivity) as well as to use it oneself, and ownership rights were freely transferable, or as lawyers say alienable (transferability), value would be maximized. This leaves out of account, however, the costs of a property-rights system, both the obvious and the subtle ones. Those costs are a particular focus of this chapter.

An example will illustrate a subtle cost of exclusivity. Suppose our farmer estimates that he can raise a hog with a market value of $100 at a cost of only $50 in labor and materials, for a net of $50, and that no alternative use of the land would yield a greater net value — in the next best use, his income from the land would be only $20. He will want to raise the hog. But now suppose his property right is qualified in two respects: He has no right to prevent an adjacent railroad from accidentally emitting engine sparks that may set fire to the hog's pen, killing the hog prematurely; and a court may decide that his raising a hog on this land is a nuisance, in which event he will have to sell the hog on disadvantageous (why disadvantageous?) terms before it is grown. In light of these contingencies he must reevaluate the yield of his land: He must discount the $100 to reflect the probability that the yield may be much less, perhaps zero. Suppose that, after this discounting, the expected revenue from raising the hog (market value times the probability that it will reach the market) is only $60. He will not raise the hog. The anticipated profit from raising the hog is now only $10 (the farmer's costs are $50). The next best use, we said, would yield a profit of $20. He will put the land to that use, which we said was less valuable ($20 versus $50), and the value of the land will fall.

But the analysis is incomplete. Removing the hog may increase the value of surrounding residential land by more than the fall in the value of the farmer's parcel; or the cost of preventing the emission of engine sparks may exceed the reduction in the value of the farmer's land when he switches from raising hogs to growing, say, fireproof radishes. But, the alert reader may interject, if the increase in value to others from a different use of the farmer's land exceeds the decrease to him, let them buy his right. The railroad can purchase an easement to emit sparks; the surrounding homeowners can purchase a covenant from the farmer not to raise hogs; there is no need to limit the farmer's property right. But . . . the costs of effecting a transfer of rights — transaction costs — are often prohibitive, and when this is so, giving someone the exclusive right to a resource may reduce rather than increase efficiency.

§3.2 Problems in the Creation and Enforcement of Property Rights

Property rights are not only less exclusive but less universal than they would be if they were not costly to enforce. Imagine a primitive society in which the principal use of land is for grazing. The population of the society is small relative to the amount of land, and its flocks are small too. No technology exists for increasing the value of the land by fertilizer, irrigation, or other techniques. The cost of wood or other materials for fencing is very high and, the society being illiterate, a system for publicly recording land ownership is out of the question. In these circumstances the costs of enforcing property rights might well exceed the benefits. The costs would be the costs of fencing to keep out other people's grazing animals, and would be substantial. The benefits might be zero. Since there is no crowding problem, property rights would confer no static benefits, and since there is no way of improving the land, there would be no dynamic benefits either. It is no surprise that property rights are less extensive in primitive than in advanced societies and that the pattern by which property rights emerge and grow in a society is related to increases in the ratio of the benefits of property rights to their costs.

The common law distinction between domestic and wild animals illustrates the general point. Domestic animals are owned like any other personal property; wild animals are not owned until killed or put under actual restraint (as in a zoo). Thus, if your cow wanders off your land, it is still your cow; but if a gopher whose burrow is on your land wanders off, he is not your property, and anyone who wants can capture or kill him, unless he is tame — unless he has an *animus revertendi* (the habit of returning to your land). (Can you think of an economic argument for the doctrine of *animus revertendi?*) It would be difficult to enforce a property right in a wild animal and pretty useless; most wild animals, as in our gopher illustration, are not valuable, so there is nothing to be gained from creating incentives to invest in them.

Suppose the wild animals *are* valuable. Unless there are property rights in valuable fur-bearing animals, such as sable and beaver, hunters will hunt them down to extinction, even though the present value of the resource will be diminished by doing so. The hunter who spares a mother beaver so that it can reproduce knows that the beavers born to her will almost certainly be caught by someone other than himself (so long as there are many hunters), and he will not forgo a present benefit to confer a future benefit on someone else. Property rights would be desirable in these circumstances but it is hard to imagine a feasible scheme for giving the hunter who decided to spare the mother beaver a property right in her unborn litter. The costs of enforcing such a property right would still exceed the benefits, though the benefits would now be substantial.

There are two possible solutions. The more common is to use the regulatory powers of the state to reduce hunting to the approximate level it would be at if the animals were hunted at an optimal rate; this is an example of how regulation can be a substitute for property rights in correcting a divergence between private and social costs or benefits. The other solution is for one person to buy up the entire habitat of the animals; he will then regulate hunting on his property optimally because he will obtain all the gains from doing so.

Another example of the correlation between property rights and scarcity is the difference in the water law systems of the eastern and western states of the United States. In the eastern states, where water is plentiful, water rights are communalized to a significant extent, the basic rule being that riparian owners (i.e., the owners of the shore of a body of water) are each entitled to make reasonable use of the water — a use that does not interfere unduly with the uses of the other riparians. In the western states, where water is scarce, exclusive rights can be obtained by appropriation (use).

Now consider the example of things, often very valuable things such as the treasure in a shipwreck, which were once owned but have been abandoned. Here the general rule is finders keepers. In a sense this is the same rule as for wild animals and for water in western states. Ownership of the thing is obtained by reducing it to actual possession. Until then the thing is unowned (the unborn beavers, the abandoned ship), and it is this gap in ownership — this interval when no one has a property right — that is the source of the economic problem.

But the problem is slightly different in the animal and treasure cases. In the case of wild animals the problem is too rapid exploitation; in the case of abandoned property it is too costly exploitation. Suppose the treasure in the shipwreck is worth $1 million and it will cost $250,000 to hire a team of divers to salvage it. Because the expected profit of the venture is so high, someone else may decide to hire his own team and try to beat the first team to it. A third and even a fourth may try, too, for if each one has the same chance (25 percent) of reaching the treasure first, then the expected value of the venture to each one ($1 million $\times$ .25) will still cover each one's expected cost. If all four try, however, the cost of obtaining the treasure, $1 million, will be four times what it would have been if only one had tried. The net social loss from this competition will, it is true, be less than $750,000, because the competition probably will result in the treasure's being found sooner (thus increasing its present value) than if only one salvager were trying. But the gain in time may be too modest to offset the additional expenditures that accelerated the search.

There would be no problem of excessive cost if the treasure had not been abandoned; for then the owner would simply have hired one of the four salvagers for $250,000. But when we call property "abandoned" in the legal sense, we mean that the cost of revesting the property in the original owner is prohibitive, either because it is impossible at a reasonable cost to find him or because he considers the property (perhaps incorrectly) to be worth less than the cost of finding or using it. The problem of too costly exploitation of a valuable resource, like the problem of too rapid exploitation, is rooted ultimately in the sometimes prohibitive costs of enforcing property rights.

The common law sometimes gives the first committed searcher for abandoned property a right to prevent others from searching so long as his search is conscientiously pursued. Another common law rule that reduces wasteful rent-seeking in the quest for abandoned property makes abandoned treasure trove (currency and bullion), if found, escheat to the government rather than becoming the property of the finder. This rule reduces the investment in finding to whatever level the government thinks proper; the government determines that level by determining how much reward to give the finder. In the case of currency (as distinct from treasure that has historical, aesthetic, or collectors' value), the optimal level is very low, perhaps zero. Finding money does not increase the wealth of society; it just enables the finder to have more of society's goods than someone else. The optimal reward may therefore be very low — maybe zero. The trend in the common law is to expand the escheat principle of treasure trove into other areas of found property and thus give the finder a reward rather than the property itself; this makes economic sense.

It might appear that nothing could be more remote from sunken treasure than patented inventions, and yet the economic problem created by patents is remarkably like that of abandoned property. Ideas are in a sense created but in another sense found. Suppose that whoever invents the widget will, if allowed to exclude others from its use by being granted a patent, be able to sell the patent to a manufacturer for $1 million. And suppose that the cost of invention is $250,000. Others will try to be first to invent the widget. This competition will cause it to be invented sooner. But suppose it is invented only one day sooner; the value of having the widget a day earlier will be less than the cost of duplicating the entire investment in invention.

As the discussion in this section shows, the *denial* of a property right can be as much an economizing device as the creation of one. . . .

§3.3 Intellectual Property: Patents, Copyrights, Trademarks, Trade Secrets, and Privacy

As the preceding section illustrated, the economist experiences no sense of discontinuity in moving from physical to intellectual property. In particular, the dynamic rationale for property rights is readily applied to the useful ideas that we call inventions. Suppose that it costs $10 million to invent a new type of food blender, the marginal cost of producing and selling the blender once it is invented is $50 (why is the $10 million not a marginal cost?), and the estimated demand is for 1 million of the blenders (we can for present purposes ignore the fact that demand will vary with the blender's price). Unless the manufacturer can charge $60 per blender, he will not recoup his costs of invention. But if other manufacturers face the same marginal cost as he, competition will (in the absence of patents) bid the price down to $50, the effort at recoupment will fail, and anticipating this the manufacturer will not make the invention in the first place; he will not sow if he won't be able to reap.... So we have patents. The law uses several devices to try to minimize the costs of duplicating inventive activity that a patent system invites. Here are five devices used:

1. A patent expires after 17 years, rather than being perpetual. This reduces the value of the patent to the owner and hence the amount of resources that will be devoted to obtaining patents. In addition, patents often are obtained before commercial development is complete, in which case the commercially valuable patent period will be shorter than 17 years. And the patentee must make public disclosure of the invention. Although competitors cannot copy the invention, they may get ideas from the disclosure as to how to invent around the patent.

2. Inventions are not patentable if they are "obvious." The functional meaning of obviousness is, discoverable at low cost. The lower the cost of discovery, the less necessary patent protection is to induce the discovery to be made, and the greater is the danger of overinvestment if patent protection is allowed. If an idea worth $1 million costs $1,000 rather than $250,000 to discover, the amount of wasteful duplication to get a patent will be greater, perhaps $249,000 greater.

3. Patents are granted early — before an invention has been carried to the point of commercial feasibility — in order to head off costly duplication of expensive development work....

4. The patent applicant must show not only that his invention is nonobvious (as well as novel — why this requirement?), but also that it is "useful." This requirement might be thought superfluous. If the invention is not useful, it will not generate significant monopoly rents. But screening out useless inventions reduces the cost of patent searches to subsequent inventors....

5. Fundamental ideas (the laws of physics, for example) are not patentable, despite their great value....An idea does not have a stable physical locus like a piece of land. With the passage of time it becomes increasingly difficult to identify the products in which a particular idea is embodied; and it is also difficult to identify the products in which a basic idea, having many and varied applications, is embodied. Here then is another example of how the costs of property rights limit their extent.

The costs of the patent system include (besides inducing potentially excessive investment in inventing) driving a wedge between price and marginal cost....Once an invention is made, its costs are sunk; in economic terms, they are zero. Hence a price that includes a royalty to the inventor will exceed the opportunity cost of the product in which the invention is embodied. This wedge, however, is analytically the same as the cost of a fence to demarcate a property right in land; it is an indispensable cost of using the property rights system to allocate resources.

NOTES AND QUESTIONS ON THE ECONOMICS OF PROPERTY RIGHTS

1. Posner self-consciously views property issues from an economic perspective. For an assessment (and critique) of the core assumptions of mainstream economics, see the selection by Jolls, Sunstein & Thaler, infra p. 62. In Posner's hands, does the economic paradigm generate important insights? This reader includes many selections by both proponents and skeptics of traditional law and economics, and should provide ample opportunities for appraisal of the approach.

2. Economists make use of two quite different definitions of *efficiency*. The first is *Pareto superiority*. An outcome is Pareto superior to the status quo if the outcome would make at least one individual better off and no one worse off. The second is the *Kaldor-Hicks* test, according to which an outcome is efficient if, after the outcome occurs, the gainers value its occurrence more than the losers disvalue it. Because the Kaldor-Hicks criterion does not require that gainers actually compensate losers, many outcomes that satisfy the Kaldor-Hicks test do not satisfy the Pareto-superiority test. Assume, for instance, that closing an utterly obsolete military base would be Kaldor-Hicks efficient. The shutdown nevertheless would not be Pareto superior unless compensation were actually paid to local merchants, base employees, and others sustaining losses, in amounts sufficient to make each loser at least indifferent to the closure.

In a prior passage in the excerpted work Posner states that because the "conditions of Pareto superiority are almost never satisfied in the real world," economists normally employ the Kaldor-Hicks standard for efficiency. Was this Posner's own practice in the passages just reproduced? For Posner's qualified defense of the Kaldor-Hicks approach, see Economic Analysis of Law pp. 12-17 (5th ed. 1998).

A person who acquires an asset tends to value it more than previously. See the discussion of loss aversion in Jolls, Sunstein & Thaler, infra p. 62. As a result, the preexisting distribution of wealth may determine whether a particular measure satisfies the Kaldor-Hicks criterion. Symposium on Efficiency as a Legal Concern, 8 Hofstra L. Rev. 485-770 (1980), is a leading collection of essays on the ethics of the Kaldor-Hicks test. See also the sources on cost-benefit analysis, infra p. 231, Note 2. The selection by Rawls, infra p. 94, rejects any system of utilitarian ethics (such as the Kaldor-Hicks criterion) because it might permit one person's welfare to be sacrificed for the greater good of others. But compare the selection by Michelman, infra p. 480, which invites attention to how individuals fare in the long run. Why does the Kaldor-Hicks approach become more appealing the longer the perspective one adopts?

3. Posner restates Blackstone's economic rationale for the alienability of resources: A trade between willing parties can be expected to generate gains for both sides. Does this rationale undergird the common law doctrine that limits the powers of bargainers and donors to create restraints on alienation? Or, contrarily, is that doctrine in tension with freedom of contract? Most legal systems sharply limit the alienation of, for example, babies, body parts, and sexual services. Could Posner account for these policies? A selection by Margaret Radin, infra p. 336, revisits issues of inalienability.

4. Posner draws on wild animals, treasure troves, and scientific inventions to illustrate how a legal system might efficiently bestow an exclusive right to *pursue* a resource. At what stage, if ever, should the editorial board of a law review give a student member an exclusive right to develop a particular Note topic?

Are Property and Contract Efficient?*

Duncan Kennedy & Frank Michelman

Introduction

This is an article about economic justifications for the legal institutions of private property and enforceable contract. There is, of course, an enormous literature addressed to such questions. . . .

This Article . . . neither argues for (nor against) any legal rules or institutions nor proposes a proper role or technique for eco-

*Source: 8 Hofstra L. Rev. 711-737 (1980).

nomic analysis. It is concerned, in the first place, with what may appear to be a task of mere intellectual housekeeping: that of cataloguing and refuting in detail a number of *false* arguments and suppositions about the economic virtues of private property and free contract. The arguments that concern us are those purporting to justify the legal institutions in question by reference only (a) to a very weak, highly plausible value judgment that we should do things that make or could make everyone affected more satisfied than they would otherwise be, and (b) to a very weak, highly plausible factual judgment that people tend most of the time to act as though they had goals and were trying to achieve them — i.e., that people are rational maximizers of satisfactions. . . .

I. Five False Arguments for Private Property

In this Part, we take up a series of arguments for private property, and show that each depends on empirical assumptions additional to that of rational maximizing behavior. Throughout, we will be contrasting the property regime, or PP, with two other regimes, since economic arguments for PP always make some implicit comparison with alternative possibilities. The two other regimes are the state of nature (SON) and the regime of forced sharing for needs (FSN).

A property regime (PP) is one in which things of value are assigned to owners, who have the following rights with respect to them: (a) they can consume them, or use them to produce other things of value, which they will also own; (b) they can get the state's help in preventing any nonowner from consuming them or using them for production without the owner's consent; and (c) owners have exclusive power to transfer ownership to others, with the state recognizing and then enforcing the transfer. This is admittedly a very rough, and in a number of respects a weasel-worded definition, but it is adequate for our present purposes. . . .

In the state of nature (SON) there is no ownership of anything, and no institution of legally enforced contract either. People may simply do as they wish, using whatever means are available to them — subject to everyone else doing likewise. Conceptually, the distinction between PP and SON is that in PP ownership rights are assumed to be automatically and universally respected — or, equivalently, perfectly and costlessly protected by an absolutely reliable and irresistible force ("the state"); whereas in SON, while there is always the contingent possibility of some people, perhaps by prearrangement, coming forcefully to the aid of others seeking protection or vindication for ownership-like positions, actual protection or vindication will always depend on the hazards of specific, concrete tests of strength (will, wit, etc.).

Forced sharing for needs (FSN) resembles private property, except that ownership is qualified in the following way. Anyone who "needs" a thing and doesn't own it (or its equivalent in cash or credit) may take or requisition it from anyone else who owns it and doesn't "need" it, and the state will intervene, if necessary, on the side of the needy taker. We can imagine rules defining need objectively, either in very general terms (e.g., having in one's ownership at this moment less than two-thirds of the per capita average share of privately held national wealth) or in terms of a series of particular situations, equally objectively described (e.g., being diabetic and lacking insulin for an overdue shot). . . .

We have cast our five arguments in terms of comparisons between PP and SON or FSN. In each case we compare the valued experiences generated, or sometimes the hours worked, under the various regimes.[7] . . .

A.   First Argument for PP: Security Increases Production

In both SON and FSN no one can expect with certainty to be able to retain the fruits of her labor. It follows, according to the First Argument, that people will not work as much as under conditions of legally guaranteed security. . . .

There are two mistakes in the First Argument. The first, par-

---

7. We have construed the several arguments for property as all designed to show that property is relatively efficient by the test variously known as "Kaldor-Hicks," or "hypothetical compensation," or "potential Pareto superiority" — i.e., that property will generate a higher-valued periodic total output of goods, services, and leisure for the members of society taken altogether than will any alternative regime. Some economists may object that such is not the sense in which they ordinarily speak of "efficiency," that in calling a regime "efficient" a careful economist would mean only that it was a "Pareto *optimum*," an arrangement that could not be altered without worsening the lot of at least one person; that, indeed, comparison of regimes in terms of *total* values *across* society is meaningless without an objective, or at least intelligible, metric for comparing one person's gain with another's loss; that the only such metric known is that of (actual or constructed) offer or asking prices, which is unsatisfactory because it suppresses the important but unfathomable effects of changes in distribution on the total of individual welfare levels.

Our response is, first, that the strict criterion of actual Pareto superiority — better for each person, or at least as good — cannot be the one intended by claims that property is relatively efficient, because it is plain without argument that the strict criterion cannot select among PP, SON, and FSN; second, that a great deal of policy analysis, as distinguished from work in economic theory, in fact aims, if only mediately, at maximization of social welfare by way of "educated guesses" about cross-personal welfare comparisons. . . .

ticularly relevant to SON, is that it confuses the legal "permission" of violence and chaos with the actual social practice of violence and chaos. Even if no one has any legal right to protection, and everyone is legally entitled to do anything they want and can get away with, it does not follow that among rational maximizers there must arise either random depredations or actual freedom to refrain from production. There might, in SON, evolve a balance of physical and social force such that both the "weak" and the "strong" have very distinct ideas about what will probably happen to them if they do or don't produce. And the particular, highly discernible pattern of force might be one that induces the population as a whole to produce more rather than less than they would under PP.

In a two-person SON, for example, the stronger won't necessarily kill the weaker. The stronger may be more interested in the consumption of products of labor than in perfect safety or in aggression for its own sake. Even according to the usual, very pessimistic models of human nature used in this kind of analysis, the stronger in that case will rather force the weaker to work, and extract from him as much surplus as is compatible with stability. It might very well be that he would impose something analogous to a tax on everything except what the weaker needed to survive at a level that permitted the kind of production the stronger desired. There is no reason to expect this arrangement to generate great "uncertainty." The weaker would know pretty well what to expect and so would the stronger.

To be sure, the weaker may receive less return for his labor than under a two-person property regime, while the stronger receives a large income without working at all. But the weaker's incentive to work will not necessarily be lessened by the low return to labor. . . .

The second objection to the First Argument, relevant to both SON and FSN, is that even if holdings and harvests are more secure under PP than SON and FSN, people may respond to the hazards of the latter regimes by working more rather than less. Under the chancy, non-property regimes people are doubtful whether they will enjoy the fruits of their productive undertakings, so the reward for each unit of work or investment is less, *ex ante*, than it would be under property. Because the reward is less, according to the First Argument, they will work less. The objection is that reducing the probable share of product retained by the producer may induce people to work more rather than less, in order to maintain the same level of welfare-from-consumption. For example, a farmer may respond to the threat of theft by planting more crops, in the hope that he can thereby offset depredations and keep his income up — with the result of increasing the consumption of society as a whole, the thieves included. In technical terms, it all depends on the relation between the income and the substitution effects of the reduced rewards from work.

The argument that property has desirable effects on productive effort thus amounts to no more than an empirical assertion. . . .

B.   Second Argument for PP: Theft Is Inefficient

Suppose a thief takes something, in the SON, that the thief would willingly have paid only five dollars for in PP, while the possessor would have offered ten dollars to the thief at the moment of theft, if it had been possible thereby to bind the thief not to steal the object. It is a common intuition that it is somehow not economically sound to let the theft happen under these circumstances. It is, one might think, inefficient because the law is sanctioning a change that makes one person worse off (the possessor, by ten dollars) while making another better off by considerably less (the thief, by five dollars).

The argument that theft is inefficient plainly depends on an assumption of substantial transaction costs, which in turn imports motivational assumptions regarding individual wants and proclivities, not at all implicit in the bare postulate of rational maximizing behavior. If there are no transaction costs, there will be no theft, even without the coercive legal institution of property, unless the property is worth more to the thief than to the victim. Otherwise, the possessor will offer the thief some sum to go away, they will negotiate, and strike a bargain in which the thief receives something between five and ten dollars in exchange for desisting. The end result is that the prior possession is respected but the possessor ends up, say, out $9.95, rather than the $10 value of the object, while the thief ends up pocketing $9.95 rather than what would have been (for him) $5.00 worth of stolen goods. The only difference between this outcome and the one that would have occurred under a property regime is "distributional." The object is finally allocated to the same use (unless the possessor's impoverishment causes him to change that use). Some are better off and some worse off than they would have been under PP, but we cannot rank either outcome as Pareto superior to the other.

Let us, however, grant arguendo that substantial transaction costs are an inevitable accompaniment of essential human nature. The theft, then, may well occur in SON but not in PP, apparently leaving society $5 poorer in SON. On the other hand, transaction costs also disrupt the functioning of a PP regime. For example, transaction costs in PP may prevent the transfer of an object from a possessor who values it at $5 to another who values it at $10; whereas in SON, the other might simply take the object. For ought the rationality postulate can tell us, the disruption in PP may on the whole be more damaging to wealth or welfare than that in SON. We cannot say a priori which way the balance of systemic advantage lies. . . .

C. Third Argument for PP: PP Reduces Uncertainty

The third argument for PP is that SON and FSN involve an unpleasant psychological state of anxiety about whether or not one will be able to keep what one has and to enjoy the fruits of one's labor. Since this anxiety is a psychic "bad," we can make everyone better off by eliminating it through a property regime. . . .

The basic response to the argument that property maximizes the psychic good of certainty is that, under all three regimes, to enhance certainty for one person is to impair certainty for another. Under a property regime people are all certain that they and no one else will receive the fruits of their labor, but all uncertain of access to the fruits of others' labor. In moving from one regime to another, some will have gained security at the expense of others, and everyone will have traded certainty and uncertainty of one kind for certainty and uncertainty of another. . . .

In the state of nature, the strong are certain that no automatic, irresistible force will stop them from exploiting the weak. Thus secure in the knowledge of their strength, they are certain of receiving benefits they cannot be as certain of receiving under property. . . .

. . . [L]ife under forced sharing will be *differently* certain and uncertain than life under property. Forced sharing ties the fortunes of the individual to the group. It therefore eliminates some fundamental uncertainties of a property regime. Under FSN, one need not fear that one's own unproductiveness will expose one to isolated deprivation as long as others are producing. But forced sharing introduces its own forms of insecurity, since the fortunes of the group depend on a complex process of interaction, with no guarantees against a disastrous slide into uncooperative behavior.

. . . [T]hose who are "good at production" under private property, or who have large holdings of property, would obviously have more to fear from forced sharing than those who are weak producers and have no property. . . . But the gainers from property . . .

are also vulnerable, in a property regime, to mischance that leaves them in need, whereas under forced sharing they would not be. . . .

D. Fourth Argument for PP: Coordinational Failure

The Fourth Argument for PP is that life under SON or FSN will be an organizational nightmare, whereas coordination under property will be easily managed. . . .

In a complex economic system, with extensive division of labor and little production for autoconsumption, the economic process as a whole requires an extraordinary amount of social cooperation. If everyone has property in his labor, and if property in the means of production is widely dispersed, this cooperation requires great numbers of complex chains of bargains among individual right holders, and these bargains will be costly to organize and vulnerable to strategic failure. The situation under property may be a "prisoners' dilemma" such that each owner rationally pursuing his view of his own interest will behave antisocially. For example, every owner may withdraw his property from production because of fear of economic collapse, and thereby fulfill as fact what began as only prophecy. If there were no transaction costs, each property owner would see that the sum of all the individual exercises of rights was a social disaster, and the group could strike a bargain to keep production going. But the atomization of control might make such a solution impossible. By contrast, a single "strong man" who controlled the whole economy might avert the disaster by forcing everyone to behave in the socially appropriate fashion. Likewise, communal ownership might result in "planning" that prevented crisis.

The point, then, is not that some or any property regime can never be superior on efficiency grounds to the state of nature. Rather, if there are no transaction costs preventing bargaining, each regime is necessarily efficient, in the sense of Pareto optimal (on the production-possibility frontier), whereas in the presence of transaction costs the question of efficiency is an empirical one. Given transaction costs, it may be that people in SON would be blocked from moving to a property regime that would unleash such a flood of commodities that the gainers could compensate the strong for their losses. But it might also work the other way around: the dispersal of control among property holders might prevent the strong from reorganizing production along lines that would produce enormous surpluses, which would in turn permit the strong to buy off the weak.

E. *Fifth Argument for PP: Distribution of the Tradeoff Between Work and Leisure*

We have now arrived at the argument for private property that seems most plausible to people who have some technical knowledge of economics. It is that a property regime maximizes welfare because it provides individuals with both the information and motivation they require to make the choices among different kinds of work and investment, and between work and leisure, that will allow the group to get the maximum of satisfaction from the resources available to them. One form of the argument is to assert that departures from private property always cause a "distortion" of incentives. The distortion argument is complex, and in order to address it we will have to elaborate our model of a property regime considerably beyond what has been necessary up to this point.

1.   THE CRUSOE ECONOMY

The idea that underlies the "distortion" argument is that of the single producer on a desert island who "owns" both his own labor and a defined set of natural resources, simply because there is no one else around to make conflicting claims. This solitary producer will spend some time at work and some time not working. The postulate of rational maximizing behavior is helpful in figuring out what particular division he will make between the two uses of time. He will work until the psychic rewards of another unit of work fall below those of a unit of leisure. In equilibrium he will arrange things so that the marginal yield of utility from work and leisure is equal.

He will follow the same procedure in deciding what to work on. In equilibrium, the marginal yield of a further minute spent on shelter will exactly equal that of a minute spent on food gathering. These marginal equalities guarantee that Crusoe is getting the most possible satisfaction out of both his time and his resources. There is a quite real sense in which the actual quantities of work of different kinds, and of leisure, that Crusoe chooses are "natural." They reflect the natural surround of physical resources, and Crusoe's "nature," in the sense in which nature means simply a set of preferences.

2.   THE MULTIPLE-CRUSOE ECONOMY

The next step in the development of the distortion argument is to imagine a multiplicity of islands, each different from the others, each with a different Crusoe on it. At first, the Crusoes are ignorant of each others' existence. Each behaves as though he were the only person in the world, producing in such a way as to generate marginal equality of satisfactions from different kinds of work, and from the mix of work and leisure. Then they become aware of one anothers' existence.

Let's suppose they respond to this knowledge by agreeing that each Crusoe will "own" his island, and by creating a state to enforce their property regime. Each will continue to produce as before, except now there is the possibility of trade and the division of labor. Imagine a first phase of trade in resources only. Two Crusoes discover that each would prefer the other's island to his own. That is, given the first Crusoe's preferences and his capacities for labor and leisure, he would prefer to own the second's island rather than his own; and vice versa for the second Crusoe. A round of trading of islands ensues, until there is no trade left that anyone wants to make. On each island, the Crusoe owner produces until the marginal equalities are achieved. . . .

It would be misleading to describe as "natural" the various quantities of different kinds of work and of leisure that the Crusoes are now doing. These amounts depend on what island each Crusoe has, and this in turn depends on the initial distribution. This is an important point, which we can illustrate as follows. Suppose three Crusoes and three islands, with the Crusoes' rankings as follows:

A prefers 1 to 2 and 2 to 3
B prefers 1 to 2 and 2 to 3
C prefers 1 to 3 and 3 to 2

Initial distribution I:
A gets 1
B gets 2
C gets 3
Result: no trades

Initial distribution II:
A gets 1
B gets 3
C gets 2
Result: A keeps 1; B gets 2; C gets 3 (same as I)

Initial distribution III:
A gets 2
B gets 1
C gets 3
Result: no trades (different from I)

Initial distribution IV:
A gets 3
B gets 1
C gets 2
Result: B keeps 1, A gets 2, C gets 3 (same as III, different from
    I and II)

It seems unnecessary to continue through all the permutations, since the result is clear: who ends with which island depends on who has which island to start with, and on the preferences as among islands of different Crusoes. After the islands have been finally distributed, each Crusoe will equalize the marginal returns of work and leisure. But the result of this equalization process, the *actual* division of time, depends on who has which island rather than on anything in "nature." There is no particular work/leisure tradeoff that is natural, any more than there is a natural distribution of islands. Another way to put the same point is to say that there are multiple possible efficient outcomes given a set of Crusoes and a set of islands. Once the trading process is completed, and each Crusoe has equalized the marginal returns of different kinds of work and leisure, the situation will be Pareto optimal. But there are as many actual contents for the optimal solution as there are post-trading distributions of islands. . . .

d.   Labor "Wasted" on Protection Against Theft — . . . [A proponent of private property might assert] that in the state of nature people will have an incentive to produce goods that the stronger cannot so easily take from them, rather than the goods they want most, and also have an incentive to spend time on devices designed to make theft more difficult. Since they would prefer to have the products of an equal amount of time spent under a property regime, it would appear that property *must* generate a net increase in welfare.

An easy answer is that PP involves its own kinds of "unproductive" activities, like lawyering, prosecuting, judging, and housing the legal system. Whether, under any particular set of circumstances, these will cost more or less than fences (etc.) is an empirical question.

Furthermore, we cannot treat the argument about precautions as conclusive, even assuming costless enforcement of legal property rights. The argument assumes that the diversion of production into theft-proof goods and into precautions is a pure loss, from the point of view of social welfare, so that eliminating the diversion is a pure gain. But it is obvious that the production is diverted because some people are trying to live off the products of others. Eliminating the diversion by introducing private property means preventing the freeloaders from freeloading, as well as reducing the wages available to those whose strongest talents are for serving as guards. It seems, on the face of it, that this should decrease the welfare of the latter groups. When the diversion argument ignores the impact of property rules on their welfare, it is patently inconclusive. The gain to the industrious from being able to produce what they most want, and from dismantling their defensive measures, may or may not be greater than the loss to former thieves and Pinkertons. In order to decide, we need a social welfare function that allows us to compare these gains and losses. . . .

NOTES AND QUESTIONS ON CRITICAL APPRAISALS OF PRIVATE PROPERTY

1. Kennedy and Michelman (K&M) seek to prove that the efficiency of private property (PP) cannot be deduced from the barebones premises of economics. If K&M think that economists need to enrich their initial assumptions, why do they assert that the traditional economic rationales for PP are "false," as opposed to "incomplete"? More broadly, is deductive logic a helpful tool for appraising the relative merits of PP and alternative institutions? How empirically inclined are K&M in comparison to, say, Blackstone and Posner?

2. K&M identify two mistakes in the argument that the security of PP serves to enhance production. First, in SON the strong may coerce the weak to produce even more than they would under PP. K&M give an example in which there is one strong person and one weak person. Does this example load the dice in their favor? Why might the weak be substantially less productive in SON if many strong persons were competing to extract the surplus of their labor? See the selection by Hardin on the "tragedy of the commons," infra p. 119. See also Thomas Hobbes, Leviathan, ch. 13 (1651), arguing that the state of nature is a more or less egalitarian war of all against all. In settled societies, why did even slaveowners sometimes give informal property rights to slaves? See Yoram Barzel, Economic Analysis of Property Rights 105-113 (2d ed. 1997).

Second, K&M argue that individuals might work *harder* if their holdings were insecure, perhaps to attain a margin of safety in consumption. Reread Posner's response to this criticism, supra

p. 55, footnote 1. Who has the better of this exchange? For a more formal economic inquiry that supports parts of Posner's rejoinder, see Stergios Skaperdas, Cooperation, Conflict, and Power in the Absence of Property Rights, 82 Am. Econ. Rev. 720 (1992). K&M's position receives reinforcement in Mark Kelman, A Guide to Critical Legal Studies 155-157 (1987).

Neither Posner nor K&M cite evidence about the effects of insecurity on work effort. Anthropological studies indicate that, in virtually all preliterate societies, an individual or kinship group that cultivates a crop is granted private property rights in that crop. See Martin J. Bailey, Approximate Optimality of Aboriginal Property Rights, 35 J.L. & Econ. 183, 191-192 (1992); Melville J. Herskovits, Economic Anthropology, 350-370 (1952). Does this empirical regularity strengthen Posner's side of the debate? Prove as a logical matter that PP inevitably increases crop production?

3. Theft is regarded as a crime in all societies. See James Q. Wilson & Richard J. Herrnstein, Crime and Human Nature 22-23, 448-450 (1985). Does the universality of this norm undermine K&M's attack on the proposition that "theft is inefficient"?

The common law doctrine of private necessity entitles a starving hiker to break into an uninhabited mountain cabin to obtain food. Does this rule support K&M's arguments about theft? Would Posner think the private-necessity doctrine inefficient? The law of adverse possession may end up rewarding thievery. Is it inefficient? Consult the selection by Merrill, infra p. 190.

4. K&M argue that PP may not reduce uncertainty. Is risk allocation a zero-sum game? If so, what explains the existence of insurance companies, which sell the service of risk-bearing? Do the selections by Goffman and Radin, supra pp. 1 and 8, show that in practice certain forms of PP enhance aggregate security? Do those selections suggest premises about human nature that economists might add to their models in order to satisfy K&M's demands for deductive rigor?

5. In their "Crusoes" discussion, K&M demonstrate the possibly profound influence of initial entitlements. For other sources on this issue, see infra pp. 207-208, Note 3.

6. Michelman provides an even richer and more expansive version of his views in Frank I. Michelman, Ethics, Economics, and the Law of Property, in Ethics, Economics, and the Law 3 (NOMOS XXIV) (J. Roland Pennock & John W. Chapman eds., 1982).

C.   Diffusion of Political Power

Capitalism and Freedom*

Milton Friedman

I.   The Relation Between Economic Freedom and Political Freedom

It is widely believed that politics and economics are separate and largely unconnected; that individual freedom is a political problem and material welfare an economic problem; and that any kind of political arrangements can be combined with any kind of economic arrangements. The chief contemporary manifestation of this idea is the advocacy of "democratic socialism" by many who condemn out of hand the restrictions on individual freedom imposed by "totalitarian socialism" in Russia, and who are persuaded that it is possible for a country to adopt the essential features of Russian economic arrangements and yet to ensure individual freedom through political arrangements. The thesis of this chapter is that such a view is a delusion, that there is an intimate connection between economics and politics, that only certain combinations of political and economic arrangements are possible, and that in particular, a society which is socialist cannot also be democratic, in the sense of guaranteeing individual freedom.

Economic arrangements play a dual role in the promotion of a free society. On the one hand, freedom in economic arrangements is itself a component of freedom broadly understood, so economic freedom is an end in itself. In the second place, economic freedom is also an indispensable means toward the achievement of political freedom.

The first of these roles of economic freedom needs special emphasis because intellectuals in particular have a strong bias against regarding this aspect of freedom as important. They tend to express contempt for what they regard as material aspects of life, and to regard their own pursuit of allegedly higher values as on a different plane of significance and as deserving of special attention. For most citizens of the country, however, if not for the intellectual, the direct importance of economic freedom is at least comparable in

*Source: pp. 7-32 (1962).

significance to the indirect importance of economic freedom as a means to political freedom.

The citizen of Great Britain, who after World War II was not permitted to spend his vacation in the United States because of exchange control, was being deprived of an essential freedom no less than the citizen of the United States, who was denied the opportunity to spend his vacation in Russia because of his political views. The one was ostensibly an economic limitation on freedom and the other a political limitation, yet there is no essential difference between the two.

The citizen of the United States who is compelled by law to devote something like ten percent of his income to the purchase of a particular kind of retirement contract, administered by the government, is being deprived of a corresponding part of his personal freedom. . . .

A citizen of the United States who under the laws of various states is not free to follow the occupation of his own choosing unless he can get a license for it, is likewise being deprived of an essential part of his freedom. So is the man who would like to exchange some of his goods with, say, a Swiss for a watch but is prevented from doing so by a quota. So also is the Californian who was thrown into jail for selling Alka Seltzer at a price below that set by the manufacturer under so-called "fair trade" laws. So also is the farmer who cannot grow the amount of wheat he wants. And so on. Clearly, economic freedom, in and of itself, is an extremely important part of total freedom.

Viewed as a means to the end of political freedom, economic arrangements are important because of their effect on the concentration or dispersion of power. The kind of economic organization that provides economic freedom directly, namely, competitive capitalism, also promotes political freedom because it separates economic power from political power and in this way enables the one to offset the other.

Historical evidence speaks with a single voice in the relation between political freedom and a free market. I know of no example in time or place of a society that has been marked by a large measure of political freedom, and that has not also used something comparable to a free market to organize the bulk of economic activity.

Because we live in a largely free society, we tend to forget how limited is the span of time and the part of the globe for which there has ever been anything like political freedom: the typical state of mankind is tyranny, servitude, and misery. The nineteenth century and early twentieth century in the Western world stand out as striking exceptions to the general trend of historical development. Political freedom in this instance clearly came along with the free market and the development of capitalist institutions. So also did political freedom in the golden age of Greece and in the early days of the Roman era.

History suggests only that capitalism is a necessary condition for political freedom. Clearly it is not a sufficient condition. Fascist Italy and Fascist Spain, Germany at various times in the last seventy years, Japan before World Wars I and II, tzarist Russia in the decades before World War I — are all societies that cannot conceivably be described as politically free. Yet, in each, private enterprise was the dominant form of economic organization. It is therefore clearly possible to have economic arrangements that are fundamentally capitalist and political arrangements that are not free.

Even in those societies, the citizenry had a good deal more freedom than citizens of a modern totalitarian state like Russia or Nazi Germany, in which economic totalitarianism is combined with political totalitarianism. Even in Russia under the Tzars, it was possible for some citizens, under some circumstances, to change their jobs without getting permission from political authority because capitalism and the existence of private property provided some check to the centralized power of the state.

The relation between political and economic freedom is complex and by no means unilateral. In the early nineteenth century, Bentham and the Philosophical Radicals were inclined to regard political freedom as a means to economic freedom. They believed that the masses were being hampered by the restrictions that were being imposed upon them, and that if political reform gave the bulk of the people the vote, they would do what was good for them, which was to vote for laissez faire. In retrospect, one cannot say that they were wrong. . . .

Fundamentally, there are only two ways of coordinating the economic activities of millions. One is central direction involving the use of coercion — the technique of the army and of the modern totalitarian state. The other is voluntary co-operation of individuals — the technique of the market place.

The possibility of coordination through voluntary cooperation rests on the elementary — yet frequently denied — proposition that both parties to an economic transaction benefit from it, *provided the transaction is bilaterally voluntary and informed.*

Exchange can therefore bring about co-ordination without coercion. A working model of a society organized through voluntary exchange is a *free private enterprise exchange economy* — what we have been calling competitive capitalism.

In its simplest form, such a society consists of a number of independent households — a collection of Robinson Crusoes, as it were. Each household uses the resources it controls to produce goods and services that it exchanges for goods and services produced by other households, on terms mutually acceptable to the two parties to the bargain. It is thereby enabled to satisfy its wants indirectly by producing goods and services for others, rather than directly by producing goods for its own immediate use. The incentive for adopting this indirect route is, of course, the increased product made possible by division of labor and specialization of function. Since the household always has the alternative of producing directly for itself, it need not enter into any exchange unless it benefits from it. Hence, no exchange will take place unless both parties do benefit from it. Cooperation is thereby achieved without coercion.

Specialization of function and division of labor would not go far if the ultimate productive unit were the household. In a modern society, we have gone much farther. We have introduced enterprises which are intermediaries between individuals in their capacities as suppliers of service and as purchasers of goods. And similarly, specialization of function and division of labor could not go very far if we had to continue to rely on the barter of product for product. In consequence, money has been introduced as a means of facilitating exchange, and of enabling the acts of purchase and of sale to be separated into two parts.

Despite the important role of enterprises and of money in our actual economy, and despite the numerous and complex problems they raise, the central characteristic of the market technique of achieving coordination is fully displayed in the simple exchange economy that contains neither enterprise nor money. As in that simple model, so in the complex enterprise and money-exchange economy, cooperation is strictly individual and voluntary *provided*: (a) that enterprises are private, so that the ultimate contracting parties are individuals and (b) that individuals are effectively free to enter or not to enter into any particular exchange, so that every transaction is strictly voluntary.

It is far easier to state these provisos in general terms than to spell them out in detail, or to specify precisely the institutional arrangements most conducive to their maintenance. Indeed, much of technical economic literature is concerned with precisely these questions. The basic requisite is the maintenance of law and order to prevent physical coercion of one individual by another and to enforce contracts voluntarily entered into, thus giving substance to "private." Aside from this, perhaps the most difficult problems arise from monopoly — which inhibits effective freedom by denying individuals alternatives to the particular exchange — and from "neighborhood effects" — effects on third parties for which it is not feasible to charge or recompense them. These problems will be discussed in more detail in the following chapter.

So long as effective freedom of exchange is maintained, the central feature of the market organization of economic activity is that it prevents one person from interfering with another in respect of most of his activities. The consumer is protected from coercion by the seller because of the presence of others sellers with whom he can deal. The seller is protected from coercion by the consumer because of other consumers to whom he can sell. The employee is protected from coercion by the employer because of other employers for whom he can work, and so on. And the market does this impersonally and without centralized authority.

Indeed, a major source of objection to a free economy is precisely that it does this task so well. It gives people what they want instead of what a particular group thinks they ought to want. Underlying most arguments against the free market is a lack of belief in freedom itself.

The existence of a free market does not of course eliminate the need for government. On the contrary, government is essential both as a forum for determining the "rules of the game" and as an umpire to interpret and enforce the rules decided on. What the market does is to reduce greatly the range of issues that must be decided through political means, and thereby to minimize the extent to which government need participate directly in the game. The characteristic feature of action through political channels is that it tends to require or enforce substantial conformity. The great advantage of the market, on the other hand, is that it permits wide diversity. It is, in political terms, a system of proportional representation. Each man can vote, as it were, for the color of tie he wants and get it; he does not have to see what color the majority wants and then, if he is in the minority, submit.

It is this feature of the market that we refer to when we say that the market provides economic freedom. But this characteristic also has implications that go far beyond the narrowly economic. Political freedom means the absence of coercion of a man by his fellow men. The fundamental threat to freedom is power to coerce, be it in the hands of a monarch, a dictator, an oligarchy, or a momentary majority. The preservation of freedom requires the elimination of such concentration of power to the fullest possible extent and the dispersal and distribution of whatever power cannot be eliminated — a system of checks and balances. By removing the organization of economic activity from the control of political authority, the market eliminates this source of coercive power. It enables economic strength to be a check to political power rather than a reinforcement.

Economic power can be widely dispersed. There is no law of conservation which forces the growth of new centers of economic strength to be at the expense of existing centers. Political power, on the other hand, is more difficult to decentralize. There can be numerous small independent governments. But it is far more difficult to maintain numerous equipotent small centers of political power in a single large government than it is to have numerous centers of economic strength in a single large economy. There can be many millionaires in one large economy. But can there be more than one really outstanding leader, one person on whom the energies and enthusiasms of his countrymen are centered? If the central government gains power, it is likely to be at the expense of local governments. There seems to be something like a fixed total of political power to be distributed. Consequently, if economic power is joined to political power, concentration seems almost inevitable. On the other hand, if economic power is kept in separate hands from political power, it can serve as a check and a counter to political power.

The force of this abstract argument can perhaps best be demonstrated by example. Let us consider first, a hypothetical example that may help to bring out the principles involved, and then some actual examples from recent experience that illustrate the way in which the market works to preserve political freedom.

One feature of a free society is surely the freedom of individuals to advocate and propagandize openly for a radical change in the structure of the society — so long as the advocacy is restricted to persuasion and does not include force or other forms of coercion. It is a mark of the political freedom of a capitalist society that men can openly advocate and work for socialism. Equally, political freedom in a socialist society would require that men be free to advocate the introduction of capitalism. How could the freedom to advocate capitalism be preserved and protected in a socialist society?

In order for men to advocate anything, they must in the first place be able to earn a living. This already raises a problem in a socialist society, since all jobs are under the direct control of political authorities. It would take an act of self-denial whose difficulty is underlined by experience in the United States after World War II with the problem of "security" among Federal employees, for a socialist government to permit its employees to advocate policies directly contrary to official doctrine.

But let us suppose this act of self-denial to be achieved. For advocacy of capitalism to mean anything, the proponents must be able to finance their cause — to hold public meetings, publish pamphlets, buy radio time, issue newspapers and magazines, and so on. How could they raise the funds? There might and probably would be men in the socialist society with large incomes, perhaps even large capital sums in the form of government bonds and the like, but these would of necessity be high public officials. It is possible to conceive of a minor socialist official retaining his job although openly advocating capitalism. It strains credulity to imagine the socialist top brass financing such "subversive" activities.

The only recourse for funds would be to raise small amounts from a large number of minor officials. But this is no real answer. To tap these sources, many people would already have to be persuaded, and our whole problem is how to initiate and finance a campaign to do so. Radical movements in capitalist societies have never been financed this way. They have typically been supported by a few wealthy individuals who have become persuaded — by a Frederick Vanderbilt Field, or an Anita McCormick Blaine, or a Corliss Lamont, to mention a few names recently prominent, or by a Friedrich Engels, to go farther back. This is a role of inequality of wealth in preserving political freedom that is seldom noted — the role of the patron.

In a capitalist society, it is only necessary to convince a few wealthy people to get funds to launch any idea, however strange, and there are many such persons, many independent foci of support. And, indeed, it is not even necessary to persuade people or financial institutions with available funds of the soundness of the ideas to be propagated. It is only necessary to persuade them that the propagation can be financially successful; that the newspaper or magazine or book or other venture will be profitable. The competitive publisher, for example, cannot afford to publish only writing with which he personally agrees; his touchstone must be the likelihood that the market will be large enough to yield a satisfactory return on his investment.

In this way, the market breaks the vicious circle and makes it possible ultimately to finance such ventures by small amounts from many people without first persuading them. There are no such possibilities in the socialist society; there is only the all-powerful state.

Let us stretch our imagination and suppose that a socialist government is aware of this problem and is composed of people anxious to preserve freedom. Could it provide the funds? Perhaps, but it is difficult to see how. It could establish a bureau for subsidizing subversive propaganda. But how could it choose whom to support? If it gave to all who asked, it would shortly find itself out of funds, for socialism cannot repeal the elementary economic law that a sufficiently high price will call forth a large supply. Make the advocacy of radical causes sufficiently remunerative, and the supply of advocates will be unlimited.

Moreover, freedom to advocate unpopular causes does not require that such advocacy be without cost. On the contrary, no society could be stable if advocacy of radical change were costless, much less subsidized. It is entirely appropriate that men make sacrifices to advocate causes in which they deeply believe. Indeed, it is important to preserve freedom only for people who are willing to practice self-denial, for otherwise freedom degenerates into license and irresponsibility. What is essential is that the cost of advocating unpopular causes be tolerable and not prohibitive.

But we are not yet through. In a free market society, it is enough to have the funds. The suppliers of paper are as willing to sell it to the Daily Worker as to the Wall Street Journal. In a socialist society, it would not be enough to have the funds. The hypothetical supporter of capitalism would have to persuade a government factory making paper to sell to him, the government printing press to print his pamphlets, a government post office to distribute them among the people, a government agency to rent him a hall in which to talk, and so on.

Perhaps there is some way in which one could overcome these difficulties and preserve freedom in a socialist society. One cannot say it is utterly impossible. What is clear, however, is that there are very real difficulties in establishing institutions that will effectively preserve the possibility of dissent. So far as I know, none of the people who have been in favor of socialism and also in favor of freedom have really faced up to this issue, or made even a respectable start at developing the institutional arrangements that would permit freedom under socialism. By contrast, it is clear how a free market capitalist society fosters freedom.

A striking practical example of these abstract principles is the experience of Winston Churchill. From 1933 to the outbreak of World War II, Churchill was not permitted to talk over the British radio, which was, of course, a government monopoly administered by the British Broadcasting Corporation. Here was a leading citizen of his country, a Member of Parliament, a former cabinet minister, a man who was desperately trying by every device possible to persuade his countrymen to take steps to ward off the menace of Hitler's Germany. He was not permitted to talk over the radio to the British people because the BBC was a government monopoly and his position was too "controversial."

Another striking example, reported in the January 26, 1959 issue of Time, has to do with the "Blacklist Fadeout." Says the Time story:

"The Oscar-awarding ritual is Hollywood's biggest pitch for dignity, but two years ago dignity suffered. When one Robert Rich was announced as top writer for The Brave One, he never stepped forward. Robert Rich was a pseudonym, masking one of about 150 writers . . . blacklisted by the industry since 1947 as suspected Communists or fellow travelers. The case was particularly embarrassing because the Motion Picture Academy had barred any Communist or Fifth Amendment pleader from Oscar competition. Last week both the Communist rule and the mystery of Rich's identity were suddenly rescripted.

"Rich turned out to be Dalton (Johnny Got His Gun) Trumbo, one of the original "Hollywood Ten" writers who refused to testify at the 1947 hearings on Communism in the movie industry. Said producer Frank King, who had stoutly insisted that Robert Rich was "a young guy in Spain with a beard": "We have an obligation to our stockholders to buy the best script we can. Trumbo brought us The Brave One and we bought it." . . .

"In effect it was the formal end of the Hollywood black list. For barred writers, the informal end came long ago. At least 15% of current Hollywood films are reportedly written by blacklist members. Said Producer King, "There are more ghosts in Hollywood than in Forest Lawn. Every company in town has used the work of blacklisted people. We're just the first to confirm what everybody knows."

One may believe, as I do, that communism would destroy all of our freedoms, one may be opposed to it as firmly and as strongly as possible, and yet, at the same time, also believe that in a free society it is intolerable for a man to be prevented from making voluntary arrangements with others that are mutually attractive because he believes in or is trying to promote communism. His freedom includes his freedom to promote communism. Freedom also, of course, includes the freedom of others not to deal with him under those circumstances. The Hollywood blacklist was an unfree act that destroys freedom because it was a collusive arrangement that used coercive means to prevent voluntary exchanges. It didn't work precisely because the market made it costly for people to preserve the blacklist. The commercial emphasis, the fact that people who are running enterprises have an incentive to make as much money as they can, protected the freedom of the individuals who were blacklisted by providing them with an alternative form of employment, and by giving people an incentive to employ them.

If Hollywood and the movie industry had been government enterprises or if in England it had been a question of employment by the British Broadcasting Corporation it is difficult to believe that the "Hollywood Ten" or their equivalent would have found employment. Equally, it is difficult to believe that under those circumstances, strong proponents of individualism and private enterprise — or indeed strong proponents of any view other than the status quo — would be able to get employment.

II.   The Role of Government in a Free Society . . .

I turn now to consider more specifically, though still in very broad terms, what the areas are that cannot be handled through the market at all, or can be handled only at so great a cost that the use of political channels may be preferable.

Government as Rule-Maker and Umpire

It is important to distinguish the day-to-day activities of people from the general customary and legal framework within which these take place. The day-to-day activities are like the actions of the participants in a game when they are playing it; the framework, like the rules of the game they play. And just as a good game requires acceptance by the players both of the rules and of the umpire to interpret and enforce them, so a good society requires that its members agree on the general conditions that will govern relations among them, on some means of arbitrating different interpretations of these conditions, and on some device for enforcing compliance with the generally accepted rules. As in games, so also in society, most of the general conditions are the unintended outcome of custom, accepted unthinkingly. At most, we consider explicitly only minor modifications in them, though the cumulative effect of a series of minor modifications may be a drastic alteration in the character of the game or of the society. In both games and society also, no set of rules can prevail unless most participants most of the time conform to them without external sanctions; unless that is, there is a broad underlying social consensus. But we cannot rely on custom or on this consensus alone to interpret and to enforce the rules; we need an umpire. These then are the basic roles of government in a free society: to provide a means whereby we can modify the rules, to mediate differences among us on the meaning of the rules, and to enforce compliance with the rules on the part of those few who would otherwise not play the game.

The need for government in these respects arises because absolute freedom is impossible. However attractive anarchy may be as a philosophy, it is not feasible in a world of imperfect men. Men's freedoms can conflict, and when they do, one man's freedom must be limited to preserve another's — as a Supreme Court Justice once put it. "My freedom to move my fist must be limited by the proximity of your chin."

The major problem in deciding the appropriate activities of government is how to resolve such conflicts among the freedoms of different individuals. In some cases, the answer is easy. There is little difficulty in attaining near unanimity to the proposition that one man's freedom to murder his neighbor must be sacrificed to preserve the freedom of the other man to live. In other cases, the answer is difficult. In the economic area, a major problem arises in respect of the conflict between freedom to combine and freedom to compete. What meaning is to be attributed to "free" as modifying "enterprise"? In the United States, "free" has been understood to mean that anyone is free to set up an enterprise, which means that existing enterprises are not free to keep out competitors except by selling a better product at the same price or the same product at a lower price. In the continental tradition, on the other hand, the meaning has generally been that enterprises are free to do what they want, including the fixing of prices, division of markets, and the adoption of other techniques to keep out potential competitors. Perhaps the most difficult specific problem in this area arises with respect to combinations among laborers, where the problem of freedom to combine and freedom to compete is particularly acute.

A still more basic economic area in which the answer is both difficult and important is the definition of property rights. The notion of property, as it has developed over centuries and as it is embodied in our legal codes, has become so much a part of us that we tend to take it for granted, and fail to recognize the extent to which just what constitutes property and what rights the ownership of property confers are complex social creations rather than self-evident propositions. Does my having title to land, for example, and my freedom to use my property as I wish, permit me to deny to someone else the right to fly over my land in his airplane? Or does his right to use his airplane take precedence? Or does this depend on how high he flies? Or how much noise he makes? Does voluntary exchange require that he pay me for the privilege of flying over my land? Or that I must pay him to refrain from flying over it? The mere mention of royalties, copyrights, patents; shares of stock in corporations; riparian rights, and the like, may perhaps emphasize the role of generally accepted social rules in the very definition of property. It may suggest also that, in many cases, the existence of a well specified and generally accepted definition of property is far more important than just what the definition is. . . .

In summary, the organization of economic activity through voluntary exchange presumes that we have provided, through government, for the maintenance of law and order to prevent coercion of one individual by another, the enforcement of contracts voluntarily entered into, the definition of the meaning of property rights, the interpretation and enforcement of such rights, and the provision of a monetary framework.

Action Through Government on Grounds of Technical Monopoly and Neighborhood Effects

The role of government just considered is to do something that the market cannot do for itself, namely, to determine, arbitrate, and enforce the rules of the game. We may also want to do through government some things that might conceivably be done through the market but that technical or similar conditions render it difficult to do in that way. These all reduce to cases in which strictly voluntary exchange is either exceedingly costly or practically impossible. There are two general classes of such cases: monopoly and similar market imperfections, and neighborhood effects.

Exchange is truly voluntary only when nearly equivalent alternatives exist. Monopoly implies the absence of alternatives and thereby inhibits effective freedom of exchange. In practice, monopoly frequently, if not generally, arises from government support or from collusive agreements among individuals. With respect to these, the problem is either to avoid governmental fostering of monopoly or to stimulate the effective enforcement of rules such as those embodied in our anti-trust laws. However, monopoly may also arise because it is technically efficient to have a single producer or enterprise. I venture to suggest that such cases are more limited than is supposed but they unquestionably do arise. A simple example is perhaps the provision of telephone services within a community. I shall refer to such cases as "technical" monopoly.

When technical conditions make a monopoly the natural outcome of competitive market forces, there are only three alternatives that seem available: private monopoly, public monopoly, or public regulation. All three are bad so we must choose among evils. . . . I reluctantly conclude that, if tolerable, private monopoly would be the least of the evils.

If society were static so that the conditions which give rise to a technical monopoly were sure to remain, I would have little confidence in this solution. In a rapidly changing society, however, the conditions making for technical monopoly frequently change and I suspect that both public regulation and public monopoly are likely to be less responsive to such changes in conditions, to be less readily capable of elimination, than private monopoly.

Railroads in the United States are an excellent example. A large degree of monopoly in railroads was perhaps inevitable on technical grounds in the nineteenth century. This was the justification for the Interstate Commerce Commission. But conditions have changed. The emergence of road and air transport has reduced the monopoly element in railroads to negligible proportions. Yet we have not eliminated the ICC. On the contrary, the ICC, which started out as an agency to protect the public from exploitation by the railroads, has become an agency to protect railroads from competition by trucks and other means of transport, and more recently even to protect existing truck companies from competition by new entrants. . . .

Technical monopoly may on occasion justify a de facto public monopoly. It cannot by itself justify a public monopoly achieved by making it illegal for anyone else to compete. For example, there is no way to justify our present public monopoly of the post office. It may be argued that the carrying of mail is a technical monopoly and that a government monopoly is the least of evils. Along these lines, one could perhaps justify a government post office but not the present law, which makes it illegal for anybody else to carry mail. If the delivery of mail is a technical monopoly, no one will be able to succeed in competition with the government. If it is not, there is no reason why the government should be engaged in it. The only way to find out is to leave other people free to enter.

The historical reason why we have a post office monopoly is because the Pony Express did such a good job of carrying the mail across the continent that, when the government introduced transcontinental service, it couldn't compete effectively and lost money.

The result was a law making it illegal for anybody else to carry the mail. That is why the Adams Express Company is an investment trust today instead of an operating company. I conjecture that if entry into the mail-carrying business were open to all, there would be a large number of firms entering it and this archaic industry would become revolutionized in short order.

A second general class of cases in which strictly voluntary exchange is impossible arises when actions of individuals have effects on other individuals for which it is not feasible to charge or recompense them. This is the problem of "neighborhood effects." An obvious example is the pollution of a stream. The man who pollutes a stream is in effect forcing others to exchange good water for bad. These others might be willing to make the exchange at a price. But it is not feasible for them, acting individually, to avoid the exchange or to enforce appropriate compensation.

A less obvious example is the provision of highways. In this case, it is technically possible to identify and hence charge individuals for their use of the roads and so to have private operation. However, for general access roads, involving many points of entry and exit, the costs of collection would be extremely high if a charge were to be made for the specific services received by each individual, because of the necessity of establishing toll booths or the equivalent at all entrances. . . .

These considerations do not apply to long-distance turnpikes with high density of traffic and limited access. For these, the costs of collection are small and in many cases are now being paid, and there are often numerous alternatives, so that there is no serious monopoly problem. Hence, there is every reason why these should be privately owned and operated. . . .

Parks are an interesting example because they illustrate the difference between cases that can and cases that cannot be justified by neighborhood effects, and because almost everyone at first sight regards the conduct of National Parks as obviously a valid function of government. In fact, however, neighborhood effects may justify a city park; they do not justify a national park, like Yellowstone National Park or the Grand Canyon. What is the fundamental difference between the two? For the city park, it is extremely difficult to identify the people who benefit from it and to charge them for the benefits which they receive. If there is a park in the middle of the city, the houses on all sides get the benefit of the open space, and people who walk through it or by it also benefit. To maintain toll collectors at the gates or to impose annual charges per window overlooking the park would be very expensive and difficult. The entrances to a national park like Yellowstone, on the other hand, are few; most of the people who come stay for a considerable period of time and it is perfectly feasible to set up toll gates and collect admission charges. This is indeed now done, though the charges do not cover the whole costs. If the public wants this kind of an activity enough to pay for it, private enterprises will have every incentive to provide such parks. And, of course, there are many private enterprises of this nature now in existence. I cannot myself conjure up any neighborhood effects or important monopoly effects that would justify governmental activity in this area.

Considerations like those I have treated under the heading of neighborhood effects have been used to rationalize almost every conceivable intervention. In many instances, however, this rationalization is special pleading rather than a legitimate application of the concept of neighborhood effects. Neighborhood effects cut both ways. They can be a reason for limiting the activities of government as well as for expanding them. Neighborhood effects impede voluntary exchange because it is difficult to identify the effects on third parties and to measure their magnitude; but this difficulty is present in governmental activity as well. It is hard to know when neighborhood effects are sufficiently large to justify particular costs in overcoming them and even harder to distribute the costs in an appropriate fashion. Consequently, when government engages in activities to overcome neighborhood effects, it will in part introduce an additional set of neighborhood effects by failing to charge or to compensate individuals properly. Whether the original or the new neighborhood effects are the more serious can only be judged by the facts of the individual case, and even then, only very approximately. Furthermore, the use of government to overcome neighborhood effects itself has an extremely important neighborhood effect which is unrelated to the particular occasion for government action. Every act of government intervention limits the area of individual freedom directly and threatens the preservation of freedom indirectly for reasons elaborated in the first chapter.

Our principles offer no hard and fast line how far it is appropriate to use government to accomplish jointly what it is difficult or impossible for us to accomplish separately through strictly voluntary exchange. In any particular case of proposed intervention, we must make up a balance sheet, listing separately the advantages and disadvantages. Our principles tell us what items to put on the one side and what items on the other and they give us some basis for attaching importance to the different items. In particular, we shall always want to enter on the liability side of any proposed government intervention, its neighborhood effect in threatening freedom, and give this effect considerable weight. Just how much weight to give to it, as to other items, depends upon the circumstances. If, for example, existing government intervention is minor, we shall attach a smaller weight to the negative effects of additional government intervention. This is an important reason why many earlier liberals, like Henry Simons, writing at a time when government was small by today's standards, were willing to have government undertake activities that today's liberals would not accept now that government has become so overgrown.

NOTES AND QUESTIONS ON PROPERTY'S RELATION TO LIBERTY

1. In Friedman's litany of legal restraints on freedom early in this selection, he leaves out several quite widespread kinds of laws that curtail voluntary transactions. Some examples are laws limiting the contractual capacities of minors (including statutory rape laws), laws restraining the use of narcotics, and laws requiring the use of automobile seat belts or motorcycle helmets. Do any of these differ from Friedman's examples? Would you expect him to accept any of these laws? Why or why not? Are there rationales for such constraints that might be compatible with an overall libertarian commitment? Consider Cass R. Sunstein, Legal Interference with Private Preferences, 53 U. Chi. L. Rev. 1129 (1986), arguing that some legislation reflects "preferences about preferences" — that is, we know we are likely to be tempted by X or Y, but wish we weren't; thus we willingly pass legislation in order to restrain ourselves from following preferences that we consider shortsighted in our more sober moments. See also Jon Elster, Ulysses and the Sirens (1984).

2. Is it in fact true that a private property/free market economic system diffuses political power? Why isn't political power more diffused if major economic assets are owned by the public, that is, by the entire citizenry, as in socialist regimes? Compare Charles E. Lindblom, Politics and Markets 170-188 (1977) (concentrations of private wealth lead to plutocracy). One response, deriving from the economics-influenced literature of "public choice," is that publicly owned or managed goods tend to be siphoned off by special interests. Two classics on this subject are Mancur Olson, The Logic of Collective Action (1st ed. 1965); and James Buchanan & Gordon Tullock, The Calculus of Consent (1962).

3. How great a concession does Friedman make when he observes that government properly may prevent violence, operate the

monetary system, enforce contracts, define property rights, provide antitrust protection, and manage at least some streets, parks, and pollution problems? Do such responses to "market failure" swallow up the claim that the market can coordinate without coercion — and with it, the claim that the market can diffuse power and protect individualism? Might not a government act quite repressively in, say, antitrust or environmental enforcement?

4. Friedman's arguments interestingly echo some political claims from an earlier time, described in Joyce Appleby's Capitalism and the New Social Order: The Republican Vision of the 1790s (1984). Appleby points out that prior to the mid-eighteenth century, most people thought that hierarchical governance was essential to the ordering of human behavior (including economic behavior) since human beings were thought to be generally too unruly to operate without detailed and intimate supervision.

Undermining this hierarchical world view, according to Appleby, was the eighteenth-century growth of commerce and an accompanying popular discussion of a single metaphoric "market." If goods that were bought and sold could reach a rough equilibrium or "market" price in this larger market, then the "market" itself appeared to be a self-regulating mechanism, operating without the need for political supervision — or as Friedman put it, capable of "coordination without coercion." In the eighteenth century, according to Appleby, the next step was an extension of this economic idea into the political arena: If human beings did not need hierarchic rulers to govern their economic affairs, then why did they need rulers in politics generally? In this way, Appleby claims that the development of free market economic thinking was a crucial step toward the early republican political theory of democracy and popular self-governance, although Appleby herself appears to think that the actual experience of capitalism should make observers less sanguine about the liberating effects of the market.

5. Friedman is of course not the only theorist to relate property to liberty, but some other theorists do so on quite different grounds. For example, Gregory S. Alexander, in Commodity and Propriety: Competing Visions of Property in American Legal Thought, 1776-1970 (1997), tracks a dialectic between the Friedman-like "commodity" version of property and a conflicting "republican" view somewhat different from that described by Appleby, supra. According to Alexander, a continuing tradition of "republican" thought has made property especially relevant for citizens' "independence," but this theory also has argued for a number of political restraints on market activities. See also Radin,

Personhood, supra p. 8, and the notes that follow it. For a somewhat skeptical review of a variety of arguments that associate
property with liberty, see Carol M. Rose, Property as the Keystone
Right?, 71 Notre Dame L. Rev. 329 (1996).

6. Friedman's references to Russia are now out of date. Was
the Soviet system bound to fail because it violated human nature?
See the Pipes selection, supra p. 20. For a thoughtful discussion of
the role of property in the new post-socialist constitutions of eastern Europe, see Cass R. Sunstein, On Property and Constitutionalism, 14 Cardozo L. Rev. 907 (1993). Sunstein is generally
considered a liberal constitutional law scholar, and while he is
sympathetic to distributional concerns, he nevertheless echoes
some of Friedman's themes. For more on distributional issues, see
the following section.

D. Distributive Justice

INTRODUCTORY NOTE ON PAST AND PRESENT THEORIES OF DISTRIBUTIVE JUSTICE

The institution of private property tends to preserve existing —
and invariably unequal — distributions of wealth. Not surprisingly, ideological opponents of private property have consistently
stressed its association with inequality. Theorists critical of private
property were especially prominent in the nineteenth century, a
period of unprecedented industrial expansion. Karl Marx, the most
influential of these critics, called for the State, once it had been
reconstituted to represent the "proletariat," to seize ownership of
capital, land, and other means of production from the "bourgeoisie." In practice, does State ownership empower individual workers? Enrich them? Decrease their alienation? Or, as critics of
Marxist regimes have asserted, entoil workers in huge unresponsive bureaucracies?

Henry George, a member of the generation following Marx's,
provided an enduringly influential critique of the justice of private
property in land. George's core concern was tax policy. He was
chary of taxes on orchards, buildings, and other *land improvements*,
on the grounds that taxes of this stripe discourage investment and
unfairly reduce returns to enterprises. George's central insight was
that *land sites*, as distinguished from improvements on land, are
almost completely inelastically supplied (at least outside Holland).

"A tax on date trees, imposed by the Mohammed Ali, caused the Egyptian fellahs to cut down their trees: but a tax of twice the amount imposed on land produced no such result." The upshot, for George, was that government should impose steep taxes to appropriate "unearned" increments in land values. As he saw it, these taxes would not crimp production and would justly transfer site values (which arise from growth of the community and not from owner enterprise) to the collectivity that created them. A concise statement of his views is Henry George, Our Land and Land Policy, 9 Writings of Henry George 108 (1898). Are there any economic or ethical differences between taxing site values and taxing the *natural* human capital that especially intelligent or athletic persons are born with?

This section includes several contemporary selections on the crucial question of distributive justice, starting with an excerpt from John Rawls's influential A Theory of Justice. Later in this volume, selections by Jolls, Sunstein & Thaler (infra p. 221) and Zerbe & Anderson (infra p. 273) consider informal norms of fair distribution.

Consider, prior to embarking on these readings, to what extent the U.S. Constitution embodies principles of distributive justice. Jennifer Nedelsky associates certain views with James Madison and the other framers, and contrasts them with egalitarianism:

> In the conception crystallized and articulated during the formation of the Constitution, the relationship between inequality, property, liberty, and limited government was as follows: The acquisition and use of property were essential elements of liberty. Given free rein, "men's different and unequal faculties of acquiring property" would result in unequal possessions. Justice required the protection of these acquisitions from the predatory claims of the less successful. The object of government was to provide both this liberty and this justice. . . .
>
> The egalitarian vision is practically a reversal of this founding conception: Whether the inequality of property is the result of liberty or not, it stands in the way of liberty and justice for all. The freedom to use and acquire property and the security of one's acquisitions are no longer defining elements of liberty and justice, but the potential objects of regulation and redistribution — aimed at assuring justice and liberty. In the stronger versions of egalitarianism, this objective entails a governmental responsibility either to assure that the ability to exercise one's rights is not contingent on wealth or to provide the resources necessary to make that exercise possible. . . .

Jennifer Nedelsky, Private Property and the Limits of American Constitutionalism 261-262 (1990).

For echoes of the views that Nedelsky associates with the framers, see Richard A. Epstein, Takings (1985); Milton Friedman, Capitalism and Freedom, ch. 10 (1962); and Robert Nozick, Anarchy, State, and Utopia (1974). In a more egalitarian vein are Bruce A. Ackerman, Social Justice in the Liberal State (1980), and Ronald M. Dworkin, Taking Rights Seriously (1977).

Nedelsky herself welcomes the eclipse of the Madisonian stress on property, in part because she sees it as resting on the flawed conception that individuals achieve autonomy on their own, not through social relationships. See Private Property and the Limits of American Constitutionalism at 264-276. According to one reviewer, "Nedelsky's failure to consider the additional material prosperity introduced by a system of private property means that, if anything, her own account of the Madisonian Constitution is 'distorted': Constitutional protection for private property is far easier to attack in a zero-sum society than in a world where private property creates incentives that encourage a better life for all." Thomas W. Merrill, Zero-Sum Madison, 90 Mich. L. Rev. 1392, 1393 (1992).

A Theory of Justice*

John Rawls

. . . I shall be satisfied if it is possible to formulate a reasonable conception of justice for the basic structure of society conceived for the time being as a closed system isolated from other societies. The significance of this special case is obvious and needs no explanation. It is natural to conjecture that once we have a sound theory for this case, the remaining problems of justice will prove more tractable in the light of it. With suitable modifications such a theory should provide the key for some of these other questions.

The other limitation on our discussion is that for the most part I examine the principles of justice that would regulate a well-ordered society. Everyone is presumed to act justly and to do his part in upholding just institutions. Though justice may be, as Hume remarked, the cautious, jealous virtue, we can still ask what a perfectly just society would be like. Thus I consider primarily what I call strict compliance as opposed to partial compliance theory (§§25, 39). The latter studies the principles that govern how we are to deal with injustice. It comprises such topics as the theory of punishment, the doctrine of just war, and the justification of the

*Source: pp. 8-22, 60-65 (1971).

various ways of opposing unjust regimes, ranging from civil disobedience and militant resistance to revolution and rebellion. Also included here are questions of compensatory justice and of weighing one form of institutional injustice against another. Obviously the problems of partial compliance theory are the pressing and urgent matters. These are the things that we are faced with in everyday life. The reason for beginning with ideal theory is that it provides, I believe, the only basis for the systematic grasp of these more pressing problems. . . .

3.   The Main Idea of the Theory of Justice

My aim is to present a conception of justice which generalizes and carries to a higher level of abstraction the familiar theory of the social contract as found, say, in Locke, Rousseau, and Kant. In order to do this we are not to think of the original contract as one to enter a particular society or to set up a particular form of government. Rather, the guiding idea is that the principles of justice for the basic structure of society are the object of the original agreement. They are the principles that free and rational persons concerned to further their own interests would accept in an initial position of equality as defining the fundamental terms of their association. These principles are to regulate all further agreements; they specify the kinds of social cooperation that can be entered into and the forms of government that can be established. This way of regarding the principles of justice I shall call justice as fairness.

Thus we are to imagine that those who engage in social cooperation choose together, in one joint act, the principles which are to assign basic rights and duties and to determine the division of social benefits. Men are to decide in advance how they are to regulate their claims against one another and what is to be the foundation charter of their society. Just as each person must decide by rational reflection what constitutes his good, that is, the system of ends which it is rational for him to pursue, so a group of persons must decide once and for all what is to count among them as just and unjust. The choice which rational men would make in this hypothetical situation of equal liberty, assuming for the present that this choice problem has a solution, determines the principles of justice.

In justice as fairness the original position of equality corresponds to the state of nature in the traditional theory of the social contract. This original position is not, of course, thought of as an actual historical state of affairs, much less as a primitive condition of culture. It is understood as a purely hypothetical situation characterized so as to lead to a certain conception of justice. Among the essential features of this situation is that no one knows his place in society, his class position or social status, nor does any one know his fortune in the distribution of natural assets and abilities, his intelligence, strength, and the like. I shall even assume that the parties do not know their conceptions of the good or their special psychological propensities. The principles of justice are chosen behind a veil of ignorance. This ensures that no one is advantaged or disadvantaged in the choice of principles by the outcome of natural chance or the contingency of social circumstances. Since all are similarly situated and no one is able to design principles to favor his particular condition, the principles of justice are the result of a fair agreement or bargain. For given the circumstances of the original position, the symmetry of everyone's relations to each other, this initial situation is fair between individuals as moral persons, that is, as rational beings with their own ends and capable, I shall assume, of a sense of justice. The original position is, one might say, the appropriate initial status quo, and thus the fundamental agreements reached in it are fair. This explains the propriety of the name "justice as fairness": It conveys the idea that the principles of justice are agreed to in an initial situation that is fair. The name does not mean that the concepts of justice and fairness are the same, any more than the phrase "poetry as metaphor" means that the concepts of poetry and metaphor are the same.

Justice as fairness begins, as I have said, with one of the most general of all choices which persons might make together, namely, with the choice of the first principles of a conception of justice which is to regulate all subsequent criticism and reform of institutions. Then, having chosen a conception of justice, we can suppose that they are to choose a constitution and a legislature to enact laws, and so on, all in accordance with the principles of justice initially agreed upon. Our social situation is just if it is such that by this sequence of hypothetical agreements we would have contracted into the general system of rules which defines it. Moreover, assuming that the original position does determine a set of principles (that is, that a particular conception of justice would be chosen), it will then be true that whenever social institutions satisfy these principles those engaged in them can say to one another that they are cooperating on terms to which they would agree if they were free and equal persons whose relations with respect to one another were fair. . . .

In working out the conception of justice as fairness one main task clearly is to determine which principles of justice would be chosen in the original position. To do this we must describe this situation in some detail and formulate with care the problem of choice which it presents. These matters I shall take up in the immediately succeeding chapters. It may be observed, however, that once the principles of justice are thought of as arising from an original agreement in a situation of equality, it is an open question whether the principle of utility would be acknowledged. Offhand it hardly seems likely that persons who view themselves as equals, entitled to press their claims upon one another, would agree to a principle which may require lesser life prospects for some simply for the sake of a greater sum of advantages enjoyed by others. Since each desires to protect his interests, his capacity to advance his conception of the good, no one has a reason to acquiesce in an enduring loss for himself in order to bring about a greater net balance of satisfaction. In the absence of strong and lasting benevolent impulses, a rational man would not accept a basic structure merely because it maximized the algebraic sum of advantages irrespective of its permanent effects on his own basic rights and interests. Thus it seems that the principle of utility is incompatible with the conception of social cooperation among equals for mutual advantage. It appears to be inconsistent with the idea of reciprocity implicit in the notion of a well-ordered society. Or, at any rate, so I shall argue.

I shall maintain instead that the persons in the initial situation would choose two rather different principles: the first requires equality in the assignment of basic rights and duties, while the second holds that social and economic inequalities, for example inequalities of wealth and authority, are just only if they result in compensating benefits for everyone, and in particular for the least advantaged members of society. These principles rule out justifying institutions on the grounds that the hardships of some are offset by a greater good in the aggregate. It may be expedient but it is not just that some should have less in order that others may prosper. But there is no injustice in the greater benefits earned by a few provided that the situation of persons not so fortunate is thereby improved. The intuitive idea is that since everyone's well-being depends upon a scheme of cooperation without which no one could have a satisfactory life, the division of advantages should be such as to draw forth the willing cooperation of everyone taking part in it, including those less well situated. Yet this can be expected only if reasonable terms are proposed. The two principles mentioned seem to be a fair agreement on the basis of which those better endowed, or more fortunate in their social position, neither of which we can be said to deserve, could expect the willing cooperation of others when some workable scheme is a necessary condition of the welfare of all. Once we decide to look for a conception of justice that nullifies the accidents of natural endowment and the contingencies of social circumstance as counters in quest for political and economic advantage, we are led to these principles. They express the result of leaving aside those aspects of the social world that seem arbitrary from a moral point of view. . . .

4. The Original Position and Justification . . .

It seems reasonable to suppose that the parties in the original position are equal. That is, all have the same rights in the procedure for choosing principles; each can make proposals, submit reasons for their acceptance, and so on. Obviously the purpose of these conditions is to represent equality between human beings as moral persons, as creatures having a conception of their good and capable of a sense of justice. The basis of equality is taken to be similarity in these two respects. Systems of ends are not ranked in value; and each man is presumed to have the requisite ability to understand and to act upon whatever principles are adopted. Together with the veil of ignorance, these conditions define the principles of justice as those which rational persons concerned to advance their interests would consent to as equals when none are known to be advantaged or disadvantaged by social and natural contingencies. . . .

. . . I have emphasized that this original position is purely hypothetical. It is natural to ask why, if this agreement is never actually entered into, we should take any interest in these principles, moral or otherwise. The answer is that the conditions embodied in the description of the original position are ones that we do in fact accept. Or if we do not, then perhaps we can be persuaded to do so by philosophical reflection. . . . We need a conception that enables us to envision our objective from afar: The intuitive notion of the original position is to do this for us.

5. Classical Utilitarianism

There are many forms of utilitarianism, and the development of the theory has continued in recent years. I shall not survey these forms here, nor take account of the numerous refinements found in contemporary discussions. My aim is to work out a theory of justice that represents an alternative to utilitarian thought generally and so to all of these different versions of it. I believe that the contrast between the contract view and utilitarianism remains essentially the same in all these cases. Therefore I shall compare justice as fairness with familiar variants of intuitionism, perfectionism, and utilitarianism in order to bring out the underlying differences in the simplest way. With this end in mind, the kind of utilitarianism I shall describe here is the strict classical doctrine which receives perhaps its clearest and most accessible formulation in Sidgwick. The main idea is that society is rightly ordered, and therefore just, when its major institutions are arranged so as to achieve the greatest net balance of satisfaction summed over all the individuals belonging to it. . . .

11. Two Principles of Justice

I shall now state in a provisional form the two principles of justice that I believe would be chosen in the original position. . . . The first statement of the two principles reads as follows:

> First: each person is to have an equal right to the most extensive basic liberty compatible with a similar liberty for others.
> Second: social and economic inequalities are to be arranged so that they are both (a) reasonably expected to be to everyone's advantage, and (b) attached to positions and offices open to all. . . .

By way of general comment, these principles primarily apply, as I have said, to the basic structure of society. They are to govern the assignment of rights and duties and to regulate the distribution of social and economic advantages. As their formulation suggests, these principles presuppose that the social structure can be divided into two more or less distinct parts, the first principle applying to the one, the second to the other. They distinguish between those aspects of the social system that define and secure the equal liberties of citizenship and those that specify and establish social and economic inequalities. The basic liberties of citizens are, roughly speaking, political liberty (the right to vote and to be eligible for public office) together with freedom of speech and assembly; liberty of conscience and freedom of thought; freedom of the person along with the right to hold (personal) property; and freedom from arbitrary arrest and seizure as defined by the concept of the rule of law. These liberties are all required to be equal by the first principle, since citizens of a just society are to have the same basic rights.

The second principle applies, in the first approximation, to the distribution of income and wealth and to the design of organizations that make use of differences in authority and responsibility, or chains of command. While the distribution of wealth and income need not be equal, it must be to everyone's advantage, and at the same time, positions of authority and offices of command must be accessible to all. One applies the second principle by holding positions open, and then, subject to this constraint, arranges social and economic inequalities so that everyone benefits.

These principles are to be arranged in a serial order with the first principle prior to the second. This ordering means that a departure from the institutions of equal liberty required by the first principle cannot be justified by, or compensated for, by greater social and economic advantages. The distribution of wealth and income, and the hierarchies of authority, must be consistent with both the liberties of equal citizenship and equality of opportunity.

It is clear that these principles are rather specific in their content, and their acceptance rests on certain assumptions that I must eventually try to explain and justify. A theory of justice depends upon a theory of society in ways that will become evident as we proceed. For the present, it should be observed that the two principles (and this holds for all formulations) are a special case of a more general conception of justice that can be expressed as follows.

> All social values — liberty and opportunity, income and wealth, and the bases of self-respect — are to be distributed equally unless an unequal distribution of any, or all, of these values is to everyone's advantage.

Injustice, then, is simply inequalities that are not to the benefit of all. Of course, this conception is extremely vague and requires interpretation.

As a first step, suppose that the basic structure of society distributes certain primary goods; that is, things that every rational man is presumed to want. These goods normally have a use whatever a person's rational plan of life. For simplicity, assume that the chief primary goods at the disposition of society are rights and liberties, powers and opportunities, income and wealth. (Later on in Part Three the primary good of self-respect has a central place.) These are the social primary goods. Other primary goods such as health and vigor, intelligence and imagination, are natural goods; although their possession is influenced by the basic structure, they are not so directly under its control. Imagine, then, a hypothetical initial arrangement in which all the social primary goods are equally distributed: everyone has similar rights and duties, and income and wealth are evenly shared. This state of affairs provides a benchmark for judging improvements. If certain inequalities of wealth and organizational powers would make everyone better off than in this hypothetical starting situation, then they accord with the general conception.

Now it is possible, at least theoretically, that by giving up some of their fundamental liberties men are sufficiently compensated by the resulting social and economic gains. The general conception of justice imposes no restrictions on what sort of inequalities are permissible; it only requires that everyone's position be improved. We need not suppose anything so drastic as consenting to a condition of slavery. Imagine instead that men forego certain political rights when the economic returns are significant and their capacity to influence the course of policy by the exercise of these rights would be marginal in any case. It is this kind of exchange which the two principles as stated rule out; being arranged in serial order they do not permit exchanges between basic liberties and economic and social gains. . . .

Now the second principle insists that each person benefit from permissible inequalities in the basic structure. This means that it must be reasonable for each relevant representative man defined by this structure, when he views it as a going concern, to prefer his prospects with the inequality to his prospects without it. One is not allowed to justify differences in income or organizational powers on the ground that the disadvantages of those in one position are outweighed by the greater advantages of those in another. Much less can infringements of liberty be counterbalanced in this way. Applied to the basic structure, the principle of utility would have us maximize the sum of expectations of representative men (weighted by the number of persons they represent, on the classical view); and this would permit us to compensate for the losses of some by the gains of others. Instead, the two principles require that everyone benefit from economic and social inequalities. . . .

NOTES AND QUESTIONS ON THE RAWLSIAN THEORY OF JUST DISTRIBUTION

1. Rawls sets his scenario by isolating his hypothetical society from all others. What if he instead supposed that all societies per-

mitted easy entry and departure, and then asked, to what society would people — in particular, the least advantaged — gravitate? Rawls asserts that people in fact cannot voluntarily choose the society in which they live. But if they could easily move about, would the quest for "justice as fairness" be an unnecessary exercise? Might we then find a plurality of just societies, perhaps having quite different characteristics?

2. Does Rawls make things too easy for himself by supposing that "everyone is presumed to act justly and to do his part in upholding just institutions"? With this assumption, can he even address some of the central problems in property and contract regimes, such as the "prisoner's dilemma" and "tragedy of the commons," where individual self-interest diverges from the common good? Do property regimes always confront problems of "partial compliance," which Rawls for the most part avoids?

3. Consider the "original position": Would a person so ignorant of herself that she did not know her status, abilities, or conceptions of the good really have any basis for choice about the just society? For a critique on the thinness of personality supposed by Rawls, see Michael J. Sandel, Liberalism and the Limits of Justice 62 (1982).

4. Elsewhere in A Theory of Justice (at §§12-13), Rawls discusses at length his central principle of just wealth distribution, which he calls "the difference principle." As Rawls states it, "[t]he intuitive idea is that the social order is not to establish and secure the more attractive prospects of those better off unless doing so is to the advantage of those less fortunate." Id. at 75. Thus, for example, an inequality in the distribution of income among social classes "is justifiable only if the difference in expectation is to the advantage of the representative man who is worst off, in this case the unrepresentative unskilled worker. The inequality in expectation is permissible only if lowering it would make the working class even more worse off." Id. at 78.

How does the difference principle differ from the principle of Pareto superiority, described supra p. 62, Note 2? How does it differ from the utilitarian (or Kaldor-Hicks) principle that Rawls rejects (for example, the principle of choosing those institutions that would "achieve the greatest net balance of satisfaction" to all participants in the society)?

5. Would people behind a veil of ignorance really choose Rawls's difference principle over the utilitarian principle? What if the difference principle entailed some loss in net social wealth due to lessened incentives, administrative costs, and so on? Might a rational person instead choose utilitarian institutions on the theory

that *ex ante*, such institutions would improve her chances for a slice of a larger pie? See James Q. Wilson, The Moral Sense 73-76 (1993). What does Rawls's difference principle implicitly presume about people's attitudes toward risk? See Carol M. Rose, "Enough, and As Good" of What? 81 Nw. U. L. Rev. 417 (1987).

6. Rawls's Theory of Justice elicited voluminous commentary. For a sampling of the early reactions, see Reading Rawls (Norman Daniels ed., 1975). Rawls updates and elaborates his views in Political Liberalism (1993). On the issue of distributive justice, he asserts:

> ... [M]easures are required to assure that the basic needs of all citizens can be met so that they can take part in political and social life.
>
> About this last point, the idea is not that of satisfying needs as opposed to mere desires and wants; nor is it that of redistribution in favor of greater equality. The constitutional essential here is rather that below a certain level of material and social well-being, and of training and education, people simply cannot take part in society as citizens, much less equal citizens.

Id. at 166.

Backlash*

Mark J. Roe

Economic systems produce wealth, and law and economics analysts try to find which systems are more likely to produce greater wealth, with that wealth distributed acceptably. But in some systems, politics may lash back at the productive arrangements, and this backlash potential complicates economic analysis. Take the following example, admittedly extreme: A rule of free contracting leads a nation to construct large organizations — call them latifundia — in which the senior controllers earn millions of dollars annually, the middle ranking overseers earn hundreds of thousands of dollars annually, and the lowest paid workers earn tens of thousands of dollars annually. In no alternative organizational configuration could any of the three "levels" earn more.

The "twist" in the latifundia system here is that the lowest ranking workers could fare no better in any known alternative system, the most obvious being a system of small-scale firms. Employees at all levels in the alternative society would earn less.

*Source: 98 Colum. L. Rev. 217-241 (1998).

Senior controllers would not be needed there, their talents would not be tapped, and their pay would be reduced, because they would run smaller, less profitable enterprises. The alternative society's per capita GNP is less than the latifundia's. Not only is the latifundia nation's GNP at its highest possible level, but its poorest citizens also live better than they would in any other system.[2]

Suppose that after a few prosperous years, this nation of latifundia becomes politically unstable. Instability was not foreordained, but it arises. Although the lowest ranking employees have a higher income in the latifundia than in any alternative business structure, after the first few placid years they change their minds. Initially they were happy, but they come to hate the system, the government, and the controllers. They start to envy the controllers, whose power and wealth they resent. They grouse on the job, complain to one another, and finally, many revolt. The controllers resist, and in the years of turmoil that ensue the nation fritters away its early economic advantages. Its GNP declines.

At the same time that the nation of latifundia enjoyed its early happy success, a nearby nation developed different institutions. It outlawed latifundia, taxed senior controllers' income at 90 percent marginal tax rates, and subsidized small businesses and family farmers. Although its people were initially poorer — less food, smaller homes, fewer clothes, no luxuries — the nation was never afflicted with the latifundia nation's later turmoil. Backlash, voters' eventually destructive resentment of the organization of production, never emerged. Employees at the lowest level — whose income initially was *less* than the income of the lowest ranking latifundia employees — identify with their small firms' owners. They never revolt; they are satisfied; and because of the scattered organization of industry and farming, they neither develop the revolutionary ideology that led the nation of latifundia to turmoil nor — because workers and managers are scattered in many small enterprises — do they find themselves working in a setting conducive to revolutionary organization.

Consider again the *ex ante* setting. One nation, that of latifundia, has a high GNP and its lowest paid workers do better than their counterparts in the nation of small enterprises. Yet the GNP of the nation of latifundia is about to decline sharply. Now suppose we seek to analyze each nation's institutions from a law and eco-

2. To get a true measure of fairness and wealth, we must adjust each system's value by its nonmonetary costs and benefits. We will do so in Part IV; that adjustment contorts but does not cut the main line of thought here.

nomics perspective. In the family farm society, we look at the marginal tax rate, the regulatory and tax subsidies to small business, the rules that stymie latifundia, and so on, and pronounce each institution inefficient.

Yet which nation is in overall terms more efficient over time? Can we analyze the efficiency of any one of the institutions in the subsidized, regulated, overtaxed nation, most of which would be suboptimal in strict efficiency terms, without considering backlash and the (possibly) politically stabilizing effects of these otherwise inefficient institutions?

I. The Efficiency of Stability

Obviously, the nation that buys immediate prosperity at the price of serious political instability later cannot be said to be more efficient over time than its less productive but more stable neighbor. The difficulty this poses for law and economics scholarship is that accounting for backlash could disable our ability to analyze the efficiency of any single institution or law. What if this law, or this institution, is the one that will tip the nation toward turmoil? Can the law or institution, even if at present productively efficient compared to the next best institution or law, be said to be overall efficient if economic turmoil might result from using it instead of using the less efficient alternative? And if backlash is potentially in play, is accounting for it so amorphous that nothing useful could be said about the law's or institution's efficiency?

We have several plausible exits from this dilemma, each of which would appeal to American law and economics analysts. First, we can assume that at the usual scale of efficiency analysis, this or that institution or law will not induce turmoil. The odds that any one specific law or its alternative would contribute to turmoil or its avoidance are too slim to consider.

Politics, according to this reasoning, is merely secondary to efficiency, and turmoil, one could assume, is unlikely. To an American, this scenario should seem plausible. After all, the United States, unlike Argentina, for example, has never gone through deep and upsetting economically based turmoil. . . .

This way out helps to explain why law and economics scholarship has taken root more deeply in the United States than elsewhere. Outside of the United States, in nations where the risk of institutionally induced turmoil is greater, politics cannot be ignored, and efficiency-based analysis is secondary to assuring stability. In the United States, because such a risk of turmoil is minimal, the efficiency analyst can proceed while ignoring these risks. . . .

For now we will rest here, satisfied that efficiency analysis (at least when the result is Rawlsian satisfactory) is still the way to go in the United States because turmoil is so unlikely for the United States that we can ignore it, because we usually cannot tell *ex ante* whether the efficient institution or the inefficient one will promote turmoil, and because we can be humble enough to limit the domain of law and economics analysis. Below I nevertheless argue that the political problem permeates even basic, ordinary American analysis of, say, takeovers and bankruptcy policy, and hence, political turmoil writ small *is* indeed an American issue. But first we shall analyze three issues in order to deepen the argument I have made so far on backlash. First, does any real society correspond, however roughly, to the latifundia hypothetical I posed in the Introduction — a society that is productively efficient and satisfactorily fair but whose efficient institutions produce political instability? We do not need to produce a real society to make the abstract argument, but producing one might make the abstractions more convincing, and I believe we can produce several. Second, we must confront a problem with the abstract latifundia model: If people are so unhappy in the productive society, why does the market alone not lead that society to the happier, more stable society of family farming? If the market can do this, then is there something wrong with the backlash abstraction? As we shall see, nothing is wrong with the abstraction, because the market cannot always cure the problem. Finally, given people's eventual unhappiness in the latifundia, can we say that the society is really Rawlsian fair as compared to the society of family farmers?

II. Argentina

Does any real society correspond to the once rich and then collapsing latifundia society? At the beginning of the twentieth century, the Argentine standard of living approximated that of western Europe; its per capita gross national product in the 1920s was the eighth highest in the world. The land was . productive; people made money. Most people ate well and were housed satisfactorily. The nation was politically stable. Massive immigration to its frontier settled some of the world's richest agricultural land. Poor people, particularly from Italy, emigrated to Argentina to improve their economic well-being and most of them did. The nation began to industrialize. The quality of Argentina's international financial obligations was not just high, but was approaching that of the world's premier international obligation, the British consol. Buenos Aires built its subway system at about the same time New York did.

Then things fell apart. The economy deteriorated, and turmoil ensued. Investors no longer could be sure of their investments; economic and political turmoil deterred progress. The economy declined, nearly to Third World status, as its per capita GNP plummeted from eighth to forty-third in the world. Juan Perón came and went, as did a military dictatorship. The puzzle of why this came to be has challenged academics, including one Nobel Prize winner, Douglass North, who noted in his Nobel Speech the vexing question of why some nations protect property and prosper while others fail economically.[9]

The received wisdom is that many Third World nations fail to develop strong civil societies with satisfactory property rights, chilling the investment climate and thereby hindering development. Entrepreneurs fear to invest and capital does not accumulate. Without institutions that basically protect property and entrepreneurial investment (or a satisfactorily run public sector), development just will not occur.[10]

But the possibility suggested in some recent scholarship on the Argentine collapse poses a more profound question for us, one that comports with the hypothetical of a politically unstable nation of latifundia that we started with at the beginning of this essay. Protection of property and investment expectations was not all that bad in Argentina at the beginning of the twentieth century. The system was not poverty-stricken and unproductive. Indeed it was quite productive. Argentina's problem was not that it failed to "take off" — to use a phrase once popular in developmental economics — but that it crashed. Here is the rub: It was the means of productivity in "latifundia" (actually, tenant farming) and urban enterprises that destabilized Argentine politics and facilitated the nation's economic decay, a decay from which Argentina has not yet recovered.

. . . While Argentina was settling the wheatfields of the pam-

9. See Douglass C. North, Economic Performance Through Time, 84 Am. Econ. Rev. 359, 364-66 (1994) (Nobel lecture).
10. See Douglass C. North, Institutions, Institutional Change and Economic Performance 110-11 (1990); Robert E. Hall & Charles I. Jones, The Productivity of Nations 2-3 (National Bureau of Econ. Research Working Paper No. 5812, 1996).

pas, some Argentine leaders sought to build instead a nation of yeoman farmers — the Jeffersonian model — and tried to imitate the American homestead plan for family farms. Recall also that the American result was reached partly by government fiat: The land was "free" or cheap, but only if the homesteader improved the land, and that improvement, once its costs were sunk, made abandonment or consolidation into large-scale farming a less immediate option than it otherwise would have been.

But historical contingencies made American-style family farm homesteading hard for Argentina. First, the homesteaders in the United States were subsidized with cheap land (a plausible productive inefficiency). Argentina, however, burdened with debts from local South American wars, lacked the luxury of a balanced budget that would have facilitated a yeoman-style land giveaway; the Argentine government needed fast cash for what land it had, and it had already promised to give away land to finance the war effort. Second, large-scale *estancias* were already common in Argentina for beef raising, making large-scale operations rather than small family farms seem normal. Third, Argentina, as part of a nation-building effort, sought to swell immigration to settle its frontier. Argentine land policy settled the land faster and more densely than a small-scale family farm policy would have, because the land-owning "entrepreneurs" needed tenants, and hence took responsibility for peopling the land.

The Peronist revolution, although primarily urban, sprang from this rural organization of production. When the market for Argentina's beef and wheat production collapsed during the Depression, dispossessed tenant farmers and others streamed into the cities to enter the lowest rungs of urban and industrial labor. Although Perón did not come to power immediately during the migration, these rural emigrants became Perón's core supporters, and by insisting both on controlling food prices and on excluding foreign business, they barred both the rural bourgeoisie from saving and foreigners from investing, thereby denying Argentina its two biggest potential sources of capital accumulation.

This account of Argentina's collapse — plausible but not incontrovertible — roughly corresponds to the latifundia hypothetical. Productive institutions led to a political backlash, eventually making the society comparatively poorer. . . .

We can profitably contrast Argentina . . . with two other societies: Germany in the 1870s and 1880s and Italy in the 1960s and 1970s. In both societies, nations experiencing unrest decided through politics to head off that unrest and quelled the backlash.

During the 1960s and 1970s, the chances were not small that Italy's communist party would win a national election and take power. To head off that result, the Christian Democratic Party sought to structure business enterprises to reduce the chances of communist victory, even at possible economic cost. Believing that employees at a small, closely held firm tended to identify with the fortunes of the owner and tended not to develop a worker-wide class consciousness, the Christian Democratic governments subsidized small firms through tax and regulatory policy. Even if organizing work in large manufacturing enterprises was sometimes more productive than organizing it in smaller, closely held firms, the large firm induced greater class consciousness and facilitated union organizing.

A similar theme of late nineteenth-century industrialization on the European continent was the belief that the evils of England's Lancashire mills were to be avoided. One reason to avoid the gloomy mills was a social preference for a different, sunnier society. A second reason was calculated and instrumental: A society needed to avoid the Lancashire mills to avoid revolution. Bismarckian cynical social policy was the practical result. . . .

III. Could the Market Prevent the Revolution?

Could the market move the latifundia from its unstable initial condition to become the stable nation of small, but less profitable businesses? The answer is maybe yes, maybe no.

The means by which the market could work are obvious. Market incentives arise when the once-happy employees change their minds and come to hate their jobs and their bosses. The employees who start to grouse would be ready to move to another, happier business. The middle level managers, who grouse a little, would leave the latifundia, set up small businesses, and hire employees who are unhappy at the larger firms. Although the smaller businesses would be less productive than the latifundia in our hypothetical world and accordingly would be unable to pay as much to their employees, the smaller businesses' employees would accept the lower wage because they would be happier. In their new settings, employees would grouse less and the revolution would never come. As long as the "price" of happiness is higher than the "cost" of slightly lower wages, the market will work.

Everybody is happy, the system is stable, and the market has worked its magic.

Must the market work this way?

No, it need not. Grousing is a private bad, for whose elimination employees will sometimes give up wages. But political stability is a public good, for which employees may quite rationally refuse to pay.

First, consider the following example: When working in the latifundia, you are offered a job at a small business at a 10 percent pay cut. Will you take it? . . . What if your resentment is directed at *everyone* in the society who has a multimillion dollar salary, whether you work for them or not? It is this resentment that starts the grousing and revolutionary organizing that leads to turmoil in this society, and your move to the smaller business will *not* make you resent your relative position any less. . . .

Second, people in the latifundia society may lack the consciousness that shifting workers to new jobs would stabilize the society. Once large-scale enterprise permeates the society, many actors may simply be unable to vividly imagine work being organized otherwise. . . .

. . . The property rights literature tends to see property rights as coming prior to production. A society protects property rights, and then it produces. Constitutionally entrenching strong property rights is seen by some as the best way to protect property, but this approach has its weaknesses. First, constitutions and their enforcement are malleable; having a rule constitutionally enshrined does not tell us whether property truly will be secure. Second, providing property rights is a public good, and public goods depend on politics and social support; if property rights are unpopular, the public (which must provide the public good) may not support them. Property rights thus in turn depend in part on production, because not all ways of organizing production will be seen as equally legitimate; some ways of producing (or of distributing) wealth will induce more turmoil and weaker property rights than others. Moreover, some forms of organization are less stable than others and which ones succeed over time can depend on social and cultural settings. Beliefs about the proper scope of government (such as Jeffersonian limits versus centralization), socialization in schools (respecting property, inculcating a belief in opportunity and in the justice of unequal outcomes), and religion (both in producing beliefs and in providing dimensions other than the economic over which politics can divide a polity) all can affect whether a system of production will or will not yield political backlash. Property rights, social preferences, and production are resolved continually, not sequentially.

IV. Definitions: Are the Latifundia Truly Rawlsian Fair?

I have thus far put off justifying the latifundia society as Rawlsian fair. True, all levels of employees have higher salaries than they would have had in their most plausible alternative, that of family farms. In that narrow sense, the latifundia are Rawlsian fair.

But how can it be Rawlsian fair if the employees are materially satisfied but become emotionally miserable? Their welfare ends up lower than what it would have been on the family farm, and the assumption of Rawlsian fairness seems contradicted.[26] Similarly, if in the long run the society decays, even a straightforward utilitarian analysis could pronounce the initially rich latifundia to be neither efficient nor fair. If the original society was not efficient and fair in normal terms, then "ordinary" efficiency and wealth maximization analysis would try to move that society from the latifundia to the family farms. "Backlash" analysis would be superfluous.

But remember how the hypothetical started out. People at all levels were initially happy; only later did the lower level employees resent the highly paid senior managers. The society of latifundia may start out as both Rawlsian fair and efficient when compared to the society of family farms. Although employees are not ecstatic about the incomes of the senior controllers, they enjoy their lives, they grouse little, and they eat well. They are merely annoyed, not angry and indignant. There is no reason for the market to transform that society to something more efficient in the long run, because everyone is as happy as he or she can be.

But the organization of production on the latifundia makes change in the employees' perceptions ripe. Perceptions do not *have* to change, but they do change. Eventually envy and resentment arise.[28] Revolutionary leaders organize better on the latifundia than they can on the family farms in the other nation. They can persuade employees that their lives are miserable (and when per-

---

26. Cf. Robert Frank, Choosing the Right Pond — Human Behavior and the Quest for Status 17-38 (1985) (arguing that an employee's utility function is partly defined by income relative to a reference group of friends and fellow workers).

28. Actually, Rawls excluded envy from his list of factors affecting utility, an exclusion that has been criticized: See . . . Robert Wolff, Understanding Rawls — A Reconstruction and Critique of A Theory of Justice 5, 28-29, 187 (1977); see also Guido Calabresi, About Law and Economics: A Letter to Ronald Dworkin, 8 Hofstra L. Rev. 553, 556 (1980) (describing how if A is made wealthier without making B poorer, B may be less happy because of A's greater wealth); Richard H. McAdams, Relative Preferences, 102 Yale L.J. 1, 4-5 (1992) (arguing that preferences for relative wealth count); Amartya Sen, The Impossibility of a Paretian Liberal, 78 J. Pol. Econ. 152, 155-57 (1970). . . .

suaded, the employees' lives "really" become miserable), and they can further inflame latent employee resentment of the rich lives that the senior controllers lead. Such organization, persuasion, and arousal are harder or impossible on the family farms, if only because the life of one family farmer does not vividly differ from that of another.

Extreme preference transformation, to use the vocabulary of economics, can occur on the latifundia, but not on the family farm. . . . [T]he result after preference transformation need not be social transformation to the newly-perceived-as-superior family farm arrangement. If the latifundia society cannot transform itself peacefully through the market or politics, the society could decay to a social state inferior *both* to the starting position for the latifundia *and* to the starting point for the family farms. . . .

V. Is Turmoil Un-American? How About Small Changes? . . .

. . . [E]ven small institutional decisions can have political repercussions. Turmoil, stopped factories, and revolution are the "dramatic" costs of unwanted political secondary effects, but the political effects need not be revolutionary. Small but real political effects are plausible for the United States, and their plausibility renders law and economics scholarship more difficult, here and now, in the United States. To show why this is so, I will look at two business institutions whose efficiency is debated: hostile takeovers and chapter 11 of the bankruptcy law.

Suppose we know that a harsh chapter 11 — say one facilitating the quick sale or liquidation of the bankrupt firm — and a freewheeling takeover market best deployed capital and minimized Rawlsian pain. That is, suppose that for takeovers we knew that (1) the immediate unemployment unleashed by hostile takeovers was small, and (2) the long-term employment result was quite positive. Similarly, suppose that we know that hostile takeovers facilitate greater employment because they encourage firms to be managed better, they lower social waste, and they economize on capital. Finally and similarly, let us hypothesize that we know that chapter 11 sales or liquidations end society's bad bets quickly. Capital moves to better uses and overall employment (both in raising the number of people employed and in raising salaries at the low end) is improved.

But — and here comes the "diluted," nonrevolutionary political side effect — a rule of chapter 11 sale and free-wheeling hostile takeovers will make the employment losses, even if temporary and offset by greater employment gains diffused through the economy, salient in the media. This media saliency could result, I hypothesize, not in an Argentine revolution, but eventually (or at least at a nontrivial level of probability) either in, say, debilitating, wealth-decreasing trade protection or in a no-fire rule for anyone in this or that broad employment category or across the board in the economy. This is not unrealistic, at least from a comparative perspective. Many European nations have difficult-to-fire policies that are seen as impeding businesses from offering entry-level employment. Japanese lifetime employment policies for important classes of employees developed as a political expedient to block off revolutionary potential and the possibility of socialist electoral victories. And trade protection becomes salient in the United States when employees and voters perceive instability in their working lives.

Add to this sequence a further assumption: Trade protection or the no-fire rule reduces the society's wealth because more enterprises stagnate. Eventually unemployment rises as some enterprises become reluctant to hire, so that, we assume, those on the lowest rungs in that society become poorer. So, (1) if both a bankruptcy rule of sale and a free-wheeling takeover policy are efficient but increase the political probability of no-fire rules or trade protection, and (2) if no-fire rules or protection would eventually reduce aggregate employment and wage levels, then (3) how can we analyze the efficiency of chapter 11 and hostile takeovers? . . .

. . . Hence we see the difficulty for law and economics scholarship, even today in the United States, and even without the alien and improbable risk of fundamental revolutionary political turmoil.[40] . . .

Conclusion . . .

. . . [B]ecause one usually cannot predict whether it is the production-enhancing rule or the inefficient rule that would promote turmoil, one who accounts for turmoil would not usually change the bottom line of the economic analysis. This indeterminacy — the potential that an otherwise efficient rule might degrade a society, because of the turmoil it could create — could lead politicized analysts to reject any economic analysis of a rule's or an

---

40. NAFTA, the North American Free Trade Association, could be analyzed similarly, with disruptions of free trade not as the backlash, but with free trade as the rule that could produce a backlash. Few economically oriented analysts doubt the efficiency of free trade in most settings. But if free trade whips up a successful political backlash — the backlash thus far has failed to influence policy deeply — then efficiency analysis becomes harder. . . .

institution's efficiency effects; indeterminacy, one might (incorrectly) conclude, makes law and economics analysis beside the point. But, even when lacking a sense of the probabilities, one should *not* jump to conclude that, because efficiency — after considering political effects — cannot be assuredly predicted, anything goes. Often the best policy is to ignore secondary political repercussions, because indeterminacy does *not* imply that efficiency cannot be predicted at all (which if so would legitimately allow politicians to decide on the basis of what makes political sense or what makes the decision maker feel good). Rather, indeterminacy adds an "error term": Without knowing more about the political probabilities, the efficient result *could* induce negative backlash, but so could the inefficient result. When we cannot assess which one is more likely to produce backlash (but we know one will produce less wealth than the other), then the policy choice is easier, and we choose the efficient wealth-enhancing one. We simply recognize that there is an error term, one involving backlash, in our calculations. . . .

This way of looking at economic problems opens up another research view. A full understanding of the origins, persistence, and disappearance of economically inefficient statutes could lead to them being seen not just as policy mistakes or interest group rent-seeking, but as efficiency interacting with backlash. As we have seen, critical statutes that seem inefficient — small farm subsidies, Robinson-Patman-style antitrust, Glass-Steagall, and the list could go on — could be seen as not just policy errors or interest-group power plays, but as ways to avoid destructive backlash (or as the products of backlash). They dampen crises and then over time — perhaps too slowly, perhaps not too slowly — they degrade and disappear.

NOTES AND QUESTIONS ON EQUALITY, PROSPERITY, AND THE DESIGN OF WELFARE PROGRAMS

1. At bottom Roe argues that an analyst of a proposed policy should take into account the secondary effects the policy would have on political and social life. Does any academic discipline train professionals to have special abilities to predict secondary effects of this sort? Is there an objective method of determining whether a program of, say, rent control would better diffuse social discontent than a program of housing vouchers? Is the "error term" that

Roe's analysis introduces simply an invitation to sloppy and self-serving policy analysis?

2. Roe cites Douglass North, who was awarded a Nobel Prize for his work on the determinants of economic growth. See especially Douglass C. North & Robert Paul Thomas, The Rise of the Western World (1973), a sweeping historical study that links prosperity to the emergence of private property rights. Does Roe adequately explain why a system of private property in the means of production led to cataclysmic backlash in Argentina (and Russia), but not in the United States (and Switzerland)?

3. Are current inequalities of income and wealth in the United States likely to trigger backlashes, large or small? How do the poor fare in material terms in the United States, compared to their counterparts in other nations? If the measure is relative poverty, that is, the percentage of households with incomes reported to be below a given percentage of the national average income, the United States has one of the highest poverty rates among industrialized nations. If the measure is equivalent purchasing power, however, the United States (along with Canada and Luxembourg) has the lowest absolute poverty rate in the world. See McKinley L. Blackburn, Comparing Poverty: The United States and Other Industrial Nations (1997). On the high, and increasing, degree of income inequality in the United States, see Sheldon Danziger & Peter Gottschalk, America Unequal (1995); James K. Galbraith, Created Unequal: The Crisis in American Pay (1998). On the dramatic improvements in the housing conditions of poor families in the United States since 1940, see the selection by Weicher, infra p. 393, and the notes that follow it.

4. Some of the statistical studies cited in the prior note make use of the "poverty rate" — the Census Bureau's official yardstick of material hardship. Data used to calculate the poverty rate are gleaned from householders' reports of their cash income. Critics assert that these householder responses underestimate the resources available to poor households. First, by counting only cash income, the official poverty rate ignores householders' receipt of *in-kind* transfers, such as food stamps, Medicaid, and Section 8 housing allowances. In 1998, government outlays on various in-kind transfers to the poor were about triple the amount of government cash transfers to the poor. (Query: From a poor person's perspective, is receipt of a dollar of, say, Medicaid benefits the equivalent of receipt of a dollar in cash?) Second, surveys of consumer expenditures suggest that many households underreport their cash income to census workers. See Morton Paglin, The Underground Economy: New Estimates from Household Income and

Expenditure Surveys, 103 Yale L.J. 2239, 2249 (1994) (estimating underground economy in 1990 at 8.4 percent of Gross Domestic Product). On how poor families actually get by, see Kathryn Edin & Laura Lein, Making Ends Meet: How Single Mothers Survive Welfare and Low-Wage Work (1997).

5. Are individuals more concerned about their absolute levels of income and wealth, or with how they stand relative to others? See the sources that Roe cites in his footnotes 26 and 28. In his tale of the latifundia society, how does he implicitly answer this question? From a Rawlsian perspective, are the relative incomes or the absolute incomes of the least advantaged more pertinent?

6. Should each citizen have a constitutional right to a minimum level of material wherewithal? As Nedelsky reports, supra p. 93, James Madison thought not. Some scholars, however, have reasoned that the post–Civil War amendments to the Constitution overturned Madison's conception. See, e.g., Akhil R. Amar, Forty Acres and a Mule: A Republican Theory of Minimal Entitlements, 13 Harv. J.L. & Pub. Poly. 37 (1990) (construing Thirteenth Amendment to require the federal government to provide all individuals with a minimum level of sustenance and shelter); Frank I. Michelman, Welfare Rights in a Constitutional Democracy, 1979 Wash. U. L.Q. 659 (restating Michelman's long-held position that the Equal Protection Clause can be construed to confer unconditional welfare rights). This scholarly position in turn has drawn criticism. See, e.g., Amy L. Wax, Rethinking Welfare Rights, 63 L. & Contemp. Probs. 257 (2000) (arguing that welfare policies must honor deeply held norms that impose reciprocal duties to be socially productive). See also Robert C. Ellickson, The Untenable Case for an Unconditional Right to Shelter, 15 Harv. J.L. & Pub. Poly. 17 (1992). Ellickson identifies two express "positive" constitutional rights: the Thirteenth Amendment guarantee of self-ownership of one's labor (and human capital), and the state constitutional conferrals of a right to receive primary and secondary education. He argues that these two particular "positive" rights were elevated to constitutional status because they reinforce work incentives, whereas unconditional constitutional rights to receive material aid would dull those incentives.

7. Progressive income taxes are logical sources of revenue for redistributive programs. Do these taxes blunt work incentives? As Kennedy and Michelman observe, supra p. 66-67, while a higher tax rate might cause some workers to choose more leisure (a substitution effect), the same taxes could induce *more* work from individuals striving to avoid diminution in after-tax income (an income effect). Which effect is greater is not obvious. Some inves-

tigators assert that higher taxes on balance do discourage work, and redistributive efforts therefore significantly diminish the total pie. See Edgar K. Browning & William R. Johnson, The Trade-Off Between Equality and Efficiency, 92 J. Pol. Econ. 175 (1984). Others think the effect is small. See Thomas MaCurdy, Work Disincentive Effects of Taxes, 82 Am. Econ. Rev. 243 (Pap. & Proc. 1992).

8. Should private law take into account the wealth of litigants involved in a particular civil case, in order to accomplish a more progressive distribution of income? Most law-and-economics scholars argue it should not, on the grounds that private-law rules are inferior distributive mechanisms compared to broader tax and welfare programs. See, e.g., A. Mitchell Polinsky, An Introduction to Law and Economics 119-127 (2d ed. 1989); Louis Kaplow & Steven Shavell, Should Legal Rules Favor the Poor?, 29 J. Legal Stud. 821 (2000). For doubts about the soundness of this position, see, e.g., Christine Jolls, Behavioral Economics Analysis of Redistributive Legal Rules, 51 Vand. L. Rev. 1653 (1998); Chris William Sanchirico, Deconstructing the New Efficiency Rationale, 86 Cornell L. Rev. 1003 (2001).

On most civil issues it is prejudicial — indeed often a reversible error — for a trial judge to allow admission of evidence concerning the wealth of the parties. Does this mean that the law on the books already comports with the economists' predominant view? Is the law in action as insensitive to distributive considerations?

9. At bottom, how important are material goods to personal welfare? A child's prospects seem to be affected less by the material prosperity of the parental household than by parents' personal attributes — on dimensions such as honesty, reliability, and diligence. See Susan E. Mayer, What Money Can't Buy: Family Income and Children's Life Chances (1997). What implications does this have for the design of welfare programs?

What does it mean for a society to be wealthy? Marshall P. Sahlins argues that "the original affluent society" was that of paleolithic hunter-gatherers, who enhanced their well-being by *wanting less* rather than *producing more*. See Sahlins, The Original Affluent Society, *in* Stone Age Economics 1-39 (1972). This relaxed attitude permitted them to meet their needs quite adequately without a great deal of labor and to spend a considerable amount of time chatting, loafing, and sleeping. James Axtell, The Invasion Within: The Contest of Cultures in Colonial North America 302-327 (1985) argues that seventeenth-century Native Americans were far more successful in wooing renegades and war-raid captives to their nomadic lifestyle than the European settlers were at "converting" Native Americans to a sedentary life; this was at least in part because of the attractions of adventure and what a pair of "white Indians" called " 'the most perfect freedom, the ease of living, [and] the absence of those cares and corroding solicitudes which so often prevail with us.' " Id. at 327.

Which society was wealthier? If hunter-gatherer ways are so appealing, why have so many former hunter-gatherer bands given them up?

Chapter 2

The Problem of the Commons

A. Tragedy or Comedy?

The Tragedy of the Commons*

Garrett Hardin

... We can make little progress in working toward optimum population size until we explicitly exorcize the spirit of Adam Smith in the field of practical demography. In economic affairs, The Wealth of Nations (1776) popularized the "invisible hand," the idea that an individual who "intends only his own gain," is, as it were, "led by an invisible hand to promote ... the public interest." Adam Smith did not assert that this was invariably true, and perhaps neither did any of his followers. But he contributed to a dominant tendency of thought that has ever since interfered with positive action based on rational analysis, namely, the tendency to assume that decisions reached individually will, in fact, be the best decisions for an entire society. If this assumption is correct it justifies the continuance of our present policy of laissez-faire in reproduction. If it is correct we can assume that men will control their individual fecundity so as to produce the optimum population. If the assumption is not correct, we need to reexamine our individual freedoms to see which ones are defensible.

*Source: 162 Science 1243-1248 (1968).

The Tragedy of Freedom in a Commons

The rebuttal to the invisible hand in population control is to be found in a scenario first sketched in a little-known pamphlet in 1833 by a mathematical amateur named William Forster Lloyd (1794-1852). We may well call it "the tragedy of the commons," using the word "tragedy" as the philosopher Whitehead used it: "The essence of dramatic tragedy is not unhappiness. It resides in the solemnity of the remorseless working of things." . . .

The tragedy of the commons develops in this way. Picture a pasture open to all. It is to be expected that each herdsman will try to keep as many cattle as possible on the commons. Such an arrangement may work reasonably satisfactorily for centuries because tribal wars, poaching, and disease keep the numbers of both man and beast well below the carrying capacity of the land. Finally, however, comes the day of reckoning, that is, the day when the long-desired goal of social stability becomes a reality. At this point, the inherent logic of the commons remorselessly generates tragedy.

As a rational being, each herdsman seeks to maximize his gain. Explicitly or implicitly, more or less consciously, he asks, "What is the utility to *me* of adding one more animal to my herd?" This utility has one negative and one positive component.

1. The positive component is a function of the increment of one animal. Since the herdsman receives all the proceeds from the sale of the additional animal, the positive utility is nearly +1.
2. The negative component is a function of the additional overgrazing created by one more animal. Since, however, the effects of overgrazing are shared by all the herdsmen, the negative utility for any particular decision-making herdsman is only a fraction of −1.

Adding together the component partial utilities, the rational herdsman concludes that the only sensible course for him to pursue is to add another animal to his herd. And another; and another. . . . But this is the conclusion reached by each and every rational herdsman sharing a commons. Therein is the tragedy. Each man is locked into a system that compels him to increase his herd without limit — in a world that is limited. Ruin is the destination toward which all men rush, each pursuing his own best interest in a society that believes in the freedom of the commons. Freedom in a commons brings ruin to all.

Some would say that this is a platitude. Would that it were! In a sense, it was learned thousands of years ago, but natural selection favors the forces of psychological denial. The individual benefits as an individual from his ability to deny the truth even though society as a whole, of which he is a part, suffers. Education can counteract the natural tendency to do the wrong thing, but the inexorable succession of generations requires that the basis for this knowledge be constantly refreshed.

A simple incident that occurred a few years ago in Leominster, Massachusetts, shows how perishable the knowledge is. During the Christmas shopping season the parking meters downtown were covered with plastic bags that bore tags reading: "Do not open until after Christmas. Free parking courtesy of the mayor and city council." In other words, facing the prospect of an increased demand for already scarce space, the city fathers reinstituted the system of the commons. (Cynically, we suspect that they gained more votes than they lost by this retrogressive act.)

In an approximate way, the logic of the commons has been understood for a long time, perhaps since the discovery of agriculture or the invention of private property in real estate. But it is understood mostly only in special cases which are not sufficiently generalized. Even at this late date, cattlemen leasing national land on the western ranges demonstrate no more than an ambivalent understanding, in constantly pressuring federal authorities to increase the head count to the point where overgrazing produces erosion and weed dominance. Likewise, the oceans of the world continue to suffer from the survival of the philosophy of the commons. Maritime nations still respond automatically to the shibboleth of the "freedom of the seas." Professing to believe in the "inexhaustible resources of the oceans," they bring species after species of fish and whales closer to extinction.

The National Parks present another instance of the working out of the tragedy of the commons. At present, they are open to all, without limit. The parks themselves are limited in extent — there is only one Yosemite Valley — whereas population seems to grow without limit. The values that visitors seek in the parks are steadily eroded. Plainly, we must soon cease to treat the parks as commons or they will be of no value to anyone.

What shall we do? We have several options. We might sell them off as private property. We might keep them as public property, but allocate the right to enter them. The allocation might be on the basis of wealth, by the use of an auction system. It might be on the basis of merit, as defined by some agreed-upon standards. It might be by lottery. Or it might be on a first-come, first-served basis, administered to long queues. These, I think, are all the reasonable possibilities. They are all objectionable. But we must choose — or acquiesce in the destruction of the commons that we call our National Parks.

Pollution

In a reverse way, the tragedy of the commons reappears in problems of pollution. Here it is not a question of taking something out of the commons, but of putting something in — sewage, or chemical, radioactive, and heat wastes into water; noxious and dangerous fumes into the air; and distracting and unpleasant advertising signs into the line of sight. The calculations of utility are much the same as before. The rational man finds that his share of the cost of the wastes he discharges into the commons is less than the cost of purifying his wastes before releasing them. Since this is true for everyone, we are locked into a system of "fouling our own nest," so long as we behave only as independent, rational, free-enterprisers.

The tragedy of the commons as a food basket is averted by private property, or something formally like it. But the air and waters surrounding us cannot readily be fenced, and so the tragedy of the commons as a cesspool must be prevented by different means, by coercive laws or taxing devices that make it cheaper for the polluter to treat his pollutants than to discharge them untreated. We have not progressed as far with the solution of this problem as we have with the first. Indeed, our particular concept of private property, which deters us from exhausting the positive resources of the earth, favors pollution. The owner of a factory on the bank of a stream — whose property extends to the middle of the stream — often has difficulty seeing why it is not his natural right to muddy the waters flowing past his door. The law, always behind the times, requires elaborate stitching and fitting to adapt it to this newly perceived aspect of the commons.

The pollution problem is a consequence of population. It did not much matter how a lonely American frontiersman disposed of his waste. "Flowing water purifies itself every ten miles," my grandfather used to say, and the myth was near enough to the truth when he was a boy, for there were not too many people. But as population became denser, the natural chemical and biological recycling processes became overloaded, calling for a redefinition of property rights. . . .

Freedom to Breed Is Intolerable

The tragedy of the commons is involved in population problems in another way. In a world governed solely by the principle of "dog eat dog" — if indeed there ever was such a world — how many children a family had would not be a matter of public concern. Parents who bred too exuberantly would leave fewer descendants, not more, because they would be unable to care adequately for their children. David Lack and others have found that such a negative feedback demonstrably controls the fecundity of birds. But men are not birds, and have not acted like them for millenniums, at least.

If each human family were dependent only on its own resources; *if* the children of improvident parents starved to death; *if,* thus, overbreeding brought its own "punishment" to the germ line — *then* there would be no public interest in controlling the breeding of families. But our society is deeply committed to the welfare state, and hence is confronted with another aspect of the tragedy of the commons. . . .

Pathogenic Effects of Conscience . . .

If we ask a man who is exploiting a commons to desist "in the name of conscience," what are we saying to him? What does he hear? — not only at the moment but also in the wee small hours of the night when, half asleep, he remembers not merely the words we used but also the nonverbal communication cues we gave him unawares? Sooner or later, consciously or subconsciously, he senses that he has received two communications, and that they are contradictory: (1, the intended communication) "If you don't do as we ask, we will openly condemn you for not acting like a responsible citizen"; (2, the unintended communication) "If you *do* behave as we ask, we will secretly condemn you for a simpleton who can be shamed into standing aside while the rest of us exploit the commons."

Everyman then is caught in what Bateson has called a "double bind." Bateson and his co-workers have made a plausible case for viewing the double bind as an important causative factor in the genesis of schizophrenia. The double bind may not always be so damaging, but it always endangers the mental health of anyone to whom it is applied. "A bad conscience," said Nietzsche, "is a kind of illness."

To conjure up a conscience in others is tempting to anyone who wishes to extend his control beyond the legal limits. Leaders at the highest level succumb to this temptation. Has any President during the past generation failed to call on labor unions to moderate voluntarily their demands for higher wages, or to steel companies to honor voluntary guidelines on prices? I can recall none. The rhetoric used on such occasions is designed to produce feelings of guilt in noncooperators.

For centuries it was assumed without proof that guilt was a valuable, perhaps even an indispensable, ingredient of the civilized life. Now, in this post-Freudian world, we doubt it.

Paul Goodman speaks from the modern point of view when he says: "No good has ever come from feeling guilty, neither intelligence, policy, nor compassion. The guilty do not pay attention to the object but only to themselves, and not even to their own interests, which might make sense, but to their anxieties."

One does not have to be a professional psychiatrist to see the consequences of anxiety. We in the Western world are just emerging from a dreadful two-centuries-long Dark Ages of Eros that was sustained partly by prohibition laws, but perhaps more effectively by the anxiety-generating mechanisms of education. . . .

Since proof is difficult, we may even concede that the results of anxiety may sometimes, from certain points of view, be desirable. The larger question we should ask is whether, as a matter of policy, we should ever encourage the use of a technique the tendency (if not the intention) of which is psychologically pathogenic. We hear much talk these days of responsible parenthood; the coupled words are incorporated into the titles of some organizations devoted to birth control. Some people have proposed massive propaganda campaigns to instill responsibility into the nation's (or the world's) breeders. But what is the meaning of the word responsibility in this context? Is it not merely a synonym for the word conscience? When we use the word responsibility in the absence of substantial sanctions are we not trying to browbeat a free man in a commons into acting against his own interest? Responsibility is a verbal counterfeit for a substantial *quid pro quo*. It is an attempt to get something for nothing.

If the word responsibility is to be used at all, I suggest that it be in the sense Charles Frankel uses it. "Responsibility," says this philosopher, "is the product of definite social arrangements." Notice that Frankel calls for social arrangements — not propaganda.

Mutual Coercion Mutually Agreed Upon

The social arrangements that produce responsibility are arrangements that create coercion, of some sort. Consider bank robbing. The man who takes money from a bank acts as if the bank were a commons. How do we prevent such action? Certainly not by trying to control his behavior solely by a verbal appeal to his sense of responsibility. Rather than rely on propaganda we follow Frankel's lead and insist that a bank is not a commons; we seek the definite social arrangements that will keep it from becoming a commons. That we thereby infringe on the freedom of would-be robbers we neither deny nor regret.

The morality of bank robbing is particularly easy to understand because we accept complete prohibition of this activity. We are willing to say "Thou shalt not rob banks," without providing for exceptions. But temperance also can be created by coercion. Taxing is a good coercive device. To keep downtown shoppers temperate in their use of parking space we introduce parking meters for short periods, and traffic fines for longer ones. We need not actually forbid a citizen to park as long as he wants to; we need merely make it increasingly expensive for him to do so. Not prohibition, but carefully biased options are what we offer him. A Madison Avenue man might call this persuasion; I prefer the greater candor of the word coercion.

Coercion is a dirty word to most liberals now, but it need not forever be so. As with the four-letter words, its dirtiness can be cleansed away by exposure to the light, by saying it over and over without apology or embarrassment. To many, the word coercion implies arbitrary decisions of distant and irresponsible bureaucrats; but this is not a necessary part of its meaning. The only kind of coercion I recommend is mutual coercion, mutually agreed upon by the majority of the people affected.

To say that we mutually agree to coercion is not to say that we are required to enjoy it, or even to pretend we enjoy it. Who enjoys taxes? We all grumble about them. But we accept compulsory taxes because we recognize that voluntary taxes would favor the conscienceless. We institute and (grumblingly) support taxes and other coercive devices to escape the horror of the commons.

An alternative to the commons need not be perfectly just to be preferable. With real estate and other material goods, the alternative we have chosen is the institution of private property coupled with legal inheritance. Is this system perfectly just? As a genetically trained biologist I deny that it is. It seems to me that, if there are to be differences in individual inheritance, legal possession should be perfectly correlated with biological inheritance — that those who are biologically more fit to be the custodians of property and power should legally inherit more. But genetic recombination continually makes a mockery of the doctrine of "like father, like son" implicit in our laws of legal inheritance. An idiot can inherit millions, and a trust fund can keep his estate intact. We must admit that our legal system of private property plus inheritance is unjust — but we put up with it because we are not convinced, at the moment, that anyone has invented a better system. The alternative of the commons is too horrifying to contemplate. Injustice is preferable to total ruin.

It is one of the peculiarities of the warfare between reform and the status quo that it is thoughtlessly governed by a double standard. Whenever a reform measure is proposed it is often defeated when its opponents triumphantly discover a flaw in it. As Kingsley Davis has pointed out, worshippers of the status quo sometimes imply that no reform is possible without unanimous agreement, an implication contrary to historical fact. As nearly as I can make out, automatic rejection of proposed reforms is based on one of two unconscious assumptions: (1) that the status quo is perfect; or (2) that the choice we face is between reform and no action; if the proposed reform is imperfect, we presumably should take no action at all, while we wait for a perfect proposal.

But we can never do nothing. That which we have done for thousands of years is also action. It also produces evils. Once we are aware that the status quo is action, we can then compare its discoverable advantages and disadvantages with the predicted advantages and disadvantages of the proposed reform, discounting as best we can for our lack of experience. On the basis of such a comparison, we can make a rational decision which will not involve the unworkable assumption that only perfect systems are tolerable.

Recognition of Necessity

Perhaps the simplest summary of this analysis of man's population problems is this: The commons, if justifiable at all, is justifiable only under conditions of low population density. As the human population has increased, the commons has had to be abandoned in one aspect after another.

First we abandoned the commons in food gathering, enclosing farm land and restricting pastures and hunting and fishing areas. These restrictions are still not complete throughout the world.

Somewhat later we saw that the commons as a place for waste

disposal would also have to be abandoned. Restrictions on the disposal of domestic sewage are widely accepted in the Western world; we are still struggling to close the commons to pollution by automobiles, factories, insecticide sprayers, fertilizing operations, and atomic energy installations.

In a still more embryonic state is our recognition of the evils of the commons in matters of pleasure. There is almost no restriction on the propagation of sound waves in the public medium. The shopping public is assaulted with mindless music, without its consent. Our government is paying out billions of dollars to create supersonic transport which will disturb 50,000 people for every one person who is whisked from coast to coast three hours faster. Advertisers muddy the airwaves of radio and television and pollute the view of travelers. We are a long way from outlawing the commons in matters of pleasure. Is this because our Puritan inheritance makes us view pleasure as something of a sin, and pain (that is, the pollution of advertising) as the sign of virtue?

Every new enclosure of the commons involves the infringement of somebody's personal liberty. Infringements made in the distant past are accepted because no contemporary complains of a loss. It is the newly proposed infringements that we vigorously oppose; cries of "rights" and "freedom" fill the air. But what does "freedom" mean? When men mutually agreed to pass laws against robbing, mankind became more free, not less so. Individuals locked into the logic of the commons are free only to bring on universal ruin; once they see the necessity of mutual coercion, they become free to pursue other goals. I believe it was Hegel who said, "Freedom is the recognition of necessity."

The most important aspect of necessity that we must now recognize, is the necessity of abandoning the commons in breeding. No technical solution can rescue us from the misery of overpopulation. Freedom to breed will bring ruin to all. At the moment, to avoid hard decisions many of us are tempted to propagandize for conscience and responsible parenthood. The temptation must be resisted, because an appeal to independently acting conscience selects for the disappearance of all conscience in the long run, and an increase in anxiety in the short.

The only way we can preserve and nurture other and more precious freedoms is by relinquishing the freedom to breed, and that very soon. "Freedom is the recognition of necessity" — and it is the role of education to reveal to all the necessity of abandoning the freedom to breed. Only so, can we put an end to this aspect of the tragedy of the commons.

NOTES AND QUESTIONS ON THE COMMONS

1. What attributes make a resource subject to commons problems? Are examples drawn from overgrazing and water pollution really comparable to the example of "freedom to breed"? Hardin himself has long been associated with population control and anti-immigration causes; for a critical commentary see Tucker Carlson, The Intellectual Roots of Nativism, Wall St. J., Oct. 2, 1997, at A22. What is a population "problem," anyway? If other resources (like grazing land, air, and water) were not subject to unrationed open access, would overpopulation be a problem?

2. Hardin mentions several ways to avoid the commons problem by rationing, including the creation of private property, auctions, merit-based allocation, lotteries, and first-come-first-served by queue. Can you think of other rationing methods? Which is best for which kinds of resources?

3. Private property is often said to avert the tragedy of the commons. But does it? Who enforces property limitations? Does another kind of "commons" problem lurk in the organization and maintenance of a property regime? See James Krier, The Tragedy of the Commons, Part II, 15 Harv. J.L. & Pub. Poly. 325, 332-339 (1992). In addition, might property rights become so over-developed that they actually prevent access to resources? Michael Heller identifies such a problem in The Tragedy of the Anticommons: Property in the Transition from Marx to Markets, 111 Harv. L. Rev. 621 (1998). For discussion of the "anticommons" problem in intellectual property, see the selection by Heller and Eisenberg, infra p. 159.

4. Hardin's article has generated an enormous literature, some of it critical of his view that the commons is inherently tragic. One critic is Elinor Ostrom. In Governing the Commons (1990), she joins with other authors in sharply distinguishing "open access" resources from "common property" resources. The latter term designates resources that are owned or controlled by finite numbers of people who manage to organize themselves (and exclude outsiders) in such a way that they use the "commons" productively. Ostrom compiles many examples from all over the world, including fisheries, irrigation works, and grazing areas. Still another example appears in the selection that follows, by James Acheson. As you read it, consider what kinds of common resources might be tragic, and what kinds might lend themselves instead to common management. Consider also the role of culture in solving (or creating) commons problems. For further reflections on the role of

culture in property, see the selection by Zerbe & Anderson, infra p. 273.

5. The "tragedy of the commons" is sometimes described as an "*n*-person prisoner's dilemma." Can you see why? For more on the prisoner's dilemma, see Axelrod, The Evolution of Cooperation, infra p. 261.

6. The phrase "tragedy of the commons" was itself a huge hit. Several similar ideas, however, were developed earlier and in a more systematic way by H. Scott Gordon, in The Economic Theory of a Common-Property Resource: The Fishery, 62 J. Pol. Econ. 124 (1954). Does Gordon's title perhaps suggest why he is not as well-known as Hardin?

*The Lobster Gangs of Maine**

James M. Acheson

While lobstermen themselves often subscribe to the stereotype of the independent man-at-sea, they are in fact part of a complicated social network. The industry has rules that all men are expected to obey, its own standards of conduct, and its own mythology. To succeed in lobstering a man not only must have certain technical skills and work hard, but also must be able to operate in a particular social milieu.

Beyond the kinship group, the most important people in a lobster fisherman's life are the men who fish from the same harbor. Such social groupings, while they are recognized by everyone in the lobster-fishing industry, have no universally accepted name. People refer to the "Monhegan boys," or the "Friendship fishermen," or the "Port Clyde gang." Sometimes men refer to those in their own harbor as "the men I fish with." I have called these groups "harbor gangs," although this term is only rarely used by the fishermen themselves (Acheson 1972).

Membership in a harbor gang strongly influences many aspects of a lobster fisherman's career. Most importantly, it controls entry into the industry. To go lobster fishing, a man must first become a member of a harbor gang. Once he has gained admission, he can go fishing only in the territory "owned" communally by

*Source: pp. 48-49, 73-76, 142-144 (1988).

members of that gang. Fishermen who place their traps in the territory of another gang can expect swift retribution, normally the purposeful destruction of their gear. Although these territories and the gangs that own them are completely unrecognized by the state, they are a longstanding reality. Fishermen identify with a particular harbor gang and are identified as members of it. Members of harbor gangs obtain a great deal of valuable information from one another on fishing locations and innovations. They also assist one another in times of emergency at sea. If a motor breaks down or someone runs out of gas, other members of the gang are called for a tow. This is one of the reasons that people in a harbor gang keep their radios on the same channel. . . .

Lobster fishermen in the same harbor gang ordinarily have long-term, multistrand ties with one another. Almost all live in the town where the harbor is located. Many are members of long-established families and share kinship ties as well. The men of the same generation have grown up together, and members of their families have known one another and intermarried for generations. . . .

Defense of Boundaries

Violation of territorial boundaries meets with no fixed response. An older person from an established family with a long history of fishing might infringe on the territorial rights of others almost indefinitely. Those being infringed upon are especially reluctant to accuse a gang leader or the member of a large family, either of whom could have a large number of allies. An unpopular person, a young fisherman, or a newcomer encounters trouble more quickly. Sooner or later, however, someone decides to take action against the interloper. Sometimes a small group of fishermen decide to act in concert, but boundary defense is often effected by one person acting alone.

The violator is usually warned, sometimes by verbal threats and abuse, but usually by surreptitious molestation of lobstering gear. Two half-hitches of rope may be tied around the spindle of the buoy, or legal-sized lobsters may be taken out and the doors of the traps left open. Fishermen have been known to leave threatening notes in bottles inside the offending traps, and one colorful islander carves a representation of female genitalia in the styrofoam buoys. Most interlopers move their gear when warned in these ways. If the violations persist, the traps are destroyed. Fishermen have destroyed traps by "carving them up a little" with a chain saw or by smashing them with sledge hammers. When such traps are pulled, the owner has little doubt as to what has happened. Usually, however, the offending traps are cut off: they are pulled, the buoy toggles and warp line are cut, and the trap is pushed into deep water, where there is little chance of finding it. There is no practical way to protect traps in the water. Removing the traps not only removes the symbol of another person's intrusion but also limits the intruder's capacity to reduce the defender's own catch. Destruction of traps does not usually lead to direct confrontation since the owner can only guess who destroyed them or even whether they were destroyed on purpose.

In a few instances, gangs defend their boundaries as a group. It is well known that anyone invading the traditional territories of such islands as Metinic, Monhegan, and Green Island can expect coordinated resistance from men fishing those islands. Once in a while, groups goaded beyond endurance launch a full-scale "cut war" in which hundreds of traps are destroyed, boats sunk, and even docks and fish houses burnt. These so-called lobster wars lead to longstanding bitterness, violence, and court action.

It is a rare day in a harbor when someone does not suspect that his traps have been tampered with. Many incidents occur as a result of feuds and competition within a particular area. Much of this small-scale molestation stems from the fact that maintaining territorial lines means constantly utilizing one's own territory and perhaps a little more — a process known as "pushing the lines." Even in slow months, a few traps are left in certain peripheral areas to maintain local territorial claims. However, fishermen touch another's gear only with great reluctance, knowing that their own gear is vulnerable to retaliation. The whole industry is aware that the individuals whose traps have been cut off may well take vengeance, but frequently against the wrong person. The result, they know, can be a comic and costly chain of events in which the innocent and the guilty retaliate blindly against one another. The norms are therefore widely obeyed, and although the entire coast is patrolled by only a few wardens, there is little trouble. Fishermen are very careful to punish intruders in ways that will not provoke a massive, violent response. According to one fisherman, "The trick to driving a man [out of the area] is to cut off just one or two traps at a time." This harassment makes it unprofitable to fish an area but does not challenge a man to open warfare, since he can only guess who cut his traps.

A conspiracy of silence surrounds all trap-cutting incidents and efforts to enforce boundaries. Those who resort to cutting traps rarely advertise their "skill with the knife," to reduce both the possibility of retaliation and the chance of losing their lobster licenses for destroying the traps of other men. Destruction of another's gear is always considered immoral, regardless of the circumstances, because it interferes with the victim's ability to feed his family. Victims may growl and threaten but they rarely report the incident to any law enforcement agency. The culprit's identity may be unknown, and chances of successful prosecution are small. Fishermen feel strongly that the law should be kept at bay and that people should handle their own problems. Any fisherman who goes to the police to complain about trap cuttings not only looks ineffectual and ridiculous but is somewhat of a threat. When a man's traps are missing, taking the law into his own hands is not only more effective but also maintains his standing among fellow fishermen. . . .

Fishermen say that a man is allowed to fish within the entire territory owned by the harbor gang to which he belongs. This statement is not strictly accurate. A man is expected to keep his distance from other fishermen and not "dump" his traps on top of another's, where they can become entangled. Fishermen with traps in a saturated location have usufructuary rights; others cannot enter until someone leaves. The older, more skilled fishermen are likely to have their traps prepositioned in the best locations. When lobsters do appear, those who have "camped out" in good spots have monopolized all or most of the available space. Younger fishermen — particularly those who have joined the gang recently — are well advised to stay out of the way of men with status in the hierarchy of skill and prestige. Men of lower status can lose a great deal by coming into conflict with highliners.

Sometimes groups of men use a particular spot or set of spots for such a long time that they begin to feel proprietary rights over these locations. Within harbor gangs in the study area, however, such men have only usufructuary rights, not permanent ownership. Should the men who regularly fish in a location move their traps elsewhere, others from the harbor gang can move their traps into it. . . .

Common-Property Resources

According to the theory of common-property resources, resources such as fish, air, water, and publicly owned parks and forests are overexploited and abused in ways that privately owned resources are not. Owners of private property protect their resources, while those exploiting publicly owned or open-access resources are locked into a system that makes unlimited exploitation rational. Why should one cattleman, logger, or polluter conserve the resources, since he cannot capture the benefits for himself? Under these circumstances, it is only logical for such a person to expand the amount of capital he uses and strive to use as much of the resources as possible and as fast as possible. The result is what Garrett Hardin has called the "tragedy of the commons." In the case of fisheries, the "tragedy" is said to result in overexploitation of fish stocks, decline of the breeding stock, "overcapitalization," and "economic inefficiency." Two different kinds of solutions have been suggested for such common-property problems. Many of the economists who have developed this body of theory see salvation in establishing private property rights of one kind or another. Hardin, a biologist, is more pessimistic. He believes such problems can be solved only by draconian government controls.

Although the theory of common-property resources has played a key role in shaping current conceptions of resource management, little empirical work has been done to verify this theory. . . . One axiom of the theory is that property rights help to conserve resources, promote economic efficiency, and result in higher incomes. This case study confirms this axiom. In the perimeter-defended areas, where access is more limited and property rights are more vigorously enforced, the stock of lobsters is larger, catches of fishermen are larger, and the breeding stock is larger. However, the theory assumes that there are really only two kinds of ownership: private ownership and having no control over access at all. As . . . a number of other authors have recently pointed out, there are really three different kinds of property: private property, communal or jointly owned property, and "open access." Maine lobstering territories are an instance of joint or communal property. Such institutions, which can be generated by local communities operating on their own, can be effective in conserving the resources. This case study reinforces [the] point . . . that the problem is not "common property" but "open access," or no controls at all on usage. It also helps to modify Hardin's theory by pointing out that governmental action and private property are not the only solutions to resource problems. An alternative solution is a communal property arrangement.

Maine lobster territories are not unique in this respect. A large number of local communities have generated a wide variety of institutions to control exploitation of the resources on which their livelihood depends. Though tragedies of the commons (more accurately, tragedies of "open access") do exist in both the third world and the developed world, they are not inevitable in the absence of private property.

Maine lobstering territories have not been an unqualified success in conserving the resource. They have limited the numbers of fishermen entering the fishery, but except in those few places where informal or formal trap limits are imposed (e.g., Swans Island), they have not helped to limit the number of traps and the escalation of fishing effort.

NOTES AND QUESTIONS ON COMMUNAL PROPERTY REGIMES

1. Acheson describes three kinds of property, locating them on a spectrum of exclusivity: private property, an intermediate communal property, and the completely nonexclusive "open access." Open-access property is thought to be particularly subject to the "tragedy of the commons." How do these categories apply to property normally considered "public"? Which kind of property is, say, a post office building? The White House? A small neighborhood park? Yellowstone National Park? Are any or all of these properties subject to the "tragedy of the commons"? What might account for differences?

2. What accounts for the intermediate communal property that Acheson posits? The Maine fishermen appear to have certain elements of individual entitlement in their practices; why have they not gone the whole way to individual property?

3. Would you describe the Maine lobstermen's territory as a kind of "property," as Acheson does? Why or why not? Does the lobstermen's example suggest that property is a creature of law, as is often argued, or rather an institution that can arise informally? See generally Robert C. Ellickson, Order Without Law: How Neighbors Settle Disputes (1991). Might law actually impede the development of efficient informal group property? See Robert Higgs, Legally Induced Technical Regress in the Washington Salmon Fishery, in Empirical Studies in Institutional Change (Lee J. Alston et al. eds., 1996), describing how the state's formal law of open access undermined efficient native fisheries.

4. Why do lobstermen generally retaliate against interlopers in a surreptitious manner? Note the danger of secret retaliation: The victim may counter-retaliate against the wrong person. Why would the community of lobster fishers engage in a "conspiracy of silence" when they themselves might bear the brunt of mistaken responses? Compare Jon Elster, Norms of Revenge, 100 Ethics 862 (1990), describing the open (and communally encouraged) practices of retaliation in certain Balkan countries, particularly in re-

sponse to slights to family honor. Under what circumstances would you expect norms of secret revenge? Open and public revenge? Are norms of revenge necessary to maintain a property regime?

5. The Maine lobstermen's retaliatory methods suggest a strong note of lawlessness, not to mention misogyny. Should one worry about the thuggish and antidemocratic features of these admittedly picturesque traditional communities? See Carol M. Rose, Common Property, Regulatory Property, and Environmental Protection, in The Drama of the Commons (Elinor Ostrom et al. eds., 2002). For an alternative vision of a nontraditional type of "liberal commons," based on democratic governance and the possibility of individual exit, see Hanoch Dagan and Michael Heller, The Liberal Commons, 110 Yale L. Rev. 549 (2001).

6. Is it true that open-access property is always "tragic"? See Sax, infra p. 537, on the "public trust" and the notes thereafter.

7. Might some "hardwired" aspect of human nature generate solutions to commons problems? See Edna Ullmann-Margalit, The Emergence of Norms (1978), arguing that prisoner's dilemmas and commons problems, or at least some of them, predictably give rise to norms that help solve the problems. If this is true, does it simply add to the mystery? Where do such norms come from? Bear this question in mind when you read the next selection by Harold Demsetz.

B.   The Economics of the Commons

Toward a Theory of Property Rights*

Harold Demsetz

When a transaction is concluded in the marketplace, two bundles of property rights are exchanged. A bundle of rights often attaches to a physical commodity or service, but it is the value of the rights that determines the value of what is exchanged. Questions addressed to the emergence and mix of the components of the bundle of rights are prior to those commonly asked by economists. Economists usually take the bundle of property rights as a datum and ask for an explanation of the forces determining the

*Source: 57 Am. Econ. Rev. Pap. & Proc. 347-358 (1967).

price and the number of units of a good to which these rights attach.

In this paper, I seek to fashion some of the elements of an economic theory of property rights. The paper is organized into three parts. The first part discusses briefly the concept and role of property rights in social systems. The second part offers some guidance for investigating the emergence of property rights. The third part sets forth some principles relevant to the coalescing of property rights into particular bundles and to the determination of the ownership structure that will be associated with these bundles.

The Concept and Role of Property Rights

In the world of Robinson Crusoe property rights play no role. Property rights are an instrument of society and derive their significance from the fact that they help a man form those expectations which he can reasonably hold in his dealings with others. These expectations find expression in the laws, customs, and mores of a society. An owner of property rights possesses the consent of fellowmen to allow him to act in particular ways. An owner expects the community to prevent others from interfering with his actions, provided that these actions are not prohibited in the specifications of his rights.

It is important to note that property rights convey the right to benefit or harm oneself or others. Harming a competitor by producing superior products may be permitted, while shooting him may not. A man may be permitted to benefit himself by shooting an intruder but be prohibited from selling below a price floor. It is clear, then, that property rights specify how persons may be benefited and harmed, and, therefore, who must pay whom to modify the actions taken by persons. The recognition of this leads easily to the close relationship between property rights and externalities.

Externality is an ambiguous concept. For the purposes of this paper, the concept includes external costs, external benefits, and pecuniary as well as nonpecuniary externalities. No harmful or beneficial effect is external to the world. Some person or persons always suffer or enjoy these effects. What converts a harmful or beneficial effect into an externality is that the cost of bringing the effect to bear on the decisions of one or more of the interacting persons is too high to make it worthwhile, and this is what the term shall mean here. "Internalizing" such effects refers to a process, usually a change in property rights, that enables these effects to bear (in greater degree) on all interacting persons.

A primary function of property rights is that of guiding incentives to achieve a greater internalization of externalities. Every cost and benefit associated with social interdependencies is a potential externality. One condition is necessary to make costs and benefits externalities. The cost of a transaction in the rights between the parties (internalization) must exceed the gains from internalization. In general, transacting cost can be large relative to gains because of "natural" difficulties in trading or they can be large because of legal reasons. In a lawful society the prohibition of voluntary negotiations makes the cost of transacting infinite. Some costs and benefits are not taken into account by users of resources whenever externalities exist, but allowing transactions increases the degree to which internalization takes place. . . .

The Emergence of Property Rights

If the main allocative function of property rights is the internalization of beneficial and harmful effects, then the emergence of property rights can be understood best by their association with the emergence of new or different beneficial and harmful effects.

Changes in knowledge result in changes in production functions, market values, and aspirations. New techniques, new ways of doing the same things, and doing new things — all invoke harmful and beneficial effects to which society has not been accustomed. It is my thesis in this part of the paper that the emergence of new property rights takes place in response to the desires of the interacting persons for adjustment to new benefit-cost possibilities.

The thesis can be restated in a slightly different fashion: property rights develop to internalize externalities when the gains of internalization become larger than the cost of internalization. Increased internalization, in the main, results from changes in economic values, changes which stem from the development of new technology and the opening of new markets, changes to which old property rights are poorly attuned. A proper interpretation of this assertion requires that account be taken of a community's preferences for private ownership. Some communities will have less well-developed private ownership systems and more highly developed state ownership systems. But, given a community's tastes in this regard, the emergence of new private or state-owned property rights will be in response to changes in technology and relative prices.

I do not mean to assert or to deny that the adjustments in property rights which take place need be the result of a conscious endeavor to cope with new externality problems. These adjustments have arisen in Western societies largely as a result of gradual changes in social mores and in common law precedents. At each step of this adjustment process, it is unlikely that externalities per se were consciously related to the issue being resolved. These legal and moral experiments may be hit-and-miss procedures to some extent but in a society that weights the achievement of efficiency heavily, their viability in the long run will depend on how well they modify behavior to accommodate to the externalities associated with important changes in technology or market values.

A rigorous test of this assertion will require extensive and detailed empirical work. A broad range of examples can be cited that are consistent with it: the development of air rights, renters' rights, rules for liability in automobile accidents, etc. In this part of the discussion, I shall present one group of such examples in some detail. They deal with the development of private property rights in land among American Indians. These examples are broad ranging and come fairly close to what can be called convincing evidence in the field of anthropology.

The question of private ownership of land among aboriginals has held a fascination for anthropologists. It has been one of the intellectual battlegrounds in the attempt to assess the "true nature" of man unconstrained by the "artificialities" of civilization. In the process of carrying on this debate, information has been uncovered that bears directly on the thesis with which we are now concerned. What appears to be accepted as a classic treatment and a high point of this debate is Eleanor Leacock's memoir on The Montagnes: "Hunting Territory" and the Fur Trade.[3] Leacock's research followed that of Frank G. Speck[4] who had discovered that the Indians of the Labrador Peninsula had a long-established tradition of property in land. This finding was at odds with what was known about the Indians of the American Southwest and it prompted Leacock's study of the Montagnes who inhabited large regions around Quebec.

Leacock clearly established the fact that a close relationship existed, both historically and geographically, between the development of private rights in land and the development of the commercial fur trade. The factual basis of this correlation has gone unchallenged. However, to my knowledge, no theory relating privacy of land to the fur trade has yet been articulated. The factual material uncovered by Speck and Leacock fits the thesis of this

3. Eleanor Leacock, American Anthropologist (American Anthropological Asso.), Vol. 56, No. 5, Part 2, Memoir No. 78.
4. Cf., Frank G. Speck, The Basis of American Indian Ownership of Land, Old Penn Weekly Rev. (Univ. of Pennsylvania), Jan. 16, 1915, pp. 491-495.

paper well, and in doing so, it reveals clearly the role played by property right adjustments in taking account of what economists have often cited as an example of an externality — the overhunting of game.

Because of the lack of control over hunting by others, it is in no person's interest to invest in increasing or maintaining the stock of game. Overly intensive hunting takes place. Thus a successful hunt is viewed as imposing external costs on subsequent hunters — costs that are not taken into account fully in the determination of the extent of hunting and of animal husbandry.

Before the fur trade became established, hunting was carried on primarily for purposes of food and the relatively few furs that were required for the hunter's family. The externality was clearly present. Hunting could be practiced freely and was carried on without assessing its impact on other hunters. But these external effects were of such small significance that it did not pay for anyone to take them into account. There did not exist anything resembling private ownership in land. And in the *Jesuit Relations*, particularly Le Jeune's record of the winter he spent with the Montagnes in 1633-34 and in the brief account given by Father Druilletes in 1647-48, Leacock finds no evidence of private land holdings. Both accounts indicate a socioeconomic organization in which private rights to land are not well developed.

We may safely surmise that the advent of the fur trade had two immediate consequences. First, the value of furs to the Indians was increased considerably. Second, and as a result, the scale of hunting activity rose sharply. Both consequences must have increased considerably the importance of the externalities associated with free hunting. The property right system began to change, and it changed specifically in the direction required to take account of the economic effects made important by the fur trade. The geographical or distributional evidence collected by Leacock indicates an unmistakable correlation between early centers of fur trade and the oldest and most complete development of the private hunting territory. . . .

The principle that associates property right changes with the emergence of new and reevaluation of old harmful and beneficial effects suggests in this instance that the fur trade made it economic to encourage the husbanding of fur-bearing animals. Husbanding requires the ability to prevent poaching and this, in turn, suggests that socioeconomic changes in property in hunting land will take place. The chain of reasoning is consistent with the evidence cited above. Is it inconsistent with the absence of similar rights in property among the southwestern Indians?

Two factors suggest that the thesis is consistent with the absence of similar rights among the Indians of the southwestern plains. The first of these is that there were no plains animals of commercial importance comparable to the fur-bearing animals of the forest, at least not until cattle arrived with Europeans. The second factor is that animals of the plains are primarily grazing species whose habit is to wander over wide tracts of land. The value of establishing boundaries to private hunting territories is thus reduced by the relatively high cost of preventing the animals from moving to adjacent parcels. Hence both the value and cost of establishing private hunting lands in the Southwest are such that we would expect little development along these lines. The externality was just not worth taking into account.

The lands of the Labrador Peninsula shelter forest animals whose habits are considerably different from those of the plains. Forest animals confine their territories to relatively small areas, so that the cost of internalizing the effects of husbanding these animals is considerably reduced. This reduced cost, together with the higher commercial value of fur-bearing forest animals, made it productive to establish private hunting lands. Frank G. Speck finds that family proprietorship among the Indians of the Peninsula included retaliation against trespass. Animal resources were husbanded. Sometimes conservation practices were carried on extensively. Family hunting territories were divided into quarters. Each year the family hunted in a different quarter in rotation, leaving a tract in the center as a sort of bank, not to be hunted over unless forced to do so by a shortage in the regular tract....

The Coalescence and Ownership of Property Rights

I have argued that property rights arise when it becomes economic for those affected by externalities to internalize benefits and costs. But I have not yet examined the forces which will govern the particular form of right ownership. Several idealized forms of ownership must be distinguished at the outset. These are communal ownership, private ownership, and state ownership.

By communal ownership, I shall mean a right which can be exercised by all members of the community. Frequently the rights to till and to hunt the land have been communally owned. The right to walk a city sidewalk is communally owned. Communal ownership means that the community denies to the state or to individual citizens the right to interfere with any person's exercise of communally owned rights. Private ownership implies that the community recognizes the right of the owner to exclude others from exercising the owner's private rights. State ownership implies that the state may exclude anyone from the use of a right as long as the state follows accepted political procedures for determining who may not use state-owned property. I shall not examine in detail the alternative of state ownership. The object of the analysis which follows is to discern some broad principles governing the development of property rights in communities oriented to private property.

It will be best to begin by considering a particularly useful example that focuses our attention on the problem of land ownership. Suppose that land is communally owned. Every person has the right to hunt, till, or mine the land. This form of ownership fails to concentrate the cost associated with any person's exercise of his communal right on that person. If a person seeks to maximize the value of his communal rights, he will tend to overhunt and overwork the land because some of the costs of his doing so are borne by others. The stock of game and the richness of the soil will be diminished too quickly. It is conceivable that those who own these rights, i.e., every member of the community, can agree to curtail the rate at which they work the lands if negotiating and policing costs are zero. Each can agree to abridge his rights. It is obvious that the costs of reaching such an agreement will not be zero. What is not obvious is just how large these costs may be.

Negotiating costs will be large because it is difficult for many persons to reach a mutually satisfactory agreement, especially when each hold-out has the right to work the land as fast as he pleases. But, even if an agreement among all can be reached, we must yet take account of the costs of policing the agreement, and these may be large, also. After such an agreement is reached, no one will privately own the right to work the land; all can work the land but at an agreed upon shorter workweek. Negotiating costs are increased even further because it is not possible under this system to bring the full expected benefits and expected costs of future generations to bear on current users.

If a single person owns land, he will attempt to maximize its present value by taking into account alternative future time streams of benefits and costs and selecting that one which he believes will maximize the present value of his privately owned land rights. We all know that this means that he will attempt to take into account the supply and demand conditions that he thinks will exist after his death. It is very difficult to see how the existing communal owners can reach an agreement that takes account of these costs.

In effect, an owner of a private right to use land acts as a broker whose wealth depends on how well he takes into account the competing claims of the present and the future. But with communal rights there is no broker, and the claims of the present generation will be given an uneconomically large weight in determining the intensity with which the land is worked. Future generations might desire to pay present generations enough to change the present intensity of land usage. But they have no living agent to place their claims on the market. Under a communal property system, should a living person pay others to reduce the rate at which they work the land, he would not gain anything of value for his efforts. Communal property means that future generations must speak for themselves. No one has yet estimated the costs of carrying on such a conversation.

The land ownership example confronts us immediately with a great disadvantage of communal property. The effects of a person's activities on his neighbors and on subsequent generations will not be taken into account fully. Communal property results in great externalities. The full costs of the activities of an owner of a communal property right are not borne directly by him, nor can they be called to his attention easily by the willingness of others to pay him an appropriate sum. Communal property rules out a "pay-to-use-the-property" system and high negotiation and policing costs make ineffective a "pay-him-not-to-use-the-property" system.

The state, the courts, or the leaders of the community could attempt to internalize the external costs resulting from communal property by allowing private parcels owned by small groups of persons with similar interests. The logical groups in terms of similar interests, are, of course, the family and the individual. Continuing with our use of the land ownership example, let us initially distribute private titles to land randomly among existing individuals and, further, let the extent of land included in each title be randomly determined.

The resulting private ownership of land will internalize many of the external costs associated with communal ownership, for now an owner, by virtue of his power to exclude others, can generally count on realizing the rewards associated with husbanding the game and increasing the fertility of his land. This concentration of benefits and costs on owners creates incentives to utilize resources more efficiently.

But we have yet to contend with externalities. Under the communal property system the maximization of the value of communal property rights will take place without regard to many costs, because the owner of a communal right cannot exclude others from enjoying the fruits of his efforts and because negotiation costs are too high for all to agree jointly on optimal behavior. The development of private rights permits the owner to economize on the use of those resources from which he has the right to exclude others. Much internalization is accomplished in this way. But the owner of private rights to one parcel does not himself own the rights to the parcel of another private sector. Since he cannot exclude others from their private rights to land, he has no direct incentive (in the absence of negotiations) to economize in the use of his land in a way that takes into account the effects he produces on the land rights of others. If he constructs a dam on his land, he has no direct incentive to take into account the lower water levels produced on his neighbor's land.

This is exactly the same kind of externality that we encountered with communal property rights, but it is present to a lesser degree. Whereas no one had an incentive to store water on any land under the communal system, private owners now can take into account directly those benefits and costs to their land that accompany water storage. But the effects on the land of others will not be taken into account directly.

The partial concentration of benefits and costs that accompany private ownership is only part of the advantage this system offers. The other part, and perhaps the most important, has escaped our notice. The cost of negotiating over the remaining externalities will be reduced greatly. Communal property rights allow anyone to use the land. Under this system it becomes necessary for all to reach an agreement on land use. But the externalities that accompany private ownership of property do not affect all owners, and, generally speaking, it will be necessary for only a few to reach an agreement that takes these effects into account. The cost of negotiating an internalization of these effects is thereby reduced considerably. The point is important enough to elucidate.

Suppose an owner of a communal land right, in the process of plowing a parcel of land, observes a second communal owner constructing a dam on adjacent land. The farmer prefers to have the stream as it is, and so he asks the engineer to stop his construction. The engineer says, "Pay me to stop." The farmer replies, "I will be happy to pay you, but what can you guarantee in return?" The engineer answers, "I can guarantee you that I will not continue constructing the dam, but I cannot guarantee that another engineer will not take up the task because this is communal property; I have no right to exclude him." What would be a simple negotiation between two persons under a private property arrangement turns out to be a rather complex negotiation between the farmer and everyone else. This is the basic explanation, I believe, for the preponderance of single rather than multiple owners of property. Indeed, an increase in the number of owners is an increase in the communality of property and leads, generally, to an increase in the cost of internalizing.

The reduction in negotiating cost that accompanies the private right to exclude others allows most externalities to be internalized at rather low cost. Those that are not are associated with activities that generate external effects impinging upon many people. The soot from smoke affects many homeowners, none of whom is willing to pay enough to the factory to get its owner to reduce smoke output. All homeowners together might be willing to pay enough, but the cost of their getting together may be enough to discourage effective market bargaining. The negotiating problem is compounded even more if the smoke comes not from a single smoke stack but from an industrial district. In such cases, it may be too costly to internalize effects through the marketplace.

Returning to our land ownership paradigm, we recall that land was distributed in randomly sized parcels to randomly selected owners. These owners now negotiate among themselves to internalize any remaining externalities. Two market options are open to the negotiators. The first is simply to try to reach a contractual agreement among owners that directly deals with the external effects at issue. The second option is for some owners to buy out others, thus changing the parcel size owned. Which option is selected will depend on which is cheaper. We have here a standard economic problem of optimal scale. If there exist constant returns to scale in the ownership of different sized parcels, it will be largely a matter of indifference between outright purchase and contractual agreement if only a single, easy-to-police, contractual agreement will internalize the externality. But, if there are several externalities, so that several such contracts will need to be negotiated, or if the contractual agreements should be difficult to police, then outright purchase will be the preferred course of action.

The greater are diseconomies of scale to land ownership the more will contractual arrangement be used by the interacting neighbors to settle these differences. Negotiating and policing costs will be compared to costs that depend on the scale of ownership, and parcels of land will tend to be owned in sizes which minimize the sum of these costs.[8]

8. Compare this with the similar rationale given by R.H. Coase to explain the firm in The Nature of the Firm, Economica, New Series, 1937, pp. 386-405.

NOTES AND QUESTIONS ON DEMSETZ'S THEORY OF PROPERTY RIGHTS

1. When Demsetz speaks of communal ownership, does he mean open-access property or property controlled by a limited group? If, as Demsetz asserts, "communal property results in great externalities," why do nations with private property systems allocate a significant fraction of their lands to streets, sidewalks, parks, and other open-access areas?

2. In sharp contrast to Hardin's pessimism, Demsetz predicts that efficient property rights tend to "emerge" after technological shocks or other events have created new cost-saving opportunities. Similarly optimistic is Terry L. Anderson & P. J. Hill, The Evolution of Property Rights: A Study of the American West, 18 J.L. & Econ. 163 (1975).

Gary Libecap is less sanguine. He argues that the likelihood of property rights evolving adaptively is positively associated with:

a. the magnitude of the aggregate gains the institutional reform could be expected to engender;
b. the smallness of the number of parties involved;
c. the homogeneity of the parties;
d. the quality of shared information about the incidence of gains and losses; and
e. the extent of concentration of wealth before the institutional reform, and deconcentration of wealth afterward.

With respect to point (e), Libecap observes that if wealth is concentrated *ex ante* few have a stake in retaining the existing regime, but if gains are concentrated *ex post*, distributional issues may keep the parties from agreeing on a new order. See Gary D. Libecap, Contracting for Property Rights 19-28 (1989). Apply these criteria to: the Labrador tribe that serves as Demsetz's chief example; Acheson's lobstermen; settlers on the American frontier; the world population (whose growth is Hardin's central concern).

Libecap's investigations into various extractive resources have led him to conclude that asymmetries in information may influence the likelihood, character, and shape of any emergent property rights regimes. See Libecap, The Conditions for Successful Collective Action, *in* Local Commons and Global Interdependence (Robert O. Keohane & Elinor Ostrom eds., 1995). For an application of Libecap's views to changes in environmental legislation, see Merrill, Understanding Market Mechanisms, infra p. 521. A painstaking inquiry into the influences on changes in range law is Shawn Everett Kantor, Politics and Property Rights: The Closing of the Open Range in the Postbellum South (1998) (finding that distributional conflicts sometimes did hold up reform).

3. "We all know that [if a single person owns land] he will attempt to take into account the supply and demand conditions that he thinks will exist after his death." Demsetz, at p. 141. Is it indeed a virtue of the institution of private property that it prompts mortal owners to consider the welfare of future generations? This issue receives fuller treatment infra in Note 5, pp. 380-381.

4. This selection concludes with Demsetz's assertion that parcels of land tend to be efficiently sized. Is his reasoning persuasive? Given your answer, should a city employ zoning ordinances to set minimum sizes for lots? Should a city invoke the power of eminent domain to assemble large land parcels for redevelopment?

Property in Land*

Robert C. Ellickson

I. The Case for Individual Ownership of Land ...

A. *Three Simple Land Regimes*

... Suppose that a close-knit group of 25 adults, identified by letters A through Y, were to control the land within the perimeter of the large square pictured in Figures 1 and 2. Suppose further that this group had to choose to govern this territory either as open-access property, group property, or individual property — regimes that it could establish either by formal rule or informal practice. Recall that under the first of these three alternatives, the open-access regime, anyone at all, including persons other than A ... Y, would be completely privileged to enter and use the land within the perimeter. Both theory and practice suggest that this regime would likely be beset by tragedy.

Under the second alternative, group ownership, the 25 members would jointly own both privileges to use the land within the perimeter and rights to exclude all others from it. The 25 would manage the land collectively by means of some relatively democratic governance system. Figure 1, in which there are no internal

*Source: 102 Yale L.J. 1315, 1322-1335, 1341-1344 (1993).

Figure 1
Group Ownership

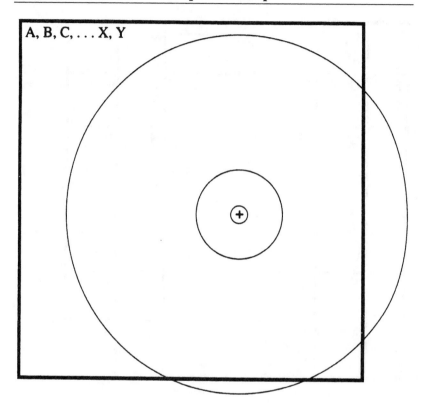

A, B, C, ... X, Y

division lines within the perimeter, illustrates group ownership by
A ... Y.

To create the third regime, individual ownership, A ... Y
would subdivide all of the land within the square into 25 parcels,
one of which would be assigned to each member. Figure 2 shows
one of the many possible divisions they might create. In this instance, all land within the perimeter of the square has been sub-
divided into 25 rectangles of unequal area, and each rectangle has
been allotted to the individual owner indicated in its upper left
corner. At this point in the inquiry, an individual owner of a parcel
can be regarded as having unfettered privileges of use as well as
absolute rights to exclude.

A person's action (or inaction) may affect the physical condition of land. To highlight the significance of differences in the spatial consequences of actions, both Figures 1 and 2 include identical

Figure 2
Individual Ownership

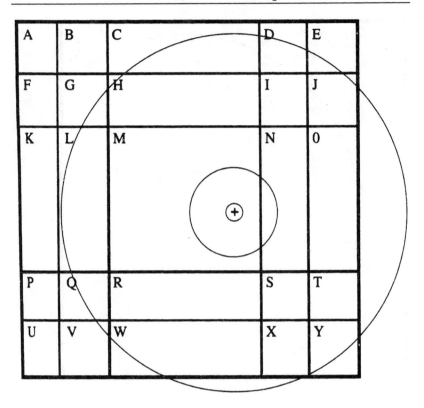

sets of concentric circles drawn around a common center at which a human action is hypothesized to occur. These circles deserve highly sophisticated adjectives. The innermost circle illustrates the minor land area that is substantially affected by a *small event*, such as the cultivation of a tomato plant. The intermediate region circumscribes the territory substantially affected by a *medium event*, such as the building of a small dam to create a pond in a stream. Lastly, the outside circle delimits the domain substantially affected by a *large event*, such as a fire that emits choking fumes over a wide-ranging area.

Before these Figures can be employed to elucidate the relative efficiency of alternative land regimes, the potentially ambiguous term *efficiency* must be clarified. The rational-actor model assumes that an individual calculatingly pursues his self-interest. This implies that a member of a social group will be tempted at times to undertake a land activity that is individually rewarding but socially wasteful. Whatever the land regime, an individual's self-interested, opportunistic act will create a *deadweight loss* whenever the costs it inflicts on others exceed the individual's benefits from the act. When land is group-owned, each group member may be tempted to grab too many of the parcel's assets, to pollute the property with wastes, and to shirk from useful work that would enhance the land's value. Conversely, when land is individually owned, a self-interested owner may be tempted to use it without regard to the costs and benefits conferred on neighbors or others. Individuals may be able to reduce deadweight losses by (1) enforcing existing property rights; (2) transferring property rights to better managers; or (3) redefining property rights so as to create better-tailored incentives for appropriate economic activity. Each of these responses, however, would give rise to *transaction costs*. Different land regimes therefore involve different combinations of transaction costs and deadweight losses. A change in land rules is *efficient* when it reduces the sum of these two sorts of costs.

B.   Small Events: The Relative Ease of Monitoring Boundaries

1.   THE GENIUS OF INDIVIDUAL LAND OWNERSHIP

In his classic work, Demsetz showed that individual ownership of land completely internalizes to owners the effects of what this article calls small events. In essence, the parcelization of land is a relatively low-transaction-cost method of inducing people to "do the right thing" with the earth's surface, the vernacular for avoiding deadweight losses. Compared to group ownership, not to mention an open-access regime, private property tends best to equate the personal product of an individual's small actions with the social product of those actions.

Suppose, for example, that the small event pictured by the innermost circle in Figures 1 and 2 was to be the cultivation of a garden of tomato plants. Under the group ownership regime portrayed in Figure 1, the 25 co-owners would be forced to use their internal governance mechanisms to prevent deadweight losses in the growing and harvesting of the tomatoes. They might succeed in doing this, but only by incurring the transaction costs of monitoring potential shirkers and grabbers within the group's membership.

For three basic reasons, monitoring tends to be cheaper under the individual ownership regime illustrated in Figure 2. First, self-control by one person (in this instance, owner *M*) by means of his own central nervous system is much simpler than the multiperson coordination entailed in intragroup monitoring. When land uses have no spillover effects, individual ownership directly and precisely punishes land misuse and rewards productive labor.

Second, individual ownership not only greatly reduces the number of instances in which people have to be watched, but it also makes that task simpler when it must be performed. Demsetz incautiously implied that an individual landowner is entirely free of the burden of monitoring others' behavior within the borders of his parcel. Not so. A landowner must still be on the lookout for wasteful grabbing by trespassers who enter land without authorization. *A key advantage of individual land ownership is that detecting the presence of a trespasser is much less demanding than evaluating the conduct of a person who is privileged to be where he is.* Monitoring boundary crossings is easier than monitoring the behavior of persons situated inside boundaries. For this reason, managers are paid more than night watchmen. To illustrate, suppose that the 25 owners in Figure 1 wanted to deter a deviant member from stealing tomatoes from one of their common gardens. Because each member would have the privilege of entering all gardens, the group might have to assign overseers to scrutinize the minute-to-minute behavior of all persons present in cropgrowing areas to guard against pilferage.[41] If the tomato garden were individually owned, by contrast, the sole owner would merely need to watch for an unauthorized entry. Upon seeing a trespasser cross a physically marked boundary, the owner in the usual case could expel him without having to marshal evidence of misconduct beyond the unauthorized entry itself.

Third, Demsetz has recently pointed out that an individual landowner is much more highly motivated than a group member to police boundaries or to carry out any other sort of monitoring fraction. A sole owner bears the entirety of any loss stemming from his slack oversight, whereas a group member bears only a function. The institution of private land ownership thus not only simplifies monitoring tasks, but also tends to ensure that those tasks are in the hands of conscientious agents.

---

41. The hypothetical is realistic. The stealing of sheaves of grain from fields was a common problem in open-field villages. See Warren O. Ault, Open-Field Farming in Medieval England: A Study of Village By-Laws 34-38 (1972).

2. TECHNOLOGIES FOR MARKING, DEFENDING,
   AND PROVING BOUNDARIES

Because private property in land necessitates the policing of boundaries, advances in surveying and fencing techniques may enhance the comparative efficiency of the institution. Preliterate societies developed many simple technologies that a landowner could use to detect and deter trespassers. During Hammurabi's reign around 1750 B.C., pegs were used to mark borders. Cairns, dikes, and stone walls are even more graphic and immovable. In social environments in which neighbors are inclined to cooperate, physically marked boundaries, if uncontroversially placed, are largely self-enforcing. A four-year-old can understand the convention that one does not cross a marked boundary. By contrast, the internal work rules that govern behavior within group-owned land are not nearly as plain to observers.

For millennia, absentee owners have employed simple technologies such as hedges, moats, and impregnable fencing to keep out persons and animals that do not respect boundaries. In addition, domesticated dogs, especially ones that instinctively bark at or attack strangers, are superb boundary defenders. By contrast, dogs are quite useless in enforcing a group's internal rules of conduct. Can a dog be trained to bark when a familiar person has shirked or pilfered? A modern-day landowner intent on detecting boundary violations can resort, in lieu of a dog, to an inexpensive electronic motion detector. "Shirking detectors" — devices that would sound an alarm when a worker was simply going through the motions — have yet to be invented.

In sum, a shift from group to individual ownership of land substitutes the relatively cheap systems of self-control and boundary monitoring for the relatively costly system of pervasive intragroup monitoring. In contexts where the satisfaction of basic human needs entails the coordination of many small events — such as the planting and harvesting of crops, caring for children and animals, and maintaining dwellings and other structures — the parcelization of land is a major institutional achievement.

Individual ownership does, however, generate some new transaction costs, mainly those arising from the proliferation of boundaries and ownership entities. The boundaries in the parcelized regime in Figure 2 are three times the length of the boundaries in the group-ownership regime in Figure 1. Disputes may arise over both the location of these boundaries and the identities of parcel owners. Because land boundaries are human artifacts, a group must develop rules concerning adequate means of delineating parcels and proving ownership. Partly to reduce outlays for erecting indestructible boundary monuments, ancient groups that had developed written languages strove to establish authoritative off-site records of boundaries and owners. Some of the earliest surviving human texts, the Mesopotamian kudurrus dating from c. 2500 B.C., record private land transfers on stone stelae about two feet high; these stones eventually came to be kept in temples. A Sumerian proverb refers to a "Registrar of Deeds." In Egypt, the vizier was keeping comprehensive land records by 2350 B.C., and by 650 B.C. an Egyptian staff of "land-measurers" was working under an "overseer of farmlands." Four thousand years after the Mesopotamian experience, the Puritans, with land becoming scarce in Massachusetts, began a major effort to improve the quality of land registries.

The efficiency thesis predicts that innovations in technologies for marking, defending, and proving boundaries lead to more parcelization because they reduce the transaction costs of private property regimes. According to this view, for example, Glidden's invention of barbed wire in 1874 should have stimulated more subdivision of rangeland in the American West. And this indeed appears to have occurred. In Shasta County, California, innovations in fencing and irrigation enhanced the cost-effectiveness of fenced pasture and spurred the parcelization of unfenced ranges on which cattlemen had previously run herds at-large. Conversely, the viability of group ownership might be enhanced by the advent of inexpensive video cameras or other technologies for monitoring behavior within a group setting.

C. Medium Events: A Simple Way to Promote Cooperative Relations

Demsetz's second major argument for private property in land rested on the social dynamics of medium events. Suppose, as Demsetz himself did, that the intermediate circle in Figures 1 and 2 were to demarcate the expected territorial effects of the proposed construction of a small dam. The parcelization of group land, Demsetz pointed out, would greatly reduce the number of persons concerned with this event. In the democratic group-ownership situation portrayed in Figure 1, all 25 co-owners would have to become knowledgeable about the proposed dam in order to help decide whether it was a cost-justified project. In the parcelized regime of Figure 2, by contrast, only the two substantially affected landowners, M and N, would have to be involved in the externality adjustment process. Embracing the consensus position that transaction costs tend to increase with the number of individuals involved, Demsetz saw land parcelization as having the virtue of increasing small-number situations. Picking up on this assertion, Michelman rightly stated that practitioners of transaction-cost economics stress avoidance of "excessive dependence of coordination on large-number transactions."[57]

When medium events are at issue, parcelization has two additional advantages that Demsetz did not mention. First, besides reducing the number of persons who must coordinate, parcelization is a low-transaction-cost device for knitting these individuals closely together, thereby inclining them toward cooperative behavior. In most societies, land ownership changes slowly. Two adjoining landowners therefore usually enjoy a continuing multiplex relationship — the sort that is most likely to engender cooperation. To be sure, a democratic commune of 25 members might be so close-knit that the average twosome of its members, chosen at random, would be even more intimate than two adjoining individual landowners. To achieve that degree of close-knittedness, however, the group might have to convene regular evening meetings of the entire membership. By contrast, two abutting landowners in a parcelized regime may be able to maintain amicable relations with only an occasional exchange of pleasantries across their common fence. The *sum* of transaction costs and deadweight losses arising out of medium events is therefore likely to be lower when land is individually owned.

Parcelization also relegates the settlement of disputes arising out of medium events to those persons most likely to be informed about the matter in controversy. A sole owner of a land parcel is apt to have better knowledge of its immediate environment than virtually anyone else does. For example, if a dam were proposed for a site on parcel M in Figure 2, M and N, the owners of the only two parcels substantially affected, probably could appraise the total costs and benefits of the dam better than could a random pair of members in the A . . . Y group.

In short, for activities that result in mostly small and medium events, individual ownership is better than both open-access and group ownership for minimizing the sum of deadweight losses and transaction costs. According to the efficiency thesis, this insight explains why family farming is ubiquitous, why collectivized agriculture almost always fails, and why virtually no dwelling units

57. [Frank I. Michelman, Ethics, Economics, and the Law of Property, in NOMOS XXIV, Ethics, Economics and the Law 3, 20 (J. Roland Pennock & John W. Chapman eds., 1982).]

are shared by groups as large as 25. Indeed, the historical record supports the following private-property thesis: *a close-knit group virtually always entitles its members to own, as private property, lands used for dwellings, crops, and other intensive activities.*

II. The Advantages of Group Ownership of Land

The discussion up to this point has given short shrift to the merits of group (and other forms of public) ownership of land. Staying entirely within Demsetz's general framework, one can enrich his analysis by explicitly incorporating the possibilities of increasing returns to scale and the desirability of spreading risks. . . .

A.   *When Returns Increase with Parcel Size*

Bigger land parcels are sometimes better. As tracts increase in area, the costs of fencing and other forms of perimeter monitoring drop per acre enclosed. This mathematical relationship has prompted many traditional societies to graze livestock on expansive group-owned pastures. A large territory also permits a landowner to use more specialized equipment and workers and to marshal gangs of workers for projects for which returns to scale exist. . . .

When Demsetz posed an example that involved a large event, he rightly qualified his enthusiasm for land parcelization. For example, if the large event pictured in Figure 2 were to be a smoky fire on parcel M, the transaction costs of large-number coordinations might prevent the many affected parcel owners from cooperating to resolve the dispute through some external institution. By contrast, if the governing body of the group portrayed in Figure 1 already had controls in place to monitor internal small and medium events, it might be able to respond to this large event much more expeditiously than the diffuse group of individual neighbors could. When a group's system of internal social control is itself characterized by increasing returns to scale, the identity of the land regime that best minimizes costs depends in part on what sorts of events — small, medium, or large — carry the highest stakes for group welfare.

The case for private ownership of farms and homesteads rests on the plausible assumption that vital agricultural, construction, homemaking, and child-rearing activities entail mostly small and medium events.[73] For the reasons just suggested, however, industrial activities that cause local air pollution might be better placed on large tracts which, because of the investment required, are likely to be group-owned. Group ownership does not necessarily imply government ownership, of course. The sorry environmental records of federal land agencies and Communist regimes are a sharp reminder that governments are often particularly inept managers of large tracts. Large events are inherently difficult to regulate. Identifying the institutions that govern them best — or, more bluntly, least badly — should be an exercise in experience, not logic. This points up the value of history. Under what circumstances, if any, have pioneers establishing land regimes from scratch chosen to own land collectively?

B.   Three Pioneer Settlements

Three of the most famous remote habitations in U.S. history were the Jamestown settlement of 1607, the Plymouth settlement of 1620, and the Mormon settlement at Salt Lake in 1847. [Discussion omitted.]

Although these three pioneer settlements differed, their land histories are remarkably similar. In each case the settlers started with group ownership of land, but after a period began parcelling out plots to individuals and households, a move that improved agricultural productivity. These events support the private-property thesis, but are unlikely to surprise anyone familiar with the history of collectivized agriculture. It is more intriguing to ask why the settlers declined to establish private property in croplands from the start. The prior section suggested one possibility. The pioneers at the three settlements may have started off with group-owned land in order to exploit returns to territorial scale presented by initial public works such as defensive palisades and, at Salt Lake, irrigation facilities. There is evidence, however, that high risks, not scale economies, were the main impetus for the initial collectivization of land at these outposts.

---

73. Marx and Engels tragically exaggerated the efficiencies of scale that are present in agriculture. See [Frederic L.] Pryor, [The Red and the Green 34-35, 372-373 (1992)]. . . . In 1987 in Cuba, an extreme case, the average state farm employed 1448 workers on 14,084 hectares (roughly 35,000 acres). [Id.] at 144 (table showing sizes of collective and state farms in Marxist regimes). By contrast, family farms still dominate American agriculture. In 1987, non-family-held corporations with eleven or more shareholders accounted for only 1.8% of the value of farm products sold in the United States. See Bureau of the Census, Statistical Abstract of the United States 647 (1991).

C. Group Ownership as a Risk-Spreading Device

A sole landowner bears the entire risk that his land will be damaged, devalued, or unproductive. Group ownership, by contrast, pools risk. Because most individuals are risk-averse, the risk-spreading feature of group property is advantageous — even decisive in certain situations.

As alternatives to group ownership of property, a group may employ numerous other risk-spreading mechanisms, including reciprocal altruism within a family or social group, insurance markets, and government welfare programs. In comparison, group ownership of land is in most contexts a mediocre method of spreading losses. It concentrates group investments in a single, highly undiversified, asset. Moreover, for reasons presented in Part I, intensive uses are usually less efficiently conducted on group land than on private land, a fact that makes group land ownership a comparatively costly insurance vehicle.

The efficiency thesis predicts that group land ownership will be more prevalent in situations in which risks are high and a group cannot employ a superior insurance mechanism. The settlers of the three pioneer communities initially faced conditions of precisely this sort. That the risks were acute cannot be doubted. All three pioneer settlements were remote outposts, located weeks or months away from civilization. The first parties of settlers faced lethal dangers, including raids by Indians, infections from exotic diseases, and difficulties in learning how to farm in their strange environments. Remoteness precluded risk-spreading through multigenerational kinship networks, insurance markets, or government welfare programs. The settlers could spread risks only among themselves, and one option was to have a collective economy that guaranteed each member some share of total group output.

Risk analysis also suggests why the pioneers would begin to parcelize their lands after a period of time. Settlers would lower their probability estimates of disaster and be less attentive to risk-spreading as they gradually learned how to prevent tribal raids, avoid disease, and grow crops. Moreover, as the months passed, the settlers could develop more efficient social-insurance mechanisms, such as informal mutual-aid relationships, tithe-supported churches, and tax-supported governments. In sum, after a few years, the risk-spreading benefits of group land ownership would no longer outweigh its familiar shortcomings, such as the shirking that notably afflicted Jamestown and Plymouth. At that point, the settlers understandably would switch to private land tenure, the system that most cheaply induces individuals to accomplish small and medium events that are socially useful.

Jamestown's history provides particular support for the proposition that high levels of risk promote group ownership. Fatalities from disease, famine, and Indian raids were higher at Jamestown than at the other [two] settlements. Historians have engaged in a spirited debate about why the Jamestown settlers bowled in the streets as they starved.... [S]eventeenth-century observers tended to stress the system of property rights in early Jamestown. At first, most land was held collectively, and each resident was fed no matter how much he worked. Later, when the colony began systematically to parcelize its lands, the reports of idleness ceased. Edmund S. Morgan, an eminent colonial historian, nevertheless has been reluctant to attribute much of Jamestown's work problem to its collectivized economy. Instead, Morgan has argued that the Jamestown settlers were handicapped by a culture of idleness that afflicted Englishmen of their background.[123]

By historical fluke, there is convincing evidence that the settlers' ideas and attitudes about work were not the problem at Jamestown. In 1609, the flagship of a Virginia Company fleet heading for Jamestown encountered rough weather and landed in Bermuda instead. Bermuda proved to be a much safer place. The island was uninhabited, and disease was far less prevalent than at Jamestown. Bermuda's first settlers had early success in growing corn. In 1612, the Virginia Company sent another 50 colonists to make the settlement permanent. In 1615, the Bermuda settlers began a process of meting out twenty-five acre plots to each member; by comparison, the Jamestown colony had endured for seven years before it officially doled out three-acre plots. Contrary to what Morgan's thesis would predict, idleness was not a problem on Bermuda, where settlers were building substantial houses at a time when the Virginians were still dwelling in "little better than shanties."[127]

Risk analysis provides a simple explanation of why events unfolded differently at Jamestown and Bermuda. In the high-risk environment at Jamestown, settlers persevered with a collectivist economy that included group land ownership partly because that institution served to spread an individual's risk of becoming in-

123. [Edmund S. Morgan, The Labor Problem at Jamestown, 1607-18, 76 Am. Hist. Rev. 595, 611 (1971).]

127. [Virginia Bernhard, Bermuda and Virginia in the Seventeenth Century: A Comparative View, 19 J. Soc. Hist. 57, 60 (1985).]

capacitated. In Bermuda, a low-risk environment, the settlers moved more promptly to the risk-concentrating regime of individual land ownership, which generated pronounced productivity gains (as a similar move eventually did at Jamestown). In short, the unusually deadly environment at Jamestown not only decimated the labor force, but also helped perpetuate institutions that spread risks but put less food on the table.

NOTES AND QUESTIONS ON LAND REGIMES

1. According to this selection, an *efficient* rule is one that minimizes the sum of (a) transaction costs, and (b) deadweight losses stemming from externalities. Is this simply a version of the Kaldor-Hicks test, described supra p. 62, Note 2? Would Demsetz concur in this usage?

2. Ellickson shares Demsetz's optimism about the evolution of property institutions, but only where social groups are close-knit. In light of Libecap's criteria, supra p. 145, Note 2, how might a close-knit group be defined?

3. Do dogs and fences warrant the attention this selection gives them? Is it indeed easier for land occupants to monitor boundary crossings by trespassers than the behavior of members who are privileged to use group lands? If communal farming is inherently inefficient, what explains the long survival of the kibbutzim of Israel and the communal Hutterite farms of the Great Plains? See Ellickson's discussion at pp. 1344-1362 of this article, and the sources cited therein. Are not most family farms communes of a sort? Two valuable essays, on the rise and fall of communal agriculture are Barry C. Field, The Evolution of Property Rights, 42 Kyklos 319 (1989), and Henry E. Smith, Semicommon Property Rights and Scattering in the Open Fields, 29 J. Legal Stud. 131 (2000).

4. While the selection asserts that the institution of private land ownership is apt to give rise to problems such as air pollution, it concludes that events of large territorial scope will bedevil a society whatever its mix of land regimes. Is this too pessimistic? On approaches to controlling pollution, see Merrill, Explaining Market Mechanisms, infra p. 521.

5. The selection highlights risk-spreading as one of the advantages of group ownership and contends that risk factors explain why land was owned communally in Jamestown longer than it

was in Bermuda. What other differences between these two settlements might have been significant?

The Kwakiutl Indians of British Columbia were renowned for potlatching, a reciprocal exchange institution that required ostentatious gift-giving by those who had enjoyed particularly bountiful salmon harvests. According to one analyst, this system evolved because it enabled the tribe's subgroups to maintain exclusive property rights in salmon fisheries. Potlatching provided each subgroup with insurance against a poor salmon harvest and thereby reduced its likelihood of encroaching on another subgroup's fishing territory. See D. Bruce Johnsen, The Formation and Protection of Property Rights Among the Southern Kwakiutl Indians, 15 J. Legal Stud. 41 (1986). Is a system of this sort likely to wither in the face of growing insurance markets and government welfare programs?

6. Efficiencies of scale may be present in the use of resources other than land. Consider money: How might a dozen poor individuals coordinate with one another periodically to provide useful clumps of capital to each of the dozen? See Ivan Light, Ethnic Enterprise in America (1972); Timothy Besley, Stephen Coate & Glenn Loury, The Economics of Rotating Credit Associations, 83 Am. Econ. Rev. 792 (1993).

C. The Problem of the Anticommons

Can Patents Deter Innovation? The Anticommons in Biomedical Research*

Michael A. Heller & Rebecca S. Eisenberg

Thirty years ago in *Science*, Garrett Hardin introduced the metaphor "tragedy of the commons" to help explain overpopulation, air pollution, and species extinction. People often overuse resources they own in common because they have no incentive to conserve. Today, Hardin's metaphor is central to debates in economics, law, and science and is a powerful justification for privatizing commons property. Although the metaphor highlights the

*Source: 280 Science 698-701 (1998).

cost of overuse when governments allow too many people to use a scarce resource, it overlooks the possibility of underuse when governments give too many people rights to exclude others. Privatization can solve one tragedy but cause another.

Since Hardin's article appeared, biomedical research has been moving from a commons model toward a privatization model. Under the commons model, the federal government sponsored premarket or "upstream" research and encouraged broad dissemination of results in the public domain. Unpatented biomedical discoveries were freely incorporated in "downstream" products for diagnosing and treating disease. In 1980, in an effort to promote commercial development of new technologies, Congress began encouraging universities and other institutions to patent discoveries arising from federally supported research and development and to transfer their technology to the private sector. Supporters applaud the resulting increase in patent filings and private investment, whereas critics fear deterioration in the culture of upstream research. Building on Heller's theory of anticommons property, this article identifies an unintended and paradoxical consequence of biomedical privatization: A proliferation of intellectual property rights upstream may be stifling life-saving innovations further downstream in the course of research and product development.

The Tragedy of the Anticommons

Anticommons property can best be understood as the mirror image of commons property. A resource is prone to overuse in a tragedy of the commons when too many owners each have a privilege to use a given resource and no one has a right to exclude another. By contrast, a resource is prone to underuse in a "tragedy of the anticommons" when multiple owners each have a right to exclude others from a scarce resource and no one has an effective privilege of use. In theory, in a world of costless transactions, people could always avoid commons or anticommons tragedies by trading their rights. In practice, however, avoiding tragedy requires overcoming transaction costs, strategic behaviors, and cognitive biases of participants, with success more likely within close-knit communities than among hostile strangers. Once an anticommons emerges, collecting rights into usable private property is often brutal and slow.

Privatization in postsocialist economies starkly illustrates how anticommons property can emerge and persist. One promise of the transition to a free market was that new entrepreneurs would fill stores that socialist rule had left bare. Yet after several years of reform, many privatized storefronts remained empty, while flimsy metal kiosks, stocked full of goods, mushroomed on the streets. Why did the new merchants not come in from the cold? One reason was that transition governments often failed to endow any individual with a bundle of rights that represents full ownership. Instead, fragmented rights were distributed to various socialist-era stakeholders, including private or quasi-private enterprises, workers' collectives, privatization agencies, and local, regional, and federal governments. No one could set up shop without first collecting rights from each of the other owners.

Privatization of upstream biomedical research in the United States may create anticommons property that is less visible than empty storefronts but even more economically and socially costly. In this setting, privatization takes the form of intellectual property claims to the sorts of research results that, in an earlier era, would have been made freely available in the public domain. Responding to a shift in U.S. government policy in the past two decades, research institutions such as the National Institutes of Health (NIH) and major universities have created technology transfer offices to patent and license their discoveries. At the same time, commercial biotechnology firms have emerged in research and development (R&D) niches somewhere between the proverbial "fundamental" research of academic laboratories and the targeted product development of pharmaceutical firms. Today, upstream research in the biomedical sciences is increasingly likely to be "private" in one or more senses of the term — supported by private funds, carried out in a private institution, or privately appropriated through patents, trade secrecy, or agreements that restrict the use of materials and data.

In biomedical research, as in postsocialist transition, privatization holds both promises and risks. Patents and other forms of intellectual property protection for upstream discoveries may fortify incentives to undertake risky research projects and could result in a more equitable distribution of profits across all stages of R&D. But privatization can go astray when too many owners hold rights in previous discoveries that constitute obstacles to future research. Upstream patent rights, initially offered to help attract further private investment, are increasingly regarded as entitlements by those who do research with public funds. A researcher who may have felt entitled to coauthorship or a citation in an earlier era may now feel entitled to be a coinventor on a patent or to receive a royalty under a material transfer agreement. The result has been a spiral of overlapping patent claims in the hands of different owners, reaching ever further upstream in the course of biomedical research. . . .

The problem we identify is distinct from the routine underuse inherent in any well-functioning patent system. By conferring monopolies in discoveries, patents necessarily increase prices and restrict use — a cost society pays to motivate invention and disclosure. The tragedy of the anticommons refers to the more complex obstacles that arise when a user needs access to multiple patented inputs to create a single useful product. Each upstream patent allows its owner to set up another tollbooth on the road to product development, adding to the cost and slowing the pace of downstream biomedical innovation.

How a Biomedical Anticommons May Arise

Current examples in biomedical research demonstrate two mechanisms by which a government might inadvertently create an anticommons: either by creating too many concurrent fragments of intellectual property rights in potential future products or by permitting too many upstream patent owners to stack licenses on top of the future discoveries of downstream users.

Concurrent fragments. The anticommons model provides one way of understanding a widespread intuition that issuing patents on gene fragments makes little sense. Throughout the 1980s, patents on genes generally corresponded closely to foreseeable commercial products, such as therapeutic proteins or diagnostic tests for recognized genetic diseases. Then, in 1991, NIH pointed the way toward patenting anonymous gene fragments with its notorious patent applications on expressed sequence tags (ESTs). NIH subsequently abandoned these patent applications and now takes a more hostile position toward patenting ESTs and raw genomic DNA sequences. Meanwhile, private firms have stepped in where NIH left off, filing patent applications on newly identified DNA sequences, including gene fragments, before identifying a corresponding gene, protein, biological function, or potential commercial product. The Patent and Trademark Office (PTO), in examining these claims, could create or avoid an anticommons.

Although a database of gene fragments is a useful resource for discovery, defining property rights around isolated gene fragments seems at the outset unlikely to track socially useful bundles of property rights in future commercial products. Foreseeable commercial products, such as therapeutic proteins or genetic diagnostic tests, are more likely to require the use of multiple fragments. A proliferation of patents on individual fragments held by different owners seems inevitably to require costly future transactions to bundle licenses together before a firm can have an effective right to develop these products.

Patents on receptors useful for screening potential pharmaceutical products demonstrate another potential "concurrent fragment" anticommons in biomedical research. To learn as much as possible about the therapeutic effects and side effects of potential products at the preclinical stage, firms want to screen products against all known members of relevant receptor families. But if these receptors are patented and controlled by different owners, gathering the necessary licenses may be difficult or impossible. . . . Unable to procure a complete set of licenses, firms choose between diverting resources to less promising projects with fewer licensing obstacles or proceeding to animal and then clinical testing on the basis of incomplete information. . . .

Stacking licenses. The use of reach-through license agreements (RTLAs) on patented research tools illustrates another path by which an anticommons may emerge. As we use the term, an RTLA gives the owner of a patented invention, used in upstream stages of research, rights in subsequent downstream discoveries. Such rights may take the form of a royalty on sales that result from use of the upstream research tool, an exclusive or nonexclusive license on future discoveries, or an option to acquire such a license. In principle, RTLAs offer advantages to both patent holders and researchers. They permit researchers with limited funds to use patented research tools right away and defer payment until the research yields valuable results. Patent holders may also prefer a chance at larger payoffs from sales of downstream products rather than certain, but smaller, upfront fees. In practice, RTLAs may lead to an anticommons as upstream owners stack overlapping and inconsistent claims on potential downstream products. . . .

. . . [S]ome universities and other nonprofit research institutions have balked at terms DuPont Corporation has offered for licenses to use patented oncomouse and cre-lox technologies, although others have acquiesced to the license terms. These patents cover genetically engineered mice useful in research that could result in products falling outside the scope of the patent claims. DuPont has offered noncommercial research licenses and sublicenses on terms that seem to require licensees to return to DuPont for further approval before any new discoveries or materials resulting from the use of licensed mice are passed along to others or used for commercial purposes. DuPont thereby gains the right to participate in future negotiations to develop commercial products that fall outside the scope of their patent claims. In effect, the license terms permit DuPont to leverage its proprietary position in up-stream research tools into a broad veto right over downstream research and product development.

As RTLAs to use patented research tools multiply, researchers will face increasing difficulties conveying clear title to firms that might develop future discoveries. . . .

Transition or Tragedy?

Is a biomedical anticommons likely to endure once it emerges? Recent empirical literature suggests that communities of intellectual property owners who deal with each other on a recurring basis have sometimes developed institutions to reduce transaction costs of bundling multiple licenses. For example, in the music industry, copyright collectives have evolved to facilitate licensing transactions so that broadcasters and other producers may readily obtain permission to use numerous copyrighted works held by different owners. Similarly, in the automobile, aircraft manufacturing, and synthetic rubber industries, patent pools have emerged, sometimes with the help of government, when licenses under multiple patent rights have been necessary to develop important new products. When the background legal rules threaten to waste resources, people often rearrange rights sensibly and create order through private arrangements. . . .

On the other hand, there may be reasons to fear that a patent anticommons could prove more intractable in biomedical research than in other settings. Because patents matter more to the pharmaceutical and biotechnology industries than to other industries, firms in these industries may be less willing to participate in patent pools that undermine the gains from exclusivity. Moreover, the lack of substitutes for certain biomedical discoveries (such as patented genes or receptors) may increase the leverage of some patent holders, thereby aggravating holdout problems. Rivals may not be able to invent around patents in research aimed at understanding the genetic bases of diseases as they occur in nature.

More generally, three structural concerns caution against uncritical reliance on markets and norms to avoid a biomedical anticommons tragedy: the transaction costs of rearranging entitlements, heterogeneous interests of owners, and cognitive biases among researchers.

Transaction costs of bundling rights.   High transaction costs may be an enduring impediment to efficient bundling of intellectual property rights in biomedical research. First, many upstream patent owners are public institutions with limited resources for absorbing transaction costs and limited competence in fast-paced, market-oriented bargaining. Second, the rights involved cover a diverse set of techniques, reagents, DNA sequences, and instruments. Difficulties in comparing the values of these patents will likely impede development of a standard distribution scheme. Third, the heterogeneity of interests and resources among public and private patent owners may complicate the emergence of standard license terms, requiring costly case-by-case negotiations. Fourth, licensing transaction costs are likely to arise early in the course of R&D when the outcome of a project is uncertain, the potential gains are speculative, and it is not yet clear that the value of downstream products justifies the trouble of overcoming the anticommons. . . .

Heterogeneous interests of rights holders. Intellectual property rights in upstream biomedical research belong to a large, diverse group of owners in the public and private sectors with divergent institutional agendas. Sometimes heterogeneity of interests can facilitate mutually agreeable allocations (you take the credit, I'll take the money), but in this setting, there are reasons to fear that owners will have conflicting agendas that make it difficult to reach agreement. For example, a politically accountable government agency such as NIH may further its public health mission by using its intellectual property rights to ensure widespread availability of new therapeutic products at reasonable prices. . . . By contrast, a private firm is more likely to use intellectual property to maintain a lucrative product monopoly that rewards shareholders and funds future product development. When owners have conflicting goals and each can deploy its rights to block the strategies of the others, they may not be able to reach an agreement that leaves enough private value for downstream developers to bring products to the market.

A more subtle conflict in agendas arises between owners that pursue end-product development and those that focus primarily on upstream research. The goal of end-product development may be better served by making patented research tools widely available on a nonexclusive basis, whereas the goal of procuring upstream research funding may be better served by offering exclusive licenses to sponsors or research partners. . . .

Cognitive biases. People consistently overestimate the likelihood that very low probability events of high salience will occur. For example, many travelers overestimate the danger of an airplane crash relative to the hazards of other modes of transportation. We suspect that a similar bias is likely to cause owners of upstream biomedical research patents to overvalue their discoveries. Imagine that one of a set of 50 upstream inventions will likely be the key to identifying an important new drug, the rest of the set will have no practical use, and a downstream product developer is willing to pay $10 million for the set. Given the assumption that no owner knows *ex ante* which invention will be the key, a rational owner should be willing to sell her patent for the probabilistic value of $200,000. However, if each owner overestimates the likelihood that her patent will be the key, then each will demand more than the probabilistic value, the upstream owners collectively will demand more than the aggregate market value of their inputs, the downstream user will decline the offers, and the new drug will not be developed. Individuals trained in deterministic rather than probabilistic disciplines are particularly likely to succumb to this sort of error.

A related "attribution bias" suggests that people systematically overvalue their assets and disparage the claims of their opponents when in competition with others. We suspect that the attribution bias is pervasive among scientists because it is likely adaptive for the research enterprise as a whole. Overcommitment by individuals to particular research approaches ensures that no hypothesis is dismissed too quickly, and skepticism toward rivals' claims ensures that they are not too readily accepted. But this bias can interfere with clear-headed bargaining, leading owners to overvalue their own patents, undervalue others' patents, and reject reasonable offers. Institutional ownership could mitigate these biases, but technology transfer offices rely on scientists to evaluate their discoveries. When two or more patent owners each hope to dominate the product market, the history of biotechnology patent litigation suggests a likelihood that bargaining will fail.

Conclusion

Like the transition to free markets in postsocialist economies, the privatization of biomedical research offers both promises and risks. It promises to spur private investment but risks creating a tragedy of the anticommons through a proliferation of fragmented and overlapping intellectual property rights. An anticommons in biomedical research may be more likely to endure than in other areas of intellectual property because of the high transaction costs of bargaining, heterogeneous interests among owners, and cognitive biases of researchers. Privatization must be more carefully deployed if it is to serve the public goals of biomedical research. Policy-makers should seek to ensure coherent boundaries of upstream patents and to minimize restrictive licensing practices that interfere with downstream product development. Otherwise, more upstream rights may lead paradoxically to fewer useful products for improving human health.

NOTES AND QUESTIONS ON THE ANTICOMMONS

1. An analyst can usefully employ the concepts of the commons and anticommons not just in biotechnology, but in any domain of modern intellectual property. For a useful survey of cyberspace issues, see Margaret Jane Radin, Property Evolving in Cyberspace, 15 J.L. & Com. 509 (1996). See also Merges, infra p. 560.

2. For the first use of the term "anticommons" in the sense of this selection, see Robert C. Ellickson, Property in Land, 102 Yale L.J. 1315 (1993), at 1322, n. 22, reproduced in part supra p. 146. As noted in the selection, Michael Heller, in The Tragedy of the Anticommons: Property in the Transition from Marx to Markets, 111 Harv. L. Rev. 621 (1998), further develops the anticommons idea in the context of post-Soviet Russia. Both Ellickson and Heller attribute the germ of the anticommons idea to Frank I. Michelman, Ethics, Economics and the Law of Property, in NOMOS XXIV: Ethics, Economics and the Law 3, 6 (1982). Michelman's article suggested that property requires a principle of "composition," and becomes unusable if unduly fragmented.

3. Is the tragedy of the anticommons really a mirror image of the tragedy of the commons as Heller and Eisenberg state? Notice that the problem of the commons is one of *under*developed property rights, while that of the anticommons is one of *over*developed rights. Does this suggest that anticommons problems might be even more difficult to overcome than commons problems? Are they more likely to be affected by such cognitive biases as the "endowment effect," a factor mentioned by Heller and Eisenberg? For more on such biases, see Jolls et al., infra p. 221.

4. The anticommons is a problem of "too much property." Are there others? For example, might the propertization of some resources, but not others, lead people to overuse those left in a common or open-access state? For examples involving both environmental resources and intellectual property, see Carol M. Rose, The Several Futures of Property: Of Cyberspace and Folk

Tales, Emission Trades and Ecosystems, 83 Minn. L. Rev. 129 (1998), where it is suggested that in theory such instances of "too much property" are really "too little property," and that harmful substitutions can be overcome if the remaining resources are propertized too. Does the Heller & Eisenberg article suggest that this theoretical solution might be impracticable?

5. In a modern society are anticommons problems really serious? Real estate dealers must constantly arrange for land assembly, but shopping centers and large buildings nevertheless do get built. In the realm of intellectual property, as the authors note, holders of rights form patent pools and copyright collectives. Even Moscow storefront kiosks have become a thing of the past. Is an unbreakable anticommons idiosyncratic to biotechnology, if it exists there? Are Heller and Eisenberg too pessimistic about people's ability to bargain around fragmented property rights? Might the rules of property law prevent fragmentation from arising? See Merrill & Smith, infra p. 360; see also Carol M. Rose, What Government Can Do for Property (And Vice Versa), in The Fundamental Interrelationships between Government and Property (N. Mercuro & W. Samuels eds., 1999). And, as a last resort, are there governmental mechanisms such as eminent domain that can help enable assemblage of rights in contexts of public importance? See Calabresi & Melamed, infra p. 233, and Krier & Schwab, infra p. 249. Might such mechanisms be adapted to mitigate other anticommons problems? See Robert C. Ellickson, New Institutions for Old Neighborhoods, 48 Duke L.J. 75 (1998).

6. Even if some aspects of law help to overcome the tragedy of the anticommons, do other aspects of the law exacerbate it? See James M. Buchanan & Yong J. Yoon, Symmetric Tragedies: Commons and Anticommons, 43 J.L. & Econ. 1 (2000), arguing that the anticommons idea captures the inefficiencies of modern regulatory bureaucracy, in which each of a number of overlapping permitting processes can stymie action.

7. Is the anticommons necessarily an evil? Reconsider Acheson's description of the complex entitlements of Monhegan lobsterfishers, supra p. 129; and consider also the even more complex and fragmented entitlements of precontact Maori, described by Banner, infra p. 321. Might such complex rights structures serve a positive function, preventing alienability and holding together a community in which the participants need to work together over time? For an argument to this effect, using the example of complex entitlements in the medieval agricultural commons, see Henry E. Smith, Semicommon Property Rights and Scattering in the Open Fields, 29 J. Legal Stud. 131 (2000). Might the anticommons be of

some use in modern bureaucratic processes as well, despite the criticisms of Buchanan & Yoon, supra? For example, might delay actually be the point of some overlapping regulatory processes, to allow for accommodation of otherwise overlooked considerations? See Sax, infra p. 537.

Chapter 3

The Significance of Possession

The Economics of Rights, Cooperation and Welfare*

Robert Sugden

5.1 Nine Points of the Law

When oil and gas reserves were discovered under the North Sea the problem arose of who had the right to exploit them. The potential claimants were nation states. Given the power of most nation states to inflict harm on most others, it was important to find some way of dividing up the reserves that would be generally acceptable. In effect, nations were involved in a variant of the division game, but with many players instead of just two.

The solution reached was to allocate each portion of the sea bed to the country whose coastline happened to be nearest. In terms of any abstract theory of justice, this seems completely arbitrary. The main beneficiaries from this arrangement were the United Kingdom and Norway. West Germany, despite its large population and its considerable length of North Sea coastline, came out badly. Why did West Germany acquiesce in such an unfair partition? Why, for that matter, should the share-out have been restricted to countries with a North Sea coastline? The poor countries of Africa and Asia might have used arguments of distributive justice to support claims to North Sea oil. If it is replied that these

*Source: pp. 87-97 (1986) (from Chapter 5, "Possession").

countries lack the military power to support such claims, how much military power does Norway have? And the United States and the Soviet Union are overwhelmingly more powerful than any of the North Sea countries; yet they too got nothing.

One answer might be that this peculiar division of the sea bed was prescribed by international law. In 1958 an international conference in Geneva had drafted a convention which was to come into force when it had been ratified by 22 states; the 22nd state signed in 1964. According to this convention, each state has a right to exploit the continental shelf adjacent to its coastline. International boundaries on the continental shelf are to be fixed by agreement between the states concerned, but in case of dispute, median lines (i.e., lines equidistant from the coasts of two countries) are to be used. In fact, however, the agreement among the North Sea countries departed from this convention quite significantly. There is a deep trench between the Norwegian coast and the North Sea oilfields; according to the Geneva Convention these oilfields were all on the British continental shelf, even though in some cases the closest coastline was Norway's. In the event the North Sea countries opted for the simpler rule of ignoring the depth of the sea bed and allocating every portion of continental shelf to the country with the closest coastline. So the partition of the North Sea was not arrived at simply by applying existing international law. And in any case, we should need to explain why the Geneva Convention was agreed in the first place. The participants in the Geneva Conference were also playing a kind of division game: Why did the median line solution appeal to them?

Suppose, suggests Milton Friedman, that:

> you and three friends are walking along the street and you happen to spy and retrieve a $20 bill on the pavement. It would be generous of you, of course, if you were to divide it equally with them, or at least blow them to a drink. But suppose you do not. Would the other three be justified in joining forces and compelling you to share the $20 equally with them? I suspect most readers will be tempted to say no. (Friedman, 1962, p. 165)

This is another example of the division game, this time with four players. Friedman suggests that if his readers played the game they would recognize the rule of "finders keepers." Although we may tell our children that the right thing to do is to take the money to a police station, I feel sure Friedman is right: most people *would* recognize that the person who finds the $20 bill keeps it. At any rate, the finder's claim is far stronger than that of the friends who happen to be with him when he finds it.

Suppose you are driving your car and approaching a long

bridge over a river. The bridge is only wide enough for one car. Another car is approaching the bridge from the other side. It reaches the bridge before you do and begins to cross. Do you stop and allow the other car to cross, or continue on in the expectation that the other driver will see you coming and reverse? My observation is that most drivers recognize a convention that the first car on the bridge has the right of way.

In each case, I suggest, a conflict is resolved by appeal to a convention. In each case the convention works by assigning each disputed object to the claimant with whom the object is already most closely associated — "associated" in some sense that is itself conventional. The first driver on the bridge has a special association with it — the relation of being the first claimant, or of being the person in possession. The person who first picks up the $20 bill has a similar relation to it. In the case of the North Sea, each portion of the sea bed is assigned to the nation whose land is closest to it.

In the rest of this chapter I shall argue that many of the property conventions that are used to resolve human conflicts work in this way: They exploit existing associations between claimants and objects. Such conventions inevitably tend to favour possessors, since to be in possession of something is to have a very obvious association with it. The maxim that possession is nine points of the law is more than a description of a feature of a particular legal system; it describes a pervasive tendency in human affairs. . . .

5.2   Asymmetries in the Structure of a Game . . .

. . . [S]uppose that at the start of every contest one individual is in possession of the disputed resource while the other is not. I shall call the first player the possessor and the second the challenger. This is an asymmetry of labelling. However, we might expect that in reality the asymmetry would go a little deeper than this, for two main reasons. First, we might expect an individual, on average, to value disputed resources more highly when he is the possessor than when he is the challenger, because at any time the things a person has in his possession are likely to be things he particularly values. (That is why he is carrying them around with him, keeping close watch on them, or whatever. And people develop habits of life around, and acquire skills to use, the things they have long possessed.) Second, we might expect that in the case of a fight, possession confers some advantage; thus an individual may be slightly more likely to win fights when he is the possessor than when he is the challenger. . . .

This line of argument supplies one reason why conventions favouring possessors might tend to be relatively successful in a world of natural selection. However, many other conventions have similar advantages. Take, for example, the convention that a disputed resource goes to the best fighter, or the convention that it goes to the person who needs it most. Either of these seems more directly connected with a relevant asymmetry than the convention favouring possessors. Wouldn't these conventions be more likely to establish themselves?

5.3   Prominence and Possession

If a convention is to develop it must first be recognized by people: Each person must come to see that there is some pattern in the behaviour of his fellows, and that it is in his interest to follow this pattern himself. In the early stages of the development of a convention, when only a small proportion of the population are following it, these patterns are likely to be hard to spot. People are more likely to find those patterns that — consciously or unconsciously — they are looking for. Thus a convention is more likely to develop if people have some prior expectation that it will.

This is not as circular as it sounds. Such prior expectations correspond with Schelling's concept of prominence. Despite the elusiveness of this concept, and the way it seems to lie beyond the reach of rational analysis, there can be no doubt that some solutions *are* more prominent than others.

Hume seems to have had in mind something like Schelling's notion of prominence when writing his Treatise on Human Nature — particularly the two penetrating passages entitled "Of the origin of justice and property" and "Of the rules, which determine property" (Hume, 1740, Book 3, Part 2, Sections 2-3). As I have pointed out before, Hume argued that rules of property are conventions that have evolved spontaneously — that have arisen, as he put it, gradually and acquired force by slow progression and by our repeated experience of the inconveniences of transgressing them. He tried to answer the question I am confronting: Why does one particular convention of property evolve rather than another? To answer this question, he wrote, we must look to "the imagination" rather than to "reason and public interest" (1740, Book 3, Part 2, Section 3).

Hume presents the following example of a division game:

I first consider men in their savage and solitary condition; and suppose, that being sensible of the misery of that state, and foreseeing the advantages that wou'd result from society, they seek each other's company, and make an offer of mutual protection and assistance. I also suppose, that they are endow'd with such sagacity as immediately to perceive, that the chief impediment to this project of society and partnership lies in the avidity and selfishness of their natural temper; to remedy which, they enter into a convention for the stability of possession, and for mutual restraint and forbearance. I am sensible, that this method of proceeding is not altogether natural; but besides that I here only suppose those reflexions to be form'd at once, which in fact arise insensibly and by degrees; besides this, I say, 'tis very possible, that several persons, being by different accidents separated from the societies, to which they formerly belong'd, may be oblig'd to form a new society among themselves; in which case they are entirely in the situation above-mention'd.

'Tis evident, then, that their first difficulty, in this situation, after the general convention for the establishment of society, and for the constancy of possession, is, how to separate their possessions, and assign to each his particular portion, which he must for the future inalterably enjoy. This difficulty will not detain them long; but it must immediately occur, as the most natural expedient, that every one continues to enjoy what he is at present master of, and that property or constant possession be conjoin'd to the immediate possession. (1740, Book 3, Part 2, Section 3)

... Hume is claiming that the rule favouring possessors has a natural prominence; this leads people to converge on it as a solution in a game in which any agreement is better than none.

Why is this solution particularly prominent? Hume appeals to what he claims is a natural tendency of the human mind to seek out relations between objects:

'Tis a quality, which I have already observ'd in human nature, that when two objects appear in a close relation to each other, the mind is apt to ascribe to them any additional relation, in order to compleat the union. . . . Thus for instance, we never fail, in our arrangement of bodies, to place those which are *resembling* in *contiguity* to each other, or at least in *correspondent* points of view; because we feel a satisfaction in joining the relation of contiguity to that of resemblance, or the resemblance of situation to that of qualities. . . . As property forms a relation betwixt a person and an object, 'tis natural to found it on some preceding relation; and as property is nothing but a constant possession, secur'd by the laws of society, 'tis natural to add it to the present possession, which is a relation that resembles it. (1740, Book 3, Part 2, Section 3)

I think there is an important truth here. If we are playing a game in which we have to agree on a way of assigning objects to persons, there *is* a natural prominence to solutions that base the assignment on some pre-existing relation between persons and objects. And the closer the resemblance between the pre-existing relation and

Figure 5.2
A Pure Coordination Game

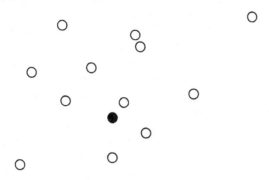

Join the black circle to one of the white circles. If you choose
the same circle as your partner, you win £10; otherwise,
you win nothing.

the one to be determined in the game, the more prominent is the
solution based on that relation.

If this sounds like a conservative rationalization of the law of
property, consider the following pure coordination game.... You
and a partner are separated and not allowed to communicate. Then
you are each shown the pattern of circles drawn in Figure 5.2. You
are told to draw a line joining the black circle to any one white
circle. If you both hit on the same white circle, you will each be
given £10; otherwise, you get nothing. Which circle would you
choose? My hunch is that most people would choose the white
circle closest to the black one. The reason, I think, is the one given
by Hume. You are asked to establish a relation between the black
circle and a white one (the relation of being linked by a line). It is
natural to look for some other relation, already there in the dia-
gram, by which one and only one white circle can be linked to the
black one; the most prominent such relation, surely, is that of being
closest. (I cannot *prove* that this is the most prominent relation.
Why not the relation of lying directly below the black circle, or of
being farthest away from it? I can only say that closeness seems
the most prominent relation to me, and hope the reader has the
same reaction.)

Prominence, as I argued in Section 3.3, is often dependent on
analogy. When people face new problems of the kind that are resolved by convention, they tend to look for prominent solutions
by drawing analogies with other situations in which conventions

are well established. Thus conventions can spread from one context to another. The conventions that are best able to spread are those that are most general (i.e., that can be applied in the greatest range of cases) and most fertile (i.e., most susceptible to extension by analogy). The idea that disputes are resolved in favour of possessors seems to be peculiarly fertile and general.

Conventions favouring possessors can be found everywhere. Perhaps the purest case is the principle, embodied in English law, that a right to a parcel of land or to a right of way can be established by a long period of undisputed occupation or use. However arbitrary this principle may be from any moral point of view, it seems to be generally recognized as a working convention, even in cases in which litigation is out of the question. Consider minor disputes between neighbours, between workmates, or between employers and employees. Think how much importance is attached to precedents, to "custom and practice." If your neighbour or workmate or employer starts doing something that annoys you, the time to complain is *straight away* — before a precedent is established. Why do precedents matter so much, if not because there is some convention that established practices are allowed to continue? And notice how very general this convention is — how many different kinds of disputes it can be used to resolve.

Closely analogous with conventions favouring possessors are conventions favouring first claimants — those people who first register, in a way that is itself defined by convention, their claims on disputed resources. Take the convention of the queue, or of "first come, first served." The principle here is that, of all the people who might dispute over something — perhaps the opportunity to use a public telephone, or to be served in a shop, or to get on a bus — the person who was there first has established the strongest claim. Or take the principle of "last in, first out" for determining who must go when someone in a factory or office has to be made redundant. Or take the convention, well established on planes and trains, that once a person has occupied a seat it is his for the rest of his journey, even if he leaves it temporarily.

The author Leo Walmsley has described a convention that was recognized on the Yorkshire coast up to the 1930s. After a storm, valuable driftwood could be washed up. The first person to go on to any stretch of the shore after high tide was allowed the pick of the driftwood; anything he collected into piles and marked with two stones was regarded as his, to carry away when he chose. This is an interesting mixture of two principles — the principle of first claims and the principle that property can be acquired by labour.

When driftwood is washed up on the shore it belongs to no one, but by gathering it into piles a person makes it his.

This latter principle is formulated most famously by Locke, who gives it the status of natural law — a moral law that is evident to the natural reason of man:

> Though the Water running in the Fountain be every ones, yet who can doubt, but that in the Pitcher is his only who drew it out? His *labour* hath taken it out of the hands of Nature, where it was common, and belong'd equally to all her Children, and *hath* thereby *appropriated* it to himself.
> Thus this Law of reason makes the Deer, that *Indian's* who hath killed it . . . And amongst those who are counted the Civiliz'd part of Mankind, who have made and multiplied positive Laws to determine Property, this original Law of Nature for the *beginning of Property*, in what was before common, still takes place; and by vertue thereof, what Fish any one catches in the Ocean, that great and still remaining Common of Mankind . . . is *by* the *Labour* that removes it out of that common state Nature left it in, *made* his *Property* who takes that pains about it. (1690, Second Treatise, Ch. 5)

Like Hume, I am not convinced that this principle of property can be discovered out of nothing, by reason alone. But Locke is surely right in saying that, in the absence of "positive laws," this principle is widely recognized as a way of resolving disputes. It is, I suggest, a convention that has evolved. . . .

Hume suggests another form of prominence that is related to possession:

> We acquire the property of objects by *accession*, when they are already connected in an intimate manner with objects that are already our property, and at the same time inferior to them. Thus the fruits of our garden, the offspring of our cattle, and the work of our slaves, are all of them esteem'd our property, even before possession. (1740, Book 3, Part 2, Section 3)

In other words, conventions may exploit two-step relations between persons and objects: If I am in possession of object X, and if there is some especially prominent relation between object X and some "inferior" object Y, then this may be enough to establish a prominent relation between me and Y. This idea may help to explain the attraction of the median-line solution to the problem of partitioning the North Sea. Among geographical features, the relation of closeness seems to have an inescapable prominence, and in this sense it is natural to associate each portion of the sea bed with the closest land mass, and thus with the nation that is in possession of that land.

An alternative explanation of the median-line solution is that it derived its prominence from the existence of longstanding conventions about fishing rights. It has long been recognized that each nation has the right to control fishing off its own coasts, although how far this right extends has often been a matter of dispute — as in the "cod wars" between Britain and Iceland. The median-line rule is a natural extension of this principle, and so this may be an example of the spread of conventions by analogy. But then why did the convention of coastal fishing rights become established? Hume's idea of accession may help to explain why this convention seems a natural solution to fishing disputes.

NOTES AND QUESTIONS ON CLAIMS DERIVED FROM PROXIMITY

1. Sugden talks as if an "association" between people and things is a matter of convention, but in discussing "prominence," does he implicitly assume some element of human nature to explain the conventions? If so, what is it? A territorial instinct? If so, how can the term "property" be extended to matters as abstract and intangible as a patent or a stock option? Toward the end of the selection, he notes the example of a person who collects a bundle of driftwood and marks it with stones. In what sense are the stones "prominent"? Does "prominence" have any unifying thread at all?

2. Sugden says that "first in time" is analogous to spatial proximity. What if anything is the analogy? Is physical likeness equally analogous to proximity? Consider, for example, the belief among some peoples that physical representations (photos, pictures, etc.) give power over the represented person (as exemplified in voodoo dolls), or the belief that naming gives power over the thing or person named. Does naming and magical representation represent a kind of property? Is allocation according to promixity (or "first in time") just our version of voodoo? On the subject of magic and property (perhaps the original voodoo economics), see Mark C. Suchman, Invention and Ritual: Notes on the Interrelation of Magic and Intellectual Property in Preliterate Societies, 89 Colum. L. Rev. 1264 (1989), describing intellectual property in magical skills.

3. Might proximity itself be a proxy for power or control over a given resource? For example, could the allocation of North Sea oil rights to nearby countries simply be a tacit recognition that those countries could sabotage anyone else's efforts to take these resources? Are those countries simply larger versions of the Mon-

hegan lobster gangs described by Acheson, supra? If so, the ability to exert control is the chief element in the "association" of things with persons, and proximity is simply one factor in such control. Compare Yoram Barzel, Economic Analysis of Property Rights 105-113 (2d ed. 1997), and Stefano Fenoaltea, Slavery and Supervision in Comparative Perspective, 44 J. Econ. History 635 (1984). These authors try to explain why slaves (who in theory owned nothing) were frequently granted formal or informal property rights in their labor; this was most likely when their work had to be done with care (with skilled carpentry, for instance), giving them a *de facto* ability to sabotage output.

4. Battles over the control of resources commonly have pay-offs structured like those in a Chicken-Hawk game, in which the two players' joint payoffs are maximized when one is submissive (like a chicken) and the other acts aggressively (like a hawk). (For an example of a Chicken-Hawk payoff matrix, see infra p. 283, a portion of the selection by Zerbe & Anderson.) A social convention may enable people to coordinate to avoid the costly timidity of Chicken-Chicken outcomes and the costly violence of Hawk-Hawk outcomes. A simple convention that achieves this desirable result is *Bourgeois*. A person who adopts this strategy is submissive with regard to resources in others' possession but fights to defend resources in his own possession. (In the animal world, the widespead adoption of this strategy leads to patterns of territoriality.) To solve Chicken-Hawk games, why would a society prefer a *Bourgeois* convention that systematically favors possessors over a *My-Place-Is-Yours* convention that would call for a possessor always to yield to an intruder? (Note that both succeed in avoiding Chicken-Chicken and Hawk-Hawk outcomes.) Which convention would better encourage investments in improvements? Better reward efforts to obtain information about the potential uses of a given resource? See Brian Skyrms, Evolution of the Social Contract 65-79 (1996).

5. Allocation of property rights on the basis of proximity seems rather arbitrary, but it is not necessarily unattractive on distributional grounds. For example, some proposals for protection of tropical rainforest resources would allocate property rights in the forest to local indigenous populations. See Lee Breckenridge, Protection of Biological and Cultural Diversity: Emerging Recognition of Local Community Rights in Ecosystems under International Environmental Law, 59 Tenn. L. Rev. 735 (1992). Similarly, a number of proposals for pharmaceutical uses of rainforest genetic materials would allocate to source-nations property shares in any products actually developed. See Roger A. Sedjo, Property Rights, Genetic

Resources and Biotechnological Change, 35 J. Law & Econ. 198 (1992). How might these allocations of property rights, based on proximity, help to preserve rainforest resources?

6. What does "possession" mean? The next selection addresses this issue.

Possession as the Origin of Property*

Carol M. Rose

How do things come to be owned? This is a fundamental puzzle for anyone who thinks about property. One buys things from other owners, to be sure, but how did the other owners get those things? Any chain of ownership or title must have a first link. Someone had to do something to anchor that link. The law tells us what steps we must follow to obtain ownership of things, but we need a theory that tells us why these steps should do the job.

John Locke's view, once described as "the standard bourgeois theory,"[1] is probably the one most familiar to American students. Locke argued that an original owner is one who mixes his or her labor with a thing and, by commingling that labor with the thing, establishes ownership of it. This labor theory is appealing because it appears to rest on "desert," but it has some problems. First, without a prior theory of ownership, it is not self-evident that one owns even the labor that is mixed with something else. Second, even if one does own the labor that one performs, the labor theory provides no guidance in determining the scope of the right that one establishes by mixing one's labor with something else. Robert Nozick illustrates this problem with a clever hypothetical. Suppose I pour a can of tomato juice into the ocean: Do I now own the seas?[5]

A number of thinkers more or less contemporary to Locke proposed another theory of the basis of ownership. According to this theory, the original owner got title through the consent of the rest of humanity (who were, taken together, the first recipients from God, the genuine original owner). Locke himself identified the problems with this theory; they involve what modern law-and-economics writers would call "administrative costs." How does

*Source: 52 U. Chi. L. Rev. 73-88 (1985).
1. Richard Schlatter, Private Property: The History of an Idea 151 (1951).
5. . . . . Anarchy, State and Utopia 175 (1974). . . .

everyone get together to consent to the division of things among individuals?

The common law has a third approach, which shares some characteristics with the labor and consent theories but is distinct enough to warrant a different label. For the common law, *possession* or "occupancy" is the origin of property. This notion runs through a number of fascinating old cases with which teachers of property law love to challenge their students. Such inquiries into the acquisition of title to wild animals and abandoned treasure may seem purely academic; how often, after all, do we expect to get into disputes about the ownership of wild pigs or long-buried pieces of eight? These cases are not entirely silly, though. People still do find treasure-laden vessels, and statesmen do have to consider whether someone's acts might support a claim to own the moon, for example, or the mineral nodes at the bottom of the sea. Moreover, analogies to the capture of wild animals show up time and again when courts have to deal on a nonstatutory basis with some "fugitive" resource that is being reduced to property for the first time, such as oil, gas, groundwater, or space on the spectrum of radio frequencies.

With these more serious claims in mind, then, I turn to the maxim of the common law: first possession is the root of title. Merely to state the proposition is to raise two critical questions: What counts as possession, and why is it the basis for a claim to title? In exploring the quaint old cases' answers to these questions, we hit on some fundamental views about the nature and purposes of a property regime.

Consider Pierson v. Post,[16] a classic wild-animal case from the early nineteenth century. Post was hunting a fox one day on an abandoned beach and almost had the beast in his gunsight when an interloper appeared, killed the fox, and ran off with the carcass. The indignant Post sued the interloper for the value of the fox on the theory that his pursuit of the fox had established his property right to it.

The court disagreed. It cited a long list of learned authorities to the effect that "occupancy" or "possession" went to the one who killed the animal, or who at least wounded it mortally or caught it in a net. These acts brought the animal within the "certain control" that gives rise to possession and hence a claim to ownership.

Possession thus means a clear act, whereby all the world un-

16. 3 Cai. R. 175 (N.Y. Sup. Ct. 1805).

derstands that the pursuer has "an unequivocal intention of appropriating the animal to his individual use." A clear rule of this sort should be applied, said the court, because it prevents confusion and quarreling among hunters (and coincidentally makes the judges' task easier when hunters do get into quarrels).

The dissenting judge commented that the best way to handle this matter would be to leave it to a panel of sportsmen, who presumably would have ruled against the interloper. In any event, he noted that the majority's rule would discourage the useful activity of fox hunting: who would bother to go to all the trouble of keeping dogs and chasing foxes if the reward were up for grabs to any "saucy intruder"? If we really want to see that foxes don't overrun the countryside, we will allocate a property right — and thus the ultimate reward — to the hunter at an earlier moment, so that he will undertake the useful investment in keeping hounds and the useful labor in flushing the fox.

The problem with assigning "possession" prior to the kill is, of course, that we need a principle to tell us when to assign it. Shall we assign it when the hunt begins? When the hunter assembles his dogs for the hunt? When the hunter buys his dogs?

Pierson thus presents two great principles, seemingly at odds, for defining possession: (1) notice to the world through a clear act, and (2) reward to useful labor. The latter principle, of course, suggests a labor theory of property. The owner gets the prize when he "mixes in his labor" by hunting. On the other hand, the former principle suggests at least a weak form of the consent theory: The community requires clear acts so that it has the opportunity to dispute claims, but may be thought to acquiesce in individual ownership where the claim is clear and no objection is made.

On closer examination, however, the two positions do not seem so far apart. In *Pierson*, each side acknowledged the importance of the other's principle. Although the majority decided in favor of a clear rule, it tacitly conceded the value of rewarding useful labor. Its rule for possession would in fact reward the original hunter most of the time, unless we suppose that the woods are thick with "saucy intruders." On the other side, the dissenting judge also wanted some definiteness in the rule of possession. He was simply insisting that the acts that sufficed to give notice should be prescribed by the relevant community, namely hunters or "sportsmen." Perhaps, then, there is some way to reconcile the clear-act and reward-to-labor principles.

The clear-act principle suggests that the common law defines acts of possession as some kind of *statement*. As Blackstone said, the acts must be a *declaration* of one's intent to appropriate. . . . [23]

Possession now begins to look even more like something that requires a kind of communication, and the original claim to the property looks like a kind of speech, with the audience composed of all others who might be interested in claiming the object in question. Moreover, some venerable statutory law obligates the acquiring party to *keep on* speaking, lest he lose his title by "adverse possession."

Adverse possession is a common law interpretation of statutes of limitation for actions to recover real property. Suppose I own a lot in the mountains, and some stranger to me, without my permission, builds a house on it, clears the woods, and farms the lot continuously for a given period, say twenty years. During that time, I am entitled to go to court to force him off the lot. But if I have not done so at the end of twenty years, or some other period fixed by statute, not only can I not sue him for recovery of what was my land, but the law recognizes him as the title owner. The doctrine of adverse possession thus operates to transfer property to one who is initially a trespasser if the trespasser's presence is open to everyone, lasts continuously for a given period of time, and if the title owner takes no action to get rid of him during that time.

Here again we seem to have an example of a reward to the useful laborer at the expense of the sluggard. But the doctrine is susceptible to another interpretation as well; it might be designed, not to reward the useful laborer, but to require the owner to assert her right publicly. It requires her to make it clear that she, and not the trespasser, is the person to deal with if anyone should wish to buy the property or use some portion of it. . . .

Possession as the basis of property ownership, then, seems to amount to something like yelling loudly enough to all who may be interested. The first to say, "This is mine," in a way that the public understands, gets the prize, and the law will help him keep it against someone else who says, "No, it is *mine*." But if the original communicator dallies too long and allows the public to believe the interloper, he will find that the interloper has stepped into his shoes and has become the owner.

Similar ideas of the importance of communication, or as it is more commonly called, "notice," are implicit in our recording stat-

23. [2 Commentaries on the Laws of England] 9, 258.

utes and in a variety of other devices that force a property claimant to make a public record of her claims on pain of losing them altogether. Indeed, notice plays a part in the most mundane property-like claims to things that the law does not even recognize as capable of being reduced to ownership. "Would you please save my place?" one says to one's neighbor in the movie line, in order to ensure that others in line know that one is coming back and not relinquishing one's claim. In my home town of Chicago, one may choose to shovel the snow from a parking place on the street, but in order to establish a claim to it one must put a chair or some other object in the cleared space. The useful act of shoveling snow does not speak as unambiguously as the presence of an object that blocks entry.

Why, then, is it so important that property owners make and keep their communications clear? Economists have an answer: Clear titles facilitate trade and minimize resource-wasting conflict. If I am careless about who comes on to a corner of my property, I invite others to make mistakes and to waste their labor on improvements to what I have allowed them to think is theirs. I thus invite a free-for-all over my ambiguously held claims, and I encourage contention, insecurity, and litigation — all of which waste everyone's time and energy and may result in overuse or underuse of resources. But if I keep my property claims clear, others will know that they should deal with me directly if they want to use my property. We can bargain rather than fight; through trade, all items will come to rest in the hands of those who value them most. If property lines are clear, then, anyone who can make better use of my property than I can will buy or rent it from me and turn the property to his better use. In short, we will all be richer when property claims are unequivocal, because that unequivocal status enables property to be traded and used at its highest value.

Thus, it turns out that the common law of first possession, in rewarding the one who communicates a claim, *does* reward useful labor; the useful labor is the very act of speaking clearly and distinctly about one's claims to property. Naturally, this must be in a language that is understood, and the acts of "possession" that communicate a claim will vary according to the audience. Thus, returning to Pierson v. Post, the dissenting judge may well have thought that fox hunters were the only relevant audience for a claim to the fox; they are the only ones who have regular contact with the subject matter. By the same token, the mid-nineteenth-century California courts gave much deference to the mining-camp customs in adjudicating various Gold Rush claims; the Forty-Niners themselves, as those most closely involved with the subject, could best communicate and interpret the signs of property claims and would be particularly well served by a stable system of symbols that would enable them to avoid disputes.

The point, then, is that "acts of possession" are, in the now fashionable term, a "text," and that the common law rewards the author of that text. But, as students of hermeneutics know, the clearest text may have ambiguous subtexts. In connection with the text of first possession, there are several subtexts that are especially worthy of note. One is the implication that the text will be "read" by the relevant audience at the appropriate time. It is not always easy to establish a symbolic structure in which the text of first possession can be "published" at such a time as to be useful to anyone. Once again, Pierson v. Post illustrates the problem that occurs when a clear sign (killing the fox) comes only relatively late in the game, after the relevant parties may have already expended overlapping efforts and embroiled themselves in a dispute. Very similar problems occurred in the whaling industry in the nineteenth century: The courts expended a considerable amount of mental energy in finding signs of "possession" that were comprehensible to whalers from their own customs and that at the same time came early enough in the chase to allow the parties to avoid wasted efforts and the ensuing mutual recriminations.

Some objects of property claims do seem inherently incapable of clear demarcation — ideas, for example. In order to establish ownership of such disembodied items we find it necessary to translate the property claims into sets of secondary symbols that our culture understands. In patent and copyright law, for example, one establishes an entitlement to the expression of an idea by translating it into a written document and going through a registration process — though the unending litigation over ownership of these expressions, and over which expressions can even be subject to patent or copyright, might lead us to conclude that these particular secondary symbolic systems do not always yield widely understood "markings." We also make up secondary symbols for physical objects that would seem to be much easier to mark out than ideas; even property claims in land, that most tangible of things, are now at their most authoritative in the form of written records.

It is expensive to establish and maintain these elaborate structures of secondary symbols, as indeed it may be expensive to establish a structure of primary symbols of possession. The economists have once again performed a useful service in pointing out that there are costs entailed in establishing any property system. These costs might prevent the development of any system at all for some objects, where our need for secure investment and trade is not as great as the cost of creating the necessary symbols of possession.

There is a second and perhaps even more important subtext to the "text" of first possession: the tacit supposition that there is such a thing as a "clear act," unequivocally proclaiming to the universe one's appropriation — that there are in fact unequivocal acts of possession, which any relevant audience will naturally and easily interpret as property claims. Literary theorists have recently written a great deal about the relativity of texts. They have written too much for us to accept uncritically the idea that a "text" about property has a natural meaning independent of some audience constituting an "interpretive community" or independent of a range of other "texts" and cultural artifacts that together form a symbolic system in which a given text must be read. It is not enough, then, for the property claimant to say simply, "It's mine" through some act or gesture; in order for the "statement" to have any force, some relevant world must understand the claim it makes and take that claim seriously.

Thus, in defining the acts of possession that make up a claim to property, the law not only rewards the author of the "text," it also puts an imprimatur on a particular symbolic system and on the audience that uses this system. Audiences that do not understand or accept the symbols are out of luck. . . .

In the history of American territorial expansion, a pointed example of the choice among audiences made by the common law occurred when one group did not play the approved language game and refused to get into the business of publishing or reading the accepted texts about property. The result was one of the most arresting decisions of the early American republic: Johnson v. McIntosh,[49] a John Marshall opinion concerning the validity of opposing claims to land in what is now a large part of Illinois and Indiana. The plaintiffs in this case claimed through Indian tribes, on the basis of deeds made out in the 1770s; the defendants claimed under titles that came from the United States. The Court found for the defendants, holding that the claims through the Indians were invalid, for reasons derived largely from international law rather than from the law of first possession. But tucked away in the case was a first-possession argument that Marshall passed over. The Indians, according to an argument of the claimants from the United States, could not have passed title to the opposing

49. 21 U.S. (8 Wheat.) 543 (1823).

side's predecessors because, "[b]y the law of nature," the Indians themselves had never done acts on the land sufficient to establish property in it. That is to say, the Indians had never really undertaken those acts of possession that give rise to a property right.

Although Marshall based his decision on other grounds, there was indeed something to the argument from the point of view of the common law of first possession. Insofar as the Indian tribes moved from place to place, they left few traces to indicate that they claimed the land (if indeed they did make such claims). From an eighteenth-century political economist's point of view, the results were horrifying. What seemed to be the absence of distinct claims to land among the Indians merely invited disputes, which in turn meant constant disruption of productive activity and dissipation of energy in warfare. Uncertainty as to claims also meant that no one would make any productive use of the land because there is little incentive to plant when there is no reasonable assurance that one will be in possession of the land at harvest time. From this classical economic perspective, the Indians' alleged indifference to well-defined property lines in land was part and parcel of what seemed to be their relatively unproductive use of the earth.

Now it may well be that North American Indian tribes were not so indifferent to marking out landed property as eighteenth-century European commentators supposed. . . . Or it may be that at least some tribes found landed property less important to their security than other forms of property and thus felt no need to assert claims to property in land. But however anachronistic the *Johnson* parties' (ultimately mooted) argument may now seem, it is a particularly striking example of the relativity of the "text" of possession to the interpretative community for that text. It is doubtful whether the claims of any nomadic population could ever meet the common law requirements for establishing property in land. Thus, the audience presupposed by the common law of first possession is an agrarian or a commercial people — a people whose activities with respect to the objects around them require an unequivocal delineation of lasting control so that those objects can be managed and traded.

But perhaps the deepest aspect of the common law text of possession lies in the attitude that this text strikes with respect to the relationship between human beings and nature. At least some Indians professed bewilderment at the concept of owning the land. Indeed they prided themselves on not marking the land but rather on moving lightly through it, living with the land and with its creatures as members of the same family rather than as strangers who visited only to conquer the objects of nature. The doctrine of first possession, quite to the contrary, reflects the attitude that human beings are outsiders to nature. It gives the earth and its creatures over to those who mark them so clearly as to transform them, so that no one else will mistake them for unsubdued nature.

We may admire nature and enjoy wildness, but those sentiments find little resonance in the doctrine of first possession. Its texts are those of cultivation, manufacture, and development. We cannot have our fish both loose and fast, as Melville might have said,[61] and the common law of first possession makes a choice. The common law gives preference to those who convince the world that they have caught the fish and hold it fast. This may be a reward to useful labor, but it is more precisely the articulation of a specific vocabulary within a structure of symbols approved and understood by a commercial people. It is this commonly understood and shared set of symbols that gives significance and form to what might seem the quintessentially individualistic act: the claim that one has, by "possession," separated for oneself property from the great commons of unowned things.

NOTES AND QUESTIONS ON FIRST POSSESSION

1. Rose presents the meaning of "possession" as culturally relative. Is it? Is Sugden more accurate when he suggests that some indicia of ownership are "found everywhere"? Consider blazes cut into trees by the Native American hunters, whose practices are described in the selection from Demsetz, supra p. 135: Would those be recognized as property claims everywhere? What about a wall or a fence? Are these universally recognizable assertions of ownership? If so, would this mean that possession is not culturally relative after all?

2. Even if one supposes that the specific indicia of property are relative, how do those indicia begin and evolve? Who thought of putting a chair in the shoveled-out parking place and how did others decipher its meaning? Are there similarities between these signaling devices and the more general evolution of language? Is there some "deep structure" of property analogous to the "deep

61. . . . Moby-Dick, ch. 89 ("Fast-Fish and Loose-Fish") (1st ed. London, 1851). . . .

structure" that some linguists (notably Noam Chomsky) detect in language and grammar? See also the selections on informal property rights, infra Chapter 6.

3. Rose slides easily from visible signals of property to "artificial" systems of property designation, such as recording systems. Are these really so similar? Might the intervention of legal institutions make the latter "marking" devices differ with respect to costs, effectiveness, and responsiveness to change?

4. Does Rose overly romanticize Native Americans' relationships to nature? Lewis and Clark's journals reported that Plains Indians routinely killed far more animals than they ate (for example, by herding buffalo over cliffs), and deliberately set fire to tall pine trees to watch them explode. More recent historical work confirms that Indians used fire extensively as a wildlife management agent, and apparently hunted some prehistoric animals to extinction. See, for instance, Stephen J. Pyne, Fire in America: A Cultural History of Wildland and Rural Fire 71-76 (1982); Shepard Krech, The Ecological Indian: Myth and History (1999). Does all this mean that Indians had a more callous and instrumental attitude toward nature than Rose suggests? If so, is it fair to suggest that the common law of property has a uniquely instrumental and domineering attitude toward nature?

5. An academic literature loosely described as "ecofeminism" also explores the relationship of nature to property. A classic work is Carolyn Merchant, The Death of Nature (1980), arguing that the post-Renaissance development of male-dominated, rationalistic, scientific thought has contributed to an estrangement from nature in modern Western thinking; interestingly enough, Merchant identifies rationalistic science with capitalist property. Are science, capitalism, and property all tied together in an instrumental and domineering attitude toward nature? Or is the "conquest of nature" simply part of what all people do in their use of natural resources? See James R. McGoodwin, Crisis in the World's Fisheries (1990), detailing attitudes and practices in small fishing communities around the world; see also Bonnie McCay & James Acheson, The Question of the Commons (1990), in which several essays deal with indigenous practices and attitudes about wildlife.

6. There is an extensive literature on how European colonists acquired, by conquest and otherwise, the lands of indigenous peoples on other continents. See, e.g., Eric Kades, The Dark Side of Efficiency: *Johnson v. M'Intosh* and the Expropriation of American Indian Lands, 148 U. Penn. L. Rev. 1065 (2000) (arguing that colonists sought to minimize the costs they incurred when dispossessing natives); Robert A. Williams Jr., The American Indian in

Western Legal Thought: The Discourses of Conquest (1990); and, infra p. 321, the selection by Stuart Banner on the English dispossession of the Maori in New Zealand. See generally Carol M. Rose, Property and Expropriation, 2000 Utah L. Rev. 1 (analyzing different types of expropriations).

7. A rule that awards ownership to a first possessor may trigger a duplicative or otherwise wasteful race to be first. How might legal rules be shaped to minimize this problem? See the selection by Posner, supra p. 54, and Dean Lueck, The Rule of First Possession and the Design of the Law, 38 J.L. & Econ. 414 (1995).

8. Under what circumstances is possession inadequate to warrant conferral of paramount title? A thief has possession of stolen goods, but not ownership of them in a legal sense. When a patron checks her coat in a restaurant, she does not relinquish ownership of it to the restaurant (which is merely a bailee). For discussion of how some leading legal minds have analyzed the relevance of the possessor's intentions in these sorts of contexts, see Richard A. Posner, Savigny, Holmes, and the Law and Economics of Possession, 86 Va. L. Rev. 535 (2000). For a comparative perspective, see James Gordley & Ugo Mattei, Protecting Possession, 44 Am. J. Comp. L. 293 (1996).

Property Rules, Liability Rules, and Adverse Possession*

Thomas W. Merrill

The law of adverse possession tends to be regarded as a quiet backwater. Both judicial opinions and leading treatises treat the legal doctrine as settled. The theory underlying the doctrine, although routinely discussed in the opening weeks of first-year property courses, is only rarely aired in the law reviews any more. Indeed, the most frequently cited articles on adverse possession date from the 1930s and earlier. Perhaps most tellingly, adverse possession seems to have completely escaped the attention of the modern law and economics movement — almost a sure sign of obscurity in today's legal-academic world.

Nevertheless, two recent events — one academic, the other judicial — are sufficiently challenging to our conventional under-

*Source: 79 Nw. U. L. Rev. 1122-1128, 1133-1135, 1152-1153 (1984-1985).

standing of adverse possession that they deserve comment. The academic event is the publication of a law review article by Professor Richard Helmholz of the University of Chicago concerning the state of mind that a possessor must have before he can obtain title by adverse possession.[3] Earlier treatments of this subject tended to proceed normatively, asserting the "correct" rule based on considerations of policy. Helmholz, however, is interested in determining what state of mind is actually demanded by courts before they will award title by adverse possession. To this end, he has surveyed "the bulk" of all reported cases dealing with adverse possession decided since 1966. His conclusion is rather startling. Although academic commentators generally argue that the subjective mental state of the possessor should be irrelevant, Helmholz finds that "where courts allow adverse possession to ripen into title, bad faith on the part of the possessor seldom exists. Where the possessor knows that he is trespassing, valid title does not accrue to him simply by the passage of years."

If nothing else, Helmholz's study casts doubt on whether we should take the common law test for acquiring title by adverse possession at face value. According to the common law, adverse possession requires, in addition to the running of the statute of limitations, that the possession be (1) actual, (2) open and notorious, (3) exclusive, (4) continuous, and (5) hostile under a claim of right. The common law test does not demand subjective good faith belief on the part of the possessor that he is entitled to the property. Nevertheless, it appears that judges and juries rather consistently manipulate the five standard elements in such a way as to award title to the possessor who entered the property in good faith, i.e., without actual knowledge of the paramount title of the true owner, and to deny title to the possessor who entered in bad faith, i.e., with actual knowledge of the paramount title. Subjective good faith is, then, an unstated sixth element — one which can be overcome perhaps if the equities strongly cut the other way, but a presumptive element all the same. This conclusion, which Helmholz convincingly demonstrates, suggests the need to reassess the common law doctrine.

The judicial event which challenges our traditional understanding of adverse possession is a decision of the California Supreme Court, Warsaw v. Chicago Metallic Ceilings, Inc.[10] con-

---

3. Helmholz, Adverse Possession and Subjective Intent, 61 Wash. U. L.Q. 331 (1983).

10. 35 Cal. 3d 564, 676 P.2d 584, 199 Cal. Rptr. 773 (1984).

cerning a first cousin of adverse possession — prescriptive easements.[11] The plaintiff had constructed a large commercial building with a narrow driveway that left insufficient room for delivery trucks to turn around and back up to its loading dock. Consequently, trucks regularly drove onto a vacant portion of the defendant's land next door in order to make this maneuver. The plaintiff was aware of the problem, and tried several times, without success, to purchase an easement from the defendant. Later, the defendant decided to develop its land, erecting a pad of earth (and, after the plaintiff was denied a preliminary injunction, a warehouse) at the point where the trucks turned onto its property. The plaintiff sued, contending that the construction interfered with an easement it had acquired by prescription. The trial court sustained this contention, finding that the plaintiff had used the subject property for the statutory period of five years, and had satisfied all of the other elements necessary for prescription. The defendant was ordered to remove the pad of earth and the structure.

What is significant about *Warsaw* is the debate about remedies which took place on appeal. The court of appeal, although sustaining the finding that the plaintiff had satisfied the requirements for prescription, declared that the plaintiff could obtain a prescriptive easement and force the defendant to remove the improvements, only if the *plaintiff* agreed to pay the defendant the fair market value of the easement thus acquired. The California Supreme Court likewise upheld the finding that the plaintiff had satisfied the requirements for prescription, but overturned this novel form of relief.

The significance of the debate in *Warsaw* emerges in terms of the typology of legal rules introduced by Calabresi and Melamed. Traditionally, adverse possession and prescription have reflected what Calabresi and Melamed call a system of "property rules." That is, before judgment the true owner's (TO's) interest is protected by a property rule: no one — including the adverse possessor (AP) — can take it from the TO without his consent. After entry of judgment awarding the AP title by adverse possession, the *AP's* interest is protected by a property rule: no one — including the TO — can take it from the AP without his consent. The court of appeal's decision in *Warsaw*, however, suggests a different kind of

---

11. Prescriptive easements involve nonpossessory *use* of property which ripens into an easement, as opposed to possession of property which ripens into a fee simple. 7 R. Powell, Real Property ¶1026 (P. Rohan ed. 1977). Generally speaking, the same legal requirements apply to both adverse possession and prescriptive easements, although the nonpossessory nature of an easement generally means that the continuity and exclusivity elements must be interpreted differently.

scheme. Before judgment, the TO's entitlement would be protected, as before, by a property rule. But after judgment, the entitlement would remain with the TO, protected now by what Calabresi and Melamed call a "liability rule." In other words, after judgment the TO would keep the property, but the AP could take it away from the TO without his consent by paying the TO the fair market value of the property taken.

In what follows, I will suggest that the research of Professor Helmholz and the remedial innovation proposed in *Warsaw* are related. After all, *Warsaw* is, in Professor Helmholz's terminology, a clear case of bad faith — there is no question that the plaintiff knew that its trucks were encroaching on land belonging to the defendant. In light of Professor Helmholz's study, therefore, it is somewhat surprising that the California courts ruled in favor of the plaintiff in the first place. This may explain why a majority of the judges who heard the *Warsaw* case, even if they felt constrained to hold that the plaintiff had established an easement by prescription, were sympathetic to the idea of making the plaintiff pay for the easement so acquired — a liability rule. More generally, it suggests that liability rules may be an appropriate mediating device between the traditional policies supporting the institution of adverse possession — all of which apply whether the possessor is acting in good faith or in bad faith — and the evident reluctance of courts to "reward" bad faith possessors by giving the AP an entitlement protected by a property rule. . . .

I. The Theory of Adverse Possession . . .

The assignment of entitlements in the period before the statute of limitations runs need not detain us for long. There is no question about who gets the entitlement during this period: Courts uniformly and automatically award it to the TO. The reasons for this are generally the same as those which support a system of private property rights, as opposed to one which recognizes only possessory, i.e., squatter's rights. First, there is a strong economic justification. If the state did not protect title but only the fact of possession, no one would ever be secure in leaving valuable things unattended or entrusting them to someone else through lease or bailment.[17] The result would undoubtedly be over-investment in security devices, and under-investment in the cultivation and de-

---

17. See 2 W. Blackstone, Commentaries ch. 1 (1766).

velopment of natural resources. In addition, there is a derivative justification based upon civic values: Cultural diversity, countervailing centers of political power, and independent institutions of scholarly inquiry may require larger accumulations of private wealth than would be possible under a system of mere possessory rights.[18] Finally, and again derivatively, there is a justification based on human personality: Accumulated material wealth may be important to an individual's identity and plans for the future, and property rights in material things protect these interests.[19] All of this, with varying degrees of emphasis on different aspects of the justification for property rights, has rarely been a matter of controversy, at least within the Anglo-American legal tradition.[20]

The problem comes in determining who should get the entitlement to the property *after* the statute of limitations runs. Clearly, courts often award the entitlement to the possessor rather than to the title holder during this period — that's what adverse possession is all about. But as Professor Helmholz's study reminds us, courts may also grant the entitlement to the TO. Given the strong case for maintaining a system of property rights, a threshold question is why we are *ever* justified in shifting the entitlement from the TO to the AP after the passage of a number of years. Surprisingly, there is very little systematic discussion of this fundamental issue in the legal literature. Nevertheless, it is possible, with some effort, to glean from that literature four different, and yet essentially complementary, rationales for the institution of adverse possession[:] ... the problem of lost evidence, the desirability of quieting titles, the interest in discouraging sleeping owners, and the reliance interests of APs and interested third persons. The important thing to note about these rationales is that, at least at the level of general justification, they are mutually supportive. One can like some and dislike others, or one can subscribe to all four, and the result is still the same — the entitlement should be transferred to the AP after the statute of limitations runs. Indeed, standing alone some of these rationales may appear too weak to overcome the presumption in favor of a system of property rights rather than

18. See M. Friedman, Capitalism and Freedom ch. 1 (1962); Reich, The New Property, 73 Yale L.J. 733 (1964).

19. Cf. Radin, Property and Personhood, 34 Stan. L. Rev. 957 (1982) (contrasting property for personhood and "fetishistic," i.e., purely accumulative, property).

20. Even the Marxist critique of private property advocates state or collectively owned property — not a system of possessory rights — as an alternative. As Demsetz has pointed out, state or collectively owned property is in many respects more like private property than possessory rights.

of possessory rights. But taken together, they represent a rather imposing case for transferring the entitlement to the AP after a significant period of time has elapsed.

All of this makes Professor Helmholz's study the more puzzling. The traditional theories suggest that the entitlement should be transferred to the AP after the expiration of the limitations period, and provide no basis for distinguishing between the good faith and bad faith possessor. Yet Professor Helmholz's findings about the importance of subjective intent cast considerable doubt on whether the traditional theories provide a complete account of the relevant concerns. Of course, his findings do not necessarily mean that the proclivities of judges and juries who decide adverse possession cases are correct. One could argue that judges and juries, absorbed in an ex post analysis of the facts of particular controversies, simply have failed to appreciate the strength of the systemic justifications for the institution of adverse possession. But it is probably unwise to denounce the voice of collective experience. A better approach would be to ask whether the inclination of the courts has some justification of its own — a justification which perhaps the legal literature has overlooked. If such a countervailing rationale exists, then the question of assigning the entitlement after the statute of limitations runs may not be so simple after all.

Actually, it is not hard to identify a countervailing concern: the interest in punishing or deterring those who engage in purely coercive transfers of property. This concern can be stated in terms of incentives. Purely coercive transfers of property are socially undesirable because they undermine incentives for productive activity, stimulate excessive precautionary measures, and generally destroy the fabric of human relations. What then will be the effect on the incidence of this activity if the dispossessor can, after the passage of a certain period of time, obtain title to the property? Obtaining title constitutes a powerful reward for such a coerced transfer. With title, the dispossessor no longer has to fear legal retribution from the TO (or the state), and can develop, sell, subdivide, or borrow against the property at will. One would expect a potential dispossessor, in calculating whether to seize someone else's property, to balance this potential reward against the probability of apprehension and the severity of the penalty if caught. If we assume any degree of rationality at all (and decisions about taking property are generally "rational," i.e., economically motivated) then the potential reward, even if it is several years in coming, should lead to a higher incidence of coerced transfers than we would expect to find in the absence of such a reward.

In the period before the statute of limitations runs, the concern with punishing or deterring coerced transfers is much in evidence. Intentional dispossession of property — whether in the form of trespass or theft — generally is regarded as a felony punishable by imprisonment. Moreover, the TO has an impressive array of civil remedies to recover the property or its value in money, often fortified by statutory provisions for multiple or punitive damages. After the statute runs, however, the concern with punishing or deterring coerced transfers disappears; or at least it *seems* to disappear in the common law doctrine and traditional legal commentary on adverse possession.

For present purposes, what is especially promising about the interest in punishing or deterring coerced transfers is that it provides a basis for distinguishing between the good faith and bad faith possessor, and thus for explaining the findings of Professor Helmholz. . . .

. . . I suggested that courts manipulate the common law doctrine of adverse possession in order to punish or deter those who intentionally dispossess others of their property. A less drastic means of achieving a similar end would be to apply a liability rule in cases of bad faith possession. A rule of limited indemnification would in effect impose a fine on bad faith dispossessors equal to the value of the property at the time of original entry. Squatters and thieves would know that, even if they could obtain title to property after the passage of the statute of limitations and the satisfaction of the common law's five elements, they would have to pay for their gain. Consequently, the incentives to engage in coerced transfers would be reduced.

There are several advantages to reflecting our disapproval of the bad faith possessor at the stage of remedy rather than entitlement. First, in cases where the TO has disappeared or the dispossession occurred so long ago that evidence of the mental state of the possessor has been lost or forgotten, an action for indemnification would simply fail, leaving the main purposes of the system of adverse possession intact. Conversely, if subjective bad faith were an express requirement for obtaining title by adverse possession, the difficulties of proof associated with this element could interfere measurably with the functions of adverse possession.

Second, by limiting the issue of subjective intent to the remedial stage, we would strengthen the extent to which APs and interested third parties could rely on an AP's continued possession of the property. Consider the case, probably not that unusual, where the AP has some inkling that the title rests in someone else — in other words, where the evidence of bad faith is ambiguous —

and yet the TO has not filed an action to regain possession. If the subjective intent of the AP were a relevant issue at the stage of entitlement, then the AP would face considerable uncertainty. If he should go ahead and improve or develop the property, he could have his entire interest wiped out by a subsequent action by the TO for possession. However, if the issue of subjective intent were relevant only to the question of remedy, the worst that could happen in this situation would be that the AP would have to pay the fair market value as of the date of original entry (plus prejudgment interest). This should encourage APs to improve and develop the property, safe in the knowledge that they would be assured at least continued possession of the property and the value of the improvements. In addition, interested third parties (who do not know whether the AP acquired the property in good faith or bad faith) should have greater confidence that the AP will remain in possession.

Finally, and perhaps most importantly, if courts knew that the bad faith possessor would be faced with an action for indemnification, they might not feel compelled to manipulate the traditional common law doctrine in order to "punish" those who acquired the property in bad faith, and "reward" those who acquired it innocently. Adoption of the limited indemnification requirement would permit the basic entitlement determination rule to take on a more mechanical cast, reducing the need for litigation to establish title by adverse possession, at least in cases where the TO has disappeared or there is no question that the AP acted in good faith. Admittedly, there is an element of speculation here. But it stands to reason that judges and juries would be much more willing to apply a mechanical rule at the stage of entitlement if they knew that there was a way of "doing justice" at the stage of remedy. Certainly, it is hard to imagine that this reform would produce greater uncertainty than exists today, when the official doctrine says one thing and the results reached by the courts say another.

NOTES AND QUESTIONS ON ADVERSE POSSESSION

1. Why are judges and juries generally unsympathetic to would-be adverse possessors who knew of, or believed in, the true owner's superior title? In particular, how much do you suppose judges and juries are influenced by what Merrill identifies as the economic inefficiencies of coerced transfer? In their hostility to

such adverse possessors, are they simply indifferent to the "desert" theory, that is, the idea that property should reward useful labor?

2. Merrill lists several rationales against shifting ownership: securing titles, encouraging investment, diffusing political power, and protecting personal projects. Can you think of ways in which some or all of these same rationales speak for adverse possession? Is this an instance in which, as the Critical Legal Studies scholars assert more generally, the legal rationales are indeterminate? Does Helmholz's study of the ways judges and juries actually behave support the charge of legal indeterminacy?

3. Doesn't Merrill's proposed solution encourage willful trespass? Note that in the *Warsaw* case that serves as his central example, the plaintiff would be entitled to "buy" an easement in the end, even though the defendant refused to sell. Is this solution simply a variation on eminent domain, which in most jurisdictions is only granted for projects that have an arguable public purpose? See the dissent in the much-cited Boomer v. Atlantic Cement Co., 309 N.Y.S.2d 312 (N.Y. 1970), and the selections by Calabresi and Melamed, infra p. 233, and Krier and Schwab, infra p. 249.

4. Suppose that the true owner (TO1) sells to a second owner (TO2) after an adverse possessor (AP) has trespassed on a portion of the property for the statutory period (so that under the Merrill proposal AP acquires an interest in the property but has to pay compensation). Who should receive the compensation, TO1 or TO2? On what does your answer depend? Does this problem suggest why courts do not necessarily find liability rules an attractive alternative to property rules?

5. John G. Sprankling, in An Environmental Critique of Adverse Possession, 79 Cornell L. Rev. 816 (1994), contends that a prodevelopment nineteenth-century ideology pervades the traditional doctrines of adverse possession law. To deter the overdevelopment of rural areas, he urges that privately owned wildlands be exempt from adverse possession. In light of the rationales for adverse possession that Merrill identifies, is Sprankling's proposed reform sound? Conversely, should the rights of squatters in urban areas be bolstered? For a review of squatters' entitlements around the globe, see Brian Gardiner, Squatters' Rights and Adverse Possession, 9 Ind. Intl. & Comp. L. Rev. 119 (1997).

6. Do the policies that underlie statutes of limitations for the recovery of property counsel against curing unjust expropriations that occurred many decades in the past? If so, why did Congress enact in 1946 the Indian Claims Commission Act, which authorized tribes to seek compensation from the federal government for ex-

propriations occurring in previous centuries? How strong a claim (and against whom) do the descendants of nineteenth-century slaves have for reparations? See, e.g., Derrick Bell, Jr., And We Are Not Saved 123-139 (1987); Boris Bittker, The Case for Black Reparations (1973).

7. Is there reason to think that the doctrine of adverse possession is simply an artifact of our untidy system of land records? Could the whole doctrine be eliminated with more strict recording requirements, as is the case in jurisdictions that rely on the Torrens system of land registration? What problems might arise? For some of these, see Rose, Crystals and Mud, infra p. 304.

Chapter 4

The Coase Theorem and Its Limitations

The Problem of Social Cost*

Ronald H. Coase

I. The Problem to Be Examined

This paper is concerned with those actions of business firms which have harmful effects on others. The standard example is that of a factory the smoke from which has harmful effects on those occupying neighbouring properties. The economic analysis of such a situation has usually proceeded in terms of a divergence between the private and social product of the factory, in which economists have largely followed the treatment of Pigou in The Economics of Welfare. The conclusions to which this kind of analysis seems to have led most economists is that it would be desirable to make the owner of the factory liable for the damage caused to those injured by the smoke, or alternatively, to place a tax on the factory owner varying with the amount of smoke produced and equivalent in money terms to the damage it would cause, or finally, to exclude the factory from residential districts (and presumably from other areas in which the emission of smoke would have harmful effects on others). It is my contention that the suggested courses of action are inappropriate, in that they lead to results which are not necessarily, or even usually, desirable.

*Source: 3 J.L. & Econ. 1-3, 6-8, 13-19 (1960).

II. The Reciprocal Nature of the Problem

The traditional approach has tended to obscure the nature of the choice that has to be made. The question is commonly thought of as one in which A inflicts harm on B and what has to be decided is: How should we restrain A? But this is wrong. We are dealing with a problem of a reciprocal nature. To avoid the harm to B would inflict harm on A. The real question that has to be decided is: Should A be allowed to harm B or should B be allowed to harm A? The problem is to avoid the more serious harm. I instanced in my previous article[2] the case of a confectioner the noise and vibrations from whose machinery disturbed a doctor in his work. To avoid harming the doctor would inflict harm on the confectioner. The problem posed by this case was essentially whether it was worth while, as a result of restricting the methods of production which could be used by the confectioner, to secure more doctoring at the cost of a reduced supply of confectionery products. Another example is afforded by the problem of straying cattle which destroy crops on neighbouring land. If it is inevitable that some cattle will stray, an increase in the supply of meat can only be obtained at the expense of a decrease in the supply of crops. The nature of the choice is clear: meat or crops. What answer should be given is, of course, not clear unless we know the value of what is obtained as well as the value of what is sacrificed to obtain it. To give another example, Professor George J. Stigler instances the contamination of a stream.[3] If we assume that the harmful effect of the pollution is that it kills the fish, the question to be decided is: Is the value of the fish lost greater or less than the value of the product which the contamination of the stream makes possible? It goes almost without saying that this problem has to be looked at in total *and* at the margin.

III. The Pricing System with Liability for Damage

I propose to start my analysis by examining a case in which most economists would presumably agree that the problem would be solved in a completely satisfactory manner: when the damaging business has to pay for all damage caused *and* the pricing system

2. Coase, The Federal Communications Commission, 2 J.L. & Econ. 26-27 (1959).

3. G.J. Stigler, The Theory of Price 105 (1952).

works smoothly (strictly this means that the operation of a pricing system is without cost).

A good example of the problem under discussion is afforded by the case of straying cattle which destroy crops growing on neighbouring land. Let us suppose that a farmer and a cattle-raiser are operating on neighbouring properties. Let us further suppose that, without any fencing between the propeties, an increase in the size of the cattle-raiser's herd increases the total damage to the farmer's crops. What happens to the marginal damage as the size of the herd increases is another matter. This depends on whether the cattle tend to follow one another or to roam side by side, on whether they tend to be more or less restless as the size of the herd increases and on other similar factors. For my immediate purpose, it is immaterial what assumption is made about marginal damage as the size of the herd increases.

To simplify the argument, I propose to use an arithmetical example. I shall assume that the annual cost of fencing the farmer's property is $9 and that the price of the crop is $1 per ton. Also, I assume that the relation between the number of cattle in the herd and the annual crop loss is as follows:

Number in Herd (Steers)	Annual Crop Loss (Tons)	Crop Loss per Additional Steer (Tons)
1	1	1
2	3	2
3	6	3
4	10	4

Given that the cattle-raiser is liable for the damage caused, the additional annual cost imposed on the cattle-raiser if he increased his herd from, say, 2 to 3 steers is $3 and in deciding on the size of the herd, he will take this into account along with his other costs. That is, he will not increase the size of the herd unless the value of the additional meat produced (assuming that the cattle-raiser slaughters the cattle), is greater than the additional costs that this will entail, including the value of the additional crops destroyed. Of course, if, by the employment of dogs, herdsmen, aeroplanes, mobile radio and other means, the amount of damage can be reduced, these means will be adopted when their cost is less than the value of the crop which they prevent being lost. Given that the annual cost of fencing is $9, the cattle-raiser who wished to have a herd with 4 steers or more would pay for fencing to be erected and maintained, assuming that other means of attaining the same end would not do so more cheaply. When the fence is erected, the marginal cost due to the liability for damage becomes zero, except to the extent that an increase in the size of the herd necessitates a stronger and therefore more expensive fence because more steers are liable to lean against it at the same time. But, of course, it may be cheaper for the cattle-raiser not to fence and to pay for the damaged crops, as in my arithmetical example, with 3 or fewer steers. . . .

IV.   The Pricing System with No Liability for Damage

I now turn to the case in which, although the pricing system is assumed to work smoothly (that is, costlessly), the damaging business is not liable for any of the damage which it causes. This business does not have to make a payment to those damaged by its actions. I propose to show that the allocation of resources will be the same in this case as it was when the damaging business was liable for damage caused. As I showed in the previous case that the allocation of resources was optimal, it will not be necessary to repeat this part of the argument.

I return to the case of the farmer and the cattle-raiser. The farmer would suffer increased damage to his crop as the size of the herd increased. Suppose that the size of the cattle-raiser's herd is 3 steers (and that this is the size of the herd that would be maintained if crop damage was not taken into account). Then the farmer would be willing to pay up to $3 if the cattle-raiser would reduce his herd to 2 steers, up to $5 if the herd were reduced to 1 steer and would pay up to $6 if cattle-raising was abandoned. The cattle-raiser would therefore receive $3 from the farmer if he kept 2 steers instead of 3. This $3 foregone is therefore part of the cost incurred in keeping the third steer. Whether the $3 is a payment which the cattle-raiser has to make if he adds the third steer to his herd (which it would be if the cattle-raiser was liable to the farmer for damage caused to the crop) or whether it is a sum of money which he would have received if he did not keep a third steer (which it would be if the cattle-raiser was not liable to the farmer for damage caused to the crop) does not affect the final result. In both cases $3 is part of the cost of adding a third steer, to be included along with the other costs. If the increase in the value of production in cattle-raising through increasing the size of the herd from 2 to 3 is greater than the additional costs that have to be incurred (including the $3 damage to crops), the size of the herd will be increased. Otherwise, it will not. The size of the herd will be the same whether the cattle-raiser is liable for the damage caused to the crop or not.

It may be argued that the assumed starting point — a herd of 3 steers — was arbitrary. And this is true. But the farmer would not wish to pay to avoid crop damage which the cattle-raiser would not be able to cause. For example, the maximum annual payment which the farmer could be induced to pay could not exceed $9, the annual cost of fencing. And the farmer would only be willing to pay this sum if it did not reduce his earnings to a level that would cause him to abandon cultivation of this particular tract of land. Furthermore, the farmer would only be willing to pay this amount if he believed that, in the absence of any payment by him, the size of the herd maintained by the cattle-raiser would be 4 or more steers. Let us assume that this is the case. Then the farmer would be willing to pay up to $3 if the cattle-raiser would reduce his herd to 3 steers, up to $6 if the herd were reduced to 2 steers, up to $8 if one steer only were kept and up to $9 if cattle-raising were abandoned. It will be noticed that the change in the starting point has not altered the amount which would accrue to the cattle-raiser if he reduced the size of his herd by any given amount. It is still true that the cattle-raiser could receive an additional $3 from the farmer if he agreed to reduce his herd from 3 steers to 2 and that the $3 represents the value of the crop that would be destroyed by adding the third steer to the herd. Although a different belief on the part of the farmer (whether justified or not) about the size of the herd that the cattle-raiser would maintain in the absence of payments from him may affect the total payment he can be induced to pay, it is not true that this different belief would have any effect on the size of the herd that the cattle-raiser will actually keep. This will be the same as it would be if the cattle-raiser had to pay for damage caused by his cattle, since a receipt forgone of a given amount is the equivalent of a payment of the same amount.

It might be thought that it would pay the cattle-raiser to increase his herd above the size that he would wish to maintain once a bargain had been made, in order to induce the farmer to make a larger total payment. And this may be true. It is similar in nature to the action of the farmer (when the cattle-raiser was liable for damage) in cultivating land on which, as a result of an agreement with the cattle-raiser, planting would subsequently be abandoned (including land which would not be cultivated at all in the absence of cattle-raising). But such manoeuvres are preliminaries to an agreement and do not affect the long-run equilibrium position, which is the same whether or not the cattle-raiser is held responsible for the crop damage brought about by his cattle.

It is necessary to know whether the damaging business is liable or not for damage caused since without the establishment of this initial delimitation of rights there can be no market transactions to transfer and recombine them. But the ultimate result (which maximizes the value of production) is independent of the legal position if the pricing system is assumed to work without cost.

V.   The Problem Illustrated Anew ...

Judges have to decide on legal liability but this should not confuse economists about the nature of the economic problem involved. In the case of the cattle and the crops, it is true that there would be no crop damage without the cattle. It is equally true that there would be no crop damage without the crops. The doctor's work would not have been disturbed if the confectioner had not worked his machinery; but the machinery would have disturbed no one if the doctor had not set up his consulting room in that particular place. . . . If we are to discuss the problem in terms of causation, both parties cause the damage. If we are to attain an optimum allocation of resources, it is therefore desirable that both parties should take the harmful effect (the nuisance) into account in deciding on their course of action. It is one of the beauties of a smoothly operating pricing system that, as has already been explained, the fall in the value of production due to the harmful effect would be a cost for both parties. . . .

. . . [I]t has to be remembered that the immediate question faced by the courts is *not* what shall be done by whom *but* who has the legal right to do what. It is always possible to modify by transactions on the market the initial legal delimitation of rights. And, of course, if such market transactions are costless, such a rearrangement of rights will always take place if it would lead to an increase in the value of production.

VI.   The Cost of Market Transactions Taken into Account

The argument has proceeded up to this point on the assumption (explicit in Sections III and IV and tacit in Section V) that there were no costs involved in carrying out market transactions. This is, of course, a very unrealistic assumption. In order to carry out a market transaction it is necessary to discover who it is that one wishes to deal with, to inform people that one wishes to deal and on what terms, to conduct negotiations leading up to a bargain, to draw up the contract, to undertake the inspection needed to make sure that the terms of the contract are being observed, and so on. These operations are often extremely costly, sufficiently costly at any rate to prevent many transactions that would be carried out in a world in which the pricing system worked without cost.

In earlier sections, when dealing with the problem of the re-arrangement of legal rights through the market, it was argued that such a rearrangement would be made through the market when-ever this would lead to an increase in the value of production. But this assumed costless market transactions. Once the costs of carry-ing out market transactions are taken into account it is clear that such a rearrangement of rights will only be undertaken when the increase in the value of production consequent upon the rearrange-ment is greater than the costs which would be involved in bringing it about. When it is less, the granting of an injunction (or the knowledge that it would be granted) or the liability to pay dam-ages may result in an activity being discontinued (or may prevent its being started) which would be undertaken if market transac-tions were costless. In these conditions the initial delimitation of legal rights does have an effect on the efficiency with which the economic system operates. One arrangement of rights may bring about a greater value of production than any other. But unless this is the arrangement of rights established by the legal system, the costs of reaching the same result by altering and combining rights through the market may be so great that this optimal arrangement of rights, and the greater value of production which it would bring, may never be achieved. . . .

The discussion of the problem of harmful effects in this section (when the costs of market transactions are taken into account) is extremely inadequate. But at least it has made clear that the prob-lem is one of choosing the appropriate social arrangement for deal-ing with the harmful effects. All solutions have costs and there is no reason to suppose that government regulation is called for sim-ply because the problem is not well handled by the market or the firm. Satisfactory views on policy can only come from a patient study of how, in practice, the market, firms and governments han-dle the problem of harmful effects. Economists need to study the work of the broker in bringing parties together, the effectiveness of restrictive covenants, the problems of the large-scale real-estate development company, the operation of Government zoning and other regulating activities. It is my belief that economists, and policy-makers generally, have tended to over-estimate the advantages which come from governmental regulation. But this belief, even if justified, does not do more than suggest that government regulation should be curtailed. It does not tell us where the boundary line should be drawn. This, it seems to me, has to come from a detailed investigation of the actual results of handling the problem in different ways. . . .

NOTES AND QUESTIONS ON THE COASE THEOREM

1. Although The Problem of Social Cost received little acclaim in the mid-1960s, by the 1970s and 1980s it had become the most cited article on law. It is regarded as the genesis of two highly influential concepts: the "Coase Theorem" and "transaction costs" (although neither phrase appears in the article). Coase's major writings are collected in Ronald Coase, The Firm, the Market, and the Law (1988), a corpus of work that won him the Nobel Prize in Economic Science in 1991. Before being influenced by the pages that follow, try to articulate Coase's central, and counterintuitive, insight in The Problem of Social Cost.

2. Is the practical upshot of Coase's analysis that legal decisions are unimportant? Or rather that, when comparing alternative rules, one should focus on the relative levels of transaction costs that parties would have to bear in managing the entitlement and in bargaining to transfer it? Coase himself has spoken on the matter: "The world of zero transaction costs has often been described as a Coasian world. Nothing could be further from the truth. It is the world of modern economic theory, one which I was hoping to persuade economists to leave." The Firm, the Market, and the Law 174 (1988). In effect, Coase revealed the importance of transaction costs by assuming them away, much as economists came to better understand the significance of restraints on trade by devising models of perfect competition.

3. The *strong* version of the Coase Theorem, sometimes called the "invariance" proposition, asserts that, in a world of zero transaction costs, a change in legal rules would have no effect on the allocation of resources. To use Coase's example, the imposition of liability for cattle trespass would not cause cattle-raisers to reduce the size of their herds or to install more fencing. It is now universally agreed that the strong version of the theorem is untenable because changes in law may have "wealth effects." For instance,

the imposition of liability on ranchers might result in a reduction of the wealth of individuals who own land especially suited for ranching. Because of these wealth effects, an allocation of resources that had previously been efficient might no longer be so. For example, if owners of ranchland were to be the primary purchasers of cowboy boots, a drop in their wealth would lead to a drop in the optimal output of cowboy boots. On the general point, see Harold Demsetz, When Does the Rule of Liability Matter?, 1 J. Legal Stud. 13 (1972), and the discussion by Kennedy and Michelman, supra pp. 70–72.

More plausible to many economists is the *weak* version of the Coase Theorem, often called the "efficiency" proposition. This weak form holds that, regardless of initial legal entitlements, in a world of zero transaction costs, individuals would bargain with one another to garner all possible gains from trade (in economic jargon, move to the Pareto frontier). What is the difference between these two formulations? Why is the second version weaker than the first?

4. The demise in 1976 of the Reserve Clause in major league baseball gave rise to a spirited debate over the realism of various versions of the Coase Theorem. The Reserve Clause prohibited a veteran player from negotiating with teams other than his current one. In When Does the Rule of Liability Matter?, 1 J. Legal Stud. 13, 16-18 (1972), Harold Demsetz, embracing a strong version of the Coase Theorem, argued that the Reserve Clause did not affect the pairing of players with teams, although it did reduce the salaries of veteran players. According to Demsetz's reasoning, if, say, Pete Rose meshed most efficiently with the Cincinnati Reds, market transactions would eventually put him there, Reserve Clause or not.

In Consumption Theory, Production Theory, and Ideology in the Coase Theorem, 52 S. Cal. L. Rev. 669 (1979), Mark Kelman observed that during 1976-1977, the first two years after the demise of the Reserve Clause, *all* 20 players who had declared themselves free agents changed teams. Kelman argued that this pattern refuted Demsetz's prediction. Kelman was promptly challenged in Matthew Spitzer & Elizabeth Hoffman, A Reply to Kelman . . . , 53 S. Cal. L. Rev. 1187 (1980). Spitzer and Hoffman asserted that a broader look at 1967-1977 data indicated that the elimination of the Reserve Clause had not significantly increased the *rate* at which players moved from one major league team to another. Spitzer and Hoffman's analysis implied that the 20 free agents who had changed teams in 1976-1977 had recognized that they were no longer efficiently paired with their old team and in effect had "traded" themselves. Kelman's rejoinder appears at 53 S. Cal. L. Rev. 1215 (1980).

5. What are the practical implications of the Coase Theorem? Robert Cooter offers the following summary, derived in significant part from Guido Calabresi, The Costs of Accidents 26-31 (1970):

> In real situations faced by policymakers, transaction costs are positive. The Coase Theorem suggests that the role of law is to assign entitlements to the party who values them the most, so that the costly process of exchanging the entitlement is unnecessary. There are many similar versions of this proposition, for example, liability for accidents should be assigned to the party who can prevent them at lowest cost, or the cost of breach of contract should be assigned to the party who is the best insurer against nonperformance. If the party who values the entitlement the most cannot be identified, then it should be assigned to the party who can initiate an exchange at the least cost. . . .

Robert Cooter, The Cost of Coase, 11 J. Legal Stud. 1, 18 (1982).

Can legislators and judges make practical use of Cooter's abstract recommendations? In the first paragraph of The Problem of Social Cost, Coase asserts that it is generally "inappropriate" to make the owner of a polluting factory liable to those injured by its smoke. Why might Cooter's guidelines suggest a contrary result under these exact circumstances? On the wisdom of emission fees on polluters, see the selection by Merrill, infra p. 521.

6. The Problem of Social Cost eventually spawned a huge literature, much of it attacking one or another of Coase's assumptions. For example, the Coase Theorem optimistically anticipates that people will succeed in bargaining to share potential gains from trade. This may be too rosy a view. According to Cooter, even if transaction costs are nil, it is possible that "private bargaining to redistribute external costs will not achieve efficiency unless there is an institutional mechanism to dictate the terms of the contract." Robert Cooter, The Cost of Coase, 11 J. Legal Stud. 1, 18 (1982). The next two readings challenge: (1) Coase's notion that the legal system is the basic source of people's entitlements; and (2) Coase's conception of human psychology, especially his statement that "A receipt forgone of a given amount is the equivalent of the payment of the same amount."

Order Without Law: How Neighbors Settle Disputes*

Robert C. Ellickson

[This work describes the resolution of animal-trespass disputes in a rural portion of Shasta County, located at the northern end of California's Central Valley. The county contains both "open range," within which owners of livestock generally are *not* liable for damage that their trespassing cattle cause upon unfenced land, and "closed range," within which they *are* liable for that damage. Before reading the selection, try to anticipate to what extent trespass law actually affects how Shasta County cattle ranchers interact with their rural neighbors, many of whom live on smaller "ranchettes."]

The Settlement of Trespass Disputes

If Shasta County residents were to act like the farmer and the rancher in Coase's parable, they would settle their trespass problems in the following way. First, they would look to the formal law to determine who had what entitlements. They would regard those substantive rules as beyond their influence (as "exogenous," to use the economists' adjective). When they faced a potentially costly interaction, such as a trespass risk to crops, they would resolve it "in the shadow of" the formal legal rules. Because transactions would be costless, enforcement would be complete: No violation of an entitlement would be ignored. For the same reason, two neighbors who interacted on a number of fronts would resolve their disputes front by front, rather than globally.

The field evidence casts doubt on the realism of each of these literal features of the parable. Because Coase himself was fully aware that transactions are costly and thus that the parable was no more than an abstraction, the contrary evidence in no way diminishes his monumental contribution in The Problem of Social Cost. Indeed the evidence is fully consistent with Coase's central idea that, regardless of the content of law, people tend to structure their affairs to their mutual advantage. Nevertheless, the findings reported here may serve as a caution to law-and-economics scholars who have underestimated the impact of transaction costs on how the world works.

*Source: pp. 52-62 (1991).

Norms, Not Legal Rules, Are the Basic Sources of Entitlements

In rural Shasta County, where transaction costs are assuredly not zero, trespass conflicts are generally resolved not *in* "the shadow of the law" but, rather, *beyond* that shadow. Most rural residents are consciously committed to an overarching norm of cooperation among neighbors. In trespass situations, their applicable particularized norm, adhered to by all but a few deviants, is that an owner of livestock is responsible for the acts of his animals. Allegiance to this norm seems wholly independent of formal legal entitlements. Most cattlemen believe that a rancher should keep his animals from eating a neighbor's grass, regardless of whether the range is open or closed. Cattlemen typically couch their justifications for the norm in moral terms. Marty Fancher: "Suppose I sat down [uninvited] to a dinner your wife had cooked?" Dick Coombs: It "isn't right" to get free pasturage at the expense of one's neighbors. Owen Shellworth: "[My cattle] don't belong [in my neighbor's field]." Attorney-rancher Pete Schultz: A cattleman is "morally obligated to fence" to protect his neighbor's crops, even in open range. . . .

Incomplete Enforcement: The Live-and-Let-Live Philosophy

The norm that an animal owner should control his stock is modified by another norm that holds that a rural resident should put up with ("lump") minor damage stemming from isolated trespass incidents. The neighborly response to an isolated infraction is an exchange of civilities. A trespass victim should notify the animal owner that the trespass has occurred and assist the owner in retrieving the stray stock. Virtually all residents have telephones, the standard means of communication. A telephone report is usually couched not as a complaint but rather as a service to the animal owner, who, after all, has a valuable asset on the loose. Upon receiving a telephone report, a cattleman who is a good neighbor will quickly retrieve the animals (by truck if necessary), apologize for the occurrence, and thank the caller. The Mortons and the Shellworths, two ranching families in the Oak Run area particularly esteemed for their neighborliness, have a policy of promptly and apologetically responding to their neighbors' notifications of trespass.

Several realities of country life in Shasta County help explain why residents are expected to put up with trespass losses. First, it is common for a rural landowner to lose a bit of forage or to suffer minor fence damage. The area northeast of Redding lies on a deer migration route. During the late winter and early spring thousands of deer and elk move through the area, easily jumping the barbed-wire fences. Because wild animals trespass so often, most rural residents come to regard minor damage from alien animals not as an injurious event but as an inevitable part of life.

Second, most residents expect to be on both the giving and the receiving ends of trespass incidents. Even the ranchette owners have, if not a few hobby livestock, at least several dogs, which they keep for companionship, security, and pest control. Unlike cattle, dogs that trespass may harass, or even kill, other farm animals. If trespass risks are symmetrical, and if victims bear all trespass losses, accounts balance in the long run. Under these conditions, the advantage of reciprocal lumping is that no one has to expend time or money to settle disputes.

The norm of reciprocal restraint that underlies the "live-and-let-live" philosophy also calls for ranchers to swallow the costs of boarding another person's animal, even for months at a time. A cattleman often finds in his herd an animal wearing someone else's brand. If he recognizes the brand he will customarily inform its owner, but the two will often agree that the simplest solution is for the animal to stay put until the trespass victim next gathers his animals, an event that may be weeks or months away. The cost of "cutting" a single animal from a larger herd seems to underlie this custom. Thus, ranchers often consciously provide other people's cattle with feed worth perhaps as much as $10 to $100 per animal. Although Shasta County ranchers tend to regard themselves as financially pinched, even ranchers who know that they are legally entitled to recover feeding costs virtually never seek monetary compensation for boarding estrays. The largest ranchers northeast of Redding who were interviewed reported that they had never charged anyone or been charged by anyone for costs of that sort. Even when they do not know to whom a stray animal belongs, they put the animal in their truck the next time they take a load of animals to the auction yard at Cottonwood and drop it off without charge so that the brand inspector can locate the owner.

Mental Accounting of Interneighbor Debts

Residents who own only a few animals may of course be unable to see any average reciprocity of advantage in a live-and-let-live approach to animal trespass incidents. This would be true, for example, of a farmer whose fields frequently suffered minor damage from incursions by a particular rancher's livestock. Shasta County norms entitle a farmer in that situation to keep track of those minor losses in a mental account, and eventually to act to remedy the imbalance.

A fundamental feature of rural society makes this enforcement system feasible: Rural residents deal with one another on a large number of fronts, and most residents expect those interactions to continue far into the future. In sociological terms, their relationships are "multiplex," not "simplex." In game-theoretic terms, they are engaged in iterated, not single-shot, play.[51] They interact on water supply, controlled burns, fence repairs, social events, staffing the volunteer fire department, and so on. Where population densities are low, each neighbor looms larger. Thus any trespass dispute with a neighbor is almost certain to be but one thread in the rich fabric of a continuing relationship.

A person in a multiplex relationship can keep a rough mental account of the outstanding credits and debts in each aspect of that relationship. Should the aggregate account fall out of balance, tension may mount because the net creditor may begin to perceive the net debtor as an overreacher. But as long as the aggregate account is in balance, neither party need be concerned that particular subaccounts are not. For example, if a rancher were to owe a farmer in the trespass subaccount, the farmer could be expected to remain content if that imbalance were to be offset by a debt he owed the rancher in, say, the water-supply subaccount.

The live-and-let-live norm also suggests that neighbors should put up with minor imbalances in their aggregate accounts, especially when they perceive that their future interactions will provide adequate opportunities for settling old scores. Creditors may actually prefer having others in their debt. For example, when Larry Brennan lost seven tons of baled hay to Frank Ellis' cattle in open range, Brennan (although he did not know it) had a strong legal claim against Ellis for intentional trespass. Brennan estimated his loss at between $300 and $500, hardly a trivial amount. When Ellis learned of Brennan's loss he told Brennan to "come down and take some hay" from Ellis' barn. Brennan reported that he declined this

51. The law-and-society literature has long emphasized that law is not likely to be important to parties enmeshed in a continuing relationship. For example, Marc Galanter has observed: "In the American setting, litigation tends to be between parties who are strangers. Either they never had a mutually beneficial continuing relationship, as in the typical automobile case, or their relationship — marital, commercial, or organizational — is ruptured. In either case, there is no anticipated future relationship. In the American setting, unlike some others, resort to litigation is viewed as an irreparable breach of the relationship." Marc Galanter, "Reading the Landscape of Disputes: What We Know and Don't Know (and Think We Know) about Our Allegedly Contentious and Litigious Society," 31 UCLA L. Rev. 4, 24-25 (1983). . . .

offer of compensation, partly because he thought he should not have piled the bales in an unfenced area, but also because he would rather have Ellis in debt to him than be in debt to Ellis. Brennan was willing to let Ellis run up a deficit in their aggregate interpersonal accounts because he thought that as a creditor he would have more leverage over Ellis' future behavior.

The Control of Deviants: The Key Role of Self-Help

The rural Shasta County population includes deviants who do not adequately control their livestock and run up excessive debts in their informal accounts with their neighbors. Frank Ellis, for example, was notoriously indifferent about his reputation among his neighbors. In general, the traditionalists who let their animals loose in the mountains during the summer are less scrupulous than the modernists are in honoring the norms of neighborliness. This is likely due to the fact that traditionalists have less complex, and shorter-lived, interrelationships with the individuals who encounter their range cattle.

To discipline deviants, the residents of rural Shasta County use the following four types of countermeasures, listed in escalating order of seriousness: (1) self-help retaliation; (2) reports to county authorities; (3) claims for compensation informally submitted without the help of attorneys; and (4) attorney-assisted claims for compensation. The law starts to gain bite as one moves down this list.

Self-help. — Not only are most trespass disputes in Shasta County resolved according to extralegal rules, but most enforcement actions are also extralegal. A measured amount of self-help — an amount that would serve to even up accounts — is the predominant and ethically preferred response to someone who has not taken adequate steps to prevent his animals from trespassing.

The mildest form of self-help is truthful negative gossip. This usually works because only the extreme deviants are immune from the general obsession with neighborliness. Although the Oak Run-Round Mountain area is undergoing a rapid increase in population, it remains distinctly rural in atmosphere. People tend to know one another, and they value their reputations in the community. Some ranching families have lived in the area for several generations and include members who plan to stay indefinitely. Members of these families seem particularly intent on maintaining their reputations as good neighbors. Should one of them not promptly and courteously retrieve a stray, he might fear that any resulting gossip would permanently besmirch the family name.

Residents of the Northeastern Sector foothills seem quite conscious of the role of gossip in their system of social control. One longtime resident, who had lived for many years in a suburb of a major California urban area, observed that people in the Oak Run area "gossip all the time," much more than in the urban area. Another reported intentionally using gossip to sanction a traditionalist who had been "impolite" when coming to pick up some stray mountain cattle; he reported that application of this self-help device produced an apology, an outcome itself presumably circulated through the gossip system.

The furor over Frank Ellis's loose cattle in the Oak Run area induced area residents to try a sophisticated variation of the gossip sanction. The ranchette residents who were particularly bothered by Ellis's cattle could see that he was utterly indifferent to his reputation among them. They thought, however, that as a major rancher, Ellis would worry about his reputation among the large cattle operators in the county. They therefore reported Ellis's activities to the Board of Directors of the Shasta County Cattlemen's Association. This move proved unrewarding, for Ellis was also surprisingly indifferent to his reputation among the cattlemen.

When milder measures such as gossip fail, a person is regarded as being justifed in threatening to use, and perhaps, even actually using, tougher self-help sanctions. Particularly in unfenced country, a victim may respond to repeated cattle trespasses by herding the offending animals to a location extremely inconvenient for their owner. Another common response to repeated trespasses is to threaten to kill a responsible animal should it ever enter again. Although the killing of trespassing livestock is a crime in California, six landowners — not noticeably less civilized than the others — unhesitatingly volunteered that they had issued death threats of this sort. These threats are credible in Shasta County because victims of recurring trespasses, particularly if they have first issued a warning, feel justified in killing or injuring the mischievous animals.[58] Despite the criminality of the conduct (a fact not necessarily known to the respondents), I learned the identity of two persons

58. Violent self-help — occasionally organized on a group basis as vigilante justice — was a tradition in the nineteenth-century American West. "The laws [in Wyoming] appeared to require that a farmer fence his land to keep cattle out, but many a farmer preferred to save the cost of a fence, then wait until cattle came in his land, and with a shot or two secure a winter's supply of beef." Daniel J. Boorstin, The Americans: The Democratic Experience 30 (1973). See also Ernest Staples Osgood, The Day of the Cattleman (1929), at 157-160 (lynching of horse thieves); at 242 (killing of trespassing cattle); and at 252-253 (describing how large cattle companies mobilized an army to invade Johnson County, Wyoming, to prevent small ranchers from using violent self-help against the companies' cattle).

who had shot trespassing cattle. Another landowner told of running the steer of an uncooperative neighbor into a fence. The most intriguing report came from a rancher who had had recurrent problems with a trespassing bull many years before. This rancher told a key law enforcement official that he wanted to castrate the bull — "to turn it into a steer." The official replied that he would turn a deaf ear if that were to occur. The rancher asserted that he then carried out his threat.

It is difficult to estimate how frequently rural residents actually resort to violent self-help. Nevertheless, fear of physical retaliation is undoubtedly one of the major incentives for order in rural Shasta County. Ranchers who run herds at large freely admit that they worry that their trespassing cattle might meet with violence. One traditionalist reported that he is responsive to complaints from ranchette owners because he fears they will poison or shoot his stock. A judge for a rural district of the county asserted that a vicious animal is likely to "disappear" if its owner does not control it. A resident of the Oak Run area stated that some area residents responded to Frank Ellis's practice of running herds at large by rustling Ellis's cattle. He suggested that Ellis print tee shirts with the inscription: "Eat Ellis Beef. Everyone in Oak Run Does!"

Complaints to public officials. — The longtime ranchers of Shasta County pride themselves on being able to resolve their problems on their own. Except when they lose animals to rustlers, they do not seek help from public officials. Although ranchette owners also use the self-help remedies of gossip and violence, they, unlike the cattlemen, sometimes respond to a trespass incident by contacting a county official who they think will remedy the problem. These calls are usually funneled to the animal control officer or brand inspector, who both report that most callers are ranchette owners with limited rural experience. As already discussed, these calls do produce results. The county officials typically contact the owner of the animal, who then arranges for its removal. Brad Bogue, the animal control officer, reported that in half the cases the caller knows whose animal it is. This suggests that callers often think that requests for removal have more effect when issued by someone in authority.

Mere removal of an animal may provide only temporary relief when its owner is a mountain lessee whose cattle have repeatedly descended upon the ranchettes. County officials therefore use mild threats to caution repeat offenders. In closed range, they may mention both their power to impound the estrays and the risk of criminal prosecution. These threats appear to be bluffs; as noted, the county never impounds stray cattle when it can locate an owner, and it rarely prosecutes cattlemen (and then only when their animals have posed risks to motorists). In open range, county officals may deliver a more subtle threat: not that they will initiate a prosecution, but that, if the owner does not mend his ways, the Board of Supervisors may face insuperable pressure to close the range in the relevant area. Because cattlemen perceive that a closure significantly diminishes their legal entitlements in situations where motorists have collided with their livestock, this threat can catch their attention.

A trespass victim's most effective protest is one delivered directly to his elected county supervisor — the person best situated to change stray-cattle liability rules. Many Shasta County residents are aware that traditionalist cattlemen fear the supervisors more than they fear law enforcement authorities. Thus in 1973 the alfalfa farmer John Woodbury made his repeated phone calls about mountain cattle not to Brad Bogue but to Supervisor John Caton. When a supervisor receives many calls from trespass victims, his first instinct is to mediate the crisis. Supervisor Norman Wagoner's standard procedure was to assemble the ranchers in the area and advise them to put pressure on the offender or else risk the closure of the range. Wagoner's successor, Supervisor John Caton, similarly told Frank Ellis that he would support a closure at Oak Run unless Ellis built three miles of fence along the Oak Run Road. If a supervisor is not responsive to a constituent's complaint, the constituent may respond by circulating a closure petition, as Doug Heinz eventually did in Oak Run.

The rarity of claims for monetary relief. — Because Shasta County residents tend to settle their trespass disputes beyond the shadow of the law, one might suspect that the norms of neighborliness include a norm against the invocation of formal legal rights. And this norm is indeed entrenched. Owen Shellworth: "I don't believe in lawyers [because there are] always hard feelings [when you litigate]." Tony Morton: "[I never press a monetary claim because] I try to be a good neighbor." Norman Wagoner: "Being good neighbors means no lawsuits." Although trespasses are frequent, Shasta County's rural residents virtually never file formal trespass actions against one another. John Woodbury, for example, made dozens of phone calls to Supervisor John Caton, but never sought monetary compensation from the traditionalists whose cattle had repeatedly marauded his alfalfa field. Court records and conversations with court clerks indicate that in most years not a single private lawsuit seeking damages for either trespass by livestock or the expense of boarding estrays is filed in the county's courts. Not only do the residents of the Northeastern Sector foothills refrain from filing formal lawsuits, but they are also strongly disinclined to submit informal monetary claims to the owners of trespassing animals.

The landowners who were interviewed clearly regard their restraint in seeking monetary relief as a mark of virtue. When asked why they did not pursue meritorious legal claims arising from trespass or fence-finance disputes, various landowners replied: "I'm not that kind of guy"; "I don't believe in it"; "I don't like to create a stink"; "I try to get along." The landowners who attempted to provide a rationale for this forbearance all implied the same one, a long-term reciprocity of advantage. Ann Kershaw: "The only one that makes money [when you litigate] is the lawyer." Al Levitt: "I figure it will balance out in the long run." Pete Schultz: "I hope they'll do the same for me." Phil Ritchie: "My family believes in 'live and let live.'"

Mutual restraint save parties in a long-term relationship the costs of going through the formal claims process. Adjoining landowners who practice the live-and-let-live approach are both better off whenever the negative externalities from their activities are roughly in equipoise. Equipoise is as likely in closed range as in open. Landowners with property in closed range — the ones with the greatest formal legal rights — were the source of half of the quotations in the prior two paragraphs.

When a transfer *is* necessary to square unbalanced accounts, rural neighbors prefer to use in-kind payments, not cash. Shasta County landowners regard a monetary settlement as an arms' length transaction that symbolizes an unneighborly relationship. Should your goat happen to eat your neighbor's tomatoes, the neighborly thing for you to do would be to help replant the tomatoes; a transfer of money would be too cold and too impersonal. When Kevin O'Hara's cattle went through a break in a fence and destroyed his neighbor's corn crop (a loss of less than $100), O'Hara had to work hard to persuade the neighbor to accept his offer of money to compensate for the damages. O'Hara insisted on making this payment because he "felt responsible" for his neighbor's loss, a feeling that would not have been in the least affected had the event occurred in open instead of closed range. There can also be social pressure against offering monetary settlements. Bob Bosworth's father agreed many decades ago to pay damages to a trespass victim in a closed-range area just south of Shasta County; other cattlemen then rebuked him for setting an unfortunate precedent. The junior Bosworth, in 1982 the president of the Shasta

County Cattlemen's Association, could recall no other out-of-pocket settlement in a trespass case.

Trespass victims who sustain an unusually large loss are more likely to take the potentially deviant step of making a claim for monetary relief. Among those interviewed were adjusters for the two insurance companies whose liability policies would be most likely to cover losses from animal trespass. The adjusters' responses suggest that in a typical year these companies receive fewer than ten trespass damage claims originating in Shasta County. In the paradigmatic case, the insured is not a rancher but rather a ranchette owner, whose family's horse has escaped and trampled a neighboring homeowner's shrubbery. The claimant is typically not represented by an attorney, a type of professional these adjusters rarely encounter. The adjusters also settle each year two or three trespass claims that homeowners or ranchette owners have brought against the ranchers. Ranchers who suffer trespasses virtually never file claims against others' insurance companies. An adjuster for the company that insures most Shasta County ranchers stated that he could not recall, in his twenty years of adjusting, a single claim by a rancher for compensation for trespass damage.

Attorney-assisted claims. — The landowners, particularly the ranchers, express a strong aversion to hiring an attorney to fight one's battles. To hire an attorney is to escalate a conflict. A good neighbor does not do such a thing because the "natural working order" calls for two neighbors to work out their problems between themselves. The files in the Shasta County courthouses reveal that the ranchers who honor norms of neighborliness — the vast majority — are not involved in cattle-related litigation of any kind.

NOTES AND QUESTIONS ON SOCIAL NORMS

1. This selection's central theme is that neighbors often trump formal law with their own informal norms. This finding is consistent with a critique of "legal centralism" that law-and-society scholars have long embraced, and that has now won widespread acceptance among legal scholars. For theoretical treatments of the nature of social norms, see, for example, Richard H. McAdams, The Origin, Development, and Regulation of Norms, 96 Mich. L. Rev. 338 (1997) (hypothesizing that norms are supported by conferrals of positive and negative esteem); Eric A. Posner, Law and Social Norms (2000) (viewing norm-compliance as a signal that one

is a trustworthy trading partner); and Symposium, Social Norms, Social Meaning, and the Economic Analysis of Law, 27 J. Legal Stud. 537 (1998).

Does a practicing lawyer have to be sensitive to the influence of nonlegal sources of rules? Are there any lessons for what law schools should teach? Does the Shasta County aphorism, "Being good neighbors means no lawsuits," necessarily imply that the practice of law is ignoble? That litigious people are deviants? For more on informal property rights, see Acheson, supra p. 129, and the selections in Chapter 6, infra.

2. In other portions of his Shasta County study, Ellickson reports that rural residents worry far more that wayward livestock will collide with highway motorists than that animals will trespass on cropland. The ruralites unhesitatingly turn to the legal system to resolve highway claims (which commonly are high-stakes disputes between strangers), but seldom use the legal system to resolve animal-trespass disputes (which commonly are low-stakes affairs arising between neighbors engaged in continuing dealings).

Footnote 51 of the selection quotes Galanter's assertion that law is primarily important when disputants lack a future relationship. If this is true, in what contexts is, say, adverse-possession law likely to be irrelevant? Landlord-tenant law? Nuisance law? The law governing relations among concurrent owners?

3. Regardless of what the formal law provides, Shasta County residents reportedly honor a norm that an owner of livestock is responsible for the acts of his animals. Why did they embrace that particular norm, as opposed to, for example, a norm obligating cropgrowers to fence out others' livestock? Ellickson speculates that a fencing-out norm *did* prevail in Shasta County during the nineteenth century, when the population was less dense, fencing more expensive, and highways free of motorists. Order Without Law 185-188 (1991). This thesis that norms evolve adaptively echoes Demsetz's notions about the evolution of property rights, supra p. 135. For a theory of how social interactions might generate this upbeat result, see Robert C. Ellickson, The Market for Social Norms, 3 Am. L. & Econ. Rev. 1 (2001).

4. Shasta County residents are reported to use mild forms of violence to enforce their norms. Are their violent acts legally privileged forms of self-help? How great is the danger that self-help violence will trigger an escalating feud? Did Acheson's lobstermen feud too much? Is it significant that Shasta County residents developed their norms while under the umbrella of an established government?

5. Why might neighbors in Shasta County prefer to square

unbalanced accounts with gifts and other in-kind payments, as opposed to cash transfers? Are urbanites just as likely to do this? See also Margaret Radin on alienability, infra p. 336. More broadly, how generalizable are the Shasta County findings?

A Behavioral Approach to Law and Economics*

Christine Jolls, Cass R. Sunstein & Richard Thaler

I. Foundations: What Is "Behavioral Law and Economics"? . . .

A. Homo Economicus and Real People

The task of behavioral law and economics, simply stated, is to explore the implications of *actual* (not hypothesized) human behavior for the law. How do "real people" differ from *homo economicus*? We will describe the differences by stressing three important "bounds" on human behavior, bounds that draw into question the central ideas of utility maximization, stable preferences, rational expectations, and optimal processing of information. People can be said to display *bounded rationality, bounded willpower*, and *bounded self-interest. . . .*

1. BOUNDED RATIONALITY

Bounded rationality, an idea first introduced by Herbert Simon, refers to the obvious fact that human cognitive abilities are not infinite. We have limited computational skills and seriously flawed memories. People can respond sensibly to these failings; thus it might be said that people sometimes respond rationally to their own cognitive limitations, minimizing the sum of decision costs and error costs. To deal with limited memories we make lists. To deal with limited brain power and time we use mental shortcuts and rules of thumb. But even with these remedies, and in some cases because of these remedies, human behavior differs in systematic ways from that predicted by the standard economic model of unbounded rationality. Even when the use of mental shortcuts is rational, it can produce predictable mistakes . . .

2. BOUNDED WILLPOWER

In addition to bounded rationality, people often display bounded willpower. This term refers to the fact that human beings

*Source: 50 Stan L. Rev. 1471, 1476-1484, 1489-1500 (1998).

often take actions that they know to be in conflict with their own long-term interests. Most smokers say they would prefer not to smoke, and many pay money to join a program or obtain a drug that will help them quit. . . . Thus, the demand for and supply of law may reflect people's understanding of their own (or others') bounded willpower; consider "cooling off" periods for certain sales and programs that facilitate or even require saving.

3. BOUNDED SELF-INTEREST

Finally, we use the term bounded self-interest to refer to an important fact about the utility function of most people: They care, or act as if they care, about others, even strangers, in some circumstances. . . . In many market and bargaining settings . . . people care about being treated fairly and want to treat others fairly if those others are themselves behaving fairly. As a result of these concerns, the agents in a behavioral economic model are both nicer and (when they are not treated fairly) more spiteful than the agents postulated by neoclassical theory. . . .

B. Testable Predictions . . .

. . . [A] fundamental principle of conventional law and economics concerns the nature of costs: "Cost to the economist is 'opportunity cost,' " and " '[s]unk' (incurred) costs do not affect decisions on prices and quantity."[25] Thus, according to traditional analysis, decision makers will equate opportunity costs (which are costs incurred by forgoing opportunities — say, the opportunity to sell one's possessions) to out-of-pocket costs (such as costs incurred in buying possessions); and they will ignore sunk costs (costs that cannot be recovered, such as the cost of nonrefundable tickets). But each of these propositions is a frequent source of predictive failures. The equality of opportunity costs and out-of-pocket costs implies that, in the absence of important wealth effects, buying prices will be roughly equal to selling prices. This is frequently violated, as is well known. Many people holding tickets to a popular sporting event such as the Super Bowl would be unwilling to buy tickets at the market price (say $1000), yet would also be unwilling to sell at this price. Indeed, estimates of the ratio of selling prices to buying prices are often at least two to one, yet the size of the transaction makes it implausible in these studies to conclude that wealth effects explain the difference. As described below, these results are just what behavioral analysis suggests. . . .

25. Richard A. Posner, Economic Analysis of Law 6, 7 (5th ed. 1998).

[A second] fundamental principle of conventional law and economics is that "resources tend to gravitate toward their most valuable uses" as markets drive out any unexploited profit opportunities.[29] When combined with the notion that opportunity and out-of-pocket costs are equated . . . , this yields the Coase Theorem — the idea that initial assignments of entitlements will not affect the ultimate allocation of resources so long as transaction costs are zero. Many economists and economically oriented lawyers think of the Coase Theorem as a tautology; if there were really no transaction costs (and no wealth effects), and if an alternative allocation of resources would make some agents better off and none worse off, then of course the agents would move to that allocation. Careful empirical study, however, shows that the Coase Theorem is not a tautology; indeed, it can lead to inaccurate predictions.[31] That is, even when transaction costs and wealth effects are known to be zero, initial entitlements alter the final allocation of resources. These results are predicted by behavioral economics, which emphasizes the difference between opportunity and out-of-pocket costs.

Consider the following set of experiments conducted to test the Coase Theorem;[32] let us offer an interpretation geared to the particular context of economic analysis of law. The subjects were forty-four students taking an advanced undergraduate course in law and economics at Cornell University. Half the students were endowed with tokens. Each student (whether or not endowed with a token) was assigned a personal token value, the price at which a token could be redeemed for cash at the end of the experiment; these assigned values induce supply and demand curves for the tokens. Markets were conducted for tokens. Those without tokens could buy one, while those with tokens could sell. Those with tokens should (and do) sell their tokens if offered more than their assigned value; those without tokens should (and do) buy tokens if they can get one at a price below their assigned value. These token markets are a complete victory of economic theory. The equilibrium price was always exactly what the theory would predict, and the tokens did in fact flow to those who valued them most.

However, life is generally not about tokens redeemable for cash. Thus another experiment was conducted, identical to the first

---

29. [*Id.*] at 11.
31. Daniel L. Kahneman, Jack L. Knetsch & Richard H. Thaler, Experimental Tests of the Endowment Effect and the Coase Theorem, 98 J. Pol. Econ. 1325, 1329-1342 (1990).
32. See *id.*

except that now half the students were given Cornell coffee mugs instead of tokens. Here behavioral analysis generates a prediction distinct from standard economic analysis: Because people do not equate opportunity and out-of-pocket costs for goods whose values are not solely exogenously defined (as they were in the case of the tokens), those endowed with mugs should be reluctant to part with them even at prices they would not have considered paying to acquire a mug had they not received one.

Was this prediction correct? Yes. Markets were conducted and mugs bought and sold. Unlike the case of the tokens, the assignment of property rights had a pronounced effect on the final allocation of mugs. The students who were assigned mugs had a strong tendency to keep them. Whereas the Coase Theorem would have predicted that about half the mugs would trade (since transaction costs had been shown to be essentially zero in the token experiments, and mugs were randomly distributed), instead only fifteen percent of the mugs traded. And those who were endowed with mugs asked more than twice as much to give up a mug as those who didn't get a mug were willing to pay. This result did not change if the markets were repeated. This effect is generally referred to as the "endowment effect"; it is a manifestation of the broader phenomenon of "loss aversion" — the idea that losses are weighted more heavily than gains — which in turn is a central building block of Kahneman and Tversky's prospect theory. . . .

II. Behavior of Agents

A. The Ultimatum Game

1. THE GAME AND ITS SUNK-COST VARIATION

We [turn to] bounded self-interest, the third bound described above. A useful first example of this bound is agents' behavior in a very simple bargaining game called the ultimatum game. In this game, one player, the Proposer, is asked to propose an allocation of a sum of money between herself and the other player, the Responder. The Responder then has a choice. He can either accept the amount offered to him by the Proposer, leaving the rest to the Proposer, or he can reject the offer, in which case both players get nothing. Neither player knows the identity of his or her counterpart, and the players will play against each other only once, so reputations and future retaliation are eliminated as factors.

Economic theory has a simple prediction about this game. The Proposer will offer the smallest unit of currency available, say a penny, and the Responder will accept, since a penny is better than nothing. This turns out to be a very bad prediction about how the game is actually played. Responders typically reject offers of less than twenty percent of the total amount available; the average minimum amount that Responders say they would accept is between twenty and thirty percent of that sum.[47] Responders are thus willing to punish unfair behavior, even at a financial cost to themselves. This is a form of bounded self-interest. And this response seems to be expected and anticipated by Proposers; they typically offer a substantial portion of the sum to be divided — ordinarily forty to fifty percent.

Economists often worry that the results of this type of experiment are sensitive to the way in which the experiment was conducted. What would happen if the stakes were raised substantially, or the game was repeated several times to allow learning? In this case, we know the answer. To a first approximation, neither of these factors changes the results in any important way. Raising the stakes from $10 per pair to $100, or even to more than a week's income (in a poor country) has little effect; the same is true of repeating the game ten times with different partners. (Of course, at some point raising the stakes would matter; probably few people would turn down an offer of five percent of $1,000,000.) We do not see behavior moving toward the prediction of standard economic theory.

Thus, the factors that many economists thought would change the outcome of the game did not. But, as we learned in a study conducted for this article, a factor that economic theory predicts will *not* have an effect, namely the introduction of a sunk cost, does have an effect. As noted above, economics predicts that decision makers will ignore sunk costs in making their choices . . . ; but in fact decision makers often do not behave in this way. Do sunk costs alter behavior in the ultimatum game? To find out, we asked classroom volunteers to bring $5 — what would become a sunk cost for them — to class. Students were given a form asking them how they would play both roles in an ultimatum game in which the $10 to be divided was contributed half by the Proposer and half by the Responder. They were told that their role would be determined by chance, so they had to decide first what offer to make if they were chosen to be a Proposer and then what minimum offer they would

47. See Werner Güth, Rolf Schmittberger & Bernd Schwarze, An Experimental Analysis of Ultimatum Bargaining, 3 J. Econ. Behav. & Org. 367, 371-372, 375 tbls.4 & 5 (1982); Daniel Kahneman, Jack L. Knetsch & Richard H. Thaler, Fairness and the Assumptions of Economics, 59 J. Bus. S285, S291 tbl.2 (1986).

be willing to accept if they were a Responder. We also ran a version of the standard ultimatum game (without sunk costs by the students) as a control.

Although economic theory says that the sunk-cost variation of the ultimatum game will have no effect on behavior (since the $5 collected from each student is a sunk cost and should therefore be ignored by the players), we predicted that in this domain sunk costs would matter. In particular, we anticipated that Responders would feel that they had an "entitlement" to the $5 they had contributed to the experiment and would therefore be reluctant to accept less. This is precisely what we found. In the original version of the game, when the $10 to be divided was provided to subjects by the experimenter, the average minimum amount demanded by Responders was $1.94. In the sunk-cost version, where the students each paid $5 to participate, the average demand was $3.21 for a group of MIT MBA students, $3.73 for a group of University of Chicago (UC) MBA students, and $3.35 for a group of UC Law students. . . .

Note that our emphasis here, as well as in the ordinary ultimatum game, is on the fairness behavior of Responders, not on affirmative concerns for fairness on the part of Proposers. (As noted above, their behavior appears fully consistent with financially maximizing responses to Responders' fairness behavior; other experimental results support this conclusion.[51])

The fairness results obtained in various experimental settings, such as the ultimatum game, cannot be explained on grounds of reputation. The parties are interacting anonymously and in a one-shot fashion. . . .

2. FAIRNESS, ACRIMONY, AND SCRUPLES

Theoretical considerations. — How can economic analysis be enriched to incorporate the behavior observed in the ultimatum game and its sunk-cost variant? As we have indicated, the first step is to relax the assumption, common to most economic theorizing, of "unbounded self-interest." This assumption implies that Proposers should offer the smallest sum possible, and Responders should accept. An alternative view is offered in the following account:

---

51. See Elizabeth Hoffman, Kevin McCabe & Vernon L. Smith, Social Distance and Other-Regarding Behavior in Dictator Games, 86 Am. Econ. Rev. 653, 653-654 & fig.1 (1996) (finding that Proposers typically offered no more than 10% of the sum to be divided — and over 60% offered nothing — when (1) the Responder had no choice but to accept the Proposer's offer and (2) anonymity was guaranteed).

In the rural areas around Ithaca it is common for farmers to put some fresh produce on a table by the road. There is a cash box on the table, and customers are expected to put money in the box in return for the vegetables they take. The box has just a small slit, so money can only be put in, not taken out. Also, the box is attached to the table, so no one can (easily) make off with the money. We think that the farmers who use this system have just about the right model of human nature. They feel that enough people will volunteer to pay for the fresh corn to make it worthwhile to put it out there. The farmers also know that if it were easy to take the money, someone would do so.[54]

We emphasize that this is *not* a story of simple altruism. As noted above, such altruism is sometimes recognized in conventional economics; our account, in contrast, is a more complicated story of reciprocal fairness. A concern for fairness is part of most agents' utility function. The results of the ultimatum game, like the behavior of the Ithaca shoppers, cannot readily be explained on grounds of simple altruism. First of all, the games are played between anonymous strangers. What reason is there to believe that these people care about one another? (Most of us give little of our wealth to anonymous strangers whom we have no reason to believe are any worse off than we are. Similarly, most people driving by a farm do not pull over and stuff two dollars through the mail slot, even in Ithaca. Fairness behavior is probably reciprocal.) Second, we observe not only apparently "nice" behavior (generous offers) but also "spiteful" behavior (Responders turning down small offers at substantial cost to the Proposers). In the ultimatum game, people appear simultaneously nicer and more spiteful than conventional assumptions predict. . . .

The sort of balanced conception of human nature suggested by the ultimatum game results and the practices of farmers in Ithaca need not be informal or ad hoc. It is possible to incorporate material and nonmaterial motives, such as the desire to be fair (to those who have been fair) and also to be spiteful (to those who have not been fair), in a rigorous analysis. An elegant formal treatment is offered by Matthew Rabin in a model of fairness.[55] Rabin's framework incorporates three stylized facts about behavior. Stated simply and nonformally:

(A) People are willing to sacrifice their own material well-being to help those who are being kind.

54. Richard H. Thaler & Robyn M. Dawes, Cooperation *in* Richard H. Thaler, The Winner's Curse: Paradoxes and Anomalies of Economic Life 6, 19-20 (1992).
55. Matthew Rabin, Incorporating Fairness into Game Theory and Economics; 83 Am. Econ. Rev. 1281 (1993).

(B)   People are willing to sacrifice their own material well-being to punish those who are being unkind.
(C)   Both motivations (A) and (B) have a greater effect on behavior as the material cost of sacrificing becomes smaller.

Rabin shows how these assumptions about behavior can explain the behavior observed in the ultimatum game as well as other games of cooperation such as the Prisoner's Dilemma. . . .

What is "fair"? — Absent acrimony, spiteful behavior — such as rejection of small offers in the ultimatum game — is typically observed in situations where one party has violated a perceived "norm of fairness." This raises an obvious question: What is "fair"? In the ultimatum game, most people regard an offer of, say, a penny to the Responder as "unfair." This perception is an illustration of a more general pattern: People judge outcomes to be "unfair" if they depart substantially from the terms of a "reference transaction" — a transaction that defines the benchmark for the parties' interactions.[60] When the interactions are between bargainers dividing a sum of money to which neither is more entitled than the other (and this is common knowledge), the "reference transaction" is something like an equal split; substantial departures are viewed as unfair and, accordingly, punished by Responders. If parties are bargaining over the division of money and both have reason to view one side as more entitled than the other, then the "reference transaction" is a split that favors the more-entitled party.[61] And if the parties are a consumer and a firm in the market, the "reference transaction" is a transaction on the usual terms for the item in question. . . .

B. Bargaining Around Court Orders

1. COASIAN PREDICTION

As noted above, an important aspect of law and economics is the Coase Theorem, which says that the assignment of a legal entitlement will not influence the ultimate allocation of that entitle-

60. See Daniel Kahneman, Jack L. Knetsch & Richard Thaler, Fairness as a Constraint on Profit Seeking: Entitlements in the Market, 76 Am. Econ. Rev. 728, 729-730 (1986).
61. See Elizabeth Hoffman & Matthew L. Spitzer, Entitlements, Rights, and Fairness: An Experimental Examination of Subjects' Concepts of Distributive Justice, 14 J. Legal Stud. 259, 261 (1985).

ment when transaction costs and wealth effects are zero. A straightforward application of this idea is that when a court enters a judgment, whether in the form of an injunction or a damage award, the parties are likely to bargain to a different outcome if that outcome is preferable to what the court did and the transaction costs and wealth effects are small. (Thus, for instance, if the court enters a prohibitively high damage award but the activity in question is efficient, the parties should bargain for a lower damage level, since this would increase the surplus to be shared between them.) To whom an entitlement is allocated after litigation, and how it is protected (by a property rule or a liability rule), are irrelevant to the ultimate allocation of the entitlement in these circumstances.

2.   BEHAVIORAL ANALYSIS

Influenced by behavioral economics, many legal commentators have observed that in light of the endowment effect described in Part I (an aspect of prospect theory, and thus an instance of bounded rationality), the assignment of a legal entitlement may well affect the outcome of bargaining, even when transaction costs (as conventionally defined) and wealth effects are zero.[65] This conclusion is suggested by the mugs experiments described in Part I, as well as by a substantial body of other evidence on the endowment effect. The mugs results were obtained in circumstances that were the most favorable to the predictions of the conventional theory. Transaction costs were zero and the sort of emotional attachments that can grow over time in the real world were absent. Mug owners had become mug owners just minutes before the markets were run. Compare that with a homeowner who has been endowed with the right to have her homestead protected from noxious fumes being emitted nearby.

Although the endowment effect suggests generally that the assignment of a legal entitlement may affect the outcome of bargaining, such an effect is especially likely when the entitlement is in the form of a court order obtained after legal proceedings between opposing parties. . . .

Data gathered by Ward Farnsworth suggest that there is much less post-trial bargaining than the economic model would predict.[71]

65. See, e.g., Elizabeth Hoffman & Matthew L. Spitzer, Willingness to Pay vs. Willingness to Accept: Legal and Economic Implications, 71 Wash. U.L.Q. 59, 99 (1993).

71. Ward Farnsworth, [Do Parties to Nuisance Cases Bargain After Judgment? A Glimpse Inside the Cathedral, 66 U. Chi. L. Rev. 373 (1999)].

Farnsworth interviewed attorneys from approximately twenty nuisance cases in which injunctive relief was sought and either granted or denied after full litigation before a judge. In not a single case of those Farnsworth studied did parties even attempt to contract around the court order, even when transaction costs were low, and even when an objective third party might think that there was considerable room for mutually advantageous deals. Conventional analysis might attribute failures to reach an ultimate agreement to asymmetric information;[72] but under such analysis it is difficult to explain the complete failure even to negotiate. It is also interesting to note that the lawyers interviewed said that the parties would not have reached a contractual solution if the opposite result had been reached. (This last point also means that the no-bargaining result cannot be explained by supposing that the court orders entered were uniquely efficient.)

The lawyers' explanations for these results are behavioral in character. Once people have received a court judgment, they are unwilling to negotiate with the opposing party, partly because of an unwillingness by victorious plaintiffs to confer advantages upon their opponents. Having invested a great deal of resources in pursuing the case all the way to court and through a trial, victors perceive themselves as having a special right to the legally endorsed status quo, and they are unlikely to give that right up, especially to their opponent, for all, or most, of the tea in China. Their investment in the entitlement gives it a distinctive character. Bargains are unlikely in the extreme; the plaintiff and the defendant tend not even to think about them. These tendencies are reinforced (according to the lawyers in Farnsworth's study) by the presence of acrimony between the parties; thus acrimony combines with the endowment effect to produce an absence of negotiation. . . .

NOTES AND QUESTIONS ON LOSS AVERSION AND BEHAVIORAL LAW AND ECONOMICS

1. Drawing on the pathbreaking work of cognitive psychologists Daniel Kahneman and Amos Tversky, Jolls, Sunstein, and Thaler (JST) assert that people tend to regard a loss as more momentous than a nominally equivalent forgone gain. If so, initial

---

72. See, e.g., Louis Kaplow & Steven Shavell, Property Rules Versus Liability Rules: An Economic Analysis, 109 Harv. L. Rev. 713, 734 & n.66 (1996) (discussing economic models in which asymmetric information leads to failed negotiations).

allocations of entitlements have some tendency to persist. To return to Coase's central example, a farmer who might offer only $400 to purchase a neighboring rancher's entitlement to open grazing, might (if entitled to prevent trespass by livestock) insist on the rancher's payment of $800 to waive that right. Usually there are fewer sales of a commodity as its price rises — in this case from $400 to $800. As a result, even apart from transaction costs and wealth effects, the ranchers' cattle are more likely to enter the farmer's fields when ranchers have a right to open grazing (and the rancher's opportunity cost is $400) than when the farmer has a right to exclude (and the rancher would have to pay $800). Because of loss aversion alone, law thus may have flypaper effects.

2. JST stress the importance of psychological dispositions, particularly whether a person frames an outcome as a loss or a forgone gain and whether a person thinks an outcome is fair. How do these psychological dispositions arise? To what extent are they hardwired in human genes? The results of "reference transactions" in markets? The products of culture, socialization, and social norms? The products of legal rules that have fed back to influence people's perceptions? On this last possibility, see, for example, Lawrence Lessig, The Regulation of Social Meaning, 62 U. Chi. L. Rev. 943 (1995); Richard H. McAdams, A Focal Point Theory of Expressive Law, 86 Va. L. Rev. 1649 (2000); and Cass R. Sunstein, On the Expressive Function of Law, 144 U. Pa. L. Rev. 2021 (1996). If law does affect people's values, is it futile for a policy analyst to undertake a cost-benefit analysis of a statute or regulation? See generally Symposium, Cost-Benefit Analysis: Legal, Economic, and Philosophical Perspectives, 29 J. Legal Stud. 837 (2000).

Experimentalists are investigating to what extent these psychological dispositions vary according to nationality and other demographic characteristics of respondents. See, e.g., Rachel Croson & Nancy Buchan, Gender and Culture: International Experimental Evidence from Trust Games, 89 Am. Econ. Rev. 386 (1999). This work promises to help reveal to what extent these psychological dispositions are not universal, but instead contingent on varying cultural norms, including law.

3. In particular, what are the sources of "psychological ownership" — that is, the disposition to regard the deprivation of an item as a loss, as opposed to a forgone gain? In the mug experiments reported by JST, of what significance was physical possession? The passage of time? The distinctiveness of the mugs? Perceptions of legal or other normative title? Past outlays of effort and expense (sunk costs)? Suppose these factors diverge, as in the case of adverse possession? Which is more influential then?

4. Consider the political implications of loss aversion. Does it help explain why Congress has been reluctant to close military bases, end agricultural subsidies, and privatize public housing? Why legislators require employers to withhold estimated income-tax liabilities from employees' paychecks? Why the local officials who support growth controls rarely push to reduce current populations? See generally Roger G. Noll & James E. Krier, Some Implications of Cognitive Psychology for Risk Regulation, 19 J. Legal Stud. 747 (1990), an exploration of the political implications of a number of psychological phenomena.

5. What are the implications for legal doctrine? If loss aversion creates a status quo bias, does it help explain the rule of *stare decisis*? Why a minor physical taking is usually more constitutionally suspect than a regulatory restriction that drastically reduces future development opportunities? In adverse possession cases, why the law eventually favors the claims of the adverse possessor, as opposed to those of the original owner? See David Cohen & Jack L. Knetsch, Judicial Choice and Disparities Between Measures of Economic Values, 30 Osgoode Hall L.J. 737 (1992); Robert C. Ellickson, Bringing Culture and Human Frailty to Rational Actors, 65 Chi.-Kent L. Rev. 23, 35-39 (1989).

6. Is equal division always the fairest result in an Ultimatum Game? How would participants react if the Proposer had "earned" that role by besting the Responder in a simple game of skill? In an experiment that JST cite in footnote 61, Hoffman and Spitzer found that participants then would be likely to honor Lockean ethics — that is, to regard the game-winner as entitled to more than half.

7. As Farnsworth notes in his study, the failure of parties in nuisance cases to negotiate after the final appellate judgment may be due in part to self-selection. A litigant who pursues a case to that stage is apt to have idiosyncratic values and to have become spiteful toward the opposing party.

8. Leading contributions to the genre are collected in Behavioral Law and Economics (Cass R. Sunstein ed., 2000). For a variety of appraisals of the approach, some of them skeptical of whether it is worth the complexities it creates, see Richard A. Posner, Rational Choice, Behavioral Economics, and the Law, 50 Stan. L. Rev. 1551 (1998), and the contributions to Symposium, The Legal Implications of Psychology: Human Behavior, Behavioral Economics, and the Law, 51 Vand. L. Rev. 1747 (1998).

Chapter 5

Property Rules, Liability Rules

Property Rules, Liability Rules, and Inalienability:
One View of the Cathedral*

Guido Calabresi & A. Douglas Melamed

I. Introduction . . .

The first issue which must be faced by any legal system is one we call the problem of "entitlement." Whenever a state is presented with the conflicting interests of two or more people, or two or more groups of people, it must decide which side to favor. Absent such a decision, access to goods, services, and life itself will be decided on the basis of "might makes right" — whoever is stronger or shrewder will win. Hence the fundamental thing that law does is to decide which of the conflicting parties will be entitled to prevail. The entitlement to make noise versus the entitlement to have silence, the entitlement to pollute versus the entitlement to breathe clean air, the entitlement to have children versus the entitlement to forbid them — these are the first order of legal decisions.

Having made its initial choice, society must enforce that choice. Simply setting the entitlement does not avoid the problem of "might makes right"; a minimum of state intervention is always necessary. Our conventional notions make this easy to comprehend with respect to private property. If Taney owns a cabbage patch and Marshall, who is bigger, wants a cabbage, he will get it unless

*Source: 85 Harv. L. Rev. 1089-1993, 1105-1121, 1124-1127 (1972).

the state intervenes. But it is not so obvious that the state must also intervene if it chooses the opposite entitlement, communal property. If large Marshall has grown some communal cabbages and chooses to deny them to small Taney, it will take state action to enforce Taney's entitlement to the communal cabbages. . . .

The state not only has to decide whom to entitle, but it must also simultaneously make a series of equally difficult second-order decisions. These decisions go to the manner in which entitlements are protected and to whether an individual is allowed to sell or trade the entitlement. In any given dispute, for example, the state must decide not only which side wins but also the kind of protection to grant. It is with the latter decisions, decisions which shape the subsequent relationship between the winner and the loser, that this article is primarily concerned. We shall consider three types of entitlements — entitlements protected by property rules, entitlements protected by liability rules, and inalienable entitlements. The categories are not, of course, absolutely distinct; but the categorization is useful since it reveals some of the reasons which lead us to protect certain entitlements in certain ways.

An entitlement is protected by a property rule to the extent that someone who wishes to remove the entitlement from its holder must buy it from him in a voluntary transaction in which the value of the entitlement is agreed upon by the seller. It is the form of entitlement which gives rise to the least amount of state intervention: Once the original entitlement is decided upon, the state does not try to decide its value. It lets each of the parties say how much the entitlement is worth to him, and gives the seller a veto if the buyer does not offer enough. Property rules involve a collective decision as to who is to be given an initial entitlement but not as to the value of the entitlement.

Whenever someone may destroy the initial entitlement if he is willing to pay an objectively determined value for it, an entitlement is protected by a liability rule. This value may be what it is thought the original holder of the entitlement would have sold it for. But the holder's complaint that he would have demanded more will not avail him once the objectively determined value is set. Obviously, liability rules involve an additional stage of state intervention: Not only are entitlements protected, but their transfer or destruction is allowed on the basis of a value determined by some organ of the state rather than by the parties themselves.

An entitlement is inalienable to the extent that its transfer is not permitted between a willing buyer and a willing seller. The state intervenes not only to determine who is initially entitled and to determine the compensation that must be paid if the entitlement is taken or destroyed, but also to forbid its sale under some or all circumstances. Inalienability rules are thus quite different from property and liability rules. Unlike those rules, rules of inalienability not only "protect" the entitlement; they may also be viewed as limiting or regulating the grant of the entitlement itself.

It should be clear that most entitlements to most goods are mixed. Taney's house may be protected by a property rule in situations where Marshall wishes to purchase it, by a liability rule where the government decides to take it by eminent domain, and by a rule of inalienability in situations where Taney is drunk or incompetent. This article will explore two primary questions: (1) In what circumstances should we grant a particular entitlement? and (2) In what circumstances should we decide to protect that entitlement by using a property, liability, or inalienability rule?

II.   The Setting of Entitlements

What are the reasons for deciding to entitle people to pollute or to entitle people to forbid pollution, to have children freely or to limit procreation, to own property or to share property? They can be grouped under three headings: economic efficiency, distributional preferences, and other justice considerations. [Discussion omitted.]

III.   Rules for Protecting and Regulating Entitlements

Whenever society chooses an initial entitlement it must also determine whether to protect the entitlement by property rules, by liability rules, or by rules of inalienability. In our framework, much of what is generally called private property can be viewed as an entitlement which is protected by a property rule. No one can take the entitlement to private property from the holder unless the holder sells it willingly and at the price at which he subjectively values the property. Yet a nuisance with sufficient public utility to avoid injunction has, in effect, the right to take property with compensation. In such a circumstance the entitlement to the property is protected only by what we call a liability rule: An external, objective standard of value is used to facilitate the transfer of the entitlement from the holder to the nuisance. Finally, in some instances we will not allow the sale of the property at all, that is, we will occasionally make the entitlement inalienable.

This section will consider the circumstances in which society will employ these three rules to solve situations of conflict. Because the property rule and the liability rule are closely related and depend for their application on the shortcomings of each other, we treat them together. We discuss inalienability separately.

A. Property and Liability Rules

Why cannot a society simply decide on the basis of the already mentioned criteria who should receive any given entitlement, and then let its transfer occur only through a voluntary negotiation? Why, in other words, cannot society limit itself to the property rule? To do this it would need only to protect and enforce the initial entitlements from all attacks, perhaps through criminal sanctions, and to enforce voluntary contracts for their transfer. Why do we need liability rules at all?

In terms of economic efficiency the reason is easy enough to see. Often the cost of establishing the value of an initial entitlement by negotiation is so great that even though a transfer of the entitlement would benefit all concerned, such a transfer will not occur. If a collective determination of the value were available instead, the beneficial transfer would quickly come about.

Eminent domain is a good example. A park where Guidacres, a tract of land owned by 1,000 owners in 1,000 parcels, now sits would, let us assume, benefit a neighboring town enough so that the 100,000 citizens of the town would each be willing to pay an average of $100 to have it. The park is Pareto-desirable if the owners of the tracts of land in Guidacres actually value their entitlements at less than $10,000,000 or an average of $10,000 a tract. Let us assume that in fact the parcels are all the same and all the owners value them at $8,000. On this assumption, the park is, in economic efficiency terms, desirable — in values foregone it costs $8,000,000 and is worth $10,000,000 to the buyers. And yet it may well not be established. If enough of the owners hold-out for more than $10,000 in order to get a share of the $2,000,000 that they guess the buyers are willing to pay over the value which the sellers in actuality attach, the price demanded will be more than $10,000,000 and no park will result. The sellers have an incentive to hide their true valuation and the market will not succeed in establishing it.

An equally valid example could be made on the buying side. Suppose the sellers of Guidacres have agreed to a sales price of $8,000,000 (they are all relatives and at a family banquet decided that trying to hold out would leave them all losers). It does not follow that the buyers can raise that much even though each of 100,000 citizens *in fact* values the park at $100. Some citizens may try to free-load and say the park is only worth $50 or even nothing to them, hoping that enough others will admit to a higher desire and make up the $8,000,000 price. Again there is no reason to believe that a market, a decentralized system of valuing, will cause people to express their true valuations and hence yield results which all would *in fact* agree are desirable.

Whenever this is the case an argument can readily be made for moving from a property rule to a liability rule. If society can remove from the market the valuation of each tract of land, decide the value collectively, and impose it, then the holdout problem is gone. Similarly, if society can value collectively each individual citizen's desire to have a park and charge him a "benefits" tax based upon it, the freeloader problem is gone. If the sum of the taxes is greater than the sum of the compensation awards, the park will result.

Of course, one can conceive of situations where it might be cheap to exclude all the freeloaders from the park, or to ration the park's use in accordance with original willingness to pay. In such cases the incentive to free-load might be eliminated. But such exclusions, even if possible, are usually not cheap. And the same may be the case for the market methods which might avoid the holdout problem on the seller side.

Moreover, even if holdout and freeloader problems can be met feasibly by the market, an argument may remain for employing a liability rule. Assume that in our hypothetical, freeloaders can be excluded at the cost of $1,000,000 and that all owners of tracts in Guidacres can be convinced, by the use of $500,000 worth of advertising and cocktail parties, that a sale will only occur if they reveal their true land valuations. Since $8,000,000 plus $1,500,000 is less than $10,000,000, the park will be established. But if collective valuation of the tracts and of the benefits of the prospective park would have cost less than $1,500,000, it would have been inefficient to establish the park through the market — a market which was not worth having would have been paid for.

Of course, the problems with liability rules are equally real. We cannot be at all sure that landowner Taney is lying or holding out when he says his land is worth $12,000 to him. The fact that several neighbors sold identical tracts for $10,000 does not help us very much; Taney may be sentimentally attached to his land. As a result, eminent domain may grossly undervalue what Taney would actually sell for, even if it sought to give him his true valuation of his tract. In practice, it is so hard to determine Taney's true valuation that eminent domain simply gives him what the land is worth "objectively," in the full knowledge that this may result in over or under compensation. The same is true on the buyer side. "Benefits" taxes rarely attempt, let alone succeed, in gauging the individual citizen's relative desire for the alleged benefit. They are justified because, even if they do not accurately measure each individual's desire for the benefit, the market alternative seems worse. For example, fifty different households may place different values on a new sidewalk that is to abut all the properties. Nevertheless, because it is too difficult, even if possible, to gauge each household's valuation, we usually tax each household an equal amount.

The example of eminent domain is simply one of numerous instances in which society uses liability rules. Accidents is another. If we were to give victims a property entitlement not to be accidentally injured we would have to require all who engage in activities that may injure individuals to negotiate with them before an accident, and to buy the right to knock off an arm or a leg. Such pre-accident negotiations would be extremely expensive, often prohibitively so. To require them would thus preclude many activities that might, in fact, be worth having. . . .

We should also recognize that efficiency is not the sole ground for employing liability rules rather than property rules. Just as the initial entitlement is often decided upon for distributional reasons, so too the choice of a liability rule is often made because it facilitates a combination of efficiency and distributive results which would be difficult to achieve under a property rule. . . .

B. Inalienable Entitlements

Thus far we have focused on the questions of when society should protect an entitlement by property or liability rules. However, there remain many entitlements which involve a still greater degree of societal intervention: The law not only decides who is to own something and what price is to be paid for it if it is taken or destroyed, but also regulates its sale — by, for example, prescribing preconditions for a valid sale or forbidding a sale altogether. Although these rules of inalienability are substantially different from the property and liability rules, their use can be analyzed in terms of the same efficiency and distributional goals that underlie the use of the other two rules.

While at first glance efficiency objectives may seem undermined by limitations on the ability to engage in transactions, closer analysis suggests that there are instances, perhaps many, in which economic efficiency is more closely approximated by such limitations. This might occur when a transaction would create significant externalities — costs to third parties.

For instance, if Taney were allowed to sell his land to Chase, a polluter, he would injure his neighbor Marshall by lowering the value of Marshall's land. Conceivably, Marshall could pay Taney not to sell his land; but, because there are many injured Marshalls, freeloader and information costs make such transactions practically impossible. . . .

Another instance in which external costs may justify inalienability occurs when external costs do not lend themselves to collective measurement which is acceptably objective and nonarbitrary. This nonmonetizability is characteristic of one category of external costs which, as a practical matter, seems frequently to lead us to rules of inalienability. Such external costs are often called moralisms.

If Taney is allowed to sell himself into slavery, or to take undue risks of becoming penniless, or to sell a kidney, Marshall may be harmed, simply because Marshall is a sensitive man who is made unhappy by seeing slaves, paupers, or persons who die because they have sold a kidney. Again Marshall could pay Taney not to sell his freedom to Chase the slaveowner; but again, because Marshall is not one but many individuals, freeloader and information costs make such transactions practically impossible. . . . [I]t might seem that the state could intervene by objectively valuing the external cost to Marshall and requiring Chase to pay that cost. But since the external cost to Marshall does not lend itself to an acceptable objective measurement, such liability rules are not appropriate. . . .

There are two other efficiency reasons for forbidding the sale of entitlements under certain circumstances: self paternalism and true paternalism. Examples of the first are Ulysses tying himself to the mast or individuals passing a bill of rights so that they will be prevented from yielding to momentary temptations which they deem harmful to themselves. This type of limitation is not in any real sense paternalism. It is fully consistent with Pareto-efficiency criteria, based on the notion that over the mass of cases no one knows better than the individual what is best for him or her. It merely allows the individual to choose what is best in the long run rather than in the short run, even though that choice entails giving up some short run freedom of choice. Self paternalism may cause us to require certain conditions to exist before we allow a sale of an entitlement; and it may help explain many situations of inalienability, like the invalidity of contracts entered into when drunk, or under undue influence or coercion. But it probably does not fully explain even these.

True paternalism brings us a step further toward explaining such prohibitions and those of broader kinds — for example, the prohibitions on a whole range of activities by minors. Paternalism is based on the notion that at least in some situations the Marshalls know better than Taney what will make Taney better off. Here we are not talking about the offense to Marshall from Taney's choosing to read pornography, or selling himself into slavery, but rather the judgment that Taney was not in the position to choose best for himself when he made the choice for erotica or servitude. The first concept we called a moralism and is a frequent and important ground for inalienability. But it is consistent with the premises of Pareto-optimality. The second, paternalism, is also an important economic efficiency reason for inalienability, but it is not consistent with the premises of Pareto-optimality: The most efficient pie is no longer that which costless bargains would achieve, because a person may be better off if he is prohibited from bargaining.

Finally, just as efficiency goals sometimes dictate the use of rules of inalienability, so, of course, do distributional goals. Whether an entitlement may be sold or not often affects directly who is richer and who is poorer. Prohibiting the sale of babies makes poorer those who can cheaply produce babies and richer those who through some nonmarket device get free an "unwanted" baby. Prohibiting exculpatory clauses in product sales makes richer those who were injured by a product defect and poorer those who were not injured and who paid more for the product because the exculpatory clause was forbidden. Favoring the specific group that has benefited may or may not have been the reason for the prohibition on bargaining. What is important is that, regardless of the reason for barring a contract, a group did gain from the prohibition.

This should suffice to put us on guard, for it suggests that direct distributional motives may lie behind asserted nondistributional grounds for inalienability, whether they be paternalism, self paternalism, or externalities. . . . For example, we may use certain types of zoning to preserve open spaces on the grounds that the poor will be happier, though they do not know it now. And open spaces may indeed make the poor happier in the long run. But the zoning that preserves open space also makes housing in the suburbs more expensive and it may be that the whole plan is aimed at securing distributional benefits to the suburban dweller regardless of the poor's happiness.

IV. The Framework and Pollution Control Rules

Nuisance or pollution is one of the most interesting areas where the question of who will be given an entitlement, and how it will be protected, is in frequent issue. Traditionally, and very ably in the recent article by Professor Michelman, the nuisance-pollution problem is viewed in terms of three rules.[53] First, Taney may not pollute unless his neighbor (his only neighbor, let us assume), Marshall, allows it (Marshall may enjoin Taney's nuisance). Second, Taney may pollute but must compensate Marshall for damages caused (nuisance is found but the remedy is limited to damages). Third, Taney may pollute at will and can only be stopped by Marshall if Marshall pays him off (Taney's pollution is not held to be a nuisance to Marshall). In our terminology rules one and two (nuisance with injunction, and with damages only) are entitlements to Marshall. The first is an entitlement to be free from pollution and is protected by a property rule; the second is also an entitlement to be free from pollution but is protected only by a liability rule. Rule three (no nuisance) is instead an entitlement to Taney protected by a property rule, for only by buying Taney out at Taney's price can Marshall end the pollution.

The very statement of these rules in the context of our framework suggests that something is missing. Missing is a fourth rule representing an entitlement in Taney to pollute, but an entitlement which is protected only by a liability rule. The fourth rule, really a kind of partial eminent domain coupled with a benefits tax, can be stated as follows: Marshall may stop Taney from polluting, but if he does he must compensate Taney.

As a practical matter it will be easy to see why even legal writers as astute as Professor Michelman have ignored this rule. Unlike the first three it does not often lend itself to judicial imposition for a number of good legal process reasons. For example, even if Taney's injuries could practically be measured, apportionment of the duty of compensation among many Marshalls would present problems for which courts are not well suited. If only those Marshalls who voluntarily asserted the right to enjoin Taney's pollution were required to pay the compensation, there would be insuperable freeloader problems. If, on the other hand, the liability rule entitled one of the Marshalls alone to enjoin the pollution and required all the benefited Marshalls to pay their share of the compensation, the courts would be faced with the immensely difficult task of determining who was benefited how much and imposing a benefits tax accordingly, all the while observing procedural limits within which courts are expected to function.

The fourth rule is thus not part of the cases legal scholars read when they study nuisance law, and is therefore easily ignored by them. But it is available, and may sometimes make more sense than any of the three competing approaches. Indeed, in one form or another, it may well be the most frequent device employed. To appreciate the utility of the fourth rule and to compare it with the other three rules, we will examine why we might choose any of the given rules.

We would employ rule one (entitlement to be free from pollution protected by a property rule) from an economic efficiency point of view if we believed that the polluter, Taney, could avoid or reduce the costs of pollution more cheaply than the pollutee, Marshall. Or to put it another way, Taney would be enjoinable if he were in a better position to balance the costs of polluting against the costs of not polluting. We would employ rule three (entitlement to pollute protected by a property rule) again solely from an economic efficiency standpoint, if we made the converse judgment on who could best balance the harm of pollution against its avoidance costs. If we were wrong in our judgments and if transactions between Marshall and Taney were costless or even very cheap, the entitlement under rules one or three would be traded and an economically efficient result would occur in either case. If we entitled Taney to pollute and Marshall valued clean air more than Taney valued the pollution, Marshall would pay Taney to stop polluting even though no nuisance was found. If we entitled Marshall to enjoin the pollution and the right to pollute was worth more to Taney than freedom from pollution was to Marshall, Taney would pay Marshall not to seek an injunction or would buy Marshall's land and sell it to someone who would agree not to seek an injunction. As we have assumed no one else was hurt by the pollution, Taney could now pollute even though the initial entitlement, based on a wrong guess of who was the cheapest avoider of the costs involved, allowed the pollution to be enjoined. Wherever transactions between Taney and Marshall are easy, and wherever economic efficiency is our goal, we could employ entitlements protected by property rules even though we would not be sure that the entitlement chosen was the right one. Transactions as described above would cure the error. While the entitlement might have important distributional effects, it would not substantially undercut economic efficiency.

The moment we assume, however, that transactions are not cheap, the situation changes dramatically. Assume we enjoin Taney and there are 10,000 injured Marshalls. Now *even if* the right to pollute is worth more to Taney than the right to be free from pollution is to the sum of the Marshalls, the injunction will probably stand. The cost of buying out all the Marshalls, given holdout problems, is likely to be too great, and an equivalent of eminent domain in Taney would be needed to alter the initial injunction. Conversely, if we denied a nuisance remedy, the 10,000 Marshalls could only with enormous difficulty, given freeloader problems, get together to buy out even one Taney and prevent the pollution. This would be so even if the pollution harm was greater than the value to Taney of the right to pollute.

If, however, transaction costs are not symmetrical, we may still be able to use the property rule. Assume that Taney can buy the Marshalls' entitlements easily because holdouts are for some reason absent, but that the Marshalls have great freeloader problems in buying out Taney. In this situation the entitlement should be granted to the Marshalls unless we are sure the Marshalls are the cheapest avoiders of pollution costs. Where we do not know the identity of the cheapest cost avoider it is better to entitle the Marshalls to be free of pollution because, even if we are wrong in our initial placement of the entitlement, that is, even if the Marshalls are the cheapest cost avoiders, Taney will buy out the Marshalls and economic efficiency will be achieved. Had we chosen the converse entitlement and been wrong, the Marshalls could not have bought out Taney. Unfortunately, transaction costs are often high on both sides and an initial entitlement, though incorrect in terms of economic efficiency, will not be altered in the market place.

Under these circumstances — and they are normal ones in the pollution area — we are likely to turn to liability rules whenever we are uncertain whether the polluter or the pollutees can most cheaply avoid the cost of pollution. We are only likely to use liability rules where we are uncertain because, if we are certain, the costs of liability rules — essentially the costs of collectively valuing the damages to all concerned plus the cost in coercion to those who would not sell at the collectively determined figure — are unnecessary. They are unnecessary because transaction costs and bargaining barriers become irrelevant when we are certain who is the cheapest cost avoider; economic efficiency will be attained without transactions by making the correct initial entitlement.

As a practical matter we often are uncertain who the cheapest cost avoider is. In such cases, traditional legal doctrine tends to find a nuisance but imposes only damages on Taney payable to the Marshalls. This way, if the amount of damages Taney is made to pay is close to the injury caused, economic efficiency will have had its due; if he cannot make a go of it, the nuisance was not worth its costs. The entitlement to the Marshalls to be free from pollution unless compensated, however, will have been given *not* because it was thought that polluting was probably worth less to Taney than freedom from pollution was worth to the Marshalls, nor even because on some distributional basis we preferred to charge the cost to Taney rather than to the Marshalls. It was so placed *simply because we did not know* whether Taney desired to pollute more than the Marshalls desired to be free from pollution, and the only way we thought we could test out the value of the pollution was by the only liability rule we thought we had. This was rule two, the imposition of nuisance damages on Taney. At least this would be the position of a court concerned with economic efficiency which believed itself limited to rules one, two, and three.

Rule four gives at least the possibility that the opposite entitlement may also lead to economic efficiency in a situation of uncertainty. Suppose for the moment that a mechanism exists for collectively assessing the damage resulting to Taney from being stopped from polluting by the Marshalls, and a mechanism also exists for collectively assessing the benefit to each of the Marshalls from such cessation. Then — assuming the same degree of accuracy in collective valuation as exists in rule two (the nuisance damage rule) — the Marshalls would stop the pollution if it harmed them more than it benefited Taney. If this is possible, then even if we thought it necessary to use a liability rule, we would still be free to give the entitlement to Taney or Marshall for whatever reasons, efficiency or distributional, we desired. . . .

. . . Assume a factory which, by using cheap coal, pollutes a very wealthy section of town and employs many low income workers to produce a product purchased primarily by the poor; assume also a distributional goal that favors equality of wealth. Rule one — enjoin the nuisance — would possibly have desirable economic efficiency results (if the pollution hurt the homeowners more than it saved the factory in coal costs), but it would have disastrous distribution effects. It would also have undesirable efficiency effects if the initial judgment on costs of avoidance had been wrong and transaction costs were high. Rule two — nuisance damages — would allow a testing of the economic efficiency of eliminating the pollution, even in the presence of high transaction costs, but would quite possibly put the factory out of business or diminish output and thus have the same income distribution effects as rule one. Rule three — no nuisance — would have favorable distributional effects since it might protect the income of the workers. But if the pollution harm was greater to the homeowners than the cost of avoiding it by using a better coal, and if transaction costs — holdout problems — were such that homeowners could not unite to pay the factory to use better coal, rule three would have unsatisfactory efficiency effects. Rule four — payment of damages to the factory after allowing the homeowners to compel it to use better coal, and assessment of the cost of these damages to the homeowners — would be the only one which would accomplish both the distributional and efficiency goals. . . .

V.   The Framework and Criminal Sanctions . . .

Beginning students, when first acquainted with economic efficiency notions, sometimes ask why ought not a robber be simply charged with the value of the thing robbed. And the same question is sometimes posed by legal philosophers. If it is worth more to the robber than to the owner, is not economic efficiency served by such a penalty? Our answers to such a question tend to move quickly into very high sounding and undoubtedly relevant moral considerations. But these considerations are often not very helpful to the questioner because they depend on the existence of obligations on individuals not to rob for a fixed price and the original question was why we should impose such obligations at all.

One simple answer to the question would be that thieves do not get caught every time they rob and therefore the costs to the thief must at least take the unlikelihood of capture into account. But that would not fully answer the problem, for even if thieves were caught every time, the penalty we would wish to impose would be greater than the objective damages to the person robbed.

A possible broader explanation lies in a consideration of the difference between property entitlements and liability entitlements. For us to charge the thief with a penalty equal to an objectively determined value of the property stolen would be to convert all property rule entitlements into liability rule entitlements.

The question remains, however, why *not* convert all property rules into liability rules? The answer is, of course, obvious. Liability rules represent only an approximation of the value of the object to its original owner and willingness to pay such an approximate value is no indication that it is worth more to the thief than to the owner. In other words, quite apart from the expense of arriving collectively at such an objective valuation, it is no guarantee of the economic efficiency of the transfer. If this is so with property, it is all the more so with bodily integrity, and we would not presume collectively and objectively to value the cost of a rape to the victim against the benefit to the rapist even if economic efficiency is our sole motive. Indeed when we approach bodily integrity we are getting close to areas where we do not let the entitlement be sold at all and where economic efficiency enters in, if at all, in a more complex way. But even where the items taken or destroyed are things we do allow to be sold, we will not without special reasons impose an objective selling price on the vendor.

Once we reach the conclusion that we will not simply have liability rules, but that often, even just on economic efficiency grounds, property rules are desirable, an answer to the beginning student's question becomes clear. The thief not only harms the victim, he undermines rules and distinctions of significance beyond the specific case. Thus even if in a given case we can be sure that the value of the item stolen was no more than X dollars, and even if the thief has been caught and is prepared to compensate, we would not be content simply to charge the thief X dollars. Since in the majority of cases we cannot be sure of the economic efficiency of the transfer by theft, we must add to each case an undefinable kicker which represents society's need to keep all property rules from being changed at will into liability rules. In other words, we impose criminal sanctions as a means of deterring future attempts to convert property rules into liability rules.

The first-year student might push on, however, and ask why we treat the thief or the rapist differently from the injurer in an auto accident or the polluter in a nuisance case. Why do we allow liability rules there? In a sense, we have already answered the question. The only level at which, before the accident, the driver can negotiate for the value of what he might take from his potential victim is one at which transactions are too costly. The thief or rapist, on the other hand, could have negotiated without undue expense (at least if the good was one which we allowed to be sold at all) because we assume he knew what he was going to do and to whom he would do it. The case of the accident is different because knowledge exists only at the level of deciding to drive or perhaps to drive fast, and at that level negotiations with potential victims are usually not feasible.

The case of nuisance seems different, however. There the polluter knows what he will do and, often, whom it will hurt. But as we have already pointed out, freeloader or holdout problems may often preclude any successful negotiations between the polluter and the victims of pollution; additionally, we are often uncertain who is the cheapest avoider of pollution costs. In these circumstances a liability rule, which at least allowed the economic efficiency of a proposed transfer of entitlements to be tested, seemed appropriate, even though it permitted the nonaccidental and unconsented taking of an entitlement. It should be emphasized, however, that where transaction costs do not bar negotiations between polluter and victim, or where we are sufficiently certain who the cheapest cost avoider is, there are no efficiency reasons for allowing intentional takings, and property rules, supported by injunctions or criminal sanctions, are appropriate.

NOTES AND QUESTIONS ON THE DISTINCTION BETWEEN PROPERTY RULES AND LIABILITY RULES

1. At places Calabresi and Melamed (C & M) imply that lawmakers should *first* decide which party in a dispute to favor, and *then* decide how to protect that favored party. At other places they argue that these decisions are to be made simultaneously. Which approach is likely to lead to better results? Are lawmakers wiser to consider rights in the abstract, or always with an eye to interrelated remedial issues?

2. The private law of property shifts from property-rule to liability-rule protection when it:

   a. entitles a single concurrent owner to force a partition sale of co-owned real estate;

   b. provides only monetary relief to owners of lands flooded by a millpond created by a private dam (an innovation of the Mill Acts, enacted as early as the eighteenth century); and

   c. restricts nuisance plaintiffs to the remedy of damages.

Under what circumstances would C & M support these shifts to liability rules?

3. Does C & M's terminology obfuscate fundamental differences in the entitlements attributable to the different "rules"? Critics have noted that an entitlement "protected" by a liability rule actually has a lesser content than one protected by a property rule; see Jules L. Coleman & Jody Kraus, Rethinking the Theory of Legal Rights, 95 Yale L.J. 1335, 1346 (1986); see also Carol M. Rose, The Shadow of the Cathedral, 106 Yale L.J. 2175, 2178-2179 (1997), describing a liability rule as dividing the entitlement, giving an op-

tion to the polluting factory while leaving the homeowner with merely a "PRSTO" (property-right-subject-to-an-option). Does the language of options make the relationship of the parties clearer? Is there any reason why C & M might have wanted to paper over the loss of rights entailed by liability rules?

4. According to C & M's analysis, should a local government be entitled to exercise the power of eminent domain when it wishes to acquire (and preserve) the birthplace of a former President? When it wishes to widen Main Street? When it wishes to acquire commercial space to house its planning department? See Thomas W. Merrill, The Economics of Public Use, 72 Cornell L. Rev. 61 (1986).

5. To what extent should C & M's "rule four" be available to a private party? Richard Epstein notes the institutional and substantive constraints that the law normally puts around the use of liability rules in general, both in tort law and in the law of eminent domain (an instance of rule four); he argues that a generalized use of rule four is in effect an attack on the basic principle of private property that generally allows an owner to sell if and when she pleases. See Epstein, A Clear View of The Cathedral: The Dominance of Property Rules, 106 Yale L.J. 2091 (1996).

6. At places C & M imply that inalienability rules are *alternatives* to property rules and liability rules. In the usual case, property rules and liability rules govern the remedies A has against B when B interferes with A's entitlements; inalienability rules, by contrast, are rights that the *state* has against A to prevent A from consensually making deals with the likes of B. In light of this difference, are C & M wise to treat the three sorts of rules as members of the same set? For more on issues of alienability, see the selection by Radin, infra p. 336.

7. On the functions of criminal law, see Alvin Klevorick, Legal Theory and the Economic Analysis of Torts and Crimes, 85 Colum. L. Rev. 905 (1985).

8. In an example on p. 244, C & M state that the proper outcome of a pollution dispute might depend on a comparison of the wealth of the homeowners suffering from the pollution and the wealth of the polluting factory's workers and customers. By contrast, others contend that distributional goals are invariably better achieved by means of broad taxation and welfare programs, rather than through private adjudication. See e.g., A. Mitchell Polinsky, An Introduction to Law and Economics, 119-127 (2d ed. 1989). Who has the better of this debate? Whose approach is more congruent with the letter of nuisance doctrine? With nuisance law "in action"?

9. Thomas Merrill, in Trespass, Nuisance, and the Costs of

Determining Property Rights, 14 J. Legal Stud. 13 (1985), has used C & M's property rule/liability rule distinction to illuminate the differences between the law of trespass and nuisance. Trespass cases, he argues, generally involve low transaction costs and lend themselves to "mechanical," all-or-nothing property-rule solutions, in which the entire right is assigned to one of the parties and the parties thereafter can bargain if they wish. On the other hand, nuisance cases as a general rule involve diffuse externalities like air or water pollution, affecting large numbers of heterogeneous parties who are unlikely to be able to bargain to a solution. According to Merrill, in such nuisance cases the courts use more vague "judgmental" rules, deciding each case themselves and assigning liability after case-by-case balancing of the various interests. Does Merrill's analysis explain why nuisance law inherently tends to be an "impenetrable jungle," as William Prosser once called it (Prosser and W. Page Keeton, The Law of Torts 616-617 (5th ed. 1984))? Although they use a different analysis, Louis Kaplow and Steven Shavell arrive at conclusions quite similar to Merrill's in arguing that liability rules are appropriate for what they call "externalities," whereas property rules are more appropriate for what they call possessory "things." See Kaplow & Shavell, Property Rules versus Liability Rules: An Economic Analysis, 109 Harv. L. Rev. 713 (1996).

10. Like Coase's famous article, supra p. 200, C & M's article continues to play a central role in legal scholarship. For a discussion of its impressive citation count over the years, see James E. Krier & Stewart J. Schwab, The Cathedral at Twenty-Five: Citations and Impressions, 106 Yale L.J. 2121 (1997).

Property Rules and Liability Rules: The Cathedral in Another Light*

James E. Krier & Stewart J. Schwab

I. Some Background

A. "Four Rules": An Intellectual History

The problem of environmental pollution is the stock example in the literature of concern to us here, so we shall use it too. As

*Source: 70 N.Y.U. L. Rev. 440, 442-464 (1995).

Calabresi and Melamed pointed out, traditional thinking about the pollution problem had envisioned three alternative ways a court might resolve an ongoing conflict, say a nuisance suit, between a polluter P and a resident R. *First*, the court could find a nuisance and issue an injunction against P in favor of R (meaning that P, in order to keep on polluting, would have to buy off R in a subsequent, post-injunction transaction). *Second*, the court could find a nuisance but permit P to go on polluting upon payment of damages to R. *Third*, the court could find the pollution not to be a nuisance and permit P to continue (meaning that R, in order to bring a halt to the pollution, would have to buy off P in a subsequent transaction). There were, in short, "three rules," the first and third of which might induce post-judgment voluntary (bilateral) transactions and the second of which might induce a post-judgment involuntary (unilateral) transaction, a sale that P could, if it chose, force upon R.

As right and complete as this set of possibilities had always seemed, Calabresi and Melamed could show easily enough that something was missing. Their method was to model the conflict between P and R in terms of its two variables: (1) an *entitlement* to the environmental resource at stake, such as air, water, peace and quiet, or a view; and (2) the *means of protecting* that entitlement. . . .

. . . In principle, there must be "four rules" for resolving matters, rather than the traditional three. What had been missing, and what Calabresi and Melamed discovered with their model, is the now rather notorious "rule four." The rule recognizes an entitlement in P protected by a liability rule. . . .

B. Efficiency and Justice

Now that we can see how judges hold four suits in their deck, not just the three that they'd played with for so long, it is reasonable to ask what this understanding adds to the game. To answer that question, we have to begin by thinking about the objectives of the game in the first place.

Here we subscribe to what seems to be the general view: In the event of conflicts arising from incompatible demands upon some resource (in our stock example, some environmental resource), the idea is to achieve resolutions that promote "efficiency" and "justice." "Efficient" resolutions are taken to be those that maximize the value of the resource (or minimize the cost of the conflict over the resource). . . . "Justice," in its turn, means essentially everything else that matters to a sensible resolution — distributional or corrective justice, for example. . . .

II. Property Rules and Liability Rules: The Conventional Wisdom

It appears to us that practitioners of Calabresi and Melamed's approach, of whom there are many, have gradually obliterated the nuanced, indeed the tentative, nature of the original analysis, substituting for it a simplistic conventional wisdom about how to assign and protect entitlements in terms of the four rules we have described.

A. Assigning Entitlements Initially

Start with the matter of initial assignment. How should a judge decide who, as between P and R, is to get the contested entitlement initially? . . . As already suggested, efficiency and justice bear on the answer, but so too do the costs of transacting. Regarding efficiency, suppose that the judge concludes from the evidence in an R $v.$ P case that it is less costly for P to avoid (abate) the pollution than it is for R to avoid or tolerate it. (In Calabresi's original and now very familiar terminology, P is the cheapest cost avoider.) Suppose also that the judge has no justice preference for either party. The efficient resolution then would be to assign the entitlement in question to R; this appears to be its cost-minimizing or value-maximizing location, and by hypothesis there is no justice reason to trump it. The entitlement could be given to R (protected by a property rule granting R injunctive relief).

But now suppose that the judge might be wrong in concluding that P is the cheapest cost avoider. Is there any way to hedge against such an error, such that if the entitlement *starts out* with R it can still *end up* with P if in fact that is its efficient location? The answer to this question goes directly back through Calabresi to Coase. As virtually everybody in the business must know by now, one item in Coase's magnificent contribution to our understanding of social cost was the demonstration that, absent any impediments to bargaining, an initial mistaken (inefficient) assignment of an entitlement can (will) always be corrected by subsequent transactions between the parties. . . .

Insignificant transaction costs is a strong assumption, but if it holds there are equally powerful consequences. . . . The judge could . . . simply assign the entitlement to R for [a] justice reason alone, knowing all along that if the entitlement's efficient location happened to be in the hands of P, it would move there. In short, when transaction costs are insignificant, efficiency concerns become irrelevant to the judge's inquiry; only justice reasons matter. . . .

[Where transaction costs are high, there] is a problem, of course, if efficiency (here in the guise of asymmetric transaction costs) cuts in favor of *P* but justice cuts in favor of *R*. Obviously, some kind of complicated tradeoff has to be made — easy for us to say, confounding for judges to do. For one thing, information about the considerations to be "traded off," efficiency and justice, is by definition rather poor. For another thing, the basic conceptions, justice in particular, have elusive meanings. And third, whatever they mean, they seem to be incommensurable.

B. Protecting Entitlements

Once the judge in an *R v. P* case has determined the initial location of the entitlement to the resource in question, there remains the matter of entitlement protection. Here, as we saw, there are two alternatives, a property rule and a liability rule. . . .

The conventional answer appears to be that the correct . . . choice depends on the level of transaction costs. If transaction costs are insignificant (low), then the judge should use property rules to resolve the *R v. P* dispute, choosing between rule one (injunctive relief to *R*) and rule three (*R* is denied all relief) by reference to justice preferences, considerations of who might value the entitlement most as between *R* and *P*, and (or) asymmetry in the costs of bargaining (tradeoffs among these might be necessary, as we have seen). . . .

But suppose, as is regularly the case, that transaction costs *are* significant (high) — whether because there are multiple *P*s and *R*s (giving rise to multi-party negotiations, and more importantly, the strategic behavior of free riders and holdouts) or even if there is only one *P* and one *R* (where bilateral monopoly may also induce strategic behavior). Here the post-Calabresi-and-Melamed commentators have presumed, almost uniformly, that the judge should opt in favor of liability rules (with the choice between rules two and four turning on justice reasons and asymmetries in information, among other factors).

The reasoning behind this typical presumption runs as follows: Take a situation where, thanks to high transaction costs, the judge's initial assignment of the entitlement is probably also going to be its final resting place if a property rule is used because bargaining impediments will stall any subsequent transfer. No problem: Use a liability rule instead. Determine the costs that *P*'s pollution works on *R* and hold that *P* may continue polluting only upon payment of that amount to R, as damages. If P's avoidance cost is lower than the damages, P will choose to avoid — the efficient result. If P's avoidance cost is higher than the damages, P will choose to pollute and pay — the efficient result again. And the just result, too, so long as the judge has a justice preference for R, or at least no justice preference at all. In short, when private bargaining is likely to fail, one can (so runs the conventional view) turn to the judge to establish a price. . . .

III. Property Rules and Liability Rules: Another View

. . . Our quarrel is with the conventional view on the issue of entitlement protection, particularly the virtual dogma that liability rules should be used when transaction costs are high.

This particular piece of the conventional wisdom seems to have begun settling in very shortly after Calabresi and Melamed published their article in 1972. Richard Posner, in the first edition of his widely used text on law and economics, cited Calabresi and Melamed's discussion in support of the assertion that "where transaction costs are high, the allocation of resources to their highest valued uses is facilitated by denying property right holders an injunctive remedy against invasions of their rights and instead limiting them to a remedy in damages. . . ."[43] The generalization has persisted since then, as one could readily enough gather from a sampling of the literature. It has become, as we said, virtual dogma. Unhappily, however (and as so commonly happens), the dogma is incorrect, and for a reason that makes the entire structure of four rules as vulnerable as a house of cards.

A. Transaction Costs and Assessment Costs

1. THE PROBLEM

It was Professor Polinsky who first suggested (at least in print) the error in the conventional wisdom, and the point, once made, is obvious. Just as obstacles to bargaining (transaction costs) might impede efficient exchanges by the parties in property rule cases, so problems in obtaining and processing information (assessment costs) might impede efficient damage calculations by the judge in liability rule cases. If, say, the judge uses liability rule two and calculates damages in a way sufficiently off the mark, then P might

---

43. Richard A. Posner, Economic Analysis of Law 29 (1st ed. 1972). . . .

well pay and pollute when it should abate, or abate when it should pay and pollute. In short, to the question "whether the arguments favoring damage remedies are logically coherent," Polinsky answered: "They are not." On real-world assumptions, "the argument could easily go either way."[46]

2. THE PROBLEM FURTHER EXAMINED

To his credit, Richard Posner seems to have recognized the problem in the conventional wisdom, but in a way that only deepens it. . . . The chief discussion in the two later editions [of Posner's law and economics text] stands essentially as it was in the two earlier editions, to the effect that "where transaction costs are high, the allocation of resources to their highest valued uses is facilitated by denying property right holders an injunctive remedy against invasions of their rights and instead limiting them to a remedy in damages." But now a footnote adds that this statement *"assumes that damages can be computed with reasonable accuracy. If they cannot, there is an argument for injunctive relief."* . . .

. . . [C]onsider the language we italicized above and notice that the conventional wisdom implicitly contains not one piece of advice, but two, each the apparent corollary of the other. The first piece says this:

> *If transaction costs are low, use property rules (and otherwise, use liability rules).*

The second advises:

> *If damages can be computed with reasonable accuracy, use liability rules (and otherwise, use property rules).*

Now take the real world and acknowledge that transaction costs are commonly high *and* that assessment costs are, too. After all, the parties will typically confront some impediments to bargaining, and the judge will typically confront some difficulties in trying to assess damages accurately. Then, if in this real-world setting we begin with the first piece of conventional advice, we will be led by it to the second. If, instead, we begin with the second, we will be led by it to the first. So it seems that whether the judge should end up using a property rule, or rather a liability rule, turns on nothing but the arbitrary matter of where the judge starts out. . . .

46. [A. Mitchell Polinsky, Resolving Nuisance Disputes: The Simple Economics of Injunctive and Damage Remedies, 32 Stan. L. Rev. 1075, 1111 (1980).]

B. Objective (Pretend) and Subjective (Real) Outlooks . . .

. . . The conventional view simply *presumes* that liability rules represent the best that can be done under the circumstances. The question then is this: Why not presume the opposite?

To understand the case for such a reverse presumption, begin with the conceit of *objective* damages, the usual measure in R v. P and related litigation. To measure R's damages objectively is to take the market price, set by the intersection of supply and demand curves, and to ignore R's actual, or real (*subjective*), reservation price — the minimum price R would accept in a bilateral (voluntary) exchange. Quite obviously, objective damages can understate the truth of the matter; they neglect R's consumer surplus or sentimental value, and hence they can promote error in a very systematic fashion. Still, the objective measure is used because subjective measures are usually too difficult to calculate (assessment costs are too high), given the likelihood that R would behave opportunistically, exaggerating sentiments when testifying and the like. So objective damages are a purely cosmetic device. We pretend they represent reality because the pretense *seems* to make liability rules work.

But if the objective damages are just cosmetic, then why not fashion things in a different way and pretend instead that the parties *can bargain*? The conventional pretense saves the liability-rule game, whereas this opposite pretense of ours would save the property-rule game. Exactly as the objective outlook on damages is simply taken to be a *real* indication of value, so our "objective" (pretend) outlook on bargaining could simply be taken to represent how the parties *really* measure their respective opportunity (damage and avoidance) costs. We need only imagine that whatever bargain the parties reach, including no bargain at all, that "whatever" is efficient. . . .

C. The Problems of Correlation and Synergy

We have seen thus far that market bargaining entails transaction costs and that judicial valuation entails assessment costs. Each is a species of what we can call *valuation costs*. Since both methods of valuing entitlements, through the market or in the courts, are ordinarily costly, either can be wrong, resulting in *error costs*. Hence the (efficiency) issue in any given case is this: Which kind of rule, property or liability, promises to minimize the sum of valuation and error costs?

That, we think, is the question for reflective judges, who should compare *their* ability (and their confidence in their ability) to overcome assessment-cost problems with the *parties'* ability (and the judges' confidence in the parties' ability) to overcome transaction-cost problems. Quite obviously, this entails another complicated kind of tradeoff among seeming incommensurables, "something like summing up an orange, the number 6, and the note F#." The need for such a tradeoff is conveniently ignored by the conventional view, even as modified by Posner, and happily enough, we suppose, because the exercise appears to be so daunting. In fact, however, two problems can make the task more complex than it thus far appears, and both problems arise for the same general reason. . . .

1. CORRELATION

Suppose that commonly enough, though not always, the very circumstances that make for high or low transaction costs also make for high or low assessment costs. Where this positive correlation holds, the conventional ground for choosing between property rules and liability rules is undermined. Both rules will work well in the circumstance of low costs, but both will work poorly in the circumstance of high costs, leaving no (efficiency) grounds for choosing between the alternative property and liability rules in high-cost cases. So let us consider briefly (the reasons are actually familiar ones) why the two kinds of valuation costs might tend to be high at the same time, and under the same circumstances.

High transaction costs are likely to arise, oddly enough, in two very different bargaining situations — bargaining between multiple parties on the one hand, and between few parties on the other. In either kind of case, then, property rules are problematic. Unfortunately, however, in either kind of case assessment costs can also be high, such that liability rules are also problematic. Moreover, in both kinds of cases, the very factors that contribute to high transaction costs can contribute at the same time to high assessment costs, such that any rule can be problematic in any case.

Consider multiple-party cases first. When many people have to bargain, their sheer numbers can prevent efficient trades because it takes longer (costs more) for a lot of people to reach accord than it does for a few. Hence high transaction costs might swamp the value of the transaction itself to the parties. . . . The consequence could be that no exchange is made, even where the value of clean air to all the Rs exceeds P's avoidance cost (the difference between the two being the potential "gains from trade").

Perhaps, then, the judge should instead award the entitlement in question to the Rs and once again protect it with a property rule (rule one), thinking that this will reduce transaction costs. Now holdouts are the problem. Suppose in fact that P's avoidance cost exceeds the sum of all the Rs' damages, such that abatement is an *in*efficient result. To avoid abating, P has to buy out everybody in order to buy out anybody, and each R will be inclined to extract from P *all* of the gains from trade.

In both of the foregoing instances, there is a so-called bilateral monopoly that arises because P and the Rs are locked into mutual dealings: each side can only sell to (or buy from) the other. The costs of the ensuing bluffs and counters can kill efficient exchange.

One can, of course, overstate the free-rider and holdout problems. Private parties sometimes manage to engage in exchange even when some people free ride or hold out, as long as the gains from trade are sufficient to make the costs of transacting worthwhile. (But beware: the larger the gains from trade, the larger the holdout problem can become because the more there is to gain from engrossing the lion's share.) Nevertheless, property rules are well known to induce just the behavior we describe.

The conventional answer, of course, is to use liability rules in these situations, in particular liability rule two. But we can now understand that rule two is unsatisfying to the extent that these very same multiple-party cases entail high assessment costs as well as high transaction costs, and this might regularly be the case. For example, to assess all the Rs' damages from pollution, the court has to figure out, ideally (that is, in terms of subjective values), how much money would make all of them just indifferent to tolerating the pollution — difficult enough in the case of one or a few Rs, heroic in the case of many. At the least, the court would have to assess damages objectively, in terms of diminished fair market value. This may make the task easier, but not necessarily easy (inexpensive) given the considerable amount of expert testimony the assessment would entail. In any event, the objective approach carries with it the cost of biased assessments, as we saw earlier.

The foregoing discussion allows us now to deal briefly with cases involving just a few parties. Here property rules will give rise to the very problems of strategic behavior (induced by bilateral monopolies) that we considered in connection with multiple-party cases. Liability rules might work satisfactorily provided objective damages are used, save for those instances where pollution damage and pollution avoidance cost are close to equal (but here the costs of error are minor in any event). Subjective damages would give rise to the assessment costs we have already discussed. Judges will have problems assessing the correct values for the same reason private bargainers would: limited, hidden information. If parties can hide their valuations from each other, they can hide them from a judge. . . .

2. SYNERGY

To see the point about synergy, return to our discussion of objective (pretend) and subjective (real) outlooks, and imagine the following criticism stated by someone as skeptical of our analysis as we are of the conventional analysis:

> It's silly what you said about judicial versus market estimations of value, because you've made matters all or nothing when in fact they are not. If transaction costs are high the parties simply can't bargain, but with objective damages assessed by the court (your well-taken point about them to the side) at least you capture a *part* of reality. So using them when transaction costs are high is, though not great, still the best way to go.[68]

Our riposte is this: Just as objective damages admittedly capture a part of the truth, so too, usually, will the parties' efforts to bargain. The conventional view tends to see value-measured-by-the-courts as a continuous function, more or less accurate in any given case, but at the same time regards value-measured-by-the-market as noncontinuous, either accurate when transaction costs are "low" or worthless when they are "high." But obviously, just as assessment costs can be low or high or somewhere in between, so too can transaction costs. Parties will often be able to bargain more or less clumsily, even if they seldom can bargain smoothly. . . .

We believe it likely that the coping and learning capacities of the parties will be in part a function of judicial attitudes about liability rules. In other words, there will be a synergistic relationship between what courts do and what parties do. To see our point and test our belief, simply imagine two alternative regimes:

> (1) *If a judge thinks the parties will not bargain effectively, the judge will step in with a liability-damages rule.*

Or, instead,

> (2) *If a judge thinks the parties will not bargain effectively, tough.*

Which regime would best promote the development of effective — say cooperative — bargaining techniques in the long run? If

---

68. This represents a stylized version of Kaplow and Shavell's point about "best estimates" of harm [referring to the draft that became: Louis Kaplow & Steven Shavell, Property Rules versus Liability Rules: An Economic Analysis, 109 Harv. L. Rev. 713 (1996)].

the answer is (2), which we think it has to be, then an obvious conclusion follows. The more ready the courts are to intervene by way of damages when bargainers might balk — on the notion that assessment costs are lower than transaction costs — the less likely the parties are to learn how to reduce the latter.

NOTES AND QUESTIONS ON THE CONTINUING DEBATE OVER PROPERTY RULES VS. LIABILITY RULES

1. Krier and Schwab (K & S) argue that liability rules not only carry assessment costs for courts but also have feedback effects (or synergistic costs) in the sense that they discourage private bargaining and the process of *learning* to bargain. Is it the case that liability rules discourage bargaining? Ian Ayres and Eric Talley make the opposite argument; that is, that the divided entitlements of liability rules should encourage bargaining by forcing at least some of the bargaining parties to reveal private information that they could otherwise conceal in the course of strategic bargaining. See Ayres & Talley, Solomonic Bargaining: Dividing a Legal Entitlement to Facilitate Coasean Trade, 104 Yale L.J. 1027 (1995); see also Ian Ayres & J.M. Balkin, Legal Entitlements as Auctions: Property Rules, Liability Rules, and Beyond, 106 Yale L.J. 703 (1996). In the context of intellectual property, Robert Merges's findings tend to support K & S's side of the argument; Merges argues that mandatory liability rules tend to depress the formation of contractual patent and copyright "pools" among rights-holders. Merges, Contracting into Liability Rules: Intellectual Property Rights and Collective Rights Organizations, 84 Cal. L. Rev. 1293 (1996). Note also that insofar as liability rules complicate entitlements, they could impede trade; see Merrill & Smith, infra p. 360.

2. K & S note that transactions may break down in two opposite situations: where there are too many parties, and where there are too few parties. The latter cases are particularly likely to involve bilateral monopolies, where parties may "hold out" and bargain strategically, each trying to gain the bulk of the gains from trade at the expense of the other. For more on strategic bargaining, see Cooter, The Cost of Coase, cited supra p. 209, Note 5, arguing that Coase neglected the small-number problems of strategic bargaining. Notice that Ian Ayres and his co-authors, supra, tend to lump the small-number and large-number problems together as variations on "transaction costs," whereas Cooter treats them as

separate matters. Which view is more accurate? Are these bargaining problems analytically similar or different? Might the differences between large-number and small-number bargaining impediments underlie basic differences between tort and contract law? For the argument that they do, and that property law may aim at still another class of bargaining impediments, namely "moral hazard," see Carol Rose, The Shadow of the Cathedral, 106 Yale L.J. 2175, 2197-2200 (1996); compare Thomas W. Merrill & Henry E. Smith, The Property-Contract Interface, 101 Colum. L. Rev. 773, 791 (2001), identifying property as a strategy of lumpy assignment of "exclusive management" rights to resources by contrast to contract law's strategy of enabling fine-grained "governance" of resources.

3. Do four "rules" cover all the possible permutations of liability and property protection? In a portion of Krier and Schwab's article not reproduced here, the authors invent a new "rule four with a double reverse twist." For still more possibilities, particularly drawing on the financial instruments of "put" and "call" options, see Madeline Morris, The Structure of Entitlements, 78 Cornell L. Rev. 822 (1993).

Chapter 6

Property Rights that Arise Outside the Legal System

The Evolution of Cooperation*

Robert Axelrod

Under what conditions will cooperation emerge in a world of egoists without central authority? This question has intrigued people for a long time. And for good reason. We all know that people are not angels, and that they tend to look after themselves and their own first. Yet we also know that cooperation does occur and that our civilization is based upon it. But, in situations where each individual has an incentive to be selfish, how can cooperation ever develop?

The answer each of us gives to this question has a fundamental effect on how we think and act in our social, political, and economic relations with others. And the answers that others give have a great effect on how ready they will be to cooperate with us.

The most famous answer was given over three hundred years ago by Thomas Hobbes. It was pessimistic. He argued that before governments existed, the state of nature was dominated by the problem of selfish individuals who competed on such ruthless terms that life was "solitary, poor, nasty, brutish, and short" (Hobbes 1651/1962, p. 100). In his view, cooperation could not de-

*Source: 3-12, 19-21, 30-35 (1984).

velop without a central authority, and consequently a strong government was necessary. Ever since, arguments about the proper scope of government have often focused on whether one could, or could not, expect cooperation to emerge in a particular domain if there were not an authority to police the situation. . . .

A good example of the fundamental problem of cooperation is the case where two industrial nations have erected trade barriers to each other's exports. Because of the mutual advantages of free trade, both countries would be better off if these barriers were eliminated. But if either country were to unilaterally eliminate its barriers, it would find itself facing terms of trade that hurt its own economy. In fact, whatever one country does, the other country is better off retaining its own trade barriers. Therefore, the problem is that each country has an incentive to retain trade barriers, leading to a worse outcome than would have been possible had both countries cooperated with each other.

This basic problem occurs when the pursuit of self-interest by each leads to a poor outcome for all. To make headway in understanding the vast array of specific situations which have this property, a way is needed to represent what is common to these situations without becoming bogged down in the details unique to each. Fortunately, there is such a representation available: the famous *Prisoner's Dilemma* game.

In the Prisoner's Dilemma game, there are two players. Each has two choices, namely cooperate or defect. Each must make the choice without knowing what the other will do. No matter what the other does, defection yields a higher payoff than cooperation. The dilemma is that if both defect, both do worse than if both had cooperated. This simple game will provide the basis for the entire analysis used in this book.

The way the game works is shown in Figure 1. One player chooses a row, either cooperating or defecting. The other player simultaneously chooses a column, either cooperating or defecting. Together, these choices result in one of the four possible outcomes shown in that matrix. If both players cooperate, both do fairly well. Both get R, the *reward for mutual cooperation*. In the concrete illustration of Figure 1 the reward is 3 points. This number might, for example, be a payoff in dollars that each player gets for that outcome. If one player cooperates but the other defects, the defecting player gets the *temptation to defect*, while the cooperating player gets the *sucker's payoff*. In the example, these are 5 points and 0 points respectively. If both defect, both get 1 point, the *punishment for mutual defection*.

What should you do in such a game? Suppose you are the row player, and you think the column player will cooperate. This

Figure 1
The Prisoner's Dilemma

Column Player

		Cooperate	Defect
Row Player	Cooperate	$R = 3, R = 3$ Reward for mutual cooperation	$S = 0, T = 5$ Sucker's payoff, and temptation to defect
	Defect	$T = 5, S = 0$ Temptation to defect and sucker's payoff	$P = 1, P = 1$ Punishment for mutual defection

Note: The payoffs to the row chooser are listed first.

means that you will get one of the two outcomes in the first column of Figure 1. You have a choice. You can cooperate as well, getting the 3 points of the reward for mutual cooperation. Or you can defect, getting the 5 points of the temptation payoff. So it pays to defect if you think the other player will cooperate. But now suppose that you think the other player will defect. Now you are in the second column of Figure 1, and you have a choice between cooperating, which would make you a sucker and give you 0 points, and defecting, which would result in mutual punishment giving you 1 point. So it pays to defect if you think the other player will defect. This means that it is better to defect if you think the other player will cooperate, *and* it is better to defect if you think the other player will defect. So no matter what the other player does, it pays for you to defect.

So far, so good. But the same logic holds for the other player too. Therefore, the other player should defect no matter what you are expected to do. So you should both defect. But then you both get 1 point which is worse than the 3 points of the reward that you both could have gotten had you both cooperated. Individual rationality leads to a worse outcome for both than is possible. Hence the dilemma.

The Prisoner's Dilemma is simply an abstract formulation of some very common and very interesting situations in which what is best for each person individually leads to mutual defection, whereas everyone would have been better off with mutual cooperation. The definition of Prisoner's Dilemma requires that several relationships hold among the four different potential outcomes.

The first relationship specifies the order of the four payoffs. The best a player can do is get T, the temptation to defect when the other player cooperates. The worst a player can do is get S, the sucker's payoff for cooperating while the other player defects. In ordering the other two outcomes, R, the reward for mutual cooperation, is assumed to be better than P, the punishment for mutual defection. This leads to a preference ranking of the four payoffs from best to worst as T, R, P, and S.

The second part of the definition of the Prisoner's Dilemma is that the players cannot get out of their dilemma by taking turns exploiting each other. This assumption means that an even chance of exploitation and being exploited is not as good an outcome for a player as mutual cooperation. It is therefore assumed that the reward for mutual cooperation is greater than the average of the temptation and the sucker's payoff. This assumption, together with the rank ordering of the four payoffs, defines the Prisoner's Dilemma.

Thus two egoists playing the game *once* will both choose their dominant choice, defection, and each will get less than they both could have gotten if they had cooperated. If the game is played a known finite number of times, the players still have no incentive to cooperate. This is certainly true on the last move since there is no future to influence. On the next-to-last move neither player will have an incentive to cooperate since they can both anticipate a defection by the other player on the very last move. Such a line of reasoning implies that the game will unravel all the way back to mutual defection on the first move of any sequence of plays that is of known finite length (Luce and Raiffa 1957, pp. 94-102). This reasoning does not apply if the players will interact an indefinite number of times. And in most realistic settings, the players cannot be sure when the last interaction between them will take place. As will be shown later, with an indefinite number of interactions, cooperation can emerge. The issue then becomes the discovery of the precise conditions that are necessary and sufficient for cooperation to emerge.

In this book I will examine interactions between just two players at a time. A single player may be interacting with many others, but the player is assumed to be interacting with them one at a time. The player is also assumed to recognize another player and to remember how the two of them have interacted so far. This ability to recognize and remember allows the history of the particular interaction to be taken into account by a player's strategy.

A variety of ways to resolve the Prisoner's Dilemma have been developed. Each involves allowing some additional activity that alters the strategic interaction in such a way as to fundamentally change the nature of the problem. The original problem remains, however, because there are many situations in which these remedies are not available. Therefore, the problem will be considered in its fundamental form, without these alterations.

1. There is no mechanism available to the players to make enforceable threats or commitments (Schelling 1960). Since the players cannot commit themselves to a particular strategy, each must take into account all possible strategies that might be used by the other player. Moreover the players have all possible strategies available to themselves.

2. There is no way to be sure what the other player will do on a given move. This eliminates the possibility of metagame analysis which allows such options as "make the same choice as the other is about to make." It also eliminates the possibility of reliable reputations such as might be based on watching the other player interact with third parties. Thus the only information available to the players about each other is the history of their interaction so far.

3. There is no way to eliminate the other player or run away from the interaction. Therefore each player retains the ability to cooperate or defect on each move.

4. There is no way to change the other player's payoffs. The payoffs already include whatever consideration each player has for the interests of the other.

Under these conditions, words not backed by actions are so cheap as to be meaningless. The players can communicate with each other only through the sequence of their own behavior. This is the problem of the Prisoner's Dilemma in its fundamental form.

What makes it possible for cooperation to emerge is the fact that the players might meet again. This possibility means that the choices made today not only determine the outcome of this move, but can also influence the later choices of the players. The future can therefore cast a shadow back upon the present and thereby affect the current strategic situation.

But the future is less important than the present — for two reasons. The first is that players tend to value payoffs less as the time of their obtainment recedes into the future. The second is that there is always some chance that the players will not meet again. An ongoing relationship may end when one or the other player moves away, changes jobs, dies, or goes bankrupt. . . .

The next chapter explores the emergence of cooperation through a study of what is a good strategy to employ if confronted with an iterated Prisoner's Dilemma. This exploration has been done in a novel way, with a computer tournament. Professional game theorists were invited to submit their favorite strategy, and each of these decision rules was paired off with each of the others to see which would do best overall. Amazingly enough, the winner was the simplest of all strategies submitted. This was TIT FOR TAT, the strategy which cooperates on the first move and then does whatever the other player did on the previous move. A second round of the tournament was conducted in which many more entries were submitted by amateurs and professionals alike, all of whom were aware of the results of the first round. The result was another victory for TIT FOR TAT! The analysis of the data from these tournaments reveals four properties which tend to make a decision rule successful: avoidance of unnecessary conflict by cooperating as long as the other player does, provocability in the face of an uncalled for defection by the other, forgiveness after responding to a provocation, and clarity of behavior so that the other player can adapt to your pattern of action.

These results from the tournaments demonstrate that under suitable conditions, cooperation can indeed emerge in a world of egoists without central authority. To see just how widely these results apply, a theoretical approach is taken in Chapter 3. A series of propositions are proved that not only demonstrate the requirements for the emergence of cooperation but also provide the chronological story of the evolution of cooperation. Here is the argument in a nutshell. The evolution of cooperation requires that individuals have a sufficiently large chance to meet again so that they have a stake in their future interaction. If this is true, cooperation can evolve in three stages.

1. The beginning of the story is that cooperation can get started even in a world of unconditional defection. The development *cannot* take place if it is tried only by scattered individuals who have virtually no chance to interact with each other. However, cooperation can evolve from small clusters of individuals who base their cooperation on reciprocity and have even a small proportion of their interactions with each other.

2. The middle of the story is that a strategy based on reciprocity can thrive in a world where many different kinds of strategies are being tried.

3. The end of the story is that cooperation, once established on the basis of reciprocity, can protect itself from invasion by less cooperative strategies. Thus, the gear wheels of social evolution have a ratchet.

Chapters 4 and 5 take concrete settings to demonstrate just how widely these results apply. Chapter 4 is devoted to the fascinating case of the "live and let live" system which emerged during the trench warfare of World War I. In the midst of this bitter conflict, the front-line soldiers often refrained from shooting to kill — provided their restraint was reciprocated by the soldiers on the other side. What made this mutual restraint possible was the static nature of trench warfare, where the same small units faced each other for extended periods of time. The soldiers of these opposing small units actually violated orders from their own high commands in order to achieve tacit cooperation with each other. A detailed look at this case shows that when the conditions are present for the emergence of cooperation, cooperation can get started and prove stable in situations which otherwise appear extraordinarily unpromising. . . .

. . . Two important facts about non-zero-sum settings . . . have to be taken into account. First, the proposition of the previous chapter demonstrates that what is effective depends not only upon the characteristics of a particular strategy, but also upon the nature of the other strategies with which it must interact. The second point follows directly from the first. An effective strategy must be able at any point to take into account the history of the interaction as it has developed so far.

A computer tournament for the study of effective choice in the iterated Prisoner's Dilemma meets these needs. In a computer tournament, each entrant writes a program that embodies a rule to select the cooperative or noncooperative choice on each move. The program has available to it the history of the game so far, and may use this history in making a choice. If the participants are recruited primarily from those who are familiar with the Prisoner's Dilemma, the entrants can be assured that their decision rule will be facing rules of other informed entrants. Such recruitment would also guarantee that the state of the art is represented in the tournament.

Wanting to find out what would happen, I invited professional game theorists to send in entries to just such a computer tournament. It was structured as a round robin, meaning that each entry was paired with each other entry. As announced in the rules of the tournament, each entry was also paired with its own twin and with RANDOM, a program that randomly cooperates and defects with equal probability. Each game consisted of exactly two hundred moves. The payoff matrix for each move was the familiar one described in Chapter 1. It awarded both players 3 points for mutual cooperation, and 1 point for mutual defection. If one player defected while the other player cooperated, the defecting player received 5 points and the cooperating player received 0 points.

No entry was disqualified for exceeding the allotted time. In fact, the entire round robin tournament was run five times to get a more stable estimate of the scores for each pair of players. In all, there were 120,000 moves, making for 240,000 separate choices.

The fourteen submitted entries came from five disciplines: psychology, economics, political science, mathematics, and sociology. . . .

One remarkable aspect of the tournament was that it allowed people from different disciplines to interact with each other in a common format and language. Most of the entrants were recruited from those who had published articles on game theory in general or the Prisoner's Dilemma in particular.

TIT FOR TAT, submitted by Professor Anatol Rapoport of the University of Toronto, won the tournament. This was the simplest of all submitted programs and it turned out to be the best!

TIT FOR TAT, of course, starts with a cooperative choice, and thereafter does what the other player did on the previous move. This decision rule is probably the most widely known and most discussed rule for playing the Prisoner's Dilemma. It is easily understood and easily programmed. It is known to elicit a good degree of cooperation when played with humans (Oskamp 1971; W. Wilson 1971). As an entry in a computer tournament, it has the desirable properties that it is not very exploitable and that it does well with its own twin. It has the disadvantage that it is too generous with the RANDOM rule, which was known by the participants to be entered in the tournament.

In addition, TIT FOR TAT was known to be a powerful competitor. In a preliminary tournament, TIT FOR TAT scored second place; and in a variant of that preliminary tournament, TIT FOR TAT won first place. All of these facts were known to most of the people designing programs for the Computer Prisoner's Dilemma Tournament, because they were sent copies of a description of the preliminary tournament. Not surprisingly, many of them used the TIT FOR TAT principle and tried to improve upon it.

The striking fact is that *none* of the more complex programs submitted was able to perform as well as the original, simple TIT FOR TAT.

This result contrasts with computer chess tournaments, where complexity is obviously needed. For example, in the Second World Computer Chess Championships, the least complex program came in last (Jennings 1978). It was submitted by Johann Joss of the Eidgenossishe Technische Hochschule of Zurich, Switzerland, who also submitted an entry to the Computer Prisoner's Dilemma Tournament. His entry to the Prisoner's Dilemma Tournament was a small modification of TIT FOR TAT. But his modification, like the others, just lowered the performance of the decision rule.

Analysis of the results showed that neither the discipline of the author, the brevity of the program — nor its length — accounts for a rule's relative success. What does?

Before answering this question, a remark on the interpretation of numerical scores is in order. In a game of 200 moves, a useful benchmark for very good performance is 600 points, which is equivalent to the score attained by a player when both sides always cooperate with each other. A useful benchmark for very poor performance is 200 points, which is equivalent to the score attained by a player when both sides never cooperate with each other. Most scores range between 200 and 600 points, although scores from 0 to 1000 points are possible. The winner, TIT FOR TAT, averaged 504 points per game.

Surprisingly, there is a single property which distinguishes the relatively high-scoring entries from the relatively low-scoring entries. This is the property of being *nice*, which is to say never being the first to defect. (For the sake of analyzing this tournament, the definition of a nice rule will be relaxed to include rules which will not be the first to defect before the last few moves, say before move 199.)

Each of the eight top-ranking entries (or rules) is nice. None of the other entries is. There is even a substantial gap in the score between the nice entries and the others. The nice entries received tournament averages between 472 and 504, while the best of the entries that were not nice received only 401 points. Thus, not being the first to defect, at least until virtually the end of the game, was a property which, all by itself, separated the more successful rules from the less successful rules in this Computer Prisoner's Dilemma Tournament.

Each of the nice rules got about 600 points with each of the other seven nice rules and with its own twin. This is because when two nice rules play, they are sure to cooperate with each other until virtually the end of the game. Actually the minor variations in endgame tactics did not account for much variation in the scores.

Since the nice rules all got within a few points of 600 with each other, the thing that distinguished the relative rankings among the nice rules was their scores with the rules which are not nice. This much is obvious. What is not obvious is that the relative ranking of the eight top rules was largely determined by just two of the other seven rules. These two rules are *kingmakers* because they do not do very well for themselves, but they largely determine the rankings among the top contenders.

The most important kingmaker was based on an "outcome maximization" principle originally developed as a possible interpretation of what human subjects do in the Prisoner's Dilemma laboratory experiments (Downing 1975). This rule, called DOWNING, is a particularly interesting rule in its own right. It is well worth studying as an example of a decision rule which is based upon a quite sophisticated idea. Unlike most of the others, its logic is not just a variant of TIT FOR TAT. Instead it is based on a deliberate attempt to understand the other player and then to make the choice that will yield the best long-term score based upon this understanding. The idea is that if the other player does not seem responsive to what DOWNING is doing, DOWNING will try to get away with whatever it can by defecting. On the other hand, if the other player does seem responsive, DOWNING will cooperate. To judge the other's responsiveness, DOWNING estimates the probability that the other player cooperates after it (DOWNING) cooperates, and also the probability that the other player cooperates after DOWNING defects. For each move, it updates its estimate of these two conditional probabilities and then selects the choice which will maximize its own long-term payoff under the assumption that it has correctly modeled the other player. If the two conditional probabilities have similar values, DOWNING determines that it pays to defect, since the other player seems to be doing the same thing whether DOWNING cooperates or not. Conversely, if the other player tends to cooperate after a cooperation but not after a defection by DOWNING, then the other player seems responsive, and DOWNING will calculate that the best thing to do with a responsive player is to cooperate. Under certain circumstances, DOWNING will even determine that the best strategy is to alternate cooperation and defection.

At the start of a game, DOWNING does not know the values of these conditional probabilities for the other players. It assumes that they are both .5, but gives no weight to this estimate when information actually does come in during the play of the game.

This is a fairly sophisticated decision rule, but its implementation does have one flaw. By initially assuming that the other player is unresponsive, DOWNING is doomed to defect on the first two moves. These first two defections led many other rules to punish DOWNING, so things usually got off to a bad start. But this is precisely why DOWNING served so well as a kingmaker. First-ranking TIT FOR TAT and second-ranking TIDEMAN AND CHIERUZZI both reacted in such a way that DOWNING learned to expect that defection does not pay but that cooperation does. All of the other nice rules went downhill with DOWNING. . . .

NOTES AND QUESTIONS ON GAME THEORY AND THE ITERATED PRISONER'S DILEMMA

1. Axelrod's computer tournament was far tidier than human affairs. The payoff matrix did not vary from round to round. Each pair of entrants knew they would play one-against-the-other for exactly 200 rounds. No contestant could find out the choices a competitor had made in his prior encounters with other entrants. Do these sorts of simplification limit the lessons one can draw from Axelrod's results? Or does simplification help reveal, to quote Axelrod, the "fundamental form" of the problem of cooperation?

For criticism of the Axelrod format, see, for instance, Jack Hirshleifer & Juan Carlos Martinez Coll, What Strategies Can Support the Evolutionary Emergence of Cooperation?, 32 J. Conflict Resolution 367 (1988), who showed that TIT FOR TAT was dominated by "mean" strategies in elimination games, in which only winners move on.

On the other hand, consider the possibility that Axelrod's analysis may be too pessimistic. Even in one-shot Prisoner's Dilemma games where anonymity is assured, players cooperate far more often than Axelrod predicts they would. One reason, perhaps, may be "bounded self-interest." Recall Jolls, Sunstein & Thaler's discussion, supra p. 225, of how Responders in Ultimatum Games are willing to sacrifice their own receipts in order to punish Proposers who have made unfair offers. Might not internalized norms of fairness constrain choices in a Prisoner's Dilemma setting? For the assertion that economists, either because of self-selection or training, are particularly likely to defect in a one-shot Prisoner's Dilemma, see Robert H. Frank, Thomas D. Gilovich & Dennis T. Regan, Do Economists Make Bad Citizens?, J. Econ. Persp., Winter 1996, at 187. But compare Anthony M. Yezer, Robert S. Goldfarb & Paul J. Poppen, Does Studying Economics Discourage Cooperation?, J. Econ. Persp., Winter 1996, at 177 (finding that economics students behave more cooperatively than others in real-world settings).

2. In Axelrod's tournament a player tended to prosper by being:

a. nice (that is, not the first to defect);
b. prepared immediately to punish a defection; and
c. willing to forgive another's past defections once accounts had been squared.

Aside from the issue of whether rational actors would choose these tactics, do they constitute a sound approach to the game of life?

What truth is there in baseball manager Leo Durocher's adage, "Nice guys finish last"?

3. Can Axelrod's work shed light on the landlord-tenant relationship? A landlord and tenant are situated in a repeated game. Each may be tempted to defect — typically, the tenant by failing to pay rent when due, and the landlord, by breaching obligations to maintain the premises. The payoffs in a landlord-tenant relationship, however, are not necessarily structured like those of a Prisoner's Dilemma. Is landlord-tenant law usefully viewed as an attempt to alter the payoff structure in order to elicit cooperation between landlords and tenants?

Game theory suggests that cooperation is most likely to break down toward the end of a relationship. Is this true in the case of leaseholds? How might landlords employ security deposits to prevent tenants from chiseling at the end of the term on rent obligations? How might tenants (or lawmakers) prevent landlords from wrongfully withholding the return of security deposits?

Reputational concerns can deter opportunism. For example, a landlord might refrain from mistreating current tenants because prospective tenants might learn of the misconduct. What might a university's student government do to enhance local landlords' reputational concerns? Conversely, in many urban markets commercial firms will provide to landlords, for a fee, reports on prospective tenants' prior involvements in housing litigation. What sorts of tenants might be *helped* by the existence of these firms?

In an ambitiously broad study of an actual housing market, the Rand Corporation found landlord-tenant relations in Brown County, Wisconsin, to be "relaxed and comfortable." Rand Corporation, Second Annual Report of the Housing Assistance Supply Experiment 69 (R-1959-HUD May 1976). Why might reported appellate cases provide a distorted lens on landlord-tenant relationships? What effect does rent control have on the level of cooperation between landlords and tenants? On rent control, see infra pp. 415-422.

4. Recall Acheson's description, supra p. 129, of how the lobster gangs of Maine created property rights in congestible fisheries. Under what conditions can the users of a limited-access commons employ strategies similar to TIT FOR TAT to forestall the sort of "tragedy" that Garrett Hardin thought to be inexorable?

In a laboratory experiment involving human subjects, Ostrom, Walker, and Gardner (OWG) simulated exploitation of a common-pool resource. The pool was vulnerable to excessive depletion unless all eight possible appropriators cooperated to limit their rates of extraction. OWG manipulated from session to session the ability

of the appropriators to communicate with one another and to sanction those who overdrew from the common pool. Generally, provision of opportunities for both communication and sanctioning
fostered cooperative behavior. OWG conclude:

> Policymakers responsible for the governance and management of small-
> scale [common-pool resources] should *not* presume that the individuals
> involved are caught in an inexorable tragedy from which there is no
> escape. Individuals may be able to arrive at joint strategies to manage
> these resources more efficiently. To accomplish this task, they must have
> sufficient information to pose and solve the allocation problems they
> face. They must also have an arena where they can discuss joint strat-
> egies and perhaps implement monitoring and sanctioning. In other
> words, when individuals are given an opportunity to restructure their
> own situation, they frequently — but not always — use this opportunity
> to make credible commitments and achieve higher joint outcomes with-
> out an external enforcer.

Elinor Ostrom, James Walker & Roy Gardner, Covenants with and
without a Sword: Self-Governance Is Possible, 86 Am. Pol. Sci. Rev.
404, 414 (1992). What are the implications for natural resources
law? For land use regulation?

 5. Axelrod's book helped trigger a boom in academic work on
cooperation, much of it from a game-theoretic perspective. For law
students, an especially suitable introduction to game theory is
Douglas G. Baird, Robert H. Gertner & Randel C. Picker, Game
Theory and the Law (1994).

Culture and Fairness in the Development of Institutions in the California Gold Fields*

Richard O. Zerbe, Jr. & C. Leigh Anderson

After 1848 thousands of relatively young, armed, male miners from
31 countries poured into California in search of gold. They entered
a region essentially devoid of government control, at a time when
"a generally applicable mining law or policy simply did not exist."
The Polynesian, a newspaper published in Honolulu, wrote at the
time:

> The love of it [gold] arouses all the baser passions of man's nature, and
> we fear the gold regions of California will be the theater of tragic events
> — the scene of bloodshed and strife. The Sun never yet shone upon a

*Source: 61 J. Econ. Hist. 114-138 (2001).

more motley crowd than will be assembled there. We tremble for the result upon the morals of the people and the peace of the country. In the confusion which must prevail there for the next twelve months, the law will be powerless, rights will be disregarded, reason dethroned and brute force will reign triumphant.

The prediction that the mines would be the scene of chaotic violence was wrong. Rather than anarchy or violent gang rule, what quickly emerged in the California gold fields were social institutions and rules for gold mining that relied upon a system of norms without unusual violence. Each mining district drew up an explicit contract, usually in writing. As one observer wrote in 1848, "It is curious how soon a set of crude regulations sprung into existence, which everybody seemed to abide by." By the spring of 1849 the custom had become a set of rules that "placed the strong and the weak upon a footing of equality, defined the claims that might be set apart, protected the tools left on the ground as evidence of proprietorship, and permitted the adventurers to hold their rights as securely as if they were guaranteed by a charter from the government."

In this essay we attempt to explain the society formed by the California gold miners in the early years of the gold rush, 1849/50. Our account supports earlier rational-choice interpretations that property arrangements settling the American Western frontier were based on the marginal costs and benefits of defining and enforcing property rights. We contend further, however, that culture mattered in these choices, not only by affecting the costs of defining and enforcing rights, but probably in the speed and nature of institutional change in response to changing prices. Culture also provided a focal point that lowered the costs of collective action necessary to supply these institutions. Our account extends John Umbeck's explanation of the gold fields, based on a theory of violence, by appealing to cultural norms to better explain the miners' behavior and by offering a theory of the evolution of institutions based on these common norms.[7]

The civil society of the California gold miners was one of many possible equilibria. How was this particular equilibrium selected? Culturally derived norms of fairness embodied in familiar

7. John A. Umbeck, Might Makes Rights: A Theory of the Function and Initial Distribution of Property Rights, 19 Econ. Inq. 38 (1981). Umbeck's account does not explain majority rule by the miners, cooperation to punish violators, the language of fairness in the miners' own accounts, the relative absence of intraethnic violence, the existence of interethnic violence, the use of judges, and the first-come, first-served allocation procedure for claims. His account predicts incorrectly that all miners on the site would receive a claim.

institutions helped to facilitate collective action and produce order among the California gold miners, by acting as focal points to solve the initial coordination problem. By embodying familiar and fair principles these institutions provided for cooperation in the gold fields.[9] . . .

The Evolution of Social Institutions

A rational-choice account of social interaction attempts to predict outcomes on the basis of reductionist assumptions about the agents' positions, strategic opportunities, and maximizing behavior. Yet many game-theoretic models, particularly ones with indefinitely repeated play, are plagued by a multiplicity of outcomes. This indeterminacy suggests that Umbeck's rational-choice account of property-rights formation in the gold fields is incomplete, as it fails to explain why the equilibrium he posits, and not some other possible equilibrium, is the one chosen.

In the absence of violence, establishing viable social institutions first requires players coordinating to provide the institutions, where coordination itself is a public good, and then ensuring that these institutions embody incentives to cooperate. . . .

Recognizing or creating focal points aids equilibrium selection by providing one way for players to coordinate.[15] A focal point provides a coordination mechanism that, prior to the play of the game, has mutual significance to the players based on their common past experiences. These experiences, socially or culturally derived, help players to "know" what to do, and to be able to predict what other players will do. . . .

We propose, contrary to Umbeck, that property rights in the California gold fields were not imposed by the strong on the weak. Rather, they were social conventions in a repeated game that were selected from among many possible ones because they were a focal point for the miners. We consider two levels of institutions or rules: the collective-choice rules through which the operational rules could be changed, which included majority rule and trial by jury;

9. This is related to field evidence on how communities can avoid the "tragedy of the commons" without recourse to a central government. Examples are offered in Elinor Ostrom, Governing the Commons: The Evolution of Institutions for Collective Action (1990); and Making the Commons Work (Daniel W. Bromley ed., 1992).

15. Thomas Schelling, The Strategy of Conflict (1960). The idea of focal points as equilibrium outcomes in repeated games has been developed by David M. Kreps, Game Theory and Economic Modeling (1990); and by Gary J. Miller, Managerial Dilemmas: The Political Economy of Hierarchy (1992).

and the operational rules that governed day-to-day decisions on claim size, rules for working claims, and claim rationing through a first-come, first-served allocation rule. . . .

The Culture and Custom of the Miners

A common culture increases the likelihood of social institutions having mutual significance to individuals and hence of being a coordinating focal point. We describe some characteristics of the miners and suggest some common cultural views on government, work, and property that formed the basis for the formation and stability of the institutions. These common cultural views, we suggest, embodied notions of just deserts that we call Lockean fairness and Jacksonian democracy. . . .

. . . [A]bout 75 percent of the miners were from the United States, and fully 90 percent were from either the United States or Europe.[21] The miners were hardly the motley crew *The Polynesian* suggested. The evidence suggests that the emigrants were generally of higher-than-average social class and education. . . .

Views of Government

Majority rule and trial by jury were part of the culture of the miners. . . . The Public Lands Commission of 1880 notes the importance of the miners' cultural background and records that instead of general lawlessness:

> . . . the adventurers of 1849 spontaneously instituted neighborhood or district codes of regulations . . . to define and protect a brief possessory ownership. . . . In the absence of State and Federal laws . . . and with the inbred respect for equitable adjustment of rights between man and man, which is the inheritance of centuries of English common law, the miners only sought to secure equitable rights . . . with a well founded confidence, that no machinery was necessary to enforce their regulations other than the swift, rough blows of public opinion. . . .

Views of Work

Gold-digging is hard work, and its rewards should go to those who earn them, according to the articles appearing in *Alta Califor-*

---

21. There is agreement among historians that the rules and customs developed in other mining jurisdictions before the California discovery were part of the stock of knowledge of some of the early miners who had experience in these jurisdictions, and that these rules influenced the developments in California. The relative influence of the Spanish practices, those in the Cornish mines, those devised by the federal government in administering leasing schemes in the 1830s and thereafter, or those developed in yet other jurisdictions remains the subject of debate. . . . [ED. — Footnote relocated.]

nia, a San Francisco newspaper that began publication in 1849 and that followed the miners very closely: "Fortunes are not to be made in the mines in a few weeks. Those who have prospered in the mines have done so by labor incessant and severe."

Lockean fairness, in the sense that one deserved what one worked for, was an explicit tenet of labor reformers in the 1830s and 1840s and of the widespread "producerism" movement, or Jacksonian democracy.... For Democrats, farmers and laborers were clearly producers, and maybe manufacturers, but certainly not banks, insurance companies, railroads, or lawyers who derived their wealth from the work of others. The Whigs felt that almost all occupational groups deserved respect and esteem.

The ideal that emerged in Jacksonian America was that of the autonomous small producer. The primary aim of the Jacksonians was to open the avenues of social advancement to all laborers, not to redistribute the property of the rich. The notion of "wage slavery," that is, "... that the wage earner was somehow less than fully free," was widespread. The idea of wage slavery, says Foner, "provided a critique of emerging capitalism in which workplace exploitation ... took center stage."[49] We predict, therefore, that the ownership and operation of mines would favor the small individual producer rather than wage or gang labor.

Views of Property

"Each man possesses himself absolutely, and therefore that with which he mixes his labor becomes his property." This emphasis on men's rights to what they produce echoed those of Thomas Paine, who, writing late in the eighteenth century, distinguished between the land itself, properly the property of all, from improvements made upon it "which should go to the individuals responsible for them."

John Reid's account, generally well regarded by historians, on the views of ownership and property held by overland emigrants from this time, applies as well to the forty-niners....

Reid notes that the emigrants carried with them, and acted upon, a sense of private property as fully developed as the one they had at home. Charity existed, but it was recognized to be charity, not a right to a more equal distribution, or even a right to steal when starving or dying of thirst.[53]

---

49. Eric Foner, Free Soil, Free Labor, Free Men: The Ideology of the Republican Party Before the Civil War xix (1970).

53. John Reid, Law for the Elephant: Property and Social Behavior on the Overland Trail 361 (1980). [ED. — Footnote relocated.]

Views of Punishment

There was, among the miners, a willingness to participate in punishing defectors. . . .

Social norms such as a sense of fairness can promote cooperation and a willingness to help sanction those who do not cooperate, helping to overcome the free-rider problem of group action. Cultural norms may also lead those who do not participate in punishing wrongdoing to feel shame or guilt. Thus, a sense of fairness — or perhaps more accurately, a sense of justice — may lead not only to a desire to see the bully punished, but to participate in his punishment. . . .

The Institutions of the Gold Fields . . .

Majority Rule

The record suggests that majority rule was a preexisting norm and was consistent with the culture and custom of the American, and many of the European, miners. . . . The following account is cited as typical by Umbeck:

> The first workers on the bar had taken up claims of a generous size, and soon the whole bar was occupied. The region was full of miners and they came pouring down upon the river, attracted by the reports of a rich strike, until their tents and campfires presented the appearance of a vast army. Those without claims far exceeded in number the fortunate ones. A miners' meeting was called to make laws. Majority ruled in a mining camp in those days, and it was voted to cut down the size of claims to forty feet. The claim owners were powerless to resist, but had to admit to the fiat of the majority. The miners were then registered in the order of the date of their arrival upon the bar, and in that order were allowed to select claims until all were taken. Even then there was a great crowd of disappointed ones.[64] . . .

Majority rule, however, was not used everywhere or by all groups, which is consistent with our prediction that majority rule was more likely to be found where the culture of the miners predisposed them in this direction. Alternative organizational principles existed in the region — some of the Latin and Chinese miners worked as contract labor for wages, with the individual miners subject to the control of a company or controlling organization without rights to strike out on their own. The numerical superiority of the majority and its consequent advantages with respect to vi-

64. From the Public Lands Commission of 1880. . . .

olence are insufficient to explain the adoption of majority rule by American and European miners in connection with the nonadoption by the Chinese and some Latin miners. A fuller and more satisfying explanation for the use of majority rule recognizes the prior acceptance and use of majority rule as a preexisting norm. . . .

. . . In the absence of fair decisions by the majority, the minority might have been more likely to fight. The following account by Charles Shinn is instructive:

> William Dougherty and a companion found gold in a canyon on the Yuba River. They were doing well when, after several days, they were visited by a delegation of miners from a neighboring camp. The visitors, six or eight in number, proposed to share the find. A meeting was held and it was decided that each miner should be allowed to own a strip of land ten feet wide on the river and three hundred feet deep. Dougherty and his companion were in the minority, and could not have objected even had they wished; but the plan was so entirely in accordance with the usual custom — the unwritten law of older camps — that they yielded a ready and cheerful acquiescence. In view of the fact that they were the discoverers, it was unanimously agreed that they should have first choice of ground.[72]

. . . [Miners were willing to take] action to ensure that the fair thing was done as in the following example:

> Two mining partners, (Sim and Sprenger) worked a claim together. Sprenger met with an accident and was crippled and helpless. Against the custom of the camp, Sim ejected Sprenger from the claim. Sprenger took the matter to the local Alcalde, or mayor. Sim, it later transpired, bribed the Alcalde to support him. Without knowing of the bribe, the miners refused to accept the Alcalde's support of Sim, and ". . . over a thousand miners threw down their picks and shovels — and came to the main camp." The miners formed a new court, reinstalled Sprenger as half owner of the claim; Sim was ordered to pay the costs of his partner, the Alcalde was deposed, and the miners, learning of the bribe, exacted the bribe from the Alcalde, and a new organization was set up to settle disputes, "The Hayden Court."[76]

. . . [T]he custom of providing for an injured miner is . . . a low-cost method of purchasing insurance against illness or injury. The miners' interest in the Sprenger case could be viewed as arising from their interest in preserving the insurance mechanism and in having an honest Alcalde.

---

72. Charles Howard Shinn, Mining Camps: A Study in American Frontier Government 165-166 (1947).

76. Shinn, ibid., pp. 190-198. Hayden later became Chief Justice of the California Supreme Court.

Trial by Jury . . .

Claim Size

In the early days of the mines, 1848 to 1850, claims were mainly held and worked individually. In the earliest period some Native Americans were hired for wages, but this did not meet with approval and was soon stopped. Similarly, attempts to bring slaves into the mines were strongly and effectively resisted. The Jacksonian ideal of the small producer governed here. Both the wage laborer and his employer were held in contempt, and the use of gang labor was a source of tension between the Chinese and some Latins, on the one hand, and Americans on the other. Claim size then was generally geared to the individual producer and not to contract or slave labor.

Our explanation of claim size is based on fairness, which contributes to political stability, and to which efficiency served as a constraint. The size of claims can be explained by the "producerism" concept that a man could only claim what he could reasonably work, and is consistent with the principle of Lockean fairness: "However, only so much as a man improves and can use belongs to him, nor may a man deprive another of the means of self-preservation by overextending his reach for property." This explanation is also consistent with the miners' own language: "The claims were made small so everyone would have a chance to get one."

What a miner could reasonably work is not dissimilar to the concept of an efficient-sized claim: "[T]he idea being in each case to afford every man a fair chance to accumulate wealth and with this object in view, to give him as much ground as he could possibly use." . . .

The evidence is consistent with a correspondence between efficiency and fairness for claim size. The efficient claim size is determined by increasing the ratio of miners to land until the miners' implicit wage rate (their opportunity cost) is equal to the marginal physical product of labor times the market price of gold. That is, the size of an original claim would be increased as long as the additional land added to the original claim was more productive as part of the original claim than as part of the new claim.

If claim sizes are efficient, the size of claims on more productive land should be smaller. Absent such an inverse relationship between productivity and claim size, this hypothesis is rejectable. Umbeck establishes that claim size varies inversely with productivity, which is consistent with the efficiency hypothesis. Efficiency considerations would also lead claim size to change with technology, and is clearly the case in the historical literature.

Neither simple equality nor an explanation ignoring group behavior explains claim size well. Simple equality, such that each miner on the spot at the time the mining district is formed receives a claim, does not explain claim size. Simple fairness leads to an equal division so that everyone receives a plot. Given a sufficient number of men, these plots would be inefficiently small. This did not happen. There were nonviolent attempts to reduce the standard 100-foot claim to 25 feet by a class of latecomers called "twenty-five-foot men," which did not succeed. The simple equality hypothesis is also inconsistent with the accounts of left-out miners noted by Nancy Farriss and Smith.

Umbeck presents a different hypothesis of claim size for individual miners but does not include a theory of group behavior. The violence hypothesis that Umbeck suggests is that "no wealth maximizer would accept less wealth than he could have through the use of his personal force, the agreed upon contract must initially endow each individual with the same amount of wealth as that which they could have had through violence." But given majority rule, a miner would have gained little but punishment from violence. . . .

. . . Certainly, the role of majority rule in setting claim size was not one of pure force. In the account cited earlier, Dougherty and his companion were clearly outgunned, but the majority gave them first choice of claim even while reducing the size of claims. The size of claim chosen, "a strip of land ten feet wide on the river and three hundred feet deep," was in fact just the norm for productive land along streams. Were a theory of violence based on group behavior the explanation, the claims of the majority would have been larger or more valuable than that of Dougherty and his companion.

Rules for Working Claims

Agreements among miners in a district provided restrictions on the number of days a miner could leave a claim or requirements for the minimum number of days a miner had to work the claim, and restrictions on the number of claims one miner could own. . . .

Claims did not have to be worked during periods of the year when weather rendered them unworkable. A requirement in the contract specified the number of days the claim had to be worked rather than the number of days the claim holder had to be present. These facts suggest that producerism, rather than maintaining a sufficient fighting force, was the primary reason for the labor requirement.

A second piece of evidence consistent with fairness but inconsistent with the violence hypothesis was provisions for excusing people who were sick, or attending others who were sick, from working their claims. For example, a provision from a Siskiyou County mining district states "[t]hat no person's claim shall be jumpable on Little Humbug while he is sick or in any other way disabled from labor, or while he is absent from his claim attending upon sick friends." Such provisions are not consistent with maximizing the number of fighting men. These provisions may be not only fair, but also efficient as insurance measures. . . .

The First-Come, First-Served Allocation Rule

First-come, first-served procedures were used by the California miners in establishing the choice of claims. Miners had to choose claims of standard size set by the mining district but choice was on the basis of their date of arrival, the first discoverer getting first choice, and so forth.[106] Why did the majority give special place to order of arrival and to first discoverers? First-come, first-served procedures can serve as focal points to avoid conflict because they appear to be fair.

The advantages of such a social rule can be illustrated with the simple game of Chicken-Hawk, and the pay-off matrix in Table 3. In the context of the miners' situation, the Chicken-Chicken interaction is a solution in which the claim size chosen is inefficiently small as, for example, when every miner receives a claim. The Hawk-Hawk encounter represents mutual defection and violence: in the mining context the Hawk-Hawk outcome is equivalent to no property rights or to violence over claims. The off-diagonal encounters, Chicken-Hawk and Hawk-Chicken, represent the greatest total joint wealth. . . .

When one considers this as a repeated game, all sorts of outcomes appear possible. The difficulty for a miner in deciding whether to be a chicken or a hawk is in knowing what the other player will do, and in knowing how one's actions in one round may affect one's reputation and thus the other players' actions in another round. It is easy to see why miners would have preferred

---

106. Sometimes the first discoverer received two claims rather than their first choice.

Table 3
Chicken-Hawk

	Chicken	Hawk
Chicken	4, 4	0, 20
Hawk	20, 0	−10, −10

a social rule that gave them an equal chance of having the first choice of claim. . . .

. . . During each turn there is a random assignment of which player gets to go first based on first discovery. It is obvious that the player going first will choose H since he can reasonably anticipate that the second player's response to the first player choosing H is to choose C. A player's choice of C or H would be random in the sense that the determination of the first player is random.

The first-come, first-served strategy appears to have the advantage of stability — a stability rooted in fairness. Neither the lottery nor other procedures such as last-come, first-served recognize the moral claim of the first discoverer or of earlier arrivals.

The first-come, first-served procedure has some local efficiencies aside from those connected with fairness. The first-come procedure encourages further, and faster, discovery of gold, as it encourages the mining of gold before others arrive; it retains the advantage for the first discoverer; it obviates the need for the earlier miners to resettle; it eliminates the problem associated with last-come, first-served that there could always be a new last person; and it recognizes that the earliest miners would develop special knowledge about particular claim sites. It also implicitly recognizes the advantage in violence to the first-comers since the miners earliest on a site will generally have known one another longer. They are, therefore, better able to form a cohesive group, to present an effective fighting force, and to constitute the core of the majority and, as the majority, to vote in favor of the self-serving first-come, first-served rule.

If Lockean notions of fairness influence outcome, not only should a moral entitlement give one a larger share, but the stronger the moral entitlement, the greater the share. This is consistent with the miners' practice of claim choice by order of arrival, and with a truly fascinating aspect of the Elizabeth Hoffman and Matthew Spitzer experiments suggesting that an egalitarian result is substantially more likely in the absence of moral differences.[112] Coming earlier to a claim seems to have been sufficient to establish the order of choice by which miners were allocated claims.

Ethnicity as a Transactions Cost: The Failure of Cooperation

The best evidence for the cultural hypothesis suggested here lies in the variance produced by culture. Culture provides a common language for cooperation and a common focal point for agreement. If culture is a device for reducing transaction costs, then transaction costs should be greater cross-culturally than within a culture. This was indeed the case. Violence and the failure of cooperation in the gold fields were primarily among racial or ethnic groups, such as between Whites and Hispanics, Whites and Chinese, Americans and non-Americans, or to a lesser extent, American and European (particularly French) or Australian miners. The American miners especially harassed the Chilean, Mexican, Chinese, Native American, and French miners, and the Australians, the latter being regarded by some as rather lawless elements. The American spirit of individualism and equality seemed to find wage labor as practiced by the Mexicans and Chinese particularly offensive. . . .

Changes in the Society of the Miners

In 1848, before the hordes of miners had descended upon the fields, disorders were rare; observers report a period of "almost Arcadian honesty" that lasted well into 1849. "The people here are civil and mind their own business," a forty-niner from Michigan wrote of conditions on the middle fork of the American River. "I hear of no thefts, robberies, or murders." There were in fact, very few. "Any miner, . . ." a second forty-niner said of Weaverville, ". . . can leave his things loose in his tent, and be gone a week, or month, and come back and find them as he left them." Similar statements could be quoted from such geographically diverse locations as the Yuba River, Mormon Island, Hangtown, Murphy's Diggings, and Mariposa.

The components of the miners' society later changed, however. "[T]he camps of 1849 are described, by those who best knew them, as on the whole remarkably orderly. By the middle of 1850 we meet with a few great disturbances, like those in the Sonora. By the begin-

---

112. Elizabeth Hoffman & Matthew L. Spitzer, Entitlements, Rights, and Fairness: An Experimental Examination of Subjects' Concepts of Distributive Justice, 14 J. Legal Stud. 259 (1985).

ning of 1851, however, complaints are general and quickly lead up to violence. . . . " The ability to form focal points around familiar institutions gave way to an influx of workers with different cultures, the pressure of greater numbers of miners relative to the claims available, and technological changes favoring more capital-intensive mining with wage labor and larger claim sizes that undermined the ideals of individual producerism. These forces changed the marginal costs and benefits of the gold field institutions, and led in Malcolm Rohrbough's words to ". . . a gradual unraveling of the consensus of the rules of behavior that characterized the first mining seasons. . . ." The work rules of the earlier miners no longer sufficed, and indeed proved to be inefficient and litigious. The break up of the consensus led first to an increase in violence and robbery, and then as order was imposed from without, to war by litigation, or what has been called "court-room mining." . . .

NOTES AND QUESTIONS ON PROPERTY RIGHTS UNDER CONDITIONS OF ANARCHY

1. In what ways were the conditions that the California gold miners faced more conducive to cooperative outcomes than the conditions faced by the players in Axelrod's Prisoner's Dilemma tournament?

2. Zerbe and Anderson (Z & A) compare the miners' situation to a Chicken-Hawk game. In Chicken-Hawk, the two players generally do best when they alternate in making aggressive plays, such as asserting mining claims. Do Z & A provide convincing reasons why the miners would have preferred to allocate claims according to a rule of first-come, first-served, as opposed to a rule of last-come, first-served? Compare the readings in Chapter 3 on why the law of property tends to favor possessors.

3. Can you reconcile Z & A's assertion that the miners embraced norms of Lockean fairness with the meagerness of the miners' rewards to discoverers of new diggings?

4. Assume Z & A are correct in their claim that cultural norms provided focal points for the miners to follow. How did these norms arise? Why did the miners' culture support norms of Lockean fairness and Jacksonian democracy, as opposed to, say, "might makes right," or deference on the basis of age or social status? Z & A include a quotation from a report of the Public Lands Commission of 1880 that attributes the miners' cultural values to "the inheritance of centuries of English common law." Did the judges

who shaped the English common law create those values? Or (mostly) derive them from popular sentiments? On the origin of norms, see the sources cited in Note 3, supra p. 220.

5. Z & A report that most miners were willing to pitch in to help punish wrongdoers. Why didn't they free-ride? A conspicuous free-rider might risk subsequent *third-party sanctions*, such as shaming by observers. Another possibility is that many miners had internalized a norm that required them to contribute to the appropriate punishment of wrongdoers, and would have experienced the *first-party sanction* of guilt even if no one else detected their free-riding. Individuals acquire internalized norms through socialization, particularly through interactions during childhood with parents, teachers, and others. On a child's development of distinct emotions of guilt and shame, see Jerome Kagan, The Nature of the Child 145-149 (1984). On the (underappreciated) role of first-party systems of social control, see Robert Cooter, Do Good Laws Make Good Citizens? An Economic Analysis of Internalized Norms, 86 Va. L. Rev. 1577 (2000); Robert C. Ellickson, Bringing Culture and Human Frailty to Rational Actors, 65 Chi.-Kent L. Rev. 23, 43-54 (1989).

6. Z & A report that ethnic divisions greatly inhibited cooperative behavior in the gold fields. What implications does this finding have about the limits of informal property rights as a subsystem of social control? On informal property on the American frontier, see generally Andrew P. Morriss, Miners, Vigilantes & Cattlemen: Overcoming Free Rider Problems in the Private Provision of Law, 33 Land & Water L. Rev. 581 (1998).

7. Z & A imply that cultural rules can constitute a kind of "social capital" that eases economic and social interactions. How and why do societies vary in their provision of this social good? See Francis Fukuyama, Trust: The Social Virtues and the Creation of Prosperity (1995); Robert D. Putnam, Bowling Alone: The Collapse and Revival of American Community (2000).

*To Each Less than She Needs, From Each More than She Can Do: Allocations, Entitlements and Value**

Hanna Papanek

Differential morbidity and mortality rates between males and females in southern Asia indicate starkly how inequalities in re-

*Source: *in* Persistent Inequalities 167-173 (Irene Tinker ed., 1990).

source allocation affect women's survival chances. The purpose of this chapter is to bring together two areas of scholarship that are beginning to show signs of convergence: (1) studies by demographers, economists, nutritionists, and health specialists that provide concrete data to document these inequalities and (2) explorations into women's sense of self-worth, their feelings about their place in family and society, and the social learning of gender differences and gender relations. Using Asia as the focus in this chapter, I will relate ideas about socially and culturally formed "entitlements" to resource shares to ideas about the process of socialization for inequality.

Gender and Inequality

Gender differences, based on the social construction of biological sex distinctions, are one of the great "fault lines" of societies — those marks of difference among categories of persons that govern the allocation of power, authority, and resources....

. . . Both gender differences and gender relations are of special importance within domestic groups, and it is within the household that children first learn their significance. The adults and older children who consciously and unconsciously teach them also reinforce their own learning in the process.

How a group or society distributes available resources among members reflects not only power and authority relations but also the moral basis of the group, its consensus about distributive justice, and its implicit priorities. Uncovering these implicit priorities is especially important in the case of gender-based inequalities for, having been learned from a very early age, they are unusually resistant to change later on. The relations between males and females are also so full of ambivalences and contradictions that change can be resisted at every turn. For example, cultural ideals in many societies prescribe high respect for women, especially mothers, yet in the same society, social norms accord women little power and authority and smaller shares of available resources. In addition, if the process of socialization for inequality has been successful, most people will not perceive inequalities for what they are — or, if they do, will argue for their moral rightness.

Children are taught very early in life about distributive justice in terms of differences in gender and age. When some get more food on their plate and others less, when some are sent to school and others not, children can see, in dramatic ways, what the differences are between boys and girls in their societies. These are lessons that they will remember, even those rebels who carry their anger over unjust treatment into adult activism for a cause. The way children are taught about shares and inequalities based on gender and age is a crucial part of the way they learn their place in family and society. The "compulsory emotions" — the way one is supposed to feel — play an important role in this learning.

Resource allocation processes within groups are, of course, closely linked to power and authority relations, but the linkage is not always obvious. Bigger shares of resources may signal a difference in power or status, rewarding those who are singled out for "the lion's share." Being able to look forward to getting bigger shares when one is older or more successful may be a goad for getting ahead or a solace while one waits, as in the stereotypical notion of the South Asian daughter-in-law in a patrilineal household who waits resentfully, doing the hard work of the house, until she can unload it on her successor. But age can also bring responsibilities, as in the equally stereotypical case of elder brothers in South Asia who forgo their privileges in favor of younger siblings for whom they are newly responsible. The expectation that mothers will sacrifice themselves for their children is another stereotype — and not only in South Asia.

. . . I emphasize resource allocations within households from the perspective of sociocultural *entitlements* to resource shares. These entitlements are based on social consensus and form an important process of childhood socialization. As noted in more detail in the sections that follow, the didactic function of entitlements has much to do with learning how one is valued by others and how one values oneself. Power and authority are also closely related to entitlements — both as a means for obtaining consensus on larger entitlements and as a reward.

A focus on social learning of inequalities is crucial to the process of change — whether this change comes about through major reorganizations of societies or by way of individuals and groups changing their ideas and behavior. One of the tasks of research on inequality is also to explain its persistence so that active attempts toward change can be more effective.

A perspective on resource entitlements and social learning, finally, helps to uncover some of the processes of women's complicity in their own inequality. The "secondary" socialization of adult women that I discuss later in this essay indicates how and why women often teach their children inequality, even if this involves their own remembered pain. . . .

Empirically measurable indicators of inequality are the first step in developing such criteria. The last two decades have seen an unprecedented accumulation of evidence about gender-based inequalities in resource allocations and access to opportunities in countries around the world. In South Asia, researchers often began by focusing on the very distorted sex ratio (proportion of males and females in a population), largely due to the excess of female over male mortality. In the most basic sense — survival — females are disadvantaged. . . . In Bangladesh, for example, detailed observations have shown that females receive less food than males in intrahousehold resource allocations and less medical care.

Other studies have focused on women's employment. . . .

In literacy and education, females are disadvantaged throughout South Asia, except in Sri Lanka and parts of southern India, but are being educated in much larger numbers in Southeast Asian countries. In South Asia, girls attend school in smaller numbers and for shorter periods than boys, with the differences most marked in Pakistan. Literacy rates are heavily skewed as a result. There are sharp differences between urban and rural areas throughout the region, in this respect, and these differences reflect not only class distinctions but also differences in family strategies of survival and mobility. Where there are no acceptable job opportunities for educated women, families must think twice before investing scarce resources in educating daughters.

In short, social scientists (both within these societies and outside them) have invoked criteria of equality that may run counter to the conventional wisdom in these societies to document inequalities between males and females in the allocation of the most basic resources. These include inequalities in food intake, medical care, and education. . . .

Value, Self-Worth, and Empowerment

Explanations of allocational inequalities in recent studies often focus on the presumed value of women in terms of the anticipated returns to female labor. In the case of excess female mortality in India, there has been a tendency to find causal connections between levels of female participation in remunerated labor (especially in agriculture) and female survival chances. For example, Barbara D. Miller argued that "where FLP [female labor force participation] is high, there will *always* be high preservation of female life, but where FLP is low, female children may *or* may not be preserved" (1981: 117). Miller based her conclusions on extensive comparisons of ethnographic and statistical sources, but problems of interpretation remain. . . .

[P]roblems in linking women's value to labor force participation arise with respect to women's indispensable — indeed "priceless" — work in household maintenance and home production. Even if a particular woman can be dispensed with, women's labor in food preparation, water and fuel collection, house maintenance, and care of children and the sick or elderly remains crucial in the absence of institutional substitutes. Many societies allow widowers to remarry quickly but often frown on the remarriage of widows and divorced women. If the value of women was measured in terms of their indispensability to the household, therefore, it might be set very high. Something else is clearly involved here.

On the borderline between strictly material and what might be called "symbolic" work lies a range of activities in the social, political, and economic realms. . . . They include unpaid assistance in the work of an earning member of the household, as in the "two-person careers" of men in professional occupations (Papanek 1973); participation in children's schooling that directly assists the efforts of teachers or is linked to upward social mobility efforts; direct "status politics" in the community; and performance of religious rituals tied to family status in the community. . . .

Social and Cultural Entitlements to Resource Shares

Women, like men, get a sense of their value to others from the way they are treated by them — a process that begins in early childhood and continues throughout life. Explicitly, as well as covertly, people get messages from those around them on which to base a sense of their value to others; in turn, their sense of self-worth is, at least in part, a reflection of the value they feel they have for others. These messages may be concrete — say, receiving smaller shares of household resources than others — but they may also be interpreted in such positively compensatory ways that some household members can still *feel* valued in spite of being shortchanged (according to outside assessments). More likely, both women and men get ambiguous messages about their value to others from their material shares and the sociocultural interpretations of the rightness of these shares. . . .

The links between resource shares and feelings of self-worth are particularly important if one is interested in changing persistent inequalities. People who are consistently shortchanged may be feeling so powerless in their situations that specific attention must be paid to mobilizing solidarity among people in similar situations. Enhanced feelings of self-worth can result from efforts to mobilize a group and from experiencing — often for the first time — that even the powerless can sometimes succeed in changing their situations.

One way of conceptualizing these linkages with a view to changing inequalities is to focus on the concept of entitlements, both in their objective, material form and in the social norms and cultural values that perpetuate differential entitlements. In this second sense, these entitlements represent the social consensus about the value of specific categories of persons as expressed in the norms governing "who gets what and why." As used here, the term "entitlement" refers to the socially and culturally recognized rights of specific categories of persons to particular resource shares. These rights are expressed in common statements, such as "a man needs more food than a woman because..." or "a girl does not have to be as well educated as a boy because...." The resources available to be shared include material resources, such as food, clothing, and shelter, as well as the resources devoted to the development of individual capacities, which result from adequate health care, education, and other ways of developing necessary skills.

The concept of entitlement to resource shares embodies the ideas of distributional justice shared by members of a group or society and can therefore be seen as a central part of its moral basis. How this consensus is developed is a process that begins in childhood as a critical feature of the process of socialization....

... Since [the] intrahousehold allocation process is of major importance in socialization for inequality and reflects the internal power relations within the household, I will stress three distinct aspects: (1) the objective consequences of an allocational pattern in terms of differences among household members in nutritional status, morbidity, mortality, and skill acquisition; (2) the psychosocial consequences for individuals in terms of how they feel about themselves and how they relate to others; and (3) the moral basis of the group of society that is reflected in the norms that govern sharing of resources. Except for the first aspect, on which there is considerable empirical evidence (especially from parts of South Asia), the discussion I present here emphasizes issues for research on the basis of their relevance to potential change in persistent inequalities....

My emphasis on social and cultural elements in the consensus about entitlements leads directly to consideration of the way gender differences are learned (and taught) in a particular group. For example, when children are told that "girls need less food than boys," they are learning something important about the value of persons and not only about feeling hungry.

For the most part, allocational inequalities have been studied largely through their objective outcomes or in terms of material differences in resource shares. The "explanations" offered to justify them are equally important, especially for those who seek to change persistent inequalities. For example, in the Indian Punjab, boys customarily get curds, the richer and more valued food, while girls get buttermilk. This is said to be based on Punjabi beliefs that rich foods are needed to withstand cold winter weather. What does this explanation imply about the effect of cold on females and about women's capacity for suffering? Similarly, in Meerut District (Uttar Pradesh, India), men and women from different castes told researchers that girls and boys got different kinds of food because rich, "heat-producing" foods like butter, milk, and meat hasten the onset of puberty in girls. Parents are, in any case, anxious about protecting the sexuality of their daughters and find this reason persuasive. The implications for physical growth are clear, but what about the psychological messages carried by these food restrictions?

The mother who follows these precepts acts according to group norms and is not simply expressing a personal preference. Of course, preference for sons is in the self-interest of all mothers in a society that measures the status of women by their reproductive performance. Sons are supposed to support parents in their old age, whereas daughters have gone to another patrilineage. But a third reason, never mentioned by researchers on son-preference, is the fact that a woman can gain the household assistance of a daughter-in-law *only* by having a son; her own daughters will marry out. The mother need not explain or justify her actions in giving better food to sons but would most likely have a lot of explaining to do in the community if she acted otherwise.

Ideas about entitlement are also part of a larger cultural repertoire containing many other ideas about the relative value of categories of persons. Entitlement ideas, in short, constitute part of a system of beliefs about distributional justice. Unequal allocations of resources not only have objective effects but also fulfill a crucial didactic function. They teach children about their rights and privileges in concrete ways that are understandable even to the very young.

Later on in a child's life, these ideas and actions are elaborated into more complex statements that fulfill multiple goals. For example, telling a child that "men work harder than women and that's why they need more (or better) food" not only justifies unequal resource allocations but also says something about the value of a task and of the person carrying it out. Children know that their mothers are always busy and that their work is often arduous. Women's work is also more salient to children because it is always

visible, whereas that of men may not be. But differential entitlements put another face on the reality that children see. The work
of men is socially defined as more valuable, not only in words but
also in terms of the concrete reward that is explicitly linked to the
value of the work and of the worker.

Girls may also receive another message from adults, however,
when unequal resource allocations are explained to them in *compensatory* terms that reflect an underlying cultural ambivalence
about the value of people and tasks. For example, an elderly Jav-
anese woman recalled from her own childhood that girls were
taught to restrain themselves not only with respect to food but also
in the enjoyment of other pleasures in life. Her mother told her
that girls needed to develop more inhibitions — also in self-
expression — because "women set the norms for civilization because men cannot control themselves." Women's role in educating
children, for instance, was defined as having more spiritual value
than men's role in making a living. . . . Ideas about entitlements, as
in this instance, are not only culturally sanctioned but also sanc-
tified in spiritual terms, a frequent occurrence in other societies
where women are charged with greater responsibilities for maintaining a family's social and religious status.

Unequal entitlements are often based on *imputed needs* that
differ for categories of persons. The anthropologist Leela Dube
(personal communication, December 23, 1987) linked these imputed needs to the anticipated life trajectories of different categories of individuals; these are, in turn, reflected in the care and
respect given by others. Dube also notes that the greater entitlement of one person often becomes the increased responsibility for
care given by another. A male infant's entitlement to more food
and more careful nurturance (as in parts of India and Bangladesh)
becomes the responsibility of his caretaker, usually a female adult
or child. The importance of differential entitlements to nurturance
is dramatically illustrated in the many studies of neglect of female
children in parts of India. . . .

Differences in imputed needs can also come to include a broad
spectrum of ideas about physiological and psychological processes
in women and men. The presumed inability of men to control their
sexual impulses is coupled in many societies with restrictions on
women's behavior and an emphasis on female self-restraint in sexual matters (for added discussion of this point see Papanek 1988
and references cited there). In addition, notions of women's greater
ability in self-restraint are found with reference to other physiological processes (e.g., excretion) and women's presumed greater
ability to tolerate pain. These imputed needs — or lack thereof —

have obvious implications for personal and public health in addition to their clear relevance to systems of strict sex segregation. But all of these ideas about imputed needs coupled with differences in entitlements are also another kind of social construction of physical realities that plays a role in the perpetuation of inequality.

The didactic importance of entitlements — in the sociocultural sense used here — is especially clear in situations of competition for household resources. Siblings, for example, may be particularly strongly affected by differential resource allocations, as when girls and boys in the same household receive different amounts and kinds of food, health care, and education, and when these differences are explained to them in terms of their entitlements. Much other learning about their society is the likely outcome. . . .

References

Miller, Barbara D., 1981. The Endangered Sex: Neglect of Female Children in Rural North India. Ithaca, N.Y.: Cornell Univ. Press.

Papanek, Hanna, 1973. Men, Women and Work: Reflections on the Two Person Career. American Journal of Sociology 78 (4) 852-872.

Papanek, Hanna, 1988. Afterword: Caging the Lion: A Fable for Our Time, in Rokeya Sakhawat Hossain, Sultan's Dream. New York: Feminist Press, 58-85.

NOTES AND QUESTIONS ON GENDER-BASED ENTITLEMENTS

1. Is it appropriate to analyze intimate intrafamilial relations by focusing on ideas of entitlement? Is a property-rights approach too hard-edged and "arm's-length" to render a realistic picture of these relationships? Or, as Papanek argues, does a failure to notice differential entitlements only naturalize and perpetuate intrafamilial inequalities? For this debate in the context of divorce settlement, see Milton Regan, Spouses and Strangers, 82 Geo. L.J. 2303 (1994), and cf. Carol M. Rose, Rhetoric and Romance, 82 Geo. L.J. 2409 (1994).

2. Does Papanek's analysis have any bearing on gender relations in more developed economies? Amartya Sen, More than 100 Million Women Are Missing, N.Y. Rev. of Books, Dec. 20, 1990, at

61, argues that the more developed countries exhibit the same kinds of phenomena, though to a less severe degree. A much-discussed subject is the unequal distribution of housework and child care duties and the effects on women's earning power. For a classic study, see Paula England & George Farkas, Households, Employment, and Gender (1991); for more recent studies, see Joan Williams, Unbending Gender: Why Family and Work Conflict and What to Do About It (2000); Myra H. Strober & Agnes Miling Kaneko Chan, The Road Winds Uphill All the Way: Gender, Work, and Family in the United States and Japan (1999). For historical studies of intrafamilial differences in entitlements, see, e.g., Viviana Zelizer, The Social Meaning of Money (1994); Reva Siegel, Home as Work: The First Woman's Rights Claims Concerning Wives' Household Labor, 1850-1880, 103 Yale L.J. 1073 (1994).

3. If there are differences in entitlements based on gender, how do these differences begin and continue? For a theoretical perspective from classical contractarianism, see Carol Pateman, The Sexual Contract 39-76 (1982). More practically, Papanek discusses the self-perpetuation of such differences through the effects on the individual sense of self-worth and through social conceptions of justice. But she also mentions other institutions that maintain gendered differences of entitlement. For example, how does the common marriage custom dictating that the wife join her husband's household enlist the self-interest of parents in favoring sons over daughters?

4. Upon what general theory of property does Papanek's approach rest? That is, what does she see as the source of entitlements generally? She does not appear to follow a labor or desert theory; as Papanek points out, a woman's labor often enhances other people's entitlements rather than her own. Papanek seems to argue that entitlements are based on general cultural expectations. How does Papanek's treatment of culture relate to Zerbe and Anderson's, supra p. 273? Those authors argue that property systems arise from "culturally derived norms of fairness," but do these *include* gender inequalities, or do gender norms *override* other cultural norms of fairness? Would any norms of fairness dictate that women disproportionately play "chicken" or "dove" vis-à-vis men playing "hawk"?

5. Once a norm of inequality is in place, does rationality undermine efforts to establish equality? For example, if a given culture excludes women from the professions and trades, does it become rational to concentrate family resources on male children? See Gary Becker, A Treatise on the Family 180, 192 (enlarged ed. 1991). If so, are members of inegalitarian cultures trapped, in the

sense that rational actors within the cultures have little choice but to replicate the distributional patterns that favor male family members? See Robert Sugden, Contractarianism and Norms, 100 Ethics 768, 779-782 (1990); Carol M. Rose, Women and Property: Gaining and Losing Ground, 78 Va. L. Rev. 421 (1992). Could the same be said of unequal distributional patterns between social groups other than men and women? See Ian Ayres, Fair Driving: Gender and Race Discrimination in Retail Car Negotiations, 104 Harv. L. Rev. 817, 827-836, 850-851 (1991), arguing that discriminatory practices in car sales result from sellers' self-fulfilling prophecies in identifying some customers as "suckers."

6. Is the family the primary source of concepts of justice, imparting ideas not only of gender roles but of hierarchical ordering in other spheres? See Susan Moller Okin, Justice, Gender and the Family (1989). If so, does Rawls also need a theory of the family?

7. Is it possible that gender differences in entitlements result from differences in men's and women's bargaining strategies? For some early explorations, see Amartya Sen, Gender and Cooperative Conflicts, in Persistent Inequalities (Irene Tinker ed., 1990), linking women's lesser entitlements to bargaining disadvantages in intrafamilial "cooperative conflicts"; Rose, Women and Property, supra. Papanek implies that the improvement of a woman's opportunities in external labor markets would tend to enhance her bargaining position within her household. For support for this proposition, and for a survey of other literature on bargaining within the household, see Shelly Lundberg & Robert A. Pollak, Bargaining and Distribution in Marriage, 10 J. Econ. Persp. 139 (Fall 1996). Bargaining models are of course only a very small part of the now-vast literature on gender equality and inequality.

Chapter 7

Transacting and Trading

A. Ground Rules for Exchange

Filling Gaps in Incomplete Contracts: An Economic Theory of Default Rules*

Ian Ayres & Robert Gertner

The legal rules of contracts and corporations can be divided into two distinct classes. The larger class consists of "default" rules that parties can contract around by prior agreement, while the smaller, but important, class consists of "immutable" rules that parties cannot change by contractual agreement. Default rules fill the gaps in incomplete contracts; they govern unless the parties contract around them. Immutable rules cannot be contracted around; they govern even if the parties attempt to contract around them. For example, under the Uniform Commercial Code (U.C.C.) the duty to act in good faith is an immutable part of any contract, while the warranty of merchantability is simply a default rule that parties can waive by agreement. . . .[10]

*Source: 99 Yale L.J. 87-100, 125-127 (1989).
10. . . . This default rule/immutable rule dichotomy also pervades other areas of the law that have contractual components. In the law of divorce, for example, wealth accrued before marriage is allocated according to default rules that can be altered in pre-nuptial agreements, while income earned after marriage is immutably divided. Similarly, the repayment priorities set by state debtor-creditor law can, like default rules, be reordered through private contract. The laws of intestacy are also default rules: they fill any testamentary gap, but can be contracted around.

There is surprising consensus among academics at an abstract level on two normative bases for immutability. Put most simply, immutable rules are justifiable if society wants to protect (1) parties within the contract, or (2) parties outside the contract. The former justification turns on parentalism; the latter on externalities. Immutable rules displace freedom of contract. Immutability is justified only if unregulated contracting would be socially deleterious because parties internal or external to the contract cannot adequately protect themselves. With regard to immutable rules, the disagreement among academics is not over this abstract theory, but whether in particular contexts parentalistic concerns or externalities are sufficiently great to justify the use of immutable rules.

When the preconditions for immutability are not present, the normative legal analysis devolves to the choice of a default rule. Yet academics have paid little attention about how to choose among possible default rules. The law-and-economics movement has fought long and hard to convince courts to restrict the use of immutable rules, but has lost most of its normative energy in constructing a theory of default choice. Economists seem to believe that, even if lawmakers choose the wrong default, at worst there will be increased transaction costs of a second order of magnitude.

Few academics have gone beyond one-sentence theories stipulating that default terms should be set at what the parties would have wanted. . . .

This Article provides a theory of how courts and legislatures should set default rules. We suggest that efficient defaults would take a variety of forms that at times would diverge from the "what the parties would have contracted for" principle. To this end, we introduce the concept of "penalty defaults." Penalty defaults are designed to give at least one party to the contract an incentive to contract around the default rule and therefore to choose affirmatively the contract provision they prefer. In contrast to the received wisdom, penalty defaults are purposefully set at what the parties would not want — in order to encourage the parties to reveal information to each other or to third parties (especially the courts). . . .

An essential component of our theory of default rules is our explicit consideration of the sources of contractual incompleteness. We distinguish between two basic reasons for incompleteness. Scholars have primarily attributed incompleteness to the costs of contracting. Contracts may be incomplete because the transaction costs of explicitly contracting for a given contingency are greater than the benefits. These transaction costs may include legal fees, negotiation costs, drafting and printing costs, the costs of researching the effects and probability of a contingency, and the costs to the parties and the courts of verifying whether a contingency occurred. Rational parties will weigh these costs against the benefits of contractually addressing a particular contingency.... Scholars who attribute contractual incompleteness to transaction costs are naturally drawn toward choosing defaults that the majority of contracting parties "would have wanted" because these majoritarian defaults seem to minimize the costs of contracting.

We show, however, that this majoritarian "would have wanted" approach to default selection is, for several reasons, incomplete. First, the majoritarian approach fails to account for the possibly disparate costs of contracting and of failing to contract around different defaults. For example, if the majority is more likely to contract around the minority's preferred default rule (than the minority is to contract around the majority's rule), then choosing the minority's default may lead to a larger set of efficient contracts. Second, the received wisdom provides little guidance about how tailored or particularized the "would have wanted" analysis should be. Finally, the very costs of *ex ante* bargaining may encourage parties to inefficiently shift the process of gap filling to *ex post* court determination. If it is costly for the courts to determine what the parties would have wanted, it may be efficient to choose a default rule that induces the parties to contract explicitly. In other words, penalty defaults are appropriate when it is cheaper for the parties to negotiate a term *ex ante* than for the courts to estimate *ex post* what the parties would have wanted. Courts, which are publicly subsidized, should give parties incentives to negotiate *ex ante* by penalizing them for inefficient gaps.

This Article also proposes a second source of contractual incompleteness that is the focus of much of our analysis. We refer to this source of incompleteness as strategic. One party might strategically withhold information that would increase the total gains from contracting (the "size of the pie") in order to increase her private share of the gains from contracting (her "share of the pie"). By attempting to contract around a certain default, one party might reveal information to the other party that affects how the contractual pie is split. Thus, for example, the more informed party may prefer to have inefficient precaution rather than pay a higher price for the good. While analysts have previously explained incomplete contracting solely in terms of the costs of writing additional provisions, we argue that contractual gaps can also result from strategic behavior by relatively informed parties. By changing the default rules of the game, lawmakers can importantly reduce the opportunities for this rent-seeking, strategic behavior. In particular, the possibility of strategic incompleteness leads us to suggest that efficiency-minded lawmakers should sometimes choose penalty defaults that induce knowledgeable parties to reveal information by contracting around the default penalty. The strategic behavior of the parties in forming the contract can justify strategic contractual interpretations by courts. . . .

[I.] B. Toward a More General Theory of Penalty Defaults

Penalty defaults, by definition, give at least one party to the contract an incentive to contract around the default. From an efficiency perspective, penalty default rules can be justified as a way to encourage the production of information. The very process of "contracting around" can reveal information to parties inside or outside the contract. Penalty defaults may be justified as (1) giving both contracting parties incentives to reveal information to third parties, especially courts, or (2) giving a more informed contracting party incentives to reveal information to a less informed party. . . .

In some situations it is reasonable to expect one party to the contract to be systematically informed about the default rule and the probability of the relevant contingency arising. If one side is repeatedly in the relevant contractual setting while the other side rarely is, it is a sensible presumption that the former is better informed than the latter. Consider, for example, the treatment of real estate brokerage commissions when a buyer breaches a purchase contract. Such contracts typically include a clause which obligates the purchaser to forfeit some given amount of "earnest" money if she breaches the agreement. How should the earnest money be split between the seller and the broker if their agency contract does not address this contingency? Some courts have adopted a "what the parties would have wanted" approach and have awarded all the earnest money to the seller. We agree with this outcome, but for different reasons. The real estate broker will more likely be informed about the default rule than the seller. Indeed, the seller may not even consider the issue of how to split the earnest money in case of default. Therefore, if the efficient contract would allocate some of the earnest money to the seller, the default rule should be set against the broker to induce her to raise the issue. Otherwise, if the default rule is set to favor the broker, a seller may not raise the issue, and the broker will be happy to take advantage of the seller's ignorance. By setting the default rule in favor of the uninformed party, the courts induce the informed party to reveal information, and, consequently, the efficient contract results.

Although social welfare may be enhanced by forcing parties

to reveal information to a subsidized judicial system, it is more problematic to understand why society would have an efficiency interest in inducing a relatively informed party to a transaction to reveal information to the relatively uninformed party. After all, if revealing information is efficient because it increases the value created by the contract, one might initially expect that the informed party will have a sufficient private incentive to reveal information — the incentive of splitting a bigger pie. This argument ignores the possibility, however, that revealing information might simultaneously increase the total size of the pie and decrease the share of the pie that the relatively informed party receives. If the "share-of-the-pie effect" dominates the "size-of-the-pie effect," informed parties might rationally choose to withhold relevant information.[57]

Parties may behave strategically not only because they have superior information about the default, but also because they have superior information about other aspects of the contract. We suggest that a party who knows that a particular default rule is inefficient may choose not to negotiate to change it. The knowledgeable party may not wish to reveal her information in negotiations if the information would give a bargaining advantage to the other side.

How can it be that by increasing the total gains from contracting (the size-of-the-pie effect) the informed party can end up with a smaller share of the gains (the share-of-the-pie effect)? This Article demonstrates how relatively informed parties can sometimes benefit by strategically withholding information that, if revealed, would increase the size of the pie. A knowledgeable buyer, for example, may prefer to remain indistinguishable from what the seller wrongly perceives to be the class of similarly situated buyers. By blending in with the larger class of contractors, a buyer or a seller may receive a cross-subsidized price because the other side will bargain as if she is dealing with the average member of the class. A knowledgeable party may prefer to remain in this inefficient, but cross-subsidized, contractual pool rather than move to an efficient, but unsubsidized, pool. If contracting around the default sufficiently reduces this cross-subsidization, the share-of-the-pie effect can exceed the size-of-the-pie effect because the informed

---

57. Withholding socially valuable private information to obtain private gains is common. Companies may withhold information about innovations from competitors to increase profits; car buyers may withhold information about particular options or accessories that they value if this information signals to car dealers a greater willingness to pay for the underlying automobile; and professional athletes may withhold information about injuries to increase their salaries, even though as a result their team may inefficiently hire reserves.

party's share of the default pie was in a sense being artifically cross-subsidized by other members of the contractual class. Under this scenario, withholding information appears as a kind of rent-seeking in which the informed party forgoes the additional value attending the revealed information to get a larger piece of the contractual pie. . . .

C. Legal Responses to Contracting Around Immutable Rules

An important difference between default and immutable rules is that if parties attempt to contract around a default rule and fail, they will simply be bound by the default, whereas if parties attempt to contract around an immutable rule and fail, the law may choose to penalize the attempt by imposing a penalty different from (and, from the parties' *ex ante* perspective, worse than) the immutable standard. From an *ex ante* perspective the possibility of receiving this *ex post* penalty is just another expected cost of contracting around the default rule.

The legal response to parties who try to contract around immutable rules can also be given a default interpretation. . . .

This . . . tension arises with covenants not to compete. Courts have established an immutable rule that parties cannot make covenants of unreasonable duration. In Fullerton Lumber Co. v. Torborg, for example, the Supreme Court of Wisconsin held that a ten-year covenant was unreasonable but then struggled in deciding whether it should reformulate the contract to impose a duty not to compete for a reasonable period or penalize the employer for transgressing the immutable limitation by allowing the former employee to compete immediately.

If the goal of an immutable rule is to discourage people from even attempting to contract around a provision, then it would seem that the penalty reconstruction would be the favored result. This is again analogous to our earlier discussion of penalty defaults, in which we suggested that courts should choose the penalty that provided "least cost deterrence." The difference is that in the earlier discussion the penalties were attempting to deter gaps and here the penalties are attempting to promote gaps (that is, deter contracting around). The preference for penalty defaults to fill the gaps left in unconscionable contracts may justify the common law "blue pencil" test which simply enforces contracts after the offending provision has been struck (with a blue pencil).

NOTES AND QUESTIONS ON DEFAULT RULES

1. Though Ayres and Gertner's (A & G) article concerns contracts rather than property, they use an example from real estate sales. Can you think of other areas in which their analysis might sort out the rules of property law?

For example, do the traditional common law rules of landlord-tenant law look so draconian in the light of A & G's analysis of default rules? What about the more modern warranty of habitability in residential landlord-tenant law? Is this a conventional fall-back rule, a penalty default rule, or an immutable rule? That is, does it reflect (a) a best guess about what most landlords and tenants would agree to, (b) an inducement to landlords (or tenants) to disclose information about expectations for repair, or (c) an iron-clad rule that overrides any bargain to which the parties may agree? What are the arguments for and against each possibility? Which view should prevail, and why?

2. What accounts for changes in default rules over time? See, for example, the transformations in the law of caveat emptor described in the next selection. Why might the law shift from a default rule that penalizes buyers who fail to investigate fully the condition of the property, to a default rule that penalizes sellers who fail to disclose information?

3. Isn't it slightly odd to find a civil court's rule described as a "penalty" when these same courts often frown on any effort by the parties to build penalties into contracts? Are penalties nevertheless a pervasive aspect of the civil law, as A & G suggest? If so, why would civil law judges try to disguise this fact? If penalties are present in the civil law, how should the size of the penalty be set? Are the considerations the same as, or different from, those that govern the penalties meted out in the criminal law?

4. What precisely is the point of immutable rules? A & G mention two standard justifications: preventing externalities (protecting third parties) and parentalism (protecting the parties in the bargain). The externality argument seems straightforward, but why should courts indulge in parentalism? Why might courts try to discourage ostensibly willing parties from bargaining over certain items of property (such as parts of one's body), or transferring some property separately from other property (such as an apartment without a warranty of quality)? Does the idea of immutable bargaining rules suggest that some property is inalienable? For a further discussion of inalienability, see the selection from Radin, Market-Inalienability, infra p. 336.

Crystals and Mud in Property Law*

Carol M. Rose

Property law, and especially the common law of property, has always been heavily laden with hard-edged doctrines that tell everyone exactly where they stand. Default on paying your loan installments? Too bad, you lose the thing you bought and your past payments as well. Forget to record your deed? Sorry, the next buyer can purchase free of your claim, and you are out on the street. Sell that house with the leak in the basement? Lucky you, you can unload the place without having to tell the buyer about such things at all.

In a sense, hard-edged rules like these — rules that I call "crystals" — are what property is all about. If, as Jeremy Bentham said long ago, property is "nothing but a basis of expectation,"[1] then crystal rules are the very stuff of property: Their great advantage, or so it is commonly thought, is that they signal to all of us, in a clear and distinct language, precisely what our obligations are and how we may take care of our interests. Thus, I should inspect the property, record my deed, and make my payments if I don't want to lose my home to unexpected physical, legal, or financial impairments. I know where I stand and so does everyone else, and we can all strike bargains with each other if we want to stand somewhere else.

Economic thinkers have been telling us for at least two centuries that the more important a given kind of thing becomes for us, the more likely we are to have these hard-edged rules to manage it. We draw these ever-sharper lines around our entitlements so that we know who has what, and so that we can trade instead of getting into the confusions and disputes that would only escalate as the goods in question became scarcer and more highly valued.

At the root of these economic analyses lies the perception that it costs something to establish clear entitlements to things, and we won't bother to undertake the task of removing goods from an ownerless "commons" unless it is worth it to us to do so. What makes it worth it? Increasing scarcity of the resource, and the attendant conflicts over it. To use the example given by Harold Dem-

---

*Source: 40 Stan. L. Rev. 577-590, 596-604 (1988).
1. J. Bentham, Theory of Legislation, Principles of the Civil Code, pt. 1, ch. 8, at 68 (Baxi ed. . . . 1975).

setz, one of the most notable of the modern economists telling this story, when the European demand for fur hats increased demand for (and scarcity of) fur-bearing animals among Indian hunters, the Indians developed a system of property entitlements to the animal habitat.[6] ... In effect, as our competition for a resource raises the costs of conflict about it, those conflict costs begin to outweigh the costs of taking it out of the commons and establishing clear property entitlements. We establish a system of clear entitlements so that we can barter and trade for what we want instead of fighting.

The trouble with this "scarcity story" is that things don't seem to work this way, or at least not all the time. Sometimes we seem to substitute fuzzy, ambiguous rules of decision for what seem to be perfectly clear, open and shut, demarcations of entitlements. I call this occurrence the substitution of "mud" rules for "crystal" ones.

Thus, in the examples with which I began, we find that, over time, the straightforward common law crystalline rules have been muddied repeatedly by exceptions and equitable second-guessing, to the point that the various claimants under real estate contracts, mortgages, or recorded deeds don't know quite what their rights and obligations really are ...

... [A] move to the uncertainty of mud seems disruptive to the very practice of a private property / contractual exchange society. Thus, it is hardly surprising that we individually and collectively attempt to clear up the mud with new crystal rules — as when private parties contract out of ambiguous warranties, or when legislatures pass new versions of crystalline record systems — only to be overruled later, when courts once again reinstate mud in a different form.

These odd permutations on the scarcity story must give us pause. Why should we shift back and forth instead of opting for crystal when we have greater scarcity? Is there some advantage to mud rules that the courts are paying attention to? And if so, why do we not opt for mud rules instead? ...

I. From Crystal to Mud and Back: Three Examples

From all appearances, and despite the obvious advantages of crystalline property rules for the smooth flow of trade and commerce, we seem to be caught in an era of intractable and perhaps even

---

6. Demsetz, [Toward a Theory of Property Rights, 57 Am. Econ. Rev. 347 (Pap. & Proc. 1967)].

increasing muddiness. One could choose any number of areas to see this, and I will briefly discuss only a few, namely the examples with which I began. . . .

A. The Demise of Caveat Emptor

For several hundred years, and right up to the last few decades, caveat emptor was the staple fare of the law of real estate purchases, at least for buildings already constructed. The purchaser was deemed perfectly capable of inspecting the property and deciding for himself whether he wanted it, and if anyone were foolish enough to buy a pig in a poke, he deserved what he got. Short of outright fraud that would mislead the buyer, the seller had no duties to disclose anything at all.

One chink in this otherwise smooth wall was the doctrine of "latent defects," which, like the exception for fraud, suggested that perhaps the buyer really can't figure things out entirely. For some time now, in at least some states, a seller has had to tell a buyer about material problems with the property known to the seller but undiscoverable by the purchaser upon reasonable inspection. The doctrine began to raise a few problems of muddiness: What defects are "material"? What does the seller "know"? To what extent should the buyer "reasonably" have to inspect for herself?

Within the last few decades, the movement to mud in this area has become even more pronounced as some courts and legal commentators maintain that builder/vendors implicitly warrant a new house "habitable." But what does habitability mean? Is the house's habitability coterminous with the local housing code, or does "habitability" connote some less definite standard? What if the defects were obvious, and just what does "obvious" mean, anyway? We don't know until we litigate the issues.

Even if builder/vendors' warranties do muddy up property rights, there are some plausible reasons for them. After all, the builder/vendors are professionals, and they should know more about their own construction; they even might have avoided the problems in the first place by building more carefully. It is somewhat more difficult to extend those arguments to sellers who are themselves merely homeowners instead of builder/vendors, yet we find that even these nonprofessional sellers have increasing obligations to anticipate the buyers' desires, and to inform buyers about disagreeable factors that might make the buyers think twice. A California court, for example, has ruled that the sellers had to inform the buyer that a mass murder had taken place a decade previously in a particular house.[28] The courts now seem to presume a buyer who can't figure out much at all, and to protect that buyer they have adopted a mud standard: like good neighbors, sellers must tell buyers about any "material" defects — whatever those may be. . . .

But there is a countermove as well: Even if the legal rules have moved toward mud, private bargainers often try to install their own little crystalline systems through contractual waivers of warranties or disclosure duties (for example, the "as is" or "no warranty" sale). These private efforts in effect move things into the pattern of a circle, from crystal to mud and back to crystal. And the circle turns once again when the courts ban such waivers, as they sometimes do, and firmly re-establish a rule of mud — only to be followed by even more artful waivers.

The back-and-forth pattern of crystal and mud is even more evident in the next example, the loan secured by landed property — a form of real estate transaction whose history has often been described as resembling a seesaw.

B. Of Mortgages and Mud

Early common law mortgages were very crystalline indeed. They had the look of pawnshop transactions and were at least sometimes structured as conveyances: I borrow money from you, and at the same time I convey my land to you as security for my loan. If all goes well, I pay back my debt on the agreed "law day," and you reconvey my land back to me. But if all does not go well and I cannot pay on the appointed day, then, no matter how heart-rending my excuse, I lose my land to you and, presumably, any of the previous payments I might have made. As the fifteenth century commentator Littleton airily explained, the name "mortgage" derived from the rule that, if the debtor "doth not pay, then the land which he puts in pledge . . . is gone from him for ever, and so dead."[35]

This system had the advantage of great clarity, but it sometimes must have seemed very hard on mortgage debtors to the advantage of scoundrelly creditors. Littleton's advice about the importance of specifying the precise place and time for repayment, for example, conjures up images of a wily creditor hiding in the woods on the repayment day to frustrate repayment; presumably,

28. Reed v. King, . . . 193 Cal. Rptr. 130 (Cal App. 1983).
35. Littleton's Tenures, . . . at §332.

the unfound creditor could keep the property. But by the seventeenth century, the intervention of courts of equity had changed things. By the eighteenth and nineteenth centuries, the equity courts were regularly giving debtors as many as three or four "enlargements" of the time in which they might pay and redeem the property before the final "foreclosure," even when the excuse was lame. One judge explained that an equity court might well grant more time even after the "final" order of "foreclosure absolute," depending on the particular circumstances.[39]

The muddiness of this emerging judicial remedy argued against its attractiveness. Chief Justice Hale complained in 1672 that, "[b]y the growth of Equity on Equity, the Heart of the Common Law is eaten out, and legal Settlements are destroyed; . . . as far as the Line is given, Man will go; and if an hundred Years are given, Man will go so far, and we know not whither we shall go."[40] Instead of a precise and clear allocation of entitlements between the parties, the "equity of redemption" and its unpredictable foreclosure opened up vexing questions and uncertainties: How much time should the debtor have for repayment before the equitable arguments shifted to favor the creditor? What sort of excuses did the debtor need? Did it matter that the property, instead of dropping in the lap of the creditor, was sold at a foreclosure sale?

But as the courts moved towards muddiness, private parties attempted to bargain their way out of these costly uncertainties and to reinstate a crystalline pattern whereby lenders could get the property immediately upon default without the costs of foreclosure. How about a separate deal with the borrower, for example, whereby he agrees to convey any equitable interest to the lender in case of default? Nothing doing, said the courts, including the United States Supreme Court, which in 1878 stated flatly that a mortgagor could not initially bargain away his "equity of redemption."[45] Well, then, how about an arrangement whereby it looks as if the lender already owns the land, and the "borrower" only gets title if he lives up to his agreement to pay for it by a certain time? This seemed more promising: In the 1890s California courts thought it perfectly correct to hold the buyer to his word in such an arrangement, and to give him neither an extension nor a refund of past payments. By the 1960s, however, they were changing their minds about these "installment land contracts." After all, these deals really had exactly the same effect as the old-style mortgages

---

39. Campbell v. Holyland, 7 Ch. D. 166, 172 (1876). . . .
40. Roscarrick v. Barton, 22 Eng. Rep. 769, 770 (1672).
45. Peugh v. Davis, 96 U.S. 332, 337 (1878).

— the defaulting buyer could lose everything if he missed a payment, even the very last payment. Human vice and error seemed to put the crystal rule in jeopardy: In a series of cases culminating with a default by a "willful but repentant" little old lady who had stopped paying when she mistakenly thought that she was being cheated, the California Supreme Court decided to treat these land contracts as mortgages in disguise.[48] It gave the borrower "relief from forfeiture" — a time to reinstate the installment contract or get back her past payments.

With mortgages first and mortgage substitutes later, we see a back-and-forth pattern: crisp definition of entitlements, made fuzzy by accretions of judicial decisions, crisped up again by the parties' contractual arrangements, and once again made fuzzy by the courts. Here we see private parties apparently following the "scarcity story" in their private law arrangements: when things matter, the parties define their respective entitlements with ever sharper precision. Yet the courts seem at times unwilling to follow this story or to permit these crystalline definitions, most particularly when the rules hurt one party very badly. The cycle thus alternates between crystal and mud.

But the subject matter that has truly defied the scarcity story, often to the despair of property professors, has not been mortgages or mortgage substitutes. It has been the recording system, to which I now turn.

C. Broken Records

In establishing recording systems, legislatures have lent support to private parties' efforts to sharpen the definition of their entitlements. The *raison d'etre* of such systems is to clarify and perfectly specify landed property rights for the sake of easy and smooth transfers of land.

But the Anglo-American recording system in fact has been a saga of frustrated efforts to make clear who has what in land transfers. Common law transfers of land required a certain set of formalities between the parties, but thereafter, conflicting claims were settled by the age-old principle, "first in time, first in right." Thus, on Tuesday I might sell my farm to you, and on Wednesday I might wrongfully purport to sell it once again to innocent Farmer Brown. Poor Farmer Brown remains landless even though he knew nothing about the prior sale to you and indeed had no way of

---

48. MacFadden v. Walker, . . . 97 Cal. Rptr. 537 (Cal. 1971).

knowing about it. This outcome was hardly satisfactory from a property rights perspective. "First in time, first in right" may work well enough in a community where everyone knows all about everyone else's transactions, but outside that context, the doctrine does little to put people on notice of who owns what, and the opportunities for conflicting claims are endless.

But the efforts to remedy this flaw have gone through new cycles of certainty and uncertainty. Henry VIII attempted — without great success — to establish public registration of land claims through the Statute of Enrollments in 1536. Versions of the Statute resurfaced in Massachusetts' 1640 recording act and in other seventeenth and eighteenth century colonial recording acts, all of which were much more widely (though still somewhat irregularly) applied than their Henrician model had been.

Henry's Statute and its original American counterparts reflected an emphatically crystalline view of property. Their literal language suggests that they were versions of what has come to be called a "race" statute: the first purchaser to record (the winner of the "race" to the registry) can hold this title against all other claimants, whether or not he was in fact the first to purchase. In such a system, the official records become an unimpeachable source of information about the status of land ownership; the law counts the record owner, and only the record owner, as the true owner. The purchaser can buy in reliance on the records without fear of divestment by some unknown interloper, and without the need to make some cumbersome extra-record search for such potential interlopers.

This system was too crystalline to last. The characters to muck up this crystalline system by now should be sounding familiar: ninnies, hard-luck cases, and the occasional scoundrels who take advantage of them. What are we to do, for example, with the silly fellow who buys an interest in property but simply forgets to record? Or with the more conscientious one who does attempt to record his interest, but whose records wind up in the wrong book? Or with the lost soul whose impeccably correct filing is dropped behind the radiator by the neglectful clerk? Some courts take a hard line, perhaps concluding that the first owner was in a better position than our innocent outsider — that is, the next purchaser — to detect and correct the flaws in the records. But our sympathies for the luckless unrecorded owner put pressure on the recording system that would divest him in favor of the later-arriving outsider.

Our sympathies are all the greater when the outsider is not so innocent after all. What shall we do, say, when the unrecorded first buyer is snookered out of his claim by a later purchaser who

knows perfectly well that the land had already been sold? Shall
we allow this nasty second buyer to perfect a claim simply because
he carefully follows the official recording rules? This thought was
too much for the courts of equity, and too much for American
legislatures as well. By the early nineteenth century, the British
equity courts had imported an element of non-record "notice" into
what had initially been a "race" system. Under these doctrines, the
later purchaser could take free of the prior claims only if he did
not *know* about those prior claims, either from the records or from
non-record facts that should put him "on notice." American legislatures followed this move to such a degree that, at present, only
a handful of states maintain a race system with any rigor. The other
states deny the subsequent claim of the person who had or should
have had notice of the earlier claim.

This development means mud: What "should" a purchaser
know about, anyway? To be sure, if someone is living on the land,
perhaps the potential purchaser should make a few inquiries about
the occupant's status. But what if the "occupant's" acts are more
ambiguous, consisting of, say, shovelling some manure onto the
contested land? Well, said one court, a buyer should have asked
about the source of all that manure — and since he didn't, and thus
did not find out about the manure shoveller's prior but unrecorded
claim, the later buyer did not count as an innocent; his title was a
nullity.

With the emergence of this judicial outlook, the crystalline
idea of the recording system has come full cycle back to mud. To
be sure, the recording system can give one a fair guess about the
legal status of any given property. But by the end of the last century, as a Massachusetts court put it, "it would be seldom that a
case could occur where some state of facts might not be imagined
which, if it existed, would defeat a title." Thus, the test of a title's
"marketability" became a question of whether the title was subject
to "reasonable" doubt — a matter, of course, for the discretion of
the court. In the meantime, a whole title insurance industry sprang
up to calm the fears of would-be purchasers who wanted to avoid
questions about which doubts were reasonable and which were
not. It is this industry, in a sense, that once again makes crystals
out of the recording system's mud; and according to the reformers,
it is this industry that now stands in the way of a more rational
method of cleaning up the mess once and for all.

Yet one must wonder whether cleaning up the mess might not
just repeat the cycle of mud/crystal/mud. One of the most popular
suggestions for reform is the so-called "Torrens" system, named
for someone who thought that shipping registry methods could be

used beneficially in real estate. In this system, all claims on a given property — sales, liens, easements, etc. — are first registered and then incorporated in a certificate. Torrens registration echoes eerily the colonial "race" statutes: No unregistered claim counts, and the owner's certificate for a given property acts as the complete record of everything that anyone might claim.

Well, perhaps not everything. Government liens, fraudulent transactions, and, according to some courts, even simple errors or neglect in registration can produce unregistered claims that count. Hence this neo-race system provides no complete relief from the recording system's mud. Even after we look at the Torrens certificate, we still have to be on the lookout for the G-men, the forgers, and the ninnies who neglected to register their claims properly. Not a lot of mud, to be sure, but just wait. In some jurisdictions with a long history of Torrens registration, courts have in effect reestablished a "notice" system, defeating the interest of one who registers his claim when he knows about a prior unregistered one — or merely when he *should* have known about the prior claim. This practice, of course, means that the registry and certificate no longer count as the complete source of information about a property's title status.

The most striking aspect of these developments is that first the title recording acts, and later the registration systems, represented deliberate choices to establish crystalline rules for the sake of simplicity and ease of land sales and purchases. People who failed to use the records or registries were supposed to lose their claims, no matter how innocent they might have been, and no matter how nastily their opponents might have behaved. Yet these very crystalline systems have drifted back into mud through the importation of equitable ideas of notice — only to be replaced by new crystalline systems in the form of private contract or public legislation.

All these examples put the scarcity story to the test: What has happened to that story, according to which our rules should become more crystalline as resources become more scarce and more valuable? Why instead do we shift back and forth between hard-edged, yes-or-no crystalline rules and discretion-laden, *post hoc* muddy rules? Why do we have, over time, *both* mud *and* crystal rules with respect to the very same things, without any notable relation to their scarcity or plenty? The following section runs through a few theories that might help to explain this mystery.

[The second part of the article discusses several alternative explanations. Two opposing arguments suggest that one side or the other has been simply mistaken; some commentators associated with the law-and-economics movement argue that "mud" rules are mistaken because they impede trade; an opposing argument, associated with the critical legal studies movement, argues that crystal rules are mistaken because they send the wrong message about social norms — that is, one of unrestrained self-interest. The article puts both of these positions to one side because the historic seesaw record suggests that, mistaken or not, we are not likely to have much choice about having both crystals and mud. The author also questions a third argument — that crystal rules are associated with low transactions costs and muddy ones with high transactions costs; again the historic record seems not to bear this out. She then rejects a historical theory that crystal rules were associated with an effort to instill labor discipline, since the correlation seems weak in different times and places.

The article finds more promising an analogy to Alfred Hirschman's Shifting Involvements (1982), an economic history of social movements, which argues that as people become satiated with public affairs they move to private satisfactions, and vice versa.]

Might this process parallel the shift between mud and crystal in property law? Hirschman's book suggests that where we see recurring patterns, we might look for some internal — or as some theorists say, endogenous — factors that lead to these circular patterns. Does such an account apply to the oscillation between crystal and mud in our definitions of entitlements? We can see its application in one area at least: the recording system, where we have so often resolved uncertainty with a crystalline system, only to muddy it so thoroughly over time that we have to start all over again with a newly-minted set of clear rules.

Let us suppose that we have a system for the clarification of property titles. Might we have a tendency to overuse the system, so that in the end it becomes so hopelessly bogged down in detail that the purpose of clarity is defeated? Certainly our traditional land records have this quality. Some early cases permitted only fee interests to be recorded, but it was the very attractiveness of the system that created pressure to allow the recordation of other interests; liens, for example, or easements. Indeed, some claims may be in the records even though they are not legally recordable. Then too, many claims are recorded and just stay put over time, and sometimes even conflict with other recorded claims. The layers of these recorded but unextinguished claims can grow so thick that it hardly seems worth the time to go back and check them all. So, in a sense, we treat our clarifying systems — in this case the recording mechanisms — as a kind of "commons." The resulting system overload, in turn, creates a certain disgust with the lush proliferation of records. In fact, one of our current recording reforms would simply extinguish claims that have not been asserted during a given period.

Thus, the very attractiveness of making clear one's claims by recording them defeats the purpose of the system, that is, to clarify all claims against a given property. One sees the same pattern in the excessively long contracts that attempt to specify all possible contingencies and that no one actually reads; however comforting it might be to "have it in writing," it really isn't worth the effort to nail down everything, and the overly precise contract may wind up being just as opaque as — and perhaps even more arbitrary than — the one that leaves adjustments to the contingencies of future relations.

The trouble, then, is that an attractively simple legal device draws in too many users, or too complex a set of uses. And that, of course, is where the simple rule becomes a booby trap. It is this booby trap aspect of what seems to be clear, simple rules — the scenario of disproportionate loss by some party — that seems to drive us to muddy up crystal rules with the exceptions and the *post hoc* discretionary judgments. I turn now to the subject of disproportionate loss, the subject to which some courts apply the shorthand label of "forfeiture."

III.   Forfeiture as Overload: The Problem and the Players

A strong element of moral judgment runs through the cases in which mud supersedes crystal. These cases are often rife with human failings — sloth and forgetfulness on the one hand, greed and self-dealing on the other. These vices put pressure on our efforts to elaborate clear and distinct property specifications, and make judges and others second guess the deals that call for a pound of flesh.

Perhaps we can get at this human element by thinking not about moral qualities that are at issue, but rather about the pound of flesh. We have already seen that in the decisions about mortgages and installment land contracts, there lurks a deep antipathy to what is explicitly called the debtor's "forfeiture." The same antipathy to "forfeiture" — a loss disproportionate to the lapse — also appears in our other examples. Thus, the non-recording (or improperly recording, or negligently recording) owner would lose the very property itself; thus, the non-inspecting (or imperfectly inspecting, or negligently inspecting) buyer would get stuck with a house that may be flooded twice a week with the neighbor's sewage.

Our law seems to find these dramatic losses abhorrent. James Gordley has written convincingly that unequal exchanges have been overwhelmingly disfavored in the western legal tradition,[117] and his work suggests that rules leading to forfeitures and penalties generally are unstable in our law. Why is this so? Gordley argues that, traditionally, exchanges centering more or less around a market price counted as "equal." Such exchanges taken collectively restored the costs to the seller, and beyond that, Gordley argues, the law has had no reason to enforce what he calls random redistributions. . . .

Forfeiture might be seen as a symptom of the overloading of crystal rules. Crystalline property doctrines yield fixed consequences, and their predictability makes these doctrines attractive; but for that very reason they may be overused or overloaded in contexts that make them *un*predictable and counterproductive.

Consider the way that the enforcement of a penalty affects the incentives of persons on either side of a property entitlement. If we were to enforce penalties against defaulters or violators, the persons involved undoubtedly would be especially careful about avoiding violations. But perhaps they would be *too* careful, and try to live up to their obligations even when circumstances changed radically, and when everyone would really be better off if someone defaulted and paid normal damages for whatever harm their default caused another. Penalties might also affect the behavior of the non-defaulting parties. Because they would gain much more than damages if penalties were enforced, unscrupulous dealers might expend efforts to find trading partners who would *fail* rather than succeed, or take measures to make them trip up, in order to take the penalty proceeds and run. These victims are the people that petty con artists in my hometown of Chicago might call "mopes," a term that undoubtedly could include the unsuspecting house purchasers who overestimate their ability to live up to the loan payments, or who never suspect that there might be rats in the basement, or who don't have a clue that they have to record their titles.

Fools on the one side and sharp dealers on the other, then, are central players in the crystal-to-mud story, because they are the characters most likely to have a leading role in the systematic overloading of crystalline rules. From this perspective, as indeed the more sophisticated economic analyses tell us, crystalline rules seem less the king of the efficiency mountain than we may normally

---

117. Gordley, Equality in Exchange, 69 Calif. L. Rev. 1587 (1981).

assume. One can argue that elaborate *ex post* allocations of responsibilities might be efficient too, even if they make people's entitlements fuzzier *ex ante*. The very knowledge than one cannot gull someone else, and get away with it, makes it less likely that anyone will dissipate time and effort in trying to find the gullible. This knowledge will also reassure those of us who fear we may be made fools; can go about our business and take part in the world of trade without cowering at home because we think we need to hire a lawyer and an accountant every time we leave the car at a commercial parking lot.

How can we fit these factors together with the scarcity story about property rights? According to that story, the driving force toward crystalline rules is the competition for resources hitherto unowned — in other words, overuse of a "commons" in a given resource. The conflicts and waste from commons overuse induce us to define boundaries around entitlements so that we can trade our entitlements instead of fighting over them.

But the driving force of the movement to mud rules seems to be an overuse in the "commons" of the crystal rules themselves: We are tempted to take rules that are simple and informative in one context — as, for example, "first in time, first in right" may be in a small community — and extend them to different or more complex situations, where the consequences may be unexpected and confusing. It is in these "overload" situations that crystal rules may ultimately impede trade. Not only might sharp dealers seek out situations in which trade will fail (allowing them to collect a forfeiture from the mopes), but the mopes themselves may be frightened out of dealing altogether. Simple boundaries and simple remedies, it turns out, may yield radically unexpected results, and may destroy the confidence we need for trade, rather than fostering it. It is forfeiture, the prospect of dramatic or disproportionate loss, that brings this home; and forfeiture — and the detailed ways in which it might have been avoided — can only be known to us *ex post*.

IV. The Context of Forfeiture: Crystals and Mud as Institutional Responses to Estrangement

What can be said to generalize the context of forfeiture, where crystal rules are overloaded? Where is it in our commercial life, for example, that we find the invocation of those crystalline rules at the cost of great forfeiture to another? Stewart Macaulay's work on contracts suggests that forfeitures and penalties are called for in one context in particular: where the parties have no long-term relationship with each other.[128] . . .

Macaulay's work, as well as that of Ian Macneil,[132] suggests that crystalline rules (and their attendant forfeitures) are only designed for people who see each other on a one-time basis, and whose temptations to dupe each other, or simply to play commercial hardball, might be strongest. By way of contrast, where two persons are members of the same community, religion, family, or ongoing business deal, there are inducements to cooperation and trust that are entirely independent of the enforcement of crystalline rules.

Modern game-theorist mathematicians buttress this point, telling us that if we can arrange things in such a manner that we have repeated contact with our opposite numbers, then we can enforce cooperation through the game of "tit for tat." Recent historical work supports the point from another direction, telling us that prior to the eighteenth century, much European commerce was dominated by Jewish and Quaker merchants, whose family and religious connections could assure their mutual reliability.

Recent historical literature also suggests that as modern property and contract law developed, it became possible for people to do business with each other on the basis of sheer promises even though they had none of these familial or other long-term relationships. The legal categories of contract acted as an artificial, officially sponsored surety for the confidence and trust that would otherwise come only through the constraints of community, religion, and family. The enforceability of clear rules enables us to deal with the world of strangers apart from these communities and to arrange our affairs with persons whom we do not know, and never expect to see again. We can do so, we think, because rules are rules are rules — we all know them, and know what to expect. Crystalline rules thus seem to perform the service of creating a context in which strangers can deal with each other in confidence.

But what is easily overlooked is that mud rules, too, attempt to recreate an underlying non-legal trading community in which confidence is possible. In those communities, the members tend to readjust for future complications, rather than drive hard bargains. Mud rules mimic a pattern of *post hoc* readjustments that people *would* make if they were in an ongoing relationship with each other. People in such relationships would hardly dupe their trading

128. See Macaulay, Elegant Models, Empirical Pictures and the Complexity of Contract, 11 Law & Soc'y Rev. 507, 509 (1977).

132. See Macneil [The Many Futures of Contract, 47 S. Cal. L. Rev. 691 (1974)].

partners out of their titles, sell them defective goods, or fail to make minor readjustments on debts. If they did such things, they would lose a trading partner (or suffer denunciation in church, or become black sheep), and everyone would know it.

Now we can see why crystal and mud are a matched pair. Both are distilled from a kind of non-legal commercial context where people already in some relationship arrive at more or less imperfect understandings at the outset and expect *post hoc* readjustments when circumstances require. Just as the parties call on courts to enforce promises and protect entitlements that would otherwise be enforced by the threat of informal sanctions, so too do they call on the courts to figure out the *post hoc* readjustments that would otherwise have been made by the parties themselves.

In our one-time dealings with strangers a wedge appears that splits a trading relationship into *ex ante* and *ex post*, crystals and mud. These dealings are the situations in which it seems most important to have clear definitions of obligations, but in which it is also important to have some substitute for the pattern of ongoing cooperation that would protect us against sudden and unexpected loss.

The split between crystals and mud from one-time dealings also falls along divisions in our legal institutions. We call for crystals when we are in what Mel Eisenberg has called our "rulemaking" mode, that is, when private parties make contracts with strangers or when legislatures make prospective law for an unknown future.[137] We call for mud and exceptions only later, after things have gone awry, but at that point we stand before judges.

. . . [J]udges, who see everything *ex post*, really cannot help but be influenced by their *ex post* perspectives. They lean ever so slightly to mud, in order to save the fools from forfeiture at the hands of scoundrels. Indeed, if judges have even an occasional preference for *post hoc* readjustments, to avoid forfeiture, this preference will gradually place an accretion of mud rules over people's crystalline arrangements. These considerations suggest a modification of claims about the efficiency of common law adjudication. We are more likely to find that judicial solutions veer towards mud rules, while it is legislatures that are more apt to join with private parties as "rulemakers" with a tilt towards crystal. . . .

[The last part of the article suggests that the choice between crystals and mud may have little practical effect on vast parts of

---

137. . . . [S]ee Eisenberg, Private Ordering Through Negotiation: Dispute-Settlement and Rulemaking, 89 Harv. L. Rev. 637, 664-665 (1976).

commercial life, given the predominant characteristics of repeat play and long-term relations in commercial dealings; the impact of the debate, the author suggests, may be largely a matter of rhetoric, and of the kinds of things people like to believe about the society they live in.]

NOTES AND QUESTIONS ON OSCILLATIONS IN LEGAL RULES

1. Rose's approach suggests pessimism about lasting reform in certain legal areas, particularly our messy land records system. Is she overly gloomy? Might there be room for improvement, in which the "mud" is cabined and restrained in a generally "crystalline" system like Torrens registration, subject to exceptions for fraud and perhaps a small number of other information sources outside the formal records? Can computers help to sort out the recording system? For an interesting and informative discussion of the potential impact of computer technology, see John L. McCormack, Torrens and Recording: Land Title Assurance in the Computer Age, 18 Wm. Mitchell L. Rev. 61 (1992).

2. If courts are reluctant to permit forfeitures or penalties, how can they themselves impose the remedies that Ayres and Gertner, Filling Gaps, supra p. 297, call "penalty default rules," effectively punishing knowledgeable parties for failing to reveal information? How do court-imposed "penalty default rules" differ from the forfeitures that Rose describes?

3. What is so problematic about forfeiture? Why does the prospect of forfeiture seem to ring so many emotional bells that it can cause judges to muddy perfectly clear rules, presumably to the collective detriment of future bargaining? Might this reaction stem from "loss aversion" or "endowment effects" — that is, attachments to the things that one has (as opposed to things one might have in the future)? Recall the discussion in Jolls et al., supra p. 221.

If loss aversion creates an urge to make rules muddy with *ex post* doctrines such as "unconscionability," does loss aversion dissipate total social wealth? Or does loss aversion instead suggest a hidden efficiency argument for muddy rules? On this issue, consider a famous article, with a title almost as catchy as The Tragedy of the Commons: George Akerlof, The Market for 'Lemons': Quality Uncertainty and the Market Mechanism, 84 Q.J. Econ. 488 (1970). Akerlof argued that certain kinds of markets (for instance, used car sales) cannot easily assure customers against defects; hence customers are frightened away, and both they and potential sellers miss opportunities for mutually beneficial sales. How might muddy rules help overcome customer fears, restore confidence in markets, and open up opportunities for beneficial trades?

4. At the end of this selection, Rose mentions the highly contested hypothesis that common law adjudication leads to the emergence of efficient rules. For some arguments in favor of this position, see, for example, George Priest, The Common Law Process and the Selection of Efficient Rules, 6 J. Legal Stud. 65 (1977); Paul H. Rubin, Why Is the Common Law Efficient?, 6 J. Legal Stud. 51 (1977). Rose, however, suggests that the oscillating patterns in property law cast doubt on this theory of evolutionary efficiency in common law adjudication, since courts play the role of muddying the crystalline rules previously established by private bargains and legislation.

Surprisingly, oscillations in legal rules have attracted little attention in legal academic literature. One exception is Jason Scott Johnston, Uncertainty, Chaos, and the Torts Process: An Economic Analysis of Legal Form, 76 Cornell L. Rev. 341 (1991). Johnston finds a similar back-and-forth pattern in the law of torts. He disagrees with Rose's institutional bifurcation, however, and concludes that the courts engage in this pattern on their own, without the input of other actors that normally operate from an *ex ante* perspective, such as private bargainers and legislatures. Might courts sometimes see matters from an *ex ante* perspective? For example, might they take into account their own after-the-fact tendency to overestimate the foresight of the parties? See Jeffrey Rachlinski, A Positive Psychological Theory of Judging in Hindsight, 65 U. Chi. L. Rev. 571 (1998), arguing that a "hindsight bias" is pervasive in after-the-fact judging, but also arguing that courts compensate for this bias through a variety of judicial doctrines. Compare Duncan Kennedy, Form and Substance in Common Law Adjudication, 89 Harv. L. Rev. 1685 (1976), which sees all legal rhetoric as choosing between "rules" that reflect individualist concerns and "standards" that reflect altruistic preferences.

B. Conflicting Paradigms of Entitlement and Exchange

Two Properties, One Land: Law and Space in Nineteenth-Century New Zealand*

Stuart Banner

The role legal thought plays in structuring perceptions of the world can be seen most clearly when peoples possessing two very different legal cultures first encounter one another. The misunderstandings that arise, particularly the strikingly different perceptions of identical events, suggest law's power to organize our awareness of phenomena before they reach the level of consciousness. This article will tell the story of one such encounter, that between the Maori and the Europeans, mostly British, who began arriving in New Zealand in the late eighteenth century.

Land occupied a fundamental position in the lives and the thought of both peoples. Each possessed a system of property law, which served to allocate rights to use land so as to prevent conflicts from arising. But those systems differed dramatically from one another. If we use the word *land* to refer to the physical substance, and reserve the word *property* for the intellectual apparatus that organizes rights to use land, we can say that the British and the Maori overlaid two dissimilar systems of property on the same land. Each side perceived land, and human activity involving land, through the lens of its own property system. The result, in the early years, was that each side systematically misperceived what the other was doing. In the long run, as the balance of power gradually swung to the side of the British over the course of the nineteenth century, they were largely able to impose their property system on the Maori. The centrality of property within the thought of both peoples, however, meant that the transformation of Maori into English property rights involved much more than land. Religious belief, engagement with the market economy, political organization — all were bound up in the systems by which both peoples organized property rights in land. To anglicize the Maori property system was to revolutionize Maori life. . . .

*Source: 24 Law & Soc. Inquiry 807-813, 823-825, 830-836, 844-847 (1999).

I. Two Properties

The earliest Europeans to reach New Zealand were astonished to discover that the Maori were farmers. "In a country that has been described as being peopled by a race of cannibals," marveled John Savage after returning to England in 1805, "you are agreeably surprised by ... the patches of cultivated ground in the neighbourhood of the bay; on each of which is seen a well-thatched hut, and a shed at a little distance." James Cook, whose 1769 visit was the second European encounter with New Zealand and the first since that of Abel Tasman over a century before, observed "a great deal of Cultivated land." Cook managed to purchase "of the natives about 10 to 15 pounds of sweet Potatous," a stroke of luck possible because "they have pretty large Plantations of these." Joseph Banks, the naturalist on board Cook's ship, was more effusive: "[S]o well was ground tilled," he noted (using the word *curious* in its eighteenth-century sense of "careful"), "that I have seldom seen even in the gardens of curious people land better broke down." Banks saw sweet potatoes "rangd in rows ... all laid by a line most regularly," and a vegetable resembling the cucumber "set in small hollows or dishes much as we do in England." Nearly 200 acres were in cultivation, "tho we did not see 100 people in all." The Maori did not just farm as in England; they also appeared to divide their farms much like the English. "These plantations were from 1 or 2 to 8 or 10 acres each," Banks found, and each "distinct patch was fenced in generally with reeds placd close by another so that scarce a mouse could creep through."

These initial reports were confirmed by the early nineteenth-century English missionaries, who were eager consumers and observers of Maori agriculture. "Throughout the island they have their potato cultivations," explained William Wade, "and in many parts grow the kumara, or sweet potato, taro, maize, pumpkins, water-melons, and the kind of gourd which forms their calabashes." Samuel Marsden rejoiced at the "incredible labour and patience" of Maori farmers, who "suffer no weeds to grow, but ... root up everything likely to injure the growing crop." The Maori even seemed to share the English view of how best to use the land and its resources. "A great work is going on here," John King approved in 1819, "in cutting down a large Forrest and burning it off in order to plant it. ... this is pleasing & promising." That the Maori could be so hard working, so skilled — so nearly civilized — in this respect was miraculous. When the "badness of their tools is considered, together with their limited knowledge of agriculture," considered Augustus Earle in 1832, "their persevering industry I look upon as truly astonishing." . . .

As both peoples would soon learn, the physical similarity of English and Maori agricultural methods masked some fundamental differences between English and Maori conceptions of property. The English tended to allocate property rights in land on a geographic basis. Land was divided into pieces, each piece was assigned to an owner, and the owner was ordinarily understood to command all the resources within that geographic space. He could harvest the plants that grew spontaneously, or plant crops, or place animals on the land, or catch fish in the water, or do virtually anything else he liked as much or as little as he pleased. An owner of land was likewise understood to control the access of others. If he wished, he could allow others to enter the geographic space within his control, on whatever terms he chose, but he could also exclude others entirely. These powers were understood to be unbounded in time. A landowner would not live forever, but his powers over the land would; he merely had to assign them to someone else, either while he was still alive or upon his death, and the new owner would assume all the rights of the old. If he failed to do so, the state would do it for him, through the rules of intestate succession.

The reality of English landholding was often more complex than this ideal. A piece of land might be owned by several people at once. Others might possess a future interest in the land, the right to assume ownership upon the death of another person or the occurrence of a future event. Still others might have rights to use the land for certain limited purposes, rights the law classified as easements, licenses, and profits. Open-field farming, though by now largely abandoned, had left its traces in the common rights still extant in some places. The state had an ambiguous power to limit the owner's discretion as to the use of his land. But these intrusions into the ideal of command over a geographic space were understood as just that — exceptions to a rule. Equally important, they were with rare exception products of a landowner's free choice, whether the current owner or one of his predecessors. Future interests, easements, and so on normally existed because they had been voluntarily created by a landowner, who presumably had chosen to give up some of his power over space in exchange for some thing he valued more highly. Governmental powers over nominally private land had been consented to as well in a less direct sense, as part of the social contract creating the state, and in the ongoing process of government, in which landowners at least had a voice.

The Maori, by contrast, tended to allocate property rights among individuals and families on a functional rather than a geographical basis. That is, a person would not own a zone of space; he would instead own the right to use a particular resource in a particular way. One might possess the right to trap birds in a certain tree, or the right to fish in a certain spot in the water, or the right to cultivate a certain plot of ground. Possession of such a right did not imply the possession of other rights in the same geographic space. The same tree, for instance, could be used for fowling by one family, for berry gathering by another, and so on. Nor did possession of a use right in one place preclude possession of use rights in other places as well. A family might be understood to have the right to one place for sleeping, another for cultivating, another for catching eels, and others for various other activities. These rights were typically handed down from generation to generation within the family, so long as each new generation continued to use the right in question. The Maori, like the English, possessed multiple rights over resources, but while the English ordinarily bundled these rights into a single geographic space, the Maori did not.

Another fundamental difference between English and Maori conceptions of property involved the means used to remember the property rights already in existence. Any property system requires some way of knowing what rights have already been allocated, to forestall disputes from arising and to resolve them when they do. The English had for centuries divided their land by written surveys and memorialized their land transactions in written agreements. The Maori, lacking writing, had developed a different method. Because property rights derived largely from one's ancestry, individuals trained themselves to remember their genealogy and the history of their kin group. The strategic use of landmarks, such as stones and marks in trees, served to aid the memory. "In going through a large forest," recalled the missionary Richard Taylor,

a Chief who was my companion, said it belonged to him. I asked how he knew his boundaries, he said he would point them out when we reached them; at last he stopped at the foot of a very large tree, whose root ran across the road; he pointed out to a hollow in it, and asked me what it was. I said, it was like a man's foot. He replied, I was right; it was the impression cut by one of his forefathers, and put his foot into it to show it fitted. This, said he, is one of my boundaries, and now we are entering on the land of another.

In a similar way when travelling over the central plains, where apparently human beings had never resided, one of my natives suddenly stopped by a stream, and said, that land belonged to his family. I expressed my doubts, and asked him how he could tell. He went into some long grass, and kept feeling about with his feet for some time, then calling me to him, he pointed out four hearth-stones, and triumphantly said, here stood my father's house, and going thence to the stream, he pointed out a little hollow in the rocky side, over which an old gnarled branch sprung, and said, in this hollow of the stream, we used to suspend our eel baskets from the branch. In fact, they have many marks which, though they might pass unnoticed by Europeans, clearly indicate to them their respective rights.

These techniques were as baffling to the English as the English method initially was to the Maori. "Now the manner of making known the boundaries of land amongst the Maories is very good amongst the Maori people," one English tenant complained to his Maori landlord, "because every man has been told by his father or relations where the boundaries of his land are. Now amongst the Europeans it is not so. I cannot understand your boundaries." He pleaded with his landlord to let the "boundaries of the runs be surveyed. Then the boundaries will be plain." . . .

The chiefs of tribal units, like European government officials, did not command more property than the ordinary people within their jurisdiction, but they had a greater than ordinary power to allocate property to others. These opportunities arose frequently. Property rights had to be maintained by use; if abandoned for long enough, sometimes only a few years, a right would revert back to the tribe, and could then be allocated to someone else. Land and natural resources were so plentiful in comparison to the number of people that it made sense for tribes to move from one block of land to another periodically, rather than continuing to exploit the same block persistently. These shifts would again have afforded the opportunity to allocate some property rights, although this opportunity would have been limited by the practice of returning periodically to each block of land and resuming the old pattern of use. Such cycling was necessary because of the requirement that rights be used in order to be maintained. As one very old man recalled in the later part of the nineteenth century, his tribe followed the custom of "living for some time on each of our blocks of land, to keep our claim to each, and that our fire might be kept alight on each block, so that it might not be taken from us by some other tribe." Finally, land could be acquired by one tribe by conquest from another, in the intermittent warfare that occurred among tribes. In this circumstance, property rights would need to be allocated from scratch. . . .

The precontact Maori economy provided very little occasion for the accumulation of personal wealth. There was no money, and few other durable goods, capable of being saved. The resources naturally present on the land far exceeded the ability of the relatively small population to consume them. Land was accordingly not understood as something that one might wish to sell. The Maori had little with which to purchase it, and had there been more to exchange for it, the price at which land might have sold would have been extremely low. Any sale, moreover, would have had to occur within the tribal group that exercised control over the land. An individual could no more alienate land outside the tribe than an English landowner could transfer his land to the sovereignty of France. . . .

Historians have sometimes been too quick to conclude, however, that the English possessed a "mechanistic view of land as a simple commodity able to be exploited by individuals pursuing material wealth," in contrast to the Maori "transcendental bond with their land which was treated as a dearly loved person." To the English, land was much more than a commodity, a truth that can be perceived most directly by considering all the connotations of the English word "home." . . . And for the English, no less than the Maori, land was intertwined with collective history. The concept of "England" — a place where one's ancestors had lived, a community whose history extended back farther than anyone could know without the aid of myths of origin — was one worth dying to defend. Some colonists recognized that the Maori felt the same way. "The pride of each tribe centers in its power to maintain its own possession against aggression," observed two early leaders of the settler community. "This spirit in the native people is closely akin to one which, if we were speaking of ourselves, we should describe as patriotism."

For the English, as for the Maori, land was also an important source of status within the community. . . . The Maori and English had serious misunderstandings over conceptions of property, but they were not caused by any failure on the part of the English to perceive the nonmonetary virtues of land. As Tom Brooking suggests, "one of the great misfortunes of New Zealand is that it has been settled by two peoples who are romantic and even sentimental about land and imbue it with magical properties that push past logic into the realms of the supernatural and transcendental."

The English struggled for several decades to understand the Maori system of property rights. Looking back on the process in the 1870s, Henry Sewell recalled: "It was as difficult for us to enter into and comprehend the tribal and communistic rights of the Natives, as it was for the Natives to enter into and comprehend our system of individual title." . . .

. . . [C]oming from a culture in which property rights were organized by geographic space, and observing many Maori exercising use rights within the same zone of land, many colonizers erroneously concluded that the land was held by all in common, and that property rights were therefore unknown. The "right of individual property has never existed in New Zealand," affirmed Edward Gibbon Wakefield before a committee of the House of Commons. Such a view lasted a long time. As late as 1879, the legislator William Rees recalled that before contact a "system of Communism prevailed, and speaking generally, no native held absolutely to himself any portion in particular, of the surrounding territory of the vicinity in which he lived." . . .

II. One Land

The recognition of Maori property rights meant that in the absence of war the English could acquire land only by purchase. Until 1865, land was purchased from tribes rather than from the Maori as individuals. . . .

A transaction cannot occur without a willing seller. In the early years, the Maori were "very anxious to sell" their land, John Flatt reported. "Yes, very anxious, even up to the time of my leaving," agreed the trader George Earp. "People frequently come from the interior, and they would come up to any one who would talk to them, and make them all sorts of offers." This willingness arose because the Maori had so "much more than they seem to require for themselves," one 1821 observer concluded. . . .

English settlement was valued primarily as a means of engaging with the market economy the English brought; land sales earned European products or the means of acquiring them. Anglo-Maori trade had its darker side. The introduction of European weapons in the early nineteenth century created, in effect, an arms race, in which tribes hastened to acquire guns in order to defend themselves against other tribes who were making the same acquisitions. This would not be the last time that the fragmented and competitive nature of Maori political authority would produce insurmountable barriers to collective action. Even the more peaceful forms of trade could be viewed as an insidious fostering of dependence. "The natives are very anxious to have the white people settled among them," Jessie Campbell wrote to her mother from Wanganui in 1843, because "they cannot live now without tobacco, blankets, etc. all of which the Pakehas or White people provide them with." The introduction of alcohol soon became widely recognized as an example of this phenomenon. In retrospect, so too was the introduction of tobacco.

But trade had its positive aspects as well. The early encounters between Maori and Europeans were an economist's dream: on one side was a group with an abundance of land and some agricultural products but few other assets; on the other was a group with surplus manufactured goods eager to obtain land. That there were enormous gains to be had from trade was evident to all. The Maori generally welcomed European products, technology, and agricultural methods. When the first European trader arrived among the Arawa in 1830, for instance, tribes came from all directions, eager to begin trade. By the 1860s, Maori all over the country owned horses, guns, European clothing, and European tools. Some of these goods could be acquired by selling food, and many tribes, upon encountering Europeans, began for the first time to produce crops for external sale rather than for their own consumption. But the Maori's dominant asset was land. Without selling land, participation in the new market economy would in most circumstances be impossible. As early as 1845, one Wellington newspaper reported, the annual value of Anglo-Maori trade in Wellington alone had risen nearly to £30,000. This "means that the natives purchase from us blankets, calicoes, tobacco, guns, flour, sugar, &c. to this amount," the paper reminded its readers. The money had to come from somewhere, and more often than not, that somewhere was land. . . .

III. One Property

In the 1850s, however, many of the North Island tribes began to organize so as to prevent further land sales. Colonial officials, facing strong public pressure to acquire more land, started casting about for alternative methods of purchase. Settlers "lusting for 'fresh fields & pastures new' will soon begin to howl" if they could not obtain more land, wrote Prime Minister Edward Stafford. "Under such a pressure . . . the existing system — were it the very wisest & best ever devised — cannot be maintained." The problem was "the necessity which it involves of obtaining the consent of a large number of the owners," argued Bishop Selwyn. One obvious alternative was finally to substitute the English for the Maori system of property ownership. If individual Maori owned geographic spaces, and had the liberty to decide for themselves whether or not to sell, a vast amount of land would be available for purchase. Tribe members dissenting from the tribe's collective decision not to sell would no longer be bound to follow; they could simply sell their own parcels. "Much of the land held by individual natives under a Crown title, would speedily come into the market and become available for purposes of colonisation," Swainson predicted. . . .

So the prospect of converting the Maori into the English system of property rights in land moved to the center of settler consciousness in the late 1850s and early 1860s, as a means of piercing Maori resistance to land sales. The project was often referred to as "individualizing title," a name that accurately enough conveyed the anticipated end result — individual Maori ownership of plots of land — but was misleading as applied to the process as a whole. The Maori already had, in a nontechnical sense, "individual titles," but they were titles to particular resources rather than geographic spaces. What the colonists anticipated was not so much individualizing Maori ownership as reorganizing it in spatial terms, to resemble English practice. That the English thought instead in terms of individualizing indicates the persistence of the myth that the Maori possessed property rights in land communally rather than as individuals and families. It also suggests how strongly the geographic paradigm was embedded in settler consciousness. Thinking in terms of physical space rather than in terms of resource use, and in that context seeing many Maori using resources within the same physical space, the English had great trouble avoiding the conclusion that the Maori owned space collectively.

The perceived need to break down Maori refusal to sell land was the catalyst for the colonial government to consider seriously the possibility of transforming the Maori system of property rights, but once the issue was on the public agenda, it provoked an outpouring of other English attitudes toward landownership that had long lain semi-dormant. These attitudes further strengthened the support for converting Maori property rights into English ones. . . .

Many colonists had an insight that would come readily today — that the Maori system of property rights was less efficient than the English system, in the sense that land could be more productive if divided spatially, because of the incentives provided by the ownership of geographic space. This insight dovetailed with a growing belief among the English, contrary to the impression received by the earliest explorers and missionaries, that the Maori were not hard workers. "So long as their lands are held in common they have, properly speaking, no individual interest in improvements," argued the Resident Magistrate Walter Buller, "and consequently there is little or no encouragement to industry or incentive to ambition." The "New Zealander seldom applies himself to his work for any length of time," remarked the missionary John Liddard Nicholas. Legislative Councillor Henry Tancred contrasted English and Maori property ownership: "The one implies a busy, active, bustling life; the other, a life of indolence and inactivity." As these examples suggest, the argument was sometimes expressed too bluntly, in terms suggesting the speaker believed the Maori to possess no individual property at all. Property owned as a true commons will, in the absence of compensating regulation, provide incentives toward inactivity, but a system of property ownership organized in terms of individual use rights need not. The owner of a right to catch birds in a particular tree does not face the collective action problem associated with a true commons. No one else can free ride on his bird-catching efforts. The more birds he catches, the more he can eat, and if there is a market for birds, the wealthier he will be. The most strongly worded condemnations of Maori property ownership on grounds of inefficiency were thus unjustified, if taken literally.

If these criticisms are understood more loosely, however, as using words like "commons" and "communal" to refer not to a nonexistent true commons but rather to the Maori system of property ownership as it actually was, and as referring not to productivity in the abstract but to productivity for certain commercial purposes, the criticisms were on target. For many land uses unknown before European contact, Maori property division probably *was* less efficient than English. Large-scale commercial farming, for instance, then as now required coordinating the activities of many people occupying a large area of land. The English normally accomplished this by uniting ownership of all the land in a single person, who was then understood to have the power to direct the activities of everyone else present on the land. For the Maori to have organized a large commercial farm without abandoning their system of property rights would have required coordinating every individual with the right to use a resource in the relevant space. This would not have been impossible, particularly if the task of organization could have been undertaken within the preexisting tribal political system, but it would most likely have been more costly than the English way. These greater administrative costs would have made Maori commercial farming, all other things being equal, less profitable than English commercial farming. The comparison may be drawn even more sharply with a land use like constructing and operating a hotel. The administrative cost of assembling the necessary land area within the English system of property rights may not have been trivial, but it was probably much lower than it would have been within the Maori system, where it might have required the consent of hundreds of individuals possessing use rights. The English, who had long inhabited a market economy, had developed a system of property ownership conducive to it. The Maori, who had not, had not. The market economy that arrived in New Zealand with the English favored the spatial division of land.

In this light, the critics on efficiency grounds were most likely right. Dividing land by resource use may not have provided a disincentive to all labor — certainly not the traditional kinds of labor that characterized the Maori economy before the arrival of Europeans — but it did provide a disincentive to certain new kinds of labor directed at the market. The more cautious of the critics emphasized the latter. They perceived a switch to the pursuit of market-oriented forms labor as progress. "As long as they hold their lands as they do at present," reported the board established in 1856 to inquire into land purchasing, "they have no incentive worthy of the name to improve their social condition or to add permanent improvements to their land." The Resident Magistrate R. S. Bush agreed: "until their communistic customs are laid aside, no very great advancement will be made by the Natives generally." . . .

A second kind of productivity argument was also frequently made in support of transforming Maori landownership. If any single proposition could have commanded near unanimity among the settlers, it was that, as the *Taranaki Herald* put it, the "want of land — open, available, accessible land — when hundreds of thousands of acres lie waste and unprofitable around, is the great misfortune under which we labor." Most Maori land was not currently being cultivated, and that, to many colonists, was an intolerable waste of the colony's most valuable asset. "They have too much land, and they do not use it," complained one minor government official. "Unless the land is in a state of production the Natives should be compelled to make it productive." Land not under cultivation was, in the telling phrase used officially throughout the century, "waste land." (Land converted from its natural state to agricultural uses was, by contrast, "improved" land.) The English found that there was something intuitively wrong about letting perfectly good land sit uncultivated, especially when back in England there were millions of people who had no land at all. The colonists' feeling was similar to that many people experience today seeing uneaten food thrown in the garbage and aware of the countless hungry people who lack access to it. . . .

The Maori were not the only ones criticized for wasting land by letting it lie uncultivated. In the early years of colonization, the settler newspapers were also unsparing in their criticism of absentee landowners, Europeans committing the same sin. . . .

IV. No Property

From 1865 on, Maori land was divided and sold. The Native Land Court, established in 1865, assigned individual titles to Maori land. Most remaining Maori land was then sold to the English, either to individuals or their government. In 1800, the Maori owned over 60 million acres of land; by 1911, they owned only 7 million, much of which was not well suited for farming. A few million acres had been confiscated by the colonial government after the mid-century wars, but the rest had been sold.

With the disappearance of the Maori system of property rights, so too went much of the traditional political structure of the tribes. When chiefs could no longer control the allocation of land, they lost much of their authority. The "chiefs then had a power they have not now," James Mackay recalled in 1891. "The Native Land Court put in all the rag, tag, and bobtail, and Jack became as good as his master. That is one of the effects of the change." "Of the old chiefs, I only am left," despaired Paora Kaiwhata, of the Ngatikahungunu. "The laws made us all equal — children and slaves stood in the same rank with the chiefs. The influence of that Court has been nothing but evil. The Maoris are no longer a people, by reason of the Native Land Court." The missionary James West Stack described meeting "an old chief who once owned a hundred slaves, reduced to the most abject state of poverty" by the loss of his authority. "[A]t one time the people of the hapus and tribes would look to their older people," Pepene Eketone recalled, "but now the feeling has changed, and the people do not look so to their chiefs."

Land tenure reform was not, of course, the only cause of the erosion of traditional authority. That had many causes, including the spread of literacy and the need to adopt new forms of labor. Traditional authority, moreover, incorporated some interpersonal relationships — slavery is an obvious example — the loss of which may be viewed as positive even by those most sympathetic to traditional Maori life. The tribes were not completely destroyed; many survived into the twentieth century, and still exist today. But much of their structure of internal governance disintegrated, to be replaced with governance by the colonial state.

As tribal authority broke down, so did the tribe's ability to enforce traditional property rights in land. The ironic result was that Maori-owned land became much closer to what the less-informed proponents of "individual" titles thought it originally was — a commons, within which no individual or family possessed any enforceable rights. . . .

... T. W. Lewis, the undersecretary of the Native Department, advised that any "Native in New Zealand ... could legally go and cut timber upon any timbered land." That was a new development: "in the old days," when the tribes were able to enforce internal property rights, "a man would be knocked on the head if he went on another's land." Now, however, a tribe trying to do the same would be deemed to be committing a crime under colonial law. Even where the tribes held onto the authority to enforce traditional rights, they found their practical ability to do so hemmed in by English law. Again, the result was the one that would be expected from a commons, the over-exploitation of communal resources. In 1872, Maori were selling timber off of reserves for five shillings a tree, when the same trees owned by Europeans sold for more than twenty. The difference was common ownership; each individual Maori timber owner would accept far less for a tree than he would have accepted had he been sure that the tree would not be sold by someone else tomorrow.

The creation of these commons reinforced settler beliefs that the Maori were simply lazy and unwilling to work, and at the same time provided a further motive for the Maori to sell land, which when a commons could produce more value by being sold (to someone for whom it would cease to be a commons) than by being exploited. The deterioration of tribal authority and the sale of land thus each promoted the other. The more land was sold, the less the tribe could take on its traditional role of enforcing Maori property rights. The less the tribe could enforce property rights, the more commons-like and hence less valuable its remaining land became, and the more likely it was to be sold.

By the end of the century, the Maori no longer had most of their land, and they no longer had their system of property either. One way of organizing rights in land had been superseded by another. The British, with the military and technological superiority to establish a government and pronounce the rules by which land would be owned and transferred, had been able to force the Maori to reconceptualize land as composed of geographic spaces rather than use rights. The colonization of land, the physical substance, could not have proceeded without the simultaneous colonization of property, the mental structure for organizing rights to land.

NOTES AND QUESTIONS ON FUNCTIONAL VERSUS GEOGRAPHIC PROPERTY

1. Does Banner's description of Maori property suggest that what appears to be "the commons" or "common property" is often a complex mixture of communal and individual elements? See Henry Smith, Semicommon Property Rights and Scattering in the Open Fields, 29 J. Legal Stud. 131 (2000), describing complex combinations of individual and common rights in medieval agricultural communities; see also Acheson, supra p. 129, describing complicated mixtures of common and individual entitlements in lobstering grounds.

2. Banner's essay is this book's second description of an encounter between European settlers and native peoples; the first appears in Demsetz, supra p. 135. Demsetz's version is much less extensive, but in what other ways does the Demsetz picture differ from that of Banner? The Canadian tribes appeared to develop geographically based private property on their own, whereas the Maori more or less succumbed to a system that was foreign to them. What factors account for this difference? What difference did it make that European traders wanted *products* from land in Canada, whereas they wanted the land itself in New Zealand? Does Banner's history suggest that perhaps the Canadian history might have been more disruptive than Demsetz suggests? Take for example the trade in guns: Might weapons trade have put both sets of tribal peoples in a Prisoner's Dilemma, in which they had to trade land (or furs) in order to defend themselves from one another?

3. Why did Europeans persist in describing the Maori land system as "communism"? While the intricacies may have been difficult to see in detail, were they really invisible? Were not Europeans aware of these intricacies? Compare Rosemary Coombe, Authorial Cartographies: Mapping Proprietary Borders in a Less-Than-Brave New World, 48 Stan. L. Rev. 1357, 1362 (1996), remarking that European settlers in Canada insisted that native peoples lived as hunters and warriors in spite of "massive evidence" of their agricultural pursuits. Coombe likens such views to the self-serving view that modern indigenous peoples simply use the products of nature without contributing to their characteristics; in neither case do Westerners have to deal with native peoples as persons of authority and ownership. Could the designation of "communism" have been similarly self-serving? For similar arguments in the context of U.S. settler relations with tribal peoples,

see the notes following Rose, Possession, supra p. 180; but see Terry L. Anderson & Fred S. McChesney, Raid or Trade? An Economic Model of Indian-White Relations, 37 J. L. & Econ. 39 (1994), arguing that native claims to property became less certain as settlers moved west, leading settlers to rely more on force than on trade.

4. From the European perspective, was the Maori land system an anticommons, in the sense that the entitlements were so complex as to preclude use? See Heller & Eisenberg, supra p. 159. This seems too strong, since Banner points out that the Maori themselves could use their entitlements. Was the problem (again from the European perspective) rather one of inflexibility? That is, were Maori entitlements so fragmented that they could not be acquired and repackaged for the new uses that Europeans desired? See Merrill & Smith, infra p. 360, describing the legal *numerus clausus* principle that prevents undue fragmentation of property rights. Was the work of the Native Land Court in assigning individual entitlements an example of the *numerus clausus* at work? Does Banner's work suggest that the *numerus clausus* itself (and the anticommons) are outgrowths of a commercial conception of property in which alienability and repackaging of rights are central features? Was the earlier system of fragmented rights a type of protection against alienation of native entitlements? For other uses of inalienability, see Radin, Market-Inalienability, infra p. 336. But might legal devices promoting alienability sometimes work in favor of disadvantaged persons, particularly by empowering them to borrow against their property? See Hernando de Soto, The Mystery of Capital: Why Capitalism Triumphs in the West and Fails Everywhere Else (2000), arguing that if poor squatters could gain formal and alienable title, many would use their property as the basis for raising capital for entrepreneurial activities.

5. Banner argues that the Maori system of "functional" and inalienable property was intimately connected to its political structure, such that the collapse of the property system meant the collapse of the polity itself. Could the same be said of the English system of "geographic" property? Is this familiar form of property itself relative to a certain political structure? See Friedman, supra p. 75, and the notes that follow.

6. After reading Banner's essay, does commerce between radically different property regimes look very different from conquest? Was there any way that these two different property regimes could have both survived?

C. Markets and Morals

Market-Inalienability*

Margaret Jane Radin

Since the declaration of "unalienable rights" of persons at the founding of our republic, inalienability has had a central place in our legal and moral culture. Yet there is no one sharp meaning for the term "inalienable." Sometimes inalienable means nontransferable, sometimes only nonsalable. Sometimes inalienable means nonrelinquishable by a rightholder; sometimes it refers to rights that cannot be lost at all. In this Article I explore nonsalability, a species of inalienability I call market-inalienability. Something that is market-inalienable is not to be sold, which in our economic system means it is not to be traded in the market.

Controversy over what may be bought and sold — for example, blood or babies — pervades our news. Although some scholars have considered whether such things may be traded in markets, they have not focused on the phenomenon of market-inalienability. About fifteen years ago, for example, Richard Titmuss advocated in his book, *The Gift Relationship*,[6] that human blood should not be allocated through the market; others disagreed. More recently, Elisabeth Landes and Richard Posner suggested the possibility of a thriving market in infants,[8] yet most people continue to believe that infants should not be allocated through the market. What I believe is lacking, and wish to supply, is a general theory that can illuminate these debates. Two possibilities for filling this theoretical gap are traditional liberalism and modern economic analysis, but in this Article I shall find them both wanting.

The most familiar context of inalienability is the traditional liberal triad: the rights to life, liberty, and property. To this triad, liberalism juxtaposes the most familiar context of alienability: traditional property rights. Although the right to hold property is considered inalienable in traditional liberalism, property rights

---

*Source: 100 Harv. L. Rev. 1849-1851, 1855-1858, 1870-1873, 1877-1881, 1885 (1987).
6. .... (1971).
8. See Landes & Posner, The Economics of the Baby Shortage, 7 J. Legal Stud. 323 (1978)....

themselves are presumed fully alienable, and inalienable property rights are exceptional and problematic.

Economic analysis, growing out of the liberal tradition, tends to view all inalienabilities in the way traditional liberalism views inalienable property rights. When it does this, economic analysis holds fast to one strand of traditional liberalism, but it implicitly rejects — or at least challenges — another: the traditional distinction between inalienable and alienable kinds of rights. In conceiving of all rights as property rights that can (at least theoretically) be alienated in markets, economic analysis has (at least in principle) invited markets to fill the social universe. It has invited us to view all inalienabilities as problematic.

In seeking to develop a theory of market-inalienability, I argue that inalienabilities should not always be conceived of as anomalies, regardless of whether they attach to things traditionally thought of as property. Indeed, I try to show that the characteristic rhetoric of economic analysis is morally wrong when it is put forward as the sole discourse of human life. My general view deviates not only from the traditional conception of the divide between inalienable and alienable kinds of rights, but also from the traditional conception of alienable property. Instead of using the categories of economics or those of traditional liberalism, I think that we should evaluate inalienabilities in connection with our best current understanding of the concept of human flourishing. . . .

I.   Market-Inalienability and Noncommodification . . .

B.   The Commodification Issue

Market-inalienability often expresses an aspiration for noncommodification. By making something nonsalable, we proclaim that it should not be conceived of or treated as a commodity. . . .

How are we to determine the extent to which something ought to be noncommodified, so that we can determine to what extent market-inalienability is justified? Because the question asks about the appropriate relationship of particular things to the market, normative theories about the appropriate social role of the market should be helpful in trying to answer it. We can think of such theories as ordered on a continuum stretching from universal noncommodification (nothing in markets) to universal commodification (everything in markets). On this continuum, Karl Marx's theory can symbolize the theoretical pole of universal noncommodification, and Richard Posner's can be seen as close to the opposite theoretical pole.[38] Distributed along the continuum are theorists we may call pluralists — those who see a normatively appropriate but limited realm for commodification coexisting with one or more nonmarket realms. Pluralists often see one other normative realm besides that of the market, and partition the social world into markets and politics, markets and rights, or markets and families; but pluralists also may envision multiple nonmarket realms. For a pluralist, the crucial question is how to conceive of the permissible scope of the market. An acceptable answer would solve problems of contested commodification. . . .

III.   The Critique of Universal Commodification

A traditional critical response to universal commodification, at least since Marx, has been a global rejection of commodification. Universal decommodification or noncommodification maintains that the market ought not to exist and that social interactions involving production and consumption should be reconceived in a nonmarket way. Even if one rejects that ideal, however, as I do because of a problem of transition, the critique of universal commodification offers a crucial insight: a world in which human interactions are conceived of as market trades is different from one in which they are not. Rhetoric is not just shaped by, but shapes, reality.

A.   Universal Noncommodification

Universal noncommodification holds that the hegemony of profit-maximizing buying and selling stifles the individual and social potential of human beings through its organization of production, distribution, and consumption, and through its concomitant creation and maintenance of the person as a self-aggrandizing profit- and preference-maximizer. Anticommodifiers tend to assume that we are living under a regime of universal commodification, with its attendant full-blown market methodology and market rhetoric. They also tend to assume that universal commodification is a necessary concomitant of commodification in the narrower sense — the existence of market transactions under capitalism. Anticommodifiers link rhetoric and reality in their assump-

---

38.   . . . See R. Posner, [Economic Analysis of Law (2d ed. 1977)], at 29-33.

tion that our material relationships of production and exchange are interwoven with our discourse and our understanding of ourselves and the world.

   1. *Alienability and Alienation: The Problem of Fetishism.* — For critics of the market society, commodification simultaneously expresses and creates alienation. The word "alienation" thus harbors an ironic double meaning. Freedom of alienation is the paramount characteristic of liberal property rights, yet Marx saw a necessary connection between this market alienability and human alienation. In his early writings, Marx analyzed the connection between alienation and commodity production in terms of estranged labor; later he introduced the notion of commodity fetishism. In his treatment of estranged labor, Marx portrayed workers' alienation from their own human self-activity as the result of producing objects that became market commodities. By objectifying the labor of the worker, commodities create object-bondage and alienate workers from the natural world in and with which they should constitute themselves by creative interaction. Ultimately, laboring to produce commodities turns the worker from a human being into a commodity, "indeed the most wretched of commodities."[81] Marx continued:

> The worker becomes an ever cheaper commodity the more commodities he creates. With the *increasing value* of the world of things proceeds in direct proportion the *devaluation* of the world of men. Labour produces not only commodities; it produces itself and the worker as a *commodity* — and does so in the proportion in which it produces commodities generally.

Commodification brings about an inferior form of human life. As a result of this debasement, Marx concluded that people themselves, not just their institutions, must change in order to live without the market. To reach the post-capitalist stage, "the alteration of men on a mass scale is necessary."[84]

   The fetishism of commodities represents a different kind of human subjection to commodities (or a different way of looking at human subjection to commodities). By fetishism Marx meant a kind of projection of power and action onto commodities. This projection reflects — but disguises — human social interactions. Relationships between people are disguised as relationships be-

---

   81. Marx, Economic and Philosophical Manuscripts of 1844, *in* The Marx-Engels Reader 70 (R. Tucker ed., 2d ed. 1984).
   84. Marx, The German Ideology: Part I, *in* The Marx-Engles Reader, . . . at 193. . . .

tween commodities, which appear to be governed by abstract market forces. I do not decide what objects to produce, rather "the market" does. Unless there is a demand for paperweights, they will have no market value, and I cannot produce them for sale. Moreover, I do not decide what price to sell them for, "the market" does. At market equilibrium, I cannot charge more nor less than my opportunity costs of production without going out of business. In disequilibrium, my price and profit are still set by "the market"; my price depends upon how many of us are supplying paperweights in relation to how many people want to buy them and what they are willing to pay for them. Thus, the market value of my commodity dictates my actions, or so it seems. As Marx put it, "[producers'] own social action takes the form of the action of objects, which rule the producers instead of being ruled by them."[87] . . .

B.   The Moral and Political Role of Rhetoric . . .

"The word is not the thing," we were taught, when I was growing up. Rhetoric is not reality; discourse is not the world. Why should it matter if someone conceptualizes the entire human universe as one giant bundle of scarce goods subject to free alienation by contract, especially if reasoning in market rhetoric can reach the same result that some other kind of normative reasoning reaches on the other grounds? Consider three possible answers: It matters because the rhetoric might lead less-than-perfect practitioners to wrong answers in sensitive cases; it matters because the rhetoric itself is insulting or injures personhood regardless of the result; or — the implicit philosophical commitment of the anticommodifiers — it matters because *there is no such thing as two radically different normative discourses reaching the "same" result.*

1.   *Risk of Error.* — The rhetoric of commodification might lead imperfect practitioners to wrong answers, even if the sophisticated practitioner would not be misled. In other words, commodification-talk creates a serious risk of error in certain cases. . . .

2.   *Injury to Personhood.* — In some cases market discourse itself might be antagonistic to interests of personhood. Recall that Posner conceives of rape in terms of a marriage and sex market. Posner concludes that "the prevention of rape is essential to protect

---

87. 1 K. Marx [Capital . . . (S. Moore & E. Aveling trans., 1984], at 79.

the marriage market . . . and more generally to secure property rights in women's persons."[109] Calabresi and Melamed also use market rhetoric to discuss rape.[110] In keeping with their view that "property rules" are prima facie more efficient than "liability rules" for all entitlements, they argue that people should hold a "property rule" entitlement in their own bodily integrity. Further, they explain criminal punishment by the need for an "indefinable kicker," an extra cost to the rapist "which represents society's need to keep all property rules from being changed at will into liability rules." Unlike Posner's view, Calabresi and Melamed's can be understood as pluralist, but like Posner's, their view conceives of rape in market rhetoric. Bodily integrity is an owned object with a price.

What is wrong with this rhetoric? The risk-of-error argument . . . is one answer. Unsophisticated practitioners of cost-benefit analysis might tend to undervalue the "costs" of rape to the victims. But this answer does not exhaust the problem. Rather, for all but the deepest enthusiast, market rhetoric seems intuitively out of place here, so inappropriate that it is either silly or somehow insulting to the value being discussed.

One basis for this intuition is that market rhetoric conceives of bodily integrity as a fungible object. A fungible object is replaceable with money or other objects; in fact, possessing a fungible object is the same as possessing money. A fungible object can pass in and out of the person's possession without effect on the person as long as its market equivalent is given in exchange. To speak of personal attributes as fungible objects — alienable "goods" — is intuitively wrong. Thinking of rape in market rhetoric implicitly conceives of as fungible something that we know to be personal, in fact conceives of as fungible property something we know to be too personal even to be personal property. Bodily integrity is an attribute and not an object. We feel discomfort or even insult, and we fear degradation or even loss of the value involved, when bodily integrity is conceived of as a fungible object.

Systematically conceiving of personal attributes as fungible objects is threatening to personhood, because it detaches from the person that which is integral to the person. Such a conception makes actual loss of the attribute easier to countenance. For someone who conceives bodily integrity as "detached," the same person will remain even if bodily integrity is lost; but if bodily integrity cannot be detached, the person cannot remain the same after loss.

109. R. Posner, [Economic Analysis of Law, 2d ed. 1977], at 202.
110. Calabresi & Melamed, [Property Rules, Liability Rules, and Inalienability: One View of the Cathedral, 85 Harv. L. Rev. 1089 (1972)], at 1124-1127.

Moreover, if my bodily integrity is an integral personal attribute, not a detachable object, then hypothetically valuing my bodily integrity in money is not far removed from valuing *me* in money. For all but the universal commodifier, that is inappropriate treatment of a person. . . .

3. *"The Texture of the Human World."** — Market rhetoric, if adopted by everyone, and in many contexts, would indeed transform the texture of the human world. This rhetoric leads us to view politics as just rent seeking, reproductive capacity as just a scarce good for which there is high demand, and the repugnance of slavery as just a cost. To accept these views is to accept the conception of human flourishing they imply, one that is inferior to the conception we can accept as properly ours. An inferior conception of human flourishing disables us from conceptualizing the world rightly. Market rhetoric, the rhetoric of alienability of all "goods," is also the rhetoric of alienation of ourselves from what we can be as persons.

One way to see how universal market rhetoric does violence to our conception of human flourishing is to consider its view of personhood. In our understanding of personhood we are committed to an ideal of individual uniqueness that does not cohere with the idea that each person's attributes are fungible, that they have a monetary equivalent, and that they can be traded off against those of other people. Universal market rhetoric transforms our world of concrete persons, whose uniqueness and individuality is expressed in specific personal attributes, into a world of disembodied, fungible, attribute-less entities possessing a wealth of alienable, severable "objects." This rhetoric reduces the conception of a person to an abstract, fungible unit with no individuating characteristics.

Another way to see how universal market rhetoric does violence to our conception of human flourishing is to consider its view of freedom. Market rhetoric invites us to see the person as a self-interested maximizer in all respects. Freedom or autonomy, therefore, is seen as individual control over how to maximize one's overall gains. In the extreme, the ideal of freedom is achieved through buying and selling commodified objects in order to maximize monetizable wealth. As we have seen, Marx argued with respect to those who produce and sell commodities that this is not freedom but fetishism; what and how much is salable is not au-

---

*This phrase comes from H. Putnam, Reason, Truth and History 139-141 (1981).

tonomously determined. Whether or not we agree with him, it is not satisfactory to think that marketing whatever one wishes defines freedom. Nor is it satisfactory to think that a theoretical license to acquire all objects one may desire defines freedom. . . .

NOTES AND QUESTIONS ON INALIENABILITY AND COMMODIFICATION

1. Blackstone and Posner both generally favored the alienability of resources, on the ground that trades can be expected to benefit both buyers and sellers. See supra pp. 45 and 54. To what extent does Radin succeed in refuting their analysis?

2. Radin's article revisits an issue discussed by Rose in Property as Storytelling and in Crystals and Mud, supra p. 28 and p. 304: Why does rhetoric matter? Why is the "texture of the world" inferior if market rhetoric is used in domains that Radin regards as inappropriate? In a passage not reproduced here, Radin cites the potential damage that a child might suffer from thinking that she might be bought or sold like "fungible" property. How does the example illuminate Radin's objections to market rhetoric?

3. Note that property rhetoric is not necessarily *commodification* rhetoric. Might one think of the parent-child relationship as a trusteeship, which is of course a kind of property relation? Kathy Baker, in Property Rules Meet Feminist Needs: Respecting Autonomy by Valuing Connection, 59 Ohio St. L.J. 1523 (1998), argues that it is appropriate to treat children as the property of their caretakers, for reasons familiar in property theory: to reward and incentivize the one who actually cares for the child, and to establish a hierarchy of authority vis-à-vis interlopers. She argues that these aspects of property are especially important for single parents, primarily mothers, who frequently face interference from others (including bureaucrats) in their child-rearing efforts. Does Radin's discussion of market rhetoric adequately account for such beneficial aspects of property rhetoric?

4. Environmental law is another area in which the rhetoric of commodification is highly controversial. The selection by Merrill, Explaining Market Mechanisms, infra. p. 521, gives the major arguments favoring pricing approaches to pollution; but environmentalists often argue that these devices convey the morally objectionable impression that one may buy the right to do a wrong. Could Radin use this as an example of the effects of inappropriate rhetoric?

5. Does Radin overly romanticize intimate domains, and thus risk misunderstanding the ways that participants actually interact? Recall that Papanek, supra p. 286, analyzed the family in terms of the allocation of entitlements among the members. Which approach is more realistic?

6. In several passages not included here, Radin notes that some items, including most body parts, may not be legally sold, even though they may be given away. Might such gift-but-not-sale rules aim to prevent a horrifying form of theft? Is there an analogy between a prohibition on the sale of kidneys and an international prohibition on the sale of elephant tusks? Despite potential dangers of organ theft to meet a market, Richard A. Epstein, Sell Your Body, Save a Life, Wall St. J., April 16, 1998, at A22, is a proponent of organ sales, arguing that legalizing this trade would vastly increase the availability and safety of needed organ transplants. Of what moral relevance is the fact that there is now a substantial illicit trade in organs, involving what appear to be large numbers of voluntary donors, recipients, medical personnel, and hospitals? See Michael Finkel, Complications, N.Y. Times Sunday Magazine, May 27, 2001, p. 27, col. 1.

7. What is the actual effect of making something inalienable? Consider once again children, and the effect of a child's inalienability on an abusive parent: Might such a child be better off if the parent could sell him or her? Might alienability mean that such children would be less likely to be abused in the first place? Does inalienability really send the signal that something is priceless, or rather that it is valueless?

8. Toward the end of the full article, Radin states that a genuine concern for the avoidance of inappropriate commodification will entail some form of wealth redistribution and income maintenance. Why?

9. Suppose we were to go to the opposite extreme from universal commodification: What would "universal noncommodification" look like? Any transfers would presumably take the form of gifts. Anthropologists who study gift-giving behavior have often noted a similarity to commercial transactions. On these accounts, gift exchange stems not from pure altruism but rather from calculation, concerns about reciprocity, and even rudimentary ideas of interest payment. The classic statement of this position is Marcel Mauss, The Gift: Forms and Functions of Exchange in Archaic Societies (Ian Cunnison trans., 1967) (1925). If gift-giving is calculated and self-interested, why do many observers hold to the view that gift exchanges are more rhetorically and socially acceptable than exchanges mediated through money? Consider Ellickson's discus-

sion of exchanges among Shasta County neighbors, supra p. 218. Why does anyone care about forms and labels if both gifts and commercial trades are simply devices for mutually beneficial exchange?

Other authors have taken the position that gift-giving and market exchange are quite different. A classic is cited by Radin: Richard Titmuss, The Gift Relationship: From Human Blood to Social Policy (1971). Titmuss studied British blood collection and argued not only that most blood is donated altruistically, but that such blood is markedly superior to blood purchased from donors. But see Rueben A. Kessel, Transfused Blood, Serum Hepatitis, and The Coase Theorem, 17 J.L. & Econ. 265 (1974), attributing the superior quality of donated blood to the exemption of suppliers of defective blood from ordinary products liability rules. (Is blood sale another instance of a "Market for Lemons"? See Note 3, supra p. 319.) Another fascinating sociological study of modern gift-giving, also rejecting the self-interest model, is David Cheal, The Gift Economy (1988); see also Carol M. Rose, Giving, Trading, Thieving, and Trusting, 44 Fla. L. Rev. 295 (1992), stressing the importance of what seems to be an irrational element of altruism not only in gifts but in commercial transactions as well.

10. Notice the similarity between inalienability rules and the "immutable rules" discussed by Ayres and Gertner, supra p. 297. How do Ayres and Gertner's reasons for immutable rules (externalities and parentalism) compare with Radin's rationales for inalienability? For the other leading work on the topic (published shortly before Radin's article), see Susan Rose-Ackerman, Inalienability and the Theory of Property Rights, 85 Colum. L. Rev. 931 (1985). For Radin's more recent views on this subject, see her Contested Commodities (1996).

Rival Interpretations of Market Society: Civilizing, Destructive, or Feeble?*

Albert O. Hirschman

Introduction

Once upon a time, not all that long ago, the social, political and economic order under which men and women were living was

*Source: 20 J. Econ. Lit. 1463-1474 (1982).

taken for granted. Among the people of those idyllic times many of course were poor, sick, or oppressed, and consequently unhappy; no doubt, others managed to feel unhappy for seemingly less cogent reasons; but most tended to attribute their unhappiness either to concrete and fortuitous happenings — ill luck, ill health, the machinations of enemies, an unjust master, lord or ruler — or to remote, general and unchangeable causes, such as human nature or the will of God. The idea that the social order — intermediate between the fortuitous and the unchangeable — may be an important cause of human unhappiness became widespread only in the modern age, particularly in the eighteenth century. Hence Saint-Just's famous phrase: "The idea of happiness is new in Europe" — it was then novel to think that happiness could be *engineered* by changing the social order, a task he and his Jacobin companions had so confidently undertaken. . . . In any event, the idea of a perfectible society was not to be nipped in the bud; to the contrary, it experienced a most vigorous development, and, soon after the French Revolution, reappeared in the guise of powerful critiques of the social and economic order — capitalism — emerging at the beginning of the nineteenth century. . . .

I.　The Doux-Commerce Thesis

To begin, let me briefly evoke the complex of ideas and expectations which accompanied the expansion of commerce and the development of the market from the sixteenth to the eighteenth centuries. Here I must return to a principal theme of The Passions and the Interests (Hirschman, 1977), with the hope of placating at least partially those of my readers who complained that, with the book tracing ideological developments in some detail only up to Adam Smith, they were left guessing what happened next, in the age — our own — that *really* mattered to them. My book dwelt on the favorable side effects that the emerging economic system was imaginatively but confidently expected to have, with respect to both the character of citizens and the characteristics of statecraft. I stressed particularly the latter — the expectation, entertained by Montesquieu and Sir James Steuart, that the expansion of the market would restrain the arbitrary actions and excessive power plays of the sovereign, both in domestic and in international politics. Here I shall emphasize instead the expected effects of commerce on the *citizen* and *civil society*. At mid-eighteenth century it became the conventional wisdom — Rousseau of course rebelled against it — that commerce was a civilizing agent of considerable power and range. Let me again cite Montesquieu's key sentence, which he placed at the very beginning of his discussion of economic matters in the Spirit of the Laws:

> it is almost a general rule that wherever manners are gentle (*moeurs douces*) there is commerce; and wherever there is commerce, manners are gentle [1749, 1961, Vol. 2, p. 8].

Here the relationship between "gentle manners" and commerce is presented as mutually reinforcing, but a few sentences later Montesquieu leaves no doubt about the predominant direction of the causal link:

> Commerce . . . polishes and softens (*adoucit*) barbaric ways as we can see every day [p. 81].

This way of viewing the influence of expanding commerce on society was widely accepted throughout most of the eighteenth century. It is stressed in two outstanding histories of progress — then a popular genre — William Robertson's View of the Progress of Society in Europe (1769) and Condorcet's Esquisse d'un tableau historique du progrès de l'esprit humain (1793-1794). Robertson repeats Montesquieu almost word by word:

> Commerce . . . softens and polishes the manners of men [p. 67].

and Condorcet, while elsewhere critical of Montesquieu's political ideas also followed his lead in this area quite closely:

> Manners (*moeurs*) have become more gentle (*se sont adoucies*) . . . through the influence of the spirit of commerce and industry, those enemies of the violence and turmoil which cause wealth to flee . . . [Condorcet, 1795, p. 238].

One of the strongest statements comes from Thomas Paine, in The Rights of Man (1792):

> [Commerce] is a pacific system, operating to cordialise mankind, by rendering Nations, as well as individuals, useful to each other. . . . The invention of commerce . . . is the greatest approach towards universal civilization that has yet been made by any means not immediately flowing from moral principles [p. 215].

What was the concrete meaning of all this *douceur*, polish, gentleness, and even cordiality? Through what precise mechanisms was expanding commerce going to have such happy effects? The eighteenth-century literature is not very communicative in this regard, perhaps because it all seemed so obvious to contemporaries. The most detailed account I have been able to find appears in a technical book on commerce first published in 1704 that must have been highly successful as it was reedited repeatedly through the next eighty years.

> Commerce attaches [men] one to another through mutual utility. Through commerce the moral and physical passions are superseded by interest. . . . Commerce has a special character which distinguishes it from all other professions. It affects the feelings of men so strongly that it makes him who was proud and haughty suddenly turn supple, bending and servicable. Through commerce, man learns to deliberate, to be honest, to acquire manners, to be prudent and reserved in both talk and action. Sensing the necessity to be wise and honest in order to succeed, he flees vice, or at least his demeanor exhibits decency and seriousness so as not to arouse any adverse judgement on the part of present and future acquaintances; he would not dare make a spectacle of himself for fear of damaging his credit standing and thus society may well avoid a scandal which it might otherwise have to deplore [Samuel Ricard, 1781, p. 463].

Commerce is here seen as a powerful moralizing agent which brings many nonmaterial improvements to society even though a bit of hypocrisy may have to be accepted into the bargain. Similar modifications of human behavior and perhaps even of human nature are later credited to the spread of commerce and industry by David Hume and Adam Smith: The virtues they specifically mention as being enhanced or brought into the world by commerce and manufacturing are industriousness and assiduity (the opposite of indolence), frugality, punctuality, and, most important perhaps for the functioning of market society, probity.

There is here then the insistent thought that a society where the market assumes a central position for the satisfaction of human wants will produce not only considerable new wealth because of the division of labor and consequent technical progress, but would generate as a by-product, or external economy, a more "polished" human type — more honest, reliable, orderly, and disciplined, as well as more friendly and helpful, ever ready to find solutions to conflicts and a middle ground for opposed opinions. Such a type will in turn greatly facilitate the smooth functioning of the market. In sum, according to this line of reasoning, capitalism which in its early phases led a rather shaky existence, having to contend with a host of pre-capitalist mentalities left behind by the feudal and other "rude and barbarous" epochs, would create, in the course of time and through the very practice of trade and industry, a set of compatible psychological attitudes and moral dispositions, that are both desirable in themselves and conducive to the further expansion of the system. And at certain epochs, the speed and vigor displayed by that expansion lent considerable plausibility to the conjecture.

II. The Self-Destruction Thesis

Whatever became of this brave eighteenth-century vision? I shall reserve this topic for later and turn now to a body of thought which is far more familiar to us than the *doux-commerce* thesis — and happens to be its obverse. According to that view which first became prominent in the nineteenth century, capitalist society, far from fostering *douceur* and other fine attitudes, exhibits a pronounced proclivity toward undermining the moral foundations on which any society, including the capitalist variety, must rest. I shall call this the self-destruction thesis.

This thesis has a fairly numerous ancestry, among both Marxist and conservative thinkers. Moreover, a political economist who was neither has just recently given it renewed prominence and sophisticated treatment. So I shall first present his point of view and then go back to the earlier exponents. In his influential book, Social Limits to Growth (1976), Fred Hirsch dealt at length with what he called "The Depleting Moral Legacy" of capitalism. He argues that the market *undermines* the moral values that are its own essential underpinnings, values that are now said to have been inherited from *preceding* socioeconomic regimes, such as the feudal order. The idea that capitalism depletes or "erodes" the moral foundation needed for its functioning is put forward in the following terms:

> The social morality that has served as an understructure for economic individualism has been a legacy of the precapitalist and preindustrial past. This legacy has diminished with time and with the corrosive contact of the active capitalist values — and more generally with the greater anonymity and greater mobility of industrial society. The system has thereby lost outside support that was previously taken for granted by the individual. As individual behavior has been increasingly directed to individual advantage, habits and instincts based on communal attitudes and objectives have lost out. The weakening of traditional social values has made predominantly capitalist economies more difficult to manage [pp. 117-118].

Once again, one would like to know in more detail how the market acts on values, this time in the direction of "depletion" or "erosion," rather than *douceur*. In developing his argument Hirsch makes the following principal points:

1. The emphasis on self-interest typical of capitalism makes it more difficult to secure the collective goods and cooperation increasingly needed for the proper functioning of the system in its later stages [Chapter 11].

2. With macromanagement, Keynesian or otherwise, assuming an important role in the functioning of the system, the macromanagers must be motivated by "the general interest" rather than by their self-interest, and the system, being based on self-interest, has no way of generating the proper motivation; to the extent such motivation does exist, it is a residue of previous value systems that are likely to "erode" [p. 128].
3. Social virtues such as "truth, trust, acceptance, restraint, obligation," needed for the functioning of an "individualistic, contractual economy" [p. 141] are grounded, to a considerable extent, in religious belief, but "the individualistic, rationalistic base of the market undermines religious support" [p. 143].

The last point stands in particularly stark contrast to the earlier conception of commerce and of its beneficial side effects. In the first place, thinkers of the seventeenth and eighteenth centuries took it for granted that they have to make do with "man as he really is" and that meant to them with someone who has been proven to be largely impervious to religious and moralistic precepts. With this realistic-pessimistic appraisal of human nature, those thinkers proceeded to discover in "interest" a principle that could replace "love" and "charity" as the basis for a well-ordered society. Secondly, and most important in the present context, to the extent that society is in need of moral values such as "truth, trust, etc." for its functioning, these values were confidently expected to be *generated*, rather than eroded, by the market, its practices and incentives.

As already noted, Hirsch is only the latest representative of the idea that the market and capitalism harbor self-destructive proclivities. Let us now trace it back, if only to find out whether contact was ever made between the two opposite views about the moral effects of commerce and capitalism that have been spelled out.

The idea that capitalism as a socio-economic order somehow carries within itself "the seed of its own destruction" is of course a cornerstone of Marxian thought. But for Marx, this familiar metaphor related to the social and economic working of the system: Some of its properties, such as the tendency to concentration of capital, the falling rate of profit, the periodic crises of overproduction, would bring about, with the help of an ever-more numerous and more class-conscious and combative proletariat, the socialist revolution. Thus Marx had little need to discover a more indirect and insidious mechanism that would operate as a sort of fifth column, by undermining the moral foundations of the capitalist system from within. Marx did, however, help in forging one key link in the chain of reasoning that would eventually lead to that conception: In the Communist Manifesto and other early writings, Marx and Engels make much of the way in which capitalism corrodes all traditional values and institutions such as love, family, and patriotism. Everything was passing into commerce, all social bonds were dissolved through money. This perception is by no means original with Marx. Over a century earlier it was the essence of the *conservative* reaction to the advance of market society, voiced during the 1730s in England by the opponents of Walpole and Whig rule, such as Bolingbroke and his circle. The theme was taken up again, from the early nineteenth century on, by the romantic and conservative critics of the Industrial Revolution. Coleridge, for example, wrote in 1817 that the "true seat and sources" of the "existing distress" are to be found in the "Overbalance of the Commercial Spirit" in relation to "natural counter-forces" such as the "ancient feelings of rank and ancestry."

This ability of capitalism to "overbalance" all traditional and "higher" values was not taken as a threat to capitalism itself, at least not right away. The opposite is the case: even though the world shaped by it was often thought to be spiritually and culturally much impoverished, capitalism was viewed as an all-conquering, irresistible force. Its rise was widely expected to lead to a thorough remaking of society: Custom was to be replaced by contract, gemeinschaft by gesellschaft, the traditional by the modern. All spheres of social life, from the family to the state, from traditional hierarchy to long-time cooperative arrangements, were to be vitally affected: Metaphors often used to describe this action of capitalism on ancient social forms ranged from the outright "dissolving" to "erosion," "corrosion," "contamination," "penetration," and "intrusion" by the "juggernaut market."

But once capitalism was thus perceived as an unbridled force, terrifyingly successful in its relentless forward drive, the thought arose naturally enough that, like all great conquerors, it just might break its neck. Being a blind force (recall the expression the "blind market forces") as well as a wild one, capitalism might corrode, not only traditional society and its moral values, but even those essential to its own success and survival. In this manner, to credit capitalism with extraordinary powers of expansion, penetration and disintegration may in fact have been an adroit ideological maneuver for intimating that it was headed for disaster. The maneuver was especially effective in an age which had turned away from the idea of progress as a leading myth and was on the contrary much taken with various myths of self-destruction, from the Nibelungen to Oedipus.

The simplest model for the self-destruction of capitalism might be called, in contrast to the self-reinforcing model of *doux-commerce*, the *dolce vita* scenario. The advance of capitalism requires, so this story begins, that capitalists save and lead a frugal life so that accumulation can proceed apace. However, at some ill-defined point, increases in wealth resulting from successful accumulation will tend to enervate the spirit of frugality. Demands will be made for *dolce vita*, that is for instant, rather than delayed, gratification and when that happens capitalist progress will grind to a halt.

The idea that successful attainment of wealth will undermine the process of wealth-generation is present throughout the eighteenth century from John Wesley to Montesquieu and Adam Smith. With Max Weber's essay on The Protestant Ethic, reasoning along such lines became fashionable once again: Any evidence that the repressive ethic, alleged to be essential for the development of capitalism, may be faltering was then interpreted as a serious threat to the system's survival. Observers as diverse as Herbert Marcuse (1965) and Daniel Bell (1976) have written in this vein, unaware, it would appear, that they were merely refurbishing a well-known, much older morality tale: how the republican virtues of sobriety, civic pride, and bravery — in ancient Rome — led to victory and conquest which brought opulence and luxury, which in turn undermined those earlier virtues and destroyed the republic and eventually the empire.

While appealing in its simple dialectic, that tale has long been discredited as an explanation of Rome's decline and fall. The attempt to account for or to predict the present or future demise of capitalism in almost identical terms richly deserves a similar fate, and that for a number of reasons. Let me just point out one: The key role in this alleged process of capitalism's rise and decline is attributed first to the generation and then to the decline of personal savings so that changes in much more strategic variables, such as corporate savings, technical innovation and entrepreneurial skill, not to speak of cultural and institutional factors, are totally left out of account.

There are less mechanical, more sophisticated forms of the self-destruction thesis. The best known is probably the one put forward by Joseph Schumpeter in Capitalism, Socialism, and Democracy (1942), whose second part is entitled Can Capitalism Survive? Schumpeter's answer to that question was rather negative, not so much, he argued, because of insuperable economic problems encountered or generated by capitalism as because of the growing hostility capitalism meets with on the part of many strata, particularly among the intellectuals. It is in the course of arguing along these lines that Schumpeter writes:

> ... capitalism creates a critical frame of mind which, after having destroyed the moral authority of so many other institutions, in the end turns against its own; the bourgeois finds to his amazement that the rationalist attitude does not stop at the credentials of kings and popes but goes on to attack private property and the whole scheme of bourgeois values [p. 143].

In comparison to the *dolce vita* scenario, this is a much more general argument on self-destruction. But is it more persuasive? Capitalism is here cast in the role of the sorcerer-apprentice who does not know how to stop a mechanism once set in motion — so it demolishes itself along with its enemies. This sort of vision may have appealed to Schumpeter who, after all, came right out of the Viennese *fin-de-siècle* culture for which self-destruction had become something totally familiar, unquestioned, *selbstverständlich*. Those not steeped in that tradition might not find the argument so compelling and might timidly raise the objection that, in addition to the mechanism of self-destruction, elementary forces of reproduction and *self-preservation* also ought to be taken into account. Such forces have certainly appeared repeatedly in the history of capitalism, from the first enactments of factory legislation to the introduction of social security schemes and the experimentation with counter-cyclical macroeconomic policies. . . .

What is surprising . . . is not that these somber ideas about self-destruction arose at the more difficult and somber moments of our century, but that there was a failure to connect them with earlier, more hopeful expectations of a market society bringing forth its own moral foundation, via the generation of *douceur*, probity, trust and so on. One reason for this lack of contact is the low profile of the *doux-commerce* thesis in the nineteenth century, after its period of self-confidence in the preceding century. Another is the transfiguration of that thesis into one in which it was hard to recognize. The story of that low profile and that transfiguration must now be told.

III. Eclipse of the Doux-Commerce Thesis After the Eighteenth Century

The most plausible explanation for the eclipse of the *doux-commerce* thesis in the nineteenth century is that it became a victim of the

Industrial Revolution. The commercial expansion of the preceding centuries had of course often been violent and had created a great deal of social and human havoc, but this violence and havoc primarily affected the societies that were the objects of European penetration in Africa, Asia, and America. With the Industrial Revolution, the havoc came home. As traditional products were subjected to competitive pressure from ever new "trinkets and baubles," as large groups of laborers were displaced and as their skills became obsolete and as all classes of society were seized by a sudden passion for enrichment, it was widely felt that a new revolutionary force had arisen in the very center of capitalist expansion.

As already noted, that force was often characterized as wild, blind, relentless, unbridled — hence anything but *doux* (gentle and soft). Only with regard to international trade was it still asserted from time to time, usually as an after-thought, that expanding transactions will bring, not only mutual material gains, but also some fine by-products in the cultural and moral realms, such as intellectual cross-fertilization and mutual understanding and peace.[3] Within the boundaries of the nation, the expansion of industry and commerce was widely viewed as contributing to the breakdown of traditional communities and to the loosening and disintegration of social and affective ties, rather than to their consolidation.

To be sure, here and there one can still find echoes of the older idea that civil society is largely held together by the dense network of mutual relations and obligations arising from the market and from its expansion which in turn is fueled by an increasingly fine division of labor. In fact, as soon as the matter is put this way one's thoughts travel to Emile Durkheim and his Division of Labor in Society (1902). Here it was argued, at least in part, that the advanced division of labor of modern society functions as a substitute for the "common consciousness" that so effectively bonded more primitive societies: "it is principally [the division of labor] which holds together social aggregates of the higher type" (p. 148). But in Durkheim's subtle thought, the transactions arising from the division of labor were not by themselves capable of this substitution. The decisive role was played by the many, often *unintended* ties that people take on or fall into in the wake of market trans-

---

3. For example, John Stuart Mill writes in Principles of Political Economy (1848): "It is hardly possible to overrate the value, in the present low state of human improvement, of placing human beings in contact with persons dissimilar to themselves, and with modes of thought and action unlike those with which they are familiar.... Such communication has always been, and is peculiarly in the present age, one of the primary sources of progress."

actions and contractual commitments. Here are some formulations of this thought which recur throughout the book:

> We cooperate because we wanted to do so, but our voluntary co-operation creates duties which we did not intend to assume [p. 192].
>
> The members [of societies with a fine division of labor] are united by ties that go well beyond the ever so brief moments during which exchange actually takes place. . . . Because we exercise this or that do-mestic or social function, we are caught in a network of obligations which we do not have the right to forsake [p. 207].
>
> If the division of labor produces solidarity, this is not only because it makes of each person an exchanger (échangiste) to speak the language of the economists; it is because the division of labor creates among men a comprehensive system of rights and duties which tie them to one another in a durable fashion [pp. 402-403].

So Durkheim's construction is a great deal more complex and roundabout than Montesquieu's (or Sir James Steuart's): Society is *not* held together directly nor is it made peaceful and *doux* by the network of self-interested market transactions alone; for that sort of doctrine Durkheim has some harsh words that contrast sharply with the seventeenth and eighteenth centuries' doctrine about in-terest:

> While interest brings people closer together, this is a matter of a few moments only; it can only create an external tie among them. . . . The consciences are only in superficial contact; they do not penetrate one another . . . every harmony of interest contains a latent or delayed conflict . . . for interest is what is least constant in the world [pp. 180-181].[4]

Durkheim was thus caught between the older view that interest-oriented action provides a basis for social integration and the more contemporary critique of market society as atomistic and corrosive of social cohesion. He never spelled out in concrete detail how he conceived a "solidary" society to emerge from the division of labor and eventually moved on to a more activist view that no longer counted on this mechanism to achieve social cohesion and instead stressed moral education and political action. But, as shall be argued later, there may be considerable virtue in his ambivalent stance; and the idea that social bonds can be grafted onto economic transactions if conditions are favorable, remains to be explored in depth.

An ambivalence similar to that of Durkheim characterizes the work of his German contemporary, George Simmel. While no one

---

4. Compare this text with the exactly opposite seventeenth- and eighteenth-century statements on the constancy and predictability of interest which I reported in The Passions and the Interests (1977, pp. 48-55).

has written more powerfully on the alienating properties of money, Simmel stressed in other writings the integrating functions of various conflicts in modern society. In this connection he gave high marks to competition as an institution that fosters empathy and the building of strong social ties, not of course among the competitors but between them and an important and often overlooked third party — the customer:

> The aim for which competition occurs within a society is presumably always the favor of one or more third persons. Each of the competing parties therefore tries to come as close to that third one as possible. Usually, the poisonous, divisive, destructive effects of competition are stressed and, in exchange, it is merely pointed out that it improves economic welfare. But in addition, it has, after all, this immense sociating effect. Competition compels the wooer . . . to go out to the wooed, come close to him, establish ties with him, find his strengths and weaknesses and adjust to them . . .
>
> Innumerable times [competition] achieves what usually only love can do: the divination of the innermost wishes of the other, even before he himself becomes aware of them. Antagonistic tension with his competitor sharpens the businessman's sensitivity to the tendencies of the public, even to the point of clairvoyance, in respect to future changes in the public's tastes, fashion, [and] interests. . . . Modern competition is described as the fight of all against all, but at the same time it is the fight *for* all . . .
>
> . . . In short, [competition] is a web of a thousand sociological threads by means of conscious concentration on the will and feeling and thinking of fellowmen. . . . Once the narrow and naive solidarity of primitive social conditions yielded to decentralization . . . man's effort toward man, his adaptation to the other seems possible only at the price of competition, that is, of the simultaneous fight against a fellowman for a third one . . . [Conflict and the Web of Group Affiliations, trans. 1955].

Simmel's thought here comes close to that of Durkheim, in that he also uncovers in the structure and institutions of capitalist society a functional equivalent for the simple bonds of custom and religion that (allegedly) held traditional society together. Elsewhere he shows that the advanced division of labor in modern society, and the importance of credit for the functioning of the economy rests on, and promotes, a high degree of truthfulness in social relations. With his effusiveness and vivid imagery, Simmel is perhaps more successful than the austere Durkheim in convincing the reader that some features of market society make for social integration rather than the opposite. . . .

So much for sociology. What about the economists? After all, here was a group of social scientists that had a tradition of either outspokenly criticizing the capitalist system or of defending and praising it. Should not the praisers, at least, have had an interest in keeping alive the thought that the multiple acts of buying and selling characteristic of advanced market societies forge all sorts of social ties of trust, friendliness, sociability, and thus help hold society together? In actual fact, this sort of reasoning is conspicuously absent from the professional economics literature. The reasons are several. First, economists, in their attempt to emulate, in rigor and quantitative precision, the natural sciences, had little use for the necessarily imprecise ("fuzzy") speculations about the effects of economic transactions on social cohesion. Second, those trained in the tradition of classical economics had only scorn for the concern of sociologists over the more disruptive and destructive aspects of capitalism. They saw in such phenomena a short-run cost necessary to achieve superior long-run gains and were not impelled by that sort of critique of capitalism to search for or invoke any compensating positive effects which the expansion of the market might have on social life and ties.

But the principal explanation is supplied by yet another point. Economists who wish the market well have been *unable*, or rather have tied their own hands and denied themselves the opportunity, to exploit the argument about the integrative effect of markets. This is so because the argument cannot be made for the ideal market with perfect competition. The economists' claims of allocative efficiency and all-round welfare maximization are strictly valid only for this market. Involving large numbers of price-taking anonymous buyers and sellers supplied with perfect information, such markets function without any prolonged human or social contact among or between the parties. Under perfect competition there is no room for bargaining, negotiation, remonstration or mutual adjustment and the various operators that contract together need not enter into recurrent or continuing relationships as a result of which they would get to know each other well. Clearly this latter tie-forming effect of markets can be important only when there are substantial departures or "lapses" from the ideal competitive model. But the fact is that such lapses are exceedingly frequent and important. In the face of this situation pro-market economists have either singled out ties among suppliers and, like Adam Smith, have castigated them as "conspiracies against the public"; or, much more frequently, they have belittled the various lapses in an attempt to present the reality of imperfect competition as coming close to the ideal. In this manner, they endeavored to endow the market system with *economic* legitimacy. But, by the same token, they sacrificed the *sociological* legitimacy that could rightfully have been claimed for the way, so unlike the perfect-competition model, most markets function in the real world.

Only in recent years have a number of approaches been developed by economists that do not look at departures from the competitive model as either sinful or negligible. To the contrary, with their stress on transaction costs, limited information and imperfect maximization, these approaches explain and justify the widespread existence of continuing relationships between buyers and sellers, the frequent establishment of hierarchies in preference to markets partly as a result of such "relational exchange," the use of "voice" rather than "exit" to correct mutual dissatisfaction, and similar phenomena that make for meaningful tie-forming interaction between parties to transactions. The stage could thus be set for a partial rehabilitation of the *doux-commerce* thesis. . . .

NOTES AND QUESTIONS ON THE MORAL QUALITIES OF CAPITALISM

1. Compare the *doux-commerce* notion with Radin's view of "commodification." Might commodification have a human face after all? The historian Thomas L. Haskell has argued (though not without controversy) that the rise of eighteenth-century commerce played a major role in the growth of worldwide humanitarian interests by introducing Europeans to very distant peoples and fostering sympathy for them. See Capitalism and the Origins of the Humanitarian Sensibility (pt. 2), 90 Am. Hist. Rev. 547 (1985). The thesis is debated in The Antislavery Debate: Capitalism and Abolitionism as a Problem in Historical Interpretation (Thomas Bender ed., 1992).

2. Hirschman's brief history places Radin's views on commodification into a historical context and reveals that the idea of capitalism's moral corrosiveness has a venerable pedigree. By relativizing the thesis, does this historical excursion undermine Radin's argument?

3. Is it true, as the thesis of capitalism's self-destructiveness supposes, that participants in commerce see themselves as relentlessly pursuing direct self-interest? Stewart Macaulay, An Empirical View of Contract, 1985 Wis. L. Rev. 467, argues against this position and stresses that business people in long-term relationships are often willing to give one another needed breaks. Could commerce survive where all participants pursued their own self-interest to the limit? Consider the network of mutual dependency and trust involved in, say, buying an airplane ticket and using it to travel. Why might commerce suffer in markets in which com-

mercial actors can take advantage of one another or their customers? See Akerlof, The Market for 'Lemons,' discussed in the notes to Rose, Crystals and Mud, supra p. 304. Why do not all markets have the failings of "markets for lemons"? Why instead (contrary to the self-destructiveness thesis) does trust enable many to operate reasonably well in markets? The preconditions and economic importance of trust as "social capital" has received considerable attention in the last decade. See Symposium on Trust Relationships, 81 B.U. L. Rev. 321-705 (2000-2001); Carol M. Rose, Trust in the Mirror of Betrayal, 75 B.U. L. Rev. 531 (1995); and the sources cited in Note 7, supra p. 286.

4. At the end of this selection, Hirschman advances the counter-intuitive suggestion that the market's contributions to social cohesion arise from market impediments — that is, transactions costs, information lapses, and the like. Why might such frictions add to sociability? Might they even keep the whole market machine itself lurching along? See Hirschman's Exit, Voice, and Loyalty: Responses to Decline in Firms, Organizations, and States 43, 55, 83-84 (1970).

5. In Shifting Involvements (1982), Hirschman argues that social interests tend to fluctuate between public affairs and private business. In each case a given individual begins with enthusiasm, then suffers disappointments or boredom, and then shifts to the alternative pursuit, whereupon the cycle repeats itself. If this is an accurate picture, does it suggest that the interests in public affairs and private business are mutually supporting? Should we expect to see, over time, that societies that have the greatest degree of public involvement are those that also have the greatest degree of private initiative? What countries would be good test cases? The United States? Japan? The old Soviet Union (a negative example)? Do these examples bear out the thesis, or do they suggest that the thesis is unduly optimistic?

Chapter 8

The Subdivision of Property Interests: Of Landlords and Tenants

A. Constraints on Decomposition

Optimal Standardization in the Law of Property: The Numerus Clausus Principle[*]

Thomas W. Merrill & Henry E. Smith

A central difference between contract and property concerns the freedom to "customize" legally enforceable interests. The law of contract recognizes no inherent limitations on the nature or the duration of the interests that can be the subject of a legally binding contract. Certain types of promises — such as promises to commit a crime — are declared unenforceable as a matter of public policy. But outside these relatively narrow areas of proscription and requirements such as definiteness and (maybe) consideration, there is a potentially infinite range of promises that the law will honor. The parties to a contract are free to be as whimsical or fanciful as

[*]Source: 110 Yale L.J. 1-8, 11-12, 24-28, 31, 34-35, 38-42, 58-61, 69-70 (2000).

they like in describing the promise to be performed, the consideration to be given in return for the promise, and the duration of the agreement.

The law of property is very different in this respect. Generally speaking, the law will enforce as property only those interests that conform to a limited number of standard forms. As it is stated in a leading English case, "incidents of a novel kind" cannot "be devised and attached to property at the fancy or caprice of any owner."[1] With respect to interests in land, for example, the basic forms are the fee simple, the defeasible fee simple, the life estate, and the lease. When parties wish to transfer property in land, they must specify which legal form they are using — fee simple, lease, and so forth. If they fail to be clear about which legal interest they are conveying, or if they attempt to customize a new type of interest, the courts will generally recast the conveyance as creating one of the recognized forms. Of course, the law freely allows customization of the more physical, tangible dimensions of ownership rights. Property comes in all sorts of shapes and sizes. But with respect to the legal dimensions of property, the law generally insists on strict standardization.

Every common-law lawyer is schooled in the understanding that property rights exist in a fixed number of forms. The principle is acknowledged — at least by implication — in the "catalogue of estates" or "forms of ownership" familiar to anyone who has survived a first-year property course in an American law school. The principle, however, is by no means limited to estates in land and future interests; it is also reflected in other areas of property law, including landlord-tenant, easements and servitudes, and intellectual property. Nor is the principle confined to common-law countries; to the contrary, it appears to be a universal feature of all modern property systems. In the common law, the principle that property rights must conform to certain standardized forms has no name. In the civil law, which recognizes the doctrine explicitly, it is called the *numerus clausus* — the number is closed. We adopt this term for purposes of our discussion here, which focuses primarily on the common law.

As befits a doctrine that has no name, the principle that property rights must track a limited number of standard forms has received very little examination in Anglo-American legal literature. . . . This is again in contrast to the civil law, where the doctrine is widely acknowledged by commentators as being a substantive lim-

---

1. Keppell v. Bailey, 39 Eng. Rep. 1042, 1049 (Ch. 1834).

itation on the definition of property, as in Germany, or a limitation on the circumstances in which property rights can be enforced against third parties, as in Japan and perhaps France, or at least an unstated design principle.

Particularly striking is the virtual absence of any treatment of the *numerus clausus* by scholars influenced by the law-and-economics movement. The principle that property forms are fixed and limited in number represents an extremely important qualification to the principle of freedom of contact — a principle widely regarded by law-and-economics scholars as promoting the efficient allocation of resources. A willing buyer and a willing seller can create an infinite variety of enforceable contracts for the exchange of recognized property rights, and can describe these property rights along a multitude of physical dimensions and prices. But common-law courts will not enforce an agreement to create a new type of property right. Remarkably, virtually no effort has been made to theorize about whether this critical qualification to freedom of contract is justifiable in economic terms.

The primary candidate for an economic explanation has been the suggestion that the *numerus clausus* is a device for minimizing the effects of durable property interests on those dealing with assets in the future,[11] and in particular the effects of excessive fragmentation of interests, or an "anticommons."[12] On this view, the *numerus clausus* serves to prevent situations in which too many individuals have a veto right over the use or disposition of a resource. But whatever the merits of this anti-fragmentarian view for other property doctrines, it does not fully explain the *numerus clausus*, which is aimed at limiting *types* of rights, not the number of rightholders. As we show below, limiting fragmentation is at best an incidental effect of the *numerus clausus*, and does not appear to be a sufficiently robust explanation to account for the universal nature of the doctrine and its tenacious hold on postfeudal legal systems.

When one turns to the snippets of commentary on the *numerus clausus* found in more conventional Anglo-American legal literature, one finds that the attitude is often one of hostility. Scholars and judges tend to react to manifestations of the *numerus clausus* as if it were nothing more than outmoded formalism. For

11. This argument is made in its most general form in Carol M. Rose, What Government Can Do for Property (and Vice Versa), *in* The Fundamental Interrelationships Between Government and Property 209, 214-215 (Nicholas Mercuro & Warren J. Samuels eds., 1999). . . .

12. Michael A. Heller, The Boundaries of Private Property, 108 Yale L.J. 1163, 1176-1178 (1999).

example, the idea that property may exist only in prescribed forms is implicitly debunked by quoting Holmes's aphorism that "it is revolting to have no better reason for a rule of law than that so it was laid down in the time of Henry IV." Taking this position one step further, Critical Legal Studies (CLS) scholars have portrayed the doctrine of fixed estates as perniciously reinforcing hierarchical social relations. As one CLS-inspired source puts it, the "formalistic, box-like structure" of property law, that is, the *numerus clausus*, reflects a "feudal vision of property relationships designed to channel (force?) people into pre-set social relationships."[15]

A related source of antipathy to the *numerus clausus* may be the perception that it is a trap for the unwary. The menu of recognized property forms is relatively complex, and any attempt to venture beyond simple sales of goods and short-term leases into the arcane worlds of future interests, easements and covenants, or intellectual property requires the advice of a lawyer. When unsophisticated or poorly advised actors enter these worlds, they may find that courts force the transaction into one of the established "boxes," with the result that the actors' intentions are frustrated. By contrast, actors who are sophisticated or well-advised can almost always manipulate the menu of options so as to realize their objectives. In this sense, the *numerus clausus* discriminates in favor of those who are well endowed with legal resources and against those who are poorly endowed.

A third source of the antagonism toward the *numerus clausus* may be the lessons supposedly learned from the reform movement in landlord-tenant law. This reform effort has often proceeded under the banner of discarding outmoded "property" concepts in favor of the greater flexibility and attention to the parties' intentions associated with "contract" precepts. By extension, other features of property law that deviate from the norms of free contract may fall under a cloud of suspicion. Here again, standardization of forms is associated with the *ancien régime*, and contractual norms are assumed to be more open, fair, and egalitarian.

These casual criticisms of the *numerus clausus* fail to confront what to us are the essential questions. Before condemning standardization of forms and embracing a regime of contractual freedom with respect to the legal dimensions of property, one must

---

15. [Curtis J. Berger & Joan C. Williams, Property: Land Ownership and Use 211 (4th ed. 1997).] The junior editor of this casebook, Joan Williams, has been influenced by CLS theory. See generally, e.g., Joan Williams, The Rhetoric of Property, 83 Iowa L. Rev. 277 (1998). . . .

first engage in a series of inquiries: What are the costs and benefits of standardization in defining property rights? To what extent should standardization of rights be supplied by the government rather than relying solely on owners' incentives to conform to the most widely used forms? If the government plays a role in standardizing rights, what is the appropriate division of labor between courts and legislatures in enforcing standardization and in making the inevitable changes to the menu of standard forms that must occur over time? . . .

II.   The *Numerus Clausus* in the Common Law of Property . . .

. . . [I]t is useful to consider an example of the principle in operation. Landlord-tenant law includes a version of the *numerus clausus* principle. Leases are limited to four recognized types: the term of years, the periodic tenancy, the tenancy at will, and the tenancy at sufferance. Suppose a landlord and tenant decide to enter into a lease that does not conform to any of the four standard types — a tenancy "for the duration of the war" being the classic example. If landlord-tenant law were just like the law of contract, then there would be no reason not to enforce this agreement in accordance with its terms; that is, the tenancy would last until the war ends. But courts typically do not proceed this way. Instead, they seek to determine which of the four recognized types of leases best fits what the parties have created. Since a term of years requires a "definite calendar ending," and wars last for an uncertain length of time, most courts have concluded that a tenancy "for the duration of the war" must be either a periodic tenancy (if the lease provides for payment of rent at periodic intervals) or a tenancy at will.[28] The result of the pigeon-holing exercise in this example is thus that the parties' intentions are frustrated, because neither a periodic tenancy nor a tenancy at will has the same security of

---

28. Natl. Bellas Hess v. Kalis, 191 F.2d 739 (8th Cir. 1951); Stanmeyer v. Davis, 53 N.E.2d 22 (Ill. App. Ct. 1944); Lace v. Chandler, 1 All E.R. 305 (K.B. 1944). But cf. Smith's Transfer & Storage Co. v. Hawkins, 50 A.2d 267, 268 (D.C. 1946) (concluding that a term of years requires only that the lease be certain to end, not that it have a definite calendar ending, and thus that a tenancy until the termination of "the present war" was a term of years). *American Law of Property* asserts that "the tendency has been to uphold such leases in accordance with the intention of the parties." 1 American Law of Property, § 3.14, at 209-210 [A. James Casner ed., 1952]. But the cases do not bear this out. The minority of courts that have upheld such leases as a term of years have generally done so by changing the definition of a term of years, e.g., Smith's Transfer & Storage Co., 50 A.2d 267, not by declaring that the parties are free to modify the available forms of leases by contract.

tenure as a tenancy for the duration of the war presumably would have if enforced according to its terms.[29] . . .

III.   Measurement Costs, Frustration Costs, and the Optimal Standardization of Property Rights

What accounts for the widespread adherence to the *numerus clausus*, not only in the common law but in postfeudal legal systems throughout the world? . . .

A.   Measurement-Cost Externalities

When individuals encounter property rights, they face a measurement problem. In order to avoid violating another's property rights, they must ascertain what those rights are. In order to acquire property rights, they must measure various attributes, ranging from the physical boundaries of a parcel, to use rights, to the attendant liabilities of the owner to others (such as adjacent owners). Whether the objective is to avoid liability or to acquire rights, an individual will measure the property rights until the marginal costs of additional measurement equal the marginal benefits. When seeking to avoid liability, the actor will seek to minimize the sum of the costs of liability for violations of rights and the costs of avoiding those violations through measurement. In the potential transfer situation, the individual will measure as long as the marginal benefit in reduced error costs exceeds the marginal cost of measurement.

The need for standardization in property law stems from an externality involving measurement costs: Parties who create new property rights will not take into account the full magnitude of the measurement costs they impose on strangers to the title. An example illustrates.[109] Suppose one hundred people own watches. *A* is the sole owner of a watch and wants to transfer some or all the rights to use the watch to *B*. The law of personal property allows

29. As usual, the clever conveyancer can get around the problem, here most likely by creating a term of years determinable. Thus, for example, one could create a lease "for fifty years unless the war ends sooner." This is not exactly identical to a lease "for the duration of the war," but in most wars it would achieve the same result. . . .

109. A more complex hypothetical involving time shares in watches can be found in Henry Hansmann & Reinier Kraakman, Unity of Property Rights 5-6 (Nov. 17, 1999) (unpublished manuscript). . . .

the sale of A's entire interest in the watch, or the sale of a life estate in the watch, or the sale of a joint tenancy or tenancy in common in the watch. But suppose A wants to create a "time-share" in the watch, which would allow B to use the watch on Mondays but only on Mondays (with A retaining for now the rights to the watch on all other days). As a matter of contract law, A and B are perfectly free to enter into such an idiosyncratic agreement. But A and B are not permitted by the law of personal property to create a *property right* in the use of the watch on Mondays only and to transfer this property right from A to B.[110]

Why might the law restrict the freedom of A and B to create such an unusual property right? Suppose, counterfactually, that such idiosyncratic property rights are permitted. Word spreads that someone has sold a Monday right in a watch, but not which of the one hundred owners did so. If A now decides to sell his watch, he will have to explain that it does not include Monday rights, and this will reduce the attractiveness of the watch to potential buyers. Presumably, however, A will foresee this when he sells the Monday rights, and is willing to bear the cost of that action in the form of a lower sales price. But consider what will happen now when any of the *other* ninety-nine watch owners try to sell their watches. Given the awareness that someone has created a Monday-only right, anyone else buying a watch must now also investigate whether any particular watch does not include Monday rights. Thus, by allowing even one person to create an idiosyncratic property right, the information processing costs of all persons who have existing or potential interests in this type of property go up. This external cost on the other market participants forms the basis of our explanation of the *numerus clausus*.

At this point, it is useful to distinguish three classes of individuals who might be affected by the decision to create idiosyncratic property rights, or fancies, as illustrated by Figure 1. First are the *originating parties*, who are the participants to the transaction creating the fancy; this is A and B in Figure 1. Second are the *potential successors in interest* to the asset that is being subjected to the fancy. This would be anyone who might purchase A's reserved rights (after the transfer to B) as well as anyone who succeeds to the interest acquired by B. Potential successors in interest are shown as Cs and Ds in Figure 1. Finally, there are the *other market*

---

110. Time shares are a creation of statute, and the various statutes appear to limit time shares to real estate. Ellen R. Peirce & Richard A. Mann, Time-Share Interests in Real Estate: A Critical Evaluation of the Regulatory Environment, 59 Notre Dame L. Rev. 9, 37-42 (1983).

Figure 1
The Classes of Affected Parties

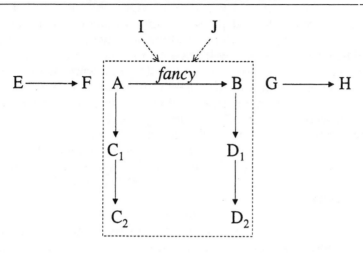

participants, people who will deal in or with watches other than the one over which A and B have transacted. Other market participants include those selling and acquiring rights in other watches such as E and F and G and H in Figure 1. They also include all who must avoid violating property rights in all watches, rights that are enforced against the world represented by I and J in Figure 1. In the hypothetical example above, the other market participants are the other ninety-nine watch owners and their successors in title, as well as anyone who potentially might violate a property right in a watch.

The difference between other possible explanations of the *numerus clausus* and our information-cost theory can be understood in terms of this three-way classification. Other explanations focus on the effect of novel property rights on the originating parties and potential successors in interests — the As, Bs, Cs, and Ds of the world. One may say that these classes of individuals fall within the "zone of privity" designated by the box with the dotted line in Figure 1. Our explanation, in contrast, focuses on the effect of unusual property rights on other market participants — the Es, Fs, Gs, Hs, Is, and Js of the world — classes of individuals who fall outside the zone of privity. As we argue, explanations based on classes of individuals within the zone of privity have difficulty identifying costs that are not impounded into the price facing those who make the decision whether to create the fancy in the first place. An explanation based on costs incurred by classes of individuals outside the zone of privity does not have this difficulty. . . .

. . . When A creates the Monday right, this can raise the information costs of third parties. If the law allows A to create a Monday interest, individuals wishing to buy watches or bailees asked to repair watches will have to consider the possibility that any given watch is a Monday-only watch (or a watch for any other proper subset of days of the week) rather than a full-week watch. While A and B might be expected to take into account the market-value-lowering effect of undesirable idiosyncratic rights when third parties like C or D consider purchasing property in this watch, they will not take into account the more general effect on processing costs created by the existence of such rights when F is considering a purchase of rights in E's watch, or I and J are worried about violating property rights. . . .

One would expect standardization to have the most value in connection with the dimensions of property rights that are least visible, and hence the most difficult for ordinary observers to measure. The tangible attributes of property, such as its size, shape, color, or texture, are typically readily observable and hence can be relatively easily measured by third parties. In the watch example, the watch can be a Timex or a Rolex and can be any size or color, and so forth. These physical attributes, and of course the price, are relatively easy for third parties to process using their senses, and thus there is less to be gained from standardizing them. The legal dimensions of property are less visible and less easy to comprehend, especially when they deviate from the most familiar forms such as the undivided fee simple. Thus, one would expect the effort to lower third-party information costs through standardization to focus on the legal dimension of ownership.

B.   Frustration Costs and the Language of Property Rights

If the only concern were in reducing third-party measurement costs, then there should be only one mandatory package of property rights, presumably a simple usufruct or an undivided fee simple. But standardization imposes its own costs. Mandatory rules sometimes prevent the parties from achieving a legitimate goal cost-effectively. Enforcing standardization can therefore frustrate the parties' intentions.

Although the *numerus clausus* sometimes frustrates parties' objectives, often those objectives can be realized by a more complex combination of the standardized building blocks of property. For example, sophisticated parties with good legal advice can create the equivalent of a lease "for the duration of the war" by entering into a long-term lease determinable if the war ends. The fact that the *numerus clausus* is in this sense "avoidable" does not mean that it is trivial: Even if the standardization effected by the *numerus clausus* principle does not absolutely bar the parties from realizing their ends, this standardization comes at a price. The effect is roughly that of price discrimination: Parties willing to pay a great deal for an objective can achieve it by incurring higher planning and implementation costs. Furthermore, the design and implementation costs imposed by the *numerus clausus* function as a sort of "pollution tax" that should deter parties from insisting on over-using hard-to-process property forms, thereby placing higher processing burdens on market participants and especially courts. . . .

C. *Optimal Standardization and the* Numerus Clausus

We are now in a position to see how the *numerus clausus* functions to promote the optimal standardization of property rights. From a social point of view, the objective should be to minimize the sum of measurement (and error) costs, frustration costs, and administrative costs. In other words, what we want is not maximal standardization — or no standardization — but optimal standardization. Fortunately, standardization comes in degrees. There is a spectrum of possible approaches to property rights, ranging from total freedom of customization on the one hand to complete regimentation on the other. Neither of these endpoints on the spectrum is likely to minimize social costs. Extreme standardization would frustrate many of the purposes to which property rights are put. On the other hand, total freedom to customize rights would create large third-party measurement and error costs and high administrative costs. Attention should focus on the middle range of the spectrum. Starting from a position of complete regimentation, permitting additional forms of property rights should reduce frustration costs by more than it increases measurement and error costs to third parties and administrative costs. Conversely, if one starts from a position of complete customization of rights, increasing the degree of standardization should lower measurement and error costs and administrative costs by more than the attendant frustration costs will rise. . . .

The *numerus clausus* principle can be seen from this perspective as a device that moves the system of property rights in the direction of the optimal level of standardization. . . . By creating a strong presumption against judicial recognition of new forms of property rights, the *numerus clausus* imposes a brake on efforts by parties to proliferate new forms of property rights. On the other hand, by grandfathering in existing forms of property, and permitting legislative creation of new forms, the *numerus clausus* permits some positive level of diversification in the recognized forms of property. We do not argue that any particular number of property forms is in fact optimal. Nor do we argue that the forms currently recognized by the common law are ideal and beyond improvement. We do submit, however, that the *numerus clausus* strikes a rough balance between the extremes of complete regimentation and complete freedom of customization, and thus leads to a system of property rights that is closer to being optimal than that which would be produced by either of the extreme positions.

D. Information Costs and the Dynamics of Property

Finally, our explanation of the *numerus clausus* generates some general predictions about the way in which property regimes will change over time: As the costs of standardization to the parties and the government shift, we expect the optimal degree of standardization to rise or fall. Consider the rise of registers of interests in real property, that is, recording acts. . . .

. . . In general, to the extent that technological change allows cheaper notice of relevant interests, the need for standardization by the law will be somewhat diminished. Just as the rise of land registers allowed some loosening of the *numerus clausus*, so too technology that lowers information costs can be expected to weaken the *numerus clausus* further. . . .

V. The *Numerus Clausus* and Institutional Choice

The *numerus clausus* also has important implications for the division of authority between courts and legislatures with respect to changes in the structure of property rights. By limiting courts to enforcing the status quo in terms of recognized property interests, the *numerus clausus* makes the courts an inhospitable forum for modifying existing forms of property or creating new ones. Consequently, parties who wish to secure changes in the pattern of available property rights must look elsewhere — most prominently, to the legislature. . . .

. . . The abolition of the fee tail, dower and curtesy, the tenancy by the entirety, and the tenancy in partnership have been accomplished in this country by legislation, not by courts. And the creation of new interests such as condominiums and time-shares has also been accomplished through legislative action rather than judicial rulings. . . .

Traditional law-and-economics scholars may regard the institutional-choice dimension of the *numerus clausus* as unfortunate. One of the tenets of early law-and-economics literature was that common-law rules are more likely to be efficient than are legislated rules. A central reason for this assumption is that legislatures were regarded as being dominated by interest groups with narrow distributional objectives, whereas common-law courts were regarded as being immune from this type of distortion. Scholars who continue to share these assumptions may regard as pernicious a doctrine that freezes further development of property forms by courts and allocates all legal change to the legislature. The *numerus clausus* from this perspective would appear to consign questions about the design of the property-rights system to the institution least likely to be motivated by concerns with economic efficiency.

Yet if we put aside for the moment concerns about the possible distortions of the legislative process associated with interest-group activity, there are a number of features of legislative decision making that make it relatively more attractive than common-law decision making as a basis for modifying or creating categories of property rights. These features can be summarized under the headings of clarity, universality, comprehensiveness, stability, prospectivity, and implicit compensation. Significantly, each of these features also bears on the explanation for the *numerus clausus* we develop in Part III — that it is designed to reduce the costs to third parties of identifying the legal dimensions of property rights. Because of these features of legislated change, it is possible that the advantages of the *numerus clausus* as a rule of institutional choice may offset or even outweigh the detriments traditionally associated with legislative decision making. . . .

VI. Conclusion . . .

The understanding that property rights by their very nature require a significant degree of standardization has a host of potentially valuable applications in assessing particular issues regarding property. These include proposals to expand the list of available intellectual property rights, proposals to use digital technology in conjunction with notice to substitute for standardization, and proposals suggesting that all landlord-tenant issues be resolved in accordance with contract law precepts. It also sheds important light on traditional disputes about the appropriate domain of freedom of contract, as well as on more contemporary debates about the significance of network effects and concern with fragmentation or an "anticommons" in assessing the development of the law. Similarly, our contention that standardization is advanced by forcing legal change to occur through legislation has important implications for fledgling efforts to devise criteria for comparative institutional analysis of courts and legislatures. Drawing out these implications must await another day. But we hope we have said enough to suggest that the *numerus clausus* is relevant to more than the driest and dustiest aspect of property — the system of estates in land. It is key to understanding one of the law's most important and dynamic institutions.

NOTES AND QUESTIONS ON THE *NUMERUS CLAUSUS* PRINCIPLE

1. The law permits a house builder to use a nearly infinite variety of floor plans and plumbing systems, including "fancy" ones. If lawmakers can assume that consumers are capable of handling the informational complexities that arise from these sorts of variations in the tangible aspects of property, why can't they assume that consumers could handle a complex menu of legal forms? Do Merrill & Smith (M & S) adequately answer this question?

2. In footnote 110, M & S observe that state legislatures have authorized time shares in real estate, but not in items of personal property such as watches. Why this distinction? In light of the existing systems of land records, why might information-processing costs be lower for real estate than for personal property? Would a public system of "watch records" be worth its costs?

3. In light of M & S's analysis, should a state ask its bar association to draft standard-form deeds, mortgages, leases, and related documents, and then require parties to real estate transactions to use those documents? Or does an optimal amount of standardization arise from the production of competing (and nonmandatory) standard forms by real estate brokers, mortgage lenders, title insurers, and other repeat players?

4. M & S admit that a skilled attorney can manipulate the conventional menu of property forms to achieve virtually any end

that a client might desire. They nevertheless defend the *numerus clausus* principle as a desirable "tax" on the creation of new types of property interests. Might it more accurately be viewed as an effort by members of the legal profession to increase demand for lawyers' services?

5. According to M & S, as technological innovations reduce the costs of storing and processing information, legislatures (and perhaps courts?) should allow an increasing diversity of legal forms. Nonetheless, some legal reformers still seek to simplify the law of property. See, for example, the opening words of the Restatement (Third) of Property: Servitudes (2000):

> This Restatement . . . substantially simplifies and clarifies one of the most complex and archaic bodies of 20th century American law. Treating the law of easements, profits, and covenants as an integrated body of doctrine, this Restatement eliminates needless distinctions. . . .

Id. at 3. Given M & S's analysis, how might the authors of the Restatement defend their project?

6. Are M & S overly sanguine about legislative, as opposed to judicial, control over the forms of property ownership? Might legislatures be more hidebound than courts? Consider the trust, widely regarded as one of the magnificent innovations of the Anglo-American common law, which has yet to win legislative authorization in Continental legal systems. See John H. Langbein, The Contractarian Basis of the Law of Trusts, 105 Yale L.J. 625, 669-671 (1995).

7. In later articles M & S have stressed that the *in rem* character of property rights is what drives lawmakers to simplify how these rights can be packaged. Because property rights must be respected by "all the world," offbeat packages may impose large informational burdens on ordinary people in the conduct of their daily lives. See Thomas W. Merrill & Henry E. Smith, The Property/Contract Interface, 101 Colum. L. Rev. 773 (2001); Thomas W. Merrill & Henry E. Smith, What Happened to Property in Law and Economics?, 111 Yale L.J. 357 (2001).

8. As M & S note, the problem of too many *types* of ownership interests is distinct from the problem of too many *owners* of given types of interests. On the latter problem, see the discussions of the commons and anticommons in Chapter 2, and also Michael A. Heller, The Boundaries of Private Property, 108 Yale L.J. 1163 (1999). Is the problem that M & S address less significant?

B.   Neighbors in Time: Of Future Interests

Economic Analysis of Law*

Richard A. Posner

§3.10 Divided Ownership — Estates in Land

More than one person may have a property right in the same thing. Our common-pool resource was an example; a more traditional one is the different "estates" in land. Property rights in real estate may be divided between a life tenant and a remainderman, between joint tenants (a special type of co-ownership), between a tenant and a landlord, and in other ways. Such divisions (whether concurrent but nonexclusive, or exclusive but time-limited) create incentives for inefficient use similar to those created by the separate ownership of the railroad right-of-way and the adjacent farmland, or the airport and the adjacent residential community. The problem has been discussed extensively in connection with the poverty of Ireland in the nineteenth century.[1] Most farmers were tenants; and it might seem that a tenant would have little incentive to improve the land because any improvement that outlasted the period of the lease would confer an uncompensated benefit on the landlord under the doctrine of fixtures (anything affixed to the property by the tenant becomes the property of the landlord on the expiration of the lease — can you think of an economic reason for this doctrine?). Yet this suggestion seems on its face to violate the Coase Theorem. Why didn't landlords agree in the leases to compensate tenants for improvements, for example by giving the tenant a percentage of the net revenues from the land after the lease expires?

There were and are landlord-tenant sharing agreements, notably share-cropping, but they don't always do the trick. Suppose the landlord agrees to provide the land, seeds, and fertilizer, and the farmer agrees to provide the labor, with the revenues from the sale of the crops to be split 50-50. The results will not be optimal, as a simple example will show. Suppose that if the farmer worked an extra hour every week on improving the land he would increase

---

*Source: pp. 82-87 (5th ed. 1998).
1. See, e.g., A. C. Pigou, The Economics of Welfare 174-175, 178-183 (4th ed. 1932); Barbara Lewis Solow, The Land Question and the Irish Economy, 1870-1903 (1971).

the dollar value of the farm's output by $2 (net of any additional cost besides his time), and that the opportunity cost — or shadow price — of his time in forgone leisure is only $1.50. Efficiency requires that he work the extra hour, but he will not, because under his deal with the landlord he will receive only $1 for work that costs him $1.50. A more complicated sharing agreement will be required for optimal results, and the more complicated it is the more costly it will be to negotiate and enforce. And the example abstracts from the problem of long-term improvements, by assuming that the tenant will still be around when his improvements come to fruition. He may not be, if the lease is short-term. The problem of the tenant's inadequate incentive to improve the land will be less serious the longer the lease; so it is not surprising that a system of tenant customary rights evolved in Ireland that made it difficult for the landlord to evict the tenant, either directly or indirectly (the latter by jacking up rents until the tenant was forced to abandon the lease). There would still have been a problem of tenant incentives if optimal tenant improvements were likely to outlast the tenants' lives; but major capital improvements, the kind most likely to outlast the current tenant, had to be made by the landlords rather than the tenants anyway, because the landlords had the capital. If anything, the problem was not that tenants lacked incentives to improve the land but that customary tenant rights made it difficult for landlords to recoup the cost of their own improvements by charging higher rents, since the tenant might complain that the rate increase violated his customary rights.

All this suggests that there is no simple solution to the problem of divided ownership except single ownership, but it is not so simple either. If the tenant is demoted to being an employee of the landlord, the problem of divided ownership disappears but is replaced by a quite analogous problem of agent shirking due to the employee's not getting to keep every dollar in added output from working — just like the tenant. And the tenant may be unwilling to buy the farm from the landlord (although this would eliminate the problem of shirking), even if he were able to do so (what would determine whether or not he was able to do so?), because of the additional risk he would incur — illustrating the important point that leasing is a form of risk-spreading.[3]

So there is an important role for law to play in regulating divided ownership. We might expect the courts to interpret leases

---

3. Steven N. S. Cheung, The Theory of Share Tenancy (1969).

as if the parties' intent had been that the property would be managed by the lessee as if he were the owner; for that presumably *was* the parties' intent, if they are rational profit-maximizers. This policy is reflected in the common law doctrine of waste, which mediates between the competing interests of life tenants and remaindermen. A life tenant will have an incentive to maximize not the value of the property, that is, the present value of the entire stream of future earnings obtainable from it, but only the present value of the earnings stream obtainable during his expected lifetime. He will therefore want to cut timber before it has attained its mature growth — even though the present value of the timber would be greater if the cutting of some or all of it were postponed — if the added value from waiting would enure to the remainderman. The law of waste forbade this. There might seem to be no need for a law of waste, because the life tenant and the remainderman would negotiate an optimal plan for exploiting the property. But since the tenant and remainderman have only each other to contract with, the situation is again one of bilateral monopoly, and transaction costs may be high. Also, the remaindermen may be children, who do not have the legal capacity to make binding contracts; they may even be unborn children. The problem of bilateral monopoly is less acute in the landlord-tenant case, because the terms of a lease are set before the landlord and tenant become locked into a relationship with each other. Very often a life tenancy is created by will, and the testator (for whom estate planning may be a once-in-a-lifetime experience) may not be alert to the potential conflicts between life tenants and remaindermen.

The law of waste has largely been supplanted by a more efficient method of administering property, one that resembles unitization: the trust. By placing property in trust, the grantor can split the beneficial interest as many ways as he pleases without worrying about divided ownership. The trustee will manage the property as a unit, maximizing its value and allocating that value among the trust's beneficiaries in the proportions desired by the grantor. Of course, it is necessary that the trustee be given the proper incentives to do this.

The tenant does not always have a shorter time horizon than the owner of the fee simple (in the case of the ordinary landlord-tenant relation) or the remainderman (in the case of a life tenancy). Take the case of an oil lease that promises the lessor a fixed royalty per barrel. Unless he expects the rate of increase of the price of oil to exceed the interest rate, he will want the oil pumped as fast as possible, whether or not the field is unitized. That will mean drilling a lot of wells. But the lessee, who has to pay for those wells, will want to pump the oil more slowly so that he can economize on the number of them. He may even drill too few wells, since in deciding how much a new well is worth he will disregard the portion of the revenues that will go to the lessor as a royalty. Therefore, most oil and gas leases contain a "development" clause that requires the lessee to drill a reasonable number of wells — "reasonable" meaning cost-justified. An interesting question that has arisen in the interpretation of such clauses is whether the lessee, in figuring the costs of a new well, may include not only his drilling and other direct costs but also the reduced revenue from the old wells, since the new well will deplete the pool from which the old wells as well as the new draw. The economic answer, for which there is some judicial support, is yes, because that depletion is a genuine opportunity cost of the new well.

We have thus far been considering vertical or temporal division of a property right. There is also horizontal division. The extreme example is the communal right, as in the pasture that is shared by a number of farmers. Communal rights differ only in degree from no rights, and thus are inefficient unless the costs of enforcing individual rights are disproportionate to the benefits.[7] Odd as it may sound, communal rights are frequently created by individuals, although in circumstances where the problem of inefficiency is minimized. For example, A may leave a plot of land to B and C, his children, in undivided joint ownership (a tenancy in common or a joint tenancy). B and C are formally in much the same position as the inhabitants of a society that does not recognize property rights. If B spends money to repair structures on the property, C will share equally in the value of the repairs, and vice versa. Although there are only two parties, there is the familiar bilateral-monopoly problem. But it is mitigated by the familial relationship; we expect more cooperation between persons united by bonds of affection. . . . In addition, the law credits the joint tenant with the value of any improvements he makes to the property up to the amount by which the improvements increase the property's value (why this qualification?). The law also, and wisely, allows any joint tenant to obtain a partition of the property into separate, individually owned parcels; this power eliminates every vestige of bilateral monopoly and communal rights.

Suppose adjacent owners of row houses, who share a party wall, are unable to agree on how to split the cost of replacing the

7. A good example is a supermarket's parking lot: It doesn't pay (outside of Manhattan!) to charge each customer for his use of a space, although doing so would enable the supermarket to have a slightly smaller lot.

wall, which is in imminent danger of collapse. One of the owners goes ahead and replaces it at his own expense and then sues the other for half the cost. There is a fair amount of judicial authority for allowing the suit, as a way around the bilateral-monopoly problem. . . .

The law's ingenuity is not limitless, and we end this section with a homely example of a case of divided ownership about which the law can do nothing: automobile rentals. As everyone who has ever rented a car knows, people do not treat the cars they rent with as much care as the cars they own; they are rougher on them, reflecting the foreshortened time horizon of their use. But because the rental company cannot supervise or monitor that use, there is no way in which it can induce the renter to take the right amount of care of the car. Here, then, is a case where transaction costs are high despite fewness of parties and no problem of bilateral monopoly. The problem is that the cost of enforcing the transaction agreed on is prohibitive.

§3.11 Problems in the Transfer of Property Rights

In order to facilitate the transfer of resources from less to more valuable uses, the law should, in principle, make property rights freely transferable. The principle must be qualified, but before doing so we must notice how divided ownership makes transfer difficult in practice even if there is no formal limitation. If 50 different people are joint tenants of a piece of property, a sale of the property will require them to agree both on the price and on the division of the proceeds among them; there will be holdout problems. The elaborate kinship networks of primitive societies forestall the emergence of property rights in such societies. Efficiency requires that property rights be transferable, and if many people have a claim on each piece of property, transfers will be difficult to arrange.

The history of English land law is a history of efforts to make land more easily transferable and hence to make the market in land more efficient. Two doctrines will illustrate this point. The "Rule in Shelley's Case" provided that if a grantor gave a life estate to A with the remainder to A's heirs, A had a fee simple (i.e., full title); the heirs were cut out. If the remainder in A's heirs were recognized, it would be very difficult to transfer the property, because his heirs would not be ascertained until his death. The "Doctrine of Worthier Title" provided that if the grantor gave property to A for life, with the remainder to the grantor's heirs, the grantor — not his heirs — owned the remainder, and thus could sell it, as his heirs apparent might not be able to do because of the uncertainty of their interest; for the grantor might have additional children, and they would be his heirs too.

The economic objection to these doctrines (besides their immense complexity, not hinted at in these descriptions) is that they imply that the grantor is not able to trade off the costs of reduced transferability against whatever benefits he derives from dividing ownership in the way the doctrines prevent. This assumption seems paternalistic and hence questionable from an efficiency standpoint. People know their interests better than courts do. But maybe the explanation is, as suggested earlier, that many of these grants are once-in-a-lifetime transactions for the grantor, and he may not have good information about the problems they create. Moreover, people who create excessively complex interests burden the courts as well as themselves and their grantees, so there is some externality that might warrant public intervention. This point explains the common law presumption that a conveyance of land to a railroad or other right-of-way company (pipeline company, telephone company, etc.) is the conveyance of a right-of-way, that is, of an easement, terminable when the acquirer's use terminates, rather than the conveyance of a fee simple. Transaction costs are minimized by undivided ownership of a parcel of land, and undivided ownership is, in turn, facilitated by the automatic reuniting of divided land once the reason for the division has ceased. If the railroad owns a multitude of skinny strips of land now usable only by the owner of the surrounding or adjacent land, then before that land can be put to its best use there must be expensive and time-consuming negotiation — that or the gradual extinction of the railroad's interest through the operation of the doctrine of adverse possession. It is cleaner to wipe out the railroad's interest upon its abandonment of railroad service.

NOTES AND QUESTIONS ON DIVIDED OWNERSHIP

1. Posner discusses a variety of co-ownership arrangements, including: (1) temporal divisions, between the owner of a present interest and the owner(s) of one or more future interests; (2) trusts, under which a trustee (the "legal owner") manages the trust assets as a fiduciary for the trust's beneficiaries (the "equitable owners"); (3) concurrent estates, under which two or more parties simultaneously share a resource, often (but not always) in equal shares;

and (4) the shared regimes that result when an easement or other nonpossessory interest is carved out of a fee simple in land.

In all these contexts there are rules of property law that deal with each co-owner's rights and duties against the other co-owners. To employ Ayres & Gertner's distinction, supra p. 297, should these rules be "immutable"? Or, should they be "defaults" that co-owners can contract around? What might Merrill & Smith supra p. 360, have to say on this issue?

2. Posner regards a short-term lease as an arrangement fraught with incentive incompatibilities, at least compared to a trust. Yet short-term leases are far more common than trusts. Why might trusts give rise to greater transaction costs? (The next selection, on farm leases, may help provide an answer.)

3. Farm sharecropping arrangements date back to ancient Mesopotamia. Posner cites Steven N. S. Cheung's theory that many tenants prefer to sharecrop in order to spread the risk of a poor harvest. See the sources cited supra p. 158, Note 5, on the risk-spreading advantages of shared ownership. An alternative theory stresses that the success of a farming venture commonly depends on both the landowner and tenant providing streams of inputs into the production process. The landlord may control offsite water sources, for example, and the tenant may control field labor. According to this latter theory, crop-sharing is a workable mechanism for deterring both sides from shirking. See Douglas W. Allen & Dean Lueck, Risk Preferences and the Economics of Contracts, 85 Am. Econ. Rev. 447 (1995). Is it more instructive to view share-cropping arrangements as landlords' instruments for suppressing subordinate classes? Cf. James C. Scott, Weapons of the Weak: Everyday Forms of Peasant Resistance (1985).

4. Is Posner overly eager to discern efficiencies in the common law? Examine his final paragraph, in which he argues that judges correctly construe ambiguous grants to right-of-way companies as easements, an interpretation that subjects these interests to the doctrine of abandonment. Could one just as persuasively argue that this interpretation is inefficient because the doctrine of abandonment engenders wasteful litigation and delays a railroad company's removal of obsolete tracks?

5. In Anglo-American law the basic estate in land is the fee simple. An owner in fee simple, although mortal himself, has ownership rights of infinite duration. Why should those presently alive have property interests that extend beyond their deaths? Note Blackstone's concern, supra p. 52, that "endless disturbances" would ensue if a decedent's property were put up for grabs at death. Why wouldn't a rule that a decedent's property escheats

to the state entirely allay Blackstone's concern? Compare Demsetz's statement, supra p. 141, that one advantage of the fee simple is that it tends to induce an owner making land-use decisions to consider economic conditions that may exist after his death. Do you understand his reasoning? Find it persuasive? Would a society be wiser to dole out only usufructuary rights in land — ones that would terminate when the usufructuary owner died or abandoned the land? How would Posner answer this question?

Infinitely long private-property rights in land were honored in the ancient Near East and ancient Greece, and have evolved within societies on every continent. See Robert C. Ellickson, Ancient Land Law, 71 Chi.-Kent L. Rev. 321, 366-368 (1995); Robert C. Ellickson, Property in Land, 102 Yale L.J. 1315, 1364-1371 (1993). Does this history prove the inherent efficiency of the fee simple? The political clout of large landowners?

A society that doles out property for infinite time periods must develop rules to govern inheritance. With remarkably few exceptions, such as Russia in 1918-1922, legal systems enable property owners to pass on property to kin. Do infinite terms of property ownership serve the interests of the young and unborn? With Demsetz's view, compare Mark L. Asher, Curtailing Inherited Wealth, 89 Mich. L. Rev. 69 (1990). Should a legal system identify particular kinfolk as successors as a matter of law, or instead entitle a decedent to designate successors by will? See James M. Buchanan, Rent Seeking, Noncompensated Transfers, and Laws of Succession, 26 J.L. & Econ. 71 (1983) (exploring the risk that testation may prompt the young to fawn for favorable testamentary treatment from the elderly).

The 'Back Forty' on a Handshake: Specific Assets, Reputation, and the Structure of Farmland Contracts*

Douglas W. Allen & Dean Lueck

It is a common scene in U.S. agriculture: A landowner and a tenant talk for a few minutes over a cup of coffee, then shake hands to clinch a one-year deal to rent a farm or piece of land. No fuss, no bother, no paperwork.

— *Jonathan Knutson*, Ag. Week *(December 11, 1989)*

*Source: 8 J.L. Econ. & Org. 366-371, 375 (1992).

1. Introduction

Many exchanges are governed by rather complicated contracts that explicitly denote dates, individuals, locations, prices, products, qualities, quantities, and contingencies for changing conditions. Transaction-cost economics has been quite successful in explaining the structure of these contracts. In particular, long-term contracts and vertical relationships have been shown to solve the contracting problems that arise in the presence of durable, transaction-specific assets. As the quote above suggests, Midwest farmers rely on farmland leases that are surprisingly simple. Contrary to focusing on why complex, long-term contracts exist, we ask the alternative and complementary question: Why do simple, short-term contracts arise when real-world contracting is costly?

In states like Nebraska and South Dakota agriculture is by far the dominant industry. On the nearly 100,000 farms in these two states, a typical farmer uses approximately 1,000 acres of farmland and $100,000 worth of farm equipment. The typical value of the land and buildings is between $300,000 and $400,000 per farm. Farmers annually sell an average of over $60,000 in annual crops such as barley, hay, oats, soybeans, and wheat. Like farmers everywhere, those in Nebraska and South Dakota do not always own all of their farmland and often lease land from other landowners. For instance, in 1982 only 59 percent of all U.S. farms were completely owner-operated, and only 35 percent of total farm acreage was cultivated by farmers that owned all their land (U.S. Department of Agriculture: Tables 536 and 537).

1.1   Contracts for Farmland

In stark contrast to the size and methods of modern farming, farmland contracts are simple and informal. Rarely are they lengthy, detailed documents, and in many cases they are not even written agreements. We use data from Nebraska and South Dakota and find that 57 percent of all contracts were oral. Those that are written tend to be simple one- or two-page documents that specify only the names of the farmer and the landowner, the dates for which the contract is binding, the location of the land, the terms of the lease in dollars or shares, and possibly conditions for contract renewal. . . . In a few cases, however, the contracts are more detailed and specify such responsibilities as paying land taxes, controlling noxious weeds, penalties for defaulting, renewal conditions, and the fraction of the land that must lie fallow.

Notably, farmland contracts tend not to stipulate in detail how the land will be farmed; rather, they require that the farmer use the land in a "thorough and farmer-like" or a "good and husband-like" manner. Farmland contracts are most often annual agreements subject to automatic renewal unless one party makes an early commitment not to renew. In our sample 65 percent of the contracts are annual. Sometimes the agreements are for several years, but rarely are they longer than five years. They are, however, typically renewed for extended periods, even up to 30 years. The markets that bring farmers and landowners together are as informal as the contracts themselves, with the most common consummation taking place on the front porch. . . .

2. Why Are Farmland Contracts So Simple?

Although farmland contracts are simple agreements, they must still be enforced. One way to enforce an agreement is for the contracting parties to stipulate and police numerous details. A second method is to specify little in an informal agreement and let market forces or the common law do the policing. Our contention is that for farmland contracts, reputations and law effectively enforce the agreements and render detailed, long-term contracts superfluous.

2.1 Specific Assets

Klein, Crawford, and Alchian [1978] and Williamson [1979] noted that contracting parties with transaction-specific assets put themselves at risk by using short-term contracts because each party could potentially extract the other's quasi-rents once the investments were made. For farmland contracts short-term leases are feasible because in general appropriable quasi-rents are absent.

Consider the assets involved in a farmland lease contract. Landowners bring just one asset to the exchange — land — and this asset is *not* specific to the exchange. There are numerous other farmers who could profitably use the land. Farmers bring several assets to the exchange, most of which are not specific to the farmland transaction. First, the farmer brings his human capital (farming skills), which are specific to the local "area" but are *not* specific to the contracted plot of land. The farmer could profitably farm other plots in the area with his present capital stock. Second, the farmer has his own land and buildings, but these can be sold and are *not* specific to a particular leased plot or leased agreement. Third, the farmer has equipment such as tractors, cultivators, and combines. Some of these implements are quite specific to the area.

For example, a potato picker has little use in western South Dakota where no potatoes are grown. But, like buildings, these machines are *not* specific to the plot in the lease contract.

In a Midwestern farmland contract only investments related to irrigation assets are potentially transaction-specific. Irrigation investments include pumps, underground pipes, wells, and other equipment that is fixed to the land as well as the farmer's skills in using a particular irrigation system on a specific plot of land. These investments are generally owned by the landowner and are not transaction-specific; but because farmers run the system, pay for daily maintenance, and often share in major repair costs, the possibility of contract hazards exists.

The crop investment is not subject to quasi-rent capture because all of the crops in this data set are annual small grains. If crops were long-term investments, such as orchards, contracts would be expected to be much longer.

2.2   Reputation and Repeated Transactions

It is well known that markets can "self-enforce" contracts. Punishment to cheaters, through lost future trade, encourages cooperation between the contract parties (Kreps [1990]). This reputation enforcement is most effective where information about cheating is good and a frequent and long-lived relationship is desired. For Midwestern farmland contracts these conditions are met. Farmers are a part of a small "community" of people who have known each other most of their lives. People would be quickly aware of anyone who cheated another and would avoid future dealings with that person. For both a landowner and a farmer there is a long-term interest in maintaining a relationship.[3]

Farmers and landowners develop reputations for honesty, fairness, producing high yields (with share contracts), and consistently demonstrating that they are good at what they do. In small farming communities reputations are well known, especially over time. As a result, over time landowners indirectly monitor farmers by observing the reported output and the quality of the soil.

The importance of repeated dealing and the minor role of transaction-specific assets influences the structure of farmland contracts. Farmer reputations act as a bond. In any growing season a farmer can reduce effort, exploit soil, or underreport the crop. However, over time an accurate assessment is made by the land-

---

3. In fact, the mean duration of the contracts in our sample is 11.5 years.

owner and others in the area as to the farmer's actual behavior. Farmers who attempt to gain at the landowner's expense will find that others may refuse to deal with them in the future.

2.3   The Common Law

When reputations are absent, farmers rely on written agreements more often, but even these contracts remain simple. This simplicity is possible because of the presence of a well-developed body of common law. For example, the prevalence of "good husbandry" clauses point to the law as a contract enforcer, since violation of such a clause provides legal grounds to terminate the lease. The use of good husbandry clauses indicates that some farming practices are similar from plot to plot in the area and that some types of "bad" farming are identifiable, and thus need not be specified in the contract. In both Nebraska and South Dakota, farming is quite homogeneous within a "locale." In such cases the law can implicitly add detail to contracts that appear to be simple.

Although contract disputes rarely end in court, there have been many cases of farming disputes, especially during the first half of this century, that established the meaning of good husbandry. These cases have involved such issues as overgrazing, destruction of trees, permitting noxious weeds to grow, plowing meadowland, removing manure rather than spreading it, damage to buildings because of overloading storage areas with crops, and extracting minerals from the soil. By now these practices are routinely held by courts to constitute poor husbandry, thus violating the terms of the farmland lease and allowing for very informal contracts, even when they are in writing.

3.   The Variation in Contract Structure

While it is true that farmland contracts are simple, they do vary: Some are oral rather than written, some are one-year rather than multiyear agreements. Given our explanation of the general simplicity of these contracts, we expect that oral contracts will be present when fewer specific assets are present and when farmers have better reputations. Likewise, annual contracts will be chosen over multiyear contracts in similar situations.

The data used to test the various enforcement cost hypotheses are taken from the 1986 Nebraska and South Dakota Land Leasing Survey. This survey collected data from farmers and landowners engaged in farmland leasing during the 1986 crop season. Each of the 3104 observations is a single contract between a farmer and a landowner, where each contract is an exchange of rights to a tract of land.

3.1   Oral or Written?

The Statute of Frauds requires that contracts that cannot be performed in one year must be written to be legally enforceable. For farmland contracts the Statute of Frauds implies that all multiyear contracts must be written contracts in order for them to be enforced in a court. If the court was a routine mechanism of enforcement, we would expect to see all multiyear contracts be written. Yet, our sample shows that only 53 percent of multiyear contracts are written, indicating the courts are not often used to enforce contracts. Instead, farmers and landowners prefer to make oral agreements independent of the contract length and rely on the market to enforce the agreements. . . .

4. Conclusion

Contract structure depends largely on the costs of enforcement. These costs vary from case to case and determine the form of contracts. For farmland leases in the American Midwest, contracts are short-term and lack all but the most rudimentary details. We have argued that this simplicity reflects the comparative advantage of enforcing these contracts through the market and the common law. The character of the farming economy — good information about reputations, desired long-term relationships, immobility of farmers and landowners, and few transaction-specific assets — lends itself to the pervasive use of what may seem to be rather naive contracts.

References

Klein, Benjamin, Robert Crawford, and Armen A. Alchian. 1978. Vertical Integration, Appropriable Rents, and the Competitive Contracting Process, 21 Journal of Law and Economics 297-326.

Kreps, David. 1990. Corporate Culture and Economic Theory, in J. Alt and K. Shepsle eds., Perspectives on Positive Political Economy. Cambridge, England: Cambridge University Press.

Williamson, Oliver E. 1979. Transaction-Cost Economics: The Governance of Contractual Relations, 22 Journal of Law and Economics 233-261.

NOTES AND QUESTIONS ON FARM LEASES

1. Allen and Lueck (A & L) observe that farm leases are extremely common. How might rural landlords and tenants overcome the risks of waste and other shortsighted land uses that Posner thinks are associated with short-term leaseholds?

2. Why might the number of appellate cases involving the meaning of "good husbandry" have declined in Nebraska and South Dakota during the latter half of the twentieth century?

3. A & L report that 47 percent of the multiyear contracts in their sample were oral and therefore unenforceable in court. What does this statistic reveal about the relative importance, in this context, of informal social controls? Are multiyear commercial leases in a suburban shopping center just as likely to be oral? What about orchard leases in rural areas?

C. Rental Housing Markets

*Poor Tenants, Poor Landlords, Poor Policy**

Irving Welfeld

A "Saturday Night Live" routine, in which Eddie Murphy (playing a convicted murderer) recites a poem entitled "Cill My Landlord," tells us a great deal about the public image of American landlords. The owner of rental property operates in a hostile environment. Although his search for profits is no different from that of other providers of goods and services, the landlord is traditionally cast in a uniquely villainous light; he is the fat cat who takes unfair advantage of the little mice who rent from him. The metaphor is unfair, however; many landlords have as good a claim to victim status as their tenants.

The landlord plays an essential role in America's housing system. There is always a substantial number of people who choose not to own, or for whom ownership may not be a good idea. In the pre-condominium past (before 1961), when apartment living and renting were synonymous, the rental sector could count on the newly married, those who were single, and inveterate urbanites.

*Source: Public Interest 110-117 (No. 92, Summer 1988).

Even today, rental housing is necessary for the highly mobile, the poor, and the financially insecure.

One would assume that the negative image of landlords derives from their rent-gouging practices, and from the high profitability of real-estate investment. But this assumption is not supported by the facts. Reviewing rent increases and the change in the value of rental property in the 1960s and 1970s, Anthony Downs concluded as follows:

> Residential rents did not increase as fast as consumer income, operating costs, or construction costs. . . . The best available estimate is that real rent levels fell about 8.4 percent from 1960 to 1980. . . . In 1980 rents would have had to be 77 percent higher than they actually were to support real market values equivalent to those in 1960. . . . Putting the conclusion another way, the real value of rental housing properties in the United States *sustainable from rents alone* appears to have fallen substantially since 1960 — perhaps by 50 percent or more. The enormous drop results from much faster increase in operating costs and rates than rents.

The phenomenon is not a new one. As Louis Winnick wrote in the 1950s,

> there is little doubt that the present generation of investors as a group has lived through a long period of relatively poor earnings as owners of rental property. On the basis of historical records of operating experience, the free and clear return on residential real estate, related to original acquisition cost, was quite unfavorable from the end of the 1920s to the 1950s.

This suggests that the bad reputation of landlords has more to do with consumer psychology and the nature of the product and service sold than with the economics of rental housing. Roger Starr makes this argument in The End of Rental Housing (The Public Interest, Fall 1979):

> The major difference between landlords and other kinds of entrepreneurs is that the landlords are involved in a long, continuing relationship with their customers, one in which the customer pays over and over again for what he already has — i.e., access to an apartment that in the very nature of things is a little bit older and worse each month. . . . The tenant cannot truly understand why he should be asked to pay again for something the landlord already made. Renewing a lease on an apartment is not like buying a new suit or a steak. . . . Perhaps they cost more than the previous suit or steak — but they are new, and the purchaser is thrilled at the prospect of eating a fresh sirloin, or wearing a new suit for the first time. An economic relationship in which the supplier cannot increase his volume except by raising his unit prices, and the customer has no psychological satisfaction to show for each new expenditure of money, inevitably produces severe tension and government intercession. As society matures and takes the productive process for granted, the intercession inevitably favors the tenant.

The Economics of Rental Property

If tenants misunderstand their landlords, economists are puzzled by them. For landlords have not acted like economic men. Operating costs rose and vacancy rates dropped in the late seventies; but landlords failed to raise rents, so as to maximize the return on their investment. How could they make a living, having ignored the economists' market models?

Landlords act as they do because for the most part they are small-scale operators. While there are few reliable national data on the subject, Anthony Downs hypothesizes that

> ownership is scattered among many small-scale landlords. My impression is based on the high percentage of rental housing containing fewer than five units [60 percent] . . . and [on conversations with] realtors and investors across the nation. . . . Small scale investors who manage their own property rarely take full account of the cost of their time. So they have lower management costs — both apparent and real — than large scale operators who employ professional management and maintenance personnel.

This subjective impression is supported by a survey of owners in New York City, the area in which one would most expect to find large-scale ownership of property. Arthur D. Little, Inc. found that 60 percent of landlords own only one building. Of those who bought buildings in the last five years, 68 percent own only one building. In over 60 percent of the cases, the owners are making less than a quarter of their income from their rental investment. The majority of the owners had incomes between $10,000 and $40,000.

Small-time operators with only a few units must act much more conservatively than large-scale operators do, or theoretical economic man would. An owner with only a few units has a stronger incentive than a landlord with more units to avoid raising rents so fast that vacancies increase. The turnover of an apartment usually involves the extra cost of repainting and/or redecorating, and the cost of finding a new tenant. More important, a vacancy for a small-time landlord involves the loss of a substantial portion of the income generated by the building. As a result, writes Anthony Downs, "this situation, plus the high rate of normal turnover among renters [in 1980, 37 percent were living in their unit for less than a year] makes most small-scale landlords *turnover minimizers* rather than *rent maximizers.*"

The eighties have seen a major change in the availability of rental housing. In the third quarter of 1987, the vacancy rate was at its highest level in over two decades. Two million and nine hundred thousand year-round rental housing units were vacant — 8.1

percent of the national inventory. In cities, the rate was even higher (8.9 percent). Nevertheless, there are cries of a housing shortage all across the land.

The Problems of the Poor . . .

When things get tough in the rental market in general, they get even tougher for the poor in particular. This is the conclusion of a memorandum from the Harvard-MIT Joint Center for Housing Studies:

> The changes in the rent burden distribution for the poorest households were particularly dramatic. . . . By 1983 the median rent burden for households in this income class had risen to 46 percent of income, and over one-quarter of the households . . . had a rent burden above three-quarters of income. . . . These results must be interpreted with great care. . . . These rent burdens are based on a household's cash income and therefore exclude income in kind, such as food stamps and Medicaid. Between 1974 and 1980, the in-kind benefits . . . increased significantly. As a result, the figures . . . overstate the increase in rent burden as a percent of total income. . . . One study estimates that including all such benefits reduces the median rent burden for the lowest one-fifth of the income distribution from 62 percent to 39 percent.

From the perspective of poor tenants the problem is excessive expenditures. From the perspective of the uneducated landlord (half of New York City's landlords never graduated from high school), the problem is insufficient revenues. The tenants with the highest rent burden are living in the lowest-priced units. In other words, the poor pay less, but doing so hurts them more. . . .

Low-Income Landlords

The most ominous occurrence in the New York City rental market is the rise in operating and maintenance expenses as a percentage of rent. In an earlier report, [Michael] Stegman pointed out that this ratio had risen from 55 percent in 1971 to 70 percent in 1981. The rise meant that the percentage of the rent dollar available to cover vacancy losses, pay debt service, and yield a profit had declined from 45 to 30 percent. Table II (which uses 1981 figures) illustrates the devastating effect of this decline on property values.

If we assume no profit, an 11 percent interest rate, and an amortization period of 15 years, $53 would support a $5,000 mortgage. If the potential buyer wanted 10 percent of the rent as profit (a reasonable amount), the resulting $27 for debt service would support a mortgage of about $2,500 a unit. Thus, while apartments along Central Park [because of rent control] may be worth up to

Table II
Median Operating and Maintenance Expenses for New York City Landlords, 1981 (in dollars)[a]

Rent (New York City Median)		265
Taxes, fees, and permits	49	
Labor	30	
Fuel and Utilities	66	
Contractor services	19	
Administration costs	11	
Other	11	
Total operating and maintenance expenses		186
Vacancy losses (assuming 10% vacancy)	26	
Total costs		212
Remaining income available for debt service and profit		53

[a]Source: Stegman, The Dynamics of Rental Housing in New York City, 1982.

fifty times the annual rent as cooperatives or condominiums, a seller a few miles uptown who obtains a price *equalling* the annual rent is doing well.

The battered but unsung heroes of the fight to provide housing for the poor are the owners who have kept many of their buildings open despite these adverse economic conditions. They are not absentee landlords living on their suburban estates. Sixty percent of New York building owners own only one building, and 61 percent of the owners of buildings with fewer than ten apartments live in their building.

These landlords are not wealthy. More than half of them were not born in the United States, and of owners who have bought within the last five years, over 35 percent are either black, Hispanic, or Asian. Thirty percent reported household incomes of under $20,000, and 9 percent incomes of less than $10,000. They did not buy their buildings because real estate provides a tax shelter. Although there are no statistics on the relation between the income of landlords and that of their tenants, people generally have landlords of their own social class.

What keeps these buildings going is quite often the "sweat" — as we saw above, there is very little equity — of the landlords. Thirty-nine percent of all New York City landlords collect the trash themselves (another 5 percent use unpaid relatives); 36 percent clean the public areas; 31.4 percent do minor plumbing repairs; 32 percent do minor electrical repairs; 23 percent repair leaky roofs;

87 percent collect the rent themselves; and 82 percent keep the books themselves. Almost half of the owners spend two to four days a week on the operations of their building, and only 16 percent receive any salary.

Yet in spite of these economies, only a third of the landlords were making money on a consistent basis, with the remainder either breaking even or losing money. Thirteen percent of the owners had to subsidize their buildings' operating expenses every month; and a further 16 percent had to inject cash during the heating season. Since these statistics cover all New York landlords, it is likely that the situation of landlords serving the poorest tenants is even worse. . . .

The conclusion to be drawn is that it is possible for landlords to make a modest profit on buildings that serve low-income tenants — if the debt service, taxes, and vacancies are low, and the owner is handy and has time on his hands. Nevertheless, the operation is marginal. All it takes is one major malfunction — a boiler that needs repair, or a roof on which there is no room for new patches — to bring the whole financial structure down, and to put the landlord and his tenants on the street. . . .

NOTES AND QUESTIONS ON RESIDENTIAL LANDLORDS

1. Many of Welfeld's statistics indicate the *percentage of landlords* possessing some characteristic; for example, "more than half [of landlords] were not born in the United States." Do these statistics necessarily reveal the *percentage of tenants* who have landlords who possess a certain characteristic? Suppose that foreign-born landlords on average own only a few units, while native-born landlords on average own many.

2. Welfeld quotes Anthony Downs's statement that most small-scale landlords are "*turnover minimizers* rather than *rent maximizers*." Downs's assertion is consistent with a number of studies finding that landlords charge long-resident tenants lower rents than they charge new tenants. For a review of the conflicting evidence on the size and existence of this discount, see J. Luis Guasch & Robert C. Marshall, A Theoretical and Empirical Analysis of the Length of Residency Discount in the Rental Housing Market, 22 J. Urb. Econ. 291 (1987). Would one expect a landlord to strive to minimize the turnover of tenants who failed to pay rent or committed waste?

3. George Sternlieb's classic, The Tenement Landlord (1966), depicts slum landlords in Newark, N.J. For a pro-landlord perspective on housing issues, see William Tucker, The Excluded Americans: Homelessness and Housing Policy (1990). For a pro-tenant view, see, for example, Barbara Bezdek, Silence in the Court: Participation and Subordination of Poor Tenants' Voices in Legal Process, 20 Hofstra L. Rev. 533 (1992).

Private Production: Has the Rising Tide Lifted All Boats?*

John C. Weicher

Housing Quality: Lifting the Boats

The United States has enjoyed a steady improvement in the quality of housing throughout the postwar period [see Table 3.1]. By every available measure, the nation has far fewer inadequate housing units than at any previous time and is close to achieving the goal of a "decent home" originally conceived in the late 1940s. . . .

Table 3.1
Measures of Substandard Housing, 1940-1980
(percentage of all occupied housing)

Problem	1940	1950	1960	1970	1980
Substandard	48.6	35.4	16.0	8.4	N.a.
Lacking complete plumbing	44.6	34.0	14.7	5.5	2.2
Dilapidated	18.1[a]	9.1	4.6	3.7	N.a.
Crowding (more than 1.0 persons per room)	20.2	15.8	11.5	8.8	4.2
Severe crowding (more than 1.5 persons per room)	9.0	6.2	3.8	2.0	1.0

Sources: Data are from the following U.S. Bureau of the Census sources: Sixteenth Census of the United States: 1940, Housing, vol. 2, pt. 1; 1950 Census of Housing, vol. 1, pt. 1; 1960 Census of Housing, vol. 2, pt. 1; 1970 Census of Housing: Components of Inventory Change, HD(4)-1; Annual Housing Survey: 1980, United States and Regions, pt. A.
N.a. = not available.
[a]"Needing major repairs" in 1940. . . .

*Source: in Housing America's Poor 45-61 (Peter Salins ed., 1987).

Quality Changes for Special Groups

All [Table 3.1] data are aggregate figures. Improvements also have occurred in the housing of various groups that have frequently received special attention in housing policy, although there are numerous gaps in the data available. The best data are presented in Table 3.5 for five major population groups: blacks, Hispanics, residents of rural areas, and two measures of poverty — the bottom quarter of the income distribution and households with real incomes of $10,000 or less in 1980 dollars. The table includes only the two traditional criteria for which there are data in 1980: units lacking complete plumbing and crowding (units with more than one person per room). For the former, disaggregated data are avail-

Table 3.5
Substandard Housing for Special Groups, 1940–1980
(percentage of occupied units)

Panel A: Lacking Complete Plumbing					
Group	1940	1950	1960	1970	1980
Blacks[a]	79.6	70.9	41.9	16.3	6.1
Hispanics	N.a.	N.a.	N.a.	6.6	2.4
Rural residents	74.8	61.6	31.5	13.8	4.8
Lowest quarter of income distribution	N.a.	60.1	33.9[b]	7.9	5.0
Real income below $10,000 in 1980 dollars	N.a.	51.6	30.0[c]	13.0	5.0

Panel B: Crowding			
Group	1960	1970	1980
Blacks[a]	28.3	19.2	9.1
Hispanics	N.a.	25.7	19.2
Rural residents	20.6	9.9	4.7
Lowest quarter of income distribution	12.1	7.1	4.3
Real income below $10,000 in 1980 dollars	12.7	8.5	4.3

Sources: Same as Table 3.1.
N.a. = not available.
[a]Nonwhites in 1940 and 1950.
[b]Estimated; correct percentage lies between 31.2 and 35.2.
[c]Estimated; correct percentage lies between 27.4 and 31.1.

able for blacks and rural residents from 1940 but for income groups only from 1950; for crowding, there are not full data for ethnic groups and income classes until 1960. But the data that are available confirm the pattern of improvement for these groups: from 1940 to 1970, these groups experienced a reduction in the incidence of dilapidated and substandard housing.

Reported changes in some of the most serious defects reported in the Annual Housing Survey further indicate physical improvement in housing for these groups. These figures, published annually since 1973 for blacks and Hispanics but only since 1978 for income classes, are reported in Table [3.6] for the two ethnic groups. In seven of the eight measures, the incidence of a defect declined between 1973 and 1980; the exception, for blacks and Hispanics, is the presence of rats or mice.

The incompleteness of the data for these and other groups do not invalidate the pattern of improvement. Housing for these major groups remains worse than for the nation as a whole. The reason for the higher incidence of housing inadequacy may be that these groups, like many other groups of interest in housing policy, are disproportionately poor. But the incidence of inadequacy is declining rapidly, indicating that housing quality is improving for the disadvantaged in general.

Table 3.6
Incidence of Housing Defects, Black and Hispanic Households, 1973 and 1983 (percentages)

Defect	Blacks		Hispanics	
	1973	1983	1973	1983
Shared or no bathroom	11.0	5.3	5.0	2.6
Shared or no kitchen	7.9	2.8	2.5	1.5
Presence of rats or mice	26.0	26.6	19.9	19.3
Exposed wiring	6.2	4.0	4.7	4.1
Lacking working out- lets in some rooms	12.6	5.8	6.4	4.3
Leaky roof	15.6	12.2	9.9	10.7
Interior wall or ceiling cracks	16.0	15.3	13.0	11.5
Holes in floors	7.2	6.3	4.4	4.3

Source: Annual Housing Survey, Part B, 1973 and 1983.

Explaining the Improvement: What Is Lifting the Boats?

There are four common explanations for the postwar improvement in housing quality: rising real incomes for American families including the poor; a falling relative price for housing; a high rate of

Table 3.7
Trends in Income, Housing Costs, and Construction, 1950-1980

	1950s	1960s	1970s
Median real income			
(percentage change over decade):			
Families	+37.5	+33.9	+ 0.8
Unrelated males	+30.2	+39.4	+13.5
Unrelated females	+31.6	+37.3	+26.9
Real housing costs			
(percentage change over decade):			
Rent (CPI)	+ 5.9	− 8.4	−18.0
Homeownership (CPI)[a]	+ 3.9[b]	+13.6	+15.1
Homeownership (Hendershott and Shilling)	+15.4[c]	−27.1	−22.6
New construction			
(millions of units):			
Total units	16.24	16.48	20.52
Total units/net household formation	1.59	1.58	1.23
Private units	15.96	15.99	19.45
Subsidized new low-income units	0.29	0.49	1.07
Subsidized existing units	0	0.10	0.77

Sources: U.S. Bureau of the Census, Statistical Abstract of the United States, various editions, for income, CPI housing costs, total new construction, and household formation; Patric H. Hendershott and James D. Shilling, "The Economics of Tenure Choice, 1955–1979," *in* C. F. Sirmans, ed., Research in Real Estate, vol. 1 (Greenwich, Conn.: JAI Press, 1982), for Hendershott and Shilling measure of homeownership cost; U.S. Department of Housing and Urban Development, HUD Statistical Yearbook, various years, for subsidized units.

[a]The sharp rise in the CPI homeownership index after 1960 is now generally recognized to misrepresent the situation confronting homebuyers: When inflation and the tax treatment of owner-occupied housing are considered, ownership became an increasingly profitable investment after 1965. These factors are omitted in the CPI. The measure developed by Hendershott and Shilling is one of several recent efforts to construct a more appropriate cost index; it is used here because it is available for the longest period.

[b]Covers 1953-1960 period only.

[c]Covers 1955-1960 period only.

new private housing production, predominantly for upper-income households, which ultimately results in better housing available to the poor ("filtering"); and government programs to clear slums and subsidize new housing production specifically for the poor.

All of these phenomena have occurred during the postwar period, concurrently with the downward trend in substandard housing (see Table 3.7). It is clear from Table 3.7 that subsidized production programs by themselves were not directly responsible for all or even most of the improvement that occurred. At best, they may have contributed to a looser housing market, reducing the demand for lower-quality housing, thereby making it possible for the poor to afford better housing.

The Concept of Filtering

This chapter is concerned with how the housing quality and economic well-being of the poor may be affected by housing policy and changes in the housing market. Therefore, the relevant question is, does the price of the modest but decent housing fall when new construction occurs? If it does, then poor people are better off in a strict economic sense; their housing costs less, and they can buy better housing, more of other goods and services, or both.

The process by which new housing production for the well-to-do results in improvement in housing quality for the poor has been called "filtering." As new housing is built, some families move into it and leave their old housing vacant. The demand for the type of housing they formerly occupied decreases, reducing its price and permitting families with somewhat lower incomes to buy or rent it. In turn, these families move out of housing that is somewhat lower in quality, reducing the demand for that type of housing and enabling families of still lower income to move in. At the bottom of the quality distribution, some households move from substandard to standard housing, and some are able to move out of the worst housing, which then drops out of the stock.

Not all new construction expedites the filtering process. Filtering occurs if there is a reduction in construction costs (because of technological progress or reduced regulation) or if there is an increase in income among the well-to-do. But units built simply to meet growth in a locality do not necessarily make the market looser; there must be construction in excess of net household formation. Also, government subsidy of the price or interest rate is not likely to cause filtering unless the subsidy induces construction that would not otherwise have occurred, using resources that would have been unemployed. This might occur during a recession. But if the resources would have been used in other economic activity, the subsidy is basically an income transfer to the new home buyers (or new apartment renters) from the rest of society, including the families who would move up. Their incomes are lower, so even if the price of better housing is lower, they may not be able to take advantage of it.

It is important to distinguish the filtering concept from general economic growth. Filtering is hypothesized to occur when the incomes of the rich increase, even if the incomes of the poor do not. Economic growth, particularly in this country, results in higher incomes throughout the population. The notion of the "rising tide" usually refers to economic growth in general; an increase in income for the rich alone is more akin to a locomotive pulling the economy. In fact, both may have been occurring recently. During the postwar period, the income distribution seems to have become slightly more equal, then after 1967 slightly more unequal, but the changes are small. Throughout the period, the poor have increasingly lived in better housing, whether or not filtering has been happening.

It is also important to identify other phenomena that are distinct from the filtering process. First is the process whereby a series of individual households replace each other in a sequence of housing moves. Several studies have identified and interviewed in sequence the specific households that moved, starting with the buyers of new houses, to see whether their housing improved. There is a "chain of moves," continuing until the chain ends, when the last family moves to its new home. The best known of these studies is by John Lansing, Charles Clifton, and James C. Morgan, written in 1969.

Second is the process whereby individual housing units deteriorate over time. Vintage models of the housing stock, such as Richard F. Muth's 1973 study, incorporate this basic assumption and trace out its implications. There is also a small but growing body of literature on housing maintenance. . . .

The Economic Argument

There has been some controversy among economists as to whether the rising tide can lift all boats in the long run. This theory was generally accepted during the 1950s, rejected in the 1960s, and resurrected in the mid-1970s. . . .

Empirical Evidence

There have been very few empirical studies of the rising tide hypothesis and no time-series analysis; the data simply do not exist. The research that has been done is cross-sectional; it usually compares either differences in the incidence of substandard housing across cities or metropolitan areas at a particular date or differential changes among cities over a period.

William Grigsby produced the first and for a long time virtually the only empirical study in 1963. He found that rents and house prices increased least during the 1950s in those metropolitan areas with the most new construction. His study was limited to nine areas, however, and he was unable to adjust for quality changes. In the early 1970s, Frank deLeeuw began to develop a housing market model to simulate various housing policy options, using census data for four metropolitan areas as prototypical markets. This model demonstrates that new private construction results in a reduction in the price and quantity of low-quality housing over a decade. More recently, Thomas G. Thibodeau and I have analyzed the Annual Housing Survey data for sixty large metropolitan areas during the early 1970s. We find a very strong negative relationship between private construction during a five-year period and substandard housing at the end of the period and a weaker but still negative effect from units built five to fifteen years earlier. The short-run impact is about one fewer substandard unit at the end of the period for every three to four built during the period. The only contrary evidence is a recent paper by Donald F. Vitaliano, who found no relationship between new private construction and the incidence of low-quality housing five to fifteen years earlier. His analysis is based on a sample of New York State communities of various sizes, rather than large metropolitan areas. There have been no other empirical investigations of the relationship between private new housing construction and the incidence of substandard housing. . . .

Subsidized Production and Quality Improvement: The "Diverted Flow"

Discussions about housing policy often contrast the filtering hypothesis with subsidized production programs such as public housing. The usual assumption is that subsidized production benefits the poor; the burden of proof thus falls on the advocates of filtering to show that new private construction also benefits the poor. In fact, when the same standards are applied to both policies, it is subsidized production that appears to be clearly inferior.

Conventional public housing, the oldest and simplest subsidized production program, has received the most attention. Analysts agree on one fundamental point — households that move directly into public housing clearly benefit. These families are removed from the private housing market and placed in better housing than they previously occupied.

Analysts have reached diverse conclusions about the effects on low-income households that are not assisted and on the housing market generally. Olsen, for example, concludes that all low-income households not assisted by the program are unaffected; they have the same incomes and face the same price for housing of a given quality as they did before the program was established. Ultimately, as many units drop from the private housing stock as there are households occupying public housing. James Sweeney, however, concludes that public housing benefits all low-income households because demand for private low-quality units declines and the rents of these units therefore fall as well; the number of households occupying the lowest quality of housing also falls. But James C. Ohls gets the opposite result. His simulation model indicates that the quality of housing deteriorates on balance for low-income households that are not assisted. Ohls does not attempt to explain his result. It is possible that public housing construction causes a decrease in private construction at the low-cost end of the housing market, leading in the long run to a reduction in the private stock and a fall in its quality. Thus the various studies allow one to conclude that the total reduction in low-quality housing (the marketwide effect) may be greater, the same as, or less than the number of new public housing units.

According to most of these studies, the effects on households other than those directly assisted occur as a result of relative price changes for different qualities of housing. Thus in this important respect, subsidized production, if effective, works to improve housing by the same filtering process as private construction.

Empirical Evidence

Whereas theoretical studies are ambivalent, empirical studies of the relationship between subsidized housing and quality in the private stock generally support the view that subsidized production has an insignificant or negative impact on the incidence of substandard housing. Studies by Davis, Eastman, and Hua and by Hirsch and Law conclude that subsidized production resulted in an improvement in housing quality only when substandard housing was defined differently at the beginning and end of the study period. When the definition was consistent over time, the subsidized production was unrelated to the incidence of low-quality housing.

My own work with Thomas G. Thibodeau [Filtering and Housing Markets: An Empirical Analysis 23 J. Urb. Econ. 21 (1988)], the most extensive study undertaken to date, found an insignificant relationship most of the time, regardless of the definition of inadequacy and using a variety of data sources on subsidized production. Disaggregating by program type and by year of construction did not improve the results. Moreover, even the most generous estimates of the benefits of subsidized production demonstrate less than a unit-for-unit reduction in substandard housing.

These results are unexpected; they fly in the face of economic theory and conventional wisdom — perhaps even of common sense. If subsidized housing helps poor people directly, it is hard to believe that its side effects can be so perverse as to negate its direct benefits and leave the poor as a whole no better off.

An important partial explanation for this apparent contradiction is that public housing occupancy is not restricted to those who have previously lived in substandard housing. Data on federal government programs show that fewer than half of new residents in assisted housing during the late 1960s and early 1970s moved on from substandard housing. Moreover, the program definition of "substandard" is not the same as criteria used in policy analyses but is an elastic, rather vague notion, based on the perceptions of the tenant and the staff of the local housing authority. Thus public housing in the real world may well have different effects from the abstract concept used in most housing market models.

A more general explanation is that subsidized housing production is in large part a substitute for private production that would probably have occurred without the program. The two most detailed studies, by Michael Murray and Craig Swan, conclude that most public housing has simply replaced private new construction in the long run, although the substitution effect takes a few years. If this is true, then one might describe public housing as a "diverted flow," in contrast to the "rising tide" of private production. . . .

Conclusions and Policy Implications

It appears that there is a rising tide, or filtering process, by which new housing built for the well-to-do ultimately results in better housing for the poor. By academic standards, the theoretical and the empirical evidence is not as conclusive as one might wish. Most recent theoretical analyses support the rising tide theory, but the most elegant ones do not definitely establish the proposition, and there is some disagreement. The preponderance of the empirical evidence, however, supports the theory, although there have not been many studies. . . .

NOTES AND QUESTIONS ON HOUSING POLICY

1. Weicher's Table 3.1 portrays steady improvements in housing quality through 1980. What has happened since? Statistics from the Census 2000 Supplementary Survey suggest a mixed picture. Nationally the percentage of occupied dwellings lacking complete plumbing plummeted from 2.2 percent in 1980 to 0.5 percent in 2000. The incidence of crowding (more than 1.0 persons per room), however, was the same in both 1980 and 2000 (4.2 percent).

2. According to "filtering" theory, why does construction of suburban housing for relatively wealthy households help low-income families living in central cities? How plausible is Weicher's paradoxical thesis that poor households as a whole benefit more from new housing built for the well-to-do than they benefit from the production of subsidized housing?

3. For further evidence on the issue of whether the production of subsidized housing projects ends up adding to the total stock of housing, see Michael P. Murray, Subsidized and Unsubsidized Housing Stocks 1935 to 1987: Crowding Out and Cointegration, 18 J. Real Est. Fin. & Econ. 107 (1999). Murray concludes that subsidized projects for the poor do add to the total stock, but that subsidized projects for moderate-income households do not.

4. Why should the federal government (or a state government) provide low-income households with in-kind housing assistance, as opposed to unrestricted cash aid? If provided at all, should housing subsidies take the form of transportable vouchers granted to households (the Section 8 program) or project subsidies that reduce rents in specific buildings (traditional public housing)? For discussion, see sources cited in Robert C. Ellickson & Vicki L. Been, Land Use Controls 1047-1070 (2d ed. 2000). The authors of a

leading work on housing economics come down emphatically on the side of vouchers because "Demand-side approaches directly attack the root of the problem in most markets — the inability of some households to afford decent-quality housing at current rents for such." Jerome Rothenberg et al., The Maze of Urban Housing Markets 349-355 (1991). For additional views, some of them more sympathetic to project subsidies, see Building Foundations: Housing and Federal Policy (Denise DiPasquale & Langley C. Keyes eds., 1990); Critical Perspectives on Housing (Rachel G. Bratt, Chester Hartman & Ann Meyerson eds., 1986); John C. Weicher, Privatizing Subsidized Housing (1997).

5. Many observers assert that the central shelter problem in the United States is not the *condition* of housing, but rather its *affordability*. See, for example, Curtis Berger, Beyond Homelessness: An Entitlement to Shelter, 45 U. Miami L. Rev. 315, 317-324 (1990-1991). But cf. Robert C. Ellickson, The Untenable Case for an Unconditional Right to Housing, 15 Harv. J.L. & Pub. Poly. 17, 28-30 (1992). Drawing on Christopher Jencks & Kathryn Edin, The Real Welfare Problem, Am. Prospect, Spring 1990, at 31, Ellickson asserts that many widely cited statistics about poor tenants' rent/income ratios exaggerate the affordability problem because the actual income of welfare families may average about three times what the Census Bureau reports.

6. Many researchers have found that homeownership enhances the welfare of both a household's residents and the larger society. See, e.g., Richard K. Green & Michelle J. White, Measuring the Benefits of Homeowning: Effects on Children, 41 J. Urb. Econ. 441 (1997); Denise DiPasquale & Edward L. Glaeser, Incentives and Social Capital: Are Homeowners Better Citizens?, 45 J. Urb. Econ. 354 (1999). What are the implications for the design of government housing assistance policies?

D.   Minimum Housing Standards

Economic Analysis of Law*

Richard A. Posner

§16.6 Wealth Redistribution by Liability Rules: The Case of Housing Code Enforcement

Housing assistance for the poor is a traditional service provided by the government. Various methods of assistance are used. One is to hire contractors to build apartment houses for the government to own and operate, renting apartments to the poor at zero or nominal rentals. Another is to give poor people money that they are allowed to spend only for housing. This method of subsidy has the attractive feature, to an economist, that it preserves a private market in housing — it just gives the poor more effective demand for the housing supplied in that market. It is true that in the short run the effect may simply be to force up rental rates, and hence to make other renters poorer, and landlords richer, as a result of the subsidy. That is the standard short-run response to a surge in demand, reflecting the fact that productive capacity is by definition fixed in the short run. . . . But in the long run the stock of housing will rise and the price will fall back toward (all the way toward?) its level before the subsidy. And public housing has even worse short-run effects than these: In the short run — before the housing is actually built and rented — the poor obtain no benefit from public housing at all. A system of rent supplements or housing vouchers not only is more flexible but works more quickly to help the intended beneficiaries.

Both public housing and rent supplements involve the taxing and spending branches of government rather than the courts. But there is a method of (purportedly) helping the poor to meet their housing needs that centrally involves the courts: the enforcement of housing codes. These codes specify minimum standards of housing — although whether in order to ensure a decent minimum level of safety and sanitation or to subsidize the building trades is a matter of debate. Legal scholarship has been imaginative in suggesting devices by which the violators of housing codes could be subjected to sanctions that would greatly reduce the incidence of

*Source: pp. 514-518 (5th ed. 1998).

Figure 16.3

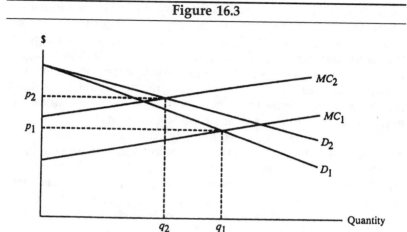

violation. To deal with the problem of substandard housing by legal sanction has the additional attraction of enabling, or seeming to enable, a principal manifestation of poverty to be eliminated without any public expenditure.

The effects of housing code enforcement are depicted in Figure 16.3. D_1 is the market demand curve for low-income housing before enforcement. It slopes downward because not all tenants would leave if rentals rose as a result of an increase in the landlords' marginal costs. MC_1 is the landlords' pre-enforcement marginal cost curve and is positively sloped to reflect the fact that the creation of low-income rental housing involves the use of some specialized resources — in particular, land — that would be worth less in any other use.

Enforcing the housing code has two main effects on the market depicted in Figure 16.3.[2] By improving the quality of the housing units it increases the demand for them. And by increasing the landlords' maintenance costs, which are marginal costs because they vary with the number of housing units provided, it shifts the marginal cost curve upward. The shift shown in Figure 16.3 is large relative to the shift in the demand curve, on the plausible assumption that if quantity demanded were highly responsive to an increase in the quality of the housing provided, the landlords would

---

2. A third effect is a reduction in the rent of land received by the landlords (assuming they are the owners of the land). The irony here is that these "rentiers" include a number of almost-poor people for whom ownership of slum property represents the first stage in the escape from poverty.

upgrade quality voluntarily and there would be no need to enforce a housing code. Both demand and supply in Figure 16.3 are depicted as being quite elastic, on the (again plausible) assumptions that slum dwellers lack the resources to pay substantially higher rentals and that slum rentals are already so depressed in relation to costs that a further reduction in those rentals would cause many landlords to withdraw from the low-income housing market (for example, by abandoning their property to the city).

Given these assumptions, housing code enforcement leads to a substantial reduction in the supply of low-income housing (from q_1 to q_2) coupled with a substantial rise in the price of the remaining supply (from p_1 to p_2). The quantity effect is actually understated (though by the same token the price effect is overstated) in Figure 16.3: Some of the higher-quality supply brought forth by housing code enforcement may be rented to the nonpoor.[3] These effects could be offset by rent supplements, but that would deprive the program of its politically attractive quality of entailing no public expenditures.

Admittedly, the magnitude of the effects shown in Figure 16.3 depends on the (arbitrary) location of the curves. It has even been suggested that demand might be perfectly elastic in the relevant region (implying no price effect of housing code enforcement) because the slightest increase would cause many tenants to double up.[6] But since doubling up is costly (it involves forgoing the value of the greater space and privacy of single family occupancy), tenants would surely be willing to pay something to avoid being forced to double up, the something being a somewhat higher rental. This implies a less than perfectly elastic demand. Empirical evidence suggests that Figure 16.3 provides a closer approximation to the actual conditions of the slum housing market than a model which assumes perfect elasticity of demand.[7]

Another suggestion is that the enforcement of a housing code

---

3. Might a covert purpose of housing codes be to increase the supply of middle income housing at the expense of the poor? Cf. George J. Stigler, Director's Law of Public Income Redistribution, 13 J.L. & Econ. 1 (1970).

6. Bruce Ackerman, Regulating Slum Housing Markets on Behalf of the Poor: Of Housing Codes, Housing Subsidies and Income Redistribution Policy, 80 Yale L.J. 1093 (1971). . . .

One court has suggested that landlords might be forbidden, on a theory of retaliatory eviction, to abandon buildings as an alternative to code compliance if they were "able" to comply. Robinson v. Diamond Housing Corp., 463 F.2d 853, 869 (D.C. Cir. 1972). Would such a prohibition increase or decrease the long-run supply of housing to the poor?

7. Werner Z. Hirsch, Law and Economics: An Introductory Analysis 71-81 (2d ed. 1988). . . .

would increase the supply of housing to the poor if enforcers focused their efforts on buildings that landlords were "milking."[8] Milking refers to the practice of maintaining a building at a lower standard than would be appropriate if the landlord intended to keep the building in operation indefinitely. He might have figured for example that because of a changing neighborhood or rising fuel costs he would probably have to abandon the building in five years willy-nilly — by that time his variable costs will exceed his rental income. It may make sense for him, once he has made this calculation, to reduce his expenditures on maintenance at once, since any long-term effects of those expenditures in preserving the building would be of little or no value to him. . . . By reducing those expenditures, he will reduce the quality of the housing, and his rental income will fall, but maybe by less than his expenditures on maintenance fall. An incidental effect may be that he abandons the building even sooner (though this will end his income stream sooner), since those expenditures would have kept the building going a little longer. If the enforcement of the local housing code prevents him from economizing in this manner, maybe he will delay abandonment, since the expenditures he is forced to make may well have some, as it were inadvertent, effect in preserving the building.

All this is terribly "iffy." Even though milking is, doubtless, sometimes rational in the real estate market when all costs and benefits are taken into account, attempting to counteract it through housing code enforcement is as likely to accelerate as to delay abandonment. The costs of compliance with the code are variable costs, which means that, as a first approximation at least, declining rental income and rising variable costs will intersect sooner, leading to earlier abandonment. It is doubtful that a court or legislature could identify those buildings where enforcement of the housing code would delay abandonment through its effect in counteracting milking rather than accelerate it through its effect in making the continued ownership of the building more expensive.

A number of cities have enacted ordinances designed to protect tenants by giving them more procedural rights in the event the landlord tries to evict them, by entitling tenants to withhold rent if landlords fail to make repairs required by the lease, by requiring landlords to pay interest on security deposits, and so forth. The effects are much like those of housing code enforcement: The ordinances raise landlords' costs and therefore increase rental lev-

8. Duncan Kennedy, The Effect of the Warranty of Habitability on Low Income Housing: "Milking" and Class Violence, 15 Fla. St. U.L. Rev. 485 (1987).

els and reduce the supply of housing (especially rental housing, since such laws encourage conversion to cooperatives and condominiums). From the standpoint of protecting poor people, the provisions regarding procedural rights and rent withholding are particularly pernicious. They are rights more likely to be invoked by the poor than by the rich. They therefore give landlords an added incentive to substitute toward more affluent tenants, who are less likely to be late with the rent or to abuse the right to withhold rent.

The reader may be reminded of our analysis . . . of the economic effects of outlawing efficient but sometimes oppressive methods of enforcing debts. Both analyses suggest that the use of liability rules or other legal sanctions to redistribute income from wealthy to poor is likely to miscarry. A rule of liability is like an excise tax: It induces a contraction in output and increase in price. . . . The party made liable, even if not poor himself (but that, as we have seen, is also possible), may be able to shift much of the liability cost to the poor through higher prices. The result may be a capricious redistribution of income and wealth within the class of poor people themselves and an overall reduction in their welfare.

NOTES AND QUESTIONS ON POSNER ON HOUSING CODES

1. Examine how Posner draws the two demand curves in Figure 16.3 on p. 405. Is it plausible to suppose, as he did, that the individuals who most highly value other attributes of housing place the lowest value on the benefits of housing code compliance? How did Posner's placement of the demand curves affect the size of the price and quantity effects depicted in Figure 16.3?

2. As Posner mentions, Duncan Kennedy has defined "milking" as a landlord's decision to stop maintaining a deteriorating residential building, with the intent of abandoning it within a few years. Should housing-code officials embrace Kennedy's advice that they act to prevent milking, or instead let it happen on the theory that landlords can best decide when investment in upkeep is no longer cost-effective? Would Posner defend a milking decision that violated a landlord's express warranties of maintenance? Should a landlord be allowed to obtain a tenant's consent to milking in consideration for charging a low rent?

3. A few examples will elucidate the economic concept of elas-

ticity. Price elasticity is measured by the proportional change in quantity divided by the proportional change in price. The supply of a good is highly elastic when a small increase in its market price would sharply increase the quantity supplied. Which is more elastically supplied: corn or Picasso paintings? The demand for a good is highly inelastic when a large change in price would not greatly affect the quantity demanded. For which is demand more inelastic: corn or cigarettes?

As Posner's discussion indicates, commentators harbor differing conceptions of the long-run elasticities of supply and demand for housing. Those who view the supply as relatively elastic worry most that laws that decimate landlords' returns will lead to housing abandonment. Jerome Rothenberg et al., The Maze of Urban Housing Markets (1991), provides a sophisticated review of research on price elasticities and other economic features of housing markets.

Regulating Slum Housing Markets on Behalf of the Poor*

Bruce A. Ackerman

II.   Slumville . . .

Imagine a city called Athens whose slums are concentrated in one geographic area that we shall call Slumville. While the residents of Slumville are extremely mobile within the confines of the slum district, Athenians living outside Slumville are extremely reluctant to move into the area even if there is a significant improvement in housing quality. Of course, if there is an enormous change in the character of the neighborhood, the city's residents may change their view of Slumville. But a moderate change will not lead them to discard their fears about the quality of life, as well as the quality of housing, enjoyed by the area's inhabitants.

While the middle-class Athenian's substantial reluctance to live in Slumville is fundamental to much of the argument that follows, several additional assumptions will be altered at subsequent stages of this essay. For purposes of the present discussion,

*Source: 80 Yale L.J. 1093, 1102-1106 (1971).

then, assume (1) both landlords and tenants act rationally in their self-interest;[11] (2) no landlord or group of landlords has successfully established a monopoly or oligopoly position in the rental market; (3) tenants are aware of the range of prices and quality levels of accommodations offered for rent in Slumville and experience no significant cost in moving from one part of Slumville to another; (4) all of Slumville's accommodations are not only slums, but are *equally* slummy; (5) similarly, all of Slumville's tenants inflict *equal* damage upon the physical structures of the houses in which they reside; (6) a significant number of poor provincials are not entering Athens from the outlands nor are Slumvillites emigrating to the hinterlands; (7) *each* and *every* landlord in Slumville earns a rate of return on his investment which substantially exceeds the return available when the property is used for other purposes; indeed (8) even if the landlords are forced to bring their residential properties up to code, their rate of return would still exceed that available for any other use of the property; and (9) no landlord will find it more profitable to abandon his building entirely when faced with the necessity of investing substantial sums to bring his tenement up to code.

The implications of these last three assumptions can be misunderstood quite easily. They do not imply that the landlords of Slumville are making exceedingly high profits on their original investments. Even if they were only making a very low rate of return after absorbing the costs of code enforcement, my description of Slumville's landlords would still be satisfied if they could only earn an even lower rate of return by converting their land to an alternative commercial use. Similarly, the ninth assumption enumerated above, which stipulates that no buildings be abandoned, does not necessarily suggest the existence of excessive returns. A landlord will seriously consider abandonment only if the discounted present value of the cost code enforcement imposes over time exceeds the capitalized value of the future profits he expects from the building. In other words, even if an investor originally purchased a building for $100,000 and is currently earning only one per cent or $1000 a year in profit before code enforcement, the only financially relevant question for him is the value the market places on the right to receive $1000. If a purchaser is willing to buy

11. The model under discussion is also restricted to a Slumville composed entirely of renters. While a subsequent portion of the essay considers certain difficulties which arise when owners themselves live in a home rented partly to tenants, considerations of length have made it impossible to consider at this time the full range of complexities raised by the fact that some slumdwellers live in houses which they own.

this future income stream for $5000, abandonment is irrational unless the anticipated stream of future code costs exceeds this amount after an appropriate discount rate is applied. Thus, the Slumville we have depicted is not one which invokes the legendary exploitative landlord; indeed, our model is compatible with a situation in which each landlord is earning an exceedingly low return on his *original* investment.[14] We have only excluded from consideration in this first simple model those landlords who are in a truly desperate financial situation in which the capitalized value of future profits is lower than the capitalized cost of code repairs.

A.

We are now in a position to trace the economic consequences of a code enforcement program in Slumville. Given the model which has been developed, it follows that when the costs of code improvements are imposed upon Slumville's landlords *none* of them will have an incentive to remove their properties from the rental housing market. For we have stipulated that even after code costs are taken into account, the return on slum investment still exceeds the rate of return available when the land is used for other purposes or not used at all. Since the imposition of code costs upon the landlords does not induce a fall in the supply of housing, rent levels will be determined by the effect of code enforcement upon the demand for housing.

Two different demand responses can be anticipated, depending upon the extent to which the housing code is enforced. First, assume that the code is enforced strictly only in one part (Area X) of Slumville and that the rest of Slumville (Area Y) is entirely ignored by the housing code inspectorate. In this case, one would expect that some of the residents of Y will find X a more attractive place than formerly and will bid the rents up in Area X. Those residents of X who find the new rent levels too steep for their taste will of course move to Y, where apartments have been vacated by those moving into the newly improved housing in X. Conse-

14. Moreover, the relationship which the owner of the fee may have with a mortgage lender is also irrelevant to this analysis. If, for example, code costs will make it unprofitable for the fee owner to meet his mortgage payment, he will simply default and the new owner of the property (generally the mortgagee) will find himself in the same position delineated in the discussion in the text: he will either incur code costs to save the remainder of his $1000 annual income stream or he will withdraw the building from the residential housing market. Since in this introductory analysis we have assumed that this second alternative is not open, only the first alternative remains.

quently, a program of selective housing code enforcement in Slum-ville will, in fact, partially fulfill the expectations of those administrators who doubt the desirability of code enforcement: Rents will increase in the target area and tenants who cannot "af-ford" the higher rents will leave the area to find new abodes in the now slummier sections of Slumville.

B.

If, however, one assumes that the housing code is enforced strictly in all of Slumville, the same result will not follow. Since we have assumed that before the code was enforced, houses in Areas X and Y were equally dilapidated, the comprehensive enforcement of the code throughout Areas X and Y will raise the quality of housing in all parts of Slumville to an equal degree, thereby pro-viding no special incentive for a resident of Area Y to want to move to Area X. Thus, rents will not rise because of competition *among* Slumville residents as occurred in the case of partial code enforce-ment just discussed.

Indeed rents will not rise *at all* in Slumville if only a single further condition is met. Paradoxically, code enforcements will have "zero rent impact" if and only if there exists a class of Slum-ville tenants who do *not* believe that code enforcement will signif-icantly improve their lives. A simple mathematical example will make this clear. Assume that, before the code is enforced, two types of families live in Slumville's 100,000 rental units: 90,000 families (the "homelovers") would be willing to pay a significant amount of money for code housing; in contrast, 10,000 families (the "luke-warm" families) would not be willing to pay extra rent for im-proved housing. This is not to say that even the lukewarm do not recognize that they will benefit from code enforcement — the im-provement is simply not significant enough in their minds to war-rant allocation of any more of their scarce funds to purchase it.

Now imagine that all of Slumville's landlords seek to pass their code costs on to tenants by raising rents by $25. While the 90,000 homelovers initially respond by paying the premium, the 10,000 lukewarm families act differently. Rather than paying the higher rent, they choose to pair up and share apartments instead, thus leaving 5000 units vacant. The lukewarm families will take this course since they believe that half an apartment at a lower rent is a better deal than a whole apartment at the inflated rental.

When the 10,000 lukewarm families decide to double-up, how-ever, the owners of the 5000 vacant apartments are faced with a serious problem. Since no new residents have (under our assumptions) been attracted to Slumville as a result of code enforcement, there is no reason to expect that they will successfully fill their apartments if they persist in demanding the $25 premium. Rather, a landlord can rent his units in only one of two ways: (a) by inducing one of the homelovers to move by cutting the premium below the $25 level or (b) by cutting the rent sufficiently to induce one of the lukewarm families to prefer an entire apartment to its more crowded quarters. It should be apparent that if a given landlord fills a vacant apartment by offering one of the homelovers a better deal than his present landlord, the competitive dynamic will continue, for the owner of the newly vacated apartment will find himself in the same bleak position as his now successful competitor once occupied. It is only when prices are set low enough to induce the lukewarm families to resume their former habits and live in individual apartments that the economic situation will regain equilibrium. But if a significant number of lukewarm families are willing to spend no additional money for the code improvements, equilibrium will not be attained until the competing landlords absorb all of the code costs and rent all of their units at the pre-code price. Q.E.D. . . .

NOTES AND QUESTIONS ON ACKERMAN ON HOUSING CODES

1. In the latter portions of his lengthy article, Ackerman drops some of the simplifying assumptions that appear in this selection. Which of the assumptions reproduced in the passage are least realistic? Some candidates:

   (a) while tenants are perfectly mobile within Slumville, no migration occurs across Slumville's borders;
   (b) because the return on slum investments is uniformly adequate, code enforcement does not prompt even the most marginally profitable landlords to abandon their buildings; and
   (c) the tenants most tepidly interested in renting in Slumville place no value on code compliance.

Which, if any, of Ackerman's assumptions are essential to his deduced conclusion, in this excerpt, that code enforcement does not push up rents? For a variety of critiques of Ackerman's analysis, see Neil K. Komesar, Return to Slumville, 82 Yale L.J. 1175 (1973)

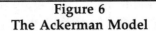

Figure 6
The Ackerman Model

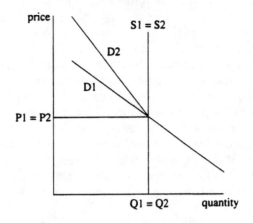

(which is immediately followed by a rejoinder by Ackerman); Werner Z. Hirsch, Joel G. Hirsch & Stephen Margolis, Regression Analysis of the Effects of Habitability Laws Upon Rent: An Empirical Observation on the Ackerman-Komesar Debate, 63 Cal. L. Rev. 1098 (1975); Richard S. Markovits, The Distributive Impact, Allocative Efficiency, and Overall Desirability of Ideal Housing Codes, 89 Harv. L. Rev. 1815 (1976).

2. Examine Figure 6, reprinted from Richard Craswell, Passing On the Costs of Legal Rules: Efficiency and Distribution in Buyer-Seller Relationships, 43 Stan. L. Rev. 361, 381 (1991). Does Craswell's graph accurately capture Ackerman's model in this selection? If so, compare how Ackerman shifts the demand curve from D1 (pre-enforcement) to D2 (post-enforcement) with how Posner makes the same shift in Figure 16.3, supra p. 405. How much does one learn from these graphs about urban housing markets? About the nature of legal scholarship?

3. How might the consequences of an implied warranty of habitability differ from the consequences of housing code enforcement? Of the many legal reforms advocated on behalf of tenants, which are most likely to achieve their goals? See generally Edward H. Rabin, The Revolution in Residential Landlord-Tenant Law: Causes and Consequences, 69 Cornell L. Rev. 517 (1984).

4. What would happen if poverty lawyers used every procedural device to delay or prevent evictions within a gentrifying neighborhood? For an optimistic assessment, see Lawrence K. Kolodney, Eviction Free Zones: The Economics of Legal Bricolage

in the Fight Against Displacement, 18 Fordham Urb. L.J. 507 (1991).

E. Rent Control

Rent Control: The International Experience*

Richard Arnott

1. The Intellectual Background

Until a decade ago, the theoretical literature modeled rent controls as a simple price ceiling (on either a housing unit or a unit of housing service) applied to a product in a perfectly competitive market. Furthermore, the analysis assumed partial equilibrium, which ignored interactions between the housing market and the rest of the economy. Under these assumptions, rent controls are unambiguously harmful. This theoretical conclusion was supported by most of the policy literature, which applied casual empiricism to describe the deleterious effects of first-generation or hard controls in frequently polemical fashion. It is on the basis of this traditional literature that North American economists are virtually unanimous in their opposition to rent controls of almost any form.

In recent years, however, there has been a wave, or at least a swell, of revisionism among housing economists and policy analysts. Most experts of the subject, while not advocating controls, are now considerably more guarded and qualified in their opposition, and some believe that a well-designed rent control program can, on balance, be beneficial. I shall discuss four strands of thought that have contributed to this change in point of view.

1. In many jurisdictions, housing economists have been participating in the policy debate on second-generation or soft rent control programs (also termed rent review). Doing so has forced them to address the question, If the political environment is unfavorable to decontrol, then how should the existing rent control program be modified to improve whatever beneficial effects rent control may have, or at least to mitigate the harmful effects? This

*Source: 1 J. Real Est. Fin. & Econ. 203-210 (1988).

experience has made housing economists realize that *the effects of a rent control program are sensitive to the details of its provisions* and that *a rent control program is a package of quite disparate policy measures.* As a result, controls are no longer regarded as a monolithic policy which simply imposes a ceiling on rents.

2. Theoretical economic models of the housing market have become considerably more sophisticated in recent years. While these models have received little practical application in housing policy analysis generally and in rent control analysis in particular, they have had some indirect influence through two avenues. First, these models can be reasonably sensitive to the details of a housing policy, and theoretical analyses employing them have reinforced the view that the effects of a policy depend on its particular provisions. Second, the new housing market models contain a significantly different conceptualization of the housing market, which has affected the way some of the younger generation of housing economists perceive the operation of the market.

3. There is increasing unease with the assumption that housing markets are perfectly competitive. While they certainly do exhibit many of the distinguishing features of the classic perfectly competitive market (notably many buyers and sellers and relative ease of entry and exit), they also have significant noncompetitive features: transactions costs (search and mobility costs), inhomogeneity of the product, consumption nonconvexities (because of transport costs, the typical household purchases all of its housing at one location), and asymmetric information (prospective tenants are poorly informed concerning unit characteristics, and landlords are uncertain of the traits of prospective tenants).

A major thrust of recent microeconomic theory has been the analysis of markets with such noncompetitive features. It is now well understood that the descriptive properties of such imperfectly competitive markets may be very different from those of perfectly competitive markets. For example, although price is the equilibrating mechanism under perfect competition, under imperfect competition there may be nonprice rationing (housing market vacancies may be a manifestation of this). Also, the law of a single price need not hold in an imperfectly competitive market; instead, equilibrium may be characterized by a distribution of prices for a homogeneous product.

The normative properties of perfectly and imperfectly competitive markets may also be markedly different. Perhaps the most celebrated and influential result in modern microeconomic theory is the First Theorem of Welfare Economics: Any perfectly competitive equilibrium is Pareto efficient. This theorem has formed the basis of countless arguments against government intervention, and is the intellectual cornerstone for the majority belief among economists that rent controls are harmful. But the theorem generally does not hold in imperfectly competitive markets, and so the potential scope for ameliorative government intervention may be considerable. The implication of this in the current context is that *because the housing market is imperfectly competitive, there is no a priori presumption that rent controls are harmful*; whether in fact they are is an empirical issue and depends on the details of the program.

4. Over the last fifteen years, there have been significant changes in the way economists think about public policy and government intervention. The traditional approach was to: 1) separate equity and efficiency, on the argument that equity considerations were best treated via lump-sum redistribution; 2) employ partial equilibrium analysis, i.e., to examine a market without reference to the rest of the economy; 3) identify classic market failures or inefficiencies (externalities and increasing returns); and 4) to support those government policies (and only those) that corrected classic market failures.

Four serious criticisms have been levelled against this traditional method of public policy analysis.

First, it has been pointed out that lump-sum redistribution is impossible because the government must base redistribution on characteristics of individuals which, because of redistribution, they have an incentive to alter. This abstract statement can be illustrated by reference to the income tax. Suppose individuals differ in terms of ability and that an individual's income is the product of his ability and hours worked. The government would like to redistribute from the more to the less able, since society deems it unfair that a person should live in misery simply because he had the misfortune to be born with little ability. But the government cannot observe ability. It can, however, observe income, and must redistribute on that basis, via an income tax. But the income tax distorts the labor-leisure tradeoff. Since any practical form of redistribution has efficiency costs, equity and efficiency are inextricably intertwined, and so government policies should be evaluated with respect to both their equity and efficiency effects. Rent controls may then be desirable because of their equity benefits, despite their efficiency costs.

Second, it has long been recognized that the conditions under which partial equilibrium analysis is fully valid are very restrictive. In particular, if there are any distortions in the rest of the economy, partial equilibrium efficiency analysis is almost never fully correct since it ignores inter-market efficiency effects. For example, partial equilibrium analysis applied to the pricing of public transit comes up with the result that transit fares should be set equal to marginal cost. When, however, consideration is given to urban auto travel, the result is modified. Because drivers do not pay for the congestion they cause, urban auto travel is typically underpriced, so that more trips are made by car than is efficient. Pricing transit fares below (partial equilibrium) marginal cost causes some drivers to switch to public transit, which reduces the efficiency loss due to underpriced car travel. Such considerations are the subject of the theory of the second best. The first best is to set all prices equal to marginal cost and to redistribute in lump-sum fashion; but given some distortions which cannot be removed, for whatever reason, what is the second best that can be done? Rent controls might be harmful in a first-best or undistorted economy, but, if they reduce the efficiency costs of other distortions in the housing market or of distortions in other markets, they may be desirable on second-best grounds. Second-best arguments work both ways, however; rent controls may be even more harmful in a distorted than in a first-best economy, by exacerbating existing distortions.

Third, the last decade has been a period of extensive and substantial deregulation. The main impetus for this was the recognition of regulatory failure and government failure. Government intervention to correct market failure may be harmful. Not only does government intervention entail administrative and compliance costs, but the intervention process itself is subject to its own kinds of inefficiency: excessive regulation, insufficiently flexible regulation, misregulation, and, in the absence of the discipline of the market, excessive and wasteful spending. Such arguments strengthen the case of those who oppose rent controls.

Fourth, the ideas of James Buchanan and his co-workers are filtering into mainstream economic thought. In the current context, of particular significance are the profound implications of two eminently reasonable statements: 1) a policy will be implemented if and only if it receives political support, and 2) which policies receive political support depends on the constitution, i.e., the body of laws and regulations concerning how social choices are made. The first statement implies that in the determination of optimal policy, account should be taken of political constraints; the second, that if the set of policies chosen is determined by the constitution, then attention should be shifted away from individual policies and instead focused on the design of the constitution. Ironically (since Buchanan is well known for his opposition to Big Government), the above line of reasoning provides an argument in favor of controls. Rent controls are generally acknowledged to be a highly inefficient method of redistribution. They may, however, be one of the most efficient methods that would receive political support.

To sum up: Ten years ago, almost all North American economists smugly regarded rent controls as the folly of the unenlightened; if all citizens were required to take a course in introductory microeconomics as part of their civics training, rent controls would disappear. Recent developments in economic thought have shaken, though not destroyed, this general belief, and have caused a reassessment and a reevaluation of rent controls, which draws on more sophisticated, but less certain, views of rent controls, the housing market, the economy, and the state. . . .

3. Themes

The Roundtable went on for four days. The topics of the four days were "Description of Different Jurisdictions' Experience" (Los Angeles, Ontario, New York City, the United Kingdom, Sweden, Israel, and Bangalore, India); "What Have We Learned about the Effects of Rent Control;" "Rent Control and Housing Policy;" and "Ontario's Options vis-à-vis Rent Control." The distillation of the discussion at the Roundtable into themes as well as my comments on them are colored by my own perceptions.

3.1   Different Jurisdictions' Experience

Despite the swell of revisionism referred to earlier concerning the effects and desirability of rent controls, the various jurisdictions' experts were unanimous in their opinion that rent controls have been harmful. In Los Angeles, where they have been mild, they have been an irritant; in Ontario, where they have been in effect for thirteen years and have been moderate, they have had a significant negative impact on the functioning of the market; in New York City, the United Kingdom, Sweden, and Israel, which have had strict controls over a long period, they have severely impeded the functioning of not only the housing market but also the labor market.

The experts were also virtually unanimous on the qualitative impacts of controls: reduced maintenance and accelerated deterioration of the rental housing stock; shrinkage of the private rental housing stock due to demolition, abandonment, conversion, and a fall in the rate of private rental construction; relatedly, a switch toward owner-occupied and public rental housing; mismatch of households to housing units; excess demand phenomena (low vacancy rates, key money and other black and grey market activities); and reduced mobility, which has caused significant distortions in the labor market.

While the evidence provided by each paper was hardly conclusive (e.g., no attempt was made to control for other housing policies or other factors) the unanimity of expert opinion made a strong impression.

A more muted theme was that long-term rent controls, while harmful, are not devastating. Politicians do not stand idly by while the housing market disintegrates; they introduce other policies to offset the deleterious effects of controls, may turn a blind eye to illegal or quasi-legal housing market activity, and may encourage selective and lax enforcement of the rent control ordinances by, for example, underfunding.

The "old lady who swallowed a fly," while not so named, played a role in all the papers. To offset the problems induced by controls, government intervention in the housing market becomes increasingly extensive, incursive, and byzantine, until, in some jurisdictions, the rental housing *market* is essentially replaced by government allocation. A related theme is that the longer controls have been in place, the harder they are to dismantle. Controls confer substantial windfall gains to sitting tenants, which they will fight hard to retain.

A final theme, which came up throughout the Roundtable, is that rent control is not a monolithic policy. A rent control policy is a package of quite disparate provisions that differ substantially from one jurisdiction to the next. The effects of different jurisdictions' programs may be significantly different.

Qualifications notwithstanding, the message from the review of different experiences was clarion: In the jurisdictions surveyed, rent controls have been harmful and have seriously impeded the functioning of the housing economy. . . .

NOTES AND QUESTIONS ON THE ECONOMICS OF RENT CONTROL

1. Arnott's essay serves as the introduction to a symposium in which members of the Roundtable appraise rent controls in various locales. The report on Ontario, which adopted rent controls in 1975, is particularly dramatic. Starts of unsubsidized rental housing fell in that province from an average of 27,999 per year during 1971-1974 (the pre-control period), to an average of 5,512

in 1975-1979. Lawrence B. Smith, An Economic Assessment of Rent Controls: The Ontario Experience, 1 J. Real Est. Fin. & Econ. 217, 222-223 (1988). What events, other than imposition of rent control, might have contributed to this sharp falloff?

2. Arnott asserts that many economists now see efficiency and equity as "inextricably intertwined." On this point, compare supra p. 117, Note 8 (sources on the relative merits of various methods of income redistribution).

3. Assess Arnott's statement that "Rent controls are generally acknowledged to be a highly inefficient method of redistribution. They may, however, be one of the most efficient methods that would receive political support." Of what plausibility and relevance are the findings in Joseph Gyourko & Peter Linneman, Equity and Efficiency Aspects of Rent Control, 26 J. Urb. Econ. 54 (1989), that the benefits of New York City's rent controls, although slightly progressive, disproportionately favor whites and are highly unequal within income groups? To what extent does political support for rent control derive from loss aversion, the psychological disposition described supra pp. 222-224? Might rent control be an effective method of forestalling political unrest that might lead to policies that are even more inefficient than rent regulation itself? See Roe, Backlash, supra p. 103.

4. In Note 3, supra p. 272, a residential leasehold is envisioned as a continuing relationship in which both the landlord and tenant are capable of employing informal sanctions, including exiting from the relationship. In practice, rent controls restrict exit opportunities. A landlord is generally prohibited from removing a sitting tenant who tenders the controlled rent. A tenant is unlikely to want to relinquish a dwelling that rents at a below-market rate, especially if the rent regulations have created shortages in the local housing market. By eviscerating social control through the threat of exit, might rent control lessen cooperation between landlords and tenants? For the hypothesis that rent control contributed to a general drop in civility in New York City, see Robert C. Ellickson, Rent Control: A Comment on Olsen, 67 Chi.-Kent L. Rev. 947, 948-949 (1991). For anecdotes that support this hypothesis, see Jeffrey Toobin, Shotgun Eviction: Did New York's Rent-Control Laws Drive a Landlord to Murder?, The New Yorker, Dec. 11, 2000, at 48.

5. In subsequent work, Arnott continues to condemn first-generation (hard) rent controls, but argues that imperfections in housing markets conceivably may justify second-generation (soft) controls. See Richard Arnott, Time for Revisionism on Rent Control?, 9 J. Econ. Persp. 99 (Winter 1995). Another (cautious) de-

fender of rent controls is Margaret Jane Radin. As the selection reprinted supra p. 8 indicates, Radin favors legal protections of "personhood" interests in property. For this reason she asserts that rent control may be justified to prolong the residencies of current tenants and to protect a community of tenants from forces of gentrification or other change. See Margaret Jane Radin, Residential Rent Control, 15 Phil. & Pub. Aff. 350 (1986).

A university town adopts rent controls. As a result, many former graduate students retain their apartments after their university connections have ceased. Incoming graduate students therefore are forced to live farther from campus. Have the rent controls advanced communitarian objectives?

6. The empirical literature on rent controls is summarized in Anthony Downs, A Reevaluation of Rent Controls (1996). A comprehensive legal overview is Kenneth K. Baar, Guidelines for Drafting Rent Control Laws, 35 Rutgers L. Rev. 723 (1983).

Chapter 9

Land Use and the Environment

A. Servitudes and Private Communities

Covenants and Constitutions*

Richard A. Epstein

Covenants and constitutions: strange bedfellows, but more than alliteration unites them. In this brief paper I shall explore the relationship between them. In order to orient the discussion, my use of the term "covenants" includes all forms of servitudes, easements, and restrictions that one person can place on another's lands. "Constitutions" are the documents that identify and entrench the fundamental law of a state or nation, on matters of both structure and individual rights.

At first blush, the two appear to be polar opposites. The law of covenants is the province only of a hardy band of real estate lawyers with the temerity to master a complex and imposing body of rules; vertical and horizontal privity; affirmative and negative covenants; matters *in esse* and *in posse*; the touch and concern requirement; notice, actual and constructive; and the ins-and-outs of recordation statutes. Constitutions, by contrast, are the province of us all, the stuff of Senate confirmation hearings, and speak to the eternal and universal truths that bind us into a nation.

Appearances can be deceiving, however. I believe that the law

---

*Source: 73 Cornell L. Rev. 906-924 (1988).

of covenants offers an intelligent blueprint for the analysis of constitutional principles. Covenants may govern party-walls and rights of way over back country roads. Their subject matter may be both well defined and permanent, and they may bind as few as two parties. But there is nothing about the logic of covenants that restricts them to two-party transactions with simple objectives. Covenants are similar in this regard to corporations, which can be closed or public. There are no external limits on the number of parties who can participate in a contract or on the type of issues that it can govern. The logic of contracting is the logic of unanimous consent. As the number of parties to a system of covenants becomes greater and the issues involved more complex, the polar differences between covenants and constitutions diminish. The closer we look at these covenants, the more they look like mini-constitutions. The common literary image of a constitution as a social contract, or even a social covenant, has more literal truth than is often supposed.

I. Covenants

Let us set the stage for analysis with a short discussion of the function and purpose of covenants. To understand their critical role in modern land transactions, it is best first to envision the circumstances in which covenants have no more than peripheral importance. Thus suppose for the moment that land is a very cheap commodity that can be effectively utilized only if owned in fairly large quantities (say for grazing or farming). Under these circumstances, there may be very little need for any system of covenants at all. Each person can live side by side with his neighbor, and each can rejoice in exclusive ownership of an unencumbered fee simple absolute in possession. The operative principle is that good fences make good neighbors. But this simple property arrangement has its Achilles heel: two people cannot share a single resource. In consequence there might be some underutilization of land. Nonetheless these losses are perhaps smaller than the costs necessary to correct them. Covenants are not cheap to draft and enforce, especially in the era before recordation. So long as transaction costs are positive, the set of efficient solutions cannot involve the realization of all possible gains from trade. Where the gains from trade are smaller than the sum of both sides' transaction costs, then the trade will not take place.

Now let us suppose that the value of land has increased dramatically, whether from an increased demand for farm produce, or from an increased demand for housing in an especially fashionable part of town. Under these circumstances, the balance shifts between the two costs identified above. The losses from the underutilization of land become very large, relative to the transaction costs of creating some legal system that allows more intensive use of the land, and the system of joint control and divided use that it requires. Once the costs of contracting become lower than the economic gains from contracting, we should expect to see voluntary contracts emerge. An increase in the frequency of covenants goes hand in hand with increases in underlying real estate values. . . .

A number of legal and institutional developments have fostered desirable voluntary exchanges. It is worthwhile to spend time on two: recordation and common plan building schemes.

A.   Recordation

The system of recordation is an indispensable aid for the effective use of any form of covenant. In the age before recordation, no one could be sure whether a restriction binding upon the immediate parties could also be enforced by or against third parties. The resulting uncertainty was very large, and it fed back into the initial willingness to control land by covenants. As land is permanent, it is only a matter of time before the original parties to the transaction sell their interests or die. Covenantees want to be able to make decisions about the construction of long-term improvements, but cannot do so if the protection they have purchased can be defeated whenever the original covenantor makes a strategic sale to a third party who is then rid of the covenant. The covenantor, for his part, will not be able, *ex ante*, to command the highest price if he cannot assure the covenantee that his successor in title will be bound by the restriction in question. The first transaction itself may therefore abort, so that the subsequent purchaser is denied the benefit of the purchase that ties the acquisition of the land to acceptance of the servitude. The point remains true, moreover, even if no cash changes hands, as frequently happens when each party's consideration is a reciprocal covenant (such as a covenant not to build above a certain height).

The concern with binding strangers did not preclude the running of covenants before the rise of recordation statutes. Roughly speaking, the rule then was that covenants could only bind subsequent takers if they had notice, actual or constructive, of the covenant.[4] The uncertainties about notice were powerful enough that they doubtless precluded many useful transactions from taking place at all. With recordation, the problem of notice disappears in all but the most unusual case. The covenantee simply records his interest in the appropriate deed or plot index; title companies then memorialize it on their own records; and all subsequent takers are now in position to assess the state of the title, and act accordingly, either by adjusting the purchase price for land to take into account the restrictions that benefit or burden it, or by not purchasing at all. The work is all routine and ministerial — a notable social triumph of the humdrum.

In my view, the recording system renders unnecessary many of the arcane features of the law of covenants that might have made sense in the prior age. The requirement that covenants "touch and concern" the land may well have made sense in an age before recordation; those covenants that did touch and concern the land were more likely to be detected by subsequent purchasers than those that were purely personal to the parties. Similarly, it might have been more difficult from an inspection of the premises to discover whether the seller had undertaken some affirmative obligation to a neighboring landowner. But now that the system of recordation is in place, the notice issue is typically solved in an explicit, sensible, and well-nigh decisive fashion, rendering unnecessary the need for the clumsy proxies that still survive in the law.

The limitation of valid covenants to those that touch and concern land, and the prohibition on affirmative obligations, are not, I believe, of much practical consequence, because there are very few persons who really would want as a business matter to tie either type of undertaking to the ownership of real property — who would want the assignee of a covenantor to prepare his income taxes? Even so, some famous institutional cases have turned on either or both these requirements. Thus the decision in Neponsit Property Owners' Association, Inc. v. Emigrant Industrial Savings Bank[8] was necessary to quell some residual doubt whether the obligation to pay money to a property owners' association touched and concerned the land, or fell afoul of New York's stringent rule against affirmative covenants. Clearly no common ownership association could survive at all without these standard covenants, any more than a government could survive without any power to

---

4. The modern law starts with Tulk v. Moxhay, 2 Ph. 774, 41 Eng. Rep. 1143 (Ch. 1848), which allowed restrictive covenants to run in equity against the purchasers who took with notice of them.

8. . . . 15 N.E. 2d 793 ([N.Y.] 1938).

tax. . . . The result in *Neponsit* is a happy one, but it could have been better reached by jettisoning the older restrictions on covenants, now that recordation statutes are in place.

A contrary position on recordation and notice is taken by Professor Alexander in his provocative paper, Freedom, Coercion, and the Law of Servitudes.[10] His attack takes place on several levels and deserves an answer here. His most general argument is that one cannot assume that interested parties are rational or understand the terms found in covenants. "[P]eople *do* engage in irrational behavior." Stated in this form, the argument extends far more broadly than the law of covenants. Indeed, if treated as a general description of human conduct, it undermines the possibilities of any form of intelligent organization whatsoever. Under this view, private bargains are unacceptable because they are doomed by ignorance and exploitation. Yet by the same token, political solutions are doomed as well, because irrationality is hardly cured in a regime that requires imperfect actors to navigate the many pitfalls of collective action. If people cannot contract intelligently, then how can they vote? The assumption of systemic irrationality is a general nonstarter from which only universal skepticism follows. . . .

B. Common Building Plans

The previous discussion shows how the rules of recordation help facilitate transactions that bind three or more persons. Recordation itself is not sufficient for that purpose and the law has also developed effective rules to allow covenants to be created that benefit and bind a large number of persons, such as the members of a subdivision, condominium, or cooperative. There is an evident transactional problem here if covenants can only exist between two persons in privity. The extent of the difficulty is fully revealed by a simple mathematical calculation. If there are n persons, then there must be pairwise contracts among all of them, so that:

$$\sum_{i=1}^{n} n - 1$$

is the minimum number of separate contracts to bind everyone to everyone else. Alternatively, if it is possible for all persons to bind

10. Alexander, Freedom, Coercion, and the Law of Servitudes, 73 Cornell L. Rev. 883 (1988).

each other by dealing with a common party (usually the developer) who stands at the middle of the circle, then n contracts (one between each person and the developer) suffice to create a network in which all persons can be bound and benefited by a set of reciprocal contracts.

Where n is very small, the transactional difference between the two methods of contracting is not significant. In order to contract with a common agent at the middle it is necessary to set up that agent but the costs of that institution can be spread only over a very small number of contracts. If the effort is to link only three people, there will have to be three contracts no matter whether they go around the sides of the triangle or through a fourth point at the middle. The system of three pairwise contracts, moreover, might be cheaper because the costs of setting up the common party at the center are avoided. As the numbers get large, as is typical with modern real estate when land becomes valuable, then there is a pronounced advantage to contracting through the central point. Thus for n equal to 100, the number of pairwise contracts required is, by the well-known formula:

$$\sum_{i=1}^{n} n - 1 = n(n-1)/2, \text{ equal to } 4950,$$

while the number of contracts through the center is only 100. At that point it would long since have been cost effective to incur the heavy front-end fixed costs of instituting a central party through whom all individual landowners are able to contract. The marginal costs of adding a single new member to the group are low when governance runs through the center, but they would be astronomical if 101 new contracts have to be separately formed. In addition, the costs of maintaining the contract network are reduced as well, for no longer is it necessary to modify, for example, 4950 existing separate contracts. Instead it should be possible to make changes in one single master arrangement in accordance with predetermined decision rules.

The law of covenants had an intuitive sense of the real economies of scale that have developed in this area. The rules for common building plans or schemes allow a promoter to insure that all purchasers of individual units stand in a position of perfect parity with one another, regardless of when they purchase their units, by inserting proper ("intent to run") language in the original deeds and faithfully recording all documents. The flexibility of this way of doing business should be manifest. The developer can now assure the first round of buyers that subsequent takers will be bound; thereafter, the developer can also assure subsequent rounds of buyers that prior takers are bound. Buyers can remain happily ignorant of the details of the scheme, precisely because it works so well. Over time, individual units may fluctuate in value, but these differences can be handled by adjustments in purchase price or financing terms without any alteration of the basic network of covenants.

In effect, the rules show the advantages of standard form contracts when there are a large number of parties. By reducing transaction costs, common building plans effectively allow vast numbers of individuals to make use of certain common areas or to benefit from the mutual restrictions and requirements on use. They become ever more important today when the high price of land makes the ideal of separate and self-contained ownership a luxury that few people who want glamour in the city or quiet at the beach can afford.

Professor Alexander sees in these rules some "particularly insidious form of coercion because it purports to effectuate private intentions rather than acknowledging that private volition is being sacrificed for the sake of some collective good." But where is the coercion or sacrifice? Of coercion there is none, unless the discrete purchase or sale is infected with duress or fraud, issues that the ordinary law of contract can handle (as it has for ages). Of sacrifice there is none either: the system of sequential contracts will only go forward if, at *every* point in the chain, both parties to the contract think that they are better off with the agreement than without it. The constant effort to conflate close choices and hard bargains with coercion is of a piece with the effort to conflate agreement with theft, and scarcity with coercion. Of course there will be some transactions in which prospective consumers find themselves making close marginal calls; that is not evidence of coercion, but only of negatively sloped demand curves.

II. The Problems of Governance: Externalities, Transaction Costs, and Intergenerational Effects

The combined effect of the recordation and building plan rules should by now be clear. Recordation is an effective way to control the externalities associated with covenants, while building plans reduce the cost of transacting among large numbers of covenantees. Nonetheless several related inquiries need still to be answered: Are there any externalities that recordation does not address? Are there any transactional difficulties that cannot be overcome by the principles of serial contracting made possible by the building plan rules? What implications do these difficulties have for the enforcement of covenants?

The most obvious way in which recordation systems control the problem of externalities is to give notice to the rest of the world of the state of the title of any person whom a network of covenants binds or benefits. Within this framework, some might fear a different kind of externality: that the substance of that network of covenants will be in some way objectionable. This fear is misplaced, because the original developer (like the corporate promoter intent upon maximizing his profit from a venture) has all the right incentives to offer the ideal mix of burdens and benefits. If he offers inferior terms, then his return from sales will suffer because the price that he can command in the market for the units will be reduced. It seems clear from common practice that few developers think that their unit owners are happy with the limited "no invasion" type restrictions that are associated with the common law of nuisance. Nuisance-type prohibitions against noise, smells, and discharges remain part and parcel of any common ownership system, but they do not begin to exhaust the class of restrictions that are routinely included in any common real estate venture. Most planned developments contain detailed restrictions concerning height, decor, and maintenance. These restrictions may look byzantine to an outsider, but they are likely to make sense because the party who imposes them has everything to lose if they are made either too stringent or too relaxed.

Some have questioned whether there are certain kinds of externalities that the above analysis does not reach. Here in particular three types should be discussed: monopoly, discrimination, and intergenerational effects — the last with reference to the doctrine of changed conditions. All involve possible harms to third persons that might not be internalized by an original owner of the land. . . .

A. Monopoly

As regards monopoly, the source of the concern is that the single developer of a large project may be able to exert some market power. The argument is always plausible with regard to land because it is an asset, fixed in location, that can have (almost by definition) only imperfect substitutes located some distance away. The question of monopoly power, however, generates different responses for different kinds of covenants. Those restrictions that are perfectly reciprocal (e.g., that relate to appearance and height) do not seem to raise any concerns under the monopoly model. If there is a monopoly problem in this context, it arises from the ability of the original developer (who may be protected by zoning restrictions on nearby parcels) to extract a monopoly price from his own purchasers. If some form of public control is found necessary, it need not be tied to the law of covenants. For in his efforts to extract monopoly rents, the developer, as already observed, has every incentive to supply the ideal set of restrictions for all his parcels: he can maximize his monopoly return in this way. The proper types of response, therefore, are numerous. The law could place some restrictions on price, for which the risks of overreaction are manifest; it could limit the size of certain subdivisions under common ownership, but only at the cost of some arguable efficiencies in operation; or ideally, it could remove whatever legal restrictions block the entry of other developers into the local market. . . .

B. Antidiscrimination

Restrictive covenants have also been used to exclude persons from certain real estate developments because of their race or religion. As a matter of American constitutional and statutory law, these covenants are now universally regarded as illegal, precisely because of their adverse effects on third parties. My purpose here is not to assess the desirability of the constitutional rules or statutes but only to stress again the general point. Any concern with antidiscrimination is best attacked head on. . . .

C. Intergenerational Effects: The Problem of Changed Conditions

The last possible source of externalities has to do with the intergenerational effects of a system of restrictive covenants. Within the traditional legal framework this problem is brought to the fore in connection with the so-called doctrine of changed conditions. This doctrine holds that a restrictive covenant is no longer enforceable, at least without modification, when the social and environmental conditions existing when the covenant was created no longer apply. In effect the doctrine of changed conditions allows the courts to expunge covenants from the records, or at least modify their provisions, once the court determines that the covenants no longer serve the purpose for which they were first introduced. In one sense, therefore, the doctrine of changed conditions is a slightly more robust form of the doctrine of frustration of purpose as it exists in the general law of contract. But the doctrine of changed conditions has a more distinctive and coercive cast.

Courts may invoke it to invalidate covenants notwithstanding the parties' express contractual intent to be bound in perpetuity unless released by contrary unanimous agreement.

The battleground here is a familiar one: Should the doctrine of changed conditions operate as a plausible default rule or as a rule of public regulation? I have already taken the position that it should fill the former, and more modest, office once the recordation system gives all parties notice of the relevant conditions. So long as all the original parties have themselves taken into account the need for future change it is highly unlikely that the legal system, which operates with very inexact knowledge of their private preferences and subjective costs, can find a rule that works better than the one that the parties themselves have agreed upon. . . .

This basic point that freedom of contract should govern is, I think, correct, but the matter of holdouts, and the bilateral monopoly problems they generate, does require more discussion. . . .

Initially, it will be instructive to draw some distinctions between the small and large number cases. Where there are, for example, only two parties to a covenant, there is much to be said for the simple rule that protects it for all time and under all circumstances. Thus the normal right of way over a servient tenement is generally regarded as valid in perpetuity, just like the fee. To be sure, there can be limitations upon the easement by contract, but as a constructional matter, the safe preference is to resist the application of the changed circumstances doctrine and to enforce the easement so long as the holder of the dominant tenement has not abandoned its use. The holder of the servient tenement who wants release from the easement must purchase it at an agreed price.

The more difficult issues arise at the other end of the spectrum when the law of covenants is pressed into the service of modern condominium and cooperative associations. In this context, should the doctrine of changed circumstances have greater sway? As is so often the case, it is critical to distinguish between the *ex ante* and *ex post* effect of the rules. *Ex post* it is clearly in some people's interest to have the right to hold out. This right may be awkward to exercise when it is apparent that consent is withheld only to extract a profit from others but it may nonetheless still have real positive value. In many cases the covenant continues to be of some value to a covenantee. As there is no ready market value for the release of the covenant, the holdout can conceal his advantage[-] taking as a defense of the subjective value he enjoys in keeping the covenant alive. Others' inability to draw a clear operational line between subjective value (thought good) and holdout value (thought bad) is great enough in practice that the determined and subtle holdout artist has a good deal of room to maneuver before he is detected and perhaps disgraced.

From the *ex ante* perspective, however, the desirability of allowing holding out takes on a very different complexion. . . . The developer who can find a way to limit holdout problems will . . . be able to command a higher total price for the units that he sells than one who cannot. We should therefore expect him to take some effort in that direction, even if preventing the holdout problem from arising is itself a task that consumes resources. The gains from investing in legal structure are likely to be substantial.

Just such an effort is made in fashioning the rules whereby covenants can be modified or removed. The holdout problem occurs in its most extreme form when unanimous consent is necessary to release lands from the restrictions imposed by covenants. The problem is identical to that which any organization, governmental or voluntary, faces when it can pass a law or resolution only by unanimous consent. Most voluntary groups recognize this problem. In response to it, they provide *by original unanimous consent* for a set of decision rules that allows some fraction, usually a majority by legal interest or number, to reverse the original decisions. So long as it is not possible to forecast perfectly, some such discretion will be needed in any system of governance. Majority rule can be introduced into networks of covenants that are part and parcel of building plans, and frequently is. In some cases where the restrictions are largely negative in type, it may be possible for any party to the covenants, upon the signature of some fraction of the total units, to free his own unit from the restrictions in question. Thus we can find majority rule provisions for modification without government command. In other cases where the interdependence between the units is greater, it might be necessary for the party to run through formal deliberation in a forum provided for in the original agreements.

The connection between covenants and constitutions should now be explicit. In both cases the ultimate task is to protect individual rights to property without inviting excessive holdout problems. A rule that allowed a majority of unit owners to do whatever it pleased with regard to restrictive covenants in place would rightly be perceived as unfair: there would be too much scope for advantage-taking. It would be quite unthinkable for the majority to be able to vote to release all its units from the force of the covenants while continuing to impose those covenants upon others; this would be indistinguishable from a corporation's majority shareholders voting a dividend for themselves and denying it to the minority, or from the majority of citizens voting to confiscate the property of some minority faction. But by the same token, any absolute protection of individual rights with an individual veto reintroduces the same problem of holdout that every system of collective governance wishes to overcome.

We therefore are driven to some mixed system of entrenched rights, compensation tests, and majority rule — all messy, and all necessary. . . .

The choices involved are both vexing and important, and I shall not try to choose in the abstract among veto rights, majority rule, compensation, and their many variations and combinations. Instead my point is more modest. So long as we know that the original owner of the property was aware of these difficulties, then the basic analysis still holds: there is no need for any public doctrine of changed conditions to limit the scope and effect of private covenants. The intermediate solutions found in the standard agreements are likely those that, in the long run, tend to minimize the total breakdown. In this light, it becomes all the more dangerous simply to invalidate a covenant on a wholesale basis, and thereby to ignore the explicit protections that the parties themselves have drafted, including those that allow for introducing some change in the existing structure.

Of course, the parties' inability to draft with perfect foresight and completeness necessarily means that courts will have to engage in some "interstitial legislation" in constructing the terms of the basic agreement. No set of agreements governs all contingencies and something has to be done to fill up the gaps. . . .

. . . While there is doubtless some small place for the doctrine of changed conditions to operate on agreements that are incomplete, it should have at best a tiny importance once [internal] governance structures are in place. . . .

NOTES AND QUESTIONS ON PRIVATE LAND RESTRICTIONS

1. Is Epstein sweeping too broadly in likening private land restrictions ("covenants") to constitutions, or even in likening simple two-party covenants to more complex multiparty ones? Is a simple two-party covenant, such as a common driveway agreement, really a close relative of the complex covenants of a condominium association or a large planned community such as Columbia, Maryland, or Reston, Virginia? Consider the feasibility of requirements for unanimous consent to alter covenant schemes:

Is it important, for example, to have nonunanimous "sunset" rules (such as "changed conditions") to extinguish two-party covenants? Is it important to have them in multiparty contexts? Do constitutions ever contemplate unanimity at all, either at the initiation or amendment stage?

2. Epstein argues that the advent of the recordation system permits courts to dispense with many of the traditional hedges around covenants, on the theory that those hedges were basically aimed at assuring notice to purchasers; presumably recordation now can take over the notice function. Is that all that the hedges can or should do? Recall Merrill & Smith's justifications of the *numerus clausus* principle that limits the proliferation of forms of property holdings. See supra p. 360. Did the traditional hedges on covenants serve to reduce the information costs of prospective purchasers of real estate? Can you imagine a less arcane set of hedges that would better serve that purpose?

3. Is Epstein's embrace of majority-rule devices a tacit concession that no one can see into the future accurately, even with the most careful planning? For an extensive development of the ways that the shortsightedness problem plays out in older servitude rules, see Stewart E. Sterk, Freedom from Freedom of Contract: The Enduring Value of Servitude Restrictions, 70 Iowa L. Rev. 615 (1985).

4. Gregory Alexander, one of the leading critics of developer-created covenant schemes, asserts that a planned community may become a "tight little island" in which an internal majority coerces an internal minority, and where community residents ignore the negative effects of their policies on outsiders. See Gregory S. Alexander, Dilemmas of Group Autonomy: Residential Associations and Community, 75 Cornell L. Rev. 1 (1989). First, on the issue of the possible coercion of an internal minority, does it matter that the unit owner's investment is in a *home*? Compare Radin, Property and Personhood, supra p. 8. Do the possible abuses of majority rule suggest that planned community self-rule should be limited in ways analogous to the constraints on majority rule in political communities? See Stewart E. Sterk, Minority Protection in Residential Private Governments, 77 B.U. L. Rev. 273 (1997), and the exchange between Robert C. Ellickson, Cities and Homeowners Associations, 130 U. Pa. L. Rev. 1519 (1982), and Gerald E. Frug, Cities and Homeowners Associations: A Reply, 130 U. Pa. L. Rev. 1589 (1982). Does the threat that a member may exit from an association adequately deter majoritarian abuse? For general praise of both majoritarianism and exit rights, see Hanoch Dagan & Michael A. Heller, The Liberal Commons, 110 Yale L.J. 549 (2001).

5. How might outsiders suffer from association rules? Do anti-discrimination laws suffice to keep planned development residents from isolating themselves from the larger community? For example, could planned community rules establish de facto income requirements that have discriminatory effects but are beyond the reach of antidiscrimination legislation? Is de facto income discrimination a greater risk in planned communities than in neighborhoods made up by individual sales of homes? In the latter, what role might be played by zoning laws that restrict homes exclusively to single-family houses? See the selections on public land use controls, infra pp. 437-469.

Assume that a developer would profit by creating a gated community that is walled off from surrounding areas. What is the risk that the gated enclave would interfere with traffic circulation in the vicinity, deflect criminal activity to unwalled areas, and create social unrest of the sort analyzed by Roe in "Backlash," supra p. 103? What (if any) legal restrictions on the developer's physical plans and the community governance system would be appropriate? See David J. Kennedy, Note, Residential Associations as State Actors: Regulating the Impact of Gated Communities on Nonmembers, 105 Yale L.J. 761 (1995). See generally Edward J. Blakely & Mary Gail Snyder, Fortress America: Gated Communities in the United States (1997).

Or do the benefits of enabling housebuyers to choose among a diverse mosaic of living environments outweigh the external costs associated with the emergence of some "tight little islands"? Compare the Tiebout hypothesis, discussed infra in Note 11, p. 502, which envisions households as "voting with their feet" among local governments. On the structural virtues of giving wide scope to private associations of all kinds, see Roderick M. Hills, Jr., The Constitutional Rights of Private Governments (Nov. 12, 2001) (unpublished manuscript).

6. Empirical studies support Epstein's prediction that the imposition of a covenant scheme typically will enhance property values within the controlled area. See William T. Hughes & Geoffrey K. Turnbull, Uncertain Neighborhood Effects and Restrictive Covenants, 39 J. Urb. Econ. 160 (1996); and the study by Janet Spreyer discussed infra Note 1, p. 468. Do these findings clinch the case in favor of covenants?

For descriptions of homeowner associations in action, see Robert Jay Dilger, Neighborhood Politics: Residential Community Associations in American Governance (1992), and Common Interest Communities (Stephen E. Barton & Carol J. Silverman eds., 1994). One of the most closely watched experiments in covenant-control is the Disney-planned town of Celebration, Florida, which draws mixed appraisals in Andrew Ross, The Celebration Chronicles: Life, Liberty, and the Pursuit of Property Value in Disney's New Town (1999), and Michael Pollan, Town-Building Is No Mickey Mouse Operation, N.Y. Times, Dec. 14, 1997, at 56.

B.   Public Land Use Controls

A Walk Along Willow: Patterns of Land Use Coordination in Pre-Zoning New Haven (1870-1926)*

Andrew J. Cappel

. . . [T]he last thirty years have witnessed a lively debate between supporters and opponents of zoning. Supporters base their arguments on the explicit or implicit assumption that rational land use decisions cannot be made without public controls. Without zoning, the argument goes, incompatible uses, such as apartments and commercial or industrial enterprises, would encroach upon low-density residential neighborhoods — thus decreasing residential property values. In addition, uncontrolled development would place severe burdens on school systems, road networks, and other aspects of urban infrastructure and could cause environmental damage. Supporters of zoning buttress their argument by relying on an historical narrative which credits the rise of zoning to the failure of the earlier, unzoned legal regime, based primarily on common law nuisance, to promote adequately coordinated land use.[9]

Opponents of zoning, on the other hand, claim that zoning diverts land to less efficient uses, is costly to administer, and is susceptible to processes of municipal corruption. Critics also argue that zoning allows communities to exclude racially or economically undesired groups and may increase the cost of available housing for such groups. They have also cast doubts upon the ability of local authorities to predict future community land use needs ac-

---

*Source: Note, 101 Yale L.J. 617-637 (1991).

9. This narrative was constructed by zoning advocates during the first decades after zoning achieved widespread implementation in the United States. See, e.g., Edward M. Bassett, Zoning 22-26 (1936); 1 James Metzenbaum, The Law of Zoning 7-11, 65-68 (2d ed. 1955). . . .

curately when drawing up a comprehensive plan.[11] Suggested reforms range from proposals to curtail sharply the role of government (especially local government) in controlling land use to outright abolition of zoning.

The assumption underlying all of these criticisms is that market forces, in conjunction with popular social and aesthetic norms, will produce a system of satisfactorily coordinated land use without the defects associated with a zoned legal regime. The pioneering work on this subject was done by Bernard Siegan, who studied land use patterns in Houston, the only major unzoned city in the United States.[13] Concentrating on representative types of commercial use, such as gas stations and automobile dealerships, and on selected residential districts, Siegan concluded that Houston had attained roughly the same degree of land use coordination — especially segregation of incompatible uses, a traditional objective of zoning — as cities operating under zoned legal regimes.[14] Results of a handful of other studies of land use patterns in major American cities prior to the enactment of zoning ordinances at least partially support the notion that coordinated land use can arise under an unzoned legal system.[15]

All of these studies concern themselves with large, metropolitan areas and thus are necessarily impressionistic; moreover, most of them focus only on selected types of land use. In contrast, this Note constitutes the first attempt to look at an unzoned regime on a microlevel, block-by-block. It examines all of the aspects of land use that zoning traditionally regulates: building coverage, height, use, lot size, yards, and setbacks. The goal of this study is not to come to a definitive conclusion concerning the desirability of zoning as compared to a less regulated system of land use control. Rather, it seeks to provide empirical evidence, on the microlevel of neighborhood development, of the ways in which a community without zoning succeeded in achieving rational land use coordi-

---

11. See Jan Z. Kranowiecki, The Fallacy of the End-State System of Land Use Control, Land Use L. & Zoning Dig., Apr. 1986, at 3.

13. Bernard H. Siegan, Non-Zoning in Houston, 13 J.L. & Econ. 71 (1970); Bernard H. Siegan, The Houston Solution: The Case for Removing Public Land Use Controls, Land Use Controls Q., Summer 1970, at 1 [hereinafter Siegan, Houston Solution].

14. See Siegan, Houston Solution, supra note 13, at 1. But cf. John Mixon, Neighborhood Zoning for Houston, 31 S. Tex. L. Rev. 1 (1990). Mixon argues that Houston's unzoned system has failed in important aspects of land use coordination, particularly in preserving residential areas (and residential property values) from damage resulting from the proximity of incompatible commercial and industrial uses.

15. See Roger W. Lotchin, San Francisco 1846-1856 (1974); Sam B. Warner, Jr., Streetcar Suburbs (2d ed. 1978) (urban development in Boston, 1870-1900). . . .

nation. This study offers a contribution to the larger contemporary debate concerning optimal forms of land use control by documenting the following: (1) the degree of land use coordination that can arise under an unzoned legal regime; (2) the extent to which any such coordinated land use may arise from economic and social forces, rather than from formal legal controls; and (3) the circumstances under which public regulations are effective in influencing private choices about land use and the circumstances under which they are relatively ineffective in doing so. In addition, this Note will cast some doubt upon the validity of the prevailing pro-zoning historical narrative: Contrary to this narrative, my research suggests that zoning might not always have been adopted in response to serious failures of the unzoned legal regime.

The subject of my research is New Haven, Connecticut, from 1870 to 1926. The study starts at the same time the city began the largest urban expansion in its history and concludes in 1926 with the enactment of its first zoning ordinance. New Haven offers a number of advantages for a study of this nature. It is representative of medium-sized cities that warmly embraced zoning during the 1920s. As an early, well-developed commercial and industrial center, as well as a center of rail transportation, New Haven possessed an abundance of the types of land uses thought to be incompatible with the preservation of residential neighborhoods. Like most medium-sized and large American cities, New Haven had a heterogeneous population composed of Yankees, Italian and Irish immigrants, and small Jewish and Black communities; it is therefore unlikely that any observed patterns of coordinated land use can be attributed to particular cultural characteristics of individual ethnic groups. Local historians have left extremely thorough documentation of the city's history, and printed records are available for all of the city's Board of Aldermen meetings during the period 1870-1926. Above all, we can trace the development of land use in pre-zoning New Haven through a remarkable series of maps, dated 1886, 1901, and 1923, that were developed for use by fire insurance companies. These maps specify the exact location, height, and mass of every structure in the city, and also specify each structure's use, such as commercial, industrial, or residential, and single or multifamily.

My research has concentrated on a seventeen block, predominantly middle class residential area in the northeast part of the city, between Lawrence and Cold Spring Streets and between Foster and St. Ronan Streets — and in particular, on the "Willow-Canner strip" which consists of the blocks between Willow Street and the south side of Canner from Foster to St. Ronan. On this strip, land use patterns have been analyzed on a lot-by-lot basis. This district has been selected because it is representative of the type of areas opened to development in the post-1870 years and because it is especially well suited for study in conjunction with the fire insurance maps, the first set of which was produced in 1886. Because the northeast residential district was one of the few in the city to remain rural until this time, it offers an exceptional opportunity to follow the growth of a neighborhood from the ground up. . . .

I. Patterns of Land Use

A cursory glance at maps of pre-zoning New Haven reveals an unmistakable pattern: Most industrial and commercial uses were segregated from residential property. In 1912, over sixty percent of manufacturing concerns, including virtually all heavy industry in the city, were located in a relatively small number of locations. . . . Within these areas, industrial concerns tended to group themselves together in discrete units, separated from neighboring housing. The resulting concentration left other portions of the city completely nonindustrial. Thus, in 1923, the northeast residential section of the city contained no manufacturing concerns; factories instead were grouped along its fringes. . . . Similarly, while State Street and the central downtown district were flourishing commercial centers, the area between Lawrence and East Rock Streets possessed only eighteen commercial sites, all but three of which were situated on corners along the north-south thoroughfares of Orange, Anderson, and Foster Streets. These sites did not encroach into the surrounding east-west residential blocks.

Examination of the northeast residential district, in particular of the Willow-Canner strip, reveals other, more subtle patterns of coordinated land use. The very existence of such patterns seems remarkable in light of how most of northeast New Haven was developed in the late nineteenth and early twentieth centuries. There are only occasional examples of developers in the modern sense of the term, who bought large parcels of land on which to build homes for public sale. More commonly, the original rural landowner sold lots directly to individual buyers or to small-scale investors who held the property — generally in groups of four lots or less — for resale. As originally surveyed, lots were of uniform size with fifty-foot frontages, but purchasers could always buy lots with greater or lesser dimensions. After purchase, owners hired their own builders or architects to design and construct their

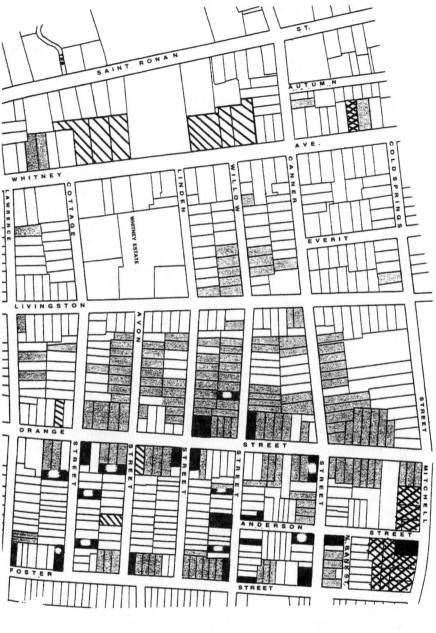

Northeast New Haven in 1923

N

→

Single Family

Two Family

Three Family

Apartments

Commercial

Undeveloped

homes. Thus, the high degree of land use coordination that we find in this area cannot, for the most part, be attributed to the actions of a single planner-owner-builder. New Haven was largely developed house-by-house with the patterns of coordination emerging out of the independent decisions of many individuals.

A. Lot Size

One of the most striking features of the pre-zoning regime was the segregation of lots according to size. From Foster to Orange Streets, lots along Willow and Canner Streets tended to be small, with the majority under 4000 square feet. Sizes increased from Orange to Livingston Streets, where a typical lot measured between 5000 and 7000 square feet. Lots between Livingston and Whitney Avenue ran larger, with half measuring 7000 square feet or more. The largest lots were those from Whitney Avenue to the west, with the majority in excess of 9000 square feet. A glance at the map confirms that this progressive east-west increase in lot size was a dominant characteristic of the entire northeast residential district.

B. Single v. Multifamily Dwellings

The location of single-family houses and two- and three-family "flats" roughly mirrored the segregation of lots, with the number of multifamily homes decreasing from east to west. A number of two-family houses, as well as some three-family, "triple-decker" buildings, were built east of Orange Street. Two-family houses predominated on most blocks between Orange and Livingston Streets, while, moving west, two-family houses appeared less frequently near Whitney Avenue. The area west of Whitney was composed almost exclusively of single-family dwellings.

By 1923, the northeast residential district, like the rest of New Haven, had undergone the phenomenon of multiple unit apartment construction. Here, as with lot size and multifamily home distribution, it is possible to observe a remarkable degree of segregation: While complexes were built along Whitney Avenue and in fringe areas on south Orange and near State, there was no sign of significant encroachment by apartments into the central portion of the residential district.

C. Building Coverage

Despite substantial variations in lot and building size, the houses along Canner and Willow Streets displayed surprising uniformity in building coverage, i.e., the percentage of a lot covered by a structure. Of the 111 sites with reliable documentation, all but twelve had buildings (excluding garages) that covered a third or less of total lot size. In fact, the majority of sites had building coverage of a quarter or less of total lot size, and no building covered more than half its site. Indeed, in the northeast residential district as a whole, only six sites had building coverage greater than fifty percent.

D. Building Height

With the exception of fourteen structures, eight triple-decker residences east of Orange Street, two stores on Foster Street, single houses on Lawrence and Everit Streets, and two apartment complexes on Whitney Avenue (all three stories high), all buildings in the northeast residential district were two and one-half stories or less.

E. Frontyards and Rearyards

Most of the structures on Willow and Canner Streets were generously set back from the street line, often with a notable degree of uniformity. On the north side of Willow Street between Livingston Street and Whitney Avenue, for example, every building was set back exactly twelve feet. On the south side of Canner Street between Whitney and Orange, the closest building stood twelve feet away from the street line, and most of the remaining houses on the block were set back twelve to fifteen feet. Frontyard setbacks were similarly spaced throughout most of the northeast residential district, although the distances diminished somewhat at the eastern edge. Rearyards throughout northeast New Haven were uniformly deeper than thirty feet, and most were greater than forty to fifty feet deep.

F. Sideyards

Sideyards also displayed a great deal of coordination, although it is superficially hard to see. At first glance, the small size of sideyards seems to reflect a weakness in New Haven's prezoning regime. In the northeast residential district, sideyards were small: along the Willow-Canner strip, more than half measured five feet or less. If the distance between houses serves as our standard of measure, however, the proportions were more ample. Few houses were closer to one another than ten feet, and most stood much farther apart than that. Indeed, the size of their separation often compared favorably to the fourteen foot minimum enacted under the 1926 zoning ordinance. Even on the small lots east of Orange Street, only two buildings extended to the lot line, and sufficient space normally existed between buildings to ensure adequate air and light. When an early buyer on a block placed his house near the lot edge, the subsequent purchaser of an adjacent lot would often place his house at the extreme opposite edge of his own lot, setting a pattern followed by subsequent purchasers. For example, prior to 1901, houses were built on the right side of lots at 285-287 and 281-283 Willow Street. When owners built in 1906-1907 on the next two adjacent lots, 279 and 277, they likewise positioned their structures at the far right side. Throughout the northeast residential district, whole lines of buildings on adjacent lots owed their site configuration to this same phenomenon. An informal social mechanism was thus created to resolve a complicated coordination problem.

In sum, on the eve of zoning, the northeast sector constituted a predominantly residential district bordered, but largely unencroached upon, by industrial and commercial sites. Lots gradually increased in size on blocks running from east to west, while the incidence of multifamily homes decreased; apartment construction remained largely confined to Whitney Avenue and areas near State Street. Building heights were low, rearyards large, and, with some exceptions, houses were situated in a roughly uniform manner an ample distance from the street. Landowners do not appear to have economized on land costs by erecting large structures on small lots; building coverage was low and remarkably uniform, and sideyards, although sometimes small, were normally sufficient for light and ventilation. Taken together, these patterns reveal a complex system of land use coordination arising out of the gradual processes of neighborhood development.

II. Land Use Controls Under a Pre-Zoning Legal Regime

The unzoned legal regime, as we have just noted, was capable of producing examples of highly sophisticated land use coordination. What is not clear from the foregoing discussion is the extent to which such coordination arose from the existence of legal rules and regulations as opposed to nonlegal forces. In order to clarify these issues, it is first necessary to outline the essential features of the pre-zoning regime.

A. Public Law: Municipal Ordinances and Regulations

As was the case elsewhere in the country, New Haven's city government underwent a transformation during the course of the second half of the nineteenth century[52] — expanding, with the creation of most of the major city departments, into roughly its current form. With these changes in the size and organization of city government came a vast enlargement in the extent and scope of municipal legislation. For example, the Building Code, which in 1870 took a mere four pages, comprised seventy-three pages of detailed regulations by 1914. Land use regulations were unusually extensive and often painstakingly detailed, with countless pages in the minutes of city council meetings devoted to such issues as whether to allow erection of billboards, theater marquises, and illuminated signs, and whether to permit building cornices to project over the sidewalk.

This did not constitute regulation in the modern sense of zoning, that is, consciously planned public control over the size and location of all types of public and private land uses. In keeping with nineteenth-century laissez faire doctrines, the city charter largely limited the scope of municipal legislation to matters of public property. To the extent that government authority extended over private property, it was restricted within the confines of the police power: prevention of fire, supervision of building safety, prohibition of private encroachment onto public streets and walks, and abatement of public nuisances.

The ordinances enacted under these charter provisions nevertheless covered a wide range of concerns touching upon problems related to land use coordination and urban development. For example, the city controlled the layout of streets in developing areas and approved the plan for private streets that landowners established before selling their parcels to the public. Similarly, the state controlled the location of street railway lines, which, by tying outlying areas to the downtown, constituted the avenues along which urban development took place.

Even before 1870, New Haven had received state authorization to establish building lines that would provide uniform mandatory

---

52. On the 19th-century transformation of urban local government in the United States, see generally Hendrik Hartog, Public Property and Private Power (1983); Robin L. Einhorn, Property Rules (1991). Einhorn's book also provides a valuable discussion of how pre-zoning legal rules, in particular the use of special assessments to finance public works, influenced development patterns in Chicago during the years 1833-1872. See Einhorn, supra, at 61-187.

minimum setbacks along each block. By 1910, however, it had become clear that the city's efforts to establish minimum legal setbacks had proven ineffective: some areas had no building lines; in other areas, there was widespread encroachment of buildings across the designated lines; and many earlier lines were established without the legally mandated assessment of damages and benefits, and were therefore unenforceable. Between 1910 and 1914, the Board of Aldermen, assisted by a newly created Commission on Building Lines, established new lines, confirmed or modified hundreds of existing ones, and passed an ordinance requiring that a building line be established for each new street at the time of its initial layout. The city designated some of these lines on its own initiative, but the majority of these lines appear to have been established in response to petitions of local landowners who desired legally mandated setbacks.

Other land use regulations appeared in the Fire and Building Codes. Most of the downtown area was designated a fire district: Within this area, owners were prohibited from erecting new wooden structures; additions to existing wooden buildings were permitted only after the owner had received special approval from the city; and no such addition could extend closer than five feet to the property line. New wooden construction was permitted outside of the fire district, but wooden houses could not be built to a height greater than three floors. In addition, no existing frame building could be converted into flats containing more than three units, and owners were prohibited from constructing multifamily housing in their rearyards. In 1905, the state enacted legislation regulating construction of "tenements" — multifamily dwellings of more than three units — that mandated maximum building coverage (ninety percent of corner lots, seventy-five percent of others), minimum rearyard sizes (ten feet), and, in most cases, minimum sideyards (four feet). At the same time, a municipal ordinance seeking to guarantee minimum levels of light and ventilation in other buildings imposed a maximum ninety-percent limit on building coverage, except for corner lots, throughout the city.

Finally, New Haven's charter empowered the city to abate nuisances injurious to health or offensive to the public. Under this grant, the city was able to regulate particularly hazardous or noxious uses: Tanneries, sellers of gunpowder and inflammable oils, slaughterhouses, and manufacturers of tallow and soap could not occupy a site without obtaining a special license. The minutes of city council meetings occasionally mention citizen complaints concerning smoke and noise were nuisances emanating from nearby railroad tracks or industrial concerns and specify the actions taken by the city for the abatement of these nuisances.

B. Private Law: Nuisance

Where public nuisance action was impossible, either because the harm was confined to a few neighbors or because those affected by the nuisance sought damages as well as abatement, aggrieved owners found a potent source of relief in the law of private nuisance. In particular, Connecticut law was unusually favorable to local residents in actions against nearby industrial concerns. In Whitney v. Bartholomew, the Connecticut Supreme Court of Errors held that even lawful uses, performed without negligence on the defendant's property, could be considered nuisances if they caused unreasonable damage to a neighbor's health or property.[80] In other decisions, Connecticut courts rejected two common defenses to nuisance actions: plaintiff's coming to the nuisance, and defendant's operating under a city license. To balance the scales somewhat, courts defined "reasonable use" in a flexible manner. Rather than applying an abstract uniform standard, courts held that reasonableness depended not only on the nature of the use, but also on its location; homeowners in industrial districts were expected to endure higher degrees of discomfort from smoke and noise than were their counterparts in more residential areas. Industry was thus protected against sensitive neighbors, and judges had the freedom to allow industrial and residential uses to coexist near one another, while still protecting homeowners from glaring abuses.[84]

III. Legal and Nonlegal Determinants of Coordination

Public and private law in New Haven had the potential to influence land use significantly. By returning to northeast New Haven,

---

80. Whitney v. Bartholomew, 21 Conn. 213, 218-219 (1851).

84. In addition to nuisance suits, the existence of private covenants among landowners could have had a significant impact on local land use patterns. By the mid-nineteenth century, Connecticut courts had upheld the enforceability of covenants running with the land. See Wright v. Wright, 21 Conn. 329 (1851). The issue of covenants need not be studied here in detail, however, since restrictive covenants were not employed in New Haven to any significant extent prior to the 1940s as a method of attaining large-scale coordinated land use. Interview with attorneys Paul North, Jr., and Daniel Dennis, Jr., in New Haven, Conn. (Nov. 20, 1990) (authorities on history of New Haven real estate). For example, with the exception of a number of right-of-way easements . . . none of the lots on the Willow-Canner strip is encumbered by title restrictions.

this Note analyzes the extent to which the existing patterns of co-ordination may have arisen as a response to the regulations of this legal regime or, alternatively, to nonlegal factors.

A. The Role of Law

1. STREET GRID

When preparing an area for development, owners were re-quired to submit plans for new streets for city approval, and such approval was almost invariably granted.[85] City officials seem to have shared with developers and individual buyers a common cul-tural notion of what a residential street should look like, and City Hall — hoping to increase the rate of private homeownership — provided a layout of streets and blocks that was attractive to po-tential buyers. A harmonious combination of public regulation and popular expectations thus gave rise to the familiar street grid of small blocks which were easily divisible into the deep rectangular lots favored by most buyers.

2. SEGREGATION OF USES

The pattern of segregation of industry away from residences appears largely to be rooted in the legal regime. Confronted with proresidential nuisance law, industry tended to congregate in iso-lated districts and blocks. The possibility of a nuisance suit also facilitated coordination between disparate uses by encouraging private abatement agreements. In addition, the flexible juridical no-tion of "reasonable uses" promoted industrial/residential coordi-nation by stimulating construction of inexpensive housing in strips alongside industrial districts whose low cost compensated for the annoyance of smoke and noise.

There are other examples of segregated uses that are attrib-utable to public decision making. In particular, government control over the location of streetcar lines profoundly influenced patterns of neighborhood development. Apartment buildings appeared near Whitney Avenue and State Street where the presence of street-cars made these areas uniquely well suited for multiunit construc-tion. Similarly, the presence of a streetcar line on State Street stimulated a concentration of commercial establishments there. As a result of such concentration, the remainder of the northeast part of the city was left free for low-density residential use.

85. During the period 1870-1926, there was only one case in which the city failed to approve a proposed street plan. . . .

3. SETBACKS

Ironically, building lines, the object of so much municipal regulation, played a relatively minor role in neighborhood development. Along the Willow-Canner strip, most residences failed to
observe the legal limit, and the same pattern can be seen elsewhere
in the city, even after the Board of Aldermen attempted to redesig-
nate the lines between 1910 and 1914. This phenomenon is partly
explained by lax municipal enforcement, but it also reflects a deep
conflict between municipal law and entrenched building custom.
When owners, usually early purchasers on a block, petitioned for
a building line, the city usually designated one a few feet behind
the line of existing structures in order to ensure larger future setbacks. Subsequent purchasers had to choose whether to follow the
mandated line or their neighbors' practice. While examples of both
decisions exist, the latter is more common, reflecting the dominance of local building customs at the time when most of the
northeast residential district was built. The power of this custom
was more evident on blocks like those at the east end of Willow
Street, where there were predominantly uniform setbacks of six to
twelve feet, despite the fact that the law permitted building up to
the street line. This suggests that the law was valuable mainly as
a reinforcement to local practice, encouraging owners to leave adequate, if not always fully legal, setbacks by building as far from
the street as their neighbors. . . .

B. Nonlegal Determinants . . .

Uniformity in height, building coverage, and yards seems
largely attributable to purchaser preferences. A number of magazines at the turn of the century published plans and descriptions
of idealized detached homes characterized by low height, limited
mass, and generous yards of the type found in northeast New Haven. These publications played an important role in shaping popular demand for a certain type of construction. Such uniformity
was furthered by the fact that New Haven possessed relatively few
residential architects and builders whom owners could ask to design their homes, and they tended to build the same type of house
over and over. For example, many of the houses on Willow Street
were designed by two men, William Allen and Frank Brown. Coordinated land use was also promoted by private agreements between individuals: when the owner of lots at 344 and 346 Willow
Street sold the 346 property in 1924, he included in the sales agreement a provision giving him an eight-foot right-of-way easement

over the land directly adjacent to his remaining property, thus preventing the neighbor from building too close to the lot line. In addition, there are examples of informal social norms exerting influence over landowner behavior: archival records reveal instances where individuals encouraged their neighbors to conform to community building standards.

IV. The Introduction of Zoning

In 1926, despite the presence of sophisticated patterns of coordinated land use, New Haven passed its first zoning ordinance. The question therefore arises whether the introduction of zoning occurred as a response to significant failings of the pre-zoning regime or was caused by factors having little or nothing to do with actual conditions of land use in the city. The paucity of source material makes it impossible to give a conclusive answer to this question, but some general observations can be made. Initial interest in zoning appears to have arisen as the result of anxieties associated with the rapid pace of urban growth in the years after 1870.

In the aftermath of the population and building booms of 1870-1910, New Haven was confronted with a shortage of land for development in reasonable proximity to downtown. At the same time, technological advances in transportation and engineering led to the introduction of automobiles and highrise construction in the city. As a result, the city began to experience problems of increased traffic, lack of parking, and congestion caused by the construction of apartments and tall downtown office buildings. Moreover, some homeowners may have become apprehensive that this congestion might force commercial enterprises to locate on residential blocks and thereby cause a decline in nearby residential property values. Concern about these problems appears to have led to fears that the formal and informal controls that had formerly determined land use decision making and safeguarded the interests of property owners might prove inadequate in the face of large-scale demographic and technological change. Such fears persuaded important elements of the city's business and political elites, above all the Chamber of Commerce, to support the City Plan Commission's proposal to adopt zoning as part of a broader scheme of planned urban development. Over time, local advocates of urban planning, armed with theories of the "City Beautiful" movement, which had become prominent throughout the country after its inception at the 1893 Columbian Exposition, came to dominate the discussion of land use controls, and the actual conditions of the city became increasingly irrelevant. Outside consultants educated residents on the theoretical superiority of zoned to unzoned land use, and in 1924 the mayor chided his fellow citizens for failing to adopt the progressive policies already enacted by more enlightened neighbors.

What got lost in this discussion was the fact that the unzoned system appeared to function fairly well. This was clearly the case in residential northeast New Haven, where there was no indication of widespread problems of traffic or of encroachment of high-density or commercial uses onto residential blocks. The scant evidence also suggests that problems of land use coordination were also not acute in the remainder of the city. For example, while several traditionally poor areas of New Haven had degenerated into slums by the 1920s, this process of urban decay appears to have been largely self-contained and did not seem to have spread significantly into surrounding areas. In addition, there is no evidence of widespread popular dissatisfaction with the pre-zoning system. Instead, the mass of small residential and commercial landowners formed some of zoning's most vociferous critics. In 1924, a group of property owners petitioned the Board of Aldermen in opposition to zoning, and public reaction at hearings held in 1925 was overwhelmingly opposed to zoning, as unduly restrictive of owners' rights to find the most profitable use for their properties.

Thus, there never appears to have been a widespread, grass roots perception in New Haven's neighborhoods that the city's pre-zoning regime did not work. Rather, new theories of urban planning fed into and complemented general fears relating to the city's growth and modernization, making zoning supporters view zoning as both necessary and inevitable. The continuing efficacy of the pre-zoning system of land use coordination, however, is confirmed by a glance at provisions of the 1926 zoning ordinance for northeast New Haven: Instead of imposing stricter requirements on the area, the ordinance, with a few exceptions, simply confirmed existing patterns of development. As a result, the great majority of buildings in northeast New Haven were already in substantial compliance with the ordinance's provisions. . . .

. . . Although the results of a single, small-scale study cannot be considered determinative, this study of New Haven casts doubt upon the prevailing assumption that coherent land use cannot take place without the type of planned public regulation represented by zoning. In particular, the results of this survey indicate that where public regulation conflicts with local economic realities or social norms — as was the case with municipal regulation of building lines — such regulation is likely to prove ineffective.[119]

In addition, this study suggests that the introduction of zoning into New Haven was not necessitated by actual conditions of local land use, but rather was the work of certain elites, particularly members of the Chamber of Commerce and City Plan Commission, who were influenced by theories developed as part of the national "City Beautiful" movement. Therefore, in contrast to the narrative traditionally advanced by supporters of zoning, the rapid spread of zoning in the 1920s may well have brought zoning to cities like New Haven where it was not really needed.

NOTES AND QUESTIONS ON THE EVOLUTION AND MERITS OF ZONING

1. How representative is New Haven? The neighborhood Cappel describes? A statistical study with results consistent with Cappel's is Daniel P. McMillen & John F. McDonald, Could Zoning Have Increased Land Values in Chicago?, 33 J. Urb. Econ. 167 (1993) ("We can state definitively that zoning did not increase land values in 1920s Chicago. . . .").

2. Does Cappel provide adequate evidence on the relative influence of custom, public and private nuisance law, and pre-zoning regulations on development in New Haven during 1870-1926? Recall the materials on informal property rights, supra Chapter 6.

How would development proceed in an environment with even fewer legal regulations than New Haven had in 1870-1926 or than Houston has today? In 1993-1994 Jane Larson studied the Mexican-American *colonias* of southern Texas. These unincorporated areas lack not only zoning controls but also building and housing codes, subdivision regulations, and requirements for water and sewer mains and other infrastructure. Her findings, in short: "As market advocates would predict, land and housing in these counties are extraordinarily inexpensive. Housing and environmental conditions, however, are deplorable." Jane E. Larson,

---

119. A similar result was reached as part of a study of patterns of urban change in New Haven several decades after the initiation of zoning. It concluded that when a community is confronted with changes either in economic conditions or in popular expectations concerning land use, "zoning probably does little more than slow down the inevitable." David L. Birch et al., Patterns of Urban Change 71-73 (1974).

Free Markets Deep in the Heart of Texas, 84 Geo. L.J. 179, 182 (1995). Community residents, however, compare life in the *colonias* favorably to their other realistic housing alternatives, in part because it enables over 80 percent of them to be homeowners. See id. at 205-208. Larson concludes by recommending a series of measures to improve life in the *colonias,* including enactment of minimal land use regulations and the mandatory extension of municipal water and sewer services. Who should pay for these service extensions?

3. Cappel's essay indicates the welter of more limited public regulations that preceded zoning. What activities do zoning ordinances govern that these prior legal measures did not? How might one argue that New Haven needed zoning more to control uses with pervasive effects (such as tall buildings) than uses with localized effects (such as backyard garages). Recall Calabresi and Melamed's thoughts on how transaction costs vary with the number of parties, supra pp. 242-243.

On embryonic land use regulations enacted in the seventeenth and eighteenth centuries, see John F. Hart, Colonial Land Use Law and Its Significance for Modern Takings Doctrine, 109 Harv. L. Rev. 1252 (1996); John F. Hart, Land Use Law in the Early Republic and the Original Meaning of the Takings Clause, 94 Nw. U. L. Rev. 1099 (2000).

4. Cappel's study terminates in 1926. What are its current implications, given intervening legal, social, and technological changes? More specifically, Cappel's New Haven lacked large-scale developers and — perhaps as a result — was almost entirely free of land-use covenants until the 1940s. (See Cappel's footnote 84.) Is zoning more or less necessary when developers are large in scale and subdivision covenants routine? Shopping centers have largely supplanted the sorts of mom-and-pop commercial outlets that appear on Cappel's map. Do bigger stores provide a greater justification for zoning?

5. Cappel asserts that members of business and political elites brought zoning to New Haven, even though popular opinion was opposed to it. How widespread is popular support for zoning today? Is it significant that the number of localities with zoning ordinances continues to mount, and that scarcely any have repudiated zoning after first embracing it?

William A. Fischel, The Economics of Zoning Laws (1985), comprehensively assesses the institution. Fischel theorizes that local officials "attempt to maximize the net worth of the median voter" in the locality. Id. at 127. If so, zoning officials can be expected to cater entirely to current residents, without regard to the welfare of nonresident households and owners of undeveloped tracts in the locality. Is Fischel's political model realistic?

6. The role of covenants in land use regulation is discussed in the preceding selection by Epstein and the following selection by Fischel. How easy is it for the residents of an existing neighborhood to create a covenant regime to control future development? Should a state legislature authorize the owners of, say, two-thirds of the acreage in a neighborhood to impose covenants that bind the entire neighborhood? Would such a scheme violate one-person, one-vote requirements? See generally Robert C. Ellickson, New Institutions for Old Neighborhoods, 48 Duke L.J. 75 (1998); Robert H. Nelson, Privatizing the Neighborhood, 7 Geo. Mason U. L. Rev. 827 (1999).

7. Although the institution of zoning is firmly ensconced in the United States, a vigorous debate rages over the merits of the institution. Virtually all commentators have been critical of suburbs' exclusionary practices that thwart construction of modest-cost housing. Most observers are comfortable, however, with the basic notion that a local government should tightly control the development of the private lands within its borders. The underlying rationale is that development tends to generate externalities that developers will not adequately take into account. Can this rationale survive the Coasean critique, supra Chapter 4?

For criticism — implicit and explicit — of the soundness of the institution of zoning, see, for example, the sources cited in the Cappel reading; Jane J. Jacobs, The Death and Life of Great American Cities (1961); Robert C. Ellickson, Alternatives to Zoning: Covenants, Nuisance Rules, and Fines as Land Use Controls, 40 U. Chi. L. Rev. 681 (1977); Douglas W. Kmiec, Deregulating Land Use: An Alternative Free Enterprise Development System, 130 U. Pa. L. Rev. 28 (1981).

8. Zoning also has many defenders. See, for example, Bradley C. Karkkainen, Zoning: A Reply to the Critics, 10 J. Land Use & Envtl. L. 45 (1994). Karkkainen admits that zoning in some instances may be unfair, corrupt, exclusionary, and inefficient, but lauds its capacity to protect a homeowner's subjective valuations of house and neighborhood.

Another staunch defense of zoning can be found in Eric Steele, Participation and Rules — The Functions of Zoning, 1986 Am. B. Found. Res. J. 709. Steele studied the piecemeal zoning change process in Evanston, an older suburban city north of Chicago. He came away impressed with the success of zoning as a participatory mechanism:

...I suggest that zoning ordinances should be viewed as procedural mechanisms to guarantee the opportunity for community participation just as much as they are viewed as rules mandating the specific details of physical design. . . .

The functioning of zoning boards makes far more sense when zoning rules are viewed as a set of criteria to identify which proposed changes may be potentially problematic to the community. The working assumption is that building more of the same is not problematic but building bigger, taller, denser, or for a different use may be damaging and therefore requires review. When potentially problematic proposals are identified, the community is notified and its members are offered the chance to come forward and state their concerns.

Id. at 749. If, as Fischel posits, local officials cater to the median voter in a municipality, does zoning serve all "community" interests? How do zoning's participatory mechanisms compare with those at work when a homeowners' association enforces covenants? When neighbors interact on a customary basis, as Cappel has described? See generally Carol M. Rose, New Models for Local Land Use Decisions, 79 Nw. U. L. Rev. 1155 (1984-1985).

9. Section 3 of the Standard Zoning Enabling Act provides that zoning "regulations shall be made in accordance with a comprehensive plan." Is comprehensive planning desirable? Possible?

The central idea of the planner is that government ought to dictate the future, and zoning is the ultimate expression of this idea. If zoning, in fact, relates to development through a series of amendments and relaxations undertaken pursuant to pressure put upon the system by application or litigation, then the attempt to control the future by describing it in detail, in advance, has failed, and reality looks more like disjointed incrementalism — a theory of planning few planners would want to embrace. . . .

The thesis of this paper is that zoning cannot work, especially in a developing community. . . .

Jan Z. Krasnowiecki, Abolish Zoning, 31 Syracuse L. Rev. 719-720 (1980). Krasnowiecki proposes a law creating "a statutory presumption that any housing project must be approved unless the approving agency gives persuasive reasons why it should not." Id. at 750. Are courts capable of reviewing local decisions under the standard that Krasnowiecki proposes?

*Do Growth Controls Matter? A Review of Empirical Evidence on the Effectiveness and Efficiency of Local Government Land Use Regulation**

William A. Fischel

... The focus of this survey is local government control of development, not national environmental policy. Growth control devices include the tightening of traditional zoning laws as well as moratoriums on the extension of water and sewer lines, non-price rationing of building permits, and tying development permits to the provision of new public facilities.... [Some commentators assert] that most of zoning's benefits could be provided by private covenants and nuisance laws. Bernard Siegan's (1972) study of Houston seems to support this claim, insofar as covenants are widely used in that city in lieu of zoning.

The covenant alternative would be most persuasive if it were easy to establish covenants in developed areas that lacked them. Janet Furman Spreyer (1989) demonstrates that they are not. Spreyer found a rare sample that enabled her to compare a zoned area with an unzoned area. The city of Houston, which still has no zoning, surrounds two municipalities that do have zoning. Within Houston are neighborhoods that are subject to private covenants and some that are not. Using a sample of homes that included all three arrangements — (a) zoned, (b) unzoned but covenanted, and (c) unzoned and uncovenanted — Spreyer was able to determine which types of property were most valuable, after accounting for the usual differences.

Spreyer found that unzoned but covenanted properties in Houston had the same value as properties in the zoned cities, but that properties that were both unzoned and uncovenanted were significantly less valuable than either of the others. In symbols, the value of (a)=(b)>(c). (To be precise, Spreyer found no statistically significant difference between (a) and (b), not perfect equality.) This could provide arguments for both sides: People who favor zoning can say it performs as well as covenants but is more easily altered, while people who dislike zoning can say that covenants do just as well as zoning with none of the governmental coercion.

Both debating points miss the cost of forming covenants. If it were easy to establish covenants in already-developed areas (or in areas in which covenants had expired ... , one should observe that

*Source: pp. 2, 13-19, 23, 29-37, 53-57 (1990).

uncovenanted land (c) has the same value as that subject to covenants (b). All it would take to convert uncovenanted land to covenanted land would be some legal fees to record the covenant in each deed. Since legal fees per housing unit would presumably be small, the reduction in land value caused by lack of covenants should be trivial. Spreyer's result, then, shows that covenants are costly to establish. This is intuitively plausible. Transaction costs of getting *all* people in an existing neighborhood to agree to restrict potential uses of their property are usually prohibitively high.

Simply to say that some zoning may be justified by the lower transaction costs of establishing it is not to say that any type of zoning is justified. Moreover, Spreyer's exclusive attention to single-family homes precludes any efficiency analysis. Lack of covenants might have permitted multifamily homes or commercial uses with values that could have been much greater than the single-family homes they displaced or devalued. But Spreyer's results do suggest that covenants are a realistic alternative to zoning only in undeveloped areas in which a single developer can acquire enough land and impose restrictions prior to sale of the homes themselves. . . .

An important pair of studies by William Stull (1975) and Ronald Lafferty and Ted Frech (1978) [addresses] the interaction between neighborhood spillover effects and local land use controls. . . . Using median home values from a 1960s sample of 40 suburban towns in the Boston metropolitan area, Stull found that nonresidential uses did adversely affect home values. Specifically, the proportion of community land devoted to the multifamily dwellings and to industrial land uses lowered single-family home values. Stull also found that the proportion of land devoted to commercial uses raised median home values when the proportion was low, but that larger proportions lowered home values. His interpretation of this is that community residents like a little commercial development for the convenience of shopping nearby, but regional commercial centers are regarded as a net cost.

Lafferty and Frech undertook to replicate Stull's study with the same sample of Boston suburbs, but they added an insightful twist. They pointed out that the avowed purpose of traditional zoning was not to exclude entire categories of uses, as Stull seemed to imply, but to concentrate them in contiguous zones. Zoning is, in principle, a municipal good-housekeeping rule: a place for everything, and everything in its place. . . . Their critique of Stull is that he looked only at community-wide effects, neglecting the adverse effects of nonresidential properties on individual properties.

Figure 1

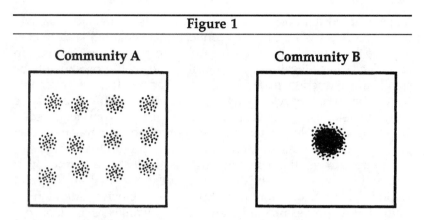

Community A   Community B

Dark areas are nonresidential uses.

To rectify this, Lafferty and Frech employed Stull's sample with an additional variable that measured the *dispersion* of nonresidential land uses. If traditional zoning theory is valid, a community that is half nonresidential but with all stores and factories concentrated in a single district will have higher average home values than similar communities that have permitted their nonresidential uses to be dispersed among the housing developments. (In fact, of course, most of the dispersed nonresidential uses might have predated the existing zoning ordinance.) In Figure 1, Community *A* should have lower average residential values than Community *B*.

Lafferty and Frech found that their dispersion index was an important overall determinant of housing values. The more dispersed a community's nonresidential land uses, the lower the value, on average, of single-family homes. The good-housekeeping theory of zoning is thus supported although the significance level of several individual variables was doubtful. . . .

One issue raised by the studies of Stull and Lafferty and Frech is the effect of undeveloped land on nearby single-family home values. In Stull's specification, a higher proportion of vacant and agricultural land reduced the average value of housing; in Lafferty and Frech's specification, the dispersion rather than the proportion of vacant land reduced the value of housing. (Dispersion is highly correlated with proportion for this variable, though.) Both findings seem entirely at odds with modern growth control rhetoric, in which preservation of open space is the *summum bonum*. If we are to take these results literally, then arguing against further residential development is irrational in the sense that maintaining open space seems to *reduce* average home values.

The problem with this interpretation (which may, even so, be a correct conclusion) is that, in the samples used, vacant land is a residual category that includes swamps and military bases as well as golf courses, parks, and wildlife refuges. Its negative impact, Stull surmises, is due to the uncertainty of future development rather than undesirability of the current use itself (1975, p. 546). Anxieties that the open space may be developed with uses that adversely affect their properties may outweigh homeowners' current enjoyment of open space. In other studies, permanently established greenbelts in other areas of the country are found to have a positive effect on nearby home values, which comports with the rhetoric of most suburban growth control advocates.[19] Thus one cannot infer that growth control is irrational from the Boston suburban studies, though it seems reasonable to surmise . . . that the enthusiasm for open space may often stem from a dislike of a specific proposal than an affection for open space itself. . . .

Gerrit Knaap (1985) conducted a study of the Portland, Oregon, urban growth boundaries. This is of special interest because it involves a modern program of comprehensive growth controls. Oregon state legislation requires that urban areas define growth boundaries around their perimeters to prevent sprawl and preserve farmland. Portland has two such boundaries: an outer perimeter beyond which no development is allowed until the year 2000 and an inner boundary outside of which development can be forbidden at local option until the land inside has been fully developed.

Knaap's 455 observations (from a sample taken during 1980) were undeveloped sites zoned for single-family homes. They were drawn from inside and outside both boundaries. His results showed that in the two Portland-area counties (Washington and Clackamas), land outside the outer growth boundary sold for significantly less than land inside the boundary. Because Knaap had already accounted for distance from the Portland CBD separately, he inferred that the twenty-year delay in development was perceived as a binding constraint and reduced the land values outside the outer boundary. His results for the effects of the inner boundary were mixed. In Washington County, the more affluent of the two counties studied, the inner growth boundary was shown also to be a constraint, but this was not so in Clackamas County. I think

---

19. Correll, Lillydahl, and Singell (1978) found this for Boulder, Colorado, and Nelson (1988) found a similar effect for Portland, Oregon.

this inconsistency may be explained by the fact that the inner boundary may be breached by local government exceptions, which may have been more readily forthcoming in less affluent and more rural Clackamas County. . . .

§6   Growth Controls and Housing Costs . . .

Seymour Schwartz at the University of California at Davis has been a coauthor of numerous studies of growth controls in the 1970s. His first event-study was Petaluma, California, which . . . had enacted a nationally famous growth control law in 1972. It was enacted specifically in reaction to new residential development, which was being built to serve commuters who took Highway 101 south toward San Francisco, forty miles away. The Petaluma Plan limited building permits to a maximum of 500 per year, well below recent and expected demand, and it rationed them with a point system that gave substantial weight to costly design features and developer-provided amenities and services to the community.

Schwartz, Hansen, and Green (1981) found that after several years, Petaluma's standard-unit housing prices had risen eight percent above those of nearby Santa Rosa, which had not adopted growth controls during that period and which had formerly had the same prices. In a follow-up study, Schwartz, Hansen, and Green . . . found that the fraction of Petaluma's housing stock that was affordable to low- and moderate-income households had dropped significantly below that of a control group. The costly design points offered by the plan overwhelmed the few points that developers got for moderate-income housing.

Schwartz, Zorn, and Hansen (1986) also examined the effects of the less famous but nearly as effective growth controls in Davis, California. As in Petaluma, house prices in Davis grew significantly more rapidly than those of a control sample of other Sacramento suburbs after growth controls were implemented. The best estimate given by the study is that growth controls caused prices in Davis to be nine percent higher in 1980 than they would have been without them.

The city of Davis attempted to mandate that the limited number of new units that were built under their controlled-growth program include some units earmarked for low- and moderate-income residents. (As a former resident of Davis, I speculate that they did this to offset the charges that growth management policies are harmful to the poor.) Growth controls were established limiting the number of building permits and requiring builders who did get permits to construct some units earmarked for low-income peo-ple.[33] According to Zorn, Hansen, and Schwartz (1986), the Davis program was successful in avoiding the skewness of the Petaluma Plan. The limited growth that did occur contained both low-income and high-income housing.

Apparent success with moderate-income housing was accom-panied by an unanticipated offset. Housing built in Davis before growth controls were adopted increased both in price and in qual-ity (more space, better accessories). Zorn, Hansen, and Schwartz expressed some puzzlement at the quality increase. They had ex-pected that older housing in Davis would increase in price as a result of the growth controls, but they did not expect the quality increase. My interpretation of this is that older housing in Davis was filtering up rather than down. Since Davis's regulations at-tempted to suppress construction for the richer side of the market, housing that otherwise would have filtered down was refitted for the more affluent buyers.

The Davis experience shows in a microcosm what econometric studies of public housing have shown at the national level. Con-struction of a million new public housing units for the poor does not augment the stock of housing for the poor by one million units. Some private housing that would have been built for the poor (e.g., mobile homes) does not get built, and some middle-class units that would have filtered down to the poor are either maintained at a higher level or diverted to other uses.[35] The housing market, like other capital markets, is subject to government crowding effects.

The other group of housing price studies was done by Lawrence Katz and Kenneth Rosen at the University of California, Berkeley. A drawback of the previous studies is their focus on two communities, both of which might be sufficiently unusual to make extrapolations unwarranted. Petaluma was a famous test case, and Davis is a university town known for its attention to environmental amenities. Notoriety itself might have sent housing prices up by signalling to house buyers the existence of an exclusive community.

Katz and Rosen (1987) overcame this problem by selecting a

33. The tie-in is a frequently employed technique of "inclusionary zoning," and it is the centerpiece of the New Jersey Supreme Court's attempt to promote low-income housing in the suburbs. See Southern Burlington Co. NAACP v. Mt. Laurel 456 A.2d 390 (N.J. 1983). A skeptical evaluation of inclusionary zoning, noting that, outside of New Jersey, it is most common in exclusive communities, is Ellickson (1981).

35. For empirical evidence supporting benefits of the filtering process to the poor, see Weicher and Thibodeau (1988). The national displacement effect was also found in an earlier study by Michael Murray (1983).

sample of over 1600 single-family home sales from 64 communities in the San Francisco Bay Area during 1979. Of these sales, 175 occurred in communities that had a growth control program (building permit moratorium or a binding rationing system) in effect for at least one year in the period 1973-1979. They found that houses selling in the growth controlled communities were 17 to 38 percent more expensive than those in other communities. Katz and Rosen thus corroborated with a broader sample (but with a larger price differential) the results that Schwartz and his coauthors found for Davis and Petaluma. . . .

What conclusions can be drawn from the housing cost studies? Their authors imply that they show that growth controls are undesirable. . . .

Let me take the role of an advocate for growth controls to show the weakness of the inefficiency implication. We know from the studies reviewed . . . above that community and neighborhood amenities raise housing values. Growth controls may create residential amenities, or, for rapidly growing communities, they may prevent impending disamenities. Hence the higher housing prices could be taken as evidence that growth controls do what they are intended to do. . . .

. . . [T]he problem caused by the focus on distributional consequences of growth controls has led to the inference that the higher housing prices that follow their imposition are a measure of their costs. In principle, the opposite is more likely true: The higher prices of housing could be a measure of their benefits. The real problem here is to identify what causes the higher prices. Higher prices of housing — or higher prices of anything else, for that matter — can occur either as a result of supply restriction (an inward shift of the supply curve, showing that lower supplies are provided at all prices) or demand stimulation (an outward shift of the demand curve, showing that higher demand exists at all prices). Inward shifts in supply smell of monopoly, and that is one efficiency objection to growth controls.

Figure 2 illustrates the problem. The panel on the left indicates a supply restriction of S to S^1, which raises the price from P_1 to P_2. The panel on the right shows the effect of making the community more attractive and thus stimulating demand from D to D^1. Just as in the inefficient supply restriction, the demand-stimulating effects of growth controls will make prices increase from P_1 to P_2. Confronted simply with evidence that prices of housing rose as a result of a public growth management program, we cannot say which scenario is the dominant case.

Of course, the two graphs [in Figure 2] are distinguished by

Figure 2

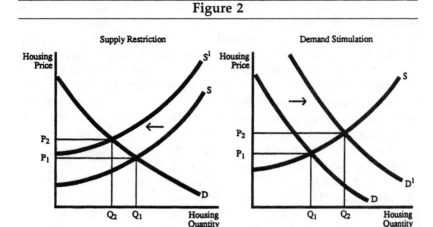

opposite effects on the quantity of housing. The supply restriction reduces the quantity of housing, while the demand stimulation increases it. The problem with evaluating growth controls as a monopoly supply restriction is that it is hard to know what the true supply curve looks like when conditions naturally change over time. Simply observing that a community declines to allow the same number of building permits as it did in the recent past is not even proof of monopoly action, much less monopoly power. A private firm with output that has expanded by ten percent per year for the last five years may find that it has reached the limits of its managerial capacities and decline to expand any more. This is not monopolistic as long as other firms can enter the industry to meet the new demand.

Growth controls are especially difficult to assess because restriction in housing supply may actually stimulate the demand for housing for reasons that have nothing to do with monopoly. With rising incomes or other shifts in demand, it may be that low-density, high-amenity communities have become relatively scarce. Growth controls may then be seen as a *positive* supply response to such demands. This statement seems odd only if one looks at a single community rather than a system of communities in a larger metropolitan market. Viewed in the metropolitan context, growth controls may be no more anomalous a supply response than a market-driven trend toward larger houses.

The key to this apologia for growth controls is the existence of alternative communities to meet other kinds of demands. If housing consumers in general or low-income people in particular do not have alternative communities in which to locate, then the reduced number of sites in the growth control communities will have extra-territorial effects on the housing market. If the supply of sites is inelastic in communities that lack growth controls, then housing prices in the metropolitan area will rise.[43] Adverse impacts from growth controls can be tested by looking at housing prices outside the restrictive communities: If they have increased, the impacts are adverse, since, presumably, the benefits of growth controls accrue exclusively to the community that enacts them.

Just such a test was conducted by Henry Pollakowski and Susan Wachter (1990). They examined the growth restrictions adopted in Montgomery County, Maryland, the northern suburb of Washington, D.C. The county had seventeen planning districts. Pollakowski and Wachter found that districts adjacent to more restrictive districts had significantly higher housing prices, though the difference was not large. This implies a spillover effect from zoning that is most probably caused by monopolistic scarcity in the more restrictive areas, since the districts were large enough that amenity effects would not have affected adjacent districts significantly. . . .

. . . Much of this essay has taken a contrary point of view. To those economists who argue that land use controls are ineffective and unnecessary, I have endeavored to show that empirical economic research does not support either conclusion, and plenty of other research points to the opposite conclusions. To those who criticize growth controls for causing high housing prices, I have pointed out that at least some of the increase in prices could result from amenity creation rather than monopolistic exclusion. On balance, however, I am inclined to believe that most growth controls impose a net cost on society. I believe that the econometric evidence discussed in this paper supports the following three conclusions:

(1) Land use controls, especially overall growth control programs, are important constraints on the land market. This in turn affects housing values, especially in suburban and exurban communities.

(2) Land use controls do provide some benefits that would be difficult to obtain under less coercive conditions. Ab-

43. Michael Elliott's (1981) study of California cities and counties shows that geographically isolated communities (e.g., Fresno) that enact growth controls have no effect on housing prices, but when several communities in one area or entire counties adopt controls, the effects are significant.

olition of zoning and related controls would create a demand for alternative controls, and it is not clear that the alternatives are less costly to administer or more efficient in their effects than zoning.

(3) Growth controls and other aggressive extensions of land use regulations probably impose costs on society that are larger than the benefits they provide. The higher housing prices associated with communities that impose growth controls are more likely the result of wasteful supply constraints than benign amenity production.

The last conclusion is more tentative than the first two because only a few studies have addressed it in a persuasive framework. . . .

Aside from their adverse effects on the cost of housing, inefficiently restrictive growth controls probably cause metropolitan areas to be too spread out. This is not to deny that growth controls may make development in *individual* municipalities more compact. My claim is that such local ordinances cause developers to go to other communities. The most likely alternative sites are in exurban and rural communities, where the political climate, at least initially, is more favorable to development. As the more rural communities become partly developed, the newcomers wrest the political machinery from the pro-growth farmers and business interests. Then these communities, too, adopt growth controls, sending development still farther from employment and commercial centers. Eventually, employment and commercial activities also disperse from traditional population centers as they find that employees and customers are harder to find.

A paradigm of modern growth control policy that illustrates the foregoing argument was recently described by Bob Narus (1990). The fifteen-square-mile town of Lincoln, Massachusetts, has for years limited growth by means of regulation, selective purchase of open land, and legal action to block regional road construction. Yet this very affluent enclave (pop. 5200) is among the few to meet the state's requirement that ten percent of the housing stock be affordable to low- and moderate-income households. Subsidized housing was built by developers as a condition for permission to build more profitable commercial buildings. The affordable units were isolated from the affluent parts of town, in which two-acre building lots recently sold for $350,000.

Its growth controls would have little effect on the housing market if Lincoln were an isolated rural town. Its open spaces, however, are maintained next to the Boston region's major employment corridor, Route 128. The town is only thirteen miles from downtown Boston. If one considers that the average gross density of most new suburbs is about four persons per acre, Lincoln's plan has displaced about 25,000 people. Given that Lincoln is not unique, merely the most successful of a group, I would conclude that at least some of the low-density, sprawling development that occurs well beyond the Route 128 corridor is caused by successful growth management by the close-in suburbs.

The long-run effect of this is a lower standard of living. People will commute more than they otherwise would, which reduces their real incomes unless they enjoy commuting. Dispersion of residences and jobs promotes more automobile travel and longer trips, creating more congestion and pollution (assuming, as is realistic, that cars are not charged for their social costs) and eventually requiring more highway construction.

The more subtle loss from inefficiently dispersed homes and businesses is the loss of agglomeration economies for firms. The basis for urban economies is the advantages of operating a business in the proximity of many other businesses. Location in a city allows firms to have access to a more skilled and flexible labor force. It also permits the face-to-face exchange of ideas, which promotes innovation. Forces that tend to disperse firms erode such advantages and reduce potential output from the industry. Telecommunications allows firms to deal with dispersion more easily now than in the past, and it is probable that advances in the electronic media have induced at least some businesses to leave urban areas without any loss in efficiency. But such firms are still the exception. Face-to-face contact is an essential ingredient of most growing businesses.

Bibliography

Correll, Mark R., Jane H. Lillydahl, and Larry D. Singell. The Effect of Greenbelts on Residential Property Values. Land Economics 54 (May 1978): 207-217.

Ellickson, Robert C. The Irony of 'Inclusionary' Zoning. Southern California Law Review 54 (September 1981): 1167-1216.

Elliott, Michael. The Impact of Growth Control Regulations on Housing Prices in California. AREUEA Journal 9 (Summer 1981): 115-133.

Katz, Lawrence, and Kenneth Rosen. The Interjurisdictional Effects of Growth Controls on Housing Prices. Journal of Law and Economics 30 (April 1987): 149-160.

Knaap, Gerrit J. The Price Effects of Urban Growth Boundaries in

Metropolitan Portland, Oregon. Land Economics 61 (February 1985): 28-35.

Lafferty, Ronald N., and H. E. Frech III. Community Environment and the Market Value of Single Family Homes: The Effect of the Dispersion of Land Uses. Journal of Law and Economics 21 (October 1978): 381-394.

Murray, Michael. Subsidized and Unsubsidized Housing Starts: 1961-1977. Review of Economics and Statistics 65 (November 1983): 590-597.

Narus, Bob. The Evolution of Growth Management in Lincoln, Massachusetts. Urban Land (January 1990): 16-19.

Nelson, Arthur C. An Empirical Note on How Regional Urban Containment Policy Influences an Interaction between Greenbelt and Exurban Land Markets. American Planning Association Journal 54 (Spring 1988): 178-184.

Pollakowski, Henry, and Susan M. Wachter. The Effects of Land Use Constraints on Housing Prices. Land Economics 66 (August 1990): 315-324.

Schwartz, Seymour I., David D. Hansen, and Richard Green. Suburban Growth Controls and the Price of New Housing. Journal of Environmental Economics and Management 8 (December 1981): 303-320.

Schwartz, Seymour I., Peter M. Zorn, and David E. Hansen. Research Design Issues and Pitfalls in Growth Control Studies. Land Economics 62 (August 1986): 223-233.

Siegan, Bernard H. Land Use Without Zoning. Lexington, Massachusetts: Heath-Lexington Books, 1972.

Spreyer, Janet Furman. The Effect of Land Use Restrictions on the Market Value of Single Family Homes in Houston. Journal of Real Estate Finance and Economics 2 (June 1989): 117-130.

Stull, William J. Community Environment, Zoning, and the Market Value of Single-Family Homes. Journal of Law and Economics 17 (October 1975): 535-557.

Weicher, John C., and Thomas G. Thibodeau. Filtering and Housing Markets: An Empirical Analysis. Journal of Urban Economics 23 (January 1988): 21-40.

Zorn, Peter M., David E. Hansen, and Seymour I. Schwartz. Mitigating the Price Effects of Growth Control: A Case Study of Davis, California. Land Economics 62 (February 1986): 47-57.

NOTES AND QUESTIONS ON GROWTH CONTROLS

1. As Fischel reports on p. 456, Janet Spreyer found that unrestricted land in Houston was less valuable, by roughly equal amounts, than land governed by either covenants or zoning. Do Spreyer's results indicate that nuisance law has been a relatively toothless method of land use regulation in Houston? To what extent do Spreyer's findings cast doubt on Cappel's conclusions about the merits of New Haven's initial zoning ordinance?

2. Fischel reviews a host of sources that indicate that growth controls push up housing prices. Do these studies help explain why local politicians are eager to manage growth? Attempt to restate Fischel's argument that price increases by themselves do not necessarily indicate that growth controls are inefficient. Why does Fischel conclude, from studies such as Pollakowski and Wachter's, that most growth controls nevertheless probably *are* inefficient?

An ambitious inquiry into the effects of land use regulations on housing prices is Stephen Malpezzi, Housing Prices, Externalities, and Regulation in U.S. Metropolitan Areas, 7 J. Housing Res. 209 (1996). Malpezzi constructed an index of the regulatory stringency of various central cities and states. The most stringent cities, according to his formula, were (in descending order) San Francisco, Honolulu, Sacramento, Boston, and New York City. The least stringent were, in ascending order, Chicago, Dayton, Gary, Dallas, and St. Louis. (Houston, despite its lack of zoning, fell roughly in the middle.) Malpezzi identified California, Massachusetts, and Minnesota as the most regulatory of states, and Alabama, Arizona, and Oklahoma as the least. Controlling for other variables, he concluded that regulation tends to raise housing prices (possibly in part on account of the benefits of regulation) and to lower homeownership rates.

3. Regional and state growth controls, which affect larger markets than local controls do, have also been found to boost housing prices. Much of the increase occurs suddenly, at the time when buyers and sellers first anticipate that the regional controls are in the offing. See, for instance, W. Patrick Beaton, The Impact of Regional Land-Use Controls on Property Values: The Case of the New Jersey Pinelands, 67 Land Econ. 172 (1991); David Dale-Johnson & Hyang K. Yim, Coastal Development Moratoria and Housing Prices, 3 J. Real Est. Fin. & Econ. 165 (1990) (on the consequences of the California Coastal Initiative). What implications do these studies have for the wisdom of state and regional land-use regulation?

4. What, if anything, is wrong with "suburban sprawl"? What policies should an advocate of "smart growth" embrace? Do developers at the urban fringe pay too little (too much?) of the costs of the infrastructure serving their developments? How would housing consumers fare if growth controls were imposed on the outskirts of a metropolitan area while interior suburbs (such as Lincoln, Massachusetts) were still permitted to pursue antigrowth policies? On these complex questions, see generally Anthony Downs, What Does 'Smart Growth' Really Mean?, Planning, April 2001, at 20; Symposium, Sustainable Growth, 35 Wake Forest L. Rev. 509 (2000); and the debate between Timothy J. Dowling and Clint Bolick at 148 U. Pa. L. Rev. 873 (2000). For an update on the effects of the urban growth boundaries that surround Portland and other Oregon cities, see Robert C. Ellickson & Vicki L. Been, Land Use Controls 989-996 (2d ed. 2000). For a broader cross-cultural and historical analysis of issues of urban form and governance, see Matthew A. Light, Note, Different Ideas of the City: Origins of Metropolitan Land-Use Regimes in the United States, Germany, and Switzerland, 24 Yale J. Intl. L. 577 (1999). Light argues that the compactness of European cities reflects a continuing tradition of urban control over the hinterland, whereas American sprawl reflects the historical weakness of American cities.

5. Fischel's footnote 33 mentions the "inclusionary zoning" program that New Jersey adopted in the aftermath of the 1983 Mount Laurel decision. Andrew G. Dietderich, An Egalitarian Market: The Economics of Inclusionary Zoning Reclaimed, 24 Fordham Urb. L.J. 23 (1996), provides a theoretical defense of this controversial practice. How well has the New Jersey program worked? See Naomi Bailin Wish & Stephen Eisdorfer, The Impact of Mount Laurel Initiatives: An Analysis of the Characteristics of Applicants and Occupants, 27 Seton Hall L. Rev. 1268 (1997), the lead article in a symposium on the subject. In Wish and Eisdorfer's sample, only 15 percent of the inclusionary units provided in the New Jersey suburbs were occupied by households who had moved there from a central city; of this subset of suburbanizing households, two-thirds were white. On the results of an analogous program in Connecticut, see Robert D. Carroll, Note, Connecticut Retrenches, 110 Yale L.J. 1247 (2001). Should racial integration be an objective of inclusionary zoning? The next selection analyzes the causes of segregated neighborhoods.

C. Housing Segregation

Micromotives and Macrobehavior*

Thomas C. Schelling

Individual Incentives and Collective Results

Economists are familiar with systems that lead to aggregate results that the individual neither intends nor needs to be aware of, results that sometimes have no recognizable counterpart at the level of the individual. The creation of money by a commercial banking system is one; the way savings decisions cause depressions or inflations is another. . . .

Some of the phenomena of segregation may be similarly complex in relation to the dynamics of individual choice. One might even be tempted to suppose that some "unseen hand" separates people in a manner that, though foreseen and intended by no one, corresponds to some consensus or collective preference or popular will. But in economics we know a great many macro-phenomena, like depression and inflation, that do not reflect any universal desire for lower incomes or higher prices. The same applies to bank failures and market crashes. What goes on in the "hearts and minds" of small savers has little to do with whether or not they cause a depression. The hearts and minds and motives and habits of millions of people who participate in a segregated society may or may not bear close correspondence with the massive results that collectively they can generate.

A special reason for doubting any social efficiency in aggregate segregation is that the range of choice is often so meager. The demographic map of almost any American metropolitan area suggests that it is easy to find residential areas that are all white or nearly so and areas that are all black or nearly so but hard to find localities in which neither whites nor nonwhites are more than, say, three-quarters of the total. And, comparing decennial maps, it is nearly impossible to find an area that, if integrated within that range, will remain integrated long enough for a couple to get their house paid for or their children through school.

*Source: pp. 140-141, 146-155 (1978).

Some Quantitative Constraints

Counting blacks and whites in a residential block or on a baseball team will not tell how they get along. But it tells something, especially if numbers and ratios matter to the people who are moving in or out of the block or being recruited for the team. With quantitative analysis there are a few logical constraints, analogous to the balance-sheet identities in economics. (Being logical constraints, they contain no news unless one just never thought of them before.)

The simplest constraint on dichotomous mixing is that, within a given set of boundaries, not both groups can enjoy numerical superiority. For the whole population the numerical ratio is determined at any given time; but locally, in a city or a neighborhood, a church or a school or a restaurant, either blacks or whites can be a majority. But if each insists on being a local majority, there is only one mixture that will satisfy them — complete segregation.

People who have to choose between polarized extremes — a white neighborhood or a black, a French-speaking club or one where English alone is spoken, a school with few whites or one with few blacks — will often choose in the way that reinforces the polarization. Doing so is no evidence that they prefer segregation, only that, if segregation exists and they have to choose between exclusive association, people elect like rather than unlike environments. . . .

Some of the processes may be passive, systemic, unmotivated but nevertheless biased. If job vacancies are filled by word of mouth or apartments go to people who have acquaintances in the building, or if boys can marry only girls they know and can know only girls who speak their language, a biased communication system will preserve and enhance the prevailing homogeneities.

A Self-Forming Neighborhood Model

Some vivid dynamics can be generated by any reader with a half-hour to spare, a roll of pennies and a roll of dimes, a tabletop, a large sheet of paper, a spirit of scientific inquiry, or, lacking that spirit, a fondness for games.

Get a roll of pennies, a roll of dimes, a ruled sheet of paper divided into one-inch squares, preferably at least the size of a checkerboard (sixty-four squares in eight rows and eight columns) and find some device for selecting squares at random. We place dimes and pennies on some of the squares, and suppose them to represent the members of two homogeneous groups — men and women, blacks and whites. French-speaking and English-speaking, officers and enlisted men, students and faculty, surfers and swimmers, the well dressed and the poorly dressed, or any other dichotomy that is exhaustive and recognizable. We can spread them at random or put them in contrived patterns. We can use equal numbers of dimes and pennies or let one be a minority. And we can stipulate various rules for individual decision.

For example, we can postulate that every dime wants at least half its neighbors to be dimes, every penny wants a third of its neighbors to be pennies, and any dime or penny whose immediate neighborhood does not meet these conditions gets up and moves. Then by inspection we locate the ones that are due to move, move them, keep on moving them if necessary and, when everybody on the board has settled down, look to see what pattern has emerged. (If the situation never "settles down," we look to see what kind of endless turbulence or cyclical activity our postulates have generated.)

Define each individual's neighborhood as the eight squares surrounding him; he is the center of a 3-by-3 neighborhood. He is content or discontent with his neighborhood according to the colors of the occupants of those eight surrounding squares, some of which may be empty. We furthermore suppose that, if he is discontent with the color of his own neighborhood, he moves to the nearest empty square that meets his demands.

As to the order of moves, we can begin with the discontents nearest the center of the board and let them move first, or start in the upper left and sweep downward to the right, or let the dimes move first and then the pennies; it usually turns out that the precise order is not crucial to the outcome.

Then we choose an overall ratio of pennies to dimes, the two colors being about equal or one of them being a "minority." There are two different ways we can distribute the dimes and the pennies. We can put them in some prescribed pattern that we want to test, or we can spread them at random.

Start with equal numbers of dimes and pennies and suppose that the demands of both are "moderate" — each wants something more than one-third of his neighbors to be like himself. The number of neighbors that a coin can have will be anywhere from zero to eight. We make the following specifications. If a person has one neighbor, he must be the same color; of two neighbors, one must be his color; of three, four, or five neighbors, two must be his color; and of six, seven, or eight neighbors, he wants at least three.

It is possible to form a pattern that is regularly "integrated"

Figure 3

```
  # O # O # O
# O # O # O # O
O # O # O # O #
# O # O # O # O
O # O # O # O #
# O # O # O # O
O # O # O # O #
  O # O # O #
```

that satisfies everybody. An alternating pattern does it (Figure 3), on condition that we take care of the corners.

No one can move, except to a corner, because there are no other vacant cells; but no one wants to move. We now mix them up a little, and in the process empty some cells to make movement feasible.

There are 60 coins on the board. We remove 20, using a table of random digits; we then pick 5 empty squares at random and replace a dime or a penny with a 50-50 chance. The result is a board with 64 cells, 45 occupied and 19 blank. Forty individuals are just where they were before we removed 20 neighbors and added 5 new ones. The left side of Figure 4 shows one such result, generated by exactly this process. The #'s are dimes and the O's are pennies; alternatively, the #'s speak French and the O's speak English, the #'s are black and the O's are white, the #'s are boys and the O's are girls, or whatever you please.

The right side of Figure 4 identifies the individuals who are not content with their neighborhoods. Six #'s and three O's want to move; the rest are content as things stand. The pattern is still "integrated"; even the discontent are not without some neighbors like themselves, and few among the content are without neighbors of opposite color. The general pattern is not strongly segregated in appearance. One is hard-put to block out #-neighborhoods or O-neighborhoods at this stage. The problem is to satisfy a fraction, 9 of 45, among the #'s and O's by letting them move somewhere among the 19 blank cells.

Anybody who moves leaves a blank cell that somebody can move into. Also, anybody who moves leaves behind a neighbor or two of his own color; and when he leaves a neighbor, his neighbor loses a neighbor and may become discontent. Anyone who moves gains neighbors like himself, adding a neighbor like them to their

Figure 4

```
- # - # O # - O      - - - # - # - -
# # # O - O # O      - - - - - - - -
- # O - - # O #      - - - - - - - -
- O # O # O # O      - - # - # - # -
O O O # O O O -      - - - - - - - -
# - # # # - - O      # - - - - - - -
- # O # O # O -      - - O - O - O -
- O - O - - # -      - - - - - - - -
```

neighborhood but also adding one of opposite color to the unlike neighbors he acquires.

I cannot too strongly urge you to get the dimes and pennies and do it yourself. I can show you an outcome or two. A computer can do it for you a hundred times, testing variations in neighborhood demands, overall ratios, sizes of neighborhoods, and so forth. But there is nothing like tracing it through for yourself and seeing the thing work itself out. In an hour you can do it several times and experiment with different rules of behavior, sizes and shapes of boards, and (if you turn some of the coins heads and some tails) subgroups of dimes and pennies that make different demands on the color compositions of their neighborhoods.

Chain Reaction

What is instructive about the experiment is the "unraveling" process. Everybody who selects a new environment affects the environments of those he leaves and those he moves among. There is a chain reaction. It may be quickly damped, with little motion, or it may go on and on and on with striking results. (The results of course are only suggestive, because few of us live in square cells on a checkerboard.)

One outcome for the situation depicted in Figure 4 is shown in Figure 5. It is "one outcome" because I have not explained exactly the order in which individuals moved. If the reader reproduces the experiment himself, he will get a slightly different configuration, but the general pattern will not be much different. Figure 6 is a replay from Figure 4, the only difference from Figure 5 being in the order of moves. It takes a few minutes to do the experiment again, and one quickly gets an impression of the kind of outcome to expect. Changing the neighborhood demands, or using twice as many dimes as pennies, will drastically affect the

Figures 5 and 6

```
    # #   O # #          # # # O       O
  # # # O O O # #      # # # O   O   O
  # # O O     O #      # # O         O
  # O   O   O O O      O   O   O   O
  O O O # O O O        O O O # O O O
    O # # # O O O          # # # O O O
      # # # #          O # # # # # # #
  O O         #        O O       # # #
```

results; but for any given set of numbers and demands, the results are fairly stable.

All the people are content in Figures 5 and 6. And they are more segregated. This is more than just a visual impression: We can make a few comparisons. In Figure 4 the O's altogether had as many O's for neighbors as they had #'s; some had more or less than the average, and 3 were discontent. For the #'s the ratio of #-neighbors to O-neighbors was 1:1, with a little colony of #'s in the upper left corner and 6 widely distributed discontents. After sorting themselves out in Figure 5, the average ratio of like to unlike neighbors for #'s and O's together was 2.3:1, more than double the original ratio. And it is about triple the ratio that any individual demanded! Figure 6 is even more extreme. The ratio of like to unlike neighbors is 2.8:1, nearly triple the starting ratio and four times the minimum demanded.

Another comparison is the number who had no opposite neighbors in Figure 4. Three were in that condition before people started moving; in Figure 5 there are 8 without neighbors of opposite color, and in Figure 6 there are 14.

What can we conclude from an exercise like this? We may at least be able to disprove a few notions that are themselves based on reasoning no more complicated than the checkerboard. Propositions beginning with "It stands to reason that . . ." can sometimes be discredited by exceedingly simple demonstrations that, though perhaps true, they do not exactly "stand to reason." We can at least persuade ourselves that certain mechanisms could work, and that observable aggregate phenomena could be compatible with types of "molecular movement" that do not closely resemble the aggregate outcomes that they determine.

There may be a few surprises. What happens if we raise the demands of one color and lower the demands of the other? Figure 7 shows typical results. Here we increased by one the number of

---

Figure 7

```
# # # # O       O
# # # # O O     O
# # # #       O
    O # O O O     O
O O O # O O O
        # # O
    O # # # O
  O   O # # #
```

---

like neighbors that a # demanded and decreased by one the number that an O demanded, as compared with Figures 5 and 6. By most measures, "segregation" is about the same as in Figures 5 and 6. The differences are in population densities: the O's are spread out all over their territory, while the #'s are packed in tight. The reader will discover, if he actually gets those pennies and dimes and tries it for himself, that something similar would happen if the demands of the two colors were equal but one color outnumbered the other by two or three to one. The minority then tends to be noticeably more tightly packed. Perhaps from Figure 7 we could conclude that if surfers mind the presence of swimmers less than swimmers mind the presence of surfers, they will become almost completely separated, but the surfers will enjoy a greater expanse of water.

Is It "Segregated"?

The reader might try guessing what set of individual preferences led from Figure 4 to the pattern in Figure 8.

The ratio of like to unlike neighbors for all the #'s and O's together is slightly more than three to one, and there are 6 O's and 8 #'s that have no neighbors of opposite color. The result is evidently segregation; but, following a suggestion of my dictionary, we might say that the process is one of *aggregation*, because the rules of behavior ascribed both to #'s and to O's in Figure 8 were simply that each would move to acquire three neighbors of like color irrespective of the presence or absence of neighbors of opposite color. As an individual motivation, this is quite different from the one that formed the patterns in Figures 5 and 6. But in the aggregate it may be hard to discern which motivation underlies the pattern, and the process, of segregated residence. And it matters!

Figure 8

```
      # #       # #
    # # #     # # #
    # # O O O # O
        O O O O O O
    O O O # O O O
        O # # # O O O
        # # #   O O
        # #
```

The first impact of a display like this on a reader may be — unless he finds it irrelevant — discouragement. A moderate urge to avoid small-minority status may cause a nearly integrated pattern to unravel, and highly segregated neighborhoods to form. Even a deliberately arranged viable pattern, as in Figure 3, when buffeted by a little random motion, proves unstable and gives way to the separate neighborhoods of Figures 5 through 8. These then prove to be fairly immune to continued random turnover.

For those who deplore segregation, however, and especially for those who deplore more segregation than people were seeking when they collectively segregated themselves, there may be a note of hope. The underlying motivation can be far less extreme than the observable patterns of separation. What it takes to keep things from unraveling is to be learned from Figure 4; the later figures indicate only how hard it may be to restore such "integration" as would satisfy the individuals, once the process of separation has stabilized. In Figure 4 only 9 of the 45 individuals are motivated to move, and if we could persuade them to stay everybody else would be all right. Indeed, the reader might exercise his own ingenuity to discover how few individuals would need to be invited into Figure 4 from outside, or how few individuals would need to be relocated in Figure 4, to keep anybody from wanting to move. If two lonely #'s join a third lonely #, none of them is lonely anymore, but the first will not move to the second unless assured that the third will arrive, and without some concert or regulation, each will go join some larger cluster, perhaps abandoning some nearby lonely neighbor in the process and surely helping to outnumber the opposite color at their points of arrival.

NOTES AND QUESTIONS
ON SEGREGATED HOUSING

1. The segregated patterns in Schelling's Figures 5 and 6 resulted from preferences to avoid being disproportionately outnumbered by "others." Preferences to be near a certain absolute number of "one's own" produced the segregated pattern in Figure 8. Should opponents of segregation be equally damning of these somewhat different preferences? Could one tell which of the two had segregated a particular neighborhood?

On actual tastes regarding the racial composition of neighborhoods, see Reynolds Farley, Elaine L. Fielding & Maria Krysan, The Residential Preferences of Blacks and Whites: A Four-Metropolitan Analysis, 8 Housing Poly. Debate 763 (1997). The authors found that whites' resistance to having black neighbors was most pronounced in the Detroit area, among the elderly, and among the less educated. Most blacks prefer integrated neighborhoods (but ones with substantial representation of blacks), but younger blacks are less willing than older blacks to pioneer in white areas.

2. Fair housing legislation seeks to deter discriminatory practices by brokers, lenders, landlords, and others on the supply side of the housing market. For evidence of discrimination on the supply side, see John Yinger, Cash in Your Face: The Cost of Racial and Ethnic Discrimination in Housing, 42 J. Urb. Econ. 339 (1997) (estimating that, because black and Hispanic households are shown fewer houses, they incur a discrimination "tax" of almost $4,000 each time they search for a house to buy). Are housing agents particularly prejudiced themselves? Or are they mainly seeking to profit by catering to the prejudices of their current and potential customers?

According to Schelling's analysis, when the tastes of housing consumers strongly support housing segregation, fair housing legislation addressed to supply-side behavior is likely to have little or no effect. See also Richard F. Muth, Cities and Housing 106-112 (1969) (attributing housing segregation mainly to household preferences). But compare Richard H. Sander, Housing Segregation and Housing Integration, 52 U. Miami L. Rev. 977 (1998) (asserting that the Fair Housing Act of 1968 did increase blacks' housing options).

3. In fact, black-white segregation has decreased somewhat in almost all U.S. metropolitan areas since 1970. See Douglas S. Massey & Nancy A. Denton, American Apartheid 222 (1993); David M. Cutler & Edward L. Glaeser, The Rise and Decline of the American Ghetto, 107 J. Pol. Econ. 455 (1999).

Schelling, who wrote this selection in the 1970s, asserts that then it was "nearly impossible" for a household to find a stably integrated neighborhood in the United States. By the advent of the twenty-first century, this was not true. See Ingrid Gould Ellen, Sharing America's Neighborhoods: The Prospects for Stable Racial Integration (2000). Examining census data through 1990, Ellen found that the percentage of metropolitan-area blacks living in census tracts that were less than half black increased from 33 percent in 1970 to 46 percent in 1990, and also that the stability of racially mixed neighborhoods rose markedly during this period. See id. at 21-34. Ellen hypothesizes that neighborhoods "tip" not because whites tend to exit as more blacks move in, but because whites looking for housing are reluctant to move into an increasingly black neighborhood (which they associate, rightly or wrongly, with poor schools and high crime).

4. Schelling suggests that race-conscious interventions targeted at keeping a few apprehensive households in place might be enough to prevent racial segregation. Ellen's analysis (see supra Note 3), by contrast, suggests that it might be more important to encourage reluctant entrants to buy in a mixed area. Either way, as a practical matter, could government officials pinpoint the households on the brink of tipping out or moving in?

These policy approaches pose the legally complex issue of affirmative action. To stem white flight, should a city be empowered to protect homeowners in transitional neighborhoods from declines in property value? Carry out race-conscious affirmative marketing? Entitle landlords and other intermediaries to use "benign quotas" that abet integration? If legal, which of these policies is apt to be most effective? See Ellen, supra, at 152-176; Comment, The Legality and Efficacy of Homeowners Equity Assurance: A Study of Oak Park, Illinois, 78 Nw. U. L. Rev. 1463 (1984); George C. Galster, Neighborhood Racial Change, Segregationist Sentiments, and Affirmative Marketing Policies, 27 J. Urb. Econ. 344 (1990); Dorn Bishop, Note, Fair Housing and the Constitutionality of Government Measures Affecting Community Ethnicity, 55 U. Chi. L. Rev. 1229-1266 (1988).

5. Not all commentators deplore segregated outcomes. See, for example, Michael R. Tein, Note, The Devaluation of Nonwhite Community in Remedies for Subsidized Discrimination, 140 U. Pa. L. Rev. 1463 (1992). Compare Sheryll D. Cashin, Middle-Class Black Suburbs and the State of Integration: A Post-Integrationist Vision for Metropolitan America, 86 Cornell L. Rev. 729 (2001) (offering a mixed assessment of segregated suburbs). Is there a communitarian defense of racial and ethnic enclaves? How should Fair Housing statutes accommodate the national commitment to an open

society with individuals' preferences for clustering with persons like themselves? Should the developer of a planned community be able to employ covenants to help ensure the community's appeal to particular racial, ethnic, or religious groups? See supra pp. 423-437.

D. The Takings Issue

Property, Utility, and Fairness: Comments on the Ethical Foundations of 'Just Compensation' Law*

Frank I. Michelman

"Taking" is, of course, constitutional law's expression for any sort of publicly inflicted private injury for which the Constitution requires payment of compensation. . . .

Such questions as those of distinguishing the "police power" from the "power of eminent domain" and of calculating "just compensation". . . seem to derive from a broader question: When a social decision to redirect economic resources entails painfully obvious opportunity costs, how shall these costs ultimately be distributed among all the members of society? Shall they be permitted to remain where they fall initially or shall the government, by paying compensation, make explicit attempts to distribute them in accordance with decisions made by whatever process fashions the tax structure, or perhaps according to some other principle? Shall the losses be left with the individuals on whom they happen first to fall, or shall they be "socialized"? . . .

II. Some Rules of Decision

Examination of judicial decisions and of legal commentary focused on them indicates that one of four factors has usually been deemed critical in classifying an occasion as compensable or not: (1) whether or not the public or its agents have physically used or

*Source: 80 Harv. L. Rev. 1165, 1168-1169, 1183-1184, 1214-1230, 1233-1238, 1245, 1253-1256 (1967).

occupied something belonging to the claimant; (2) the size of the harm sustained by the claimant or the degree to which his affected property has been devalued; (3) whether the claimant's loss is or is not outweighed by the public's concomitant gain; (4) whether the claimant has sustained any loss apart from restriction of his liberty to conduct some activity considered harmful to other people.

There follow some brief comments on each of these four "tests." The discussions are, at this point, tentative and incomplete. Their purpose is the limited one of showing that none of the standard criteria yields a sound and self-sufficient rule of decision — that each of them, when attempts are made to erect it into a general principle, is either seriously misguided, ruinously incomplete, or uselessly overbroad. The discussions tend to overlook certain redeeming qualities in the criteria — their cores of valid insight and their embodiment (and concealment) of quite relevant, even if not necessarily conclusive, inquiries. These aspects are developed at a later point. . . .

IV.   Utility, Fairness, and Compensation

A.   Compensation and Utility

A strictly utilitarian argument leading to the specific identification of "compensable" occasions would have a quasi-mathematical structure. Let us define three quantities to be known as "efficiency gains," "demoralization costs," and "settlement costs." "Efficiency gains" we define as the excess of benefits produced by a measure over losses inflicted by it, where benefits are measured by the total number of dollars which prospective gainers would be willing to pay to secure adoption, and losses are measured by the total number of dollars which prospective losers would insist on as the price of agreeing to adoption. "Demoralization costs" are defined as the total of (1) the dollar value necessary to offset disutilities which accrue to losers and their sympathizers specifically from the realization that no compensation is offered, and (2) the present capitalized dollar value of lost future production (reflecting either impaired incentives or social unrest) caused by demoralization of uncompensated losers, their sympathizers, and other observers disturbed by the thought that they themselves may be subjected to similar treatment on some other occasion. "Settlement costs" are measured by the dollar value of the time, effort, and resources which would be required in order to reach compensation settlements adequate to avoid demoralization costs. Included are the costs of settling not only the particular compensation claims presented, but also those of all persons so affected by the measure in question or similar measures as to have claims not obviously distinguishable by the available settlement apparatus.

A measure attended by positive efficiency gains is, under utilitarian ethics, prima facie desirable. But felicific calculation under the definition given for efficiency gains is imperfect because it takes no account of demoralization costs caused by a capricious redistribution, or alternatively, of the settlement costs necessary to avoid such demoralization costs. When pursuit of efficiency gains entails capricious redistribution, either demoralization costs or settlement costs must be incurred. It follows that if, for any measure, both demoralization costs and settlement costs (whichever were chosen) would exceed efficiency gains, the measure is to be rejected; but that otherwise, since either demoralization costs or settlement costs must be paid, it is the lower of these two costs which should be paid. The compensation rule which then clearly emerges is that compensation is to be paid whenever settlement costs are lower than both demoralization costs and efficiency gains. But if settlement costs, while lower than demoralization costs, exceed efficiency gains, then the measure is improper regardless of whether compensation is paid. The correct utilitarian statement, then, insofar as *the issue of compensability* is concerned, is that compensation is due whenever demoralization costs exceed settlement costs, and not otherwise.

Let us now focus on the problem of appraising demoralization costs. Since we are looking ultimately to the specification of practical methods for identifying compensable occasions, we may begin by saying that it obviously will not do to interview every potential compensation claimant and ask him how demoralized he expects to be if a given measure is adopted without provision for compensation. The objections to such a solution run far deeper than the obvious one about the costs of conducting such interviews. The interviewee probably will not himself know the answer to the question (putting aside the difficulty of his attaching a dollar value to his outrage and his loss of incentive even if he could appraise those subjectively) and, for strategic reasons, would not reveal the true answer if he knew it.

We are compelled, then, to frame the question about demoralization costs in terms of responses we must impute to ordinarily cognizant and sensitive members of society. Utilitarian algebra, it appears, cannot specify a sound compensation practice — the equation cannot be solved for that "value" of compensation which yields a maximum excess of efficiency gains over demoralization or settlement costs — until supposed facts about human psychology and behavior have been plugged into the equation as independent variables.

If we hypothesize a utilitarian defense of currently observable social practices pertaining to compensation, we can make some interesting deductions about the behavioral assumptions which must have entered into the utilitarian calculation. One clear characteristic of current practices is their reflection of a special urgency in the demand for publicly financed compensation when a loss has evidently been occasioned by deliberate social action. Society has not yet placed itself under any systematic discipline designed to assure people of compensation for all economic losses inflicted by forces regarded as beyond social control, such as earthquake or plague. If, then, the just compensation requirement is supposed to rest on strictly utilitarian grounds — if, that is, it is supposed to rest on a purpose of forestalling demoralization which impairs the output of goods — there must be at work a tacit assumption that losses which seem the proximate results of deliberate collective decision have a special counterproductive potency beyond any which may be contained in other kinds of losses. It cannot, in other words, be simply uncertainty — awareness of the possibility of unpredictable and unpreventable future loss — which utilitarians engaged in rationalizing the just compensation practice judge to be intolerably demoralizing.

We are thus led to inquire whether there is any reason to suppose that a visible risk of majoritarian exploitation should have any greater disincentive effect than the ever-present risk that accidents may happen, this being the only supposition which seems, on utilitarian premises, to justify a constitutional guaranty aimed specially against the former sort of risk. If I am able to mobilize my productive faculties under the general conditions of uncertainty which prevail in the universe, why should I be paralyzed by a realization that I am at the mercy of majorities?

There seems only one possible way to defend this behavioral supposition. The defense must begin with an imputation to human actors of a perception that the force of a majority is self-determining and purposive, as compared with other loss-producing forces which seem to be randomly generated. The argument must then proceed to the effect that even though people can adjust satisfactorily to random uncertainty, which can be dealt with through insurance, including self-insurance, they will remain on edge when contemplating the possibility of strategically determined loses. For when the bearing of strategy is evident, one faces the risk of being *systematically* imposed upon, which seems a risk of a very different order from the risk of occasional, accidental injury. One faces also the rational necessity of devoting a large proportion of his energies and resources to counterstrategy aimed at fending off the risk; where the possibility of loss will visibly be determined by strategy, that possibility cannot be conveniently dismissed from consciousness on the ground that, being uncontrollable, it is not worth thinking about.

Whatever the empirical verity of this behavioral picture, it does seem implicit in any attempt to rationalize current compensation practices in utilitarian (product-maximizing) terms. Accordingly, it seems in order to ask what criteria of compensability will emerge if the practice of compensating is taken to have the purpose of quieting people's unease about the possibility of being strategically exploited.

It seems obvious, to begin with, that this unease will be stirred by any spectacle of capricious redistribution which could easily have been avoided. Capricious redistributions will not be tolerated, even as accidental adjuncts of efficiency-dictated measures, when compensation settlements can be reached without much trouble, that is, when settlement costs are low. The clearer it is that the claimant has sustained an injury distinct from those sustained by the generality of persons in society, and the more obviously there appears to be some objectively satisfactory measure of his disproportionate or distinctive injury, the more compelling will his claim to compensation become.

Society, moreover, will have to avoid not only those capricious redistributions which a compensation payment could easily offset, but also those practically noncompensable ones which cannot plausibly be said to be necessitated by the pursuit of efficiency. Thus, measures whose efficiency is open to grave question will have to be rejected unless attended by compensation even though their arguable efficiency is enough to justify their adoption in some form. Payment of compensation in such cases may furnish a necessary assurance that the measure is not simply a disguised attempt to redistribute deliberately, by confirming the hypothesis that society deems the measure a "gainful" (efficient) one in the only ethically sure sense. Therefore, as the collective allocational measure approaches the limit of doubtful efficiency, the claim for compensation will become more compelling.

Other intertwined branches of a compensability inquiry could grow out of a utilitarian purpose to cater to the sense of security by preserving an illusion of long-run indiscriminateness in the distribution of social burdens and benefits. Thus the magnitude of the imposition would plainly be relevant: is it of quotidian variety, or is it once in a lifetime mayhem? But magnitude of individual burden, no matter how purposively conceived, reveals only a fragment, meaningless by itself, of the whole picture. We need additional information. For example, is the burden for which compensation is sought a rare or peculiar one, or do like burdens seem to have been widely, even though not uniformly, scattered about the community? Is there implicit in the measure some reciprocity of burdens coupled with benefits (as, for example, in a measure restricting a large area to residential development) or does it channel benefits and burdens to different persons? How likely does it seem that members of the class burdened by the measure were able to wield enough effective influence in the process leading to its adoption to have extracted some compensatory concession "in kind"?

B. Compensation and Fairness

It is not the purpose of this essay to make a case for utilitarian ethics. Unquestionably, the provisional assumption of a utilitarian stance towards efficiency, property, and security is clarifying to a critical study of actual compensation practices. But there is no basis for concluding that the question of compensability is intelligible only when compensation is regarded as an instrument of utilitarian maximizing. Many observers, though they may admit that the question of compensability can logically be viewed as a question of efficiency, will insist that it can also be viewed as a question of justice to be decided without regard to the effect of the decision on the net social product. We must consider whether, in the name of justice, a person might not claim compensation (or society might not refuse compensation) regardless of the consequences for the net social product.

Since I am not prepared to embark on a general canvassing of philosophies of justice, I have selected for examination one recent, nonmaximizing account of justice which seems to hold forth special promise of illuminating the compensation problem, namely the account given by John Rawls of "justice as fairness."[104]

Rawls's theory attracts our attention because it is concerned with inequalities in the treatment — the quota of powers, honors, and incomes — received by individuals under collectively main-

104. [Ed. — See Rawls's book, A Theory of Justice (1971), excerpted supra p. 94.]

tained arrangements. A cogent attempt is made to clarify the idea of justice as the special virtue of social arrangements within which such inequalities become acceptable. They are said to be acceptable — the arrangements producing them are deemed just — if those arrangements are consistent with principles which could command the assent of every member of a group of rational, self-regarding persons, convening under circumstances of mutually acknowledged equality and interdependence, to hammer out principles by which they will judge complaints against whatever rules and institutions may come to characterize their association. All of these persons are presumed to be aware that each is powerless either to impose his preferences on any other or to claim for himself, in advance, any particular position which may be constituted by a rule or institution. Social practices, then, are to be judged by principles which a person would favor if he had to assume that he might occupy the least advantageous position distinguishable under any rule or institution which might emerge. . . .

Rawls finds that two fundamental principles would emerge from this convention of the circumspect. The first principle is a general presumption that social arrangements should accord no preferences to anyone, but should assure to each participant the maximum liberty consistent with a like liberty on the part of every other participant. The second principle defines a justification for departures from the first: An arrangement entailing differences in treatment is just so long as (a) everyone has a chance to attain the positions to which differential treatments attach, and (b) the arrangement can reasonably be supposed to work out to the advantage of every participant, and especially the one to whom accrues the least advantageous treatment provided for by the arrangement in question.

For illustration of these principles we may begin by imagining, as a mode of basic organization in which the principle of "equal liberty" is strictly adhered to insofar as economic life is concerned, a society where product is distributed to all in equal shares of purchasing power. If "equal liberty" were an unqualified principle we might have to choose some such form of organization. Rawls's second principle, however, permits us to opt for some other mode of organization which departs from the strict equality principle, as long as the occupant of each position constituted by the preferred mode should be able to see that the arrangement, precisely because it involves inequalities, improves his long-run prospects over what they would have been under the "equality" mode. So, under private property institutions, product is distributed in part according to an inevitably unequal pattern which reflects the fortuity of "fac-

tor endowments" — the morally accidental and unequal distribution among individuals of strength, skill, ambition, and ownership
of physical resources (and, derivatively, of training, position, and
influence). Such inequalities are deemed just, however, as long as
it is clear that permitting distribution to take the form of returns
to factors of production enhances the volume of production so significantly that (taking into account the society's other distributional
practices) even the least well-endowed participant winds up better
off than he could reasonably count on being under any version of
strict equality. The justice of "capitalism" depends, then, on the
beliefs that markets are essential to sound resource allocation, and
that allowance of negotiated returns is essential to productive incentive. . . .

Although it is not easy to convert Rawls's second principle
into a specific test of the fairness of a given compensability decision
— in part because the principle is a great deal more complex and
subtle than may appear on the surface — it will be worthwhile to
make the effort for the added insight it may give us into the idea
of fairness as it bears on the compensation problem.

What we want to know, then, is whether a specific decision
not to compensate is fair. By the very asking of the question we
adopt the vantage point of the disappointed claimant and assume
on his part a capacity (a) to appraise his treatment and calculate
his advantage over a span of time (that is, he is not without patience) and (b) to view the particular decision in question as a
specific manifestation of a general practice which will be applied
consistently to situations involving other people. If he is unable to
extend his thinking in those two dimensions, there is no possibility
that immediately disadvantageous treatment will be acceptable to
him because it is fair.

The relevant comparison, then, is between the general practices respectively represented by specific decisions to compensate
and not to compensate in this particular case; and the crucial question is which of these general practices maximizes our claimant's
opportunities over the time span covered by his patience, imagination, and ability to project a sense of continuing selfhood. Since,
however, the claimant is supposed to understand that he may turn
out to be the person who fares worst under whatever compensation scheme is adopted (a fair arrangement, remember, is one
which is best for whoever turns out to be worst off), it is more
straightforward to ask which of the two practices minimizes his
risks.

Previous discussion helps us identify the relevant risks. The
risk associated with the more stringent compensation practice is

that its settlement costs will force abandonment of efficient projects. Opportunities to augment social output will, then, be missed, and this is matter of concern to our claimant because, no matter what distributional pattern eventuates, if there is more to be shared he stands to get more. The risk associated with the less stringent compensation practice is that of sustaining concentrated losses from efficiency-motivated social projects which otherwise would not have been sustained — losses which may partially or totally exclude their bearer from sharing in the general gains from social activity.

The question, then, is whether the more or the less stringent compensation practice minimizes the sum of these risks; or, retranslating the inquiry into one about the fairness of a particular decision not to compensate, the question is whether the practice represented by such a decision involves a greater or a less total of the two risks — of missed opportunities for augmenting shareable social output and of losses which impair the claimant's participation in such aggregate increments as are achieved — than does the practice represented by the opposite decision. But since a compensation practice is of complex and indeterminate composition — since, that is, its nature cannot be inferred by a simple process of generalizing from a single manifestation — the question of fairness must be reformulated one last time. A decision not to compensate is not unfair as long as the disappointed claimant ought to be able to appreciate how such decisions might fit into a consistent practice which holds forth a lesser long-run risk to people like him than would any consistent practice which is naturally suggested by the opposite decision.

If we set about to make practical use of this approach, we shall find ourselves asking much the same questions to determine whether a compensability decision is fair as were suggested by the utilitarian approach. The relevant risks plainly are minimized by insistence on compensation when settlement costs are low, when efficiency gains are dubious, and when the harm concentrated on one individual is unusually great. They are also minimized if insistence on compensation is relaxed when there are visible reciprocities of burden and benefit, or when burdens similar to that for which compensation is denied are concomitantly imposed on many other people (indicating that settlement costs are high and that those sustaining the burden are probably incurring relatively small net losses — else, being many, they probably could have been mobilized to deflect the measure which burdens them).

It is important, however, to note here the possibility that the utilitarian approach and the fairness approach will yield sharply inconsistent results in some situations. Whether they do will depend on the behavioral assumptions which are plugged into the utilitarian equation, and on whether utilitarian decision makers are required to assume that their decisions will be widely publicized and sensitively constructed. Consider first a case involving impact of a superficially unusual sort, perhaps not likely either to cause a great stir in the community or to recur; for example, one in which conservation officials of the United States forbid travel across a wilderness area, first by air and then by overland vehicle, with the result that the claimant is left with no practical access to his small hunting and fishing camp and is forced to close it down. Fairness rather clearly requires compensation here. But the Great Administrator who presides over the utilitarian controls might calculate that, while the settlement costs of recognizing compensability could turn out to be substantial because of a liberalizing effect on precedents governing compensability of access impairments in general, he could reasonably count on holding down the demoralization costs of a failure to compensate either by preventing the matter from becoming widely known or by not revealing the general implications of this particular decision. . . .

. . . If . . . there are circumstances where a decision not to compensate would greatly demoralize men as they are supposed actually to be, even though that decision would be fully acceptable to the patient, far-seeing, reasonable folk who inhabit the fairness model, utility and fairness will yield different results — and utility, oddly enough, will favor the more liberal compensation practice. . . .

V. The Rules of Decision Revisited . . .

. . . We should . . . consider carefully the extent to which the "fairness" or utility rationale is already reflected, even if inexplicitly, in the judicial doctrines which presently compose the main corpus of our just compensation lore. My conclusion is that these doctrines do significantly reflect the line of thought which has been elaborated in these pages, and that this approach, indeed, derives some indirect support from its power to explain much that is otherwise mysterious about the doctrines. Nevertheless, the courts fall too far short of adequate performance to be left without major assistance from other quarters.

A. Physical Invasion

It will be recalled that the factor of physical invasion has a doctrinal potency often troublesome on two counts. First, private losses otherwise indistinguishable from one another may, as in the flight nuisance cases, be classified for compensability purposes according to whether they are accompanied by a physical invasion, even though that seems a purely fortuitous circumstance. Second, purely nominal harms — such as many which accompany street-widenings or subterranean utility installations — are automatically deemed compensable if accompanied by governmental occupation of private property, in apparent contradiction of the principle that the size of the private loss is a critically important variable. Both these seeming oddities may now seem easier to understand.

Actual, physical use or occupation by the public of private property may make it seem rather specially likely that the owner is sustaining a distinctly disproportionate share of the cost of some social undertaking. Moreover, there probably will be no need, in such a case, to trace remote consequences in order to arrive at a reasonable appraisal of the gravity of the owner's loss — a loss which is relatively likely to be practically determinable and expressible as a dollar amount. Furthermore, to limit compensation to those whose possessions have been physically violated, while in a sense arbitrary, may at least furnish a practical, defensible, impersonal line between compensable and noncompensable impositions — one which makes it possible to compensate on some occasions without becoming mired in the impossible task of compensating all disproportionately burdened interests.

The most obvious argument, then, for physical invasion as a discriminant of compensability would be that it combines a capacity to hold down settlement costs — both as to determining liability and as to measuring damages — with at least some tendency to draw the line so that compensable losses do, as a class, exceed in magnitude those deemed noncompensable. To the extent that the physical invasion criterion really does have these attributes, it should satisfy the test of fairness whether viewed as independent of or as subservient to a test of utility.

. . . A rule that no loss is compensable unless accompanied by physical invasion would be patently unacceptable. A physical invasion test, then, can never be more than a convenience for identifying *clearly compensable* occasions. It cannot justify dismissal of any occasion as *clearly noncompensable.* . . .

. . . The psychological shock, the emotional protest, the symbolic threat to all property and security, may be expected to reach their highest pitch when government is an unabashed invader. Perhaps, then, the utilitarian might say that as long as courts must fend with compensability issues, to lay great stress on the polar circumstances of a permanent or regular physical use or occupation by the public is sound judicial practice — even though, at the same time and in a broader view, to discriminate on such a basis seems unacceptably arbitrary. . . .

B.   Diminution of Value

Earlier we found it hard to understand why compensability should be thought to turn on a comparison of the size of the claimant's loss with the preexisting value of that spatially defined piece of property to which the loss in value seems to be specifically attached. It can now be suggested that judicial reliance on such comparisons reflects a utilitarian approach to compensability, as qualified by some special behavioral assumptions.

The method of identifying compensable harms on the basis of the degree to which "the affected piece" of property is devalued offers several parallels to that of discriminating on the basis of physical invasion. Both methods, though they seem obtuse and illogical so long as the purpose of compensation is broadly stated to be that of preventing capricious redistributions, gain in plausibility given the more refined statement that the purpose of compensation is to prevent a special kind of suffering on the part of people who have grounds for feeling themselves the victims of unprincipled exploitation. Moreover, the appeal of both methods rests ultimately in administrative expediency, in their defining classes of cases whose members will (a) usually be easy to identify and (b) usually, under certain behavioral suppositions, present a particularly strong subjective need for compensation.

As applied to the diminution of value test, these statements require explanation. We may begin by noticing a refinement, not mentioned earlier, which might initially seem only to deepen the mystery. . . . Justice Holmes, writing for the Court in the famous *Pennsylvania Coal* case,[111] held that a restriction on the extraction of coal, which effectively prevented the petitioner from exercising certain mining rights which it owned, was a taking of property and so could be enforced only upon payment of compensation. Holmes intimated strongly that the separation in ownership of the mining rights from the balance of the fee, prior to enactment of the restric-

---

111. Pennsylvania Coal Co. v. Mahon, 260 U.S. 393 (1922).

tion, was critically important to the petitioner's victory. But why should this be so? We can see that if one owns mining rights only, but not the residue of the fee, then a regulation forbidding mining totally devalues the owner's stake in "that" land. But is there any reason why it should matter whether one owns, in addition to mining rights, residuary rights in the same parcel (which may be added to the denominator so as probably to reduce the fraction of value destroyed below what is necessary for compensability) or residuary rights in some other parcel (which will not be added to the denominator)? . . .

. . . [T]he common way of stating the test under discussion — in terms of a vaguely located critical point on a sliding scale — is misleading (though certainly a true representation of the language repeatedly used by Holmes). The customary labels — magnitude of the harm test, or diminution of value test — obscure the test's foundations by conveying the idea that it calls for an arbitrary pinpointing of a critical proportion (probably lying somewhere between fifty and one hundred percent). More sympathetically perceived, however, the test poses not nearly so loose a question of degree; it does not ask "how much," but rather (like the physical-occupation test) it asks "whether or not": Whether or not the measure in question can easily be seen to have practically deprived the claimant of some distinctly perceived, sharply crystallized, investment-backed expectation.

The nature and relevance of this inquiry may emerge more clearly if we notice one other familiar line of doctrine — that which enjoins special solicitude, when a new zoning scheme is instituted, for "established" uses which would be violations were the scheme applied with full retrospective vigor. The standard practice of granting dispensations for such "nonconforming uses" seems to imply an understanding that simply to ban them without payment of compensation, thus seriously reducing the property's market value, would be wrong and perhaps unconstitutional. But a ban on potential uses not yet established may destroy market value as effectively as does a ban on activity already in progress. The ban does not shed its retrospective quality simply because it affects only prospective uses. What explains, then, the universal understanding that only those nonconforming uses are protected which were demonstrably afoot by the time the regulation was adopted? The answer seems to be that actual establishment of the use demonstrates that the prospect of continuing it is a discrete twig out of his fee simple bundle to which the owner makes explicit reference in his own thinking, so that enforcement of the restriction would, as he looks at the matter, totally defeat a distinctly crystallized expectation. Here, then, is a case in which functional division of spatially unitary property makes the same kind of difference it made in *Pennsylvania Coal* although the division here exists only within the eye of the beholder whose feelings we are concerned about, and is not reflected in any title papers.

The worth of this kind of analysis in a utilitarian compensation program depends on a number of assumptions which, while not void of plausibility, are surely debatable. The assumptions are (1) that one thinks of himself not just as owning a total amount of wealth or income, but also as owning several discrete "things" whose destinies he controls; (2) that deprivation of one of these mentally circumscribed things is an event attended by pain of a specially acute or demoralizing kind, as compared with what one experiences in response to the different kind of event consisting of a general decline in one's net worth; and (3) that events of the specially painful kind can usually be identified by compensation tribunals with relative ease.

If these propositions are accepted, the parallelism between the physical occupation and diminution of value tests will be clear. Of the three propositions, the second surely is the most suspect. The first seems self-evident, and the third seems probably true. Thus, the claimant in *Pennsylvania Coal*, which supposed itself to own a mining interest before the incidence of the regulation, owned nothing of consequence afterward, but a residential owner in the regulated district still had essentially what he had before (though its market value may have been reduced). The zoned-out apartment house owner no longer has the apartment investment he depended on, whereas the nearby land speculator who is unable to show that he has yet formed any specific plans for his vacant land still has a package of possibilities with its value, though lessened, still unspecified — which is what he had before.

C. Balancing

Earlier it was argued that while the process of striking a balance between a compensation claimant's losses and "society's" net gains would reveal the efficiency of the measure responsible for those losses and gains, it would be inconclusive as to compensability. By viewing compensation as a response to the demands of fairness we can now see that the "balancing" approach, while certainly inconclusive, is not entirely irrelevant to the compensability issue.

What fairness (or the utilitarian test) demands is assurance that society will not act deliberately so as to inflict painful burdens on some of its members unless such action is "unavoidable" in the interest of long-run, general well-being. Society violates that assurance if it pursues a doubtfully efficient course and, at the same time, refuses compensation for resulting painful losses. In this situation, even a practical impossibility of compensating will leave the sense of fairness unappeased, since it is unfair, and harmful to those expectations of the property owner that society wishes to protect, to proceed with measures which seem certain to cause painful individual losses while not clearly promising any net social improvement. In short, where compensability is the issue the "balancing" test is relevantly aimed at discovering not whether a measure is or is not efficient, but whether it is *so obviously* efficient as to quiet the potential outrage of persons "unavoidably" sacrificed in its interest. This conclusion does not, of course, detract from our earlier conclusion that even the clear and undisputed efficiency of a measure does not sufficiently establish its fairness in the absence of compensation.

D. Harm and Benefit

For clarity of analysis the most important point to be made about asking whether a restrictive measure requires a man to "benefit" his neighbors or only stops him from "harming" them is that this distinction (insofar as it is relevant and valid at all) is properly addressed to an issue different from, and antecedent to, the issue of "compensation" as we have now come to view it. We concluded earlier that the harm-benefit distinction was illusory as long as efficiency was to be taken as the justifying purpose of a collective measure. But we have for many pages past been treating the compensation problem as one growing out of a need to reconcile efficiency with the protection of fair, or socially useful, expectations. The issue we have been trying to clarify does not exist apart from the collective pursuit of efficiency. In this scheme of things, the office of the harm-benefit distinction cannot be to help resolve that issue. But the distinction, properly understood, does have a related use. It helps us to identify certain situations which, although in most obvious respects they resemble paradigm compensability problems, can be treated as raising no compensation issues *because the collective measures involved are not grounded solely in considerations of efficiency.*

The core of truth in the harm-prevention/benefit-extraction test — and the reason for its strong intuitive appeal — emerges when we recognize that some use restrictions can claim a justification having nothing to do with the question of what use of the available resources is the most efficient. If someone, without my consent, takes away a valuable possession of mine, he is said to have stolen and is called a thief. When the theft occurs, society usually will do what it can to make the thief restore to the owner the thing stolen or its equivalent, either because "commutative justice" so requires or because it is felt that there will be an intolerable threat to stable, productive social existence unless society sets its face against the unilateral decisions of thieves that they should have what is in the possession of others. The case is not essentially different if I own a residence in a pleasant neighborhood and you open a brickworks nearby. In pursuit of your own welfare you have by your own fiat deprived me of some of mine. Society, by closing the brickworks, simply makes you give back the welfare you grabbed; and, since you were not authorized in the first place to make distributional judgments as between you and me, you have no claim to compensation. The whole point of society's intervention negates any claim to compensation.

The point, then, is that the appeal of the tendered distinction between antinuisance measures and public benefit measures lies in the fact that the activities curbed by the first sort of measure are much more likely to have been "theft-like" in their origin than are activities restricted by the second sort. Measures of the "public benefit" type can usually be justified *only* in terms of efficiency, a justification which leaves the compensation issue unresolved, while "antinuisance" measures may be justified by considerations of commutative justice, or of the protection of orderly decision making, which negate any possible claim to compensation.

It should be clear, however, that no sharp distinction is thus established between the two types of measures. Activity which is obviously detrimental to others at the time regulations are adopted may have been truly innocent when first instigated. Failure to act upon this plain truth is responsible for some of the most violently offensive decisions not to compensate. The brickyard case is the undying classic.[121] The yard is established out of sight, hearing, and influence of any other activity whatsoever. The city expands, and eventually engulfs the brickyard. The brickmaker is then ordered to desist. That order reduces the market value of his land from 800,000 dollars to 60,000 dollars. There is no question here of disgorging ill-gotten gains: Brick-making is a worthy occupation, and at the time of its establishment the yard generated no nuisance. No incompatibility with any use of other land was apparent. To

---

121. Hadachek v. Sebastian, 239 U.S. 394 (1915).

say that the brick-maker should have foreseen the emergence of the incompatibility is fantastic when the conclusion depending from that premise is that we may now destroy his investment without compensating him. It would be no less erratic for society to explain to a homeowner, as it bulldozed his house out of the way of a new public school or pumping station, that he should have realized from the beginning that congestion would necessitate these facilities and that topographical factors have all along pointed unerringly in the direction of his lot.

Just as the compensation issue raised by an ostensibly nuisance-curbing regulation cannot always be dismissed by assuming that the owner's claim is no stronger than a thief's or a gambler's, so conversely it will often be wholly appropriate to deny compensation because that assumption does hold, even though the measure occasioning the private loss seems to fall within the class of restrictions on "innocent" activity for the enrichment of the public.

Suppose I buy scenic land along the highway during the height of public discussion about the possibility of forbidding all development of such land, and the market clearly reflects awareness that future restrictions are a significant possibility. If restrictions are ultimately adopted, have I a claim to be compensated in the amount of the difference between the land's value with restrictions and its value without them? Surely this would be a weak claim. I bought land which I knew might be subjected to restrictions; and the price I paid should have been discounted by the possibility that restrictions would be imposed. Since I got exactly what I meant to buy, it perhaps can be said that society has effected no redistribution so far as I am concerned, any more than it does when it refuses to refund the price of my losing sweepstakes ticket. . . .

VI. Institutional Arrangements for Securing Just Compensation . . .

A serious objection to the habit of leaving fairness discipline to the courts is that we may thereby miss opportunities to make good use of settlement methods too artificial or innovative for judicial adoption. A court, it seems, must choose between denying all compensation and awarding "just" compensation; the loss is either a "taking" of "property" or it is not. If "just" compensation is essentially incalculable, or if the cost of computing it is very high, the court may be led to classify a situation as noncompensable. If choice must be relegated to this framework, we shall not be able to exploit the substitutability of settlement costs and demoralization costs. It may be that even though that settlement which would reduce demoralization costs to zero would be prohibitively costly, there exists some relatively cheap form of settlement which would reduce demoralization costs so effectively that, by using it, we can reduce the total of settlement plus demoralization costs below what they would be in the absence of any settlement. Such a settlement technique, if one exists, is very likely to require legislative adoption.

For illustration, consider the problem of "relocation payments" to people uprooted by various public development programs, particularly urban renewal. When land is appropriated for clearance and redevelopment, its owner is, of course, compensated in the amount of its "fair market value." But, by the generally received doctrines, tenants are not constitutionally entitled to anything (unless nonsalvageable tenant-owned fixtures are destroyed), and tenant-owners are not constitutionally entitled to be compensated for the disruptive effects of changing neighborhoods and sinking new roots, or even, in case a business is uprooted, for good will destroyed, or, very possibly, for the cash outlay entailed in moving. Justification is not hard to come by for judicial abstinence from such claims. Valuation of good will is a formidable problem. How far away is a person "entitled" to move? How do you translate into dollars the shock of changing neighborhoods and the damnable inconvenience of moving, or appraise the educational damage inflicted by midstream changes in schools? All these problems are multiplied a hundred or a thousandfold where large scale programs scatter large numbers of families. The imponderable and idiosyncratic nature of the losses involved, and the interminable wrangling over amounts which would result from imposing a legal requirement of "just compensation," furnish a classic instance in which compensation claims are defeated largely because of sheer impenetrability.

Yet the violent unfairness of many such operations is manifest. The social gains hoped for from some urban redevelopment programs, while plausible enough to override any "public purpose" objection, nevertheless depend on a still controversial conception. Easily identified, relatively small numbers of people are being handed a distinctly disproportionate and frequently excruciating share of the cost of whatever social gain is involved. Redevelopment has been typically sporadic and probably will be infrequent over the long run — a few explosions here and there in the community in the course of a lifetime. There is no palpable reciprocity;

the sufferers rarely double as special gainers, and they must submit to the spectacle of private land developers (or new residents) moving in for what looks like a publicly subsidized benefit. Those dislocated are likely to be members of a social class which comes increasingly to be identified as a faction — "the urban poor." Yet their influence and organization is not so great, certainly less than their numbers might indicate; and so the sense of having bargained for compensatory concessions probably brings little satisfaction. Altogether, the spectacle of uncompensated dislocations under these circumstances is an oppressive one.

Here is a situation in which a legislature can impose a useful fairness discipline which eludes the grasp of courts. There has, indeed, been a steadily expanding congressional solicitude for persons displaced by federally financed redevelopment activities. . . .

NOTES AND QUESTIONS ON MICHELMAN'S ANALYSIS OF TAKINGS

1. Before asking any questions about this article, let us be sure we understand Michelman's utilitarian argument. In Section IV.A. of the selection, Michelman appears to divide the problem of governmental regulation into two basic elements. First it must be decided whether the program should be adopted at all. This, Michelman suggests, requires a decision whether the costs of the program are greater than its benefits. In other words, the program should be rejected if *both:*

$$(1)\ B - C - D < 0$$

and

$$(2)\ B - C - S < 0$$

where B = project benefits
       D = demoralization costs
       S = settlement costs
       C = all project costs other than S or D.

It is only after determining that the project's benefits are greater than its costs, that a second question must be reached. This is the question whether those who lose as a result of regulation should be compensated for their losses. Here, Michelman suggests, the fundamental issue is whether $D > S$, in which case compensation should be paid, or $S > D$, in which case not.

Given this skeletal outline, consider the following question:

Which institutions, in Michelman's judgment, should be involved in resolving the first of the two basic questions? Which, the second? Can the legislature resolve the first question without knowing how the second will be resolved?

2. Although "demoralization costs" is Michelman's phrase, its intellectual source was Jeremy Bentham, who counted among the losses from confiscation not only the direct loss of the confiscated thing itself but also the fear of losing more in the future, the discouragement of friends and well-wishers, and the resulting "deadening of industry." Bentham, Principles of the Civil Code, in The Theory of Legislation 115-116 (C.K. Ogden ed., 1987) (1789).

3. Virtually all the writing on loss aversion (see e.g., Jolls, Thaler & Sunstein, supra p. 221) appeared after Michelman wrote this famous article. Does loss aversion make compensation even more important? Or might loss aversion argue instead for a more relaxed attitude about compensation, on the grounds that people are overly attached to the status quo and demand irrationally high compensation for losses, impeding needed social change? How would you expect loss aversion to affect the *politics* of takings and compensation issues? Roger G. Noll & James E. Krier, Some Implications of Cognitive Psychology for Risk Regulation, 19 J. Leg. Stud. 747, 769 (1992), suggest that the outcomes of political debates may be affected by the ways that the issues are framed, for example, as losses or as gains with respect to what is described as the status quo.

4. Michelman claims that compensation issues (and demoralization costs) are especially likely to arise in the context of losses inflicted by "deliberate social action," since accidental losses are less likely to be seen as the outgrowth of a systematic collective strategy. Why should the source of the loss matter? By analogy, would a loss due to theft cause a farmer more discouragement than a loss from flooding or insect damage? If human agency is so important, why do governments frequently subsidize flood control and flood insurance, while theft is usually compensated only by private insurance? Is it the *collective* nature of the confiscation, rather than the loss resulting from the confiscation itself, that especially matters in takings jurisprudence?

5. Do owners passively submit to governmental actions that seem to single them out? Note, for example, that arson is a widespread problem among buildings designated for special preservation as historic landmarks. A forest owner similarly may cut timber prematurely if mature trees would attract nesting by endangered species of birds, and the nesting would lead to government prohibitions on timbering. See Dean Lueck & Jeffrey Michael, Pre-

emptive Habitat Destruction Under the Endangered Species Act (Apr. 2000) (unpublished manuscript). But compare Jeffrey J. Rachlinski, Protecting Endangered Species Without Regulating Private Landowners: The Case of Endangered Plants, 8 Cornell J.L. & Pub. Poly. 1 (1998). Rachlinski agrees that endangered plants would fare best if private landowners were compensated, but contends that these species fare better with uncompensated regulatory protection than with no regulatory protection at all. For the argument that environmentalists should favor more generous compensation of regulatory losses in order to reduce landowners' incentives to harvest or develop early, see David A. Dana, Natural Preservation and the Race to Develop, 143 U. Pa. L. Rev. 655 (1995).

6. In an unexcerpted portion of this article Michelman appears to present a supplemental reason for noncompensation, stating that "it seems we are pleased to believe that we can arrive at an acceptable level of assurance that *over time* the burdens associated with collectively determined improvements will have been distributed 'evenly' enough so that everyone will be a net gainer." 80 Harv. L. Rev. at 1225. Does this gradual spreading-out of public risks raise other problems? For example, locally undesirable public facilities are often sited with little or no compensation to neighboring uses. Is a sewage treatment plant in your neighborhood the equivalent of a prison halfway house in someone else's neighborhood? Why have so many neighborhoods joined NIMBY (Not in My Backyard) movements to avoid *any* unwanted land uses? See Peter Margulies, Building Communities of Virtue: Political Theory, Land Use Policy, and the 'Not in My Backyard' Syndrome, 43 Syracuse L. Rev. 945 (1992). Does this phenomenon suggest a distrust of governmental even-handedness? A collective action problem among neighborhoods?

Another issue concerns timing: What is a fair time span within which burdens might be evened out? May the process take several generations? Note the acerbic treatment of remote compensation in the old Wobbly tune: "There'll be pie / in the sky / when you die / by and by." Does the answer depend on the discount rate — that is, how one calculates the present value of future gains and losses?

7. Is Michelman's approach to fairness faithful to Rawls? Michelman seems to consider the condition of persons made worse off as a result of particular governmental actions. Is this the relevant "worst off" grouping in a Rawlsian scheme? Might Rawls think it appropriate that a better-off group come out worse with respect to a particular measure, if the effect were to advance the larger social welfare and particularly to advance the least advantaged group?

8. How satisfactory do you find Michelman's psychological justification for the "physical invasion" test? Does it suggest some innate human characteristic, such as territoriality? Is there any relationship between Michelman's psychological explanation and Sugden's description of property based on "association" in the selection from Sugden's Economics of Rights, supra p. 170?

9. Michelman identifies a crucial problem in the "diminution of value" test of takings, that is, the choice of the denominator, or the underlying property to which the loss is compared. "How much is taken" entails understanding how much *of what*. Unfortunately, the definition of the "original" or "underlying" property turns out to be quite tricky.

Suppose your corporation owned (1) a beautiful old railroad station in Manhattan, (2) other real estate in the area of the station, and (3) the railroad operation itself. Suppose further that a new city historic-preservation ordinance made it nearly impossible for you to redevelop the station to fill up the zoning "envelope" enjoyed by all other owners in the area. If your loss — the value of airspace above the station — is to be placed in the numerator, what is the denominator? Should it be the lost airspace itself? The full station site? The corporation's real estate assets in the larger area? All the corporation's assets? Can you see why this issue affects the question of "the extent of the diminution"?

A curiously dismissive treatment of this central issue appears in the case upon which this hypothetical is based, Penn Central Transportation Co. v. City of New York, 438 U.S. 104, 130 (1978); but the problem of defining the underlying property interest is noted in Lucas v. South Carolina Coastal Council, 505 U.S. 1003, 1016 n.7 (1992).

10. Consider the "balancing" and "harm and benefit" takings tests that Michelman identifies. With respect to "balancing," do you agree that an owner suffering a property loss might be mollified by the consideration that the loss is offset by a larger public gain?

With respect to "harm and benefit," how does one know whether a building ban along a scenic highway, to use one of Michelman's examples, prohibits harms or forces benefits? Can ordinary language help? Michelman suggests that a brick-maker who moves to a remote location can thereby insulate himself from a later charge that his activity harms the property of newcomers to the area. Is a long-standing harm no longer a harm? Nuisance law may provide a guide. Cases invoking a "coming to the nuisance" defense seem to support this proposition, but some courts are more subtle, allowing "coming to the nuisance" as a defense only in nuisance suits asking for injunctive relief, and not in suits for damages. What is the point of this distinction? Would Calabresi and Melamed approve? For some modern permutations, see Spur Indus., Inc. v. Del E. Webb Dev. Co. 494 P. 2d 700 (Ariz. 1972).

11. Is "exit" a viable self-help solution to threatened takings problems? Can the implicit threat of citizen departures (or *ex ante* refusals to move in) diminish the risk of confiscatory legislation in the first place? Might this particularly apply to the takings issues presented by local governments, since those governments are most likely to compete for desirable residents? See Vicki Been, Exit as a Constraint on Land Use Exactions: Rethinking the Unconstitutional Conditions Doctrine, 91 Colum. L. Rev. 473 (1991); but for a critique, see Stewart E. Sterk, Competition Among Municipalities as a Constraint on Land Use Exactions, 45 Vand. L. Rev. 831 (1992) (stressing the immobility of real estate assets). Much of the debate on the issue of "regulatory competition" revolves around the seminal article by Charles Tiebout, A Pure Theory of Local Expenditures, 64 J. Pol. Econ. 416 (1956). According to Tiebout, just as firms compete for customers by offering varying packages of goods and services, local governments compete for residents by offering varying regulatory programs and public goods. Tiebout argued that this competition produces ideal results, but only if some highly restrictive conditions are met. Can you guess what some of them are?

12. In this excerpt Michelman doesn't discuss whether takings law should systematically favor poor claimants over rich claimants. On how takings law might be reshaped to accommodate the values of social responsibility and equality, see Hanoch Dagan, Takings and Distributive Justice, 85 Va. L. Rev. 741 (1999). Should those values instead be pursued only through broad tax and welfare programs, and not in a particularized doctrinal area such as takings? See sources cited in Note 8, supra p. 117.

Takings, Insurance, and Michelman: Comments on Economic Interpretations of 'Just Compensation' Law*

William A. Fischel & Perry Shapiro

I. The Noncompensation Controversy

Under the takings clause of the Constitution, the state is required to pay just compensation whenever it takes private property for

*Source: 17 J. Legal Stud. 269-293 (1988).

public use. Yet the explicit command of the Fifth Amendment does not foreclose asking whether, on balance, this rule is a good thing. If pressed on the question, most economists and lawyers would, we believe, conclude that the government should pay for the property that it takes. The argument, especially that of economists, might be that forcing the government to pay for the resources it gets promotes efficiency. In a world lacking any compensation requirement, the obvious fear is that private investors will be inhibited by the thought that government will snatch away or unthinkingly destroy the fruits of their venture. The fears of what will happen at the end of the process work themselves into the calculation of property owners at the beginning of that process, so that too little capital will be invested in productive enterprises. The compensation requirement thus serves the dual purpose of offering a substantial measure of protection to private entitlements, while disciplining the power of the state, which would otherwise overexpand unless made to pay for the resources that it consumes.

This conventional economic wisdom has been challenged by Blume, Rubinfeld, and Shapiro (henceforth, BRS).[2] Their article offered a model that proved that compensation for takings is inefficient in that such compensation encourages landowners to overinvest in private capital. The basic logic of their position is that compensation allows landowners to ignore the opportunity cost of their land for efficient government projects. This finding will be called the noncompensation result.

The noncompensation result is not merely an economist's curiosity. Since its articulation in 1984, the BRS result has become the focus of two law journal articles that advance it as the basis for a substantial reevaluation of compensation practice in American law.[3] Two of the authors of the article, Blume and Rubinfeld, have offered an analysis of compensation as insurance, and they have suggested that courts distinguish their awards of compensation on the basis of the risk preferences of those affected by takings. Their rule is that people whose property is taken should be awarded compensation only if they did not have an opportunity to reduce the risk of a taking by purchasing private insurance (presumably available once the rule was adopted) or by spreading risks through diversification and contingent contracts. Compensation by govern-

2. Lawrence E. Blume, Daniel L. Rubinfeld & Perry Shapiro, The Taking of Land: When Should Compensation Be Paid? 99 Q.J. Econ. 71 (1984).

3. Lawrence E. Blume & Daniel L. Rubinfeld, Compensation for Takings: An Economic Analysis, 72 Cal. L. Rev. 569 (1984); and Louis Kaplow, An Economic Analysis of Legal Transitions, 99 Harv. L. Rev. 509 (1986). . . .

ment agencies is thus viewed as a last-resort substitute for private insurance. As a practical matter, Blume and Rubinfeld suggest that wealthier people are more likely to be able to insure privately, and thus government compensation for takings might be reserved for poor people.

Louis Kaplow adopts a premise that is similar to that of Blume and Rubinfeld — that compensation serves the function of insurance — but arrives at a different policy conclusion. He argues that because moral hazard problems identified by BRS are less efficiently controlled by the government, only private insurance is needed to provide compensation for takings and, more generally, for all legal transitions, such as tax reform and deregulation. The noncompensation result thus forms an economic rationale for reading the just compensation clause out of the Constitution, although Kaplow professes to be agnostic about the application of his discussion.

In Section II we explore the logic of the noncompensation result using the distinction between property rules and liability rules developed by Calabresi and Melamed.[6] It is shown that the source of the inefficiency created by compensation is similar to the moral hazard found in many other economic policies. Section III explicates Frank Michelman's utilitarian standard and places the noncompensation result in that context.[7] We argue that the insurance model does not fit into this framework because its promoters ignore or misinterpret Michelman's demoralization costs. It is shown that the noncompensation result, which occasioned the development of the insurance model, can be incorporated in Michelman's model, and that it does militate against compensation in many instances. Section IV shows that misinterpretation of demoralization costs is also the source of confusion about whether capitalization of expected takings into land value militates against compensation for purchasers. The conclusions are given in Section V.

II. Compensation and Moral Hazard

A. A Tale of Four Floods

The following example is intended to capture the salient points of the BRS article by extending one of their examples. A

---

6. ... Property Rules, Liability Rules and Inalienability: One View of the Cathedral, 85 Harv. L. Rev. 1089 (1972).

7. Frank Michelman, Property, Utility, and Fairness: Comments on the Ethical Foundations of 'Just Compensation' Law, 80 Harv. L. Rev. 1165 (1967).

Table 1
Summary of the Scenarios in Section II

Scenario (and Rule)	Outcome	Efficiency
1. Natural disaster (no compensation)	Campground	Efficient
2. Natural disaster (government compensation)	Hotel	Inefficient
3. Public dam (government compensation)	Hotel	Inefficient
4. Private dam (landowner consent)	Campground	Efficient

family owns land in a river valley on which they contemplate establishing a business to provide overnight accommodations. They must choose between a campground and a hotel. The campground requires investments of small amounts of capital that depreciate quickly. The hotel involves more capital, which lasts longer and provides more guest services per year. Prior to investigating the geology of the region, the family concludes that the hotel is more profitable.

The only thing that would make the hotel less profitable would be to have the level of the river in the valley rise to such an extent that it would inundate the hotel, in which case all capital would be lost because the hotel would be "immovable" (too costly to move). In that case, the campground would have been more profitable, since only a trivial amount of capital would have been lost. What causes the river to rise, and what knowledge the landowners have or should have about such events, will be discussed under different scenarios. It is assumed throughout that the landowners are risk neutral. (The scenarios are summarized in Table 1 to facilitate comparison of the results.)

Scenario 1 involves a natural disaster. The landowners are made aware that there is a 20 percent probability that their land will be inundated when a natural lake is formed as a result of a rockslide on government-owned land downstream from the proposed hotel. Nothing can be done to reduce the probability of this event or to mitigate the damages it will cause once it happens, and the government is known not to be responsible for the consequences of this "act of God." As a result, the landowners decide to build the nondurable hotel (the campground), a decision which is assumed to maximize social welfare.

In scenario 2, suppose that prior to the landowners' decision to build the campground the government enacted a flood compensation bill that offers to pay those affected by natural disasters for the market value of their losses. No payment in advance, other than an increase in taxes spread among all citizens, is necessary to acquire this guarantee of compensation.

This bill will induce the landowners to erect the hotel rather than the campground. This outcome is inefficient because it guides capital into ventures with negative expected value. The risk to the landowner is removed by the promise of compensation, but the cost to society remains, since capital is removed from safer places to riskier ones. The incentive created by the flood compensation bill is an example of moral hazard.[8] Moral hazard arises from any entitlement that divorces the consequences of people's actions from their decisions. The phenomenon is pervasive in any society. Companies that provide fire insurance worry that policyholders may ignore efficient fire prevention measures; payments to victims of pollution may induce them to live too close to its source; and colleges that grant tenure to professors may find that they work relatively little thereafter. As these examples suggest, moral hazard is not confined to insurance companies or to government programs, nor does moral hazard alone deter governments from undertaking otherwise desirable actions.

Scenario 3 assumes that no natural disaster can inundate the land on which the hotel construction is planned, but the land may be submerged by a dam built by a local government granted the power of eminent domain. The government finds it socially profitable to build the dam only if some exogenous event, such as a rise in the price of oil, occurs to make hydropower profitable. Both the would-be hotel owners and the government dam builder know that the probability of such an event is 20 percent (the same as in the natural disaster case), and both parties know that the value of the dam if this event occurs will exceed the value of the durable hotel.

Assume, moreover, that the government does only projects whose benefits exceed their costs, and everyone knows that when oil prices exceed a certain level, the government will build the

---

8. Blume & Rubinfeld, supra note 3, at 618 n. 144, use this term, as do BRS, supra note 2, at 86. Moral hazard may also be thought of as an externality in the sense that it induces people to ignore some of the costs of their actions. Kaplow, supra note 3, at 551, uses this term to describe the BRS characterization of compensation. Our subsequent use of the term "moral hazard" in the text refers solely to the landowner incentives identified by BRS.

dam. The government cannot be swayed from this decision by any political activity or legal manipulations. We call this relentless dedication to benefit/cost principles the Pigovian assumption.[9] It allows the landowners to regard the government's decision to build the dam as an exogenous event. The government will seize the property if the aforementioned increase in oil prices occurs; otherwise the property is safe.

Under these conditions, BRS prove that it is inefficient to compensate the landowner for the taking. "Just compensation" is, under these conditions, a form of moral hazard. Advance knowledge of a rule that the government would pay for damages to structures would be inefficient for the same reason that disaster payments are inefficient in the second scenario: durable private capital is unnecessarily put at risk of destruction. The essence of the BRS result is that government takings are analogous to these problems. We shall examine this analogy in the next scenario and in the next section.

The BRS moral hazard problem could not arise if the private capital could be costlessly removed from the site. This result follows because the social cost of landowners who ignore the possible government taking of their land is not their loss of the land but the destruction of the capital they put there. It follows, then, that there is no inefficiency entailed in paying full compensation for government takings of labor services or portable capital. Indeed, the very mobility of such resources induces rational governments to pay full compensation for their services regardless of any constitutional requirements. This observation helps explain why real estate is the focus of a disproportionate number of taking cases.

The inefficiency of compensation is not necessarily caused by strategy. The BRS result does not depend on landowners' deliberately overbuilding, which would in any event be unprofitable unless compensation for excessive structure were for more than its market value. The BRS efficiency problem is simply that the landowners rationally disregard the probability that the government may have alternative uses for their land that require the destruction or costly removal of private capital. . . .

Scenario 4 involves a private dam. (This case does not track BRS or other aforementioned papers.) It involves the same facts as in scenario 3: A dam will become profitable if and only if there is

---

9. That Pigou may not have been a Pigovian is argued by Victor Goldberg. Pigou on Complex Contracts and Welfare Economics, 3 Res. L. & Econ. 39 (1981). We instead refer to the "Pigovian tradition" identified by Ronald H. Coase, The Problem of Social Cost, 3 J.L. & Econ. 1 (1960).

a rise in oil prices, an exogenous event whose probability is 20 percent. The difference is that the prospective dam builder is a private party who cannot exercise the right of eminent domain.

The government's role is solely to enforce contracts and protect private property from being taken by another without *consent*. Consent implies that ownership of resources is protected by a property rule, meaning that the owner can refuse to trade. The contrasting protection, under the distinctions developed by Calabresi and Melamed [see supra p. 233], is a liability rule, in which resources must be exchanged as long as the purchaser pays compensation judged by a third party to be equal to the value of the property taken. The typical example of liability rule protection for landowners is eminent domain, under which the government may take their property if it pays for it. It is this rule, of course, that is being examined in this section.

The upstream landowners in the present scenario must give their consent to the building of the dam. What will they do in this situation with regard to their business decision? They will build the campground, just as they would in the case of an uncompensated disaster. This is the efficient decision, which they will make because they can bargain with the dam builder for some of the profits of his dam in exchange for their not building the hotel. (Recall that we assumed that the dam was more profitable than the hotel, so such an exchange is feasible if transaction costs are low enough.)

It would be irrational for the upstream landowners to build the hotel to establish a better bargaining position. Property rule protection puts them in an unimprovable position: they can refuse any offer by the dam builder regardless of the current state of their land. They are thus able to collect all of the surplus value of the dam, and they have no incentive to ignore the probability that a lake may be the most profitable use of their land. This example shows that the BRS result depends on the nature of property rights as well as on the nature of government. Both issues are explored in the next section.

B. Moral Hazard, Liability Rules, and Pigovianism

The BRS noncompensation result is counterintuitive because most economists expect that attaching market prices to things induces economic agents to behave efficiently. But their result becomes more plausible if we note two differences between their models of takings and ordinary exchange. One of the actors, the government, is constrained by the Pigovian assumption to act optimally. The government does not need to be constrained by prices, since, by assumption, it has all the information and incentives to act correctly. Pigovianism suppresses any concern with inefficient levels of government.

Pigovianism alone is not sufficient to get the counterintuitive result, though, since the landowner could be protected by a property rule against government invasions as well as against invasions by other people. In such a case, the government would have to negotiate with the landowners. Because of the security of their position, the landowners would not be induced to ignore the alternative uses for their land that the government might have in mind. The sufficient (and reasonable) condition for the BRS noncompensation result is that the landowner be protected only by liability rules.

The essential problem of a liability rule is that it attempts to limit the entitlements of private property owners. The economic rationale for a liability rule is that it avoids the holdout problem. Under property rule protection, private landowners may strategically refuse to sell their property at values that may be acceptable to them in ordinary transactions in an effort to extract some of the government's surplus from the project. This is inefficient because some such strategies may result in no exchange at all, or they may involve additional resources not otherwise employed in normal market transactions. This rationale, which we accept for this article, precludes the solution suggested by scenario 4 in the previous section.[14]

Our emphasis on compensation as a liability rule also explains the problem with the traditional argument (in Section I) that compensation will improve the allocation of resources because it protects private property. The answer is that eminent domain itself is, in one perspective, a reduction in property rights, not a protection of them. The Fifth Amendment concludes, "nor shall private property be taken for public use, *without just compensation*" (our emphasis). If this clause were intended solely to protect private property, the last three words would be omitted, and *without the consent of the owner* would be substituted (as it is in the Third Amendment's prohibition of quartering peacetime troops in pri-

14. Some research has suggested that eminent domain is not less costly to the government than voluntary market transactions. See Patricia Munch, An Economic Analysis of Eminent Domain, 84 J. Pol. Econ. 473 (1976); and A. Mitchell Polinsky, Controlling Externalities and Protecting Entitlements: Property Right, Liability Rule, and Tax Subsidy Approaches, 8 J. Legal Stud. 1 (1979). If these findings held generally, however, governments would forgo the use of eminent domain, and there is little evidence that they do.

vate homes). Just compensation forces a sale on prearranged terms, something no private person could do without government authority. Those who argue that protecting private property rights improves efficiency are not contradicted by the BRS result; they have only misidentified the just compensation clause as an absolute protection for property rights. . . .

III. Michelman's Demoralization Costs and Insurance

This section explicates Frank Michelman's utilitarian approach to the taking issue and compares it to the view of takings as insurance outlined in Section I. Michelman's article is widely cited, but its economic implications are not fully appreciated.[15] Part of our purpose is to place his contribution in terms of normative economic theory, and part is to show why the aforementioned insurance rationales for takings are inconsistent with Michelman's criteria.

In addition to the utilitarian approach, Michelman advances a Rawlsian fairness criterion, which he implicitly prefers. He suggests, however, that the fairness and utilitarian criteria usually yield the same rules for compensation. For this reason, we confine ourselves in this article to the criterion based on philosophical utilitarianism, which was the original basis of normative economic theory and retains important links to modern welfare economics.

A. The Utilitarian Standard

According to Michelman, in deciding whether a government action was a taking that requires compensation, a utilitarian would consider three factors: efficiency gains, demoralization costs, and settlement costs. . . .

Michelman combines these factors into a utilitarian "felicific calculation." A government measure whose dollar benefits (B) exceed costs (C) as determined by willingness to pay and be paid, respectively, should nevertheless *not* be adopted if the net benefit is exceeded by both demoralization costs (D) and settlement costs (S). In symbols, a utilitarian does not do the project if $(B - C) <$ min (D, S). Michelman does not say what course should be followed if the government decides to go ahead with a project in which $B < C$. However, in subsequent discussion of demoralization costs, he notes that taking on an inefficient project would raise demoralization costs and compel compensation. This would, as a practical matter, discourage a budget-conscious government from performing such a project.

If net benefits are positive and greater than *either* settlement or demoralization costs (or both), the lower of S or D should be endured by the government. Thus, in this latter situation, if settlement costs are lower than demoralization costs, compensation should be paid in order to avoid the greater cost (demoralization). But if settlement costs are higher than demoralization costs, compensation should be denied on this utilitarian calculus. In symbols, the government should pay if $(B - C) > S$, and $S < D$. On the other hand, the government does *not* have to pay if $(B - C) > D$, and $D < S$.

B. Pareto, Kaldor-Hicks, and Michelman

Michelman's utilitarian standard is sometimes called an efficiency criterion. This can be misleading. It is not a rule that all government decisions must involve Pareto-superior moves, because it allows that in some situations (that is, when $[B - C] > D$, and $D < S$), some people can be left worse off if it is too costly to compensate them. In fact, it may even be possible for the government to make compensation and still do the project profitably ($B > C + S$) but still not be compelled to pay, because demoralization costs are relatively low ($D < S$). Thus, Michelman's criterion is more permissive to the government than the Pareto-superiority criterion.

On the other hand, Michelman's standard is less permissive than the Kaldor-Hicks criterion, which says simply that the government should take on projects if the gainers can compensate the losers, but does not require that it actually make the compensation. This is simply Michelman's efficiency gain, that $B > C$. The Kaldor-Hicks criterion was developed in response to the notion that settlement costs of the Pareto-superiority criterion may be so large as to prohibit all projects. But Kaldor-Hicks does not address the troubling possibility that the government may thereby impose large burdens on particular individuals.

Michelman's path-breaking contribution was to define an intermediate standard. The appeal to economists of Michelman's utilitarian formulation is that it offers a coherent, efficiency-based (cost minimization) standard for choosing between the rigid Pareto-superiority criterion, which disallows consideration of settlement costs, and the permissive Kaldor-Hicks criterion, which ignores the distribution of utility gains. . . .

C. Demoralization and Majoritarianism

The source of the demoralization cost for Michelman is the risk of "majoritarian exploitation." He is explicit in keying demoralization costs to the distinction between this political hazard and risk due to random events such as natural disasters. Majoritarianism is said to have greater disincentive effects because of a "perception that the force of a majority is self-determining and purposive. . . . The argument [for the existence of demoralization costs as distinct from other risks] must then proceed to the effect that even though people can adjust satisfactorily to random uncertainty, which can be dealt with through insurance, including self-insurance, they will remain on edge when contemplating the possibility of strategically determined losses."

Why should people feel worse about majoritarian exploitation than about other hazards? Michelman suggests it is because they are strategically determined. People can adjust to strategic losses, but these adjustments are more costly (or involve greater disutility) than adjustments to random losses, which can be "conveniently dismissed from consciousness on the ground that, being uncontrollable, it is not worth thinking about."

Regardless of the source of demoralization costs, our critical point at this juncture is that Michelman regards them as distinct from natural hazards. This is further emphasized by his list of causes of demoralization costs. They include government actions in which (a) settlement costs are low (that is, people feel worse about not being compensated if it would have been easy to do so); (b) losers perceive that their burdens are large relative to others' (disproportionate impact); (c) the efficiency of the project itself is so doubtful that it is a thin veil for unprincipled redistribution; (d) the loss is not likely to be recouped by benefits tied in some way to the project (that is, lack of reciprocity); (e) those who lose now have little confidence that they will gain from similar projects in the future; (f) losers lack political influence to be able to extract concessions to mitigate their burdens in the future.

Our private analogy of Michelman's demoralization distinction is the difference between one's feelings about a watch that is stolen and a watch that is lost. The watch is gone in both cases, but the very knowledge that it was stolen may make you feel worse and thus expend more real resources in avoiding this particular kind of loss, in part because such deliberate acts may be repeated.[31] The ability to purchase insurance against theft does not dispose of such costs, since insurance simply spreads them out over a period of time through insurance premiums. Note that the stolen watch's demoralization is net of the utility gain of the person who now has the stolen watch — and what victim has not wished that a thief's booty bring him ill fortune?

The direct disutility of the citizens whose losses are not compensated to their satisfaction is not the only demoralization cost for Michelman's utilitarians. They also count the disappointment of the losers' sympathizers, who are not necessarily losers themselves but who are made anxious (suffer disutility) as a result of the noncompensation. Add to this the "value of lost future production (reflecting either impaired incentives or social unrest) *caused by demoralization* of uncompensated losers, their sympathizers, and other observers disturbed by the thought that they themselves may be subjected to similar treatment on some other occasion."

The emphasis is added to indicate that Michelman considers these long-run costs to be caused specifically by demoralization; they are not merely prudent responses to random risks. These longrun costs arise not only from "impaired incentives" but also from social unrest. Social unrest costs could include direct public and private outlays to guard against antisocial actions, but they could as well include disaffection with the entire political process.

D. Why Insurance Models Overlook Demoralization

Given Michelman's specific disavowal of the analogy of the risk of a taking to the risk of a natural disaster, we must ask why those who advert to Michelman's principles nonetheless adopt the analogy. . . . BRS, Blume and Rubinfeld (in their joint article), . . . and Kaplow each adopt, for the noncompensation result, a Pigovian model of government. This model assumes that government is an unimpeachable benefit-cost machine. It does not inquire about the distribution of benefits, nor can it be manipulated by any faction of those governed. Thus, losses incurred by individuals whose property is taken should be regarded as analogous to those

---

31. The context of the theft may make a difference. A watch left unattended in a public washroom for a time may be stolen, but its owner may feel less demoralized from that than if it were stolen from a bedroom or by an identifiable individual. Surveys of perceptions of fairness indicate that people most strenuously object to transfers that involve deliberate exploitation of one person's utility by another. See Daniel Kahneman, Jack L. Knetsch, & Richard Thaler, Fairness as a Constraint on Profit Seeking, 76 Am. Econ. Rev. 728, 735 (1986).

that occur through such unsystematic and noncompensable events as market forces or natural events.[37] There are no majoritarian excesses possible, because government decisions do not depend on the will of *anyone*, let alone the majority. Demoralization costs in such a world should be zero.

The Pigovian model, which is adopted in most public policy models as an innocent *ceteris paribus* assumption, turns out to dispose of the taking issue entirely. Since BRS show that settlement costs are always positive (due to the moral hazard problem), $S > D$ for all projects, since $D = 0$ in the Pigovian model. Thus compensation would never be called for in a Pigovian application of Michelman's utilitarian framework.

IV. The Temporal Error of Insurance and Capitalization

A. Private Insurance and Demoralization Costs

It has been argued in the previous section that Michelman's utilitarian criterion forms a coherent framework to accommodate the moral hazard issue, and that no additional efficiency rationale is needed. Now we ask whether, if one accepts this conclusion, one could not accept also private insurance for takings, which Kaplow argues is more efficient. If landowners whose property is taken are paid, why should they feel greater loss if the payment comes from private insurance rather than from the public purse? Why does a check from a private insurer not soothe demoralization costs as well as public compensation?

One response to this line of reasoning is its impracticality. Kaplow does not attempt to explain the absence of a private, third-party insurance market for losses not covered by current eminent domain practices. We know of no legal inhibitions on such insurance, and uncompensated costs such as relocation, attorneys' fees, and lost business goodwill are often substantial and accrue to those who seem to be in a poor position to self-insure. An explanation for lack of private taking insurance, suggested to us by Robert

---

37. That members of society may regard losses incurred by deliberate acts as worse than those that occur randomly is not to argue that compensation should never be paid to the victims of random events who may not have insured themselves (for example, flood victims or destitute retirees). Our argument is only that the reasons for the latter programs do not rest on demoralization costs, but on something else, perhaps empathy with the victims. While demoralization costs are increased by the empathy of those who see others being involuntarily exploited, the basic source is the losers' knowledge that they are being involuntarily used for another's gain.

Ellickson in a letter, is adverse selection. A public planner might tip off landowners of an impending taking and encourage them to apply for insurance in order to reduce political opposition to his project. Insurance losses would mount as a result, and private insurers would withdraw. Another problem involving purely private insurance against takings is how to secure the assets of insurance companies. If the government can seize any private property without compensation, what would prevent it from seizing the assets of insurance companies?

Even if these practical problems could be overcome, however, there remains a fundamental flaw in relying on private insurance. Kaplow's proposal looks for the taking at the wrong moment in time. If landowners are risk averse, they can avoid the *risk* of a prospective taking by purchasing insurance or self-insuring. But demoralization costs are not imposed at the moment the property is taken. Demoralization costs, properly understood, arise when landowners *realize* that their wealth is reduced, not when the legal taking occurs. Even if they were risk neutral, so that they had no demand for insurance, landowners would be demoralized by the uncompensated reduction in wealth, which is the value of the property prior to the risk, times the probability that it will be taken. An insurance payment simply spreads this loss over time and reduces variance in the insured's income stream. The existence of insurance does not dispose of the issue of uncompensated transfers of wealth, and it is no more an argument for legalizing uncompensated takings than it is for legalizing the theft of watches.

To drive this point home, consider another analogy. Suppose that copyright laws were suspended. Authors who once relied on royalties from published works would realize at once that their wealth has been reduced. But because not all books may be pirated, there will be uncertainty about future incomes. Risk-averse authors may then insure. They will pay to their insurers premiums, the capitalized value of which is at least equal to the expected loss incurred as a result of copyright suspension. In the end, some authors will receive payments from their insurers for what used to be called copyright infringement. But few economists (and no commercial authors!) would argue that such private insurance amounts to the same thing as copyright law. The fundamental change was the loss of rights previously held. Insurance did not restore those rights. . . .

B.   *Capitalization and Notice Arguments Against Compensation*

Looking at takings at the wrong moment in time is the source of another problem that causes persistent confusion in the takings literature. This is the argument that expectations of a taking are capitalized in the value of property so that purchasers of the property pay less for it and thus should not be compensated. Our argument is that capitalization does not satisfy anxiety about takings because it again views the problem at the wrong moment in time.

If Brennan, expecting that a taking of Alchian's land will not be compensated once Alchian sells it, nonetheless purchases it for $100 instead of the $300 it would command absent the prospective taking, it is true that Brennan does not lose in an expected-value sense if the land is subsequently taken without compensation. But *Alchian* surely lost from the prospective taking. If he had been guaranteed compensation for takings that, like other property entitlements, ran with the land, Brennan would have had to pay Alchian $300.

To say that Brennan should not be compensated because he "moved to the taking" or "purchased with notice" or "assumed the risk" or "had rational expectations" is to make one of *Alchian's* property entitlements inalienable, if Alchian would have received compensation by holding on to it. (If neither Alchian nor Brennan would have been compensated, it is simply a taking of Alchian's property.) Insofar as alienability is regarded as an essential aspect of normal property rights, a rule that purchasers are not compensated is itself a taking of the seller's property.

One of the reasons for confusion about this point is the ambiguity of Michelman's treatment of it. He offers an example in which those who purchase land they know may be taken should not be compensated. His example is a purchaser (our Brennan) of land that is among parcels that are the subject of active public debate to prevent development in order to preserve the scenery along the highway. Michelman indicates that Brennan should not be compensated if the regulations are subsequently adopted because the price he paid for the land reflected the possibility of restrictions.

But it is not clear from the scenic highway example alone whether Michelman believes that the original owner (our Alchian) should have been compensated had he not sold it. If Alchian would not have been entitled to compensation, then there is no reason to compensate Brennan or any other successor in title for the same regulation, and Michelman's example is unexceptionable. If, on the other hand, Alchian would have been compensated but Brennan would not, Michelman makes the error of looking at the taking at the wrong moment in time. The taking's demoralization occurred when Alchian realized that his right to compensation was made inalienable, not when Brennan was denied compensation. . . .

V. Conclusion

Michelman's utilitarian standard offers a method for evaluating compensation questions that is consistent with principles of economic efficiency. It provides a normative guide for when to choose the Pareto-superiority criterion (at least insofar as just compensation is consistent with that criterion) and when to settle for the Kaldor-Hicks criterion. Michelman's framework permits incorporation of the BRS noncompensation result into settlement costs while retaining a view of government more realistic than the Pigovian assumption. Insurance rationales for compensation are inadequate in this framework, because insurance does not address demoralization cost, which plays a pivotal role in Michelman's standard. This is not to argue that the utilitarian standard is the only one consistent with economic reasoning. We argue only that those who advance the insurance rationale for compensation have not addressed the central normative question of compensation, which is when to respect individual property entitlements in a world of less-than-ideal governments.

Failure to address demoralization cost does not itself condemn all insurance rationales for compensation. It may turn out that demoralization is related to risk aversion and can be analyzed with the same methods. We need to know more about the sources of demoralization (if it exists as a distinct cost at all). We also need to know what a "majoritarian" government encompasses and why demoralization costs arise from it rather than from other types of government actions. For this reason, we conclude by pointing out two aspects of Michelman's framework that require more investigation.

"Majoritarianism" points to democratic models, of which there are a wide variety. In a separate article, we model a constitutional choice of compensation levels made in the face of a simple majority-rule government. We find that compensation would be called for if risk-neutral, utility-maximizing constitution framers anticipate a majority-rule government rather than a Pigovian government. This suggests a congruence with Michelman's result, although we cannot identify a specific factor in our model analogous to demoralization cost.

We need to know whether decisions of governments that are perceived as dominated by bureaucrats or by special-interest groups give rise to demoralization costs in the same way as more obvious examples of majority rule, such as town meetings and plebiscites. Existing commentary on this is mixed. Richard Epstein makes no distinction between takings that result from the politics of special interest or majority rule.[54] Taking a little from many people (for example, taxpayers) is regarded as the same as taking a lot from a few people (for example, outvoted owners of undeveloped land). Robert Ellickson, on the other hand, found that just-compensation remedies for excessive suburban zoning laws were especially appropriate because of the majoritarian structure of local government.[55] One reason for this distinction is that in larger governments the special-interest model of politics more likely applies, so that losers from uncompensated actions may be less demoralized by failure to compensate because they can recoup their losses in a later coalition.

We suggest that modern survey research and psychological experiments may provide insights into the extent to which random losses differ from government-imposed losses, and how different types of government-imposed losses are perceived by those who bear the costs. . . .

NOTES AND QUESTIONS ON EFFICIENCY AND THE TAKINGS ISSUE

1. Fischel and Shapiro's (F & S) analysis suggests that liability rules (unlike property rules) tend to make landowners ignore the most socially valuable uses of their property; under a liability rule for compensation, they are likely to overexpend on capital projects. This is the moral hazard problem. Does it follow that land should be protected by a property rule instead of a liability rule, either favoring the owner (government may only purchase with the consent of the owner) or favoring the government (government need not compensate and has a property right to use any land at will)? What speaks for a liability rule instead of one or the other of these property rules? See Calabresi & Melamed, supra p. 233. What speaks against it? See Krier & Schwab, supra p. 249.

2. F & S stress that Michelman's concept of demoralization costs has special concern for "majoritarian exploitation" of minorities. Is this concern itself well placed? Compare Bruce Ackerman, Beyond Carolene Products, 98 Harv. L. Rev. 863 (1985), arguing that modern public-choice theory upends the concern about exploita-

---

54. Epstein, [Takings: Private Property and the Power of Eminent Domain (1985)], at 93-96.
55. Robert C. Ellickson, Suburban Growth Controls: An Economic and Legal Analysis, 86 Yale L.J. 385, 404-420 (1977).

tion of small, identifiable minorities. According to this theory, members of such groups are most likely to be able to identify each other, organize around their narrow interests, and influence legislation — unlike the relatively passive members of wide majority groups, who feel costs and benefits only diffusely. Does Ackerman's analysis suggest that "takings" problems (where harms are imposed by the many on the few) are less important than problems of "givings" (where the few extract special benefits to the detriment of the many)? If a government must pay "just compensation" for a taking, why shouldn't it be required to collect a "fair charge" when it confers a giving? See Abraham Bell & Gideon Parchomovsky, Givings, 111 Yale L.J. 547 (2001); Eric Kades, Windfalls, 108 Yale L.J. 1489 (1999).

F & S surmise that majoritarian abuse is particularly likely at the municipal level because in that setting minority factions are less able to obtain political protection through logrolling. Should courts be particularly sympathetic to takings claims asserted against local governments, as opposed to states and the national government? Compare William A. Fischel, Regulatory Takings: Law, Economics, and Politics 100-141 (1995) (answering yes), with James E. Krier, Takings from Freund to Fischel, 84 Geo. L.J. 1895, 1910-1911 (1996) (expressing doubts). For more on the relation of public choice considerations to takings law, see Daniel A. Farber, Public Choice and Just Compensation, 9 Const. Commentary 279 (1992).

3. In their Alchian-Brennan example, F & S assert that a policy of barring the purchaser of a regulated property from pursuing a takings claim is likely to impose a loss not on the purchaser but rather on the person who owned the regulated property when this policy was adopted. They reason that the purchaser would pay less for the property because the constitutional claim would not be transferable. F & S's argument implicitly assumes that sellers and buyers are knowledgeable about both takings law and the existence of confiscatory regulations. Is that assumption plausible? For a fractured judicial debate over how the Alchian-Brennan issue should be resolved, see Palazzolo v. Rhode Island, 121 S. Ct. 2448 (2001).

4. In what ways if any do governmental confiscations resemble normal insurable risks? Can an insurance company predict the probabilities of "takings" risks in a given community in the same way that it predicts, say, the incidence of automobile accidents? If there are differences, how might they affect insurance markets?

In the literature on insurance, Frank Knight, in Risk, Uncertainty, and Profit (1921), drew a well-known distinction between *risk* (which may be estimated probabilistically) and *uncertainty* (which may not). Crudely speaking, risks are thought to be amenable to private insurance, but uncertainties are not, unless they can be grouped in such a way as to permit probabilistic estimates. Can you see why? How do the problem of moral hazard and the related problem of adverse selection (discussed in F & S's text at Section IV. A.) turn risks into uncertainties? For a lucid explanation, see George Priest, Insurability and Punitive Damages, 40 Ala. L. Rev. 1009, 1020 (1989).

Are potential governmental takings risks or uncertainties? Does the answer depend on whether governmental agents correctly weigh costs and benefits on the basis of the public interest (designated by F & S as the "Pigovian assumption")?

5. Might insurance companies themselves take on the role of defending and defining the property rights of the insured? For example, in the nineteenth century, fire insurance companies organized firefighting companies that would respond only to calls from insured property owners. See Fred McChesney, Government Prohibitions on Volunteer Fire Fighting in Nineteenth Century America: A Property Rights Perspective, 15 J. Legal Stud. 69, 73-75 (1985). Though this particular arrangement died out, can you see the reasons for integrating the services of insurance and property protection? In modern environmental law, insurance companies play a considerable role in "regulating" the activities of insured hazardous waste facilities, linking insurance coverage to compliance with various safety measures; see Steven A. Kunzman, The Insurer as Surrogate Regulator of the Hazardous Waste Industry: Solution or Perversion? 20 The Forum 469 (A.B.A. 1985). How does this role help to control the problems of moral hazard and adverse selection?

Do these examples of insurers' defense and management of property undercut F & S's argument that insurance cannot take the place of undefended property rights? Would an insurance company be able to prevent the copying of an author's creations? The overregulation of a developer's site?

6. Does making a government liable for the costs of its regulatory actions actually serve to discipline the government against excessive regulation? What if government officials respond more to political incentives than to financial ones? See Daryl J. Levinson, Making Government Pay: Markets, Politics, and the Allocation of Constitutional Costs, 67 U. Chi. L. Rev. 345 (2000). Might it make sense to uncouple the issue of government-agency liability from the issue of compensating the aggrieved property owner? See Michael A. Heller & James E. Krier, Deterrence and Distribution in

the Law of Takings, 112 Harv. L. Rev. 997 (1999). Heller and Krier identify contexts where agency liability is appropriate but victim compensation is not, and where victims warrant compensation, but not from the agency's own budget.

E. Environmental Protection

*Explaining Market Mechanisms**

Thomas W. Merrill

I. Introduction

Of the various innovations in environmental policy in the last twenty-five years, one of the most controversial has been the effort to replace traditional command-and-control regulation with market mechanisms.

Command-and-control regulation refers to a system of pollution control based on uniform standards of performance for sources of pollution. Most typically, regulators adopt standards that specify for a particular category of sources how much of a given pollutant a source is permitted to emit over a given unit of time. All sources that fall within the category are then required to achieve compliance with this standard, unless granted a variance. Often, but not always, these standards are fixed on the basis of the degree of control that can be achieved using existing technology.

Market mechanisms, in contrast, are systems of pollution control based on the imposition of a money charge on the emission of a quantity of a given pollutant over a given unit of time. The charge can take the form of a fee or tax imposed by the regulator, often referred to as a Pigovian tax, after the early proponent of the idea, economist Arthur Pigou. Alternatively, the charge can be imposed by requiring sources to purchase permits, from either the government or other sources, authorizing the emission of a quantity of a given pollutant over a given unit of time.

As befits a controversial subject, the literature on command-and-control versus market mechanisms is primarily normative. The partisans of market mechanisms stake their case on the superior

*Source: 2000 U. Ill. L. Rev. 275-298.

efficiency of a system that sets a price on the emission of pollutants and thereby creates an incentive for sources to reduce those emissions. Such a system gives regulated firms a great deal of flexibility. Each firm can choose either to pay the pollution charge or to not pollute, whichever is cheaper. This flexibility permits a given level of emissions reduction to be achieved at the lowest cost: the emissions reduction will be carried out by the firms in a position to do so with the least expenditure of resources. . . .

The defenders of command and control generally marshal two types of arguments in opposition. First, they express skepticism about whether market mechanisms would work as advertised. They point out that these mechanisms require a foolproof method of monitoring the emissions of all sources to make sure that no firms are cheating by emitting more pollution than the amount for which they have paid. Moreover, pollution taxes or tradable permits require the creation of elaborate institutional infrastructures, which may not be adequately funded. Second, command-and-control defenders argue that market mechanisms send the wrong message about environmental protection. Market mechanisms treat pollution as just another cost of doing business, whereas pollution should be treated as morally objectionable behavior that must be eliminated to the greatest extent possible. . . .

II. Two Positive Theories for the Emergence of Market Mechanisms

Within the existing positive literature on market mechanisms, it is possible to discern two general types of explanations for their emergence: wealth-maximization theory and distributional theory.

A. Wealth-Maximization Theory

The wealth-maximization theory traces its provenance to the property rights literature of neoinstitutional economics and in particular to the pioneering work of Harold Demsetz.[8] The basic insight is that property rights emerge and recede in accordance with a criterion of societal wealth maximization, in effect a type of cost-benefit analysis. The benefits of a property regime come in reducing wasteful competition to capture the economic rents associated with scarce resources (what the neoinstitutionalists call "rent dis-

8. See Harold Demsetz, Toward a Theory of Property Rights, 57 Am. Econ. Rev. 347 (1967).

sipation") and by making it easier to control the external costs associated with resource use by reducing the number of parties affected by such uses. The costs of such a regime include the costs of defining property rights, identifying the owners of such rights, and protecting the rights against interference by others. According to wealth-maximization theory, if the social benefits of a property regime exceed the social costs of creating and enforcing such a regime, then society will recognize property rights over a resource. Conversely, if the social benefits of a property regime do not exceed the social costs of creating and enforcing such a regime, then society will not recognize property rights over the resource.

A corollary to the wealth-maximization theory is that property regimes will exist in varying degrees of complexity in terms of the number of "sticks" that are recognized as belonging in the bundle of rights of the property owner and will exist with varying degrees of formality in terms of how such rights are enforced. If the net benefits of a property regime are positive but small, then this may result in the creation of a rudimentary property rights regime, such as one based on simple usufructuary rights and enforced by informal social norms. As the surplus of benefits relative to costs grows larger — that is, as the resources become more scarce or externalities become more severe or as the costs of creating and enforcing property rights fall — then we should expect to see more elaborate property regimes emerge. For example, usufructuary rights may evolve toward full ownership rights including the rights to transfer and inherit. Similarly, enforcement through social norms may be supplemented with common law remedies and criminal penalties.

Carol Rose, in a provocative article, has adopted this property rights framework to explain the evolution of different forms of environmental protection.[12] She describes four general control strategies, starting with DO-NOTHING (leaving the problem unregulated), followed by KEEPOUT (prohibiting new polluting sources), then RIGHTWAY (command-and-control regulation), and lastly PROP (market mechanisms). She suggests that, as a general matter, these four strategies are characterized by progressively higher management costs, both in terms of the costs of administrating the system and the costs to users of complying with the system. However, again as a general matter, these strategies are also progressively more effective in controlling rent dissipation and reducing externalities. The combination of these general features — higher management costs but greater effectiveness — means that

12. [Citing Rose, Rethinking Environmental Controls, 1991 Duke L.J. 1.]

as a rule, as pressure on resources increases, the political system will tend to shift to progressively more expensive but more effective control mechanisms.

Rose's adaptation of wealth-maximization theory to environmental controls yields a fairly straightforward explanation for the emergence of market mechanisms. In terms of air pollution, for example, her model suggests that the solution to the relative-cost controversy depends on how congested our air really is. If we are far enough out on the horizontal line of resource pressure, then PROP may be preferable because at that pressure level it minimizes total costs, despite its arguably higher system-wide costs of organization and policing. More generally, as the external costs of a particular form of pollution rise — that is, as particular environmental goods like clean air or water become increasingly scarce — we should expect to see the control strategy for dealing with this problem shift from RIGHTWAY (command and control) to PROP (market mechanisms). Alternatively, if the costs of administering a system of market mechanisms were to fall, perhaps because of the invention of inexpensive and effective monitoring devices, then this drop might also trigger a movement from RIGHTWAY to PROP. These possibilities, of course, are not mutually exclusive. In many instances one would expect to see a combination of increasing benefits (because of increasing pressure on resources) and reduced costs (because of new monitoring technology or the like) causing a move from command-and-control regulation to market mechanisms.

B. Distributional Theory

The distributional theory traces its provenance to the interest group theory of politics, the leading figure in this case being Mancur Olson.[16] The starting point here is not the efficiency of an institutional arrangement but rather its distributional implications. Different policy instruments will favor different social groups, and these groups are assumed to compete in an effort to persuade regulators to adopt those instruments that distribute the greatest wealth to themselves. . . .

Notice that the distributional theory suggests that society may adopt regulatory regimes that fail to maximize societal wealth. It will adopt those regimes whose distributional features are most

---

16. See generally Mancur Olson, Jr., The Logic of Collective Action: Public Goods and the Theory of Groups (1965). . . .

favorable to the groups that can organize most effectively to influence the political process. These outcomes may well result in a decrease in total societal wealth relative to other regimes, but because of the high costs of bargaining and disparities in influence among groups, a shift to a more efficient regime may not occur. . . .

III. The Use of Market Mechanisms in Environmental Law — An Overview . . .

According to Svendsen, there have been eight fully implemented environmental enforcement programs in the U.S. that rely on market mechanisms.[27] Five of these programs have arisen under various provisions of the Clean Air Act, and three were stimulated by the water quality standards mandated by the Federal Water Pollution Control Act. . . .

Several potentially significant generalizations about these market mechanism programs can be drawn from Svendsen's survey.

First, it is clear that market mechanisms play a distinctively secondary role in the overall American pollution control scene. Among the five air programs, two were transitional programs no longer in use, and one is a regional program. . . . The three water pollution programs are essentially local pilot programs; they have generated a grand total of two trades after nearly two decades of operation. Perhaps more significantly, the eight market mechanisms are wholly confined to the air and water pollution contexts. Other areas of pollution control, such as hazardous waste management and reclamation, evidently remain innocent of market mechanisms.

Second, the eight market mechanism programs all adopt the same method for putting a price on pollution. In each case, the programs rely on what have been called "grandfathered" permits — a system of tradable permits in which permits are allocated free of charge to existing pollution sources. None of the eight programs relies on any form of pollution fees or taxes or on tradable permits allocated by auction. . . .

Third, each of the programs arises in a context where the standard for acceptable levels of pollution has been independently and authoritatively established before the market mechanism was put in place. . . .

27. [Citing Gert Tinggaard Svendsen, Public Choice and Environmental Regulation 72 (1998).]

Fourth, there is no consistent theme regarding the scope and severity of the external costs addressed by these various market mechanisms. . . .

In sum, Svendsen's survey shows that command-and-control regulation continues to dominate in all areas of U.S. pollution control policy; market mechanisms are exceptional. As to the handful of market mechanisms that exist, two generalizations hold true. First, these programs always proceed by creating grandfathered transferable permit programs. Second, they are based on pollution control standards that have been authoritatively established before the market mechanism is put in place. Otherwise, the scope and severity of the pollution problems addressed and the technology used to monitor compliance and otherwise implement these programs defy generalization.

IV. What Form Market Mechanisms Take . . .

The first candidate for an explanatory theory — the wealth-maximization theory — cannot account for the strong and consistent preference for grandfathered permits over pollution taxes and auctioned permits. In terms of effectiveness in reducing pollution, the calculus as to whether taxes or tradable permits are preferred depends in part on assumptions about the slope of the marginal benefit and marginal control cost curves, making a priori judgments impossible. Taxes are sometimes said to have an advantage when we know the marginal costs of pollution but do not know the marginal control costs because we can set the tax at a rate equal to the marginal costs of pollution and allow polluters to compare the tax to their own marginal control costs. On the other hand, when the desired level of pollution is established on some basis other than the marginal costs of pollution, tradable permits have the advantage: we can reach the desired level of pollution simply by printing the right number of permits, whereas the use of taxes in this context may make it necessary to adjust tax rates before the right level of pollution is reached. Whatever we make of these differences, however, they at most explain a preference for Pigovian taxes over permits (or vice versa). They cannot explain why one type of permit system (for example, grandfathered permits) is consistently preferred to the other options. . . .

The distributional theory, in contrast, provides a ready explanation for the uniform preference for grandfathered permits over Pigovian taxes and auctioned permits. . . . [U]nder the distributional theory, the factors that determine a group's influence in the political process include (1) the costs of organizing the group for political action; (2) the per capita stakes among the members of the group with respect to the particular issue; and (3) whether the interests of the group members are uniform or in conflict with respect to the issue.

One group that has a vital interest in any effort to establish market mechanisms is the firms that engage in polluting activities. Adoption of any market mechanism means these firms henceforth will have to pay (either through taxes or purchased permits) for the privilege to pollute. The foregoing factors suggest that this group will exert strong political pressure in opposition to any proposal for Pigovian taxes or auctioned permits but is likely to have a much more equivocal response to grandfathered permits. Thus, if market mechanisms are to be adopted, grandfathered permits will encounter less resistance than the other types of market mechanisms. . . .

Although the regulatory effect of a permit system is generally the same as that of a pollution tax, the distributional consequences can be very different. Under a tax scheme, the charges for engaging in residual pollution are paid to the government. Under a permit scheme, the charges for engaging in residual pollution are paid to the holders of unused permits. If permits are auctioned by the government, then the distributional consequences of the two programs are the same. But if the permits are issued on a grandfathering basis — that is, they are given away free of charge to incumbent polluters in proportion to some baseline of emissions that exists before the scheme is initiated — then the incumbent polluters receive new wealth from the system. . . .

In short, distributional theory suggests that tax schemes and auctioned permit schemes fail because they encounter the strong and united opposition of existing sources of pollution. Grandfathered permit schemes succeed — at least some of the time — because the subsidy inherent in the distribution of free permits leaves some segments of industry better off, which shatters the industry's united opposition. . . .

V. The Why Question

Let us now turn to the more difficult question: why market mechanisms are utilized so infrequently in environmental law. Here, the wealth-maximization theory makes a more serious bid for explanatory superiority. Recall that under Professor Rose's framework, market mechanisms not only are assumed to be more effective in

reducing pollution than command and control but also are assumed to be more expensive in terms of management costs. . . . It
follows that in those areas where market mechanisms have been
adopted, we should find that pressure on environmental resources
is especially intense or that new monitoring devices or other administrative innovations have occurred that have reduced the costs
of adopting market mechanisms or both.

Some of the American experience with market mechanisms is
consistent with the wealth-maximization hypothesis. Here, it is important not to lose sight of the big picture. There is no question
that new regulatory regimes to control pollution have emerged in
the last twenty-five years, and these regimes are a response to the
public perception that environmental degradation is a more serious
problem than earlier generations had believed. Broadly speaking,
therefore, the environmental revolution that started in the 1970s —
featuring a new public sensitivity to the importance of environmental values followed by the adoption of elaborate regulatory
regimes designed to improve environmental quality — is consistent with the wealth-maximization theory. . . . Moreover, there is
some evidence suggesting that market mechanisms are associated
with especially severe environmental problems, such as the lead
additives scheduled for elimination by the Lead Additives Program and the ozone-depleting gases scheduled for elimination under the Montreal Protocols. Finally, evidence exists that market
mechanisms have been facilitated by the development of new and
more effective monitoring technology. . . .

Overall, however, it would be a considerable stretch to insist
that there is any kind of consistent correlation between the severity
of pollution or the adoption of new administrative technologies
and the use of market mechanisms. Market mechanisms have been
adopted in circumstances where the evidence of harmful health
effects is equivocal at best (acid rain and state water quality standards), and they have been adopted in circumstances where administrative techniques, including monitoring, remain primitive if
not nonexistent (the Lead Additives Program, the CFC/Halon Program, and the water programs). Thus, our experience with market
mechanisms to date (admittedly too limited to provide conclusive
proof one way or another) offers little support for the hypothesis
that market mechanisms emerge because of increasing pressure on
environmental resources and/or innovations that reduce the costs
of implementing such programs.

Can the distributional theory do better? Building on the discussion in part IV, I think it can. As we saw in that discussion,
there will be some industry opposition to any type of market mech-

anism. Opposition to pollution taxes and auctioned permits will be intense because the stakes in such a program are uniformly negative for industry. These programs face tough sledding. Opposition to grandfathered permits will be more muted and mixed. . . .

. . . To explain why command and control remains the dominant mode of environmental regulation, we must introduce the interests of other relevant actors. I will here consider two: local service providers, of whom unionized labor is the most prominent but not the only example, and environmentalists. . . .

Under a command-and-control regime that applies nationwide and places all its emphasis on new sources, the optimal strategy for a polluting firm is to stay put and to continue to operate older polluting plants as long as possible. This, of course, also protects the interests of local service providers in older polluting industries, which tend to be concentrated in the "rustbelt" states of the Midwest and North Atlantic. . . .

Note that grandfathered permits do not protect against industrial out-migration the same way that nationally uniform command-and-control regimes do. Grandfathered permits contain a local protectionist element. Incumbents receive subsidies, new entrants from the outside do not, and these subsidies clearly give incumbents a financial advantage. But grandfathered permits provide no incentive for incumbents to stay put. Indeed, they provide something of the opposite incentive, insofar as firms that shut down or move no longer need their permits and hence can sell them for cash. . . .

In light of this critical difference in the nature of the subsidies to polluters associated with the typical command-and-control regime (with its new/old distinction) and the typical market mechanism (with its grandfathered permits), it is not surprising that local service providers strongly prefer command and control. Local service providers above all else want incumbent polluters to stay put and remain in operation. Command and control creates just such an incentive. Market mechanisms, in contrast, create an incentive for plant closures. . . .

How do the environmentalists fit into the picture? Traditionally, environmentalists have embraced command and control and have opposed market mechanisms. Economists who tout market mechanisms have been puzzled by this, since market mechanisms are in theory more effective than command and control in achieving any given emissions standard. A permit scheme, for example, will always achieve its stated goal as long as permit conditions are enforced, and new permits are not printed. In contrast, command

and control rarely achieves its stated objectives because variances and incomplete enforcement result in some slippage from regulatory standards. If environmentalists really care about the environment, the economists ask, why would they oppose what promises to be the more efficacious regulatory tool? . . .

I would draw the following tentative conclusion from these reflections about the environmentalist position. Environmentalists have long opposed and continue to oppose setting emissions standards based on cost-benefit analyses. They prefer that standards be set without regard to economic costs on the basis of adequate protection of the public health, ecosystems, or particular species. In the formative years of the environmental movement — the 1970s — market mechanisms were espoused by persons who also espoused cost-benefit analyses. Hence, environmentalists opposed market mechanisms because they saw them as legitimizing cost-benefit analyses. Command and control, in contrast, was espoused by persons who supported health-based or environment-based standards. Thus, environmentalists were naturally more comfortable with the advocates of command and control.

As the years went by, particular situations arose in which environmentalists had already won the debate over standards, or the debate had already been resolved via political compromise. Environmentalists came to see that in these situations it was safe to endorse or at least acquiesce in the usage of market mechanisms, since they would function solely as a means to an end and would not undermine the environmentalist position regarding the proper metric for setting standards. Thus, in these situations, and these alone, we see significant environmentalist support for market mechanisms.

When we combine these accounts of the positions of three major institutional players — industry groups, local service providers, and environmentalists — we can patch together a somewhat complex but plausible account of why market mechanisms today play a small but not entirely inconsequential role in American environmental law. Environmental law began in the 1970s with a kind of "bootleggers and Baptists"[83] alliance centered on support for command-and-control regulation. Incumbent industry sup-

---

83. Bruce Yandle, Bootleggers and Baptists in the Market for Regulation, in The Political Economy of Government Regulation 29, 33 (Jason F. Shogren ed., 1989). The phrase "bootleggers and Baptists" is based on the claim that Sunday closing laws are enacted with the political support of two otherwise antagonistic groups — distributors of illegal liquor and teetotalers.

ported the regime because it imposed higher costs on new entrants and thus granted a measure of protection to incumbents. Local service providers supported the regime because it discouraged out-migration of industry and hence protected existing demand for unionized workers and other local inputs. Environmentalists supported the regime because it avoided any suggestion that standards should be fixed with economic costs in mind.

When we flash forward twenty-five years later, we see that this alliance has frayed considerably, but the result is more deadlock than a new consensus for action. Local service providers remain fully committed to command and control and dislike grandfathered permits because they underwrite out-migration. Much of industry has been weaned from command and control and now supports grandfathered permits. This change occurred because industry realized that it had to modernize or move to lower cost production areas, and grandfathered permits provide portable subsidies. Environmentalists hold the balance of power. They remain unalterably opposed to any injection of economic reasoning into the standard-setting process. But in select areas where standards have been fixed and are no longer contested, they are willing to back the use of market mechanisms. Thus, the moderate movement toward market mechanisms in recent years more or less parallels the moderate degree of support for these instruments we find in the environmental community.

VI. Conclusion: Toward an Explanatory Synthesis

My search for an explanation of the role of market mechanisms in environmental law has been framed in terms of a sharp dichotomy between wealth-maximization theory and distributional theory. But it may have occurred to the astute reader that there is no necessary conflict between these two explanations. To the contrary, it may be that both explanations are right, or at least partially right, and that the best explanation would entail some synthesis or combination of the two theories. Such a synthesis is intuitively plausible. It seems unlikely that society would devote substantial resources to establishing a new type of environmental control regime if the benefits of such a regime did not exceed or at least cover the relevant costs. On the other hand, it also seems plausible that society will not embrace a new type of environmental control regime if powerful groups stand opposed to such a transformation.

We have a model of sorts for such a synthesis in the work of

Gary Libecap. Especially in his work on the history of property rights in natural resources,[85] Libecap has stressed both the importance of the aggregate gains from changes in the structure of property rights and the importance of "devising politically acceptable allocation mechanisms to assign the gains from institutional change while maintaining its production advantages." As he has argued, it is not enough to identify an alternative institutional arrangement, such as unitization of oil and gas pools, that promises to increase aggregate social welfare. If powerful groups have a stake in a system of separate ownership of oil and gas rights, they will resist such a change unless they can be assured that they will end up at least as well off after unitization as they were under separate ownership. In other words, wealth-maximizing changes in institutional arrangements cannot be secured unless some device for solving distributional issues is included in the mix.

A similar analysis applies to environmental law regimes. Take a phenomenon like transboundary pollution. It may well be that some sort of regulatory regime that limits transboundary pollution would increase the joint welfare of the source state and the affected state. But if such a regime creates net benefits for the affected state but only net burdens for the source state, the source state will resist cooperating in the creation of such a regime unless some mechanism for compensating it — for transferring a portion of the affected state's gains back to the source state — can be devised. Again, distributional problems must be overcome to achieve joint wealth maximization.

The slow emergence of market mechanisms in environmental law may perhaps also be best explained using a similar synthetic model. Carol Rose has made an important contribution in reminding us that even regimes that appear to be more cost-effective in limiting pollution will usually not be adopted if the management costs of operating those regimes exceed the allocative efficiency gains. Thus, one reason market mechanisms have not been more widely adopted may be that the management costs are just too high. Achieving a significant increase in social wealth is probably a necessary condition for any movement from command-and-control to market mechanisms, and it may be that the gains in social wealth are not as large as the enthusiastic proponents of market mechanisms have made them out to be, once the management costs are fully considered.

On the other hand, the distributional theorists are surely cor-

85. [Citing Libecap, Contracting for Property Rights 4-7 (1989).]

rect that to achieve a transformation in regulatory policy from command-and-control to market mechanisms, it will be necessary to "buy off" the most important affected groups that have a vested interest in the command-and-control regime. . . .

The best prognosis overall is probably that market mechanisms will see relatively limited use in the near future, notwithstanding the overwhelming consensus among economists that they are more efficient at achieving any desired level of pollution control than is command-and-control regulation. One problem with the economic argument is that it ignores the management costs of market mechanisms. Another problem is that it ignores distributional realities. Both problems will occasionally be overcome, but it will require considerable ingenuity to find solutions that apply across the board.

NOTES AND QUESTIONS ON MARKET MECHANISMS

1. The idea of market mechanisms for environmental protection is not new; a well-known early proponent was J.H. Dales, Pollution, Politics and Prices (1968). Nevertheless, the idea has had only limited political success, as Merrill's article notes. The largest, best-known, and ostensibly most successful program is the Acid Rain program introduced in the 1990 Amendments to the U.S. Clean Air Act, placing a national cap on total sulfur dioxide emissions and allowing trades of individual emission allowances. Tradable allowances under this Act are often analogized theoretically to property rights, though the Act itself explicitly negates their designation as legal property rights (can you guess why?). Elsewhere, tradable allowance programs have been established for certain fish catches, notably in Australia and New Zealand, and they are much-discussed in connection with controlling the greenhouse gases that contribute to global warming. For a survey and analysis of these cap-and-trade programs, see Thomas Tietenberg, The Tradable Permits Approach to Protecting the Commons: What Have We Learned?, in The Drama of the Commons (Elinor Ostrom et al. eds., 2002). Still other examples of property thinking have emerged in the efforts to give local communities an economic stake in wildlife preservation, through jobs or other payoffs; see Carol M. Rose, Expanding the Choices for the Global Commons: Comparing Newfangled Tradable Allowance Schemes to Old-Fashioned Common Property Regimes, 10 Duke Envtl. L. & Poly. Rev. 45 (1999).

2. Despite Merrill's preference for the "distributional" or public choice theory, does he concede at the end of his account that currently affordable environmental market mechanisms are simply too crude to work well? One frequent criticism of tradable environmental rights, for example, is that because they use *emissions* as a surrogate for *damage*, they may do little to reduce damage and indeed may even exacerbate damage by concentrating pollutants in locations where they do more harm. See, e.g., Richard L. Revesz, Federalism and Interstate Environmental Externalities, 144 U. Pa. L. Rev. 2314 (1996). Another recurring criticism is that the "things" traded are often not comparable; for example, a new wetland may be created to "mitigate" a wetland filled for development, but the two wetlands may have considerably different wildlife, fishery, and/or flood control characteristics. For this problem and others relating to the different "currencies" in environmental values, see James Salzman & J. B. Ruhl, Currencies and the Commodification of Environmental Law, 53 Stan. L. Rev. 607 (2000). Merrill also briefly mentions objections based on monitoring: whereas command-and-control regulations typically require specific observable pollution control devices, emissions that are taxed or traded are much less subject to observation. Do such practical difficulties account for the slow pace of market mechanisms in environmental law? Are they just as persuasive as distributional considerations?

3. In his "distributional" account, Merrill attributes a critical political role to environmentalists. What distributional motivations drive this group? Is it realistic to suggest that they are attempting to preserve jobs or profits or some other private good, as the distributional theory suggests? Does the presence of what appear to be public interest motivations cast doubt on the persuasiveness of the interest group theory? Or are environmentalists' motivations simply private goods in disguise?

4. Merrill attributes environmentalists' dislike of market mechanisms to their distrust of cost-benefit analysis. What could account for this? Might it be that environmentalists fear that cost-benefit analysis systematically underprices nonmarket values like wildlife and scenery? Heroic efforts have been made to find "shadow prices" for such goods, spearheaded by the Washington think tank Resources for the Future. These efforts often require asking people how much they would pay, for example, to have the opportunity to see certain wildlife in the future ("option value") or simply to know that it exists ("existence value"). Some of the critics argue that such surveys ignore the kinds of cognitive biases discussed in Jolls et al., supra p. 221. Can you see why? For a much-cited survey, with articles for and against, see the sympo-

sium in 8 J. Econ. Persp. 3-63 (1994). An interesting leftist critique is John M. Heyde, Comment, Is Contingent Valuation Worth the Trouble? 62 U. Chi. L. Rev. 331 (1995), arguing that contingent valuation attempts to monetize values "incommensurable" with money. For an alternative approach, applying the more conventional valuation technique of "replacement value" to environmental benefits, see James Salzman, Valuing Ecosystem Services, 24 Ecology L.Q. 887 (1997).

5. Merrill briefly mentions one pervasive moral objection to market mechanisms: that the commodification of pollution sends the message that it is all right to pollute if one simply pays for it, undermining the voluntary compliance upon which much environmental protection depends. For a discussion of this objection and a provocative critique, see Lior Jacob Strahilevitz, How Changes in Property Regimes Influence Social Norms: Commodifying California's Carpool Lanes, 75 Ind. L.J. 1231 (2000). Strahilevitz found that the creation of a paying express lane actually reduced commuter cheating in this lane, and he argues by analogy that market mechanisms might increase voluntary compliance with environmental initiatives.

Chapter 10

The Public
Domain

INTRODUCTORY NOTE ON PUBLIC PROPERTY

Chapter 2, "The Problem of the Commons," includes readings that contrast private property with other forms of resource management. The selections there mainly compare private property with communal property arrangements in which the members of a defined group — say a lobster gang in Maine — share a resource. This chapter, by contrast, focuses on the underexplored realm of public property, which typically involves a larger and more indefinite set of claimants than does communal property.

Public property appears in a variety of forms. In carrying out its proprietary activities, a government may use resources much like a private owner would. For example, a citizen cannot casually enter a municipal sewage treatment plant or obtain access to a secret military code. Many government-held assets, however, are open to all comers. As the readings on the commons indicate, when a resource is exhaustible or depreciable, an "open-access" regime may lead to overuse and underinvestment. Nevertheless, even a society strongly committed to a market economy invariably holds a significant portion of its resources in open-access form. In most cities in the United States, for instance, at least one-third of the land area is devoted to streets, sidewalks, parks, and other open-access uses. Similarly, some of the most magnificent intellectual achievements, such as Shakespeare's plays and Einstein's theory of relativity, are in the public domain.

Why does the legal system make these particular resources open to all, rather than subjecting them to private, communal, or government-proprietary ownership? Should the use of open-access

536

resources be unfettered, or constrained by rules-of-the-road designed to coordinate conflicts among the horde of potential users? In an ideal world, how much public property would there be, in what resources, and in what form? On this metaquestion, compare Karl Marx & Friedrich Engels, The Communist Manifesto (1848) (urging the centralization of all instruments of production in the hands of the state) with, e.g., Robert C. Ellickson, Property in Land, 102 Yale L.J. 1315 (1993) (favoring a system of private land parcels embedded in a network of public accessways).

A.   The Governance of Public Lands

The Public Trust Doctrine in Natural Resource Law: Effective Judicial Intervention*

Joseph L. Sax

Public concern about environmental quality is beginning to be felt in the courtroom. Private citizens, no longer willing to accede to the efforts of administrative agencies to protect the public interest, have begun to take the initiative themselves. One dramatic result is a proliferation of lawsuits in which citizens, demanding judicial recognition of their rights as members of the public, sue the very governmental agencies which are supposed to be protecting the public interest. . . .

Of all the concepts known to American law, only the public trust doctrine seems to have the breadth and substantive content which might make it useful as a tool of general application for citizens seeking to develop a comprehensive legal approach to resource management problems. If that doctrine is to provide a satisfactory tool, it must meet three criteria. It must contain some concept of a legal right in the general public; it must be enforceable against the government; and it must be capable of an interpretation consistent with contemporary concerns for environmental quality. . . .

The source of modern public trust law is found in a concept that received much attention in Roman and English law — the nature of property rights in rivers, the sea, and the seashore. That

*Source: 68 Mich. L. Rev. 471, 473-490, 547, 556-560 (1970).

history has been given considerable attention in the legal literature, and need not be repeated in detail here. But two points should be emphasized. First, certain interests, such as navigation and fishing, were sought to be preserved for the benefit of the public; accordingly, property used for those purposes was distinguished from general public property which the sovereign could routinely grant to private owners. Second, while it was understood that in certain common properties — such as the seashore, highways, and running water — "perpetual use was dedicated to the public," it has never been clear whether the public had an enforceable right to prevent infringement of those interests. Although the state apparently did protect public uses, no evidence is available that public rights could be legally asserted against a recalcitrant government. . . .

As carried over to American law, this history has produced great confusion. Our system has adopted a dual approach to public property which reflects both the Roman and the English notion that certain public uses ought to be specially protected. Thus, for example, it has been understood that the seashore between high and low tide may not be routinely granted to private owners as was the general public domain under the Homestead Act and similar laws. It has rather been a general rule that land titles from the federal government run down only to the high water mark, with title seaward of that point remaining in the states, which, upon their admission to the Union, took such shorelands in "trusteeship" for the public.

Whether and to what extent that trusteeship constrains the states in their dealings with such lands has, however, been a subject of much controversy. If the trusteeship puts such lands wholly beyond the police power of the state, making them inalienable and unchangeable in use, then the public right is quite an extraordinary one, restraining government in ways that neither Roman nor English law seems to have contemplated. Conversely, if the trust in American law implies nothing more than that state authority must be exercised consistent with the general police power, then the trust imposes no restraint on government beyond that which is implicit in all judicial review of state action — the challenged conduct, to be valid, must be exercised for a public purpose and must not merely be a gift of public property for a strictly private purpose.

The question, then, is whether the public trust concept has some meaning between the two poles; whether there is, in the name of the public trust, any judicially enforceable right which restrains governmental activities dealing with particular interests such as shorelands or parklands, and which is more stringent than are the restraints applicable to governmental dealings generally.

Three types of restrictions on governmental authority are often thought to be imposed by the public trust: first, the property subject to the trust must not only be used for a public purpose, but it must be held available for use by the general public; second, the property may not be sold, even for a fair cash equivalent; and third, the property must be maintained for particular types of uses. The last claim is expressed in two ways. Either it is urged that the resource must be held available for certain traditional uses, such as navigation, recreation, or fishery, or it is said that the uses which are made of the property must be in some sense related to the natural uses peculiar to that resource. As an example of the latter view, San Francisco Bay might be said to have a trust imposed upon it so that it may be used for only water-related commercial or amenity uses. A dock or marina might be an appropriate use, but it would be inappropriate to fill the bay for trash disposal or for a housing project. . . .

The most common theory advanced in support of a special trust obligation is a property notion; historically, it is said, certain resources were granted by government to the general public in the same sense that a tract of public land may be granted to a specific individual. If that were the case, the government's subsequent effort to withdraw the right would confront the same barrier that the government faces when it condemns private property. The test is no longer whether the government is acting for a public purpose within the legitimate scope of regulatory powers, but rather whether it is taking property.

There are several serious problems with such a formulation. . . .

. . . [One] difficulty becomes apparent from an analysis of the rationale which supports the constitutional provision that "private property [shall not] be taken for public use without just compensation." The rationale is that economic benefits are to be protected against certain kinds of public acquisitiveness lest the cost of public progress be unfairly thrust upon certain individuals or groups instead of upon the general community which benefits from public enterprises. Thus, it is thought that although an individual may have an automobile which the police department would find useful, the cost of supporting law enforcement should not be borne more heavily by him than by his neighbors; if the police department wants the car, it must pay for it and thereby spread the cost among all taxpayers. Any attempt to apply this concept to property assertedly owned by the whole public is plainly incongruous. It makes economic sense to prevent the government from taking the property of an individual owner, but it is difficult to understand why the government should be prevented from taking property which is owned by the public as a whole. . . .

To accept such claims of property rights would be to prohibit the government from ever accommodating new public needs by reallocating resources. Certainly any such notion strikes at the very essence of governmental power, and acceptance of such a theory by a court would be as unwise as it is unlikely. It is important to recognize that the assertion of a taking is not a mere claim to compensation, for the objectors do not want cash; rather, it is a claim that when a resource is dedicated to public use, that dedication is irrevocable. However strongly one might feel about the present imbalance in resource allocation, it hardly seems sensible to ask for a freezing of any future specific configuration of policy judgments, for that result would seriously hamper the government's attempts to cope with the problems caused by changes in the needs and desires of the citizenry.

Although it would be inappropriate for a court to declare that governmental resource allocations are irreversible, the government may certainly make less binding commitments which discourage certain reallocations. An example of such commitments is found in the "forever wild" clause in the New York constitution, which reserves the Adirondack forest as a wilderness — a dedication to public uses which cannot be abrogated without a constitutional amendment repealing that clause. Similarly, many statutory dedications, such as those creating public parks, will be interpreted as immune from changes without specific statutory authorization. . . .

Other than the rather dubious notion that the general public should be viewed as a property holder, there is no well-conceived doctrinal basis that supports a theory under which some interests are entitled to special judicial attention and protection. Rather, there is a mixture of ideas which have floated rather freely in and out of American public trust law. The ideas are of several kinds, and they have received inconsistent treatment in the law.

The approach with the greatest historical support holds that certain interests are so intrinsically important to every citizen that their free availability tends to mark the society as one of citizens rather than of serfs. It is thought that, to protect those rights, it is necessary to be especially wary lest any particular individual or group acquire the power to control them. The historic public rights of fishery and navigation reflect this feeling; and while the particular English experience which gave rise to the controversy over those interests was not duplicated in America, the underlying concept was readily adopted. Thus, American law courts held it "inconceivable" that any person should claim a private property interest in the navigable waters of the United States. It was from the same concept that some of the language of the Northwest Ordinance was taken:

> [T]he navigable waters leading into the Mississippi and St. Lawrence and the carrying places between the same, shall be common highways, and forever free, as well to the inhabitants of the said territory as to the citizens of the United States . . . without any tax, impost, or duty therefor.

An allied principle holds that certain interests are so particularly the gifts of nature's bounty that they ought to be reserved for the whole of the populace. From this concept came the laws of early New England reserving "great ponds" of any consequence for general use and assuring everyone free and equal access. Later this same principle led to the creation of national parks built around unique natural wonders and set aside as natural national museums.

Finally, there is often a recognition, albeit one that has been irregularly perceived in legal doctrine, that certain uses have a peculiarly public nature that makes their adaptation to private use inappropriate. The best known example is found in the rule of water law that one does not own a property right in water in the same way he owns his watch or his shoes, but that he owns only an usufruct — an interest that incorporates the needs of others. It is thus thought to be incumbent upon the government to regulate water uses for the general benefit of the community and to take account thereby of the public nature and the interdependency which the physical quality of the resource implies.

Of all existing legal doctrines, none comes as close as does the public trust concept to providing a point of intersection for the three important interests noted above. Certainly the phrase "public trust" does not contain any magic such that special obligations can be said to arise merely from its incantation; and only the most manipulative of historical readers could extract much binding precedent from what happened a few centuries ago in England. But that the doctrine contains the seeds of ideas whose importance is only beginning to be perceived, and that the doctrine might usefully promote needed legal development, can hardly be doubted. . . .

One who searches through the reported cases will find many general statements which seem to imply that a government may never alienate trust property by conveying it to a private owner and that it may not effect changes in the use to which that property has been devoted. . . .

The most celebrated public trust case in American law is the decision of the United States Supreme Court in Illinois Central Railroad Company v. Illinois.[59] In 1869 the Illinois legislature made an extensive grant of submerged lands, in fee simple, to the Illinois Central Railroad. That grant included all the land underlying Lake Michigan for one mile out from the shoreline and extending one mile in length along the central business district of Chicago — more than one thousand acres of incalculable value, comprising virtually the whole commercial waterfront of the city. By 1873 the legislature had repented of its excessive generosity, and it repealed the 1869 grant; it then brought an action to have the original grant declared invalid.

The Supreme Court upheld the state's claim and wrote one of the very few opinions in which an express conveyance of trust lands has been held to be beyond the power of a state legislature. It is that result which has made the decision such a favorite of litigants. . . .

. . . The Court's decision makes sense only because the Court determined that the states have special regulatory obligations over shorelands, obligations which are inconsistent with large-scale private ownership. The Court stated that the title under which Illinois held the navigable waters of Lake Michigan is

> different in character from that which the state holds in lands intended for sale. . . . It is a title held in trust for the people of the state that they may enjoy the navigation of the waters, carry on commerce over them, and have liberty of fishing therein freed from the obstruction of interferences of private parties.

With this language, the Court articulated a principle that has become the central substantive thought in public trust litigation. When a state holds a resource which is available for the free use of the general public, a court will look with considerable skepticism upon *any* governmental conduct which is calculated *either* to reallocate that resource to more restricted uses *or* to subject public uses to the self-interest of private parties. . . .

[After an extensive review of state cases, Professor Sax observes:] Most states have had, and regretted, experience with the disposition of public trust properties to private developers and the public agencies which work in collaboration with them. Indeed, it

---

59. 146 U.S. 387 (1892).

seems fair to describe the evolution of much public trust law in the United States as an effort to retreat from the excessive generosity of early legislatures and public land management agencies. The techniques adopted are by now very familiar: constitutional and statutory restraints have been placed on the disposition of trust properties; it has been required that the public trust be reserved in any grants which are permitted; restrictions have been placed on sales or leases in order to ensure that they are consistent with the public interest; it has been stipulated that such dispositions may be made only for full market value and that revenues from them must be devoted to replacement of specific trust uses or to statewide public purposes; and authorizing legislation has been narrowly read in order to limit the scope of governmental conveyances or the authority of administrative agencies to which the power of disposition has been granted. . . .

It is clear that the historical scope of public trust law is quite narrow. Its coverage includes, with some variation among the states, that aspect of the public domain below the low-water mark on the margin of the sea and the great lakes, the waters over those lands, and the waters within rivers and streams of any consequence. Sometimes the coverage of the trust depends on a judicial definition of navigability, but that is a rather vague concept which may be so broad as to include all waters which are suitable for public recreation. Traditional public trust law also embraces parklands, especially if they have been donated to the public for specific purposes; and, as a minimum, it operates to require that such lands not be used for nonpark purposes. But except for a few cases . . . it is uncommon to find decisions that constrain public authorities in the specific uses to which they may put parklands, unless the lands are reallocated to a very different use, such as a highway.

If any of the analysis in this Article makes sense, it is clear that the judicial techniques developed in public trust cases need not be limited either to these few conventional interests or to questions of disposition of public properties. Public trust problems are found whenever governmental regulation comes into question, and they occur in a wide range of situations in which diffuse public interests need protection against tightly organized groups with clear and immediate goals. Thus, it seems that the delicate mixture of procedural and substantive protections which the courts have applied in conventional public trust cases would be equally applicable and equally appropriate in controversies involving air pollution, the dissemination of pesticides, the location of rights of way for utilities, and strip mining or wetland filling on private lands in a state where governmental permits are required.

Certainly the principle of the public trust is broader than its traditional application indicates. It may eventually be necessary to confront the question whether certain restrictions, imposed either by courts or by other governmental agencies, constitute a taking of private property, but a great deal of needed protection for the public can be provided long before that question is reached. Thus, for example, a private action seeking more effective governmental action on pesticide use or more extensive enforcement of air pollution laws would rarely be likely to reach constitutional limits. In any event, the courts can limit their intervention to regulation which stops short of a compensable taking. . . .

The principal purpose of this Article has been to explore the role of the courts in shaping public policy with respect to a wide spectrum of resource interests which have the quality of diffuse public uses. . . . [The courts] may effectively overrule a questionable policy decision by requiring that the appropriate agency provide further justification; alternatively, the courts may, in effect, remand the matter for additional consideration in the political sphere, thus manipulating the political burdens either to aid underrepresented and politically weak interests or to give final authority over the matter to a more adequately representative body.

The very fact that sensitive courts perceive a need to reorient administrative conduct in this fashion suggests how insulated such agencies may be from the relevant constituencies. A highway agency, for example, which has a professional bureaucracy, which performs its function within a large geographic area rather than within a particular community, and which is rarely the subject of attack in political campaigns, may feel quite free to hold perfunctory and essentially predetermined public hearings. In such circumstances, the decision-making process may be inadequate even though a proceeding called a public hearing has been held. These realities imply that there is a need for the more searching sort of judicial intervention described above.

Understandably, courts are reluctant to intervene in the processes of any given agency. . . .

. . . [I]n theory there is no reason that the judiciary should be the ultimate guardian of the public weal. In the ideal world, legislatures are the most representative and responsive public agencies; and to the extent that judicial intervention moves legislatures toward that ideal, the citizenry is well served. Certainly even the most representative legislature may act in highly unsatisfactory ways when dealing with minority rights, for then it confronts the problem of majority tyranny. But that problem is not the one which arises in public resource litigation. Indeed, it is the opposite problem that frequently arises in public trust cases — that is, a diffuse majority is made subject to the will of a concerted minority. For self-interested and powerful minorities often have an undue influence on the public resource decisions of legislative and administrative bodies and cause those bodies to ignore broadly based public interests. Thus, the function which the courts must perform, and have been performing, is to promote equality of political power for a disorganized and diffuse majority by remanding appropriate cases to the legislature after public opinion has been aroused. In that sense, the public interests with which this Article deals differ from the interests constitutionally protected by the Bill of Rights — the rights of permanent minorities. That realization, in turn, lends even greater support for the rejection of claims that public trust problems should be considered as constitutional issues which are ultimately to be resolved by courts even if there is a clear legislative determination.

Not all the situations which have been examined in this Article fit directly into the majority-minority analysis suggested above, but, if properly understood, they do meet the principle of that analysis. For example, in a dispute between advocates of parks and those who would take parkland for highways, it often cannot be said that one group constitutes a majority and the other a minority. It can, however, be said that one interest is at least adequately represented in its access to, and dealings with, legislative or administrative agencies while the other interest tends to face problems of diffuseness and thus tends to be underrepresented in the political process. In such cases, all that is asked of courts is that they try to even the political and administrative postures of the adversaries; if that equalization can be done judicially, the courts may properly withdraw and leave the ultimate decision to a democratized democratic process.

NOTES AND QUESTIONS ON THE PUBLIC TRUST

1. Sax's article envisioned the public trust as a primarily procedural doctrine, through which diffuse environmental concerns receive a thorough airing in appropriate judicial processes. The background reasoning comes from the public choice theory of the 1960s, for example, Mancur Olson, The Logic of Collective Action (1965), which argues that concentrated interests can overcome

much more widespread but diffuse interests. Might Sax's procedural safeguards create a different problem, that is, an anticommons? See Heller & Eisenberg, supra p. 159.

2. Does Sax's procedural approach specify closely enough which subjects should receive public trust safeguards? In a recent critique, William D. Araiza likens Sax's version of the public trust to John Hart Ely's Democracy and Distrust: A Theory of Judicial Review (1980), in that Sax's idea is to preserve adequate representation. However, Araiza criticizes Sax's version of the public trust for failing to delineate specific subjects to which the "trust" applies. See Araiza, Democracy, Distrust, and the Public Trust: Process-Based Constitutional Theory, The Public Trust Doctrine, and the Search for a Substantive Environmental Value, 45 UCLA L. Rev. 385 (1997).

3. Araiza also asserts that if the public trust doctrine's purpose is to ensure a hearing for diffuse environmental interests, it may now be passé, since modern environmentalists are sufficiently organized to get a hearing for their concerns in legislative and administrative decision-making procedures. Is this the case? Merrill, Market Mechanisms, supra p. 521, suggests that it is. Might this be true only for some environmental interests but not others? See, e.g., Eric Biber, The Application of the Endangered Species Act to the Protection of Freshwater Mussels: A Case Study, 33 Envtl. L. ___ (forthcoming Spring 2002), arguing that environmental groups, like all others engaged in development decisions, almost universally ignore these uncharismatic species. Are environmentalists just as prone as other interest groups to focus on flashy or dramatic situations?

4. Richard Epstein, a scholar usually noted for his attentiveness to private property, has rather surprisingly supported the idea of a public trust. See Richard A. Epstein, The Public Trust Doctrine, 7 Cato J. 411, 418-421 (1987). Like Sax, Epstein focuses on the political process, but in a quite different way, building on Sax's observation that the public trust doctrine has been deployed to cabin legislative giveaways. Epstein argues that the doctrine puts limits on legislators who would collude with private "rent-seekers," that is, interests who use the political process to enrich themselves at the cost of the public. Is Epstein's anti–rent-seeking approach also vulnerable to Araiza's criticism for lacking specificity?

5. Is there a substantive version of the public trust doctrine, such that some properties are inherently public rather than private? One of the editors of this reader studied the historic subject of public trust doctrine, along with closely related public claims of prescription and custom; as Sax noted, these centered over-

whelmingly on roads and waterways and the immediately adjacent lands, with an occasional foray into spaces used for public gatherings. She concluded that the primary concerns of the traditional doctrines were transportation, travel, communication, and especially commerce. Open access to transportation lanes creates positive network effects by broadening trade and fostering learning. Thus it is not tragic to permit open access to the lanes of commerce but rather "comedic," as in the phrase "the more the merrier," because open lanes of commerce invite an ever-expanding participation in commerce and communication that enhances the welfare of all. Such rationales, however, suggest why modern versions of the "trust" have expanded to locations used for public speech and recreation, since these activities also connect diverse peoples, widen experiences, and contribute to civic education, all of which also have positive network effects. See Carol M. Rose, The Comedy of the Commons: Custom, Commerce, and Inherently Public Property, 53 U. Chi. L. Rev. 711 (1986). In a retrospective of Sax's work, she suggests that in a modern context, the underlying concerns of the public trust doctrine might be less relevant to natural resources than to new communications media, where open access may create positive network effects in education and cultural exchange; see Carol M. Rose, Joseph Sax and the Idea of the Public Trust, 25 Ecology L.Q. 351, 360 (1998). But see Araiza, supra Note 2, arguing that Rose's substantive approach, like Sax's procedural one, is still insufficiently specific. Araiza argues that the positive environmental protections of state constitutions provide a more satisfactory substantive basis for the public trust. Does Araiza's rationale answer the question *why* states adopt these provisions?

6. Do the historic rationales for open access to roads and waterways really support Sax's arguments for environmental protection? Alison Rieser argues that they do, at least for ecosystem preservation. Ecosystems, she says, resemble transport and communications networks in that they too have network effects, since the preservation of any one resource may positively benefit many others. Thus, she argues, there is a case for public management of ecosystems because governments may have the requisite scale to encompass an entire ecosystem. See Alison Rieser, Ecological Preservation as a Public Property Right: An Emerging Doctrine in Search of a Theory, 15 Harv. Envtl. L. Rev. 393 (1991).

7. Sax's article mentions briefly that applications of the public trust doctrine may raise the takings issue. Can you see why? Conversely, might the public trust doctrine act as a defense for regulatory bodies against some takings challenges, insofar as the public

trust implies an inherent public easement over certain private lands? See, e.g., Just v. Marinette County, 201 N.W.2d (Wis. 1972), suggesting that the public trust may act as a defense to a takings charge against a wetland regulation. Does such a defense suggest a reason for special concern about the scope of the public trust?

8. While Sax argued that the public trust does not imply any property right in the general public against their own legislatures, a number of historic cases took the opposite position, notably Arnold v. Mundy, 6 N.J.L. 1, 71-78 (N.J. 1821), prominently cited in Matthews v. Bay Head Improvement Assn., 471 A.2d 355 (N.J. 1984). Such cases have held that legislatures cannot alienate public trust property, effectively turning the public trust doctrine into a non-constitutional constraint on legislatures. Other cases have rejected this approach. See Rose, Comedy, supra Note 5. If the people at large have an inherent and inalienable right to use certain properties, do tragedies of the commons lurk in the background? For example, if the trust means that beaches are inalienably open to the general public, who will manage congestion, trash, and other elements of upkeep? Does the public trust ultimately imply that the people can compel their legislatures to manage trust property in their behalf?

9. Sax's article generated an enormous volume of case law and commentary. For a partial count, in addition to the sources cited above, see Richard J. Lazarus, Changing Conceptions of Property and Sovereignty in Natural Resources: Questioning the Public Trust Doctrine, 71 Iowa L. Rev. 631 (1986). While much commentary has been positive, some is also sharply negative. One persistent critic is James L. Huffman, who criticizes the public trust as extraconstitutional and as an unacceptable intrusion on private property rights. See Huffman, A Fish Out of Water: The Public Trust Doctrine in a Constitutional Democracy, 19 Envtl. L. 527 (1989).

Controlling Chronic Misconduct in City Spaces: Of Panhandlers, Skid Rows, and Public-Space Zoning*

Robert C. Ellickson

. . . [The] unprecedented level of legislative and judicial attention to issues of misbehavior in public spaces makes it timely to

*Source: 105 Yale L.J. 1165, 1168-1169, 1171-1175, 1194-2000, 1219-1226, 1243-1248 (1996).

explore the appropriate social controls that pedestrians, religious leaders, police officers, legislators, and others should place (and, in the case of judges, allow to be placed) on users of streets, sidewalks, and parks.

These open-access public spaces are precious because they enable city residents to move about and engage in recreation and face-to-face communication. But, because an open-access space is one everyone can enter, public spaces are classic sites for "tragedy," to invoke Garrett Hardin's famous metaphor for a commons. The media are quick to report the gravest problems of the streets, such as armed robberies, drug trafficking, and drive-by shootings. This Article focuses on problems that by comparison seem trivial: chronic street nuisances. Chronic street nuisances occur when a person regularly behaves in a public space in a way that annoys — but no more than annoys — most other users, and persists in doing so over a protracted period. Two hypothetical examples of street nuisances recur during the analysis that follows. The first involves a panhandler, by assumption a mild-mannered one, who repeatedly stations himself on a sidewalk in front of a particular restaurant. The second involves a mentally ill bench squatter who, morning after morning, wheels a shopping cart full of belongings to a bench in a downtown plaza, stretches out a sleeping bag on the bench, and dozes there intermittently until dark. The street behavior in both cases is assumed to result in a net decrease in the use of these public spaces. Because the panhandler's presence inhibits pedestrians, the sidewalk is less used and the restaurant's business suffers; although the bench squatter himself contributes to the daytime population in the plaza, the average headcount falls because fewer pedestrians wish to linger there.

Chronic street nuisances pose practically knotty and normatively perplexing questions about the management of public spaces. Most courts have held that a city can prohibit more aggravated nuisances, such as *aggressive* panhandling[13] and *overnight* sleeping in parks not designated for camping.[14] Conversely, there is universal agreement that every person, no matter how scorned, is entitled, assuming he behaves himself, to walk on every public sidewalk and to sit on every bench in every public park. The ex-

---

13. See, e.g., City of Seattle v. Webster, 802 P.2d 1333 (Wash. 1990) (rejecting battery of constitutional attacks on ordinance intended to limit aggressive begging and obstruction of sidewalks), *cert. denied*, 500 U.S. 908 (1991). . . .

14. See, e.g., Clark v. Community for Creative Non-Violence, 468 U.S. 288 (1984) (rejecting argument that First Amendment entitled protesters to sleep overnight in tents in Lafayette Park across street from White House). . . .

amples of protracted panhandling and bench squatting fall in the baffling normative terrain that lies between these easier cases. . . .

. . . Urbanologist Jane Jacobs and criminologist Wesley Skogan have both stressed that maintaining the invitingness of streets, sidewalks, and parks is essential to the viability of an urban neighborhood.[22] The well-known "broken windows" thesis of James Q. Wilson and George L. Kelling also sounds this theme. Wilson and Kelling assert that the persistence of a minor disorder not only disturbs a neighborhood on its own account, but also, like an unrepaired broken window, signifies that social controls are attenuated at that locale. Passersby, sensing this diminished control, become prone to committing additional, perhaps more serious, criminal acts.[23] According to Wilson and Kelling, unchecked street misconduct thus has a multiplier effect.

A specialist in property law approaches the issue of street order as a problem not of speech or of crime, but of land management. Many lawmakers and scholars have treated municipal lands as an undifferentiated mass. City spaces, however, are highly diverse in character and are subject to hugely varied demands. A central normative thesis of this Article is that a city's codes of conduct should be allowed to vary spatially — from street to street, from park to park, from sidewalk to sidewalk. Just as some system of "zoning" may be sensible for private lands, so may it be for public lands. . . .

II.   Chronic Nuisances in Public Spaces

In large cities in the United States, governments own as much as 45% of the developed land area and allocate most of these public

22. Jane Jacobs, The Death and Life of Great American Cities (1961). Jacobs begins what is perhaps the most influential book ever written on cities with three chapters on the functions of sidewalks, stating:

> The bedrock attribute of a successful city district is that a person must feel personally safe and secure on the street among all these strangers. He must not feel automatically menaced by them. A city district that fails in this respect also does badly in other ways and lays up for itself, and for its city at large, mountain on mountain of trouble.

Id. at 30. Skogan sets out his views in Wesley G. Skogan, Disorder and Decline: Crime and the Spiral of Decay in American Neighborhoods (1990), and similarly notes that "[v]isible physical and social disruption is a signal that the mechanisms by which healthy neighborhoods maintain themselves have broken down. If an area loses its capacity to solve even seemingly minor problems, its character becomes suspect." Id. at 48.

23. James Q. Wilson & George L. Kelling, Broken Windows: The Police and Neighborhood Safety, Atlantic Monthly, Mar. 1982, at 29, 31-32. . . .

lands for use as streets and highways. In a society that not only accepts, but exalts, private property in land, why does one observe so much open-access land? The basic reason is that private firms cannot feasibly collect tolls from entrants who use spaces for no more than a few moments. As a result, market forces alone cannot supply an adequate number of transportation corridors such as streets and sidewalks. Nor can markets readily provide, in down-town areas, squares and parks for pedestrians to use briefly for gathering and relaxation.

Democratic ideals provide another rationale for public spaces. Mass gatherings and mixings occur more frequently where there are numerous sites that all can enter at no charge. To socialize its members, any society, and especially one as diverse as the United States, requires venues where people of all backgrounds can rub elbows. In Carol Rose's memorable phrase, there must be sites for "the comedy of the commons."[32] For a romantic, the ideal is to have some spaces that replicate the Hellenic agora or the Roman forum. A liberal society that aspires to ensure equality of oppor-tunity and universal political participation must presumptively en-title every individual, even the humblest, to enter all transportation corridors and open-access public spaces.

A.   The Tragedy of the Agora . . .

William H. Whyte, one of the most creative observers of the urban scene, convincingly asserts that the downtowns of many central cities have "[t]oo much empty space and too few people." In his pursuit of the commendable goal of drawing more pedes-trians back downtown, however, Whyte proceeds to imply that cities should exert *no* controls on "undesirables," including beggars and aggressive eccentrics. In his words:

> The biggest single obstacle to the provision of better spaces is the un-desirables problem. They are themselves not too much of a problem. It is the actions taken to combat them that is the problem. Out of an almost obsessive fear of their presence, civic leaders worry that if a place is made attractive to people it will be attractive to undesirable people. So it is made defensive. There is to be no loitering . . . and . . . no eating, no sleeping. So it is that benches are made too short to sleep on, that spikes are put in ledges. . . .[40]

Whyte's view of street life is overly romantic. He fails to discuss crime, aggressive panhandling, squeegee men, graffiti, and the

---

32. See Carol Rose, The Comedy of the Commons: Custom, Commerce, and Inherently Public Property, 53 U. Chi. L. Rev. 711, 768-771, 774-781 (1986).
40. [William H. Whyte, City: Rediscovering the Center 156 (1988).]

other forms of street disorder that deeply concern most urbanites. In many public spaces, especially ones less dense than midtown Manhattan (Whyte's main focus), the arrival of true "undesirables" may trigger an exodus that results in a net loss of street users overall. Because bringing back pedestrians is Whyte's main objective, he should not ignore the difficult problem of identifying the sorts of "undesirables" — surely muggers and armed robbers, for example — whose presence would impair progress toward that objective. This Article seeks to confront that issue not with the easy cases of muggers and robbers, but with the hard ones of panhandlers and bench squatters. . . .

III. The Many Sources of Street Order

If a perpetrator of a chronic street nuisance were deemed an appropriate target for a sanction, who should apply the punishment? Although "legal centralists" think first of the state, another enforcer often would be preferable. An individual's behavior toward another person can be constrained by: first-party controls that the individual imposes on himself; second-party controls that the other person applies; and third-party controls administered by either (a) unofficial onlookers, (b) private organizations, or (c) the state. The suitability of the candidates varies with the information they possess about street behavior, and with their incentives and capacities to act on that information. When making street law, legislators and judges should be aware of the full panoply of enforcers and be sensitive to the relative aptitude of each. . . .

A chronic street nuisance is a nearly intractable social problem largely because an affected pedestrian is highly unlikely to do anything in response to it. . . . A pedestrian who unilaterally attempts to enforce social norms during a particular encounter on the street bears all the risks of a confrontation with the street person, but ineluctably shares the prospective benefits of nuisance abatement with all other users of the same public space. The private costs of pedestrian self-help far exceed the private benefits. As economists would say, public order is a "public good," and an almost pure one at that.[152] . . .

Many private third parties have stronger incentives to monitor public spaces than ordinary pedestrians do. Landlords and tenants of street-level properties tend to be especially attentive because the

152. For an introduction to this concept, see Richard A. Musgrave & Peggy B. Musgrave, Public Finance in Theory and Practice 49-55 (5th ed. 1989).

external benefits of greater street civility are capitalized into the value of their assets. For example, a restaurateur with a multi-year lease would want to shoo away sidewalk panhandlers who had chronically annoyed his patrons. . . . Small wonder that streetfront merchants earned Jane Jacobs's glowing admiration as "eyes upon the street." . . .

. . . [R]esidents of a neighborhood may form organizations for the specific purpose of governing public spaces. Familiar examples are residential block associations and groups such as "Friends of the Park." In commercial districts, where panhandlers most commonly congregate, merchants' associations are key players. A voluntary merchants' association, such as a Chamber of Commerce chapter, may face a free-rider problem and consequently be ineffective at providing public goods. One solution to the free-riding problem is formation of a Business Improvement District (BID), a government-approved organization empowered to levy assessments on all landowners within district boundaries. Although BIDs also engage in sanitation and business promotion, the control of disorderly street people has emerged as one of their central functions. . . .

Members of close-knit social communities commonly are able to dispense with government peacekeepers. Indeed, police departments were unknown in the United States prior to the mid-nineteenth century. Today, because large cities are far from close-knit, even Jane Jacobs would acknowledge that police officers play an essential role in monitoring downtown spaces. In these social environments, other types of enforcers simply are unable to provide enough of the public good of street order. . . .

V.   The Informal and Formal Zoning of Public Spaces

Some scholars, judges, and advocates apparently believe that provisions of the Federal Constitution tightly and uniformly constrain city policies in *all* open-access public spaces. This monolithic conception is reflected in Justice Roberts's famous dictum in *Hague v. CIO*:

> Wherever the title of streets and parks may rest, they have immemorially been held in trust for the use of the public and, time out of mind, have been used for purposes of assembly, communicating thoughts between citizens, and discussing public questions. Such use of the streets and public places has, from ancient times, been a part of the privileges, immunities, rights, and liberties of citizens.[303]

303. 307 U.S. 496, 515 (1939). . . .

Justice Roberts's sweeping characterization of the uses of streets and public places is descriptively false. For example, most cities treat *street pavements* primarily as transportation corridors, and thus give transportation functions priority over citizens' efforts to use those pavements for parades, gatherings, solicitations of drivers, and other speech activities that interfere with traffic flows. Justice Roberts's broad dictum is also suspect as a statement of constitutional doctrine; the municipal priorities just mentioned have long been held not to violate the First Amendment.[304]

Charles Tiebout has indicated the theoretical advantages of enabling people of disparate tastes to "vote with their feet" among local governments that offer distinct packages of public goods and taxation policies.[305] Consumer sovereignty is also served by the provision of an array of physical and social environments within a single political unit. . . .

A. A Hypothetical Division of City Public Spaces into Red, Yellow, and Green Zones

As a mental experiment, imagine that it would be desirable for a city to have three codes, of varying stringency, governing street behavior. Borrowing from the system of traffic signals, let's call these codes Red, Yellow, and Green. Each of the city's public spaces would be assigned to a zone paired with just one of these colors. (Who is to do this zoning will be addressed shortly.) As with a traffic signal, Red would signal extreme caution to the ordinary pedestrian; Yellow, some caution; and Green, a promise of relative safety. It must be stressed that these color codes are chosen with an eye to pedestrians of ordinary tastes, not to those inclined to engage in nuisance behavior. This usage is consistent with the phrase "Red Light District," which connotes disorderliness to an ordinary citizen, but not necessarily to a brothel patron.

In Red Zones (say, 5 percent of a city's downtown area), normal standards for conduct in public spaces would be significantly relaxed. The rule would hardly be "anything goes," of course; even in these places, violence to person or property, for example, would be subject to sanction. But many sidewalk behaviors that would be considered disorderly in the rest of the city would not violate Red-Zone rules-of-the-road. In these relatively rowdy areas, a city

---

304. See, e.g., Cox v. New Hampshire, 312 U.S. 569, 575-576 (1941) (permit requirement for street parade is valid time, place, and manner restriction). . . .

305. Charles M. Tiebout, A Pure Theory of Local Expenditures, 64 J. Pol. Econ. 416 (1956). . . .

might decide to tolerate more noise, public drunkenness, soliciting by prostitutes, and so forth. More pertinently for the topic at hand, chronic panhandling and bench squatting would be permitted in a Red Zone. Red Zones, in short, would be designed as safe harbors for people prone to engage in disorderly conduct.

Yellow Zones would comprehend, say, 90 percent of a city's downtown public spaces. The city's civic center, plazas, central business district, and other principal agoras would be placed under this large umbrella. The applicable code of conduct would aim to make a Yellow-Zone space serve as a lively mixing bowl. . . . A Yellow Zone's rules of public decorum therefore would be stricter than a Red Zone's rules. There would be constraints on excessive noise, drunkenness, and other disorderly conduct. For present purposes, let's assume that *chronic* (but not episodic) panhandling and bench squatting — permitted in a city's Red Zones — would be prohibited in its Yellow Zones.

Green connotes unusually pleasant environmental conditions. In Green Zones, the remaining 5 percent of downtown, social controls would be tailored to create places of refuge for the unusually sensitive: the frail elderly, parents with toddlers, unaccompanied grade-school children, bench sitters reading poetry. To accomplish this goal, the Green-Zone code would be relatively strict in its regulation of mildly disruptive activities such as radio playing, walking a dog, leafleting, and street performances. Let's also suppose that even *episodic* panhandling and bench squatting would be banned in these locations. A large Green Zone would offer real respite from the ordinary hurly-burly of the streets. A city might also create scattered pockets of refuge, perhaps around all bus stops. . . .

B. *Alternative Zoners of Public Spaces*

A city government could zone its public spaces top-down in the manner that it zones private spaces: by means of an official map that designates zones and an ordinance text that articulates the rules-of-the-road that apply in the various districts. The Skid Rows of the 1950s are a reminder, however, that the zoning of public spaces can also occur bottom-up.

1. INFORMAL ZONING

Members of a close-knit group who repeatedly make use of an open-access public space often are able to control misconduct there without direct help from the state. They do this by developing and enforcing social norms to deter an entrant into a space from using it in a way that would unduly interfere with the opportunities of other members. City dwellers, recognizing the crazy-quilt physical character of urban spaces and the myriad demands of pedestrians, tend to vary their informal norms from public place to public place. Profanity may be improper on the shuffleboard court, but not on the handball court. Panhandling may be seen as wrong on sidewalks near school grounds, but not on Skid Row. . . .

In open-access spaces thronged with strangers, however, free-riding is apt to afflict the informal sector. When this occurs, a hybrid social-control system may develop, under which police officers, without any legislative authorization, enforce informal neighborhood rules of conduct. Police officers help create informal Green Zones, for example, when they are tougher on street nuisances in public spaces near elementary schools. Conversely, casual police practices can help turn Skid Rows into unofficial Red Zones. For example, as early as 1868, the New York police informally exempted the Bowery from a citywide Sunday-closing law; in the 1920s, they exempted it from the full rigors of Prohibition.

2. MUNICIPAL ZONING

At first blush, the formal zoning of public spaces may seem an offbeat, even bizarre, idea. However, cities routinely differentiate their application of rules-of-the-road in this fashion. Consider the municipal laws that govern conduct on *street pavements*. In a large city, these pavements range from narrow local streets to major arteries. City officials, recognizing the differences among these public spaces, vary the applicable speed limits and parking regulations. A narrow cul-de-sac becomes, so to speak, a Green Zone usually safe for tricycle riders, while an interstate highway functions as a Red Zone where motorists can expect to encounter disorderly eighteen-wheelers. . . .

The administrators of public parks commonly use a similar approach. They design and control special subzones for use as tot-lots, picnic areas, playing fields, and so on. . . . A few cities have experimented with officially designating Red Zone parks as safe harbors for unusually disorderly activity. Zurich's failed experiment with Needle Park, where the enforcement of drug laws was relaxed, is an example. Dallas, Jacksonville, and Orlando have designated specific sections of certain public parks as safe zones where the street homeless can bed down outdoors without fear of arrest. . . .

A city might move beyond these patchwork measures to a comprehensive system of Red, Yellow, and Green Zones. . . .

Once the Red, Yellow, and Green Zones had been established,

individual citizens might spontaneously enforce the varying rules of decorum. A pedestrian in a Yellow Park might be more likely to tell a chronic panhandler to desist. . . .

VII. The Relative Merits of Informal and Municipal Zoning of Public Spaces

. . . [F]ederal constitutional law is indirectly encouraging cities to bring back Skid Rows, but in a form far more official than the 1950s version. By designating particular districts where minor street misconduct would be decriminalized, a city would be providing "alternative channels" for First Amendment expression. If the right of travel or the Eighth Amendment requires a large city to provide indigent individuals with safe havens for camping, drinking, and bench squatting, these zones would satisfy that obligation. No doubt partly on the advice of city attorneys, Orlando, Dallas, Jacksonville, and other cities have begun to set up official Red Zones for the destitute.

The constitutional revolution in street law that occurred between 1965-1975 was aimed largely at limiting police discretion. While police misconduct is unquestionably a serious and legitimate concern, it is worth considering whether informal zoning is in some respects superior to the formal zoning approach that the courts currently seem to be forcing on cities. . . .

One yardstick for an institution's performance is its capacity to make optimal rules — in this context, the various street codes and boundary lines for zones. For example, is "city hall" or "civil society" better at locating a Skid Row and deciding what can go on there? In a city that formally zoned public spaces, politicians would have to draw numerous boundary lines, some at the sub-block level. Experience with conventional municipal zoning of private lands indicates that this might prove to be a capricious process, dominated by warring special interests. Politicians might distribute Green Zones as pork-barrel. Neighborhood groups could be expected to fight against Red-Zone designations nearby. If a poor minority neighborhood were targeted with more than its share of these unruly places, its residents understandably might perceive environmental racism at work. Official safe zones also tend to stigmatize the destitute users who go there and may conceivably violate constitutional rights of other citizens.

On the other hand, loosely knit social groups such as downtown pedestrians and merchants are often ineffectual norm makers and, when they do overcome their free-rider problems, may treat minorities and outsiders more viciously than a city would. Informal rulemakers also cannot produce a code as detailed as a government's. Normmakers, for example, are likely to be incapable of establishing specific hours and time limits for activities in public spaces. . . .

. . . [I]f it could be achieved, the first-best solution to the problem of street misconduct would be the maintenance of a trustworthy police department, whose patrol officers would be given significant discretion in enforcing general standards against disorderly conduct and public nuisances. Certain administrative reforms could contribute to this end. Selection, training, and supervision methods can be shaped to help make police officers more trustworthy agents of constitutional values. The continuing racial integration of police forces should tend to cure some of the racist aspects of the Skid Row system of the 1950s. In some contexts, community-based policing, which assigns a particular officer to a particular neighborhood, might make a beat-patrol officer more averse to gaining a reputation for capriciousness and excessive violence.

Many observers understandably regard a street regime premised on trustworthy police officers as unrealistic. In some cities, it unquestionably is. In these locales especially, the official zoning of public spaces — which elsewhere would be a second-best approach — may be the best that lawmakers can do. . . .

VIII.   Conclusion . . .

. . . In a handful of cases in the first half of the 1990s, federal district judges struck down ordinances and statutes that cities such as Berkeley, New York, and San Francisco used to police street misconduct. That courts are aggressively second-guessing the policies of cities as historically tolerant as these three demonstrates that federal constitutional doctrine has become far too restrictive.

Disorderly people are not the only citizens with liberty interests at stake in these instances. Street law must also attend to the privacy and mobility interests of pedestrians of ordinary sensibility, not to mention the rights of the unusually delicate. Because demands on public spaces are highly diverse, city dwellers have historically tended to differentiate their rules of conduct for specific sidewalks, parks, and plazas. . . . A constitutional doctrine that compels a monolithic law of public spaces is as silly as one that would compel a monolithic speed limit for all streets.

The reconciliation of individual rights and community values on the streets is a profoundly difficult problem. For a problem so intractable, a pluralistic legal approach is advisable. Judges should refrain from using the generally worded clauses of the United States Constitution to create a national code that denies cities sufficient room to experiment with how to grapple with street disorder. . . .

NOTES AND QUESTIONS ON THE MANAGEMENT OF URBAN PUBLIC SPACES

1. What benefits are there, if any, of thinking about panhandling on a sidewalk as an issue of resource management as opposed to, say, an issue of criminal law or civil liberties law? Does the Supreme Court's tolerance of reasonable "time, place, and manner" restrictions on speech on public lands presuppose some theory of the desirable allocation of public property? Many law review articles on the rights of sidewalk users give primacy to the entitlements of a particular subgroup — sometimes ordinary pedestrians, sometimes those who approach or confront them. See, e.g., Helen Hershkoff & Adam S. Cohen, Begging to Differ: The First Amendment and the Right to Beg, 104 Harv. L. Rev. 896, 903-904 (1991) (discussion of "self-realization" that considers only the rights of beggars, with no regard to the self-realization prospects of, say, elderly people whom beggars might scare off the streets); Cynthia Grant Bowman, Street Harassment and the Informal Ghettoization of Women, 106 Harv. L. Rev. 517 (1993) (urging governmental regulation of wolf whistles and other harassments of women by strangers in public spaces). Does conceptualizing these conflicts as "property" issues help deepen an analyst's perspective? Or is, say, a torts or First Amendment analysis more cogent?

2. Ellickson's analysis of chronic panhandling and bench squatting is premised on the notion that those behaviors annoy and repel ordinary users of public spaces. How plausible is this premise as a factual matter? For criticism of the theory that public disorder is infectious, see Bernard E. Harcourt, Reflecting on the Subject: A Critique of the Social Influence Conception of Deterrence, the Broken Windows Theory, and Order-Maintenance Policing New York Style, 97 Mich. L. Rev. 291 (1998).

3. Does Ellickson make a persuasive case for the desirability of varying street rules according to spatially demarcated zones, informal or formal? Would it be better to enact general standards of street conduct or more particularized rules? On how much leeway to give police officers, see Debra Livingston, Police Discretion and the Quality of Life in Public Places: Courts, Communities, and the New Policing, 97 Colum. L. Rev. 551 (1997).

4. Is Ellickson right to conclude that the enforcement of informal norms by pedestrians is seldom a wholly adequate system for controlling sidewalk behavior? For case studies of the interplay between law and social norms in a variety of public arenas, see Richard A. Epstein, Allocation of the Commons: Parking and Stopping on the Commons, 31 J. Legal Stud. ___ (forthcoming 2002) (examining parking practices on Chicago streets); Brandt J. Goldstein, Panhandlers at Yale: A Case Study in the Limits of Law, 27 Ind. L. Rev. 295 (1993) (depicting social controls on panhandling on New Haven sidewalks); Strahilevitz, supra p. 535, Note 5 (on motorists' norms). See also the readings in Chapter 6 on informal property rights.

5. What useful role might submunicipal governments play in managing urban spaces? See generally Richard Briffault, A Government for Our Time? Business Improvement Districts and Urban Governance, 99 Colum. L. Rev. 365 (1999).

6. Ellickson urges relaxation of many federal legal constraints on the ways that states and municipalities manage their public spaces. Might greater state and local autonomy lead to a "race to the bottom" — that is, to efforts to drive street people into neighboring jurisdictions? Compare Fischel's discussion of municipal growth controls, supra p. 456.

7. For a broad variety of measured but pointed criticisms of this selection, see Stephen R. Munzer, Ellickson on "Chronic Misconduct" in Urban Spaces: Of Panhandlers, Bench Squatters, and Day Laborers, 32 Harv. C.R.-C.L. L. Rev. 1 (1997).

B. Intellectual Achievements: Public Domain, Private Property, or Limited Commons?

Property Rights Theory and the Commons: The Case of Scientific Research*

Robert P. Merges

For some time now, commentators in and out of the scientific community have been expressing concern over the direction of sci-

*Source: 13 Soc. Phil. & Poly. 145, 147-152, 155-166 (1996).

entific research. Cogent critics have labeled it excessively commercial, out of touch with its "pure," public-spirited roots, and generally too much a creature of its entrepreneurial, self-interested times. In most if not all of this hand wringing, the scientific community's growing reliance on intellectual property rights, especially patents, looms large. Indeed, for many the pursuit of patents is emblematic of just what is rotten in the republic of science today. . . .

For most people, the description of science as an innately public enterprise comes quite naturally. This is most likely a function of two attributes widely associated with scientific research: government funding and open dissemination. . . .

The large volume of privately funded basic research apparently does not undercut the view of science as an inherently public undertaking. Because of this, it might even be argued that the open dissemination of research results — which is, of course, common to most basic science, who ever funds it — is thought by most to be the key indicator of basic or pure science.

The point here is not to quibble with this, but to unpack it. That is, I am concerned in this section with a brief description of how and under what circumstances basic research results are shared with the world. As we shall see, it is a much more limited, and closely regulated, form of disclosure than is usually imagined. The many limitations on truly public dissemination lead, in fact, to the conclusion that science is not so much given freely to the public as shared under a largely implicit code of conduct among a more or less well-identified circle of similarly situated scientists. In other words, we will come to see that science is more like a limited-access commons than a truly open public domain. . . .

Science is a highly competitive enterprise regulated by a complex set of professional norms.

[These include the norm that sociologist Robert Merton describes as "communism."[4]] "Communism" means that scientific findings are made open to all, immediately, with no sense that they are or should be proprietary in any way. "Disinterestedness" means that scientists pursue truth rather than self-interest, that they are ideally indifferent to the success of an experiment or the reception of a research finding. "Organized skepticism" means that the scientific community should rigorously test research results before accepting them as true, and that all research is in some sense "born in doubt," false until dispositively proven true.

4. Robert K. Merton, The Sociology of Science (Chicago: University of Chicago Press, 1973).

Of course, norms (in the sense in which Merton used the term) are aspirational. . . . Consequently, it is not surprising that sociologists of science have documented a set of practices that deviate in many respects from the norms Merton identified. Of most interest to us here is a set of observations made by the sociologist Warren O. Hagstrom[5] on what might be called proprietary practices in science. Hagstrom states:

> Scientists who are concerned about the possibility of being anticipated as a result of the theft of their ideas tend to be secretive. An organic chemist [in an interview] said that he only communicated with persons he was friendly with and could trust. . . .
> To the extent that scientists can establish property rights over work in progress, they need not fear anticipation. Such property rights may be more or less explicit and formal. . . . When it becomes evident to two [scientists in the same field] that their research will probably produce the same results, they may informally agree on a division of labor. . . . [Another way scientists treat their work as proprietary is by publishing a preliminary version of research in an abstract.] The latent function of publishing abstracts is to permit individuals to "stake a claim," establish property rights on research in progress.

Hagstrom concludes with the observation that "[s]cientific knowledge is community property. Discoverers have limited rights, but among them are rights to be recognized for their discoveries." Thus, we can summarize Hagstrom's findings by saying that he found certain proprietary impulses at work beneath the surface of the otherwise Mertonian world of shared, or public, science.

More recently, the practice of asserting informal property rights appears to have become even more prominent. In cutting-edge biotechnology research, for example, pre- and even post-publication practices with respect to biological materials useful to fellow researchers (such as genetically engineered mice, or particularly useful cell lines) reflect greater reluctance to share widely. While it is difficult to trace the contours of a practice that few scientists admit to, and that few even seem willing to discuss openly, several operational principles can be traced, if somewhat speculatively. First, the more expensive and difficult it is to create a given biological material, the less likely it is that it will be shared widely and quickly. Second, the creator of a biological material is more likely to share quickly with those in fields unrelated to the creator's central interests; property rights are asserted most forcefully, in other words, with direct competitors. Third, despite the increased assertion of informal property rights, these rights still fall

---

5. Warren O. Hagstrom, The Scientific Community (New York: Basic Books, 1965).

far short of absolute exclusivity. A recent investigation of sharing practices in the field of recombinant DNA research "reveals that while no makers of [mice] simply refuse to share them, some researchers substitute their own policies for those of [the National Institutes of Health, which mandates free access after publication]: not sharing mice until long after publication, or sharing mice selectively." In practice, then, this example suggests that scientists fall short of the ideal of instantaneous, widespread disclosure.

Of course, the most obvious illustration of creeping propertization is the now widespread practice of seeking *formal* property rights — in the form of patents — over research results. Nothing could be further from the aspirational norm of openness. Indeed, the absolute exclusivity of a patent would seem entirely inconsistent with the earlier observation that science is characterized by informal property rights. Yet the truth is that in general, within the community of researchers, potentially patentable and even patented research results are often shared, though on a more limited basis. . . .

. . . [P]atents have affected the way science is done. Even so, in many cases scientist-patentees assert far less than the full exclusionary force bestowed by the legal system via their patents. A limited set of rights is asserted against the community, even though the patentee holds a greater set of rights. Indeed, it is not stretching too far to argue that conduct in today's scientific community in many cases approximates the effect achieved under the older practice of establishing "informal" property rights. The difference is that, now, the "informalness" of the rights is achieved by relinquishing (or at least not asserting) some of the scientist's formal rights. It is as if the old practice of establishing minimal property out of a background of zero formal rights has been replaced by relinquishing some rights against a background of a strong, formal entitlement. . . .

. . . Most scientists seem to think that the optimal policy entails maintaining some of the traditional practices that sociologists have identified with an informal set of property rights in research results, even in an era when *formal* property rights have been widely adopted.

For example, a number of brushfires have broken out in recent years regarding the extent to which a researcher must make his or her results available to other members of the community prior to, or even after, publication. Since major research results — finding a gene, or identifying the active portion of a protein coded for by a gene of interest, for example — are usually published very quickly, they are not usually at issue. Instead, the arguments are over another issue: the dissemination of assays, reagents, and other research tools of the trade, which have come to be known generically as biological materials. Very often these are developed as an interim step on the way to the final goal of obtaining the gene or protein subunit or whatever. Since most of the basic research funding that goes into the creation of these tools is public money, the question arises: When must they be shared?

Often the discussion takes the form of back-channel gossip regarding a certain lab's unwillingness to share a research tool. Interestingly, for our purposes, the point of this gossip-induced social pressure is *not* that the tool must be described in a formal, printed publication. It is simply that the tool be provided, on a reasonable basis, to other interested labs so that they can use it in the course of their research. Indeed, other labs understand that they will almost always be required to use the biological material under a duty not to disclose it to others, and certainly not to disclose it to the public generally, until its originator has published a full account of it. . . .

The same pattern holds when the patenting of research results is at issue. Normally, the criticism of excessive patenting activity or inappropriate licensing practices does not start from the assumption that complete public access should be the norm. For example, the outcry over certain large-scale research funding arrangements between private industry and prominent research institutions does not assume that the research output of the institutions would be freely available to all in the absence of the funding agreement. Implicit is the notion that the agreements exceed standard limits on the *degree* of privatization that is acceptable in science. No one assumes that a modest degree of privatization is against the working norms of the community. . . .

Traditionally, the findings of pure scientific research have been excluded from patent protection. . . .

An . . . objection to patents in scientific discoveries is that they are not necessary to spur scientific research. As Judge Jerome Frank put it:

> Epoch-making "discoveries" or "mere" general scientific "laws," without more, cannot be patented. . . . So the great "discoveries" of Newton or Faraday could not have been rewarded with such a grant of monopoly. Interestingly enough, apparently many scientists like Faraday care little for monetary rewards; generally the motives of such outstanding geniuses are not pecuniary. . . . Perhaps (although no one really knows) the same cannot be said of those lesser geniuses who put such discoveries to practical uses.[26]

26. Katz v. Horni Signal Mfg. Corp., 145 F.2d 961, 63 U.S.P.Q. (BNA) 190 (2d Cir. 1944).

On this view, granting patents for discoveries that scientists *would have made anyway* would be socially wasteful.

For many, this latter assumption would be far less defensible in today's environment of tight federal budgets. Regardless of what *motivates* a scientist, the argument would surely run, he or she cannot make any progress in the vast majority of scientific disciplines without a great deal of money. Equipment, personnel, and the like — all essential to the performance of modern science — are very expensive. Thus, since adequate funding is essential to science, society will not receive the results of scientific research without either extensive public support or some other revenue source. It follows that if property rights can secure this alternative revenue source, they may well provide a necessary impetus for the performance of research. Far from being redundant — an unnecessary reward, heaped on a researcher who would have done the same work without it — they may well be essential. This of course moots Judge Frank's objection to the granting of rights for pure scientific finding.

If it is true that property rights are increasingly essential to the research endeavor, it is no less true that these rights will bring with them a host of problems....

[Earlier] proposals to explicitly allow patents for the results of basic scientific research eventually faced a resounding defeat. Given that the only occasion on which the appropriateness of these patents was discussed in detail yielded such negative results, it is perhaps surprising that basic research is now considered an entirely proper source of patentable subject matter. Although broad statements of scientific truth — such as $E = MC^2$ — are still considered unpatentable, many of the fruits of contemporary basic science find their way into patent claims of one variety or another these days. To some extent, this is a result of growing sophistication by patent lawyers, who have learned to state a scientific finding in terms of an at least nominally useful application. Apart from this, however, what happened to produce this de facto change in policy?

For the most part, the answer lies with changes in the relationship between science and technology since the 1930s. In the 1930s, the important science-based industries were centered around the electrical and chemical fields. Because electrical engineering and modern analytic chemistry were still very young, the findings of basic science were very basic indeed. The conceptual distance between basic research and applied technology, in other words, was very large. As a consequence, huge investments were required to translate the findings of the basic research laboratory into viable commercial products.

By the 1970s and 1980s, however, the relationship between science and technology had grown a good deal closer in many fields. In important fields such as biotechnology and certain branches of physics, the jump from lab result to commercial product was much shorter than it had been in the past. Thus, for example, the basic Cohen-Boyer research on gene-splicing led to a commercial product (genetically engineered insulin) in only a few short years. The early work on lasers, to take another example, yielded commercial results after a relatively short time as well.

In addition, a host of subsidiary factors contributed to the hastening rate of commercial application. One important factor — often overlooked — is the change in the ease of capital formation for science-intensive industries. In the 1930s, it was widely thought that only large, integrated companies could afford the "luxury" of long-term-oriented basic scientific research. By the 1970s, however, with the advent of the venture-capital industry and related support institutions, start-up companies based on new scientific findings often found a ready supply of capital from firms specializing in such speculative investments. Genentech, founded in the mid-1970s, is of course the paradigm. It is also an example of a technology-intensive start-up that was later highly touted by investment analysts when it made the jump from "private" to public financing, via an initial public offering of stock.

As the Genentech story illustrates, capital markets — together with the changing interplay between science and technology — played a crucial role in the commercialization of basic science. It is important to recognize that extensive university involvement in technology licensing — another recent development often said to be at the heart of the commercialization process — is in fact closely related to the growing sophistication of capital markets with regard to basic science. For it is quite clear that without a prospective market, fueled by the idea of significant returns on investments in the basic findings of science, the university licensing offices founded with such frequency in the 1980s and 1990s would have no one to sell to. . . .

Despite the fact that, for a variety of reasons, patents are now available for an increasing proportion of the results of basic research, the community norm of open access remains strong. Thus, it is perhaps not clear why, even though the operative legal standard has changed vis-à-vis modern science, scientists and the institutions that employ them today are seeking so many patents for their research. In other words, just because they *can* obtain patents, it does not follow that all of them *will*. Why then is everyone, in fact, making more and more use of the patent system?

The answer as I see it is fairly simple. The increasing value of patents makes adherence to the traditional community norm of nonproprietary open access implicitly more expensive. Thus, even if a particular scientist believes strongly in adherence to the norm, he or she knows that others will be tempted to ignore it because of the higher payoff that stems from seeking a patent. Since many scientists believe that although the norm is still the "correct" mode of behavior, many of their colleagues will abandon it, even those scientists who believe in the norm may well abandon it. Only a scientist who would revel in the thought that he or she was the last one remaining who adheres to the norm would continue to adhere to it.

Those familiar with the logic of game theory will recognize the basic structure of this situation. Although most players attribute the greatest value to continued shared access — to "cooperation," in game theory lingo — even many of these, fearing the inevitable abandonment of the shared norm in light of the higher individual payoffs from "defecting," will themselves defect from the prior cooperative arrangement. Others, anticipating this, will also defect. In this way, even though everyone would be better off if the cooperative behavior continued, the "equilibrium strategy" will be to defect. The problem, to put it simply, is that there is no way to enforce the norm of shared access, and no way to bind other members of the community to the cooperative arrangement. The players must rely on each other to continue to do the right thing without formal sanctions for doing otherwise. Once the payoffs from defecting increase, however, there is less assurance that the other players will continue to do the right thing. One way of stating this is that the implicit costs of the informal sanctions brought to bear on defectors — negative gossip, loss of reputation, etc. — are outweighed by the benefits, in the form of greater payoffs due to the enhanced returns provided by the formal property rights. As one highly astute observer of these matters put it recently:

> For years biomedical research has flourished while investigators have drawn heavily upon discoveries that their predecessors left in the public domain. Even if exclusive rights enhance private incentives to develop further research tools, they could do considerable damage to the research enterprise by inhibiting the effective utilization of existing ones.[32]

There is already evidence that this dynamic has begun to set in. . . .
Even if this account of the motivations of individual scientists

32. Rebecca Eisenberg, A Technology Policy Perspective on the NIH Gene Patenting Controversy, 55 U. Pitt. L. Rev. 646 (1994).

is correct (and it is admittedly highly stylized), some important questions remain. Just because patent law has in effect dropped its objections to patenting what comes out of certain basic-research labs, and just because scientists might have an incentive to patent, does that mean that the science community, or society at large, should encourage widespread patenting of these results? . . .

A recent development illustrates how scientists and research labs are responding to the incentives they face. In March 1995, a group called the Association of University Technology Managers (AUTM) announced a new, standardized form for the transfer of biological materials between nonprofit (i.e., government-funded) research labs. . . .

. . . [I]n the "nonprofit to nonprofit" form, free use is given of the research tool in its original form, but adaptations, modifications, and alterations are not covered. Indeed, modifications intended for ultimate commercialization are to be the subject of negotiations with the original provider of the material. And, perhaps most relevant here, the relatively permissive treatment of transfers applies only if the transferee does not intend a subsequent transfer to a private, for-profit firm. These private firms, being outside the common in some sense, must negotiate formal, commercial licenses. . . .

This description of contemporary trends and understandings in science should give some hint of why I have come to see science as a limited-access commons, rather than a truly open public domain. [The author goes on to discuss some recent research on the "limited-access commons" and cooperative resource management within close-knit communities, mentioning the work on informal norms in Robert C. Ellickson's *Order Without Law* (1991) and particularly citing Elinor Ostrom's *Governing the Commons* (1990).]

One could agree that the baseline in science is not complete openness, and still resist the analogy between common-property regimes and contemporary norms of science. After all, unlike water or common pasture land, scientific research is not a product of nature, waiting to be exploited. It has to be created. Thus, the thought might be that the institutions that operate in the realm of science cannot be legitimately compared to those that allocate access to preexisting natural resources such as water. . . .

This shared assumption stems, at least in part, from the fact that although science itself is not a freely given asset, such as water or pasture land, it is based on a resource that the members of the relevant community treat as a given: public money. Thus, public funding produces science, which therefore carries with it some of the attributes of a public (or, I would argue, common) resource.

True, unlike with a physical resource, where the only issue is allocation, science must first be produced by participants. And true, once it is produced, it must be disclosed in order for other members of the community to use it. Nevertheless, in many ways the practice of science makes these distinctions less important than they might at first appear. First, the production of science is a highly cooperative venture. Those who produce it understand that the community always has extensive claims on it, because without shared knowledge, research techniques, and even biological materials, there would often be no results, no progress, and hence nothing to argue about. Second, and most importantly, in the absence of shared norms, science, like water, would be subject to highly deleterious forms of self-serving behavior. A lab that always "takes" research results, but that never "gives" in return, for example, is like a municipality that pumps water as fast as it can, at the expense both of its neighbors and ultimately of rational water use. Thus, in science, as with open-access water resources, cooperation produces very large gains. . . .

In science, as we have seen, emerging pro-commercialization practices coexist (sometimes uneasily) with traditional "Mertonian" norms. . . .

In essence, the new practices can be explained — roughly and preliminarily — in the following terms. They seek to preserve the old norms while recognizing a fundamentally changed landscape. They do this by dividing potential transactions into two classes: those with other pure scientists, in which efforts are made to preserve the old rules of scientific discourse; and those with commercial entities, in which more-explicit insistence on property rights, and the attendant element of immediate compensation, are both expected. Consistent with the earlier explanation, it is important to notice that the former set of transactions are not in any sense *devoid* of property rights. Instead, they rely on informal property rights. The latter transactions, by contrast, depend on formal property rights, and are conducted "in the shadow of" these rights. This explains, for example, why transfers of as-yet-unpatented materials to commercial labs come with greater restrictions. The possibility that a patent might be sought leads to greater safeguards, such as an insistence that any commercialization, publication, or property right claims growing out of the commercial recipient's use of the materials come only after the sender has received notice and has time to respond. (This can preserve the sender's right to file his or her own patent, for instance, a right that might be endangered if the recipient makes the sender's invention public before the sender acts, e.g., by filing a patent application.)

Although I believe the two-tiered property right concept properly captures an important feature of contemporary science, I would add some warnings about its continued relevance. In general, science is in such a rapid state of flux that the differential treatment of pure and commercial science may only be a way station on the road toward a totally new set of practices. Perhaps the destination will be the complete specification and enforcement of property rights, against all comers, pure and commercial. Perhaps it will be a return to the old patterns of interaction, fueled by a declining interest in funding from commercial entities. The point here is that the two-tiered system I observe currently is only one possible configuration in the long term. . . .

What policy recommendations flow from the fact of "creeping propertization" of science, and the emergence of a two-tiered system? And what do we gain, in formulating policies, by seeing scientific research both as a common asset shared under strict rules by a close-knit community, and as a marketable product? . . .

In pursuing . . . policy goals . . . , I propose that we keep one important thought in mind: we must show respect for the internal rules of the scientific community. This will take the form, primarily, of *refusing* to adopt flat requirements that all federal scientific research, or even some portion of it, be made instantaneously available to the general public, or even to all other scientists. In other words, we must show an understanding that even if formal property rights are prohibited, a set of norms in the scientific community will continue to regulate access and related issues in ways that might be described as the imposition of certain *informal* property rights. Where this is so, we must respect it. Instead of conceiving of science as innately public, and therefore viewing any and all restrictions on public availability as inherently wrong, we should ask why the community does things the way it does.

NOTES AND QUESTIONS ON SCIENTIFIC RESEARCH AND THE PUBLIC DOMAIN

1. How do you account for scientists' norms of sharing openly with other noncommercial researchers but not with commercial users? If their scientific research is truly pure, why should scientists care whether others make a profit? Are they practicing a tit-for-tat strategy, in that they expect to get something back from other noncommercial researchers but not from commercial users? See Axelrod, supra p. 261. Or do they regard other noncommercial re-

searchers as part of the same close-knit community? See Ellickson, Order Without Law, supra p. 210. Is there any parallel to the practices of market-inalienability described by Margaret Radin, supra p. 336? That is, do scientific norms permit gift but not sale of intellectual products within the noncommercial scientific community? Do Radin's explanations hold here?

2. Why are scientists so anxious to get credit for their discoveries, even vis-à-vis other scientists? Does this suggest that scientists are "paid" in a currency different from money, namely fame? Or does fame itself translate into money?

3. Compare Merges's description of modern scientific research to the premodern view of ideas, held well into the eighteenth century: Ideas and innovations are gifts from God rather than creations of particular individuals, and hence they should be open to all. Though many inventors did try to keep secrets, musicians, writers, and others borrowed freely from one another's work, not to speak of cribbing from their own prior work. For an account of this view of creativity as a common legacy, as well as the development of a cult of "genius" to establish rudimentary property rights in intellectual products, see Martha Woodmansee, The Genius and the Copyright: Economic and Legal Conditions of the Emergence of the "Author," 17 Eighteenth Century Stud. 425 (1984). Which regime fosters creativity more effectively: open access or intellectual property? Are the musical works of Bartok and Bernstein, for example, superior to those of Bach and Handel?

4. Western intellectual property law has been accused of embracing a mythical idea of the Romantic author or inventor as an individual hero of gigantic intellect. See, e.g., James Boyle, Shamans, Software and Spleens: Law and the Construction of the Information Society (1996). Mark Rose, in Authors and Owners: The Invention of Copyright (1993), points out that Shakespeare, often cited as the quintessential Romantic creator, in fact wrote his plays in a highly collaborative environment. Does Merges depict scientific research in the same collaborative light? Do these descriptions of the creative process make Western scientific and artistic production seem to resemble traditional communal societies' creative processes when they produce folklore or new plant varieties? If so, why has it been so difficult to extend the protections of intellectual property to folklore and traditionally produced genetic resources? See Boyle, supra; see also Rosemary J. Coombe, The Cultural Life of Intellectual Properties: Authorship, Appropriation and the Law (1998).

5. Compare Merges's description of the scientific community to the selections on the commons in Chapter 2. Can there be any

"Tragedy of the Commons" in ideas, as Hardin suggested that there can be in grazing fields? Notice that an idea, unlike a grassy field or fishery, can be shared without the decimation of any underlying resource. What then would be the "tragedy" in open access to intellectual achievements? Why do scientists behave like Acheson's lobstermen and organize themselves into limited common property regimes, from which they exclude outsiders and create a blend of common responsibilities and individual entitlements among insiders? If individual property rights were to grow stronger in scientific research, would the anticommons loom as a potential problem? See Heller & Eisenberg, supra p. 159. Which poses the greater threat of "tragedy" in this arena, open access or anticommons?

6. Suppose there were no intellectual property law. Could scientists and other creators still create communities from which they exclude others and generate their own internal norms of reward and punishment? At the end of this selection, Merges seems to suggest that they could, whatever the state of intellectual property law. Analysts of cyberspace have made similar suggestions, often drawing on Ellickson, Order Without Law, supra p. 210, to argue that cyberspace should be free of both private property and governmental intrusion, because communities of users can develop their own governance norms. See, e.g., David R. Johnson & David Post, Law and Borders — The Rise of Law in Cyberspace, 48 Stan. L. Rev. 1367 (1996). For a more skeptical view, see Lawrence Lessig, The Zones of Cyberspace, 48 Stan. L. Rev. 1403 (1996).